Herman W. Siemens
Agonal Perspectives on Nietzsche's Philosophy of Critical Transvaluation

Monographien und Texte zur Nietzsche-Forschung

Herausgegeben von
Christian J. Emden
Helmut Heit
Vanessa Lemm
Claus Zittel

Begründet von
Mazzino Montinari, Wolfgang Müller-Lauter, Heinz Wenzel

Advisory Board:
Günter Abel, R. Lanier Anderson, Keith Ansell-Pearson, Sarah Rebecca Bamford,
Christian Benne, Jessica Berry, Marco Brusotti, João Constâncio, Daniel Conway,
Carlo Gentili, Oswaldo Giacoia Junior, Wolfram Groddeck, Anthony Jensen,
Scarlett Marton, John Richardson, Martin Saar, Herman Siemens,
Andreas Urs Sommer, Werner Stegmaier, Sigridur Thorgeirsdottir,
Paul van Tongeren, Aldo Venturelli, Isabelle Wienand, Patrick Wotling

Band 74

Herman W. Siemens

Agonal Perspectives on Nietzsche's Philosophy of Critical Transvaluation

—

DE GRUYTER

The research for this book and its open access publication were funded by the Dutch Research Council (NWO).

ISBN 978-3-11-126672-5
e-ISBN (PDF) 978-3-11-072229-1
e-ISBN (EPUB) 978-3-11-072231-4
ISSN 1862-1260
DOI https://doi.org/10.1515/9783110722291

This work is licensed under the Creative Commons Attribution-NonCommercial-NoDerivatives 4.0 International License. For details go to https://creativecommons.org/licenses/by-nc-nd/4.0/.

Library of Congress Control Number: 2021943973

Bibliographic information published by the Deutsche Nationalbibliothek
The Deutsche Nationalbibliothek lists this publication in the Deutsche Nationalbibliografie; detailed bibliographic data are available on the Internet at http://dnb.dnb.de.

© 2023 Herman W. Siemens, published by Walter de Gruyter GmbH, Berlin/Boston.
This volume is text- and page-identical with the hardback published in 2021.
The book is published with open access at www.degruyter.com.

Printing and binding: CPI books GmbH, Leck

www.degruyter.com

Para la aurora de mi vida

'Philosophers who are not opposed to one another are usually
joined only by sympathy, not symphilosophy'
– Fr. Schlegel, *Athenaeum Fragment* 112

'*De wetenschap, inclusief de wijsbegeerte, is uit haar aard polemisch,
en het polemische is van het agonale niet te scheiden.*'
– Johan Huizinga, *Homo Ludens*

'Enemies are of more use to the wise man than friends are to the fool. Ill will usually levels mountains of difficulty which goodwill would balk at tackling. The greatness of many has been fashioned thanks to malicious enemies. Flattery is more harmful than hatred, for the latter is an effective remedy for the flaws that the former conceals. Sensible people fashion a mirror from spite, more truthful than that of affection, and reduce or correct their defects, for great caution is needed when living on the frontier of envy and ill will.'
– Baltasar Gracián, *Oráculo* 84

Acknowledgements

Much of the work on this book was made possible by the Open Competition grant awarded by the NWO (Netherlands Organisation for Scientific Research): *Between Deliberation and Agonism: Rethinking Conflict and its Relation to Law in Political Philosophy*.

The chapters of this book draw in different ways on published and unpublished material, as indicated below. The author would like to thank the publishers for permitting the use of published material. Chapter 1 is based on a revised version of "Nietzsche's Hammer: Philosophy, Destruction, or The Art of Limited Warfare", in *Tijdschrift voor Filosofie* 60/2, 1998, pp. 321–347. Chapter 2 is based on a revised and expanded version of the chapter "Nietzsche's Agon", first published in *The Nietzschean Mind*, ed. Paul Katsafanas (Routledge, 2018). © 2018, 2021 Herman Siemens. Chapter 3 draws on unpublished work and "Agonal Writing: Towards an Agonal Model for Critical Transvaluation', in *Logoi.ph – Journal of Philosophy*, Nr. I/3, 2015 – Playing and Thinking, pp. 1–29. Chapter 4 is based on a revised and expanded version of "The first Transvaluation of all Values: Nietzsche's *Agon* with Socrates in *The Birth of Tragedy*", in *Nietzsche and Ethics*, ed. Gudrun von Tevenar, 2007, pp. 171–196, republished with permission of Peter Lang; permission conveyed through Copyright Clearance Center, Inc. Chapter 5 draws on "Agonal Configurations in the *Unzeitgemässe Betrachtungen*: Identity, Mimesis and the *Übertragung* of Cultures in Nietzsche's Early Thought", in *Nietzsche-Studien* 30, 2001, pp. 80–106; "Nietzsche contra Kant on Genius, Originality and Agonal Succession", in *Nietzsche's Engagements with Kant and the Kantian Legacy*, ed.s Brussotti, M., Siemens, H., Constancio, J., Bailey, T., vol. III: *Aesthetics, Anthropology and History*, ed.s Branco, M. & Hay, K. (Bloomsbury Academic, an imprint of Bloomsbury Publishing Plc., 2017), pp. 15–42; and "Nietzsche's '*Agonale Betrachtungen*': On the Actuality of the Greeks in the *Unzeitgemässe Betrachtungen*", in *Rethinking the Nietzschean Concept of 'Untimely'*, ed. A. Caputo (Mimesis International, 2018), pp. 23–39. Chapter 6 is based on a revised version of "(Self-)legislation, Life and Love in Nietzsche's Philosophy", in *Neue Beiträge zu Nietzsches Moral-, Politik- und Kulturphilosophie*, ed. I. Wienand (Press Academic Fribourg, 2009), pp. 67–90. Chapter 7 is based on unpublished work and draws partly on "Agonal Communities of Taste: Law and Community in Nietzsche's Philosophy of Transvaluation', in *Journal of Nietzsche Studies* 24, 2002, pp. 83–112, Copyright © 2002. This article is used by permission of The Pennsylvania State University Press. Chapter 8 draws partly on "Nietzsche's Agon with Ressentiment: Towards a Therapeutic Reading of Critical Transvaluation", reprinted by permission from Springer Nature Customer Service Centre GmbH in *Continental Philosophy Review* 34/1, 2001, pp. 69–93, Copyright (2001), and expanded with unpublished work. Chapter 9 is based on a revised version of "Umwertung: Nietzsche's 'war-praxis' and the problem of Yes-Saying and No-Saying in *Ecce Homo*", in *Nietzsche-Studien* 38, 2009, pp. 182–206.

Contents

Translations of Nietzsche's Writings —— XV

References to Nietzsche's Writings —— XVII

Abbreviations and References for Nietzsche —— XIX

Introduction —— 1
    Introducing the Agon —— 1
    I   Critical Transvaluation (*Umwertung*) —— 7
    II   Saying, Yes-Saying and Unsaying —— 9
    III   The Chapters —— 13

Chapter 1
The Art of Limited Warfare: Nietzsche's Hammer and the Need to Find a Limit in Negation —— 23
    Introduction —— 23
    I   Finding a Limit in the Negation of the Past —— 28
    I   Nietzsche's 'War-praxis' or the Art of Limited Warfare —— 32
    III   Nietzsche's Agonal Model of Warfare —— 36

Chapter 2
Nietzsche's Agon and the Transvaluation of Humanism —— 42
    Introduction —— 42
    I   Origin of the Idea —— 42
    II   Nietzsche's Transvaluation of Humanism in *Homer's Wettkampf* —— 50
    III   The Problem of Measure —— 55
    III.1 Agonal Affects: Envy, Jealousy, Ambition —— 58
    III.2 The Medial sense of measure —— 59
    IV   Nietzsche's Counter-Ideal of Humanity: the Agon between the 'Human' and the 'Inhuman' —— 63

Chapter 3
Performing the Agon: Towards an Agonal Model for Critical Transvaluation —— 66
    Introduction —— 66
    I   Nietzsche's Fictional Communities and Culture as Deception —— 69
    II   Formal and Dynamic Features of the Agon —— 73
    II.1   Agonal Envy and Jealousy —— 78
    II.2   Agonal Ambition and Egoism —— 80
    III   Agonal Culture as the *Übertragung* of War —— 83

Chapter 4
The First Transvaluation of All Values: Nietzsche's Agon with Socrates in *The Birth of Tragedy* —— 89

    I   Overcoming Socrates: *The Birth of Tragedy* as Nietzsche's first Transvaluation —— 90
    II   Plato's Socrates: Art, Philosophy and the Practice of Dying in the *Phaedo* —— 94
    III   Nietzsche's Socrates: the Practice of Music in *The Birth of Tragedy* —— 97
    IV   The Problem of Inversion and Nietzsche's Duplicitous Optic in Art —— 101
    IV.1   The Epistemic Reading —— 101
    IV.2   The Agonal Reading —— 103
    Conclusion: Agonal Critique —— 106

Chapter 5
Agonal Configurations in the *Unzeitgemässe Betrachtungen*: The Problem of Origins, Originality and Mimesis in Genius and Culture (Nietzsche and Kant) —— 111

    Introduction —— 111
    I   Schopenhauer as Kantian Genius —— 114
    II   The Problem of Originality and Precedent in Kant's Account of Genius —— 116
    Intermezzo: Nietzsche's Programme of Aesthetic Perfectionism —— 122
    III   Nietzsche's Engagement with Wagner: Daemonic Transmissability or Agonal *Betrachten* —— 127
    IV   Agonal Jealousy: Originality and Mimesis —— 130
    V   The Problem of German Culture and the Actuality of the Greeks —— 133
    VI   Succeeding to (*Nachfolgen*) the Greeks —— 136
    VII   Learning from the Greeks and the *Übertragung* of Alien Cultures —— 143
    VIII   The Greek Agon —— 148
    IX   Overcoming the Greeks —— 151

Chapter 6
Of (Self-)Legislation, Life and Love —— 153

    Introduction —— 153
    I   The Problem of Legislation: Sources and Features —— 156
    II   Schopenhauer and Wagner as Legislators —— 160
    II.1   *Schopenhauer als Erzieher* (SE/UB III) —— 160
    II.2   *Richard Wagner in Bayreuth* (UB IV/RWB) —— 166

III   Zarathustra as Legislator-Type: Nietzsche's Agonal Model of Self-Legislation —— 169
Appendix: Zarathustra as Legislator-Type: The Texts —— 179

Chapter 7
Law and Community in the Agon: Agonal Communities of Taste and Lawfulness without a Law —— 184

Introduction —— 184
I   Immanent DIKE —— 187
II   Agonal Communities of Taste —— 197
II.1   Wisdom as Taste —— 199
II.2   The Normativity of Taste —— 203
II.3   Taste as Lawfulness without a Law —— 205
III   Agonal Measure or the 'Measure of Judgement' —— 210
III.1   Justice and Measure in Nietzsche's Agon and Homer's *Iliad* —— 210
III.2   Agonal Measure and Hannah Arendt on Freedom under Laws or 'Principles' —— 214

Chapter 8
Nietzsche's Agon with *Ressentiment*: Towards a Therapeutic Reading of Critical Transvaluation (Nietzsche and Freud) —— 220

Introduction: The Problematic of Sickness, Health and Redemption —— 220
I   Dreams of Annihilation: the Problem of Repetition —— 222
II   Agonal Transvaluation as Therapy —— 227
II.1   Agonal Hermeneutics and Beyond: the Problem of Energy —— 229
II. 2   Agonal Transference (*Übertragung*) as Therapy —— 233
III   Nietzsche and Freud: Agonal and Analytic Transference —— 237
III.1   Analytic and Agonal Transference Therapy: Affinities and Differences —— 240
III.2   The Goals of Therapy: Affinities and Differences between Nietzsche and Freud —— 241
III.3   Sublimation, Play and the Mastery over *Ressentiment* —— 246

Chapter 9
Umwertung: Nietzsche's 'War-Praxis' and the Problem of Yes-Saying and No-Saying in *Ecce Homo* —— 255

Introduction —— 255
I   On War —— 256
II   Nietzsche's War-Praxis (EH Warum ich so weise bin 7) —— 266
III   Nietzsche's War-Praxis and the Standpoint of Total Affirmation —— 267
IV   Consequences for *Umwertung*: the Question of 'gegen' —— 276

Agon-Related Publications by the Author —— 280
    Books —— 280
    Chapters/Articles —— 280

Bibliography —— 282

Name Index —— 289

Subject Index —— 290

Translations of Nietzsche's Writings

The translations are mine, but I have also drawn on existing translations in the following:

The Gay Science, tr. Walter Kaufmann, New York: Vintage (1974); *Daybreak,* ed.s Maudemarie Clark and Brian Leiter, tr. R.J. Hollingdale. Cambridge: Cambridge University Press (1997); *The Anti-Christ, Ecce Homo, Twilight of idols,* ed. Aaron Ridley, tr. Judith Norman. Cambridge: Cambridge University Press (2005); *Writings from Late Notebooks,* ed. Rüdiger Bittner, tr. Kate Sturge, Cambridge: Cambridge University Press, 2006; *On the Genealogy of Morality,* ed. Keith Ansell-Pearson, tr. Cariol Diethe. Cambridge: Cambridge University Press, 2007; *Twilight of the Idols/The Anti-Christ,* tr. R.J. Hollingdale, London: Penguin, (1990); *Ecce Homo,* tr. R.J. Hollingdale, London: Penguin. (1992); *Daybreak,* tr. R.J. Hollingdale, Cambridge: Cambridge University Press (1993); *Untimely Meditations,* tr. R.J. Hollingdale, Cambridge: Cambridge University Press (1994); *Human, All Too Human,* tr. R.J. Hollingdale, Cambridge: Cambridge University Press (1996); *Philosophy in the Tragic Age of the Greeks,* tr. Marianne Cowan, Washington: Regnery Publishing, (1998); *Beyond Good and Evil,* tr. Marion Faber, Oxford: Oxford University Press (1998); *On the Genealogy of Morality,* tr. Maudemarie Clark and Alan J. Swensen, Indianapolis: Hackett Publishing Company (1998); *Twilight of the Idols,* tr. Duncan Large, Oxford: Oxford University Press (1998); *The Birth of Tragedy,* tr. Ronald Speirs, Cambridge: Cambridge University Press (2000); *The Birth of Tragedy (and Other Writings),* ed. Raymond Geuss and Ronald Speirs, Cambridge: Cambridge University Press (1999); *Thus Spoke Zarathustra,* tr. Graham Parkes. New York: Oxford University Press (2005); *Beyond Good and Evil: Prelude to a Philosophy of the Future.* R.-P. Horstmann and J. Norman (eds.), tr. Judith Norman, Cambridge: Cambridge University Press (2002); 'On Truth and Lies in a Nonmoral Sense', in: *Philosophy and Truth: Selections from Nietzsche's Notebooks of the Early 1870s,* tr. and ed. Daniel Breazeale. Atlantic Highlands, N.J.: Humanities Press (1979).

References to Nietzsche's Writings

References to Nietzsche's published/titled texts: follow the standard abbreviations given in *Nietzsche-Studien* under 'Siglen' and are listed here. German abbreviations have been used, followed by the section/aphorism number (e.g. JGB 12, M 54, GM I 13). The single exception is HW = *Homer's Wettkampf*. For sections/chapters that are not numbered but named, the abbreviations from *Nietzsche-Studien* have been used. Page references, where given, are to the relevant passage in the *Kritische Studienausgabe* (KSA) if possible, otherwise to the *Kritische Gesamtausgabe* (KGW), but not to any translations. The format is as follows:

JGB 12, KSA 5.76 (= *Jenseits von Gut und Böse*, aphorism 12, KSA volume 5, page 76);
M 95, KSA 3.86f. (*Morgenröthe*, aphorism 95, KSA volume 3, page 86f.).

References to the Nachlass: follow the notation in KSA, followed by volume and page, for example: 15[44], KSA 10.491 = note 15[44] in KSA volume 10, page 491.
2[15], KSA 12.74 = note 2[15] in KSA volume 12, page 74.

References to Nietzsche's letters (sent or received): include date, volume and page number in KSB (*Sämtliche Briefe. Kritische Studienausgabe*) or KGB (*Nietzsche Briefwechsel. Kritische Gesamtausgabe*).

Emphases in Nietzsche's writings: normal emphases (= 'gesperrt' in KSA) are rendered in *italics*. Further emphases ('halbfett' in KSA for the *Nachlass*) are rendered in ***bold italics.***

Interventions/omissions: any interventions in citations by the author, including insertions of original German words, are indicated by square brackets: []. Omissions by the author in mid-sentence are also inserted in square brackets […] in order to distinguish them from Nietzsche's own ellipses.

Quotations marks: single quotation marks ' ' are used for quotes from Nietzsche (and other authors), except for block quotes. Double quotations marks " " are used for quotes inside quotes. (This formula has been used for all quotations.)
Where texts are not rendered in their original format in KSA, forward slash / is used for paragraph breaks.

Abbreviations and References for Nietzsche

All references to Nietzsche's writings are from the following editions:

BAW Nietzsche, F. (1933–1940), *Historisch-kritische Gesamtausgabe*, Hans Joachim Mette/Carl Koch/Karl Schlechta (eds.), Munich: C.H. Beck'sche Verlagsbuchhandlung. Reprinted as: *Frühe Schriften 1854–1869*, Munich: DTV 1994.
KSA Nietzsche, F. (1980), *Sämtliche Werke. Kritische Studienausgabe in 15 Bänden*, Giorgio Colli/ Mazzino Montinari (eds.), Munich /Berlin / New York: DTV / De Gruyter.
KSB Nietzsche, F. (1986), *Sämtliche Briefe. Kritische Studienausgabe in 8 Bänden*, Giorgio Colli/ Mazzino Montinari (eds.), Munich /Berlin / New York: DTV / De Gruyter.
KGB Nietzsche, F. (1975–), *Briefwechsel. Kritische Gesamtausgabe*, established by Giorgio Colli and Mazzino Montinari, continued by Norbert Miller and Annemarie Pieper, Berlin / New York: De Gruyter.
KGW Nietzsche, F. (1967–), *Werke Kritische Gesamtausgabe*, established by Giorgio Colli and Mazzino Montinari, continued by Wolfgang Müller-Lauter and Karl Pestalozzi (eds.), Berlin / New York: De Gruyter.

Where possible the KSA references were used.

Abbreviations or 'Siglen' for Nietzsche's Writings in German (in alphabetical order)

AC	Der Antichrist. Fluch auf das Christenthum
CV 1	Ueber das Pathos der Wahrheit
CV 3	Der griechische Staat
EH	Ecce homo. Wie man wird, was man ist
EH Vorwort	Ecce Homo, Vorwort
EH Motto	[An diesem vollkommnen Tage … mir mein Leben.]
EH weise	Warum ich so weise bin
EH klug	Waum ich so klug bin
EH Bücher	Warum ih so gute Bücher schreibe
EH (GT)	see GT
EH (UB)	see UB
EH (MA)	see MA
EH (M)	see M
EH (Z)	see Z
EH (JGB)	see JGB
EH (GD)	see GD
EH Schicksal	Warum ich ein Schicksal bin
FW	Die fröhliche Wissenschaft ("la gaya scienza")
FW Vorrede	Vorrede zur zweiten Ausgabe
GD	Götzen-Dämmerung oder Wie man mit dem Hammer philosophirt
GD Alten	Was ich den Alten verdanke
GD Deutchen	Was den Deutschen abgeht
GD Epilog	Der Hammer redet
GD Fabel	Wie die "wahre Welt" endlich zur Fabel wurde

GD Irrthümer	Die vier grossen Irrthümer
GD Moral	Moral als Widernatur
GD Sokrates	Das Problem des Sokrates
GD Streifzüge	Streifzüge eines Unzeitgemässen
GGL	Geschichte der griechischen Litteratur (KGW II/5)
GM	Zur Genealogie der Moral. Eine Streitschrift
GM Vorrede	Zur Genealogie der Moral. Vorrede
GT	Die Geburt der Tragödie
GT Versuch	Die Geburt der Tragödie, Versuch einer Selbstkritik (1886)
HW	Homer's Wettkampf
JGB	Jenseits von Gut und Böse. Vorspiel einer Philosophie der Zukunft
M	Morgenröthe. Gedanken über die moralischen Vorurtheile
M Vorrede	M Vorrede von 1886
MA	Menschliches, Allzumenschliches. Ein Buch für freie Geister. Erster Band
MA I Vorrede	Vorrede von 1886
NW	Nietzsche contra Wagner. Aktenstücke eines Psychologen
NW Antipoden	Wir Antipoden
PHG	Die Philosophie im tragischen Zeitalter der Griechen
UB	Unzeitgemässe Betrachtungen
UB I	Unzeitgemässe Betrachtungen, Erstes Stück: David Strauss der Bekenner und der Schriftsteller
UB II/NNHL	Unzeitgemässe Betrachtungen, Zweites Stück: Vom Nutzen und Nachtheil der Historie für das Leben
UB III/SE	Unzeitgemässe Betrachtungen, Drittes Stück: Schopenhauer als Erzieher
UB IV/RWB	Unzeitgemäße Betrachtungen, Viertes Stück: Richard Wagner in Bayreuth
VM	(MA II) Erste Abtheilung: Vermischte Meinungen und Sprüche
VPP	Die vorplatonischen Philosophen (KGW II/4)
WA	Der Fall Wagner. Ein Musikanten–Problem
WS	(MA II) Zweite Abtheilung: Der Wanderer und sein Schatten
Z	Also sprach Zarathustra. Ein Buch für Alle und Keinen
Z I Verbrecher	Also sprach Zarathustra, Vom bleichen Verbrecher
Z II Erlösung	Von der Erlösung
Z II Taranteln	Von den Taranteln
Z III Tafeln	Von alten und neuen Tafeln

Introduction

On the evening of the 8th of June 1870, Nietzsche went together with his best friend Erwin Rohde and his new colleague from Basel, the well-known historian Jacob Burckhardt, to a tavern in Muttenz, a village outside the city. They spent the evening into the small hours drinking and conversing on their shared passion: ancient Greek culture. This conversation was the birthplace of the idea of the 'agon', which in Rohde's hands became a philologeme, in Burckhardt's hands the fulcrum of the history of Greek culture, and in Nietzsche's case a powerful philosopheme.

Introducing the Agon

This book is a record of my engagement with Nietzsche's concept of the agon over the past 20 years or so. The agon has attracted a good deal of attention among scholars and philosophers both within and outside Nietzsche-studies.[1] Already in the 1930s, it was in circulation among Nietzsche-interpreters, including Alfred Baeumler's fascist appropriation.[2] More recently, it has gained popularity in the hands of so-called 'ag-

---

[1] The agon entered the contemporary academic and popular lexicon in the late 1970s and early 1980s through Jean-François Lyotard's *The Postmodern Condition* (1979) and, in literary theory, Harold Bloom's *Agon: Towards a Theory of Revisionism* (1982). While both authors reference Nietzsche, their accounts have little to do with his concept of the agon. Drawing on the late Wittgenstein, Lyotard (1979, 10, 16f., 66) celebrates the pluralization of heterogeneous language games in postmodernity for their emancipatory effects, forming 'agonistic' networks oriented towards dissent. For his part, Bloom draws on Freud's drive theory, conceived as a dualistic / 'agonistic' struggle between Eros and Thanatos, to cast literary history as a neurotic agon with precursors, in which creativity is haunted by an Oedipal 'anxiety of influence' and 'contaminated' by 'negation, contraction and repression' (Bloom 1982, 98f.). Both authors have drawn much criticism, which has only served to stimulate interest in the concept of the agon and extend its influence over a range of disciplines from continental philosophy, intellectual history, gender studies, Jewish studies, psychology, and sports studies to political science, zoology, art history, neurochemistry, materials science, and law. Some of these developments are recorded in the volume edited by Janet Lungstrum and Elizabeth Sauer, *Agonistics: Arenas of Creative Contest* (1997), which is concerned above all with the creative force of agonistic processes in various arenas. However, it must be said that, while lip-service is paid to Nietzsche, we learn little, if anything about his concept of the agon, or its fruitfulness for current issues and debates, since most of the authors use the 'agon' very loosely for conflicts, confrontations or struggles of various kinds (e.g. psychic conflicts, 'socio-sexual agons', 'agonal dialectic', 'the classical tragic agon', 'agonistic existence', 'agonal dialogism', 'communal agonal outreach', 'agonal demonization' etc.). As I try to show in this book, Nietzsche's 'agon' is primarily a *dynamic* concept and as such is quite elastic. The problem is that the looser the concept of the agon, the greater its extension and range of application, but the weaker its explanatory power.

[2] See Baeumler 1931, esp. 17, 64ff., 75f. In the third edition of *Der Begriff des Politischen* (1933), Carl Schmitt criticises Baeumler's interpretation of Nietzsche and Heraclitus under the sign of '[d]er große metaphysische Gegensatz *agonalen* und *politischen* Denkens' ('the great metaphysical opposition of *agonal* and *political* thinking'), whereby the latter conceives war as geared towards conclusive victory

onistic' democratic theorists, who have used it in order to formulate a critique of, and alternative to mainstream liberal democratic theories.[3] This wide-ranging interest is rather puzzling, given that the most significant treatment of the agon is in a short, unpublished text, *Homer's Wettkampf* (HW),[4] given to Cosima Wagner in January 1873 as one of 'Five Prefaces to Five Unwritten Books'. Thereafter, it makes few explicit appearances in Nietzsche's published works, and it was never promoted by Nietzsche himself as a signature concept of his philosophy, as were for example 'gay science', 'the eternal return', 'the will to power' etc. In Nietzsche's unpublished notes, 'agon', 'Wettkampf' and related terms do receive more sustained attention across his work. But the philosophical significance of the concept far exceeds the 'agon' terminology. Indeed, while the concept of the agon was by no means original to Nietzsche, his achievement was to turn it into a powerful *philosopheme* with wide-ranging implications for fundamental questions in ontology, ethics, culture and politics, but also, as I argue in this book, with *performative* implications for Nietzsche's own philosophical practice.

As a measured and productive form of conflict, the agon is part and parcel of Nietzsche's life-long philosophical engagement with the problem of conflict, struggle and tension. As such, it undergoes a series of reformulations and permutations in line with the development of this problematic across his work: from his early engagements with Schopenhauer, Heraclitus and Greek culture, to the origins of justice and social life in an equilibrium of forces (MA I and II); the feeling of power and its role in agency, interaction and art (MA, M, GD); the naturalization of morality through the turn to the body and Nietzsche's philosophical physiology (Z, FW and the *Nachlass* of

---

in the sense of peace and is concluded by a peace accord, whereas the former is not oriented toward peace and knows no peace accords, since no victory is conclusive (Schmitt 1933, 10 ff., esp. note 1). This distinction informs his critique of liberalism for failing to distinguish 'war' from 'peace' clearly and advancing instead 'endless [economic – HS] competition and endless discussion [i.e. deliberation – HS], an endless contest [*Wettkampf*], which is never permitted to become "bloody" or "inimical"' (Schmitt 1933, 52). For a Nietzschean critique of the Hobbesian notion of power underpinning Schmitt's concept the political, see Siemens 2012a, 221–223. In the following chapters, I argue that it is precisely the dynamic of endless repeatability, the exclusion of conclusive peace / victory on one side, and the exclusion of destruction of the other on the other side, which make the agon a valuable device for philosophical critique and transvaluation.

3 Political interpretations / appropriations of Nietzsche's thought on the agon for a revitalised 'agonistic' democratic theory abound, most notably by David Owen, Lawrence Hatab, William Connolly, Christa Acampora and Bonnie Honig. See e.g. Hatab 1995; Acampora 2013; Connolly, 1991; Honig 1993a, 1993b; Owen 1995; Schrift 1999, 2000. For critical overviews of agonistic readings see Siemens 2001c and 2012b.

4 Together with the notebook PII8b (=16[ ], KSA vol. 7), *Homer's Wettkampf* is the most important source for Nietzsche's thought on the agon. As one of *Five Prefaces to Unwritten Books* given to Cosima Wagner, it was 'finished on the 29. December 1872' (KSA 1.792). But the drafts in notebook 16[ ] show that Nietzsche was working on it in the period summer 1871 – early 1872, i.e. during latter stages of GT. The folder MpXII 3 (=20[ ], KSA 7), containing the first draft, is dated summer '72.

1880 onwards); the question of rule and legislation in the wake of the overcoming of morality (Z and the *Nachlass* of 1883 onwards); the origins of slave morality in enmity (AC); and the problems of spontaneous activity and power-enhancement in the context of the will to power thesis, to name a few. But the agon is a multi-faceted concept, and individual facets have their individual trajectories across his work as well, such as the problem of life-affirmative idealization or sublimation; the concepts of envy and vanity and their place in our affective life and interactions; the drive for distinction (*Auszeichnung*) and the pleasure of victory; the concept of resistance as a stimulant, rather than an inhibitor; and the concept of freedom under pressure, to name a few.

In this book, my interest lies not in the trajectory of the 'agon' across Nietzsche's thought, nor in its significance for democratic theory, but in its potential as a model or cypher for his philosophical practice, and its implications for a number of key problems in his philosophy.[5] From the beginning, when I first encountered this concept in the short text *Homer's Wettkampf*, it struck me that the agon had a tremendous resonance in Nietzsche's thought, a significance for him that went well beyond ancient Greek culture, and great potential as a hermeneutic key or cypher for his philosophy. In the succeeding period, I have tried to work this intuition out by conducting a series of studies in which the concept of the agon is applied in different ways to a number of key problems in his thought across a broad range of texts. Some of the results of these studies have been published in different journals and volumes over the years. In this book, I bring revised and expanded versions together with unpublished material from these and other studies under one cover, in order to make the case as best I can for the fruitfulness of the agon as a way to understand Nietzsche's thought. My hope is to open new lines of research by stimulating others to go further than I have and extend the agon to other problems and domains of his thought.

In broad terms, my main contention is that Nietzsche draws on the agon in a variety of ways in response to problems he locates in modernity. Specifically, I propose the agon as a model for Nietzsche's philosophical practice of critical transvaluation (*Umwertung*) and ask: To what extent does it afford insight into his contestation of European (Christian-Platonic) values in the name of life, its affirmation and enhancement? While Nietzsche's strengths as a critic are widely acknowledged, his peculiar, antagonistic style of critique is usually ignored as mere rhetoric, or dismissed as violent and uncontrolled or simply incoherent. In this book, Nietzsche's concept of the agon, a measured and productive form of conflict inspired by ancient Greek culture, is advanced as the dynamic and organising principle of his philosophical practice, enabling us to make sense of his critical confrontations and the much-disputed con-

---

5 My work on political agonism has been excluded from this volume, so as to keep the focus on Nietzsche's philosophical practice and problems internal to his thought, rather than the problems in contemporary democratic theory and institutions that motivate political agonisms. So far, this work has been published in: Siemens 2001c; 2002; 2005; 2006; 2008a; 2008h; 2009b; 2009d; 2012a; 2012b; 2013; 2015b.

cept of transvaluation or *Umwertung*, and also to understand better how he addresses a number of key problems intrinsic to the project of transvaluation.

I do not aspire in this book to offer a systematic or exhaustive account of Nietzsche's philosophy, covering all the 'key concepts' and their development across his works. Nor do I claim that the agonal model can be fruitfully applied to all his texts or even all his transvaluative texts. Rather, as the title states, the book offers agonal perspectives on a number of texts and problems within Nietzsche's philosophy of critical transvaluation. Topics and problems treated include: critical history and the need to find a limit in the negation of the past (*Unzeitgemässe Betrachtungen II*); Nietzsche contra Socrates and the problem of closure (*Die Geburt der Tragödie*); Nietzsche contra humanism and the problem of humanity (*Homer's Wettkampf*); Greek classicity and the problem of original German culture (*Unzeitgemässe Betrachtungen I*); Nietzsche contra Kant on genius and the problem of legislation (*Unzeitgemässe Betrachtungen III*); the problem of self-legislation in relation to life and the overcoming of morality (*Unzeitgemässe Betrachtungen* and the *Zarathustra Nachlass*); Nietzsche's sense of community and its articulation with law, understood as a normativity of taste; *ressentiment* and the question of therapy in Nietzsche and Freud; and the problem of total affirmation in relation to total critique (*Ecce Homo*).

My approach is marked, above all, by attention to the *dynamic* and *relational* qualities of Nietzsche's conception of the agon: What is the specificum, in *dynamic* terms, of agonal interaction? How best to understand the dynamics of reciprocal agonal engagement? At the same time, attention is also paid to the 'lower' and 'upper' limits of Nietzsche's agon: What are the conditions of possibility for the agonal dynamic to arise and be sustained? And under which conditions does the agonal dynamic become impossible and slide into the wrenching, violent conflict that Nietzsche calls the 'struggle for annihilation' or *Vernichtungskampf*? For Nietzsche, the agon is not a self-sufficient good, but presupposes and depends on what he comes to call 'approximately equal power'. What exactly this means is discussed in chapter 2. Of importance here is that 'equal power' is not the concept of equality criticised by the later Nietzsche as the tendency for democracy to promote uniformity. Rather, it designates a relational or relative notion of power that *includes* the qualitative diversity that is lost under modern democratic values, and *includes* relative differences of power. Mistaking 'approximately equal power' for 'equality' is, I believe, what has led some commentators to associate 'hierarchy' or 'order of rank' with Nietzsche's agon, instead of attending to his dynamic sense of approximate equality and the way it includes (relative) difference and diversity.[6] In Nietzsch-

---

[6] See e.g. Turner 2015, 12–14, 24 f., 28; Tuncel 2009, 147, 169 note 55, 175 (in connection with power as commanding and obeying). Tuncel (2014, 355) writes that the 'hierarchical universe of agon consists of gods, demigods, heroes, priests and poets, officials and judges, trainers, victors, contestants and spectators' (also Tuncel 2009, 169) and suggests that it was familiar to Nietzsche, without giving any references. The only 'agonal universe' that Nietzsche knows is that of Heraclitus, where 'hierar-

e's concept of agonal interaction, as I take it, the difference in power between the 'weakest' and the 'strongest' is relative and never such that the former does not feel equal to the act of challenging the latter; by the same token, the 'strongest' or current victor is never more than *primus inter pares*. In other words, Nietzsche's agon precludes radical inequality, and radical inequality precludes agonal struggle in Nietzsche's sense, as some agonistic democratic theorists today would have it.[7]

As a dynamic concept, Nietzsche's agon is inherently elastic, and the agonal dynamic takes a variety of different forms in the different contexts and texts discussed in the following chapters. Indeed, I prefer to think of the concept along the lines of Kant's notion of reflective judgement, as so many attempts on Nietzsche's part to describe conceptually the dynamic relations of tension specific to the contexts he considers in their qualitative singularity, and with their own affective signature, for which there are no concepts at hand. In this vein, each chapter presents a separate study of a specific problem in Nietzsche's thought and the way(s) in which the agon throws light on the problem, as well as Nietzsche's response to it. Each chapter should therefore be intelligible on its own. At the same time, some cross-references to other chapters have been necessary in order to minimise repetition of some of the recurrent themes and concepts, or in order to indicate where the detailed exposition of a given point can be found. While, for this reason, the book does not present a cumulative argument, the sequence of chapters does approximate the chronology of my research into the agon and so tracks a trajectory of thought. The principal trajectory is from the subject-position – the antagonists' affects, goals, desires, dispositions, the agonal 'experience' – as the key to understanding agonal interaction, to an *impersonal*, medial position in the relations *between* them. This move goes against the grain of the literature on the agon, in which agonal agency is thought exclusively from the subject-position, and its unique qualities as a measured form of antagonism are derived from agential dispositions, such as self-restraint, 'agonistic respect', 'equal regard' or even 'empathy'.[8] The argument for a medial reading of the agon

---

chy' or 'rank' are not mentioned (even where he comes closest to Heraclitus in 38[12], KSA 11.610). In Tuncel 2009 (169, note 55) he explains that he is 'simply referring to the different functions of the same culture of agon; there is agon at all the levels of the hierarchy, that is to say, gods, heroes, demigods, and judges are all agonistic', again without references to Nietzsche. In this article, however, Tuncel (2009, 175) does at least relate his hierarchy to equality: 'agon takes place in a highly hierarchical world although the contest is among approximate equals.'

7 I first raised this difficulty in Siemens 2001c, 518f. This goes not just for agonistic democratic theory, but for any struggle against radical inequality, as when Bullock (1997, 100) writes of Benjamin's views on class struggle that he 'finally abandons the element of agonism, of direct struggle by human agency against the ruling context that constrains and reduces the domain of human experience.'

8 For 'agonistic respect' see Hatab 2013, 68–70, 189, 191, 220; also 60, 97–107 on 'equal regard', and Schrift 1999 for a response. For respect as 'empathy for what we are not', a 'care for difference' see Connolly 1991, 159, 166, 178. For a non-Nietzschean version of agonistic respect as a prerequisite for

is introduced in chapter 2 and is tracked in relation to key concepts such as agonal measure, law and justice in succeeding chapters, so that the book can be read as an

---

agonistic democracy, see Mouffe 2005, 14, 102. For a discussion of agonistic respect centered on Mouffe and Connolly, see Minkkinen 2020, 438 f. This is a brief and uncritical discussion, in which he tries in vain to connect both authors back to Nietzsche's agon and accepts at face value Mouffe's claim that respect is sufficient to turn the figure of an enemy into an 'agonistic adversary', ignoring existing criticisms of Mouffe. For a critique of agonistic respect, see Siemens 2013. The only other author I have come across who formulates a Nietzschean critique of respect in all too 'tame' political versions of agonism is Brandon Turner, who rightly argues that 'from the *fact* of difference the claim of respect does not follow; and [...] that the agon is not an institution of respect' (Turner 2015, 7). His attempt to capture the experience of the agon includes interesting remarks on e.g. the 'bounded fervour' of the contestants (Turner 2015, 11), but he overplays his hand by claiming that the agon is motivated by 'a desire for *disrespect:* a desire to test oneself against another, *to order oneself vertically, hierarchically*' (Turner 2015, 8). 'Disrespect' misrepresents Nietzsche's account of jealousy in HW (see chapter 5, p. 130 ff.), and Turner's emphasis on hierarchy underestimates the importance of approximate equality of power as a precondition for the agon (see chapter 2, p. 61 ff.). His paper is moreover marred by a tendency – shared with many readers – to read notions specific to the later Nietzsche, such as will to power, back into his early thought on the agon, as if it was already there in all but name, rather than a later development in his thinking. Clearly, connections between the early concept of the agon and Nietzsche's later thought are important, but they need to be made in ways that do not negate changes and the development of his thought.

Two cases in the literature are worth mentioning.

Acampora (2013, 98 f.) draws on GD Alten 3 to argue that Nietzsche's early account of the Greek agon 'foreshadows' the idea of will to power. But there are at least four salient differences between them that go unmentioned: 1. Nietzsche's Greek agon does not share the expansionist dynamic of the will to power. 2. Nor is it bent on power and overpowering, but is oriented instead towards excellence, greatness, honour and fame through victory. 3. Nietzsche's emphasis on inequality as the normal condition for will to power contrasts with the accent on approximate equality of power in the Greek agon. And 4. Nietzsche's Greek agon or *Wettkampf* is marked by a sense of measure, precluding destruction (unlike will to power), which is aligned instead with the *Vernichtungskampf* and the 'evil Eris'. The tension between the agon and will to power is perhaps most evident in JGB 259 (see Siemens 2001c, 515 f.).

In his effort to show 'agon symbolism' throughout Nietzsche's thought, Tuncel (2009) projects not just his later concern with *Rangordnung* or hierarchy into his concept of the agon (see note 6), but also the will to power with claims about 'a relation of obedience and command' among agonal contestants, and claims about the weak having to 'serve the strong; the losing contestants must accept their defeat and look up to the strong' (Tuncel 2009, 175 f.). Commanding and obeying are utterly alien to Nietzsche's concept of the agon and were born of Nietzsche's dissatisfaction in 1884 with mechanistic and teleological explanations of self-regulation, as Müller-Lauter (1978, 209 ff.) has shown. Furthermore, the view of the weak 'having to serve the strong' is not only alien to Nietzsche's understanding of obeying, which is intrinsically related to commanding and marked by activity and resistance (see e.g. 11[134], KSA 9.491; 36[22] 11.560; 37[4], KSA 11.577; 38[7], KSA 11.606; 40[55], KSA 11.655); it is also utterly alien to the Greek contestants' experience of losing, which was marked by shame. See e.g. Pindar's 8th Ode and Adkins 1960, 158 f.; see also Burckhardt (1999, esp. 81 ff.) and Gouldner (1965, esp. 49–51, 81 ff.) on the agon for honour and status as a zero-sum game, on the shame of losing, and on shame culture.

argument for the necessity of thinking about this particular form of conflict from a 'third' standpoint in the agonal relations between the agents.

Another, related trajectory is traced in the book, which begins with a programmatic account of the agon and its promise for deciphering the dynamics of Nietzschean critique, and ends by confronting the limits of the agon and its limitations as a hermeneutic device. The problem of total affirmation – one of the most intractable problems in Nietzsche's thought – is the rock against which the agon founders. The total affirmation of reality as antagonistic (and not just agonal) multiplicity marks the point at which we need to move beyond the confines of the agon and understand better Nietzsche's *ontology of conflict*. As such, the problem of affirmation also marks the point at which my work moved into Nietzsche's broader thought on conflict, some of the results of which will appear in a forthcoming book on *Nietzsche contra Kant as Thinkers of Conflict*.

All the chapters in the book share a number of presuppositions concerning Nietzsche's philosophical project (I) and the character of Nietzsche's texts (II), which I would like to spell out in advance. Together they constitute the basic frame of reference for the book.

I Critical Transvaluation (*Umwertung*)

Throughout the book, I take Nietzsche to be a philosopher of life, whose project from the beginning to the end of his productive life is to contest the prevailing values of European culture in the name of life. Drawing on Nietzsche's own characterization of his life-long task from the late writings, I call this Nietzsche's project *of critical transvaluation (Umwertung)*.[9] Against the prevailing values of European – i.e. Christian-Platonic – culture, whether metaphysical, moral or religious, Nietzsche attempts, time and again, *to raise life as the highest value*. At stake in the project of transvaluation is the problem of *overcoming*: how to overcome theoretical discourse (meta-

---

[9] For 'Umwerthung' or 'Umwerthung aller [OR der (bisherigen)] Werthe' as a label for Nietzsche's task, see: GD Vorwort, KSA 6.57f. (with reference to AC); GD Irrthümer 2, KSA 6.89; GD Alten 5, KSA 6.160 (with reference to GT); AC 13, KSA 6.179; AC 62, KSA 6.253; EH Motto, KSA 6.263 (with reference to AC; cf. 23[14], KSA 13.613); EH weise 1, KSA 6.266 (cf. 24[1], KSA 13.631); EH klug 9, KSA 6.294; EH Bücher (MA 6), KSA 6.328 (with reference to MA); EH Bücher (M 1), KSA 6.330 (with reference to M); EH Bücher (JGB 1), KSA 6.350 (with reference to JGB); EH Bücher (GM), KSA 6.352 (with reference to AC?); EH Bücher (GD 3), KSA 6.355f. (with reference to AC); EH Schicksal 1, KSA 6.365 (cf. 25[6], KSA 13.640); 26[284], KSA 11.225; 6[25], KSA 12.242; 9[66], KSA 12.370; 9[77], KSA 12.375f.; 11[38], KSA 13.20; 16[43], KSA 13.501; 23[3], KSA 13.603.

For 'Umwerthung aller [or: der] Werthe' as the title / subtitle of the planned work 'Der Wille zur Macht', see: GM III 27, KSA 5.409; 2[100], KSA 12.109; 5[75], KSA 12.111; 6[26], KSA 12.243; 9[164], KSA 12.247; 11[411], KSA 13.190; 11[414], KSA 13.192f.; 14[78], KSA 13.257; 14[136], KSA 13.320; 14[156], KSA 13.321; 15[100], KSA 13.466; 16[86], KSA 13.515; 18[17], KSA 13.537; 25[11], KSA 13.642.

physics), morality and religion *in the name of life*, its affirmation and elevation, intensification (*Steigerung*) or 'greatness'.

Nietzsche's transvaluative project has its sources in a sustained critique of moral values, culminating in a critical diagnosis of modernity. His style of critique receives its clearest formulation in the Preface to GM, as a questioning of the value of our most cherished, unquestioned values in the light of an investigation into their provenance (*Herkunft*):

> [W]e are in need of a *critique* of moral values, *the value of these values itself is for once to be put in question* – and for that a knowledge is needed of the conditions and circumstances out of which they grew, under which they have developed and shifted [...] (GM Vorrede 6, KSA 5.253)

The question of provenance (conditions, circumstances) serves to undermine the self-understanding of morality as a sovereign sphere of validity by collapsing values onto the plane of immanence. Given Nietzsche's negatively-derived one-world hypothesis, values are viewed as immanent to life, not transcendent, as really lived or 'grey' values; they are placed in relation to the life-forms or types (individual and collective) that produce them and which they inform, guide and sustain, as well as the broader (socio-physiological-political) conditions under which they emerge and thrive.[10] These considerations bear on the question of *the value* of these values, which comes down to a *differential evaluation* of values in terms of the value or quality of life they make possible. Nietzsche's questioning concerns the forms of life, the dispositions, attitudes, or types that flourish under the rule of a given value or set of values: What form of life is conditioned, preserved, or fostered by the values in question, and what quality of life does it exhibit?

> Have they until now inhibited or furthered human thriving [*Gedeihen*]? Are they signs of need, impoverishment, degeneration in life? Or, on the contrary, does the fullness, strength, the will of life betray itself in them, its courage, its confidence, its future? (GM Vorrede 3, KSA 5.250)

---

10 In a *Nachlass* note he calls this the 'real [*wirkliche*] critique of the moral ideal' and goes on to refer to three human types:
'"*Wir Immoralisten*"
wirkliche Kritik des moralischen Ideals
– des guten Menschen, des Heiligen, des
Weisen
– von der Verleumdung der sogenannten
bösen Eigenschaften
– welchen Sinn haben die verschiedenen
moralischen Interpretationen?
– was ist die Gefahr der jetzt in Europa
herrschenden Interpretation?
– was ist das Maaß, woran gemessen werden
kann? ("Wille zur Macht")' (2[185] , KSA 12.158f.)

The upshot of Nietzsche's critique of Christian-Platonic values is that they derive from, and sustain, forms of life and willing that are *turned against life* and specifically: its sources in the body, the drives and the passions. Moreover, two thousand years of life-negation, he contends, have had devastating consequences for those forms of life,[11] afflicting them with a pathology designated as 'nihilism', 'degeneration' and 'décadence', and diagnosed variously as: moral bankruptcy; the death of God and the ensuing crisis of authority; the devaluation of our highest values; the loss of 'organising powers' and its consequences in processes of disgregation, dissolution (*Auflösung*), exhaustion (*Erschöpfung*) and an incapacity to create or 'posit productively a goal for oneself' (9[35], KSA 12.350 f.); the depletion of voluntaristic resources; the debilitation and contraction (*Verkleinerung*) of the human being. It is against this background that Nietzsche's vocation to be a philosopher of life and his project of transvaluation must be understood: as an attempt to raise life as the highest value against life-negating values, to take a standpoint in life, its affirmation and enhancement, so as to question, resist and overcome the forms of life-negation underpinning Christian-Platonic values and their devastating consequences for the value and quality of those life-forms. The task, in Eric Blondel's words, is to make his texts be the 'saying of life' and a 'yes-saying to life'.

II Saying, Yes-Saying and Unsaying

In the opening chapters of *Nietzsche: The Body and Culture* (1991), Blondel offers an introduction to reading Nietzsche which is valuable in at least two respects: first, for the way he characterises the peculiar, unique quality of Nietzsche's texts vis-à-vis the philosophical tradition, what he calls the 'enigma' of Nietzsche's text; and then for the way he connects this to the concern that dominates Nietzsche's thought from beginning to end – how to say life, and how to say yes to life. The 'enigma' points to a tension between two qualities or tendencies in Nietzsche's texts. On the one hand, the texts exhibit a clearly recognizable philosophical will to truth – an effort to make philosophical claims by means of a coherent, univocal discourse. On the other hand, there is 'the rest', 'what *inside* Nietzsche's text remains *outside* discourse, whatever we call it, be it drives, rhetoric, breaks, incoherences, *Versuch*, music, comedy, solemnity, art, allusions or language games' (Blondel 1991, 5, 7); in short, that which is heterogeneous to discourse and resists discursive analysis and synthesis. But why, we may ask, should Nietzsche's texts take this enigmatic form? What is at stake? And how are we, as readers, to deal with these texts, which contain, yet also exceed, discourse?

---

11 See note 2[184] 1.158, where Nietzsche calls this '*My problem*':
'*Mein Problem:* Welchen Schaden hat die Menschheit
bisher von der Moral sowohl wie von ihrer Moralität gehabt?
Schaden am Geiste usw.'

To begin with the second question: A purely discursive analysis, typical of philosophical readings, seizes on what is a product of discursive thought – the thematic dimension of the text – at the price of writing off everything else as mere rhetoric or artistry. In so doing, it effaces the uniqueness of Nietzsche's texts, their standing both within and outside the philosophical tradition. On the other hand, aestheticist readings that place the text wholly outside philosophical discourse – as a prophetic *Schwärmerei*, an eclectic *Phantasieren* or a higher kind of gossip – miss the point that Nietzsche does maintain a discourse. Against these two extremes, Blondel calls for 'an open confrontation with the *enigma* of Nietzsche's text' (Blondel 1991, 4), and that means: to find ways *to connect* what is open to discursive formulation – the *thematic* dimension of the text – and what resists and mocks discursive treatment – the *performative* dimensions of the text (Blondel 1991, 7). Until we are able to link Nietzsche's discourse with the rest without reduction, we have failed to address the unique status of his texts vis-à-vis the philosophical tradition.

As for the first question, the 'why' of Nietzsche's enigmatic style, Blondel proposes a two-fold response. On the one hand, he appeals to Nietzsche's vocation to be the philosopher of life and to make his text be the saying of life. On the other hand, Blondel points to the profound contradiction or gap that divides thought, theory and discourse – the discourse that would enable the saying – from the life to which this saying is to refer. Without doubt, it is from Schopenhauer that Nietzsche receives the shock that determines the direction his thought will take. It is Schopenhauer who first formulated the questions unleashed by the demise of Christian faith, questions which 'an astronomer of the soul could have calculated to the day and hour' (FW 357, KSA 3.599 f.): What is the sense (*Sinn*) or purpose of living (*Wozu Leben*)? And what is the value (*Werth*) of living? What is existence worth? Against Schopenhauer, however, Nietzsche takes it as his task, not to answer in the negative – because living has no meaning, it has no value – but to take the side of life and make his writing become the saying and yes-saying of life. However, this vocation confronts him with an insurmountable difficulty, a problem that afflicts the constitution of meaning through stable signification; that is, the very discourse that would be the saying and yes-saying of life.

Following Blondel (1991, 22 ff.), the problem can be formulated as follows: Philosophical discourse – exemplified by classical rational discourse – is characterised by three aims: univocity ('clarity'); logical continuity (i.e. coherence); and architectonic structure (systematic and demonstrative linkage of terms, based on fundamental principles and/or axioms). The first aim, clarity, requires an unambiguous correspondence between the key terms in the text and the concepts they signify. The univocal meaning of a discourse is to be established by ensuring that each term or signifier brings to presence a single conceptual signified. This is achieved by inscribing a code that fixes the links between signifier and signified, and so regulates our understanding of the text. The code can be explicit – in the form of definitions and/or axioms – or implicit. As an attempt to master and contain within discourse the code that regulates its understanding, this procedure seeks to stabilise discourse as a self-contained, closed and perfectly coherent signifying whole which imposes a fixed meaning on its external referent; a procedure that is reinforced by the further aims of philosophical discourse, logical continuity and architectonic structure. In this manner, the exteriority of the text is to be 'reduced', its exposure to contingency and to disruption from the surge of life is to be minimised.

Against this background, the problem of life-affirmation can be recast as a problem of closure. For the upshot of Nietzsche's genealogical critique of western values, beginning with the figure of Socrates, is that the 'will to discursive closure' in the name of stable signification and eternal truth (metaphysics), is in fact an attempted *closure against time and against life* that originates in a willing that is turned against the will. Now, if Nietzsche is right that our values originate in a life-form that is turned against life: the attempted closure of theoretical discourse against time and the senses *in the name of eternal truth* (as in metaphysics), and the concurrent war of annihilation against the instincts *in the name of virtue* (as in the moral demand of religion and metaphysics); if, in short, these values originate in a willing that is turned against the will, then they cannot be effectively challenged by a purely theoretical discourse that suppresses the body and closes itself off against the will. Such a discourse – even if it pitted life, its affirmation and elevation, against western values – would fall prey to a *performative* contradiction: that is, in its performance – as a discourse of values – it would undermine its discursive intention. So how, at the level of discourse, is Nietzsche to engage the entire problematic of values that issues from his genealogical critique? A strictly conceptual discourse of values will just replicate what Nietzsche is contesting – the illusory closure against time and the life of the body, the theoretical and moral denial of the will on the part of the Christian-Platonic will. What Nietzsche needs to do is confound the 'will to closure' endemic to discourse, to open up his discourse towards life – *without* undoing its discursive force. He needs to *complement* or *supplement* his discursive challenge with a *performative* challenge that *enacts* the concept of life raised and pitted against western values.

Blondel offers a paradoxical but compelling account of Nietzsche's response to this task with the claim that his text enacts a dynamic of saying and unsaying (*dire et dédire*), a dynamic that also signifies life as an essentially ambiguous, ever-shifting, open-ended play of forces in conflict, and so enables the text to say life, to 'live':

> If a truth can be articulated about the body, life, reality, it can signify only through the text's saying (*le dire*), but also in the sense that it is a recanting or unsaying (*un dédire*). If, for discourse, a text can be considered 'false' since it is plurivocal, for Nietzsche, on the contrary, it is discourse which, in the face of the text as the saying of becoming, is a fiction: a repression of textual movement, a degraded text. (Blondel 1991, 29f.)

As a 'saying', Nietzsche's text enables him to maintain a discourse and so to speak up against metaphysics and life-negating values, while in 'unsaying' what is said he avoids repeating the closure against life that he criticises discursively.¹² At the same time, the dynamic of saying-unsaying 'signifies' the dynamic character of life and the body – less as a sequence of signifieds than through the signifying *process:*

> In Nietzsche, the text is charged, not with designating signifieds (whose discourse has the task of reducing exteriority as much as possible), but with being the signifying process of the body and life, operating as the movement and labour of the text. (Blondel 1991, 29)

Since the text, unlike discourse, does not master or contain the code or codes that regulate understanding it, there is no 'in-itself' of the text, no 'explanation' of it in this sense, but only interpretation, that is, the imposition of codes exterior to the text (cf. Blondel 1991, 241).

Blondel's distinction between text and discourse is compelling because it takes up the discursive and anti-discursive aspects of Nietzsche's writing, enabling us to connect and make sense of them against the problem-background of life-affirmation and closure sketched above. The movement of 'saying and unsaying' enables us to see how Nietzsche maintains a discourse, while breaking the contrived closure of discourse and opening it up to its Other by supplementing it with a *performative* challenge that *enacts* the concept of life to be affirmed. The movement of 'saying and unsaying' is also compelling because it captures a characteristic or recurrent feature of Nietzsche's style of writing, all-too familiar to any reader: his tendency to contest a position and then retract his contention, to oppose a claim only to undo his counter-claim, to posit and then throw his posit in question. In the course of this book, we will have occasion to see the variegated forms this dynamic takes in his work, but common to all is a double-movement of 'Absolutsetzung' and 'Nicht-Absolutsetzung'.¹³

From a discursive point of view, all of this is hard to make sense of, and it makes Nietzsche's style look confused or simply incoherent. In *The Body and Culture*, Blondel's response is to appeal to metaphor Indeed, his book is a detailed study of the ways in which Nietzsche uses metaphors. It is, he argues, through metaphor that Nietzsche subverts and loses what he builds conceptually, so as not to fix and lose the dynamic character of the body and life (Blondel 1991, 28f.). And it is Nietzsche's metaphors that give a coherence to his thought that escapes the trap of discursive closure on one side, and the charge of incoherence on the other. In this book, the concept of metaphor or *Übertragung* also plays an important role in

---

12 'It cannot be denied that Nietzsche maintains a discourse. But Nietzsche knows that maintaining this discourse means getting trapped in a closed ('metaphysical' or 'moral') concept of life and so of culture. He must therefore unsay or retract what he says.' (Blondel 1991, 248).
13 Müller-Lauter 1971, 113. Chapter 5 establishes this motif with regard to the will to truth, chapters 6 and 7 then trace it to the figure of the *Übermensch* and the thought of Eternal Recurrence. See also the illuminating discussion focused on the problem of struggle in van Tongeren 1988, chapter 5, § 3.1 and chapter 6. My agonal account of this double-movement offers a response to these authors, both of whom see it as deeply problematic.

a number of chapters, but it is Nietzsche's concept of the Greek agon, not metaphor, that serves as the 'master key' to his texts. From a perspective in agonal contention, the movement of 'saying and unsaying' begins to make sense as a coherent practice governed by a dynamic of empowerment-disempowerment. Instead of isolating utterances and identifying Nietzsche with 'contradictory' positions, this book invites you to situate his thinking within an agonal 'play of forces' (*Wettspiel der Kräfte*) that implicates us as readers, not just his chosen adversary, in a collective contestation of values.

My thesis in this book is three-fold:

First, that Nietzsche does not just oppose morality, religion, metaphysics or Platonism from *within* theoretical discourse. His opposition takes the form of an artistic-cultural practice – the agon –which sustains, regulates and organises his discourse.

Second, that agonal culture represents or pre-figures the *highest form of life* for Nietzsche, and it does so as a pluralistic, affirmative practice of life-as-art.

Third, that Nietzsche's text *is itself* agonal culture, as the *affirmative interpretation of life* thematised in his work as the highest form of life – the rebirth of tragic culture.

III The Chapters

The book opens by taking up the popular image of Nietzsche as a philosopher of unbridled violence who glorifies power and the pathos of aggression. This image is confronted, not by trying to subtract violent, destructive impulses from his thought, but by asking whether they make for destruction as a necessary element of his life-project of critical transvaluation. Nietzsche's project, I argue, involves a total critique of western values in the name of life, yet he is acutely aware of the self-referential implications of total critique and the logic of self-destruction that threatens it. Drawing on Nietzsche's reflections on 'critical history' in UB II, I argue that Nietzsche seeks a 'limit in the negation of the past'. In order to examine what form this might take in practice, I draw on Nietzsche's own account of his 'war-praxis' in *Ecce Homo*, with an emphasis on the moments of limitation. Against this background, the agon is introduced as a style of confrontation that allows for the total critique of values, while arresting the logic of self-destruction through a code of limited violence; 'agonal mastery' displaces destruction as the goal of critique. In the final section, the agonal pathos of envy is used to explicate the dynamic of agonal critique as an alternative to total warfare, and to flesh out the concept of mastery that separates the two.

The next **chapter (2)** is devoted to Nietzsche's concept of the Greek agon through a close interpretation of its most celebrated appearance: *Homer's Wettkampf* (and surrounding notes). At issue in this text is the question 'What is humanity?' For Nietzsche, this is at once an ontological question concerning the 'human' and its relation to the 'inhuman' or 'nature', as well as an ethical question concerning agonal agency: the 'great deeds and works' that enhance the concept 'human' by extending the range of human capacities and possibilities. Against the humanist / neo-humanist separation of the 'human' from nature and its opposition to the 'inhuman' or 'natural', Nietzsche advances the agon as a political and cultural regime that acknowledged their entwinement: the brutal and destructive sources of the great achievements of Greek civilization, but was able to measure them and turn them into creative forces. Behind Nietzsche's anti-humanist polemic are two key problems: the affirmation of life in its irredeemably cruel and conflictual character, what Nietzsche calls the all-pervasive war of annihilation or *Vernichtungskampf*; and how to co-ordinate life-affirmation with the measure needed for social life. For Nietzsche, agonal measure is not imposed from the outside; it is immanent to agonal contestation. The agon is valued as a form of conflict that co-ordinated excess and measure (*Übermaas* and *Maass*) through an institution that *both* stimulated the creative freedom of a plurality of individuals *and* limited its forms of expression. The question is how the agon generates this non-coercive form of measure. In response, the agonal affects of envy and ambition are analysed as sources of both reciprocal stimulation and reciprocal limitation, but the case is then made for the medial sense of agonal measure. The argument for the medial sense of agonal measure passes through the concept of play (*Wettspiel der Kräfte*), the social ontology of tension in agonal culture, and the medial concept of equilibrium (*Gleichgewicht*), understood as the condition *sine qua non* for agonal agency. (This argument is taken further in different contexts in chapters 7 and 8.) But Nietzsche's transvaluation of humanism would remain incomplete without a positive answer to the question 'What is humanity?' and the chapter concludes by considering what his constructive counter-ideal of humanity might look like. In order to reconnect what humanism separates – the 'human' from the 'inhuman' or 'natural' – an *agonal model of human nature* is proposed, a dynamic tension of ever-changing relations of antagonism between 'spirit' (*Geist*) and the passions, consciousness and the instincts, *Maass* and *Übermaass*. Each provokes or invokes the (resistance of the) other as a necessary counter-force or counter-position (*sich gegenseitig reizen*), while limiting or delimiting the forms its antagonism can take. This 'vertical' agon *within* each antagonist is proposed as the 'inner' or phenomenological dimension of the 'horizontal', social agon *between* individuals, grounded in the medial concept of approximate equilibrium. It is a social, not an individual achievement.

Chapter 3 draws on the first two chapters in order to introduce the performative dimension of Nietzsche's engagement with the agon. The case for a performative reading of the agon, as the dynamic principle regulating Nietzsche's transvaluative discourse, is made against the background of Nietzsche's critical diagnosis of the present as a condition of décadence and nihilism. If, as Blondel argues, philosophical discourse is governed by the will to closure for the sake of stable signification, how can Nietzsche avoid replicating in *his* discourse what he would contest? – the will to closure against time and the life of the body, the theoretical and moral denial of the will that culminates in décadence? And how is he to authorise the affirmative discourse of life that he would raise against life-negating values, given the crisis of authority brought on by the death of God? In response, I argue that Nietzsche looks for ways to open up his discourse towards life, to *supplement* his discursive challenge with a *performative* challenge that *enacts through agonal confrontation* the highest concept of life: the pluralistic, affirmative practice of life-as-art. As an artistic-cultural practice that sustains, regulates and organises Nietzsche's discourse, the agon is adopted by him as a fiction, a feint of writing, but one that is pluralistic and can only work by engaging a community of readers in a collective contestation of values. Like Zarathustra, Nietzsche is dependent on a human community to authorise his affirmative discourse, but in the absence of such a community, he can only create fictional communities which would stimulate and guide actual readers in the collective creation of affirmative values beyond good and evil. In the next part of the chapter, the implications of the agon for Nietzsche's transvaluative discourse are examined in detail. The formal and dynamic qualities of the agon make for a complex interplay of limited negation and affirmation. They also give an open-ended, inconclusive turn to transvaluation, as a project that puts the question of overcoming, as well as the very standard or measure of overcoming, into play. In the concluding section, the question of agonal culture is taken up and examined. As the transposition or transference *(Über-tragung)* of the excessive, destructive affects of the *Vernichtungskampf* (personified as the 'evil' Eris goddess) into the measured, constructive cultural forces of the *Wettkampf* (the 'good' Eris goddess), agonal culture is analysed as an aesthetic *techne* inspired by the poets and placed in opposition to the war against the passions waged by 'morality as anti-nature' (GD), characteristic of the church, as well as humanism.

The topic of **chapter 4** is Nietzsche's critique of Socrates in *Die Geburt der Tragödie* (GT), understood as his 'first act of transvaluation' (GD). At issue in GT is the relation between theory (*Wissenschaft*), art and life, and the transvaluation of their Platonic/Socratic configuration in the name of life-affirmation. In Plato's *Phaedo*, I argue, *art serves as an ancilla of philosophy, understood as a preparation for wisdom-in-death*. In GT, however, death is displaced by life-as-art as the end of philosophical desire. Nietzsche engages in a narrative contest with Plato and effectively rewrites the *Phaedo* around the figure of the music-practising Socrates, such that now *philosophy or theory serves as an ancilla or preparation for art-as-life / life-as-art*. This narrative contest allows for two readings of Nietzsche's critique. On the first reading, Nietzsche's *Phaedo* 'encodes' an immanent critique of Socrates: while critical of others' claims to knowledge, Socrates fails to put his own form of questioning (*ti esti?*) into question and so fails to realise his own demand to limit knowledge – until he practices art. At issue on this interpretation is not just the question of critique, but also Nietzsche's demand for life-affirmation or 'aesthetic justification', which he raises against the Socratic vision of philosophy as a preparation for dying, understood as closure: the closure of thought (or *Wissenschaft*) against life and the body. At issue in the second, agonal reading is Socrates' theoretical optimism and the problem of closure raised by his belief in the possibility of a completely closed and coherent interpretation of life. By tracking an agonal dynamic of reciprocal empowerment-disempowerment in Nietzsche's account of Socrates, I argue that Nietzsche is able to contest the Socratic claim to closure – *without* falling into the trap of closure in negating the possibility of closure. On this basis, a general model of agonal critique is proposed in the last section, comprising two moments: the active contention of a given claim, driven by the Socratic demand to limit knowledge (suspicion), followed by the recoil of critique on the critic, a retraction or unsaying (Blondel) that inscribes a limit in its negation of the other. This model of critique is then exemplified in a number of interpretations of Nietzsche's later texts.

Chapter 5 is devoted to the problem of modernity as set out in the *Unzeitgemässe Betrachtungen*, and two of Nietzsche's formulations in particular: the demand for original values or norms in the form of radically individual self-legislation (UB III), and the demand for an original German culture (UB I). At stake in both is a problem of origins, of unprecedented birth and formation (*Bildung*). Indeed, both are very much a problem of originality as developed by Kant in his reflections on genius in the *Critique of Judgement*, and in this chapter I argue that Nietzsche approaches his problems in the UB through an engagement *with and against* Kantian genius. Both thinkers face the same problem of thinking originality together with classical precedent, tradition and historicity, shifting the question of origins towards that of creative succession (*Nachfolge*). Drawn by the *radical freedom* of Kantian genius, Nietzsche seeks to break Kant's opposition between creative freedom in *Nachfolge* and passive mimesis (*Nachahmung*), which precludes creative originality. Taking up the moment of antagonism implicit in Kantian *Nachfolge*, he develops a notion of *agonal mimesis* (between one genius and another, one culture and another) that conjugates creative originality with tradition or classical precedent in a way that eludes Kant.

The first part of the chapter focuses on the relation between one (would-be) genius and his exemplar, as the key to self-legislation in UB III. Nietzsche casts Schopenhauer, his exemplar, in the image of Kantian genius, as a *disposition of nature that makes itself into the law*. A discussion of Kant's attempts to reconcile originality with classical precedent through the notion of *Nachfolge* culminates in the thesis that Nietzsche takes up the antagonistic moment in Kantian *Nachfolge*, but supplements and corrects it through a notion of agonal *Betrachtung*, comprising three moments: (1) an *antagonistic* moment of emancipation and overcoming with (2) a *mimetic* moment of creative reception and learning (excluded by Kant) and (3) an *affirmative* moment of gratitude or honouring (*Dankbarkeit, Verehrung*), which is absent in Kant. The dynamic of mimetic overcoming and acknowledgement in Nietzsche's agonal concept of *Betrachten* is worked out through an examination of his confrontation with Wagnerian genius in UB IV and then fleshed out through an analysis of agonal jealousy. Drawing on Nietzsche's account in *Homer's Wettkampf*, I argue that jealousy combines the demand for originality and the freedom to create a new rule or law with the need to receive, imitate or appropriate the rules and works of others.

In the second part of the chapter, the agonal concept of *Betrachten* is brought to bear on the problem of original German culture. For Nietzsche, the problem of German culture is ontological: the *non-existence* of the German, and the question I raise concerns Nietzsche's appeal to the Greeks: Why the Greeks? And how to engage with them in a way that can give birth to German culture? Against Philippe Lacoue-Labarthe (1990, 223), I argue that it does not involve 'a non-historical relation to the being, itself unhistorical, of the Greeks'. On the contrary, Nietzsche emphasises the non-autochthonous character of Greek culture and the Greeks' extraordinary ability to learn from other cultures, past and alien. What Nietzsche calls their 'art of fruitful learning' involves an agonal mimesis of past and alien cultures – the mimetic appropriation and overcoming of their neighbours' achievements in the creation of their own philosophies, gods and values. Indeed, Nietzsche's own agonal style of *Betrachten* is best understood as a mimetic doubling of the agonal Greeks and their agonal *techne* of appropriation through contention. It is just such a relation of antagonistic or *agonal mimesis* between German and Greek culture, analogous to that between one genius and another, that Nietzsche proposes in response to the problem of German culture; a relation that conjugates creative freedom and originality with receptivity and openness to what is alien (*das Fremde*). Thus the questions of origin and identity devolve into a matter of antagonistic exchange or 'agonal mimesis' with past and alien cultures. For Nietzsche, then, the 'origin' of German culture lies in *learning from the Greeks, as a past and alien culture, how to learn from cultures past and alien*. It is therefore *as a consequence* of his engagement with the Greeks that Nietzsche overcomes and goes beyond Greek culture to investigate its multiple sources; for we are, in his words, a 'multiplication of many pasts'.

Chapters 6 and **7** investigate the problems of legislation and law in their intersections with the concept of the agon, while asking what light these problems throw on the agon. In Nietzsche's thought, the concept of (self–)legislation or (*Selbst–*)*Gesetzgebung*, discussed in **chapter 6**, is profoundly ambivalent. On the one hand, it is part and parcel of his ontology of life, conceived as an incessant and multiple positing or *Setzen* of being; on the other hand, the traditional concepts of law (universal, unifying, eternal), especially the moral law, are radically life-negating. But *Gesetzgebung* is also the only resource we have against the moral law, as we see in Nietzsche's repeated attempts to formulate naturalistic, life-affirming counter-models of legislation, which are dynamic, active and pluralistic. In line with the psychologization of power in the nineteenth century, Nietzsche sees legislation as a function of individuated power, so that his thought revolves around the legislator as a type. The problematic of legislation is therefore studied in this chapter by considering three legislator-types, and reconstructing their chronological and systematic relations.

I begin with Schopenhauer (SE), whom Nietzsche casts as a legislator of laws that are radically individual and perfectionist in an Emersonian sense. This concept of self-legislation, I argue, is best understood as Nietzsche's response to the problem of modernity, construed as a crisis of dis-orientation and dis-integration. However, under the pressure of his divided loyalties to Wagner and Schopenhauer, Nietzsche is unable to formulate a life-affirming concept of legislation that addresses the problem of modernity, capitulating instead to a metaphysical affirmation of being against becoming. In *Richard Wagner in Bayreuth*, Nietzsche then tries to address this failure by casting Wagner as the 'organizational genius', capable of binding and containing a multiplicity of elements. Through this figure, I argue, Nietzsche describes a 'legislation from nowhere', which does justice to the demand for radically individual legislation in a way that overcomes the transcendence of becoming towards being in SE. However, this model remains flawed as a life-affirming and –enhancing form of legislation, since it fails to articulate the pluralistic character of life. The question is, then, what kind of legislation could articulate the temporal and pluralistic qualities of life?

This question is addressed by Nietzsche in the *Nachlass* of 1883, where Zarathustra is cast as a 'model of how to behave towards the law, insofar as he sublates the law of laws, morality, through higher ones'. At stake here is an agonal model of legislation designed to enhance the pluralistic and active qualities of life against the moral law: Zarathustra is to act as 'herald for many legislators', whose law serves not to subjugate and level a plurality of subjects, but to provoke them into self-legislation 'so that the particular individual discovers and strengthens itself through contradiction with it'. I examine the dynamic-pluralistic structure of Nietzsche's agonal model of legislation, and the extent to which it turns the 'unavoidable act of violence' in legislation into a stimulant towards self-legislation. However, these *Nachlass* notes culminate in a deferral of the task of legislation to the future, and the chapter ends by considering the motivations for this move towards 'legislators of the future', as well as the gains of Nietzsche's agonal model of legislation – above all, his insight into the *relational* character of self-legislation. This insight is taken up in the examination of law and community in the next chapter.

In **chapter 7** the notions of agonal culture and community (from chapter 3) and agonal measure (from chapter 2) are re-examined from a perspective in law. What is the nature and status of law in an 'agonal community'? In what sense can we speak of justice (*Gerechtigkeit, Dike*) as a standard of adjudication binding the public with agonal contestants, us as readers with Nietzsche's critical confrontations? The question of law is considered from a perspective in justice (Heraclitus' 'immanente dike'), from a perspective in ethics (Is there an agonal law of measure? A law of perfection?), and from a perspective in *sapientia* or wisdom-as-taste (PHG 3). Since for Nietzsche, the relation between law and life is profoundly ambivalent, the question concerns the right form or measure (*Maass*) of law, so that law works not just *against* life, but *with and against* it. My contention in this chapter is that Nietzsche locates the right measure of law in the concept of taste (*Geschmack*). Various features ascribed to taste in the philosophical tradition prior to Kant are traced to Nietzsche's texts, invoking a sense of community with substantive ethical and epistemic dimensions: an 'agonal community of taste'.

The argument begins by examining the concept of 'immanent lawfulness' (*immanente Gesetzmässigkeit*) that Nietzsche claims Heraclitus drew from the agon. In grappling with the problem of how a unitary and eternal law or justice (*Dike*) can be immanent to *polemos* (war) and multiplicity, Nietzsche appeals to the socialising, unifying powers of the agon evinced by the Panhellenic festivals, and the gradual emergence of a shared sense of justice and Hellenic identity among the Greek cities. The emergence of unitary justice, I argue, is best understood as a function of the festival character of the Panhellenic agons, and the temporal structure of the festival: as something that has its being or meaning (unitary justice) only in becoming and recurring (the ever different celebrations of the agonal festival). The implication is that unitary justice is immanent to the course taken by every agon (qua festival), as an 'infinitely sure measure of adjudicating judgement', which 'decides where victory is leaning'. The standpoint of adjudication, I argue, can only be *in the agonal relations between the contestants*. Nietzsche's agon is marked by a *medial sense of justice*.

The main topic of chapter 7 is the sense of community informing Nietzsche's project of transvaluation, which is examined under the sign of taste (*Geschmack*), understood as a *lawfulness without a law*. In order to examine the epistemic dimension of Nietzsche's sense of community, I turn to Nietzsche's discussion of pre-Socratic wisdom (PHG) as an episteme of taste, which is normative or law-like, without there being any actual laws or norms that could be used to ground or demonstrate its judgements. Wisdom is conceived by Nietzsche as a necessary supplement of science or *Wissenschaft*, which reaches in thought what science cannot think. I then turn to his perfectionism and the question of ethical law, which I interpret in line with the Kant's *sensus communis*, as a merely 'indeterminate norm' that authorises judgements of taste: Nietzsche's perfectionism works as a radically indeterminate norm that authorises transvaluative discourse by way of a futural ideal of humanity, pre-figured in agonal communities of taste. The argument passes through the seventeenth-century Spanish Jesuit philosopher Baltasar Gracián and a series of analogies between his concept of taste or *gusto* and the agon. Gracián's *gusto* is a social ideal, and the variety and conflict of *gustos* is the essence of taste. Like the agon, conflicts of taste cannot be resolved through fixed, explicit rules or standards; yet every judgement, Gracián insists, is right and complete. This paradox of justice, I argue, can only be grasped from the medial position, like Nietzsche's agonal concept of justice.

In the last part of the chapter, I revisit the agonal concept of measure (from chapter 2) and propose two analogies with Nietzsche's medial sense of law, both of which incorporate a medial sense of measure. The first situates the Greek agon in an important moment of human self-awareness, what the philologist Karl Reinhardt called the *transition from the heroic-superhuman to the problematic-human* – a diremption and conflict of the psyche clearly visible in agonal envy. This moment of human self-awareness, between the two poles of the possible and its limits, is enacted through the agonal dynamic of reciprocal provocation and reciprocal limitation within the bounds of measure. Reinhardt associates it, not with tragedy, but with the *Iliad*, where measure is not dictated by morality or a transcendent concept of justice, much less an act of self-restraint, but is the result of a diremption or 'equilibrium of sympathy' personified by Zeus. His place, the seat of adjudication, is located somewhere between human particularity and the universality of law, and it describes well the medial sense of measure as a lawfulness without a law. The second analogy is with Hannah Arendt's concept of political action, and the notion of 'principles' that she takes from Montesquieu. For Arendt, principles are the passions that animate free action, bringing political spaces into being, and there are some striking similarities between them and Nietzsche's medial sense of law. Arendt's central claim is that principles do not precede or guide performative actions in the manner of the intellect and will, but appear belatedly, as it were, in the performative act itself, and remain in force as long as the action itself. Like the laws of the agonal festival, principles only gain normative force through enactment; their identity of meaning over time is constituted through always-different acts. As the interactional sources of law necessary for action to be free, principles displace the meaning of free action from the subjective domain of intellectual deliberation and willing towards a medial position in the relations between agents.

Chapter 8 raises the question of therapy in the light of the self-referential implications of Nietzsche's critique of revenge and *ressentiment:* Is there a therapeutic dimension to the project of transvaluation comparable to Freudian psychotherapy? If we suppose that Nietzsche's thought repeats the logic of revenge in a *ressentiment* against *ressentiment*, the challenge for a therapeutic reading is to think through the *transformation* of revenge on the basis of *repetition*. With this formula, we have the key to Freud's psychoanalytic practice: repetition-compulsion in its manifestation as transference (*Übertragung*). Under the compulsion to repeat repressed experience patterns, the patient unwittingly transfers forgotten episodes onto the analytic relationship. As a *forgetful re-enactment* of hidden thought contents, transference (*Übertragung*) inhibits therapy by maintaining neurotic symptoms. Yet it also offers the analyst a displaced, metaphorical commentary on the unconscious text of hidden pathogenic instincts, as well as sources of energy for overcoming resistances and transforming sickness along the paths of remembering. In a similar vein, I argue, Nietzsche's transvaluative discourse provides an oblique metaphorical commentary on the 'unconscious text' of embodied *ressentiment:* a repetitive re-enactment or transference (*Übertragung*) of pathogenic, destructive impulses that harnesses their energy for transformative purposes. By superimposing the agon, as a model for Nietzsche's textual confrontations, on the *ressentiment* animating them, a therapeutic perspective emerges. As the transference (*Übertragung*) of Hesiod's 'evil Eris' into the 'good Eris' the agonal regime allows a *reactive* regime of *internalised* aggression to be *externalised* in *active* deeds of limited philosophical aggression – a therapeutic transformation of (self–)destructive impulses into constructive, philosophical impulses. Agonal transvaluation *enacts a compulsive-repetitive contestation of the sickness animating it*, releasing energy for an open-ended contestation of sickness that would empower us to *master* it; a goal akin to the analytic task of 'binding' or 'taming' (*Bändigung*) pathological drives.

At the same time, there are also significant differences, both theoretical and practical, between agonal and analytic therapy. In both, the pleasure principle is contested by the reality principle by exposing desire to the alterity and disorder of becoming. Yet Nietzsche replaces the healing power of consciousness (anamnesis) in Freud with processes of forgetful experience (*Einverseelung*) and incorporation (*Einverleibung*). The analytic goal of ego-development / –domination is displaced by an agonal tension between integrated, autonomous control and the disorder of affective multiplicity, between the relative unity of discourse and the multiplicity of the body. Nonetheless, the chapter ends by highlighting important affinities in the areas of sublimation, play and the goal of a *binding mastery (bändigende Herrschaft)* over pathological forces. The notion of mastery is explained in three stages, as: (1) the adaptation of vengeful, destructive desires to a reality that frustrates their satisfaction; (2) a *dynamic* sublimation of destructive human energies that both frees *and* binds them, affirms *and* limits them; and (3) the mastery over negativity and unsatisfied revenge through recourse to *play*, conceived as a non-pathological aspect of the death instinct.

In the **final chapter (9)**, I address one of the most intractable problems in Nietzsche's thought: the total affirmation of reality, as set out in one of his most perplexing books, *Ecce Homo*. This chapter rounds the book off with an attempt at self-critique that takes up the model of agonal critique from the opening chapter and inscribes its limits. The focus is on the relation between yes-saying and no-saying at the core of critical transvaluation: How can total affirmation be combined with the total critique of life-negating values? Nietzsche's favoured idiom of warfare (*Krieg, Kampf*) exhibits the incommensurability of these positions, but it also points to a deeper problem: Nietzsche's chosen target in EH is idealism, yet in waging war against idealism, he risks repeating idealism itself, which he characterises as a war to the death (*Todkrieg*) against other forms of life and thought.

The chapter begins by analysing idealist warfare as a form of oppositional thinking that seeks (1) to *separate* positively valued from negatively valued terms, in order (2) to *destroy* the negatively valued terms, and thereby (3) to eliminate opposition or war altogether, so as to make an absolute claim for its positive values. Nietzsche's own declared 'war-praxis' is then analysed as an *agonal* form of confrontational thinking that avoids repeating idealism by (1) *binding together* (not separating) opposed terms, (2) *preserving* (not destroying) its opponents or counter-values, thereby (3) preserving the dynamic or necessity of opposition or war. This model of warfare is, however, undermined by the affirmative and destructive excesses of *Ecce Homo*, catalogued in the third section of the chapter. These excesses motivate a different approach to the problem of yes– and no-saying, one that accommodates them by breaking with any single model or standpoint for Nietzschean transvaluation. On this approach, the affirmation of reality, understood as conflictual multiplicity, demands *first* the adoption of antagonistic positions with destructive intent against life-negating positions (idealism), but *then* the overcoming of any antagonistic position in favour of an 'impossible' or fictional standpoint in the *relations between* antagonists;

for only from a relational standpoint, I contend, can *all* antagonistic positions be affirmed. This approach is then generalised as a way to make sense of many of the idiosyncrasies of *Ecce Homo* – its fictional qualities, its excesses and incongruities. The chapter ends by applying this approach as a corrective to the account of *Umwertung* in EH proposed by philosopher-philologist Gerd Schank. Through a historical-philological analysis of the word 'gegen', he argues for a comparative, agonal reading of transvaluation that precludes destructive excesses. This account, I argue, can only make sense of the affirmative and destructive excesses of Nietzsche's text if supplemented by a fictional standpoint in the relations *between* the antagonistic positions of 'Dionysos against [*gegen*] the Crucified'.

Chapter 1
The Art of Limited Warfare: Nietzsche's Hammer and the Need to Find a Limit in Negation

Introduction

It is not unusual, following the subtitle of *Twilight of the Idols*, to see Nietzsche as one who 'philosophises with a hammer'. In the foreword, he writes of warfare as a kind of panacea:

> A *transvaluation of all values:* this question mark, so dark and so monstrous that it casts a shadow over the one who poses it – a destiny of a task like this forces him to run out into the sunlight every moment to shake off a seriousness that has become heavy, all too heavy. All means are justified, every "case" is a case of luck. Above all *war.* War has always been a great kind of prudence for spirits who have become too inward and profound; even in wounding [*in der Verwundung*] there is healing power. I have had as my motto for a long time a maxim, whose source I withhold from scholarly curiosity:
>
> increscunt animi, virescit volnere virtus. [...]
> [The spirit grows, strength is restored in wounding]
>
> This work too [...] is above all a recuperation, a sunspot, an escapade into the idle hours of a psychologist. And perhaps also a new war? And will new idols be sounded out? . . . This little work is a *great declaration of war* [...] (GD Vorwort, KSA 6.57 f.)

If *Twilight of the Idols* is 'a great declaration of war', *Ecce Homo* goes on to describe Nietzsche's 'war-praxis':

> Another thing is war. I am in my way warlike. Attacking belongs to my instincts. To *be able* to be an enemy, to be an enemy – that perhaps presupposes a strong nature, it is in any case conditioned in every strong nature. It needs resistances, consequently it *seeks* resistances: the *aggressive* pathos belongs as necessarily to strength as do vengefulness and vindictiveness to weakness [...] (EH weise 7, KSA 6.274)

It is this popular image that I wish to address in this book: Nietzsche as the philosopher of unbridled violence and destruction; the one who not only engages in a virulent, uncompromising polemic with western civilization – Christianity in particular – but also glorifies power and the pathos of aggression. As is well known, it is this image that was cultivated by Nazi interpreters and enabled them to appropriate Nietzsche as a militarist, Aryan philosopher.[1] This appropriation has probably done more than any to discredit his philosophy.

---

[1] On the role of Nietzsche's sister in nazifying his writings see Kaufmann 1974, 4 – 8, 15 – 18, 442 – 445. Documentation on the Nietzsche anthologies prepared by Nazi philosophers is to be found in: Kuenzli 1983, 428 – 435.

In this book, I argue that this image is a distortion of Nietzsche's philosophy. I propose to correct it by retaining certain features and rejecting others as a falsification of Nietzsche's philosophical practice. To be retained is the understanding of Nietzsche's project as a hard and uncompromising confrontation – a *total* critique of western values from which nothing is exempt:

> The Hammer Speaks.
> *Thus Spoke Zarathustra.* 3,90
>
> Why so hard! – the kitchen coal once said to the diamond: for are we not close relations?"
> Why so soft? O my brothers, I ask you as well: are you not – my brothers?
> Why so soft, so submissive and yielding? Why is there so much denial and abnegation in your hearts? so little destiny in your glances?
> And if you will not be fates, if you will not be inexorable: how will you ever be able to join me – in triumph?
> And if your hardness will not flash and cut and cut to pieces: how will you ever be able to join me – in creating? (GD Epilog, KSA 6.161. From Z III Tafeln 29)

To be rejected, on the other hand, is any confusion of Nietzsche's hammer with a project of uncontrolled or total violence bent on destruction. The task is, therefore, to think through Nietzsche's project of total critique *without* destructive violence as a necessary ingredient. This does not mean, at the other extreme, to subtract struggle – *Kampf* – from Nietzsche's project altogether, as some contemporary responses to Nazi appropriations would have us do. It is striking that Gilles Deleuze, who thematises the notion of total critique and uses destruction and violence repeatedly to characterise Nietzsche's project, should also write:

> One cannot over-emphasise *the extent to which the notions of struggle, war, rivalry or even comparison are foreign to Nietzsche and to his conception of the will to power*. It is not that he denies the existence of struggle: but he does not see it as in any way creative of values. At least the only values that it creates are those of the triumphant slave. Struggle is not the principle or motor of hierarchy but the means by which the slave reverses hierarchy. Struggle is never the active expression of forces, nor the manifestation of a will to power that affirms – any more than its result expresses the triumph of the master or the strong. Struggle, on the contrary, is the means by which the weak prevail over the strong, because they are the greatest number. (Deleuze 1983, 82)

Unlike Deleuze, Nietzsche has a highly differentiated understanding of conflict and struggle, and a rich vocabulary to match it (*Agon, Auseinandersetzung, Concurrenz, Dissonanz, Gegensätzlichkeit, Kampf, Konflikt, Krieg, Streit, Wettkampf, Wettspiel, Wettstreit, Widerspruch, Widerstreit, Zwist, Zwietracht, Zwiespalt* i.a.).[2] Among the various forms of conflict thematised by him, two paradigmatic cases or types

---

[2] For a volume that explores the integral role of conflict in Nietzsche's philosophy, not only as a theme, but as a dynamic and structural principle that cuts across the different domains of his thought, see Siemens and Pearson 2019.

stand out as distinct historical formations that have shaped European civilization. On the one hand, there is the 'slave-revolt in morality' (GM I 7, 10) at the heart of Christian morality, a reactive struggle of one class or caste in the face of an overpowering caste of 'masters'. Born of passive, impotent hatred or *ressentiment*, it seeks revenge in absolute victory, the annihilation (*Vernichtung*) of the other, but can only manage an 'imaginary revenge' that degrades the masters in order to accuse them, and overturns their values. As Deleuze points out, Nietzsche sees the slave revolt as the genetic blueprint for the reactive systems that have come to dominate European morality and thought – Darwinism, Eugen Dühring's theory of justice, Utilitarianism and democracy, to name a few.

The other paradigmatic type conflict concerns the active struggle *inter pares* of the contest or agon (*Wettkampf*) in archaic Greek culture, explored by Nietzsche and his colleague at Basel, Jacob Burckhardt, in his famous lectures on *Griechische Kulturgeschichte*.[3] In Nietzsche's most concentrated reflections on the agon, *Homer's Wettkampf* (1872) and surrounding notes, struggle *is* – pace Deleuze – an active expression of forces: agonal rivalry is, to use Nietzsche's words, a 'competitive play of forces' (*Wettspiel der Kräfte*) set in motion by a plurality of forces or geniuses playing at war.[4] This dynamic is, moreover, profoundly creative: as the institution governing all areas of life, from education to poetry and politics, the agon is the master key to archaic Greek culture, its 'impulses, deeds and works' (HW, KSA 1.783). From a dynamic point of view, agonal culture effects an affirmative displacement (*Übertragung*) or transformation of powerful, destructive impulses into constructive cultural forces. As a form of *Kampf*, agonal struggle (*Wett-kampf*) is inseparable from the pervasive struggle for annihilation (*Vernichtungs-kampf*), but also distinct from it, as a regime of limited aggression oriented towards temporary, inconclusive victory or mastery, not the absolute victory of annihilation.

Against Deleuze, I contend that Nietzsche knows, affirms and *practises* an active, creative form of struggle in agonal contestation. If the reactive sciences and philosophies of modernity all repeat the slave revolt of morality as their genetic blueprint, then Nietzsche knows only one case of a truly active thinking, modelled on active, agonal struggle – the world-view of Heraclitus:

---

[3] In Burckhardt 1929–34, volumes 8–11. Translation: Burckhardt 1998. In connection with Nietzsche's philological work on the fictitious contest between Homer and Hesiod (KGW II/1.271–339), the classicist Hugh Lloyd-Jones writes: 'it is more interesting to note that in this study we see the origins of Nietzsche's important observation of the significance in Greek life of contests and competitions. This is emphasised in the history of Greek culture of Jacob Burckhardt, a senior colleague of Nietzsche at the University of Basel; and though Burckhardt always kept his distance from Nietzsche, and later came to mistrust him, it seems certain that this feature of his work was due to Nietzsche's influence.' (Lloyd Jones 1976, 7).

[4] HW, KSA 1.789. See also 16[26], KSA 7.404: 'The contest emerges from war? As an artistic game and mimesis [*künstlerisches Spiel und Nachahmung*]?'.

> [E]s ist der Wettkampfgedanke des einzelnen Griechen und des griechischen Staates, aus den Gymnasien und Palästren, aus den künstlerischen Agonen, aus dem Ringen der politischen Parteien und der Städte mit einandander, in's Allgemeinste übertragen, so dass jetzt das Räderwerk des Kosmos in ihm sich dreht. (PHG 5, KSA 1.825)[5]

Nietzsche, I will argue, is the modern heir to Heraclitus. In Nietzsche's writing, the thought of the contest is transferred (*übertragen*), not into the cosmos, but into the task of critical transvaluation, as the principle governing his critical confrontations with prevailing values. In this chapter, this thesis will be advanced against the image of total, unlimited violence associated with Nietzsche's hammer by interrogating the goal of his total critique and its dynamic form: Is it really destructive? Does it really seek to annihilate certain pernicious values and consign them to oblivion?

The argument begins with the proposition that Nietzsche is first and foremost a *philosopher of life*. This means at least two things for his critical practice:

1) Nietzschean critique takes shape as a *contestation of values:* In examining and evaluating values, Nietzsche's text seeks to take the side of life – its affirmation and intensification. Every value – whether 'pity', 'truth', 'love' … – is therefore measured and evaluated against life, as the highest value and standard of evaluation. The preface to GM offers a typical sequence of Nietzschean questions:

> Under what conditions did the human being discover for itself those values good and evil? And *what value do they themselves have?* (GM Vorrede 3, KSA 5.249f.)

But to question the value of values in a meaningful way presupposes a standard of evaluation. That 'life' constitutes this standard for Nietzsche can be seen in the unfolding of his initial questions:

> Have they until now inhibited or furthered human thriving? Are they signs of need, impoverishment, degeneration in life? Or, on the other hand, does the fullness, strength, the will of life betray itself in them, its courage, its confidence, its future? – (GM Vorrede 3, KSA 5.250)

The pattern that emerges from Nietzsche's work is that life is raised and pitted against prevailing values of western culture. His hostility towards Christianity, for instance, derives from an analysis of Christianity as a form of life that is hostile to life: Nietzsche's hostility, here, is a hostility towards the hostility to life.

2) Life has an *existential* bearing on Nietzschean critique. As a philosopher of life, Nietzsche commits himself not just to a total critique of values in the name of life; he commits himself to critique *as a way of life*, to a *style* of critique that can be lived with. Nietzsche learns very early on that a philosophy of destruction can

---

[5] '[I]t is the contest-idea of the individual Greek and the Greek state, transferred from the gymnasia and the palaestra, from the artistic agons, from the struggles between the political parties and the states, [transferred] into the most universal terms, so that now the wheels of the cosmos turns within it.' See also 16[18], KSA 7.399f.

slip and get ensnared in the very same hostility to life that it would destroy; he is only too aware of how damaging the project of total critique can be to the health of the critic, how easily the knife of vivisection can slip and cut into one's own flesh. This problem is often thematised in his writing as a conflict between knowledge and life.[6] But it also appears as a self-referential thread that weaves its way in and out of his texts and the larger philosophical narratives they recount. In a passage discussing the philosopher's complicity with 'our whole modern mode of being', he ends with the question of life – the worth or value of the philosopher's life:

> Hubris is today our whole attitude towards nature, our violation of nature with the aid of machines and our so thoughtless [unbedenklich] inventiveness of the technician and the engineer; hubris is our attitude towards god [...]; hubris is our attitude towards *ourselves*, – for we experiment with ourselves as we would never permit ourselves with any animal, and slit open the souls of our still-living bodies, content and curious: what do we care for the "salvation" of the soul! Afterwards, we do our own self-healing: being sick is instructive, we've no doubt, far more instructive than being healthy, – the *makers of sickness* seem even more necessary for us today than the medicine-men and "healers". We now violate ourselves, there is no doubt, we nutcrackers of the soul, we questioning and questionable ones, as if life were no more than cracking nuts; in this way we must necessarily become daily yet more questionable, *more worthy* of questioning, in this way perhaps also more worthy – of living?... (GM III 9)

In this chapter, I shall dwell on another such moment, which, in response to the inescapably historical or temporal character of life, recounts our inevitable complicity, as critics, in the sins of our fathers.

The upshot of Nietzsche's existential commitment to a total critique that can be lived with is a concern to find a *limit in negation*; that is, a style of critique that remains uncompromising, but limits and contains this logic of self-destruction, the recoil of critique upon the critic. My claim in this book is that Nietzsche finds it in *agonal critique* – a form of critique modelled on the central institution of pre-Socratic Greek culture: the contest or agon. In this chapter, I examine Nietzsche's self-declared 'war-praxis' in EH in order to sketch a model of critique that retains the basic impulse of Nietzsche's total critique: to *overcome* values hostile to life, yet transforms the *destructive orientation* of total warfare into the *productive* orientation of *mastery*. For Nietzsche, 'mastery' designates a posture that, far from seeking to de-

---

[6] At stake in GT, for example, is the conflict between truth and life as the highest value (see chapter 4). The conflict between knowledge and life is first thematised in MA 31–34 and is perhaps most acute in the period of FW: see FW 107 and 11[162], KSA 9.504:
> 'Leben ist die Bedingung des Erkennens. Irren die Bedingung des Lebens und zwar im teifsten Grunde Irren. Wissen um das Irren hebt es nicht auf! Das ist nichts Bitteres!
> Wir müssen das Irren lieben und pflegen, es ist der Mutterschooß des Erkennens. Die Kunst als die Pflege des Wahnes – unser Cultus.'

stroy antagonistic values, *preserves* them as a stimulus towards the creation of new values beyond good and evil. Nietzsche's 'war-praxis', I argue, is modelled on his conception of the Greek agon, which I introduce in the last section, and will elaborate upon further in succeeding chapters, exploring in detail its implications for Nietzsche's philosophical practice as a form of *agonal critique*.

I Finding a Limit in the Negation of the Past

One of many places where Nietzsche voices a hesitation concerning the aggressive impulse celebrated in GD and EH comes in *On the Uses and Disadvantages of History for Life* when Nietzsche speaks of the necessity for a *critical* mode of history. This passage is particularly important, since his hesitation can be referred to a problem afflicting the project of total critique. He writes:

> If he is to live, the human being must possess, and from time to time employ, the strength to break up and dissolve a past: he does this by bringing it before a tribunal, scrupulously examining it and finally condemning it; every past, however, is worthy to be condemned – for that is the nature of human things: human violence and weakness have always played a mighty role in them. (NNHL 3, KSA 1.269)

Critical history, then, involves the critical evaluation or judgement of the past: What does Nietzsche have to say on this necessary form of judgement?

> Then its past is regarded critically, then one takes the knife to its roots, then one cruelly tramples over every kind of piety. It is always a dangerous process, especially so for life itself: and men and ages that serve life by judging and destroying a past are always dangerous and endangered men and ages. For since we are the outcome of earlier generations, we are also the outcome of their aberrations, passions and errors, and indeed of their crimes; it is not possible to free oneself wholly from this chain. If we condemn these aberrations and regard ourselves as above them [*enthoben*], this does not alter the fact that we stem from them. The best we can do is to contest [resist: *Widerstreite*] our inherited and hereditary [*angestammte*] nature with our knowledge of it, and through a new, severe discipline, combat our inborn heritage and implant in ourselves a new habit, a new instinct, a second nature, so that our first nature withers away. It is an attempt to give oneself, as it were *a posteriori*, a past from which one would like to stem, in opposition to that from which one does stem: – always a dangerous attempt because it is so hard to find a limit in the negation of the past [...] (NNHL 3, KSA 1.270)

The predominance of *life* in this passage is unmistakable. The pattern of argumentation is controlled throughout by the interests of life: it is life – that 'dark, driving power insatiably thirsting for itself' (NNHL 3, KSA 1.269) – that necessitates the occasional deployment of critical history, a cruel and merciless purging of errors we inherit from the past. But it is also life – the life of the critic or the culture of critique – that is threatened in the process and demands that we 'find a limit in the negation of the past' (NNHL 3, KSA 1.270). As such, this passage clearly demonstrates both elements of Nietzsche's philosophy of life introduced earlier. His *existential* commitment to critique is seen in the preoccupation with a measure of critical history that serves life and does not succumb to the destructive forces it unleashes. In the second place, the kind of judgement we are called on to make takes the form of a *contestation of values*: life necessitates these critical judgements, not merely as an external condition, but as the ground and standard of judgement. Critical history *means* measuring given life-forms or values against the interests of life as the highest value, and condemning them precisely to the degree that best serves life's interest.

But why exactly is critique such a dangerous undertaking? Critical reflection may provoke the demand to overcome a past form of life on account of its aberrations and crimes, but it does not remove the fact that we stem from it; we remain, in Nietzsche's words, 'chained' to the very errors and crimes we would condemn. Thus the danger would seem to lie in punishing crimes of which we too – on account of some genealogical fatality – are guilty. This is all rather mystifying – more like a scene from one of Aeschylus' tragedies than a philosophical problem. What, in particular, are we to make of the hereditary curse being invoked here?

Let me suggest two interpretations of Nietzsche's thought:

i) The first takes the Aeschylean pathos of the passage as its clue and asks: How does a tragic hero, such as Orestes, succumb to the hereditary curse afflicting his family? One answer is, of course, that he has always already succumbed to it by virtue of the ancestral act of transgression that first brought the curse upon his family.[7] The curse is a divine fatality, which dictates that the original crime will be repeated and avenged indefinitely: Agamemnon's sacrifice of Iphigeneia, Clytaemnestra's revenge on her husband, Orestes' revenge on his mother.[8] Yet the invocation of a divine order and divine, omnipresent time is combined by Aeschylus with a tentative exploration of human will that takes place in the opaque and confusing temporality of human action.[9] It is not until Orestes actually commits the murder of his mother that he succumbs to the hereditary curse.[10] It is his *act of destruction* which, provok-

---

7 Atreus, Agamemnon's father, slaughtered his brother's children, roasted and offered them to their unknowing father as a feast.
8 Walter Otto is a strong advocate of this reading. See Otto 1962, 178–9 on 'the opening situation, in which the demise in which it culminates, is already sealed [*beschlossen*].' Also on Clytaemnestra's murder of Agamemnon: 'the decisive action, even when it takes place in the drama itself, appears as something that is, as it were, already there a long time [*längst schon da*]' (Otto 1962, 173).
9 This is the position of J.-P. Vernant & P. Vidal-Naquet in *Myth and Tragedy in Ancient Greece* (1988). See especially 'Intimations of the Will in Greek Tragedy', and 'Aeschylus, the Past and the Present' therein. The point has been put forcefully by Karl Reinhardt (1949, 13), who writes of 'Gottes Allmacht und Vorausbestimmung, die gleichwohl ein Mitwirken des Menschen fordert [...]'. See also Nietzsche on the 'dark feeling of reciprocal dependence' between men and gods, symbolised in Aeschylus' Prometheus (GT 9, KSA 1.68).
10 Although the demise in which tragedy culminates is already sealed in the opening scene, it is, according to Otto, 'essential that it is not yet a finished catastrophe with which the play begins [...] What must follow in the second place is an occurrence, superhumanly ordained, but naturally realised through the deed of a human being, whereby what was a tearful threat in the opening scenario, first emerges, "appears" as reality and certainty' (Otto 1962, 178–9). Or again: 'Was langst

ing the Erinnies into persecuting him, prolongs the vicious circle of revenge, not broken until human justice is established with the Areopagus at the end of the drama.

Nietzsche's point, by analogy, would be that *we become enchained to the past through the very act of destroying it*. The act of critical destruction, by which we would overcome a past on account of its crimes and errors, turns out to be a futile *repetition* of the very crimes and errors we condemn. But if it is the act of critical judgement that implicates us in the crimes and errors of the past, then these crimes and errors must themselves involve acts of critical judgement. An Aeschylean reading of the scene of critical history suggests that the hereditary curse or fatality invoked by Nietzsche means something like a *dialectic of Enlightenment:* the process whereby an emancipatory impulse, which would overcome a given regime of oppression through rational critique, ends up replicating oppression in the new regime it establishes. Thus, Adorno and Horkheimer[11] describe how Plato's critique of myth ends up replacing the tyranny of superstition with the tyranny of the concept; by the same logic of (self-)destruction, the attempt to destroy Platonism would in turn replicate Plato's crimes against myth. From this perspective, Nietzsche's call for a 'limit in the negation of the past' stems from an insight into the self-defeating consequences of emancipatory critical negation.

This interpretation finds support in the 'remarkable consolation' offered in Nietzsche's closing lines on critical history:

> But here and there victory is nonetheless achieved, and for those combatants [*Kämpfenden*] who employ critical history for the sake of life, there is a remarkable consolation: namely, to know that this first nature was once a second nature and that every victorious second nature will become a first nature. (NNHL 3, KSA 1.270)

By 'first nature', Nietzsche means of course 'our inherited and hereditary nature', to be replaced by the second nature implanted by our critical practice (see the preceding lines cited on p. 28 above). By aligning this first nature, in its coming-to-be, with the second nature that is to replace it, he assimilates both critical history and its object to a single process of critical confrontation (*Kampf*) with past values and life-forms.

ii) For an alternative reading of the fatality or curse afflicting critical history, we can appeal to another hereditary curse Nietzsche invokes a few years later in *Human, All Too Human*. In MA 2, entitled the 'The congenital failure [*Erbfehler*] of philosophers', he argues that a 'lack of historical sense' has driven philosophers to look for constant, eternal truths as their starting point and the basis for their judgements. Against this, Nietzsche proposes a new kind of 'historical philosophising', whose vir-

---

schon da ist, tritt ans Licht, enthüllt sich in der Verwirklichung. Müssen wir nicht sagen, dass auch für Aischylos, wie für Sophokles, die Enthüllung selbst das tragische Geschehen ist?' (Otto 1962, 173).
11 Adorno & Horkheimer 1969.

tue is the virtue of 'modesty', and whose motto runs: 'Alles ist [...] geworden': 'Everything has become; there are *no eternal givens* [Thatsachen]: just as there are no absolute truths' (MA 2, KSA 2.24 f.). Historical philosophising calls on us to think *in the light of the insight* that there is nothing absolute, no stable and unchanging ground for judgement, no eternal and immutable standpoint in being, which would remove us from the historical reality we interrogate.

I suggest that it is this same insight that informs Nietzsche's warnings in the passage on critical history: the critic does not have the metaphysical privilege of a standpoint 'above' or beyond the forms of life he is condemning; he is not free to look outside the process of *life-as-becoming* for a ground of judgement in being, which would secure him against his own criticisms. This may well seem an untenable interpretation of a text that culminates in an appeal to the 'suprahistorical', as

> the powers which lead the eye away from becoming, towards that which bestows upon existence [*Dasein*] the character of the eternal and stable [*Gleichbedeutend*], towards *art* and *religion*. (NNHL 10, KSA 1.330)

But when Nietzsche introduces critical history, he does so against the background of the dangers of antiquarian history and the value of monumental history: the former 'knows only how to *preserve* life, not to engender it'; unlike the latter, it 'undervalues becoming [*das Werdende*]' and 'hinders the powerful resolve for what is new'; accumulating pieties and reverences for the past, antiquarian history resists piety or reverence for 'what is becoming and present [*Werdende, Gegenwärtige*]' (NNHL 3, KSA 1.268 f.). The very next line speaks of the necessity for critical history, aligning it with becoming and the active struggle for novelty (monumental history) against preservation, stasis and the stability of being.

The problem raised by critical history, then, concerns the ground or site of critique. Because of the inescapably historical or temporal character of life-as-becoming, the critic who puts the knife to a past always already cuts into his own flesh. Recognising the temporal character of life and our historical finitude binds us to the historical life-context we are to judge, exposing our complicity in the errors we would condemn. So how are we to practise a total critique of the past in the knowledge of our historical finitude? In the interests of life, critical history would condemn outright those values from the past that are hostile to life. But how can we condemn them *in the interests of life*, when that very judgement threatens *our life* – the life of the critic or the culture of critique?

Whether we follow the first or the second interpretation offered above, Nietzsche's existential commitment to critique is expressed as an anxiety concerning the destruction of past forms of life – that it will consume the life of the critic in its uncontrolled violence. How *is* this logic of self-destruction to be contained? In the context of 'historical philosophising', Nietzsche spoke of the virtue of 'modesty'. In the context of critical history, the concern with self-destruction culminates in the call 'to find a limit in the negation of the past'. The question is: what form is this practice of *lim-*

ited negation to take? It certainly cannot take the form of a compromise, or a compact that would insulate certain values from critical reflection in advance. For critical history demands that 'one cruelly tramples over every kind of piety' (NNHL 3, KSA 1.270).

The curious suggestion in the text is, in fact, that we give our critical reflection the form of a severe discipline that would enable us to contest who we are (or: who we have become) with who we would like to be (or: who we would like to become or have become):

> The best we can do is to contest [*Widerstreite*] our inherited and hereditary nature with our knowledge of it, and through a new, severe discipline, combat our inborn heritage and inplant in ourselves a new habit, a new instinct, a second nature, so that our first nature withers away. It is an attempt to give oneself, as it were *a posteriori*, a past from which one would like to stem, in opposition to that from which one does stem [...] (NNHL 3, KSA 1.270)

A new regime of the self which, in its *severity*, combats who we are with a counterfactual phantasy of the self, a dream of who we wish we were? A new art of judgement that stages an oneiric, fictive contest with one's self? Is Nietzsche really suggesting that we cannot avail ourselves of a standpoint in being, because it is a fiction *... so the best we can do is to invent an altogether fictive form of judgement?*

It does seem difficult to take this seriously as a solution to the problem of the site of critique. But in my view, this passage is programmatic for Nietzsche's subsequent critical practice: it is just such a strategy of a fully-conscious fiction, a contestation of the contemporary values we have inherited *from a fictive standpoint in archaic Greek culture*, that I shall pursue under the name of 'agonal critique'. My proposal is that Nietzsche's text deploys an *agonal* regime to regulate its critical practice, and that this fiction offers a way out of the impasse of critical history explored earlier: It creates a theatre for the total critique of values in the name of life, in which the logic of self-destruction is arrested through a code of limited violence. The first step will be to focus on a key passage in Nietzsche's oeuvre, where his style of philosophical critique is described as a form of limited warfare.

I Nietzsche's 'War-praxis' or the Art of Limited Warfare

I began this chapter with a few passages that would support fascist readings of Nietzsche, in which he appears to advocate a philosophy of warfare or total violence. It now appears that Nietzsche did after all have one or two reservations about violence. If we suppose – as I think we can – that the targets of Nietzsche's warfare are precisely the objects of critical history – those forms of life and values from the past that continue to inform the present – then there does some seem to be a serious equivocation here. Was Nietzsche simply too violent and uncontrolled a thinker to heed his own warnings? Or do those warnings betray an unfortunate lapse, a moment of weakness in an otherwise exemplary philosopher of violence?

In fact, we need not choose between these equally false alternatives, if instead we choose to read carefully. In support of this response, I shall go over the *Ecce Homo* passage on warfare cited at the start, pointing out the places where the apparent advocation of destruction is attenuated. This will serve as an introduction to the model of limited war or agonal contestation that I will then propose as the most appropriate model for Nietzschean critique.

> Another thing is war. I am in my way warlike. Attacking belongs to my instincts. To *be able* to be an enemy, to be an enemy – that perhaps presupposes a strong nature, it is in any case conditioned in every strong nature. It needs resistances, consequently it *seeks* resistances: the *aggressive* pathos belongs as necessarily to strength as do vengefulness and vindictiveness to weakness [...] The **strength** of the attacker finds in the opposition he needs a kind of *measure* [Maass[12]: (i) limit (ii) gauge, measure]; every **growth** betrays itself in the search for a powerful opponent – or problem: for a philosopher who is warlike also challenges problems to a duel. The task is to become **master**, *not* over any resistances, but over those against which one has to bring one's entire strength, suppleness and mastery of weapons to bear, – over *equal* opponents... Equality in the face of the enemy – first presupposition of an *honest* duel [...] My war-praxis can be summarised in four principles. First: I attack only those things that are victorious, – I wait, under circumstances, until they are victorious. Second: I attack only those things where I would find no allies, where I stand alone, – where I only expose [risk, compromise: *compromittire*] myself... Third: I never attack persons, I make use of the person as a strong magnifying glass with which one can make visible a general, but evasive and barely tangible state of need [...] Fourth: I attack only things where any personal differences are excluded, where there is no background in bad experiences. On the contrary, to attack in my case is a proof of good-will, under circumstances of gratitude. I bestow honour, I confer distinction insofar as I bind my name with that of an issue, a person: for or against – in this respect that counts as the same for me. If I wage war on Christianity, I have a right to do so, because I have no experience of a fatality or frustration from that direction – the most serious Christians have always been well-disposed towards me. I myself, an opponent of Christianity *de rigueur*, am far from bearing a grudge against an individual for what is the fatality of millennia. – (EH weise 7, KSA 6.274 f.: HS)[13]

This somewhat fuller account of Nietzsche's war-praxis informs us of (a) the causes of war, (b) the goals and presuppositions of war, and (c) two constitutive moments in the logic of Nietzschean warfare. Examining each in turn will remove Nietzschean warfare from the *absolute negativity* of destruction in three stages, revealing at

---

[12] In his writings and lectures, Nietzsche uses a range of different spellings for this important term (and compounds): *Maass, Maaß, Mass, Maß*. When quoting, the spelling in the text quoted is used; otherwise *Maass* and *Übermaas* are used for 'measure' and 'excess' (lit. 'overmeasure').

[13] Tuncel (2009, 165 ff.) also draws on this passage to describe 'a certain kind of agon' that Nietzsche practises. He argues that Nietzsche's language of warfare and aggression draws on the Greek sense of agon in its proximity to war and gives him 'a way of positing his destructive instincts as in a war-game'. He goes on to situate Nietzsche's agonal practice in 'an agonal world-interpretation', attacking 'the world-conception of those who contribute to the making of culture'. This move is unwarranted by Nietzsche's texts, since he is not a *Weltanschauungs*-philosopher.

each stage how a 'limit in the negation of the past', as demanded of critical history, is found.

To begin with (a) the causes of war: Nietzsche is at pains to point out that he is concerned, not with persons, but with the philosophical problems that they name.[14] These problems are, in turn, pitched at the general level of cultural conditions, so that he can deny any personal animosity towards individual Christians while being an opponent of Christianity *de rigueur*. If Nietzsche attacks Plato, Paul or Wagner, he is using them as a 'magnifying glass' to expose a general crisis of modern culture – and as a name for the 'victorious' or prevailing values of modernity that legitimate and prolong that crisis. Nietzsche's pathos of aggression as a critic, and his call for a transvaluation of all values, respond to a *cultural* problematic. They are *not* levelled at individuals, as if they were the motors of change. The principles of agency are located instead at the level of mores – collective schemas or regimes of evaluation forming types according to specific bodily economies.[15] This will become important when we come to look at Nietzsche's *agonal* response to that demand in chapter 3.

Turning to (b) the goals of warfare, we find nothing on destruction in this passage. Instead of negating the opponent, a concern with self-affirmation and –empowerment seems uppermost in Nietzschean warfare. It is an interest in *strength*, or rather an interest in *growth* or empowerment on the critic's part that drives his search for a (more) powerful opponent: he wants to attain *mastery* over a worthwhile resistance, not its destruction. Whatever mastery means, it clearly represents a *limited*, rather than *absolute negation* of the opponent. In this concern with mastery over and against destruction, we encounter the first 'limit in the negation of the past'.

The second moment of limited negation comes to light by exploring the (c) logic of warfare *qua* mastery. The text is marked by a logic of need and relativity that precludes destruction. A strong nature 'needs resistances' and so seeks resistance. In

---

14 Cf. 16[9], KSA 7.396 on the 'denial [*Verleugnung*] of the individual' in the Greek agon, and the claim: 'Es kämpfen keine Individuen, sondern Ideen mit einander.'

15 Blondel (1991, 66) rightly identifies Nietzsche's distinctive and enduring concern with *values* ('axiological forms') and a set of problems that do not fall under a (Marxist) socio-economic perspective, nor a strictly individual perspective (like the early Freud), 'since it places itself more on the level of what the eighteenth century called "mores"'. Values, for Nietzsche, are not just representations, and they occur, not in isolation, but in cultures, understood as '*collections of evaluations based on corporeity*'. As such, cultures are 'not objects (in the sense that scientific sociology confers on this concept) or, as Durkheim would call them, *things:* they are neither individual nor collective'. In the context of Nietzsche's genealogical project, Blondel (1991, 69) writes that 'culture is conceived as the collected values that govern the practice, ideals and mores of a given sociohistorical totality (the Greeks, India, Christianity, the tragic vision of the world, the superhuman). But [...] these values are evaluations: they are no longer just representations; they are also the collected means assumed by the body, according to a certain typological economy, within this totality, in order to make it master of life, obliquely (the "weak" body) or openly (the "strong" body).' In the case of certain cultures – the Greeks, the Italian Renaissance – they also act as normative models for Nietzsche. In this book, I explore the normative force of agonal Greek culture.

order to measure its strength, the attacker needs the kind of opposition that forces it to *exercise* its strength, to deploy its full range of capabilities in order to master the opponent; for only 'in the opposition that it needs' does it have a real measure (*Maass*) of what it can do. This implies that mastery requires the *preservation* of what it masters, precisely as a standard or gauge that enables it to measure and *affirm* its capacities. Clearly the need to preserve one's opponent further attenuates the absolute negativity of destruction.

This implication is then spelled out and intensified into an out-and-out affirmation of the other when, in the fourth rule of his war-praxis, Nietzsche explains his rationale for attacking:

> I bestow honour, I confer distinction insofar as I bind my name with that of an issue, a person: for or against – in this respect that counts as the same for me. (EH weise 7, KSA 6.275)

Here, the interest in preserving the opponent is expressed in the *binding of names*. The positive value of this bond is evidently such that the negative evaluation of the other is subordinate – to the point of irrelevance: critical negation of the other 'counts for the same' as an affirmative evaluation. The binding of names is, at the same time, the forging of a *genealogical* bond, where Nietzsche's opponent is a figure from the past (as often they are). By preserving the opponent's name, it expresses an interest in historical or genealogical *continuity* that confirms the sense of historical finitude troubling the critical historian. Attack, then, far from intending the absolute negativity of destruction and oblivion, intends to *affirm* the opponent in forging a bond of continuity with it. How far this bond is from the 'chain' that afflicted the critical historian comes out in the preceding line: 'With me to attack is a proof of good-will, under circumstances, of gratitude.' (EH weise 7, KSA 6.275)

Earlier we saw that the aggressor needs to *preserve* its opponent as a standard or gauge that enables it to measure and *affirm* its strength and capacities against it. We can now see that attacking, in *its* turn, constitutes a kind of *affirmation* of the opponent. It seems, therefore, that Nietzsche's fourth rule removes the rationale for warfare from a blind, one-sided logic of destruction towards *a dynamic of reciprocal affirmation or empowerment*.

But with this remark, Nietzsche appears to overplay his hand, for we seem to have lost sight of warfare altogether. The destructive negativity of Nietzschean critique has not just been limited; it has been *reversed* into affirmative gestures of gratitude and good-will. So what of the negativity of warfare? What kind of negativity is involved in Nietzsche's declared interest in mastery? According to the first rule of Nietzschean warfare, he attacks only those cultural forces that are *victorious*. The purpose, we have seen, is to gain *mastery* over them. A note from 1888 helps to explain what this means:

> I have declared war on the anaemic Christian ideal (including what is closely related to it), not with the intention of annihilating [*vernichten*] it, but only of putting an end to its *tyranny* and making place for new ideals, more *robust* ideals... The *continued existence* of the Christian

> ideal belongs to the most desirable things that there are: and just for the sake of the ideals that wish to assert themselves next to it and perhaps over it – they must have opponents, *strong* opponents in order to become *strong*. – Thus we immoralists need the *power of morality:* our drive for self-preservation wills that our *opponents* retain their strength – wills only to become *master over them*. – (10[117], KSA 12.523)[16]

We could say, then, that Nietzschean critique seeks, not to destroy the ideals it attacks, but to *place a limit or measure on their tyranny*, so as to make room for competing ideals. Now, this formulation does appear in the *Ecce Homo* text on warfare. In this text, however, it is referred to the critic, *not* his opponent:

> The strength of the **attacker** finds in the opposition he needs a kind of *measure* [or *limit*]. (EH weise 7, KSA 6.274:**HS**)

At the beginning of the passage on mastery, this line suggests that Nietzschean critique may *begin* with destructive, tyrannical intent, but finds itself limited by the resistance it seeks and encounters to a posture of *mastery*. That is: it finds itself limited to limiting the tyranny of the ideals it seeks out (for this is what mastery means in note 10[117] cited above). From this analysis it is clear that the thought of limited negation is governed by a dynamic, reciprocal structure that mirrors the *dynamic of mutual affirmation or empowerment*. In this case, Nietzsche removes the rationale for warfare from a blind, one-sided logic of destruction *towards a dynamic of mutual negation, limitation or disempowerment*. Combining both affirmative and negative moments, Nietzsche's art of warfare can be described as *a dynamic of mutual affirmation or empowerment, and mutual limitation or disempowerment*.

III Nietzsche's Agonal Model of Warfare

With this formulation we have a precise characterization of the dynamics of limited warfare used by Nietzsche to characterise the Greek agon. In *Homer's Contest*, he writes that the agon presupposes that

---

[16] 'Ich habe dem bleichsüchtigen Christen-Ideale den Krieg erklärt (sammt dem, was ihm nahe verwandt ist), nicht in der Absicht, es zu vernichten, sondern nur um seiner *Tyrannei* ein Ende zu setzen und Platz frei zu bekommen für neue Ideale, für *robustere* Ideale... Die Fortdauer des christlichen Ideals gehört zu den wünschenswerthesten Dingen, die es giebt: und schon um der Ideale willen, die neben ihm und vielleicht über ihm sich geltend machen wollen – sie müssen Gegner *starke* Gegner haben, um *stark* zu werden. – So brauchen wir Immoralisten die *Macht der Moral:* unser Selbsterhaltungstrieb will, daß unsere *Gegner* bei Kräften bleiben, – will nur *Herr über sie* werden. – ' (10[117], KSA 12.523). See also 7[53], KSA 12.312: 'Nicht ein Kampf um Existenz wird zwischen den Vorstellungen und Wahrnehmungen gekämpft, sondern um Herrschaft: – *vernichtet* wird die überwundene Vorstellung *nicht*, nur *zurückgedrängt* oder *subordinirt*. Es giebt im Geistigen keine Vernichtung ...'.

there are *several* geniuses who stimulate one another to action [mutual empowerment – HS], as they also hold one another within the bounds of measure [mutual disempowerment, limitation – HS].[17]

The cue for this interpretation is, in fact, given right at the start of the *Ecce Homo* text with the *presuppositions* for a just or honest form of warfare:

> The task is to become master, *not* over any resistances, but over those against which one has bring one's entire strength, suppleness and mastery of weapons to bear, – over *equal* opponents… Equality in the face of the enemy – first presupposition of an *honest* duel […]. (EH weise 7, KSA 6.275)

This is a reference to Hesiod's *Works and Days* where, for the first time, it is observed that 'all rivalry, all *eris* presupposes a relationship of equality'.[18] *Works and Days* is important because it forms the sub-text to *Homer's Wettkampf* (HW), the text in which Nietzsche offers his most concentrated account of the ancient Greek agon. An oblique entry into his conception of agonal culture in this text can be found in the account of the ancient Greek institution of banishment or ostracism. In the passage from which the lines cited above were drawn, he writes:

> The original sense of this peculiar institution [ostracism – HS] is not, however, that of a vent [escape-valve], but rather that of a stimulant: one removes the outstanding individual so that the play of forces [*Wettspiel der Kräfte*] may reawaken: a thought that is inimical to the "exclusivity" of genius in the modern sense, but presupposes that in a natural order of things there are always *several* geniuses who rouse [stimulate] one another to action, as they also hold one another within the bounds of measure. That is the crux of the Hellenic notion of contest: it abhors one-man rule [*Alleinherrschaft*] and fears its dangers; it desires, as a *protection* against genius – a second genius. (HW, KSA 1./89)

In the figure of the '"exclusivity of genius"' and the 'outstanding individual' one can hear the 'victorious forces' which Nietzsche singled out for attack in *Ecce Homo* (KSA 6.274). In the present context, the outstanding individual is the one who holds 'one-man' or 'absolute rule' (*Alleinherrschaft*), *the absolute and conclusive victor*, i.e. that contestant – symbolised by Nietzsche in the figure of Alexander – to whom none are equal. Nietzsche quotes the Ephesians:

> "Amongst us no-one should be the best; if someone is, then let him be elsewhere and amongst others." For why should no-one be the best? Because the contest would fail and the eternal life-ground of the Hellenic state would be jeopardised. (HW, KSA 1.788)

---

17 'daß, in einer natürlichen Ordnung der Dinge, es immer *mehrere* Genies giebt, die sich gegenseitig zur That reizen, wie sie sich auch gegenseitig in der Grenze des Maaßes halten.' (HW, KSA 1.789).
18 See Vernant 1982, 47.

This passage allows for a preliminary definition of the agon: if the outstanding individual (the absolute and conclusive victor) is ostracised for the sake of the agon, then the agon can only thrive where *a plurality* of more-or-less equal antagonistic forces (*Kräfte*) or 'geniuses' are engaged in an *inconclusive, open-ended contestation of victory or excellence.*

The agon does not admit absolute victory, but only *mastery* between the contests – temporary, intermittent victors like the Olympic champion or the winner of the contest of tragedies *this year*. The emergence of an absolute victor kills the agon and, since it is the life-blood of the Greek city-state and community, it also annihilates the state.[19] In short, *the agon gives absolute precedence to comparatives over absolute superlatives.* That the agon is intrinsically open-ended, inconclusive and repeatable can be heard in Nietzsche's formulation: *Wettspiel der Kräfte*. As the competitive play of forces, it combines the notion of a contestation of power with the endless repeatability of play.

As the model for an open-ended contestation of values, the agon offers the ideal arena for total critique; at the same time, its productive orientation promises to deflect the logic of self-destruction afflicting total critique. Now Nietzsche's critical impulse, as we saw in Ecce Homo, unfolds at a *collective* level, in response to a cultural problematic. Here too, the agon is helpful in elucidating how Nietzsche's demand for change, and the requisite response, can operate at this level. As we have seen, the agon presupposes a *plurality of forces or geniuses who rouse (reizen) one another to action (That), as they also hold one another within the bounds of measure*. The agonal dynamic is one of mutual stimulation, arousal, provocation, empowerment and mutual disempowerment, limitation within the bounds of measure. The contest will only arise out of mutual provocation and stimulation, while mutual limitation tempers and contains the victory of a single force so that the contest may continue. As the complex interplay of positive and negative postures, reciprocal affirmation and negation described in Ecce Homo, it is distinguished on one side from a redemptive scheme of peace, harmony, reconciliation;[20] and on the other, from the unmeasured antagonism of war, or mutual annihilation (*Vernichtungskampf*).

In HW, *agonal drives or affects* serve as the key to the agonal dynamic of mutual empowerment-disempowerment – and hence are a clue to the distance separating Nietzschean critique from the logic of destruction. Agonal affects are distinguished from another set of affects – those that drive men to struggle for annihilation – according to Hesiod's distinction between the 'good' and the 'evil Eris' goddesses. The 'evil Eris', referred by Nietzsche to affects such as hate, cruelty, lust, deceit and vindictiveness 'drives men towards the inimical struggle for annihilation [*Vernichtungskampf*]'. By contrast, the 'good Eris' is she

---

[19] In HW, the figure of Alexander serves as an example of the superlative victor of the agon, to whom none are equal, who therefore kills the agon and, with it, the polycentric political form of the city-states in favour of a centralised empire.
[20] Nietzsche's construal of the socialist state, for example: 5[178], [180], [188], KSA8.

who, as jealousy, wrath, envy, rouses [stimulates] men to deeds, not of mutual destruction [*Vernichtungskampf*], but rather the deed of *contest* [*Wettkampf*]. The Greek is *envious* and feels this quality not as a flaw, but rather as the effect of a *beneficent* deity [...] (HW, KSA 1.787)

But agonal affects do not just provoke contestation; they also ensure the second moment of mutual limitation. This can be seen through a consideration of envy. Envy will also serve to flesh out the agonal model of critique, as an alternative to unmeasured warfare, and in specific, to give body to the notion of *mastery* separating the two.

Envy
Nietzsche describes envy and jealousy (*Neid, Eifersucht*) as agonal affects that rouse men to contestation (*Wettkampf*), rather than mutual destruction (the *Vernichtungskampf*) (HW, KSA 1.787). Citing Aristotle, Nietzsche recalls Xenophanes' relation to Homer as an example 'that even one who is dead can rouse one who is alive to a consuming jealousy [*Eifersucht*]'. But he sees in this the desire, not to annihilate Homer's achievement, but to limit it, to outbid Homer by treating it as a stimulant to a new deed or work, a new 'greatness'; that is, a new value and a new standard of evaluation that is binding on others. Like Plato's attack on Homer, it is rooted in

> the monstrous desire to take the place of the fallen poet oneself and to inherit his fame [reputation]. Every great Hellene passes on the torch of the contest; every great virtue kindles a new greatness. (HW, KSA 1.788)

Agonal jealousy is the desire to take the place of the opponent and 'inherit his fame', that is, to appropriate his cultural authority. *At the same time* it is also envy that, on the other side, provokes the Greek's vertiginous fear of victory and its fruits. Nowhere is this moment of *self-negation, self-limitation* or *sacrifice* as pronounced as in the victor's fear of divine envy:

> Because he is envious [*neidisch*] he also feels, with every excess [*Übermaaß*] of honour, wealth, glory and happiness, the envious eye of a god resting upon him, and he fears this envy; in this case it reminds him of the transience of every human lot, his happiness fills him with dread and, sacrificing the best of it, he bows to the divine envy. (HW, KSA 1.787)

This account can be used to tie up various elements of Nietzschean critique we have encountered into a cohesive concept of *mastery* in which it culminates. Mastery was first encountered in EH as the 'limited negation' through which Nietzschean critique contains the logic of self-destruction. Nietzschean critique may *begin* with destructive, tyrannical intent, but finds itself limited by the resistance it encounters to a posture of *mastery*, which means: limiting the tyranny of the values it challenges. It is just such a confrontation that agonal envy describes – the envy of, say, a Xenophanes or Plato vis-a-vis Homer's tyrannical hold over Greek culture and education. In specific, envy traces a movement beginning in tyranny and ending in mastery. Under the sign of envy, the tyranny in so many of Nietzsche's attitudes; but more than that, the *necessary* tyranny in any judgement, becomes the 'monstrous desire to take the place' of what is being contested. At the same time, agonal envy grounds the limiting or curbing of this tyrannical drive in the two relationships it informs: 1) the contestant's relation to the gods; and 2) his relation to his antagonist. I shall consider each in succession:

1) In first instance, the tyrannical drive finds its limit in a gesture of 'sacrifice' or renunciation in the face of divine envy. This *does* seem an unpromising direction to look for insight into a modern atheistic critic like Nietzsche – until we call the character of Greek gods to mind. Far from transcendent, they are only too prone to human, all too human passions, such as envy. Indeed, their only real difference from human beings is immortality; their only real affliction, to remind us of our mortality. It is this sense of historical finitude, our bondage to life-as-becoming, familiar as the problem of critical history, that Nietzsche again emphasises in the context of agonal envy: the contestant 'fears [the god's] envy; in this case it reminds him of the transience of every human lot'.

Leaving the gods behind, we can refer the contestant's or critic's fear of envy to the other agonal contestants instead, as an equally transient plurality of active, antagonistic forces vying with one another to create a new standard of excellence, 'a new greatness'. The envious desire to appropriate for oneself the authority of another, to create a new value or rule and lay claim to a new truth, is sanctioned, indeed encouraged. But as a plurality of equally active, antagonistic forces, the agon also afflicts this desire with a sense of its own vulnerability, an anxiety to discharge hard-won satiety into badly-needed innocence.[21] Agonal envy limits the tyrannical drive in a gesture of 'sacrifice' provoked by an open-ended public contest: the submission of one's claim to a collective process of contention that ensures its mortality, the passage of each hard-won 'truth' into memory. The 'agonal play of forces' is, in other words, the source of multiple resistances that limit the tyrannical impulse of each into a posture of mastery. But what exactly does mastery mean in this context?

2) Here the second relationship of envy needs to be considered: the contestant's consuming jealousy of the reigning champion – Homer, in Plato's case. Agonal envy is *not* the desire to annihilate the champion; it seeks to limit his achievements by surpassing them, so as to 'inherit his fame'. In this formulation, the contestant's or critic's urge to destroy his opponent is checked by two familiar impulses. The first is a greater concern with self-affirmation and the empowerment of his own life – what Nietzsche called '*growth*' in EH; what here appears as the desire to outbid the opponent through an new deed or work of human 'greatness'. The other check involves a limited affirmation of the opponent, and it follows from the first impulse according

---

[21] Concerning the agonal victor, Walter Benjamin writes in 'Das Glück des antiken Menschen': 'Visible to all, praised by the people, the victor stands there: *he* is in desperate need of innocence *[Unschuld tut* ihm *bitter not]*, holding the cup of victory in upheld hands like a shell full of wine, from which a spilt drop would taint him eternally.' (Benjamin 1977, 129).

to the logic of mastery (see p. 34 f. above). The contestant's new work or deed of greatness may provide the new standard of evaluation or measure that *limits* his opponent's achievements; but it also needs to *preserve* those achievements as a measure of its superiority. As the desire to 'inherit his fame', the new work or deed affirms and preserves the opponent's achievement through a *binding of names*, a genealogical bond that would subtend the contestant's attempt to intensify and surpass the other's achievements. These are conserved, not just as a measure, but as a *stimulant* for a new deed or work, a new 'greatness'. Agonal envy brings to the notion of mastery an emphasis on *production* that reorients the destructive impulse of Nietzschean critique towards the creation of new life-affirmative values beyond good and evil.

Chapter 2
Nietzsche's Agon and the Transvaluation of Humanism

Introduction

In this chapter, I address the agon as a Nietzschean philosopheme by focussing on *Homer's Wettkampf* (HW), Nietzsche's most extended treatment of the agon, some other early texts and the surrounding *Nachlass*, asking what the agon means for Nietzsche, and why he values it. I will argue that in HW Nietzsche performs one of his earliest transvaluations, combining in his conception of the agon some key critical themes from his later thought with positive ethical impulses that animate his thought from this early stage onwards: the affirmation of life and human passions in the face of their conflictual and 'immoral' character; perfectionism, in the sense of the enhancement, intensification (*Steigerung*) and extension of human capacities; a form of measure (*Maass*) or moderation that makes social life possible without stifling creative spontaneity; particularism or radical individualism and pluralism, as well as an emphasis on openness, visibility and appearance.[1] Asking how the agon conjugates the conflicting demands for intensification and measure, for pluralism and general welfare, will enable me to show how important it is to understand agonal agency not just from the subject-position of the antagonists, but from a 'medial' position in the relations *between* them. In effect, the argument in this chapter, in shifting the explanans of agonal agency from the subject-position to the relations between them, recapitulates ontogenetically the phylogenetic evolution of my thought on the agon as reflected in the sequence of chapters that follow.

The present chapter begins by setting out the philosophical problem-background to Nietzsche's engagement with the agon in HW, and turns then to the conditions for agonal agency. The formal and dynamic qualities of the agon are then taken up in the next chapter, as a way into the question of how it is actualised in Nietzsche's philosophical practice. But I begin with a brief account of the origin of the idea.

I Origin of the Idea

In Homer, the word AGON (from AGEIN) is used primarily to mean 'gathering', 'place for gatherings' or 'arena', from which is derived the second meaning, 'contest', since it was common to hold contests or dances at various kinds of gatherings (Weiler 1974,

---

[1] In the present context I will pass over two further ethical problems central to Nietzsche's concept of the agon. They concern justice and the conditions for just judgement; and freedom under the pressure of law. For the former see Siemens (2002) and chapter 7; for the latter, see Siemens (2006).

25f.; but also Ellsworth 1981). While both meanings persist in Greek literary usage until the end of the 5th century B.C., there is a noticeable shift from the first meaning (as location) to the second (as action, in line with its etymology in AGEIN), and a significant expansion in usage to all manner of confrontation between persons, groups or peoples (in the case of war), from athletic-musical and literary-rhetorical contests to legal proceedings, but also to war and murder (Weiler 1974, 35). Characteristic of Greek usage is its deployment across the entire scale from play to serious altercation – from musical contests, horse races and marriage, to war or the murder of one's own mother or children – so that even intellectual or sporting contests carry bloody-bellicose connotations (Weiler 1974, 24, 32). The dual meaning of the word for (location of) gatherings and action indicates the profoundly social character of the agon *qua* contest, and its extensive semantic range suggests the thesis, first put forward by the German philologist Ernst Curtius, that the pervasiveness of the agon in all domains of life was specifically Greek.[2] But the best-known and most influential advocate of this thesis is Jacob Burckhardt, Nietzsche's colleague at Basel, who coined the neo-latin term 'agonal' (substantive: 'das Agonale') to describe the principle governing all areas of social and cultural life in Greece, particularly in the period after the Doric invasions to the late 6th century B.C. (approx. 1000–520 B.C.). Burckhardt gave his lectures on *Griechische Kulturgeschichte* in the years when Nietzsche was in Basel, and the agon was without question a topic of intense discussion between them.[3] Indeed, their views on the agonal character of Greek culture in this period are in many respects so close as to be indistinguishable, and the agonal principle is best understood as their shared intellectual legacy.[4] This legacy had a

---

2 According to Weiler (1974, 202), the first to raise the agon to a scientific level was Johann Heinrich Krause, author of *Die Gymnastik und Agonistik der Hellenen*, Leipzig 1841.
3 For Burckhardt's account of the agon, see especially Burckhardt 1929 vol. III chapter 2: 'Der koloniale und agonale Mensch'. The lectures were first given in the summer semester of 1872, and Nietzsche's excitement at the prospect is recorded in a letter to Carl von Gersdorff dated 1st of May 1872: 'Das Sommerkolleg von Burckhardt wird etwas Einziges: es entgeht Dir viel, daß Du es nicht erleben kannst.' (KSB 3.317). According to Salin (1979, 80), however, Nietzsche was denied entry to the lectures by Burckhardt, but waited outside to discuss them with his colleague on his way home (see Weiler 1975, 205f. and note 17). Nietzsche was later given three transcripts of the lectures, one by Baumgartner, one by Kelterborn (dated May 1875), the other by Köselitz (dated April 1976). See letter to Overbeck: 30th May 1875 (KSB 5.58).
4 As Salin shows, Greek cultural history was a topic of repeated discussions between Nietzsche and Burckhardt in the period 1871 to 1873. Nietzsche's high spirits after their first such discussion are evident in his letter to Rohde of 20/12/20th December, 1871, where he writes: 'Mit Jakob Burckhardt habe ich einige schöne Tage erlebt, und unter uns wird viel über das Hellenische conferirt. Ich glaube, man kann jetzt in dieser Hinsicht Einiges in Basel lernen.' (KSB 3.257). Salin also shows that these meetings stimulated Burckhardt to plan and write his first draft of the *Griechische Kulturgeschichte* lectures; indeed, Salin goes so far as to write that many features of these lectures only become understandable when one hears 'the preceding and simultaneous conversations with Nietzsche, especially when one hears also the uninterrupted inner *Auseinandersetzung*' (Salin 1938, 102).

considerable impact on German philological-historical studies of Greece[5] and was first seriously challenged by Huizinga in his 1939 book *Homo Ludens*, in which he argued for the universal, cross-cultural character of agonism. Huizinga's argument has been taken further by the historian of antiquity Ingomar Weiler who, through cross-cultural comparative studies, has criticised Burckhardt's conception of the Greek agon and challenged the specificity of the agon to the Greeks.[6] Nevertheless, the specificity of the Greek agon remains an open issue, as can be seen from the recent comparative study of science and medicine in early China and Greece by Lloyd and Sivin (2002). They argue that the adversarial structures of Greek public life and the model of competitive debate in front of a lay audience had a profound impact not just on the presentation, but on the content of Greek philosophy and science, in marked contrast with their Chinese counterparts.

In certain respects, Curtius' view of the ancient Greek agon bears similarities with Nietzsche's. In a letter to his brother from 1856, Curtius writes of his plan to show 'the agonistic [*agonistisch*] character of Greek life' and 'how the whole of Greek life was a contest of unleashed forces [*Wettkampf entfesselter Kräfte*], a contest between tribes and cities, in war and in peace, in art and science' (cited in Weiler 1975, 205). This plan was soon realised in his lecture *Der Wettkampf* of June 4th 1856,[7] in which the idealising, disciplining powers of the Greeks are emphasised: 'they sought to cleanse their fervour of all selfishness, they ordered and ennobled [*geordnet und veredelt*] the wild drive of ambition through the discipline of law and religion' (Weiler 1975, 204f.). Curtius also sees the Greek agon as exemplary of the 'competitive pleasure in action [*wetteifernde Tatenlust*]' characteristic of Aryan peoples, thereby feeding the agon into the ideology of German-Greek affinity that culminated in Alfred Rosenberg's notion of the 'Nordic Hellas' (Weiler 1975, 205). Burckhardt and Nietzsche both knew Curtius' work and were no doubt influenced by his view of agonistic striving as the engine of Greek culture, but they were highly critical of his classicistic-idealised vision of the Greeks.[8] In line with Greek usage of the word, Nietzsche's conception of agonal agency is decidedly ruthless, and inseparable from 'a streak of cruelty' and a 'tiger-like rage for destruction' (HW, KSA 1.783)[9]

---

5 Weiler 1969, 6 note 6; Billeter 1911, 213f.
6 See Weiler 1974 ch 6 (272–313).
7 Curtius 1877, 132–147.
8 Letter from Rohde to Nietzsche 22nd April 1871, KGB II/7/1.427 ff.
9 This point is picked up by Hoberman (1997, 295): 'In addition to its status as a civic virtue, the ancient ideal of competitive struggle possessed, in Nietzsche's view, an element of ferocity that modern people cannot contemplate without dread.' Equally by Sax (1997, 50), who writes: 'In "Homer's Contest", Nietzsche emphasises that violence is not merely pre-Homeric; it is *hinter*, both prior to and ever-present in the highest achievements of the Greeks. In stressing the constancy of violence, Nietzsche reverses his earlier interpretation in *The Birth of Tragedy*. Violence and cruelty are no longer identified solely with Dionysus, who is understood as a relatively late Asiatic intruder into an essentially Apollonian world. Cruelty is now understood as the source of and constant background to Greek culture.'

passed over by Curtius. Unlike Curtius, however, both Nietzsche and Burckhardt emphasise the measured character of the agon.[10]

For Burckhardt, the agon is first and foremost a 'driving force that no other people knows', the 'general element that brings all willing and doing to fermentation as soon as the necessary freedom is there', and which eventually comes to dominate every sphere of activity and everyday life (Burckhardt 1929 III, 68, 85). He emphasises its aristocratic origins and character, as a 'will to distinction among one's equals [*seinesgleichen*]', to 'measure oneself with others of equal standing [*Gleichstehenden*]', an institution that was open to 'every born Greek' (Burckhardt 1929 III, 68). Agonal victory is cast as 'the noble victory without passion', expressive of 'the peaceful victory of an individuality' first achieved by the Greeks (Burckhardt 1929 III, 70). The performative, non-instrumental character of the Greek agon is concentrated in Burckhardt's claim that it is 'goalless', by which he means that the only 'true goal of the contest is victory in itself [*der Sieg an sich*]', disconnected from any further goals (Burckhardt 1929 III, 77). The agonal mind-set is hereby distinguished from that of the Romans, who 'can do nothing "goalless"', but also from that of the hero, who 'fulfils great goals and mostly on solitary journeys' (Burckhardt 1929 III, 68f.). Ingomar Weiler has objected to this 'fiction of the absoluteness of victory', emphasising the complex of goals and interests at play in the Greek agon, from fame and honour to social standing and material gain (Weiler 1969, 8). Against Burckhardt's restriction of the agon to those of the equal standing, he draws on Greek mythology, where the contests are mostly between *unequals*,[11] as a record of the Greek experience of agon. Weiler's approach brings a realist corrective to Burckhardt's idealising tendencies, reminding us of the role of hubris, immoderation (*Maßlosigkeit*) and arrogance in the Greek agon (Weiler 1974, 252; 1969, 28); the dread of defeat and the shame and ignominy that accompanied it (Weiler 1969, 10); the frequency of brutal violence and the brutal treatment of the vanquished (e.g. the fate of the satyr Marsyas. Weiler 1969, 10), including death; and the importance of the prize, including material gain and, in the case of wedding agons, the bride and/or inheritance (Weiler 1969, 28f.; Weiler 1974, 264–271). Weiler's most important achievement is to have dismissed crass aristocratic ideals from the Greek agon, especially anachronistic ideals of 'fair play' – an invention of 18th and 19th century British public schools[12] – by reminding us of the

---

10 For Burckhardt and Nietzsche on the agon, see the papers by Enrico Müller and Ritchie Robertson in Siemens and Pearson 2019. For an overview of the views on the agon among 19th century German scholars, see Billeter 1911, 212–215, cf. 44f.
11 Typically gods and heroes, or heroes and mortals who challenge them. Weiler (1969, 12 note 36) refers to Pindar's world-order, in which 'the nobler must always triumph over the inferior, thus the son of Zeus Hercules over the giant Geryoneus just like Polydeukes over Lynkeus'.
12 'Sport historians like Manfred Lämmer, Ingomar Weiler, David Young and several others have dispelled the myth that the ancient Greeks were the inventors of fair play. The French archeologist and historian Paul Veyne (cited in Weiler 1991, 55) stated that the concept of playing within a predefined set of rules referred to as *game* seems to be an Anglo-Saxon invention, whereas the ancient Games were trying to imitate the brutal reality of war instead of trying to respect a set of artificial rules.' (Re-

frequent recourse to cunning and deception, and the brazen cheating endemic to the Greek agon (Weiler 1969, 27 ff.; Weiler 1974, 258–264).

In broad terms, Nietzsche's approach to the Greek agon lies somewhere between those of Burckhardt and Weiler. In line with Weiler's realism, he brings out the deeply passionate, often ruthless character of Greek agonism; the hubristic tendencies animating contestants, their tyrannical impulses,[13] and the ever-present dangers of excess (*Maßlosigkeit*) and transgression; the tremendous vulnerability and anxieties of victory; as well as the compulsive cheating, exemplified by Pericles, who, when thrown to the ground in a wrestling match, denies it and convinces those who

---

nson 2009, 6; see also Weiler 1991). This proximity to war is captured well by Nietzsche's remark 'Die Gymnastik der idealisirte Krieg.' (16[15], KSA 7), and the genealogical question: 'Der Wettkampf entsteht aus dem Kriege? Als ein künstlerisches Spiel und Nachahmung?' (16[25], KSA 7).

For a contrasting view of fair play and a regularity interpretation of the agon in archaic Greece, see Tuncel 2009, 146, 168–175; Tuncel 2013b, 83; Tuncel 2016, 355–358. He discusses the roles of the judges or *hellenodikai* at some length in enforcing rules, maintaining discipline, punishing violators and adjudicating victory. A few comments are, however, in order. First, the existence of such judges certainly presupposes that there were cheats; cheating can, however, be brazen and need not presuppose a notion of fair play. Consider, for example, the story of Pericles cheating in a wrestling match (see note 14 below), mentioned by both Nietzsche and Burckhardt. For the most part, Nietzsche was more interested in the relation of the contestants to the public, rather than the judges (or the public *as* the judges). Second, it is not a coincidence that Tuncel's remarks on fair play and justice concern *only* athletic contests. This is because much more is known about them than the kinds of agon that interest Nietzsche in HW. As Tuncel (2009, 171) concedes, 'when it comes to non-athletic contests such as music, poetry and drama and how they were judged, we are still clueless' – although Nietzsche does offer some clues in the *Philologica*, where, for example, he claims that noble families were the first judges (GGL III, KGW II/5.323). Curiously, Tuncel also ignores MA 170, where Nietzsche does discuss the standard of victory in dramatic agons. Instead, Tuncel tries to connect the agon to two well-known passages on justice in Nietzsche's work (UB II 6 and GM II 11) without adducing any textual support for the connection. Where he does adduce textual support for the claim that Nietzsche was aware of fairness in the agon, his use of the texts in question is contentious. In Tuncel 2009, 170 note 59, he cites Nietzsche's reference to 'stern judges' (*strenge Kampfrichter*) in his account of Heraclitus (PHG 6), but omits the rest of the sentence, in which the distinction between judge and player is collapsed: when Heraclitus '[…] could no longer consider the struggling pairs and the judges as separate from each other, the judges themselves seemed to struggle, the antagonists themselves seemed to judge themselves' (PHG 6, KSA 1.826 f.). In the following note (60), Tuncel mistranslates the word 'Nichtgeneigtsein' as 'not to be pre-disposed' (i.e. biased) in a *Nachlass* note on the agon in Greek court proceedings (not athletic contests!): 'Das Nichtgeneigtsein, auf den speziellen Fall einzugehn (sondern die ganze Vergangenheit und die Person zu beurtheilen) einer der wesentlichen Züge der versammelten athenischen Dikasten.' (16[36], KSA 7.406). Nietzsche's point here is that judges were 'not inclined' to go into specific cases, but instead judged the whole person and the entire past. This is fully in line with what he writes about judgement in poetic contests, in which the poet was treated as 'a teacher of what is true [*des Wahren*]' and was judged 'as "highest human being", his song as true, good, beautiful' (16[5], KSA 7.394 f.). Similarly, in MA 170, he writes that the tragic poets 'want really *to be* more excellent'.

13 See 6[7], KSA 8.99 f.; cf. MA 261; 4[301], KSA 9.174 f.; cf. M 199, M 360.

saw him fall.[14] Realism also characterises his lectures as philology professor at the time in Basel, where the agon figures frequently as an explanatory principle – for the origins of the Platonic dialogues (Plato vs. the Sophists; Plato vs. the prose writers: Plato vs. Aeschenes, Antistheneus and Xenophon);[15] for rhetoric (Demosthenes' agonistic vs Isocrates' graphic style);[16] for the emergence of prose from poetry;[17] for the relations between the rhapsodes, and Terpander's hostility to Homer; and for Thucydides' relation to Herodotus and the oral tradition in history,[18] to name a few. Nietzsche's realism extends to the ulterior motives animating contestants, emphasised by Weiler, such as earnings, honour and the furthering of political plans.[19] But there is also a strong deflationary tendency in Nietzsche's realism. In his *History of Greek Literature* lectures (*Geschichte der griechischen Litteratur*), we read of the prevalence of degeneration in Greek art;[20] of the stifling of talent[21] at the hands of publics utterly incapable of sound aesthetic judgement; of the fear of innovation in art in the polis and the resistance to it through harsh repressive laws;[22] and how, for a long time, the agon repressed the emergence of individuals.[23]

All of this reminds us how stylised Nietzsche's *philosophical* concept of the agon is in HW and surrounding notes, where he is much closer to Burckhardt. Like Burckhardt, he emphasises the aristocratic character of the Greek agon and the ideal it embodies, as the drive for distinction and excellence inter pares, as well as the concom-

---

14 HW, KSA 1.788. Also cited by Burckhardt from Plutarch (rei publ. ger. Praec. 5) in Burckhardt 1921 I, 220 note 2.
15 *Einführung in das Studium der platonischen Dialoge* (SS 1871/72 – WS 1874/75, KGW II/4.122 ff.
16 *Geschichte der griechischen Beredsamkeit* (WS 1872–1873), KGW II/4.372 ff. (Protagoras); 161 (Phaedrus and Symposium); GGL I & II, KGW II/5.196.
17 GGL I & II (WS 1874–75; SS 1875) KGW II/5.30, 196.
18 GGL I & II, KGW II/5.401 f., 228 f., 235 ff., 251.
19 GGL III, KGWI I/5.292.
20 '[...] daß die *Entartung auch in Hellas überwiegend, das Gute selten ist*, daß die Entartung hinter jeder großen Erscheinung her ist, daß in jedem Augenblick der Ansatz zum Ende da ist, daß die Linie zwischen einem Genius u. dem andern selten eine gerade Linie ist, daß eine Menge von Formen der Entwicklung erdrückt wor-den sind u. daß es überhaupt sehr gefährlich hergieng.' (GGL III, KGW II/5.310, 315).
21 Compare Harold Bloom and Nietzsche on this point: 'The anxiety of influence cripples weaker talents but stimulates canonical genius' (Bloom 1994, 11), and Nietzsche's question: 'Ob nicht sehr viele herrliche Möglichkeiten im Keime erstickt sind?' ('Whether a great many wonderful possibilities were not nipped in the bud?') after a paragraph on the agon among geniuses: 'Das Agonale ist auch die Gefahr bei aller Entwicklung; es überreizt den Trieb zum Schaffen. – Der glücklichste Fall in der Entwicklung, wenn sich mehrere Genie's gegenseitig in Schranken halten.' ('The agonal is the danger in all development: it overstimulates the drive to create. – The most felicitous case in development when several geniuses keep each other in check.') (5[149], KSA 8.78).
22 GGL III, KGW II/5.298.
23 'das siegreiche Individuum gilt as Incarnation des Gottes, tritt in den Gott zurück' (GGL III, KGW II/5.299).

itant prohibition on competing with the gods.[24] The exceptional fertility of the agon is also central to Nietzsche's account, as a stimulant to great deeds, works and the proliferation of extraordinary individuals. But of equal importance for Nietzsche is the moment of measure, which excludes violence and death from the agon. Like Burckhardt, he construes the agon as specifically Greek in HW, but he does so without falling into the crass opposition between Greeks and barbarians, to which Burckhardt is prone (see esp. Burckhardt 1929 I, 289 f.). Instead, he engages in a thought-experiment of 'subtraction': 'If [...] we take away the contest from Greek life, we gaze immediately into that pre-Homeric abyss of a gruesome savagery of hatred and pleasure in destruction [*Vernichtungslust*]'[25] – where 'pre-Homeric' means 'not-Greek'.[26] This formulation points towards a fundamental difference between Nietzsche's concept of the agon and Burckhardt's, best seen in their different genealogies of the Eris goddesses. While Greek usage of 'agon' typically blends seriousness and play, conflict and contest, Hesiod does differentiate two kinds of conflict under the sign of the two Eris goddesses in the *Erga* (*Works and Days*). According to Burckhardt, the good Eris 'is the earlier born (according to which the evil [Eris] would be only a kind of amplified degeneration [*Ausartung ins Große*], into war and strife)' (Burckhardt 1929 III, 70). In Nietzsche's version, by contrast, it is the evil Eris – 'promot[ing] wicked war and feuding, the cruel one!' – who is older, and the good Eris younger, who 'as jealousy, grudge [or wrath: *Groll*] and envy, goads men to deeds, not, however, the deeds of the struggle for annihilation [*That des Vernichtungskampfes*], but deeds of the contest [*That des Wettkampfes*]' (HW, KSA 1.787).[27] For Burckhardt, who in the end remains captive to the classical ideal, competition and the noble drive for excellence come first, and destructive conflict is a kind of grotesque deformation of those impulses. For Nietzsche, inveterate opponent of classical ideal, the unmeasured pathos of conflict – what he calls the destructive *Vernichtungskampf* –

---

24 See 16[9], KSA 7.396: 'Der Wettkampf! Und das Aristokratische, Geburtsmäßige, Edle bei den Griechen!' Also HW, KSA 1.787 on the prohibition on competing with the gods. The drive for distinction (*Auszeichnung*) and victory over others is a sustained topic for Nietzsche: see WS 31, 50, 226; VM 152, 166, 222, 291; M 30, 571 and 7[200], KSA 10.305.
25 Or again: 'without envy, jealousy and competitive ambition, the Hellenic state, like Hellenic man, deteriorates. It becomes evil and cruel, it becomes vengeful and godless, in short, it becomes "pre-Homeric"' (HW, KSA 1.792).
26 It is, however, interesting to note that in his lectures *Encyclopedia of Classical Philology*, Nietzsche draws on comparative linguistics to argue that the pre-Homeric Greeks were originally 'in the Orient' and counts 'contests' (*Wettkämpfe*) as part of their culture at that time (KGW II/3.425). In short: the agon came from pre-Homeric Asia! This is fully in line with his repeated emphasis on the allochthonous sources of Greek culture, understood by Nietzsche as a 'grand synthesis' (M 272; 41[7], KSA 11.682; see also Siemens 2001b and chapter 5).
27 See Nietzsche's lectures on Hesiod (WS 1869; SS 1870; WS 1870–1; SS 1871; SS 1873; SS 1876), where he asks which goddess is the older and contests the generally accepted version of the *Erga* used by Burckhardt, in which the good Eris is the older: 'Es ist eine Art Widerspruch. Wie soll die gute die ältere sein? Gerade die böse ist nach der Theog. Uralt' (KGW II/2.361). It is Nietzsche's corrected version that then appears in HW (KSA 1.786).

comes first, and the achievement of the Homeric and post-Homeric Greeks was to bend this pathos into affects that allowed for the social life of the polis and stimulated creative deeds through measured contests (*Wettkampf*). With this construction, Nietzsche introduces a tension into the word 'agon', between the serious business of murder and destructive conflict (*Vernichtungs-kampf*, as a variant of 'Ernstkampf') and the creative play of contestation (*Wett-kampf*), which remain nonetheless 'inseparably entwined' as forms of conflict or struggle (*Kampf*).[28] And with the pessimistic presupposition of a generalised war of annihilation, Nietzsche breaks decisively with the agon as an historical problem and his own historical-philological work on the agon[29] in favour of a philosophical problematic that will inform the rest of his work.

Without doubt, it is important to consider Nietzsche's concept of the agon in the light of contemporary scholarship in ancient philology, history, sports history and archaeology, and to see that much of what he wrote has since been confirmed and extended by it (even if in current scholarship the agon is, perhaps appropriately, subject to widespread disagreement).[30] Nietzsche's agon is not, after all, pure philhellenic fantasy, but takes off from and bears on the really lived reality of archaic Greece, or rather: of the male, mostly noble citizens in that period. But it is not an empirical or historical concept, to be gauged and evaluated against 'what we know' of archaic Greece. It is equally important to keep in mind that the concept of the agon, where we encounter it outside Nietzsche's strictly philological work, is primarily of interest to him (and to us, I would say) because it addresses fundamental *philosophical* problems concerning human existence and culture in their highest possibilities. As the gap between Nietzsche's deflationary realism in the *Phi-*

---

28 Compare Sax 1997, 58: 'Although good Eris offered an alternative to annihilating violence, she did not abolish or suppress cruelty in all its forms. The two goddesses of Eris are, in fact, not two separate deities. They are two faces of the self-same goddess. In these faces, the Greeks mythically perceived not an opposition of nature and culture but a double face of nature.'

29 Nietzsche's philological engagement with the concept of the agon goes back as far as 1867 when he prepared a talk for the *Philologische Verein* called 'Über den Sängerkrieg auf Euböa' (Janz 1981 I, 193). This concerns a text from the period of Hadrian – the so-called 'Certamen' – recounting a purported agon between Homer and Hesiod, which Nietzsche investigated over a period of several years. In 1867 he argues for the historical authenticity of this contest and already points to the fundamental role of the agon in Greek culture: that 'der ἀγών selbst aber von den ältesten Zeiten griechischer Geschichtsschreibung ein wirkendes Element ist' (quoted in Janz 1981 I, 193). Vogt (1962) charts the transformation of the Homer-Hesiod agon as a philological problem into a philosopheme in HW and argues that Nietzsche's views on the function and meaning of the agon in the world of the early Greeks developed out of his unorthodox interpretation of the Homer-Hesiod agon.

30 Tuncel 2009, 146. In this regard, Yunus Tuncel has gathered a useful collection of current scholarly literature on the agon and archaic Greece from numerous sources (see Tuncel 2009, 2013a, 2013b, 2016). But he does not investigate or indicate the extent to which the evidence and sources available to contemporary scholars were available to Nietzsche, nor do we learn anything about his agon in relation to 19th century philology. We would really need both to gauge Nietzsche's agon as an empirical or historical concept. More importantly, they would help us to understand better how he turned a philologeme into a philosopheme.

lologica and the highly stylised concept of the agon in HW makes clear, we are presented in this text with a philosopheme, not a philologeme.

II Nietzsche's Transvaluation of Humanism in *Homer's Wettkampf*

From the very first paragraph, it is clear that *Homer's Wettkampf* is not just an essay on ancient Greek culture, but one that raises the fundamental question: What is humanity?[31]

> When one speaks of *humanity* [Humanität], it is on the basis of the idea that it is that which *separates* and distinguishes human beings from nature. But there is in reality no such separation: the "natural" qualities and the so-called "human" [*menschlich*] are inseparably entwined. Human beings, in their highest and noblest capacities, are wholly nature and bear her uncanny double-character in themselves. Their frightening capacities, those considered inhuman [*unmenschlich*], are perhaps even the fruitful soil from which alone all humanity [*Humanität*] can grow forth [*hervorwachsen*] in impulses, deeds and works. (HW, KSA 1.783)[32]

By embedding the 'so-called "human"' qualities in nature, Nietzsche is clearly opposing the traditional conception of the human as the being that stands out over and above nature, with its roots in the Aristotelian conception of the *animal rationale*.[33] 'None of us knows how deep or how high physis extends' (16[42], KSA 7.408): this is how Nietzsche puts the ontological problem of human nature in a preparatory *Nachlass* note. But in this opening paragraph of HW, the ontological problem of human physis or being is bound up with a normative problem and the polemic he is announcing with humanism – or rather: the neo-humanism of Winckelmann, Goethe, Schiller, Humboldt and the entire philological guild. Nietzsche's claim is

---

[31] The *Vorstufe* to HW ('Erster, vorläufiger Entwurf von "*Homer's Wettkampf*". Angefangen den 21. Juli 1872': 20[1], KSA 7.521) opens with the questions: 'Was ist Humanität? Da liegt die Vorstellung zu Grunde, es möge das sein, was den Menschen von der Natur abscheidet und auszeichnet?' (KGW III 5/1.832f.).

[32] 'Wenn man von *Humanität* redet, so liegt die Vorstellung zu Grunde, es möge das sein, was den Menschen von der Natur *abscheidet* und auszeichnet. Aber eine solche Abscheidung giebt es in Wirklichkeit nicht: die "natürlichen" Eigenschaften und die eigentlich "menschlich" genannten sind untrennbar verwachsen. Der Mensch, in seinen höchsten und edelsten Kräften, ist ganz Natur und trägt ihren unheimlichen Doppelcharakter an sich. Seine furchtbaren und als unmenschlich geltenden Befähigungen sind vielleicht sogar der fruchtbare Boden, aus dem allein alle Humanität, in Regungen Thaten und Werken hervorwachsen kann.' (HW, KSA 1.783).

[33] This point is made by Sax (1997, 57f.) with regard to the notion of agonal culture in HW: 'The Greeks never considered culture as the opposite of nature. The agon—the unity of their entire culture—constantly combined the two. Through the agon they directed violence into positive action, and formed a culture that did not separate nature from culture. In the agon a culture was created that was, in a remarkable combination, at once nature and culture.'

that the 'highest and noblest capacities' of the ancient Greeks, the great 'impulses, deeds and works' so prized by the philhellenic humanists, are inseparable from their sources in terrifying capacities or impulses they prefer to ignore or condemn as 'inhuman'.[34] At stake in Nietzsche's question and his quarrel with humanism is not just the works of art they admired and their presuppositions in human nature. At stake is human perfection – our 'highest and noblest capacities'. While Nietzsche's perfectionism refers to individual 'impulses, deeds and works', it is important not isolate it as a concern for a few select individuals from a generic orientation towards 'humanity' and its 'growth' (*Hervorwachsen*), enhancement or intensification (*Steigerung*). Nietzsche's perfectionism, here and throughout his work, is a concern to extend the range of human capacities and possibilities by way of individual deeds and works that enhance the concept or species 'human'.[35] In these terms, the problem of humanity is not how to distinguish ourselves as humans by insulating ourselves against our natural impulses, but the question: how to bend the terrifying, destructive impulses on the ground of human existence into creative forces that extend the range of human capacities in 'impulses, deeds and works'? For Nietzsche, the question 'what is humanity?' to which the agon answers in HW, is both the ontological question of *human physis* and the normative question of *human perfection: What ought humankind to become?* These questions are, to borrow Nietzsche's words, 'inseparably entwined'.

In the succeeding paragraphs of *Homer's Wettkampf*, Nietzsche opposes the 'soft concept of modern humanity' to the 'tiger-like pleasure in destruction' of the Greeks, 'the most human of ancient people', their 'abysses of hatred', 'wanton cruelty', and their Homeric predilection for bloody battle scenes of agonising death and hubristic triumph.[36] Nietzsche's purpose in describing these scenes with such relish is to take the side of the ancient Greeks against the 'soft' humanism of modernity by connecting their greatest human achievements to their presupposition in a blood-soaked existence and a pessimistic view of life governed by 'the *children of the night*, conflict, lust, deception age and death' (HW, KSA 1.785). This move raises the problem that divides Nietzsche from Schopenhauer: How to oppose the negation of existence and the will, given its character as struggle, cruelty, pain and suffering?

---

34 See the later critique of the 'niaiserie allemande' in GD Alten 3, KSA 6.157; also 24[1], KSA 13.626, and 11[312], KSA 13.131f. Goethe, Schiller, Winckelmann, Herder and Hegel are criticised for their false naturalism (confusion of cause and effect), their lack of psychology and their exclusion of the Dionysian, as the explosive ground against which the classical ideal was erected, as both a protective measure and a celebration.
35 Nietzsche draws on various formulations throughout his work to emphasise this generic or general orientation, not just 'Species', 'Gattung', but also 'die Pflanze Mensch', 'der Begriff "Mensch"', 'der Typus Mensch', etc. See Regent 2008, 654 on Nietzsche's source for the expression 'die Pflanze Mensch' (also used by Burckhardt) in Alfieri's *pianta 'uomo'*, which he gleaned from Stendahl, not Burckhardt.
36 See Sax (1997, 55) on 'the contrast between the ancient struggle for humanity in a violent world and our modern, weak concept of so-called humanity'.

The problem of life-affirmation lies at the very epicentre of Nietzsche's thought from GT onwards. In GT, completed shortly before HW, this problem informs Nietzsche's account of Greek tragedy when he asks how 'the Hellene, by nature profound and uniquely susceptible to the finest and most severe suffering, who with penetrating vision has gazed into the midst of the terrifying destructiveness [*Vernichtungstreiben*] of so-called world history, as well as nature's cruelty', avoids succumbing to a 'Buddhistic negation of the will' (GT 7, KSA 1.56)? The answer he gives there turns on art and its capacity to bend (*umbiegen*) the revulsion at the horror and absurdity of existence into representations 'that can be lived with': the sublime and the comic (GT 7, KSA 1.57). In HW, the all-pervasive war of annihilation or *Vernichtungskampf* stands as a shorthand for this pessimistic view of life, both ancient and modern,[37] and his answer to the same problem turns on the *Wettkampf* or agon, when he writes:

> The names of Orpheus, Musaeus and their cults reveal what were the conclusions to which a continual exposure to a world of conflict and cruelty [*des Kampfes und der Grausamkeit*] led – to revulsion at existence, to the view of existence as a punishment to be expiated, to the belief in the identity of existence and guilt [indebtedness: *Verschuldetsein*]. But precisely these conclusions are not specifically Hellenic: in them, Greece meets India and the Orient in general. The Hellenic genius had yet another answer ready to the question 'What does a life of conflict and victory want?', and gives this answer in the whole breadth of Greek history.
>
> In order to understand it, we must assume that Greek genius acknowledged the existing drive, terrible as it was, and regarded it as *justified:* whereas in the Orphic turn of thought there lay the thought that a life rooted in such a drive was not worth living. Conflict and the pleasure of victory were acknowledged [*anerkannt*]: and nothing divides the Greek world so

---

37 Schopenhauer's 'self-lacerating will'; Darwin's 'struggle for existence'; Heraclitus' 'father of all things'; and, in the context of HW, the 'evil Eris' and the 'Children of the Night' described in Hesiod's *Works and Days*. For Darwin: 'The poet overcomes the struggle for existence by idealising it into a free agon [contest]. Here is the existence, for which there is still a struggle, existence in praise, in undying fame. The poet *educates* [erzieht]: he knows how to transpose [*übertragen*] the Greeks' tiger-like drives to ravaging devastation into the good Eris.' (16[15], KSA 7). For Heraclitus' 'father of all', see fragment 53: 'War is the father of all (beings) and the king of all.' (in H. Diels, *Die Fragmente der Vorsokratiker*, ed. W. Kranz, Berlin: 1960: 9th ed.). For a useful list of references to this principle in Nietzsche, see Herschbell & Nimis 1979, 22–26. One important reference not mentioned by them is in GT 4 (KSA 1.39), where Nietzsche writes of 'eternal contradiction' as the 'father of things'. The insight into war or destructiveness (*Vernichtungstreiben*) as the fundamental character of life is attributed to all Greeks in GT 7, KSA 1.56. Nietzsche's favoured expression of Greek pessimism is of course the line attributed to Silenus in GT 3 (KSA 1.35) that the best is never to have been born. Nietzsche will have come across these lines already in his school days from various sources: Theognis, Sophocles and the 'Certamen' document on the agon between Homer and Hesiod (see note 29 above and Vogt 1962). Another source, not mentioned by Vogt, is Calderon, quoted in *Schopenhauer's World as Will and Representation*.

sharply from ours as the resultant *colouring* [Färbung] of individual ethical concepts, for example of the *Eris* and *envy*. (HW 1.785)[38]

The philosophical problem driving Nietzsche's interest in the agonal Greeks is how to articulate a form of life-affirmation that does justice to the irredeemably cruel and conflictual character of life without simply succumbing to its senseless destructiveness. In HW, the agon represents the Greeks' best response to this problem, not in the form of a doctrine, teaching or particular work of art, but as a collective practice imbued with a certain ethos. What Nietzsche sees and values in the Greek agon is an institutionalised form of interaction that (1) allows for an *affirmation* of life as struggle and conflict, and the hostile drives and affects that feed it – cruelty, hatred, envy, grudge – but also (2) *transforms* the unmeasured destructiveness of the war of annihilation (*Vernichtungskampf*) into the measured and creative force of the contest (*Wettkampf*), thereby enhancing the concept or species 'human' through exceptional deeds and works.

These thoughts are given sharper, more polemical contours a few years later in a *Nachlass* note from the period of VM (1875):

> The pleasure of *intoxication*, the pleasure of *guile*, of *revenge*, of *envy*, of *slander*, of *licentiousness* [*Unzüchtigkeit*] – all of this was *acknowledged* [*anerkannt*] by the Greeks as human, and on that basis integrated into [*eingeordnet*] the edifice of society and mores. The wisdom of their institutions lies in the lack of distinction between good and evil, black and white. Nature, as it shows itself, is not denied [*weggeleugnet*], but only *ordered* [*eingeordnet*], restricted to determinate cults and days. This is the root of all freedom of mind [*Freisinnigkeit*] in antiquity; a measured discharge [*mässige Entladung*] was sought for the forces of nature, not their annihilation or negation [*Vernichtung, Verneinung*].[39]

Nowhere is Nietzsche's polemic with modern humanism sharper than in these lines: what soft humanists condemn as 'inhuman' (recall the opening paragraph of HW) – our frightening, natural impulses and capacities – were affirmed and 'acknowledged [*anerkannt*] by the Greeks as human'. Here the *affirmative transformation* of destructive, unmeasured impulses into measured, constructive forces effected by the mores and institutions of the Greek polis is polemically opposed to the attempt to negate or annihilate (*Verneinung, Vernichtung*) these destructive, natural impulses through

---

[38] The identification of individuated existence with punishment, guilt or a debt to be expiated is familiar from the problem of affirmation articulated in Z II Erlösung. These are a references to Anaximander and Schopenhauer, as can be seen in PHG 4, KSA 1.818.

[39] 'Die Lust am *Rausche*, die Lust am *Listigen*, an der *Rache*, am *Neide*, an der *Schmähung*, an der *Unzüchtigkeit* – alles das wurde von den Griechen *anerkannt*, als menschlich, und darauf hin eingeordnet in das Gebäude der Gesellschaft und Sitte. Die Weisheit ihrer Institutionen liegt in dem Mangel einer Scheidung zwischen gut und böse, schwarz und weiss. Die Natur, wie sie sich zeigt, wird nicht weggeleugnet, sondern nur *eingeordnet*, auf bestimmte Culte und Tage beschränkt. Dies ist die Wurzel aller Freisinnigkeit des Alterthums; man suchte für die Naturkräfte eine mässige Entladung, nicht eine Vernichtung und Verneinung.' (5[146], KSA 8.78; cf. VM 220).

their denial (*Wegleugnung*). At stake in this opposition is that between the *amoral* 'freedom of mind' or 'liberality' (*Freisinnigkeit*) informing the institutions and mores regulating the Greeks' practice of affirmative transformation, and a morality of judgement that seeks to annihilate our destructive, natural impulses as something that 'nicht sein soll', employing black-and-white value oppositions: human vs. inhuman, good vs. evil etc.

Nietzsche's later critique of our belief in the opposition of values from JGB 2 is unmistakable in these lines, as is his critique of Christianity in GD Moral as a morality of enmity or 'castratism' bent on annihilating our natural passions ('"il faut tuer les passions"': KSA 6.82). It is striking how the young Nietzsche's engagement with the Greek agon leads him not only to articulate the positive (life-affirmative and perfectionist) impulses that will dominate his thought throughout his work, but also to anticipate *in nuce* some key critical themes of his later thought. In HW, Nietzsche anticipates his later genealogies by tracing modern humanist values – the deeds and works they value – to their sources in dangerous natural passions they negate as inhuman and evil, confronting humanism with the demand to affirm life beyond good and evil. Indeed, the agonal Greeks provoke in Nietzsche one of his earliest attempts at transvaluation (*Umwertung*): the transvaluation of humanist values. As the opening paragraph makes clear, it is not about abolishing the concept or term 'human', but about giving it new meanings and value by re-connecting and reapportioning the so-called 'natural' and 'human', conscious and unconscious, purposive and affective determinants of human agency and transvaluating them in the name of human perfection and life affirmation.

Nietzsche's guiding thread for his transvaluation of humanism is the Otherness of agonal Greek ethics. He writes of the particular 'colouring' or 'hue' (*Färbung*) of individual ethical concepts (like Eris and envy) that divides their world from ours. What contemporary scholars cannot understand, he asserts, is how the Greeks could have seen jealousy, envy and grudge as the gifts of a beneficent deity, the goddess of the contest or 'good Eris'; and he goes on to remark that 'another ethics than the Hellenic [one] must have inspired them unawares' (HW, KSA 1.787).[40] For Nietzsche, the key to the Otherness of Greek ethics lies in the all-pervasive war of annihilation or *Vernichtungskampf* that he presupposes as a shorthand for their pessimistic view of life (nature and history). Against this background, what he values is the amoral 'liberality' (*Freisinnigkeit*) that enabled them to affirm this reality and to integrate (*Einordnen*) it into civic life through the measuring influence of the *Wettkampf*.

---

40 Cf. Finley (1982, 121): 'The *Iliad* in particular is saturated in blood, a fact which cannot be hidden or argued away, twist the evidence as one may in a vain attempt to fit archaic Greek values to a more gentle code of ethics. The poet and his audience lingered lovingly over every act of slaughter.' He goes on to quote HW and then (1982, 122 f.) to distinguish Homeric competition from the contest that would play such an important part in Greek public life in later centuries. Homer's world was 'unprepared to socialise the contest', for which 'the almost pure egoism of heroic honor' had to give way to 'civic pride'.

The agonal Greeks' freedom of mind or liberality (*Freisinnigkeit*) goes hand-in-hand with a certain openness, passionateness, and a desire to appear in public that Nietzsche calls 'the entire visibility of the soul [...] without shame' (3[49], KSA 8.28; cf. 5[70], KSA 8.60). For Nietzsche, moral judgement is part of the practical regime fostered by humanism to educate or form (*bilden*) our nature by bringing it under the control of reason, identified as both the *differentia specifica* and normative *telos* of being human. But to subject our 'nature' to universal rational principles (*das vernünftig Allgemeine*) is to suppress particularity and spontaneity in favour of universal, uniform models of practice. And against this, Nietzsche appeals to the extraordinary wealth of individuals or individual types fostered by agonal Greek culture:

> Remarkably many individuals, ought that not count as a higher morality [*Sittlichkeit*]? If one conceives of their character as having emerged slowly, what is it then that in the end engenders so much individuality? Perhaps vanity in relation to one another, competitiveness [*Wetteifer*]? Possible. Scant pleasure in convention. (3[49], KSA 8.27)

For Nietzsche, as for Burckhardt, the agon explains the Greeks' achievement of human plurality, the extraordinary proliferation of diverse individuals unequalled by any culture except perhaps the Renaissance. Despite the intensity of communal life, despite the harsh, repressive laws of the polis, Nietzsche notes that 'the agon unleashes [*entfesselt*] individual' (16[22], KSA 7.402): 'The individual intensified to the highest power by the polis. Envy, jealousy as with those of genius' (5[70], KSA 8.60). What Nietzsche values in the agon, then, is the way it fosters particularity and creative spontaneity among a plurality of individuals. The agonal polis was a kind of breeding ground or hothouse for human excellence, or rather: for human excellences, a regime of power that offers the best conditions for experiments in human excellence.

III The Problem of Measure

Yet, all of this is just one side of Nietzsche's fascination with agon. On the other side is the problem of measure (*Maass*) or limits. We saw earlier that Nietzsche's perfectionism, while embodied in individual 'impulses, deeds and work', should not be isolated, as a concern for a few select individuals, from a generic concern with 'humanity' and its growth (*Hervorwachsen*), enhancement or intensification (*Steigerung*). For Nietzsche, it is equally important not to isolate human perfection and its embodiments from the demands of social and political life. The agon is the 'life-blood' (*Lebensgrund*) of the polis, and what Nietzsche values, as we saw, is how it affirms the 'forces of nature' as human, but limits them through 'measured discharge' (*mässige Entladung*) so as to make social life possible. In HW,[41] Nietzsche's fascination with

---

41 In the *Nachlass* surrounding HW, one can see that Nietzsche equivocated on the question of mea-

the agon lies precisely in the co-ordination of excess and measure (*Übermaas* and *Maass*) through an institution that *both* stimulated the spontaneity and development of the individual *and* limited its forms of expression:

> The contest unleashes [*entfesselt*] the individual: and at the same time it restrains [*bändigt*] the latter according to eternal laws. (16[22], KSA 7.402)

The key to this thought lies in the dynamic, pluralistic character of the agon explored by Nietzsche in response to the problem of genius he inherited from Wagner. This is the principal source of his preoccupation with the question of measure at this time. Nietzsche's early thought is dominated by the figure of genius, embodied by the pre-Socratic philosophers, the great tragedians, and their contemporary avatars: Schopenhauer and Wagner. Drawing on Wagner's concept of genius, Nietzsche places the figure of genius at the apex of cultural and political life and gives him the task of creating powerful illusions (*Illusionen, Wahngebilde*) that make it possible for the human community to live and to affirm life.[42] But for Nietzsche, this position depends on the capacity of genius to limit or measure itself, what he calls 'creative self-restraint' (*schöpferische Selbstumschränkung*) with reference to Schopenhauer (SE 3, KSA 1.350 f.). And with the breakdown of his relationship with Wagner in the mid 1870's, Nietzsche loses confidence in the power of self-restraint on part of individual genius. Wagner is increasingly cast as a tyrannical force,[43] and there is a marked shift in Nietzsche's thought from the standpoint of genius and the ideal of self-limitation, to those who suffer under genius and the problem of measure or limits: How to impose limits on genius? What is best source of measure against tyrannical concentrations of power?

One answer explored by Nietzsche is contemporary democracy, identified in MA as a site of pluralism, of resistance to, and emancipation from tyrannical forces.[44] But Nietzsche's best answer, and his clearest formulation of the problem, are given in HW, in the passage on the Greek custom of ostracism cited in chapter 1:

> The original sense of this peculiar institution [ostracism –HS] is not, however, that of a vent [escape-valve], but rather that of a stimulant: one removes the outstanding individual so that the competitive play of forces [*Wettspiel der Kräfte*] may reawaken: a thought that is inimical to the "exclusivity" of genius in the modern sense, but presupposes that in a natural order of things there are always several geniuses who rouse [stimulate] one another to action [lit. deed], as

---

sure: at times it is associated with the agon and with myth, at others with myth and love *against* the naked egoism fostered by the agon (see Siemens 2017). In HW, however, he has settled for reciprocal provocation and measure as the hallmark of agonal interaction.
42 See e.g. 6[3], KSA 7.130 and 5[25], KSA 7.98.
43 See 32[22], KSA 7; 32[32], KSA 7, 32[34], KSA 7, 32[61], KSA 7 and MA 577.
44 See Siemens 2009b. From around 1880 on, Nietzsche increasingly links democracy with tyranny in the form of popular sovereignty, and with the promotion of uniformity, to the exclusion of genuine pluralism.

they also hold one another within the bounds of measure. That is the crux of the Hellenic notion of contest: it loathes one-man rule [*Alleinherrschaft*] and fears its dangers; it desires, as a protection against genius – a second genius. (HW, KSA 1.789)

The trauma of Wagner's megalomania is clearly legible in the '"exclusivity"' of genius in the modern sense'[45] and the loathing (*Abscheu*) of one-man rule (*Alleinherrschaft*) that Nietzsche shares with the agonal Greeks. Their shared response is to seek protection (*Schutzmittel*) or limits on the exclusive claims of individual genius in a plurality of more-or-less equal geniuses or forces. By banishing the towering individual to whom none are equal, ostracism secures a dynamic plurality of more-or-less equal forces or geniuses, and under these conditions a form of interaction unique to the agon comes into play: what Nietzsche calls the 'competitive play of forces' or *Wettspiel der Kräfte*, consisting of relations of reciprocal stimulation or provocation (*zur That reizen*) on one side, and reciprocal limitation within the bounds of measure (*in der Grenze des Maaßes halten*) on the other. Here, limits are not imposed on the agon by extraneous factors or affects; instead, it is in the nature of agonal interaction to generate both the perfectionist dynamic of reciprocal stimulation *and* the limits or measure on individual action needed for social life. Like Huizinga and Simmel,[46] Nietzsche was struck by the paradox that (institutionalised) conflicts like the agon house unique generative social powers. With Hartmut Schröter,[47] we can therefore speak of Nietzsche's agon as the 'element of commonalty', in which the conditions for unleashing the individual also generate the limits needed for general welfare. This is the chief paradox presented by the agon and the crux of Nietzsche's fascination with it: How is it able to conjugate the particularity and spontaneous, creative freedom of a plurality of individuals on one side, with the measure needed to secure general welfare and strong communal life on the other? How can the agon generate this non-coercive form of measure – one that does not preclude or foreclose the unleashing of spontaneous and unpredictable individual impulses?

---

[45] On Nietzsche's attitude to Wagner, see the remark by Kelterborn, a student of Nietzsche's, that he honoured Wagner 'in the first instance not just as the genial musician and *dramatist*, but above all else as a cultural force, a *fellow fighter next to him* (not above him) in the struggle for a higher German culture [einen *Mitstreiter neben*, (nicht über ihm): original emphasis]'. Dated 1875, from the *Nachbericht*, Beck'sche Ausgabe der Briefe (*Friedrich Nietzsche: Werke und Briefe. Historisch-kritische Gesamtausgabe*, C.H.Beck'sche Verlagsbuchhandlung, München, 1933–1940), Bd. 4, 351.
[46] Huizinga 1939 Ch 3: 'Spiel und Wetteifer als kulturschaffende Funktion', esp. 78, 82f. Cf. Simmel 1964.
[47] Schröter 1982, 106–122.

III.1 Agonal Affects: Envy, Jealousy, Ambition

One answer suggested by *Homer's Wettkampf* turns on the kinds of affects Nietzsche ascribes to agonal antagonists. In chapter 1 (p. 39 ff.) we saw that envy and jealousy (*Neid*, *Eifersucht*) are described as agonal affects that rouse men to contestation (*Wettkampf*), rather than mutual destruction (the *Vernichtungskampf*); that is, to displace the opponent and inherit his fame, not to destroy him. (HW, KSA 1.787). *At the same time* it is also envy, fear of divine envy, which provokes the Greek's vertiginous fear of victory, provoking a self-limiting gesture of sacrifice. On this account, then, agonal envy binds the contestants in relations of *appropriation* ('to take the place of') *and sacrifice* that generate the agonal dynamic of reciprocal provocation and limitation. Having considered envy and jealousy in the previous chapter, I will now concentrate on Nietzsche's account of egoism (*Selbstsucht*) and the agonal affect or drive of ambition (*Ehrgeiz*).

In the case of ambition, the agonal dynamic turns on the contestant's relation to the community or city-state. Whereas modern educators fear ambition as "'the evil in itself'", the Jesuits have a different attitude, much closer to the Hellenes, Nietzsche contends:

> They seem to believe that egoism [*Selbstsucht*], that is, the individual factor is just the most powerful agent which, however, receives its character as "good" or "evil" essentially from the goals towards which it reaches out. Now for the ancients the goal of agonal education was the welfare of the whole, the state society. Every Athenian, for example, was supposed to develop his self [*sein Selbst*] in the contest to that degree which would be of greatest advantage to Athens and do it the least harm. (HW, KSA 1.789)

The contestant's driving ambition was for personal glory and fame *(Ruhm)*, but for the agonal individual, this was inseparable from that of his state or community:

> [I]t was of the well-being of his maternal city that a youth thought when running or throwing or singing in competition; it was her fame that he wanted to increase through his; [and] the wreaths which the judges of the contest placed in honour upon his head, he dedicated to the gods of his city. (HW, KSA 1.789)

Nietzsche's point seems to be that a pre-reflective identity between the self and the community was pre-formed on an affective level in the agonal affects such as ambition: the agon is based on social or communal drives, what Nietzsche sometimes calls 'allgemeine Triebe' (3[44], 19[21], KSA 7).[48] Their effect is to place the individual actions which they drive into the service of the state-community:

---

48 In 19[21], KSA 7.422 Nietzsche writes of the Greeks' 'general drives' (*allgemeinen Triebe*) weakening over time, so that the individual could no longer be held in check.

> Every Greek felt from childhood on the burning wish within himself to be an instrument [*Werkzeug*] for the good [salvation] of his city in the contest of the cities: therein was his egoism [*Selbstsucht*] enflamed, therein was it also checked and bounded [*gezügelt und umschränkt*]. (HW, KSA 1.789 f.)

Or again:

> The agon unleashes the individual and at the same time it binds [restrains] the same according to eternal laws. (16[22], KSA 7)

Thus, both moments of stimulation and limitation are pre-formed on an affective level. It is the communal or social character of Hellenic ambition that determines not just the measure or limits needed for social life, but also the moment of stimulation and its dynamic relation to limitation. The contestant's driving ambition for personal glory and fame is inseparable from that of his maternal city, so that in effect he acts as an instrument (*Werkzeug*) for the good his city. In the archaic Greek context, then, the community is constitutive of individual agency at the affective level of drives, in sharp contrast to a capitalist community of bourgeois individuals or a liberal community of possessive individuals, who, as asocial individuals, are motivated to compete by strictly egoistic drives.

III.2 The Medial sense of measure

Envy and ambition go some way to explaining the paradoxical quality of agonal interaction that Nietzsche values. They are, however, of limited value. For one, these affects are culturally and historically specific, and it is hard to see how they could serve Nietzsche's polemical end and unsettle the moral self-assurance of modern humanists, who no longer fear divine envy, or of bourgeois, possessive individuals who are utterly dispossessed of anything like communal drives. In the second place, Nietzsche, like Burckhardt, emphasises *not* self-limitation, but the *unmeasured*, tyrannical character of the Greeks' drives and desires, maintaining that '[i]n his secret wishes, every Greek was a tyrant; and everyone who could be, was in fact a tyrant' (6[7], KSA 8; cf. MA 261).[49] In the third place, neither affect actually captures the dynamic of reciprocal stimulation and limitation described by Nietzsche as the 'com-

---

[49] 'The hardness, the arrogance [*Übermut*], the tyrannical' in the blood of Greek philosophers (6[7], KSA 8; 23[1], KSA 7) was not unique to them. If the agon is inimical to any monarchic or tyrannical principle, it is so in spite of the antagonists' impulses. For Nietzsche, '*All* Greeks (fr. Gorgias in Plato) believed the possession of power as tyrant to be the most enviable happiness' (4[301], KSA 9). As I shall argue, this note contains in nuce Nietzsche's response to the problem of measure in HW, when he writes: 'The equality [*Gleichheit*] of citizens is the means for avoiding tyranny, their reciprocal invigilation and restraint.' (*Die Gleichheit der Bürger ist das Mittel zur Verhinderung der Tyrannei, ihre gegenseitige Bewachung und Niederhaltung*).

petitive play of forces' (*Wettspiel der Kräfte*): one turns on the antagonists' relation to the gods, rather than each other, and so lacks any genuine reciprocity; the other turns on their relation to the community, rather than the opponent.

Perhaps the clue to a better explanation lies in the concept of play (*Spiel*) in Nietzsche's formulation *Wettspiel der Kräfte*. This suggests a deeper problem with envy and ambition, since it puts in question any attempt to explain the dynamics of agonal interaction from the subject-position of the antagonists, their affects, goals or intentions. For, as Hans-Georg Gadamer has pointed out, the dynamics of play cannot be adequately explained from the standpoint of the players. What distinguishes play as a mode of interaction is that it has its being independently of the players' consciousness, attitudes and intentions: 'the mode of being of play is not such that there must be a subject who takes up a playing attitude so that the game can be played. Rather, the most original sense of play is the medial sense.'[50] In this medial sense, play acquires a structure of repetition that is impersonal and anti-teleological. Whatever the player's intentions, their outcome is determined in the space of play or confrontation, so that the real subject of play is not the player, but play itself, which holds the players in thrall (Gadamer 1996, 106). From this perspective, the dynamics of play are freed from the players' intentions, goals, affects and efforts, which are themselves played out within a to-and-fro movement detached from any telos: 'the movement which is play, has no goal which brings it to an end; rather it renews itself in constant repetition' (Gadamer 1996, 103).

In HW, the medial or relational sense of the agon can be seen in the *social ontology of tension* presupposed by Greek pedagogy. When Nietzsche writes: 'Every gift must unfold through antagonism, this is what Hellenic popular pedagogy demands' (*Jede Begabung muss sich kämpfend entfalten, so gebietet die hellenische Volkspädagogik*: HW, KSA 1.789), this implies a necessary (*muss*), conflictual (*kämpfend*) relation of particular gifts or capacities to others. It is worth noting that, just as in the formulation 'Wettspiel der Kräfte', Nietzsche here abstracts from the agonal subject, focusing instead on 'gifts' (*Begabung*), capacities or qualities. These formulations already suggests that human subjects are not the prime movers or real subjects of the agon. If we ask why '[e]very gift or capacity must unfold through antagonism', it is, I suggest, because – according to ancient Greek educators – *each particular gift, capacity of force (Kraft) can only become what it is (sich entfalten) through (ant)agonistic striving against others*. This statement makes for a relational, pluralistic and dynamic social ontology grounded in (ant)agonistic interdependence. It is relational in the sense that the relations of antagonism or tension determine the relata – whether they are capacities, forces or subjects – and not vice versa: each capacity, force or subject needs antagonistic relations with others in order to become what it is. This is because the resistance offered by others compels me to assert myself, to define myself against it. And since the resistance I encounter is unpredicta-

---

50 Gadamer 1996, 103–104 (translation modified).

ble, continuous and contingent in origin, my identity – who I am and what I can do – turns out to be highly dynamic and contingent. New and unexpected forms of antagonism compel me to act and define myself in new and unexpected ways. We can therefore say that *each particular capacity, force or subject (1) becomes what it is through (ant)agonistic striving against others, and (2) is continuously transformed through (ant)agonistic striving against others.*

It is therefore to these relations that we must look for the moment of measure. If, as Nietzsche writes, each force or subject encounters the other as both a stimulant to deeds and a source of resistance or limits in the agon, we can say that it is *via* the antagonists *in the relations of conflict* that limits are encountered. In this medial sense, agonal measure is not a subjective achievement: the result of an inner agony of conscience, an ascetic regime of 'inward-turned aggression' of that kind that Nietzsche will later criticise in GM, nor the result of self-subjection to a universal-rational law, as advanced by humanist morality. In these cases, measure *precedes* action within coercive regimes of self-regulation that inhibit spontaneity and suppress particularity. In the agon, by contrast, the 'play of forces' precedes measure, which is itself engendered in the course of contestation (cf. Schröter 1982, 114). As such, agonal measure is dynamically bound to risks that humanism seeks to preclude through regulation under a pre-established law.

It is because the agon cannot of itself guarantee the achievement of measure that the Greeks recurred to ostracism, as a way to enforce limits by excluding those forces or geniuses whose absolute supremacy over others dissolved the possibility of measure through contention (HW, KSA 1.789). In fact, the concept of ostracism tells us something essential about the presuppositions or conditions for the agon. If superlative forces or geniuses must be ostracised, it is because the agon depends on there being a *plurality of more or less equal forces, capacities or geniuses.*

The Equilibrium of Forces (Gleichgewicht)
It is important not to confuse the concept of equality presupposed by the agon with the kind of equality Nietzsche criticises so vehemently in the context of modern democracy. In the agon, first of all, 'equality' is a dynamic term for equal forces or capacities, not equal rights or equality as an ideal. Secondly, it does not exclude qualitative diversity in favour of uniformity (*Gleichheit als Gleichmachung*), which is Nietzsche's main worry regarding democratic equality.[51] Nor does it exclude relative differences or inequalities of power; on the contrary, an agon only takes off when there is a current victor or champion, whose deed or work provokes or stimulates (*reizen*) others to challenge it. *The agon gives absolute precedence to comparatives over absolute superlatives.*

This concept of equality is most succinctly expressed in JGB 259 (KSA 5.207), where Nietzsche describes the conditions (*Bedingungen*) for a healthy aristocracy

---

51 See Siemens 2009b.

as 'actual similarity of force and value-standards' (*tatsächliche Ähnlichkeit der Kraftmengen und Werthmaassen*), enabling its members to 'treat each other as equal' or 'posit [their] will as equal to that of others'. Two things are important about this formulation: first, unlike strict equality, the concept of similarity (*Ähnlichkeit*) does not preclude differences; and second, equality is referred, not to a quantitative or external measure, but to the way each individual (*Einzelne*) estimates and treats the others. Nietzsche's thought here goes back to the concepts of equality and equilibrium first developed in MA to argue for the origins of law and justice in a dynamic equilibrium of forces.[52] As Volker Gerhardt has pointed out in his paper 'Das Prinzip des Gleichgewichts',[53] it is important to understand these concepts in their properly Nietzschean sense:

Equality does not name a quantitative measure of objective magnitudes, but 'a correspondence of real social factors, between which there can never be a quantitative equality in the strict sense' (Gerhardt 1983, 116); hence Nietzsche's qualification 'more-or-less' (*ungefähr*). Equality is not determined from an external, neutral standpoint: 'it is the expression of an estimated correspondence between the powers themselves'. The standpoint of judgement is strictly immanent: 'it lies *in* power which *judges itself* in relation to another power' (Gerhardt 1983, 117). At stake is a complex, *communicative interaction of powers* involving perception, anticipation and evaluation, announcement and symbolic understanding.

However, unlike equality, *equilibrium* can*not* be understood from the 'subject-position', the standpoint of the single antagonists or forces as a conscious goal. Antagonists do not *aim* for equilibrium; each strives for supremacy (*Übermacht*) or victory. Equilibrium, therefore, is not a subjective achievement, but an 'intersubjective' achievement, a function of the *relations between* forces, each striving for supremacy: 'to be the best'. It is from a relational standpoint in the crossing and clashing of interpretations – the medial position – that the achievement of agonal equilibrium is determined. It is, I would argue, the achievement of equilibrium that Nietzsche means when he writes in the above-cited texts of the presupposition (ostracism in HW) or conditions (JGB 259) for agonal relations. But, if it is from the achievement of equilibrium that agonal interaction takes off, then we can say: the medial concept of equilibrium inserts a disjunction between subjective intentions (to win) and the resulting equilibrium of forces that is the actual source of action and its limits or measure.

Both the social ontology of tension and the medial concept of equilibrium point towards the insufficiency of a 'subjectivist' or 'expressivist' understanding of agonal action. They insert a disjunction between the 'subject-position' of the antagonists – their desires, intentions and claims – and the qualities of their resulting agonal interaction: each contestant wants to be the best, yet an equilibrium is, or at least

---

52 See MA 92, 93; WS 22, 26, 28, 29, 33, 39.
53 Gerhardt 1983, 111–133.

can be, achieved; each is tyrannical and prone to hubristic excess, yet limits or measure can be found; each fights 'as if he alone were in the right', yet 'an infinitely sure measure of judgement determines in each instant where victory is leaning' (PHG 5, KSA 1.825f.). The implication in each case is that agonal action/interaction – and the identities it exhibits – cannot be adequately understood by starting from the subject *qua* relatum, but needs to be grasped from a medial position in the relations holding *between* a plurality of forces (*Kräfte*) *qua* social factors. Nietzsche's concept of the agon reminds us that, the individualistic pathos of his texts notwithstanding, he is a profoundly social thinker who addresses fundamental ethical questions in relational terms.

IV Nietzsche's Counter-Ideal of Humanity: the Agon between the 'Human' and the 'Inhuman'

In Nietzsche's polemic with humanism, as we saw, the amoral freedom of mind (*Freisinnigkeit*) informing the institution of the Greek agon is opposed to the morality of judgement of humanism and its value oppositions (human-inhuman, good-evil etc.) (see p. 53f.). At stake in this confrontation, as note 5[146] makes clear, is the affirmative transformation of the unmeasured, destructive drives of the *Vernichtungskampf* into the measured, constructive forces of the *Wettkampf*, over and against a morality of condemnation, which negates or annihilates (*Verneinung, Vernichtung*) the value of 'the forces of nature' as 'inhuman' (p. 53). But Nietzsche's transvaluation of humanism would remain incomplete without a positive answer to the question raised by the opening paragraph of IIW: What is humanity? So what is his constructive counter-ideal of humanity to the moral condemnation or 'annihilation' of our unbridled passions and drives? How can the humanist opposition between the so-called 'human' and the 'inhuman' be rethought in the name of life-affirmation and human perfection? At issue is the 'inner' or 'vertical' relation between spirit (*Geist*) and the passions; between discourse and desire; between purposive reason, consciousness and the forces of the unconscious; and between values, ideals, and their origin in the evaluating body and affects. What, in these terms, distinguishes agonal culture and an agonal community of readers from Christian culture – the moral community of the church – as well as from the neo-humanist culture of Nietzsche's peers? In the next chapter this question will be tackled by drawing on Nietzsche's concept of transposition (*Übertragung*). At this juncture, I will pick up on the language of annihilation in note 5[146] and explore its striking resonance with Nietzsche's critique of the church in *Götzen Dämmerung: Moral als Widernatur*.

> Formerly one made war on passion itself on account of the stupidity inherent in it: one conspired for its annihilation [*Vernichtung*] – all the old moral monsters are unanimous that "il faut tuer les passions" [...] *To annihilate* the passions and desires, merely in order to forestall their stupidity and the disagreeable consequences of their stupidity, seems to us today to be it-

self merely an acute form of stupidity. We no longer admire the dentists who pull out teeth so that they stop hurting ... [...] The church battles passion with excision [*Ausschneidung*], its "cure" is *castratism*. It never asks: "how does one spiritualise, beautify, divinise a desire?" – it has at all times placed the stress of discipline upon extermination [*Ausrottung*] (of sensuality, of pride, of the desire to rule, of greed, of the desire for revenge). – But to attack the passions at their roots means to attack life at its roots: the praxis of the church is *hostile to life*. (GD Moral 1, KSA 6.82f.)

This passage puts into sharp relief Nietzsche's critique of humanist culture in note 5[146]: like the church, humanism wages a war of annihilation *(Vernichtungskampf)* against our 'natural' impulses and passions – a war of 'excision', 'castration' or 'extermination'. Necessarily unsuccessful, this war does deny any value to our affective life and foster life-negating regimes of repression. So what alternative does Nietzsche have to propose?

It is important to remember that the opening paragraph of HW does not contest the concept of humanity. It contests its forced, dualistic separation from nature in the conception of the human being as 'animal rationale', proposing instead a radically immanent picture of humanity as part of nature and her uncanny duplicity (*Doppel-Charakter*). The humanist/Christian *Vernichtungskampf* involves *first* an absolute and false separation of ('so-called "human"' and '"natural"' or 'inhuman') qualities that are in reality 'inseparably entwined' (HW, KSA 1.783) – the division of the human into rational and appetitive elements (the half-god, half-animal of Christianity); and on this basis, *secondly*, the 'negation' or 'annihilation' of our 'natural' impulses on behalf of our 'human' qualities; that is, the moral condemnation of the appetitive animal as 'evil' – the priestly work of bad conscience, or the Socratic practice of dying. As we saw, Nietzsche contrasts this morality of judgement with the 'openness', 'passion' (*Offenheit, Leidenschaft*: 3[49], KSA 8) and 'freedom of mind' (*Freisinnigkeit*) that he so values as the Otherness of ancient Greek ethicality. If the humanist morality of judgement is criticised for waging a *Vernichtungskampf* against our 'natural' qualities, Nietzsche's amoral, anti-humanist conception of humanity is modelled on a *Wettkampf* between our 'human' and supposedly 'inhuman', natural impulses. His agonal counter-ideal also involves two claims: *first*, that each – 'human' and 'natural', spiritual and affective – aspect of human nature is what it is only through antagonism towards the other; and *second*, that each is continually transformed through its antagonistic relations to the other. I shall deal with each claim in turn.

1. The first names the *inclusive* moment of agonal relations, since it claims that each element or opponent needs antagonistic relations to the other in order to be(come) what it is. This is illustrated by the most celebrated agon in Nietzsche's writing: the Apollinian only comes to signify *Maass* in antagonism with dionysian *Übermaas* dionysian *Übermaas* in turn only comes to signify the 'truth' in antagonism with Apollinian illusion (GT 4, KSA 1.41). It is when each asserts itself absolutely *through separation and exclusion of the other* that the relation degenerates into the

Socratic vs. the Dionysian.[54] In the context of HW, we can say that it is only as a striving against human *Maass* that the heroic pathos of victory comes to signify *Übermaas* and hubris, and it is only in striving against heroic *Übermaass* that the human comes to signify *Maass* in the creation of bounded works. Without the resistance of human *Maass*, the heroic dissolves into chaos, the pervasive, lawless *Vernichtungskampf* (bellum omnia contra omnes);[55] in the absence of hubristic impulses, human works calcinate into positive law, rigid conventions, moral ideals or imperatives. This brings us to the second claim.

2. The sequence of transformations on both apollinian and dionysian sides is charted in GT and need not detain us here. In HW, Nietzsche is at pains throughout to show how excessive natural drives like hatred, revenge etc. are transformed from destructive forces into constructive agonal affects, such as envy and ambition, which stimulate (*reizen*) cultural production (HW, KSA 1.786f. Also: 16[18], KSA 7; 16[26], KSA 7). Similarly, a human work that provokes agonal envy is transformed from being the prevailing standard of taste or convention into a stimulant (*Reiz*) to deeds and works that surpass and limit its authority (HW, KSA 1.788).

Nietzsche's agonal conception of humanity is marked by dynamism and tension: ever-changing relations of antagonism between 'spirit' (*Geist*) and the passions, consciousness and the instincts, *Maass* and *Übermaass*. Each side provokes or invokes the (resistance of the) other as a necessary counter-force or counter-position (*sich gegenseitig reizen*), while limiting or delimiting the forms its antagonism can take (*sich gegenseitig innerhalb der Grenzen des Maasses halten*). This agon of human and natural impulses provides a measure of the amoral 'freedom of mind' (*Freisinnigkeit*) of Hellenic ethics and its Otherness, when set against the repressive *Vernichtungskampf* against the passions instigated by the priest and the church.

It is important to see that this dynamic of human nature is not simply an individual task or achievement. It is predicated on an approximate equilibrium of forces (*ungefähres Gleichgewicht der Kräfte*), a *Wettspiel der Kräfte* engaged in a social dynamic of reciprocal stimulation and reciprocal limitation. Nietzsche's *agonal model of human nature* is bound up with the agon, as a *model of social interaction*, and its presupposition in the medial concept of approximate equilibrium. Indeed, the interdependence of these two dimensions of the agon – the 'horizontal' agon *between* individuals and the 'vertical' agon *within* them – is one of the central ideas proposed in HW. The exceptional human achievements made possible by agonal interaction are a function of agonal regimes of human nature; such regimes, in turn, are a function of agonal interrelations among social beings.

---

54 On this difference, see Jaehnig 1972 64f.
55 HW, KSA 1.787. Cf.: CV 1, esp. KSA 1.772; 10[1], KSA 7.344; 16[15], [18], [26], [28], KSA 7.

Chapter 3
Performing the Agon: Towards an Agonal Model for Critical Transvaluation

Introduction

Having introduced Nietzsche's concept of the agon in the first two chapters, I turn now to the main thesis of this book and consider the agon as a dynamic principle regulating Nietzsche's philosophical practice of critical transvaluation. A number of formal and dynamic features of Nietzsche's concept of the agon will be singled out, in order to ask what they imply for Nietzsche's critical transvaluative discourse if, indeed, it is governed by the agon. But first, the collective, cultural presuppositions of Nietzschean critique, viewed as an agonal practice, are set out and situated in the context of Nietzsche's diagnosis of the present as a condition of nihilism. Given the generalised crisis of authority that is nihilism, Nietzsche, like Zarathustra, is dependent on contingent, historical communities to authorise his affirmative discourse. In the absence of the 'right' community, he can only create fictional communities that might stimulate and guide actual readers in the collective creation of affirmative values beyond good and evil. In the last part of the chapter, I return to the question of agonal culture and examine it as an aesthetic *techne* of measure and transformation inspired by the poets, in opposition to the war against the passions waged by the 'morality as anti-nature' of the church (GD) and humanism.

The case for an agonal reading of Nietzsche's philosophical practice rests largely on the results of reading his texts in this way. In other words, 'the proof is in the pudding', and in this book I hope to demonstrate that the agon is a fruitful model for Nietzsche's writing in at least two senses. The first is that the dynamic form peculiar to the agon allows us to make sense of Nietzsche's polemical style – of certain puzzling, yet recurrent features of his textual confrontations that tend to get ignored or written off as inessential. In the second place, the agon is also philosophically fruitful because it addresses certain problems intrinsic to transvaluation itself; problems that threaten the very coherence of Nietzsche's philosophical project. I begin with the latter.

Nietzsche's life-project of critical transvaluation (*Umwertung*) involves the critical contestation of European, life-negating values *in the name of life* as the highest value. The basic and recurrent task is to overcome theoretical discourse (metaphysics), morality and religion in the name of life, its affirmation and enhancement.[1] Now this task originates in a critical diagnosis of the present, which in turn raises a number of problems for it. If Nietzsche is right that western values originate in a 'decadent' form of life, a sick and impoverished will, then the task of overcoming re-

---

[1] See Introduction p. 7 ff.

quires not just new life-affirmative and –enhancing values, but new *forms* of evaluating, new processes of idealization that are not grounded in the negation of life.[2] Nietzsche's strategy for overcoming must somehow address not just the prevailing values, but their origins in the body, the affects, a dissolute will. The problem is, how can this be done through discourse, given the closure of discourse against the body?[3] Even if we grant that Nietzsche's discourse *can* somehow address the body, it is unclear *how* he is it to engage the condition of décadence. If, as Nietzsche claims, it is not possible to 'screw back humankind towards an *earlier* measure of virtue' (GD Streifzüge 43), to reverse décadence, then how is his writing to serve the elevation or enhancement of life? What exactly would it mean to 'overcome' décadence?

If Christian-Platonic values represent an attempt at *closure against time and against life* that originates in a willing that is turned against the will (see p. 11 f.), it is hard to see how they can be effectively challenged. If they are to be opposed philosophically, Nietzsche must engage in discourse. Yet, given that the purpose of discourse is to reduce the exteriority for the sake of stable signification, his discourse will only replicate what he is contesting – the illusory closure against time and the life of the body, the theoretical and moral denial of the will. Nietzsche therefore needs to confound the will to closure endemic to discourse and find ways to open up his discourse towards life *without* undoing its discursive force. He needs to *complement* or *supplement* his discursive challenge with a *performative* challenge that enacts the concept of life raised and pitted against western values.

The thesis of this book is three-fold:

First, that Nietzsche does not just oppose morality, religion, metaphysics or Platonism *within* theoretical discourse; his opposition takes the form of an artistic-cultural practice – the agon –which sustains, regulates and organises his discourse.

Second, that agonal culture represents or pre-figures the *highest form of life* for Nietzsche; and it does so as a pluralistic, affirmative practice of life-as-art.

Third, that Nietzsche's text *is* itself agonal culture, as the *affirmative interpretation of life* thematised in his work as the highest form of life – the rebirth of tragic culture.[4]

The claim is not that Nietzsche revives ancient Greek culture or is somehow able to embody agonal drives and express them in his text. This would be to overlook the

---

[2] This is the issue treated by Heidegger (1961, 242 ff.) as Nietzsche's 'neue[.] Auslegung des Sinnlichen aus einer neuen Rangordnung von Sinnlichem und Nichtsinnlichem', and whether it constitutes a mere 'Umdrehung' of Platonic metaphysics or a genuine 'Herausdrehung'.
[3] For closure, see the Introduction p. 11 f. and chapter 4.
[4] See GT 16, KSA 1.103 and EH (GT) 4, KSA 6.313. Also: GT 15, KSA 1.97; GT 17, KSA 1.111; GT 19, KSA 1.129; 7[78], KSA 7.156; 9[34], KSA 7.283; RWB 5, KSA 1.453; M 172, KSA 3.152; FW 382, KSA 3.637 ('der Zeiger rückt, die Tragödie *beginnt* ...'); 14[50], KSA 13.243 ('Wiederherstellung des Begriffs "tragisch"'). On art as 'Gegenbewegung': 14[117], KSA 13.293 ff.; 14[169], KSA 13.355. Also FW 283 and FW 285 for agonal visions of the future.

feint of writing, the emphatically fictive style of his agonal confrontations. What I *do* maintain is that the dynamic form peculiar to the Greek agon operates as a principle that organises and regulates his critical confrontations with his chosen adversaries. As the productive and organising principle of Nietzsche's confrontations, the agon is a good model for confronting what Blondel has called the 'enigma' of Nietzsche's text[5] and for trying to think the discursive *and* performative aspects of his critical transvaluation of values *together*. If we restrict ourselves to a discursive analysis, not only do we condemn Nietzsche to repeating the discursive closure against life that he is attempting to overcome; we also find ourselves repeating dualisms such as life-truth, becoming-being, health-sickness, active-reactive etc.; that is, repeating the metaphysical 'belief in the opposition of values' (JGB 2) Nietzsche is attempting to overcome. Until we find a way to link the discursive themes with the 'rest' in his texts, we have failed to engage their unique status in the history of European philosophy and culture. Only if we consider Nietzsche's discursive critique *together* with the performative dimension of his writing – the attempt to *enact through agonal confrontation* the concept of life pitted against metaphysics and morality – can we break decisively with these dualisms, and reach a fuller, more adequate understanding of his challenge.

Yet, the Greek agon did not take place between two adversaries in a vacuum, and there is more to Nietzsche's agonal texts than dyadic confrontations. The agon was a collective, creative practice in which the public played a crucial role in adjudicating performances and outcomes. 'The contest among artists presupposes the *right* public. *If this public is lacking*, then he is in *exile* (*Philoctetes*)', Nietzsche writes in a *Nachlass* note.[6] But what *is* the 'right public' (*das* rechte *Publikum*)? From what standpoint can this matter be adjudicated, and by what standard of judgement or justice (*Gerechtigkeit*)? With regard to Nietzsche's textual agons, the question concerns the 'right' kind of readership – the kind of readers who would save him from philosophical exile. What is an *agonal community of readers?* These questions receive their urgency from another aspect of Nietzsche's critical diagnosis of the present: the death

---

5 See Introduction p. 9f. and Blondel 1991, 7f.
6 'Cap. VII. *Das aesthetische Urtheil.*
  Was ist das aesthetische
  Urtheil? Das Richterthum in
  der Tragödie.
  Der Wettkampf unter Künstlern
  setzt das *rechte* Publikum
  voraus.
  Fehlt dies Publikum, dann
  ist er im Exil (Philoktet).
  Alle Kunstgesetze beziehn sich nur
  auf das Übertragen (nicht
  auf die originalen Träume und
  Räusche).' (16[21], KSA 7.402)

of God, understood as a crisis of authority, and the nihilistic crisis of meaning and values that comes in its wake – 'that the highest values devalue themselves' (9[35], KSA 12.350).[7] For Nietzsche, the problem of nihilism constitutes a very real and imminent threat to human life and its future, one that gives increasing urgency to his transvaluative project. But as a crisis of authority, it also poses a direct threat to the affirmative discourse he seeks to articulate.

I Nietzsche's Fictional Communities and Culture as Deception

As the Prologue to *Also sprach Zarathustra* makes clear, the death of God raises acute difficulties for an affirmative discourse seeking to reinvest life and human nature with value. If nihilism issues in a generalised crisis of authority, how is Nietzsche to authorise his own affirmative discourse? As Pippin and others[8] have shown, Zarathustra's need to 'go down' stems from a recognition that a life-affirmative discourse *depends* on contingent, historical communities for its sense and its justifying force (– a book 'for all'). The problem, as Zarathustra rapidly discovers, is that the appropriate community is absent (a book 'for none'). We crave redemption, a new belief (e.g. the Cripples), or are indifferent, content to gently rub shoulders (the Last Man); either way, we have no ears for his teaching. While Zarathustra himself fails conspicuously to resolve this problem, Nietzsche's response can be discerned in his character's interminable wandering, as a politics of resistance: 'The narrative itself strongly implies that Zarathustra is fated eternally to go "up" or beyond man and "down" into the human community. He can neither accept nor fully transcend the context that produced him.'[9] To accept would be to renounce his ideal, to resign himself to the redemptive needs of the modern 'herd animals' as their 'shepherd'; to transcend or will his audience away would be to assert his will and his ideal against time – the very gesture of revenge to be overcome. In resisting either temptation, it seems Nietzsche's Zarathustra can only wait for the historical community he 'cannot create but cannot do without'.[10]

Nietzsche cannot create the audience he needs for his affirmative discourse; that much is clear. Yet, this does not exhaust the *strategic* value of creating fictive or virtual communities of readers. Such a strategy ('[…] to enforce, falsify and invent an appropriate fiction for myself')[11] is described in the late preface to MA as a 'cunning

---

7 At the physiological level, 'nihilism' names a loss of tension (*Spannung*) attending the loss of 'organising power' and its consequences in processes of dissolution (*Auflösung*), exhaustion (*Erschöpfung*) and an incapacity to create or 'posit productively a goal for oneself' (16[21], KSA 7.402).
8 Pippin 1988; Pippin 1983. See also Conway 1988.
9 Pippin 1988, 55.
10 Pippin 1988, 63.
11 '[…] wo ich nicht fand, was ich *brauchte*, es mir künstlich erzwingen, zurecht fälschen, zurecht dichten […]' (MA I Vorrede 1, KSA 2.14).

of self-preservation', given the fearful isolation of a life dedicated to critical transvaluation. Yet in this passage there is more at stake than Nietzsche's survival or respite from solitary travails. A curious exchange occurs between Nietzsche's life-affirmative discourse and his fictive communities:

> [...] the belief that I was *not* thus isolated, not alone in *seeing* as I did – an enchanted surmising of relatedness and identity in eye and desires, a reposing in a trust of friendship, a blindness in concert with another without suspicion or question-marks, a pleasure in foregrounds, surfaces, things near and nearest, in everything possessing colour, skin and apparitionality. (MA I Vorrede 1, KSA 2.14)

Here the utopic community is not just the occasion or site for Nietzsche's affirmative discourse; his rapprochement with sensuality and desiring life *is* his immersion in this longed-for friendship. It is as if his affirmative discourse, on the point of formulation, bursts at the mere image of the lightest, friendly touch, dissolving into pulsion, the pure pleasure of attunement. In the absence of an actual community that would give sense and authority to Nietzsche's affirmative discourse, the question of affirmation devolves into that of the identity ('the Greeks'? 'the Germans and their future'?) and shape of the imaginary community which *would* make affirmation possible.

In this context, the imaginary 'we''s and 'you''s populating Nietzsche's pages serve to open up his affirmative discourse to time, to expose his ideal to the historical contingencies of readership *without* abandoning it to them. Clearly, this is more than a strategy for survival or a form of resistance. Through the forms and identities he gives to his imaginary communities of readers, Nietzsche does not just resist or exclude certain redemptive misreadings; he seeks positively to cultivate appropriate responses to the task of overcoming. He himself describes this positive, formative impulse as 'acceleration':

> [...] and perhaps I shall do something to accelerate [*beschleunigen*] their coming if I describe in advance under what vicissitudes [lit. fates] I *see* them arising, upon what paths I *see* them coming? – – (MA I Vorrede 2)

It is this strategy of acceleration or cultivation *(Bildung)* which, as I shall argue, agonal readings of Nietzsche's texts bring to light. Nietzsche's agons do not just engage the values he is contesting on the page; they engage a community of readers in a collective contestation of values that is open-ended, yet regulated and law-like. Pitched somewhere between prescription and *laissez-faire*, between prophecy and a fatalistic waiting, Nietzsche's agonal practice serves to stimulate and guide actual readers in the collective construction of radically new evaluations of life 'beyond good and evil'.

Even in sympathetic readers, however, the fictional mode of Nietzsche's formative impulse must surely arouse suspicion. The cultivation of affirmative communities in their absence is, on Nietzsche's own admission, 'false-coinage', the desperate 'self-deception' of someone irredeemably isolated (MA I Vorrede 1). How seriously are we to take an affirmative discourse virtually devoid of content and reduced to imagining those who could respond to it? What, in short, is the *value* of such fictions? This question is, in fact, pre-empted in the preface to MA, where the text undergoes a crucial turning from one perspective into another, a transaction which completes the exchange between Nietzsche's life-affirmative discourse and his fictive communities. If the question of affirmation virtually collapses into the question of feigned affirmative readers, the question of feint or fiction and its value is now translated back into *the language of life* –

> [...] what do *you* know, what *could* you know, of how much cunning of self-preservation, how much reason and higher safeguarding, is contained in such self-deception – or of how much falsity I shall *require* if I am to continue to permit myself the luxury of *my* truthfulness?... Enough, I am still living; and life is, after all, not a product of morality: it *wants* [lit. *wills*] deception, it *lives* on deception... (MA I Vorrede 1, KSA 2.14)

In these lines, the moral language of truth versus lie, 'self-deception' or 'falsity' is translated back into the amoral or extramoral language of life 'beyond good and evil'.[12] At stake in this translation is the *standard* by which we evaluate fiction. When measured against truth as the highest value, fiction *means* deception (suspect), falsity (base). But the text effects a transition or transvaluation from truth ('you') to ('my' – our?) life as the highest value – a move which throws the meaning and value of fiction wide open: What would fiction *mean* from a perspective in life? – Certainly more than falsity (as opposed to truth). What is its value when measured against life? – Certainly not the stigma of untruth and deception castigated by Plato for its pseudo-reality. Transvaluation requires that we overcome the prevailing set of meanings, so as to open a new space of meaning that would allow for life-affirmation. This is the *collective* challenge issued by Nietzsche's text, the cultural work to which it invites us.

Within the space it clears, the text opens play with the claim that there is a complicity between life and fiction at the level of surface, 'skin and apparitionality'. From this angle, fiction acquires a positive value: life '*wills* deception, it *lives* on deception'. This provocation suggests a response to our original question concerning the value and meaning of Nietzsche's fictional communities. Here, fiction, as the product of the will to deception, *means* culture as metaphor or 'vita femina' (FW 339) – the transference (*Über-tragung*, meta-phor) or repressive displacement of the body (instincts) towards the conscious surface of thought and language (expression), on the basis of the primal scission of life into unconscious instincts and conscious

---

12 The passage continues: '[...] but there you are, I am already off again, am I not, and doing what I have always done, old immoralist and bird-catcher that I am – speaking unmorally, extra-morally, "beyond good and evil"? –' (MA I Vorrede 1, KSA 2.14)

life or 'Geist'[13] – what Nietzsche goes on to call 'bad conscience' in the *Genealogie der Moral*. We are familiar with bad conscience and its priestly manipulators as the 'womb' of man as a cultural being (GM II 18, KSA 5.326). We are also familiar with its ambivalent value: in turning the 'instinct of freedom' back against itself and shattering the instinctive unity of our 'animality', it brought about the constitutive 'sickness' of culture that culminates in décadence. Yet, this 'sickness which is [...] like a pregnancy' (GM II 19) has also been productive, giving '*depth*' to the human soul, making the human into '*an interesting animal*' (GM I 6), one that arouses 'an interest, a suspense [or tension: *Spannung*], a hope' in it, as if it 'were not a goal, but a path', 'a bridge' – the 'great promise' of self-overcoming (GM II 16).

If the account of culture in GM (inspired by Judeo-Christian culture) is marked by profound ambivalence, Nietzsche's early reflections on culture from 1872–73, inspired by Greek culture, are not. Focused on culture as deception (*Täuschung*), they are unequivocal in affirming the tragic necessity of deception and error:

> Without untruth [there can be] neither society nor culture. The tragic conflict. All that is good and beautiful hangs on deception [*Täuschung*]: truth kills – it even kills itself (insofar as it recognises that error is its foundation). (29[7], KSA 7)

Here, as in the following note, the value of untruth, deception or veiling derives from its complicity with art, virtue and life – as against the complex: truth/death/self-destruction:

> Every kind of *culture* begins with the *veiling* [verschleiert] of a great many things. Human progress hangs on this veiling – life in a pure and noble sphere and the closing off of baser impulses [*Reizungen*]. The struggle against "sensuality" through virtue is essentially of an aesthetic nature. (19[50], KSA 7)

In his reflections on *agonal* culture from the same period, Nietzsche explores another form of bad conscience – perhaps its Other: 'good conscience'[14] – mediated, not by

---

13 The best account I know of 'vita femina' as a metaphor for metaphor, or life as culture, is Blondel 1985.
14 The association of good conscience with art and deception / veiling / semblance (*Schein*), exhibited in the above quotes, recurs twice in Nietzsche's writings. In FW 107 art is the 'cult of the untrue', the 'good will to semblance' (*der gute Wille zum Scheine*), which gives us 'eye and hand and above all the good conscience' to be able to make of ourselves an aesthetic phenomenon, to make of ourselves 'a goddess'. The 'good will to semblance', then recurs in GM III 25 as 'the will to deception' (*der Wille zur Täuschung*), where art is said to oppose the ascetic ideal because it sanctifies the lie with a 'good conscience'. In FW 297 the 'ability to contradict' someone (*das Widersprechen-Können*), which is the requisite capacity for agonal critique *par excellence*, is called 'the attained good conscience in the hostility towards what is habitual, traditional, sanctified' (*das erlangte gute Gewissen bei der Feindseligkeit gegen das Gewohnte, Ueberlieferte, Geheiligte*) and is the signature capacity of the freed spirit (*des befreiten Geistes*). These associations of good conscience with the (artistic) will to semblance, on the one hand, and with (agonal) antagonism, on the other, are then conjoined under the sign of life-

priests, but by a *public* institution regulating all forms of cultural life: the agon. In the agon, understood by Nietzsche as a political institution inspired by the poets, he sees an aesthetic *techne* for excluding destructive conflict from social life without the life-negating and repressive techniques of Judeo-Christian morality – through the metaphorical transference *(Übertragung)* of war: 'The poet educates [*erzieht*]: he knows how to transfer [*übertragen*] the Greeks' tiger-like drives to ravaging devastation into the good Eris' (16[15], KSA 7.398). In the last part of this chapter, I will take up Nietzsche's suggestions that agonal culture *means* the transference *(Über-tragung)* of the 'evil' Eris (goddess of war and hatred) into the 'good' Eris (goddess of envy and ambition); that is, the affirmative transformation of destructive affects into constructive cultural forces. To the extent that Nietzsche's textual confrontations convoke agonal communities of readers, this fiction or deception *means* his texts become works of agonal culture which enact the highest affirmation of life: the transference of (self–)destructive instinctual resources into productive forces of culture. But I begin by considering some of the formal and dynamic features of Nietzsche's concept of the agon, and what their implications are for Nietzsche's transvaluative texts.

II Formal and Dynamic Features of the Agon

Three features of Nietzsche's agon, above all, are of importance for their performative implications:

1. As we saw in the first two chapters, at the heart of Nietzsche's fascination with the ancient Greek agon is the dynamic of reciprocal stimulation or provocation to deeds *(zur That reizen)* and reciprocal holding within the bounds of measure *(in der Grenze das Maaßes halten)* among a plurality of geniuses or forces. We can speak of a dynamic of *reciprocal empowerment-disempowerment* or a reciprocal dynamic of *limited affirmation and limited negation:* the opponent is good, but I can

---

affirmation in a late *Nachlass* note on the (Greek) heathen cult, and opposed (as in GM III 25) to ascetic life-negation or '*non-nature*':

Die Geschlechtlichkeit, die Herrschsucht, die Lust am
Schein und am Betrügen, die große freudige Dankbarkeit
für das Leben und seine typischen Zustände – das ist am
heidnischen Cultus wesentlich und hat das gute Gewissen
auf seiner Seite. – Die *Unnatur* (schon im griechischen
Alterthum) kämpft gegen das Heidnische an, als
Moral, Dialektik. (11[35], KSA 13.19)

(Sexuality, the desire for rule [or mastery], the pleasure in semblance and in deceiving, the great, joyful gratitude for life and its typical states – that is essential to the heathen cult and has good conscience on its side. – *Non-nature* (already in Greek antiquity) fights against the heathen, in the form of morality, dialectic.)

do better and take his place (limited empowerment or affirmation of other); the other is not good enough, worth less than is thought (but *not* worth-less: a limited negation of the other, where the other is not emptied of value or completely disempowered). Taking the agonal dynamic as the model for Nietzsche's critical confrontations, this suggests that he will contest Christian-Platonic values through a double-movement of critical negation and the recoil of critique upon the critic, op-position and retraction, contention and self-limitation, questioning and putting his form of questioning into question – what in broad terms was called 'Absolutsetzung' and 'Nicht-Absolutsetzung' (Müller-Lauter) or 'saying and unsaying' (Blondel) in the Introduction (see p 11 f.). These moves are hard to make sense of in discursive terms or simply incoherent, but as instantiations of the agonal dynamic of empowerment-disempowerment, I shall argue, they constitute a coherent philosophical practice which we can interrogate as a style of critique.

2. The agon is open-ended and counter-final in character: no results are permanent, all settlements remain open to contestation, so that the contest is repeatable and incessant. As we saw in chapter 1, ostracism was directed at the 'towering individual' (*den überragende Einzelnen*), the one who threatened to attain a position of absolute rule *(Alleinherrschaft)*. This superlative individual is *the absolute and conclusive victor*, i.e. that contestant – symbolised by the figure of Alexander in HW – to whom none are equal[15] and who therefore puts an end to the agon. The agon can only thrive where *a plurality* of more-or-less equal 'forces' (*Kräfte*) or 'geniuses' are engaged in an *inconclusive, open-ended contestation of victory*.

As the principle regulating Nietzsche's text, the agon therefore gives an *open-ended, inconclusive* orientation to transvaluative discourse. Despite its popular image, Nietzschean critique is not out to destroy its opponents (life-negating values or attitudes) and assert a single-handed victory (conclusive counter-values) over them. Nietzsche's confrontations serve, not to establish absolute victory or a personal hegemony over his opponents, not to destroy and be finished with truth, good and evil, equality, or whatever values he is contesting, and consign them to oblivion. Rather than resolve the problem of overcoming once and for all, they serve to *open and re-open* the question: What would be the overcoming of prevailing (life-negating) values? What would be a standpoint beyond good and evil? What would constitute an affirmative practice beyond the hostility to life? The principal orientation of agonal texts is not destructive, but productive and experimental: to inaugurate and stimulate radical new challenges to hegemonial ideals, and to multiply new postures and radical alternatives.

This brings us back to question of 'the *right* public'. For in putting the question of overcoming into play, Nietzsche's texts can only work if this question is contested in a 'play of forces', if a plurality of antagonistic forces are drawn, challenged, pro-

---

15 Not equal in a quantitive or 'objective' sense, but in the sense that no one feels equal to the task of challenging him. See chapter 2 on the concept of equilibrium, p. 61 ff.

voked to contest the question. Just as the Greek agon is conditional upon a plurality of antagonistic forces, so agonal writing can only thrive where 'we' – an agonal community of 'scholars', 'artists', 'free spirits', 'immoralists and anti-Christians', 'philosophers of the future' or any other readers who respond to the imaginary communities that populate Nietzsche's texts – are drawn into the fray. As a model for Nietzsche's writing or a principle of production for his texts, the agon is inseparable from questions of reading, response, interpretation. It compels us to recognise that critical transvaluation is the plural affair of a community of readers, whose constitution and multiple determinations must be drawn into our interrogation of the text: Who are we? What is the 'right' public or readership?

3. There is, however, an important difference between the 'agonal play of forces' (*Wettspiel der Kräfte*) and other competitive games. Normally victory and defeat in a particular bout are firmly defined, prescribed by a rule or set of rules that give a standard or measure of victory *outside and independently* of the course taken by a particular bout. The agon, by contrast, is a form of contestation that takes place not just *within* a set of rules, but *over* those rules as well; it does not just follow a set of rules, procedures and standards, but also opens those very rules and standards to contestation.[16] In the agon, the prevailing work, and the rule or standard of victory it embodies, are thrown into question, and the judgement of what constitutes victory and defeat is determined *immanently* by the dynamic course of each contest. This is because, as Nietzsche describes it in MA 170, the agon is an open-ended contestation of excellence, in which contestants strive, not just for excellence according to prevailing standards, but for a 'new greatness' (HW, KSA 1.788); that is, to establish a new standard of excellence. Nietzsche writes:

> *Artistic ambition.* –The Greek artists, the tragedians for example, poetised in order to win; their entire art cannot be conceived without the contest: the Hesiodic Eris, ambition, gave wings to their genius. Now this ambition demanded above all else that their work should attain the highest excellence *in their own eyes*, that is, as *they* understood this excellence, without concern for the dominant taste and the general opinion concerning excellence in a work of art; thus Aeschylus and Euripides remained unsuccessful for a long time, until they had finally *educated* the judges, who appreciated their work according to the standards that they themselves set. In this way they strive for victory over rivals in their own estimation, before their own seat of judgement, they really want *to be* more excellent; they then demand consent on this their own estimation from others outside, confirmation of their judgement. Striving for honour here means "to make oneself superior and to wish that it also appears like this in public". If the former is lacking and the latter is nonetheless desired one speaks of *vanity*. If the latter is lacking and it is not missed, one speaks of *pride*.[17]

---

[16] On the ancient Greek attitude to rule-bound games, see Renson 2009 (quoted in chapter 2 note 12).

[17] *Künstler-Ehrgeiz.* – Die griechischen Künstler, zum Beispiel die Tragiker dichteten, um zu siegen; ihre ganze Kunst ist nicht ohne Wettkampf zu denken: die hesiodische gute Eris, der Ehrgeiz, gab ihrem Genius die Flügel. Nun verlangte dieser Ehrgeiz vor Allem, dass ihr Werk die höchste Vortrefflichkeit *vor ihren eigenen Augen* erhalte, so wie *sie* also die Vortrefflichkeit verstanden, ohne Rück-

Not only does the agonal antagonist want to win; in striving for victory in his own eyes, before his own seat of judgement, his ambition is to redefine what counts as winning by raising a new standard of excellence embodied in his work.[18] In this light, our initial definition of the agon needs to be revised. The agon is not just an inconclusive, open-ended contestation of victory or excellence (see p. 38), but an *inconclusive, open-ended contestation of judgements or justice, that is, of the very standard of victory or excellence*. Since the standard of victory is immanent to the dynamic course taken by each agon, we can say that each bout puts the questions 'What constitutes excellence?', 'What constitutes victory' into play.

The peculiar scope of agonal contestation gives a particular turn to the question of overcoming in Nietzsche's transvaluative discourse. If Nietzsche engages in agonal contests with the metaphysical, moral and religious values of European culture under the sign of their representatives – whether the priest, Socrates, Rousseau or any other of Nietzsche's chosen adversaries – then at issue in every confrontation is not just the question of overcoming, but also: of the very standard or measure of overcoming. Not just: What would be a standpoint beyond good and evil? But also: How to evaluate the value of these values? By what standard of evaluation? Not just: What would be an affirmative practice beyond the hostility to life? But also: How to judge what counts as an affirmative discourse? What standards does life, as the one and only reality, afford?

In the generalised crisis of authority that is modern nihilism, agonal texts cannot prescribe or authorise a new, contesting set of values from above, a new table of values etched in stone, as it were, beyond time. Instead, agonal authorship opens its

---

sicht auf einen herrschenden Geschmack und die allgemeine Meinung über das Vortreffliche an einem Kunstwerk; und so blieben Aeschylus und Euripides lange Zeit ohne Erfolg, bis sie sich endlich Kunstrichter *erzogen* hatten, welche ihr Werk nach den Maassstäben würdigten, welche sie selber anlegten. Somit erstreben sie den Sieg über Nebenbuhler nach ihrer eigenen Schätzung, vor ihrem eigenen Richterstuhl, sie wollen wirklich vortrefflicher *sein*; dann fordern sie von Aussen her Zustimmung zu dieser eigenen Schätzung, Bestätigung ihres Urtheils. Ehre erstreben heisst hier "sich überlegen machen und wünschen, dass es auch öffentlich so erscheine." Fehlt das Erstere und wird das Zweite trotzdem begehrt, so spricht man von *Eitelkeit*. Fehlt das Letztere und wird es nicht vermisst, so redet man von *Stolz*. (MA 170, KSA 2.158 f.)

18 As the above text indicates, Nietzsche does not regard the judgement to be aesthetic in a narrow or technical sense when he writes that the poet 'really wants *to be* more excellent'. In a *Nachlass* note, he speaks of a 'universal' judgement with regard to the poet and his work, which is judged to be 'true, good, beautiful':

'Der Dichter als Lehrer des Wahren.
Symbolische Deutung, weil er durchaus recht behalten soll.
7. Das Urtheil im Wettkampfe ist nicht ästhetisch, sondern
universal.
7. Der Dichter wird beurtheilt als "höchster Mensch", sein
Lied als wahr, gut, schön.
7. Gerecht ist das Urtheil nur, solange der Dichter und sein
Publikum alles gemein haben.' (16[5], KSA 7.394 f.).

counter-values, together with the very standard of evaluation or judgement, to contestation *as an attempt (Versuch), a provocation and a question;* it puts the entire 'questionable question' of overcoming to a plural readership that would respond to the task. The new rule for art or standard of excellence created by each of the great tragedians, Nietzsche tells us in MA 170, required the consent (*Zustimmung*) of the public in order to prevail. In the context of modern nihilism, Nietzsche, like Zarathustra, can *only* authorise his transvaluative discourse, if at all, in human terms, by the consent of a community of readers. And by modelling his transvaluative discourse on the agon, he in effect opens his standard of judgement and evaluation to contestation by his readership. This is not, however, to consign it to the interpretations and evaluations of *any* historical community, much less to those of any historical individual. Where the *Zustimmung* of the Greek public was wanting, we read in MA 170, Aeschylus and Euripides had first to 'educate' the public into the 'right' public receptive to their new rule for tragedy. In Nietzsche's case, as we saw, this formative impulse is likened to a kind of 'acceleration' (see p. 70), which we can now describe more precisely: agonal texts engage their readers in *an inconclusive, open-ended contestation of values – together with the very standard of evaluation*. If the agon is not just a contest of deeds or works, but also of judgements concerning those deeds or works, the contestants are, at the same time, the public, indeed the 'right' public. And if the public has the final say, and sides with the winner (this year) against the other standards, they are drawn into the agon of judgements as contestants. To engage with Nietzsche's text as an agonal readership is to be both contestants of values, and members of the adjudicating public engaged in contesting the standard of evaluation. Agonal writing gives a public turn to the individual accent in Nietzsche's thought and style, and that personal, almost muscular attraction-repulsion it provokes. As a pluralistic and reciprocal interplay of forces that excludes the absolute dominance of a single force or 'genius', the agon compels us to think the personal through in collective terms, to find one's own voice with and against those of others; or, as Nietzsche remarks, 'to recognise oneself in the antagonist' (*am Gegner sich erkennen:* 16[19], KSA 7).

At stake here are the collective, cultural presuppositions and implications of Nietzschean critique. Nietzsche reacts to the status quo with the demand that things be changed or transformed. Only, this demand is not addressed to individuals as the prime movers and agents of this change; as noted in the context of Nietzsche's self-declared 'war-praxis' in EH, it is pitched, rather, at a trans-individual level of mores – customs and habits, practices and shared belief-structures that shape individual values and action. Culture – shared *doxai* and mores, or regimes of evaluation forming types according to specific bodily economies[19] – is the ground of values and of trans-

---

[19] On Nietzsche's concept of culture or cultures as collections of evaluations, based on corporeity, which govern the practice, ideals and mores of a given sociohistorical totality, see Blondel (1991, 66, 69) and chapter 1, note 15.

valuation, the site for Nietzsche's critique of values and the site for the new values that would replace them. Although his work is characterised by a personal, individual pathos[20] and a sustained concern with the individual – its constitution and disintegration, its pathology and potential – this does not exclude a trans-individual, cultural dimension from his thought. Only, this unfolds more at a performative, than a thematic, level: in his agonal confrontations and the 'we''s and 'you''s that occupy the pages of his texts – and in the way his readership responds to them.

II.1 Agonal Envy and Jealousy

Having considered three important formal-dynamic features of Nietzsche's agon, and their performative implications for his philosophical practice, I turn now to agonal affects, such as envy, jealousy, wrath and ambition (*Neid, Eifersucht, Groll, Ehrgeiz*), and their consequences for the dynamic character of Nietzsche's agonal confrontations. As we saw in chapter 1, agonal envy and jealousy are not restricted to living peers – an important point if we consider that this goes also for the majority of Nietzsche's antagonists. Envy stimulates an individual to outbid the current victor, to limit his achievement and create a new 'greatness' so as to 'take his place' and 'inherit his fame', his cultural authority. But it is also envy that provokes the Greek's fear of divine envy, leading him to sacrifice the fruits of victory to the gods.[21]

As a model for Nietzsche's textual confrontations, agonal envy binds the act of critical interpretation to a dynamic of *appropriation* ('to take the place of') *and sacrifice*. Envy describes the tyrannical element in so many of Nietzsche's attitudes. But more than that, it describes the *necessary* tyranny in any attempt at interpretation, as the 'monstrous desire to take the place' of what is being contested and appropriate its authority.[22] At the same time, agonal envy grounds the *limiting* or curbing of this tyrannical drive, *not* in a solipsistic agony of conscience, but in a gesture of 'sacrifice' or renunciation. The gods remind the contestant of the transience of his victory; but more than that, of its *necessary* transience within an open-ended public agon – the submission of one's claim to a pluralistic process of contention that ensures its mortality, the passage of each hard-won 'truth' into memory. To appropriate for oneself the authority of another, to create a new value or rule and lay claim to a new

---

[20] Recall the second rule of Nietzsche's war-praxis: 'I attack only those things where I would find no allies, where I stand alone, – where I only expose [risk, compromise: *compromittire*] myself ...' (EH weise 7, KSA 6.274).
[21] Cf. 20[7], KSA 8.362, where the belief in divine envy is referred to the Greeks' jealousy of others' happiness, and WS 30 where it is explained in social terms as the demand that happiness be proportionate to social standing.
[22] Recall 6[7], KSA 8.99: 'In his secret wishes, every Greek was a tyrant; and everyone who could be, was in fact a tyrant' and 4[301], KSA 9, quoted on p. 59, note 49.

truth, while sanctioned and fostered by the agon, is also afflicted by a sense of vulnerability and anxiety.

Envy also provides an interesting model for the fundamentally *productive orientation* which agonal texts give to the question of overcoming. If agonal envy limits the champion's deed or work, while conserving it as a stimulant for a new achievement or 'greatness', this takes form as a *strategy of exploitation and mastery* in Nietzsche's texts, as can be seen from a number of passages spanning seventeen years of Nietzsche's productive life:

> It is not a matter of annihilating [*Vernichtung*] *Wissenschaft* but rather of *mastery* [*command*: Beherrschung]. For *Wissenschaft*, in all its goals and methods, depends through and through upon philosophical views, but *forgets this easily. But the commanding* [beherrschende] *philosophy has also to reflect upon the problem to what degree Wissenschaft may grow: it has to determine its **value!*** (19[24], KSA 7)

> I have declared war on the anaemic "Christian ideal" (including what is closely related to it), not with the intention of annihilating it [*vernichten*], but only of putting an end to its *tyranny* and making place for new ideals, *more robust* ideals... The *continued existence* of the Christian ideal belongs to the most desirable things that exist: and that for the sake of the ideals, which want [will] to assert themselves next to it and perhaps over it – they must have opponents [*Gegner*] *strong* opponents, in order to become *strong*. In this way, we immoralists need the *power of morality:* our drive for self-preservation wills that our *opponents* remain strong, – it wills only to become *master over them* [Herr über sie]. – (10[117], KSA 12)

And finally, in GD Moral als Wideratur 3, Nietzsche describes 'our' posture vis-à-vis Christianity and the moral community of the church as a 'spiritualization of enmity':

> It consists in profoundly grasping the value of having enemies: in short, that one acts and thinks in the reverse of the way in which one formerly acted and thought. The church has at all times desired [willed] the destruction [*Vernichtung*] of its enemies: we, we immoralists and anti-Christians, see that it is to our advantage that the church exists [...] A new creation in particular, the new Reich for instance [or agonal community – HS] has more need of enemies than friends: only in opposition does it feel itself as necessary, only in opposition does it *become* necessary ... (GD Moral 3)

Under the sign of 'mastery' or 'the spiritualization of enmity', these texts express an instrumental interest in the existence and power of the critic's opponents, or rather, in their enmity or opposition, as a stimulant. We can speak of a *limited affirmation* or *empowerment* of the opponent, where it is taken as the necessary condition for what Nietzsche variously calls '*growth*' (EH weise 7, KSA 6.274; see p. 33 f.), '*strength*' (EH weise 7, KSA 6.274; 10[117], KSA 12), '*self-preservation*' (10[117], KSA 12) or simply 'our advantage' in the above passage. When viewed from a perspective in agonal envy, this impulse involves the desire to surpass the opponent by creating a new work of human 'greatness'. The new work or deed of greatness provides the new standard of evaluation or measure that limits his opponent's achievements (*limited negation*);

but it also needs those achievements to be preserved as a measure of its superiority (*limited affirmation*).

Clearly, to ascribe instrumental value to the other's deed or work falls short of anything like a genuine acknowledgement of the specificity of its content.[23] This may well be a consequence of power-relations, where what is valued is the opposition or resistance of the other for the sake of one's empowerment or growth. But perhaps the problem here runs deeper. Perhaps it comes from trying to think the agonal dynamic from the subject-position, rather than the medial position. For it is not at all clear whether wanting to win a game and wanting to preserve one's opponent's accomplishment makes for a coherent practice. To play a competitive game is to play to win, and the 'Wettspiel der Kräfte' is no exception; anyone seeking to relativise this goal (for the sake of playing, for the sake of the opponent's achievement) weakens their position and becomes a 'spoilsport' who does not take the game seriously.[24]

II.2 Agonal Ambition and Egoism

As we saw in chapter 2, it is the communal or social character of Hellenic ambition that determines the moments of mutual stimulation or empowerment *and* constraint or limitation, characterising agonal interaction:

> Every Greek felt from childhood on the burning wish within himself to be an instrument for the good [salvation] of his city in the contest of the cities: therein was his egoism [*Selbstsucht*] enflamed, therein was it also checked and bounded [*gezügelt und umschränkt*]. (HW, KSA 1.789f.)

In considering the implications of agonal ambition for critical transvaluation, I will focus on two moments: its communal orientation, and its pre-reflective, affective character.

As a model for agonal writing, *ambition* suggests that the postures Nietzsche adopts only find their limit in an agonal community of readers. If Nietzsche models his confrontations on agonal ambition, as that which drives and regulates his discourse, then they are driven by an ambition for glory and fame *as the instrument* of the agonal community, its fame and well-being.[25] In GD Moral 3, as we saw,

---

23 See Müller-Lauter 1971, 122.
24 See Gadamer 1986, 108.
25 To the extent that his personal ambition exceeds, excludes or conflicts with the well-being of his community, it forfeits its agonal character for the imperialism of Alexandrian ambition or the nihilism of Socratic ambition. On Alexander, as the 'grotesque' of the Hellene and the 'caricature' of Achilles, see HW, KSA 1.783f., 792 and 16[16], KSA 7. As the 'absolute victor' whose ambition exceeded the limits of the polis, he destroyed the agon. Together with Alcibiades, Socrates' famous pupil and lover, he represents a 'deification of the individual' (3[73], KSA 7.80). It is no coincidence that Alcibiades betrayed Athens in the Peloponnesian War; for it was Socrates, according to Nietzsche, who first alienated that individual from the state-community. He displaced the latter's authority with

Nietzsche claims that the continued existence of the church is to 'our advantage'. In the final lines of *Moral als Widernatur*, he takes this up again when describing the immoralists' confrontation with the church. 'We immoralists', he writes, have come to appreciate

> that economy in the law of life that derives advantage even from the repellent species of the bigot, the priest, the virtuous man – *what* advantage? – But we ourselves, we immoralists, are the answer to that [...] (GD Moral 6)

These lines effect a shift in the authorial standpoint. At issue is not just 'our advantage', the advantage we immoralists derive from the existence of our opponent, the church; at issue is rather the advantage that *life* derives from *our existence* as a community of immoralists and anti-Christians, radically opposed to the life-negating and destructive influence of the priest. If, as I have argued, Nietzsche's agonal confrontations serve to open the question of overcoming *in the name of life, its affirmation and enhancement*, then the agonal community of immoralist readers, served by Nietzsche's agonal ambition, is best understood as a *preliminary, experimental realization* of what he calls 'the *great* life':

> One is *fruitful* only at the cost of being rich in antagonisms [or oppositions: *Gegensätze*]; one remains *young* only on condition that the soul does not relax, does not long for peace... Nothing has grown more alien to us than that desideratum of former times, "peace of soul", the *Christian* desideratum; nothing arouses less envy in us than the moral cow and the fat contentment of the good conscience. One has renounced the *great* life when one renounces war ... (GD Moral 3)

Under 'war' we should read, not the destruction (*Vernichtung*) of enemies practised by the church, but what Nietzsche calls 'our spiritualization of enmity' or the agon; and in spurring us to contest life-negating values and practices, the agon does not *allow* the soul to relax. The sustained antagonism, both within and between members of an agonal community, driven by agonal ambition, is itself an experimental enactment, a performative anticipation of the concept of the life to be affirmed in its 'greatness' against the moral and religious values contested on the discursive level.

Agonal ambition also has important implications for Nietzsche's readers. In addressing its readers as an agonal community, agonal ambition is quite distinct from modern ambition. As Nietzsche notes in HW, modern ambition, being abstracted from any communal goals, is limitless and self-defeating (HW, KSA 1.789; cf. JGB 224, KSA 5.160). Agonal writing, by contrast, encounters limits in the community, and it does so in a way that is quite distinct from modern forms of community, say, a

---

the 'sovereign concept' (16[17], KSA 7.399), and, with his '*individual-eudaemonological*' 'pretension to happiness', focused his redemptive energies on isolated individuals, rather than the 'common weal' (19[20], KSA 7; 6[13–15], KSA 8).

capitalist community of bourgeois individuals or a liberal community of possessive individuals. This is because agonal texts do not address its readers on the level of discourse – ideas and values – alone; they also move at the level of desires, drives, affects and bodily postures. It is the pre-reflective communal orientation of agonal ambition that distinguishes its readership from these modern communities, predicated as they are on the modern concept of the individual as an antecedently individuated, asocial person,[26] possessed of sovereign reason and freedom of choice. At the same time, this affective, pre-reflective communal orientation also distinguishes the agonal community from a Hegelian community, grounded in the meeting of selves through the dialectic of mutual recognition. If, as Tracy Strong has argued, 'the Hegelian politics of recognition and the search for mutuality suffice as long as selfhood is possible',[27] then it can find no place in Nietzsche's view of modernity, where selfhood is dirempt, and we are estranged from our 'selves', not to mention 'others'.[28] At issue for us moderns is the very constitution or creation of the self, the character of the self to be attained and the kinds of relations to others we wish to cultivate.

What, then, happens when 'we', caught in this condition of self- and mutual alienation, are addressed as agonal individuals whose attitudes and deeds are governed by the community at an affective level? Nietzsche is, of course, well aware that 'communal drives' no longer exist or move individual agency; indeed, in one early note, his critique of the present rests on their demise.[29] But what happens if this pre-reflective communal orientation is *simulated* by using agonal ambition as

---

26 I am referring to the individual, understood as: 1. a person that is *antecedently individuated* (a person is what it is as a person independently of the ends or values it freely chooses; the ends I choose are not constitutive of my identity or who I am) and 2. a person that is *asocial* (a person's ends are formed prior to, or independently of, society; society does not inform a person's identity, values or ends, but is rather the outcome of a contract between individuals whose ends are already given). This concept of the individual or person has been ascribed – rightly or wrongly – to Rawls and has a long history in modern moral and political thought, especially the kinds of democratic liberalism, contract theory and morality that Nietzsche was familiar with. It also informs our everyday self-understanding as moral and political agents, as it did for Nietzsche's contemporaries. What is more, it is often ascribed to Nietzsche himself by those who see him as a champion of autarkic or aristocratic individualism. It is in fact the principal target of Nietzsche's critical thought.
27 Strong 1988, 162.
28 On the modern individual: 'Die Häßlichkeit bedeutet *décadence eines Typus*, Widerspruch und mangelnde Coordination der inneren Begehrungen [...]' (14[117] 13.293) and W Epilog, KSA6.52f.: 'Der moderne Mensch stellt, biologisch, einen *Widerspruch der Werthe* dar, er sitzt zwischen zwei Stühlen, er sagt in Einem Athem Ja und Nein. Was Wunder, dass gerade in unsern Zeiten die Falschheit selber Fleisch und sogar Genie wurde? dass *Wagner* "unter uns wohnte"? Nicht ohne Grund nannte ich Wagner den Cagliostro der Modernität ... Aber wir Alle haben, wider Wissen, wider Willen, Werthe, Worte, Formeln, Moralen *entgegengesetzter* Abkunft im Leibe, – wir sind, physiologisch betrachtet, *falsch* ...'.
29 'Der maaßlose unwählerische Erkenntnißtrieb, mit historischem Hintergrunde, ist ein Zeichen, daß das Leben alt geworden ist: die Gefahr ist groß, daß die Individuen *schlecht* werden, deshalb werden ihre Interessen gewaltsam an Erkenntnißobjekte gefesselt, gleichviel welche. Die allgemeinen Triebe sind so matt geworden und halten das Individuum nicht mehr im Zaume.' (19[21], KSA 7.422).

a model for writing? What consequences does it have? What response does it provoke from shattered, self-alienated readers? What agonal ambition teaches us is that individuality in the Greek context was relational. It did not precede and determine one's relations to others; rather, it was *constituted* by the community and one's relations to others at the affective level of agonal drives.[30] If this condition is simulated at a performative level, by addressing 'us' *as if* we were agonal individuals, does it not serve to pitch the question of individual constitution, the creation of selves, *at the level of shared affects?* Through the feint of agonal ambition, I suggest, we are compelled to recognise that the creation of our 'selves' is a matter of a *collective ordering of willing* by way of relations of mutual stimulation and limitation; in short, that it is a matter of agonal culture.

III Agonal Culture as the *Übertragung* of War

In the last part of this chapter I return to Nietzsche's suggestions that agonal culture *means* the transference *(Über-tragung)* of the 'evil' Eris (goddess of war and hatred) into the 'good' Eris (goddess of envy and ambition); that is, the affirmative transformation of destructive affects into constructive cultural forces. In chapter 2, the war of annihilation or *Vernichtungskampf* against the passions instigated by priests and humanists was set against Nietzsche's dynamic and antagonistic counter-ideal of humanity, inspired by the amoral 'freedom of mind' (*Freisinnigkeit*) of Hellenic ethics, as a *Wettkampf* between 'human' and 'inhuman', 'natural' impulses. It therefore comes as no surprise, if we ask with Nietzsche, whence this freedom of mind (*Woher?*), that his answer rules out a priestly moral law. In the Greek polis, the constitution, mores and the state cults were not dictated by a priestly caste and their moral law; instead it was from Homer and the poets that the state-founders learned their freedom of mind or *Freisinnigkeit*:

> It was not a narrow priestly *moral law* [*Sittengesetz*] that was in command in the grounding of the state. Whence do the Greeks draw this freedom? No doubt already from *Homer*; but whence does he draw it? – The poets are not the wisest and logically most cultivated beings; but they take pleasure in the particulars of reality of every kind and do not want to negate it, but still to measure it [*mässigen*] so that it does not kill everything else around it. (5[146], KSA 8.78)[31]

---

[30] That Nietzsche, *contra* liberal individualism, understands the emergence of the autonomous individual as 'possible only within the context of a well-ordered community' is persuasively argued by Daniel Conway (1988, especially 258–259). Curiously, he identifies this view with Socrates, which runs counter to Nietzsche's own view of Socrates as 'individual-eudaemonological' (see note 25 above for references). Unfortunately, Conway does not address this disagreement.

[31] 'Es war nicht ein beschränktes priesterliches *Sittengesetz*, welches bei der Gründung des Staates befahl. Woher haben die Griechen diese Freiheit? Wohl schon von *Homer*; aber woher hat er's? – Die Dichter sind nicht die weisesten und logisch gebildetsten Wesen; aber sie haben die Lust am einzeln

The Otherness of Hellenic ethics lies in its amoral character as *an ethics of sensibility* (*Sinnlichkeit*) rooted in aesthetic capacities – the poets' '*sharpness of observation and the sense for the matter-of-fact* [Schärfe der Beobachtung und der Sinn für das Thatsächliche]' (5[146], KSA 8.79), their 'depth in grasping and glorifying what is nearest [*Tiefsinn im Erfassen und Verherrlichen des Nächsten*]' (5[70], KSA 8.60). In the agon, understood by Nietzsche as a political institution inspired by the poets, he sees an aesthetic *techne* for excluding destructive conflict from social life, one that offers an alternative to the *Vernichtungskampf* against the passions waged by humanism, the priest and Judeo-Christian morality – through the metaphorical transference or transposition *(Übertragung)* of war:

> 7. Finale: Dithyramb to art and the artist: because they first create [*herausschaffen*] the human and transpose [*übertragen*] all its drives into culture. (16[18], KSA 7.400)
>
> The poet overcomes the struggle for existence by idealising [*idealisirt*] it into a free agon [*Wettkampfe*]. Here is the existence, for which there is still a struggle, existence in praise, in undying fame [...]
>   The poet educates [*erzieht*]: he knows how to transpose [*übertragen*] the Greeks' tiger-like drives to ravaging devastation into the good Eris. (16[15], KSA 7.398)

At the time of HW, Nietzsche supposed humans to be possessed of a 'metaphorical drive' (*Trieb zur Metapherbildung*),[32] and the concept of metaphorical transference or *Übertragung* plays a key role in many of his philosophical endeavours. The term has a rather bewildering range of meanings. Depending on the context, it can mean: metaphor, untruth, deception or veiling; imitation or play; spiritualization, idealization, or sublimation; the exploitation, harnessing or mastery of destructive energies; and their regulation, codification or measured discharge. Several of these meanings are at play in the agonal *Übertragung* of the 'evil' into the 'good' Eris. Above all, agonal *Übertragung* instantiates Nietzsche's displacement of 'metaphor' from the linguistic-conceptual register into the physiological register, as an aesthetic process or drive at the origin of human culture.

In the present context, I shall concentrate on Nietzsche's suggestion that the artist, as architect of the agon, 'imitates' or 'plays' at war: 'The contest [*Wettkampf*] arises from war? As an artistic play [*Spiel*] and imitation [*Nachahmung*]?' (16[26] KSA 7). Here 'play' might be contrasted with 'war', and 'imitation' might be contrast-

---

Wirklichen jeder Art und wollen es nicht verneinen, aber doch so mässigen, dass es nicht alles todt macht.'

32 See WL 2, KSA 1.887 on 'Jener Trieb zur Metapherbildung, jener Fundamentaltrieb des Menschen, den man keinen Augenblick wegrechnen kann, weil man damit den Menschen selbst wegrechnen würde [...].' Also 19[230], KSA 7.492: 'Der Lügner gebraucht die Worte, um das Unwirkliche als Wirklich erscheinen zu machen, d.h. er mißbraucht das feste Fundament. / Andrerseits ist der Trieb zu immer neuen Metaphern da, er entladet sich im Dichter, im Schauspieler usw., in der Religion vor allem.'

ed with 'denial' 'negation' and 'annihilation', the terms used in note 5[146] (KSA 8) to describe the *Vernichtungskampf* against excessive, destructive affects. Agonal culture, by contrast, is described as a regime of *Einordnung*, a term that combines the notions of accommodation, appropriation, integration (*ein–*), and regulation, re-ordering (*ordnen*). Base – destructive, disruptive – impulses of human nature are 'transferred' into cultural life by way of codification, the master code being the contest or agon regulating all areas of cultural life. As a dynamic of mutual provocation and empowerment driven by affects like envy and ambition, the agon 'plays' at the *Vernichtungskampf*; yet it *merely* 'plays' at war, for as a dynamic of mutual *dis*empowerment or limitation it excludes the absolute victory of annihilation.

Like Christian and humanist cultures, the agonal 'play' of 'transference' excludes destructive forces from communal life; only it does not do so by seeking to turn them against themselves, through moral condemnation, ascetic disciplines or the inner agonies of conscience. Such regimes of self-destruction constitute what Nietzsche calls 'anti-natural morality' in *Moral als Widernatur*: it 'turns precisely *against* the instincts of life – it is a now a secret, now loud and impudent *condemnation* of these instincts' (GD Moral 4, KSA 6.85). Agonal culture, by contrast, is what Nietzsche there calls a 'naturalism in morality'; it is

> mastered by an instinct of life – some commandment of life is fulfilled through a certain canon of "ought" and "ought not", some hindrance and hostile element on life's road is thereby removed. (GD Moral 4, KSA 6.85)

Destructive instincts (e. g. revenge) are not condemned, but acknowledged as human and affirmed (the "ought") in the agon, as a stimulus to great deeds, an energizing force that provokes and empowers each antagonist to contest the other. Their destructive *effects* are, however, excluded; *not* through condemnation, the "ought not" of moral judgement and solitary struggles of conscience, but in practice – the dynamic of mutual disempowerment intrinsic to the agon. In agonal contestation the 'naturalistic' canon of "ought" and "ought not" is unreflective and somatic – played out in the postures and counter-postures of agonal contestation. And through the play of mutual limitation, destructive affects are effectively transformed, translated or transposed (*übertragen*) into constructive, agonal affects. Thus the agon effects a transformation of destructive passions – one that is based on affirmation, rather than repressive negation, and results in a measured discharge, rather than suppression.

The kind of limited, transformative affirmation of destructive forces described through *Übertragung* can also be understood through the categories of *use* and *exploitation*:

> How *Greek nature knows how to make use* [benutzen] *of all **terrifying** qualities:*
> the tiger-like rage for destruction (of the tribes etc.) in the agon
> the unnatural drives (in the education of the youth by the man)

the Asiatic *orgiastic* ways (in the Dionysian)
the hostile isolation of the individual (Erga) in the Apollinian.
    The application of the harmful towards useful [ends] is idealised in the world-view of *Heraclitus.*
    7. Finale: Dithyramb to *art and the artist:* because they first create [*herausschaffen*] the human and transpose [*übertragen*] all its drives into culture. (16[18], KSA 7.399f.)

The agon is not just one instance of the harnessing and exploitation of destructive forces described here; in HW, it is the paradigmatic and pervasive cultural form, regulating education (the 'unnatural drives') and tragedy (the 'orgiastic ways') inter alia. There is, moreover, an unmistakable parallel between the exploitation of natural forces here and the strategy of exploitation that emerged from Nietzsche's account of envy above. The exploitation of prevailing values ('the current victor') as a stimulant for counter-values (a 'new greatness') is mirrored in the exploitation of natural drives for the sake of spiritual production. This parallel highlights the isomorphic relation between the 'vertical' and 'horizontal' dimensions of agonal contestation: only through an agon between *Geist* and the passions in each contestant can an agon between them take place, and only through an agonal contest *between* them can the agon of *Geist* and passions *within* each contestant be sustained.

The notion of agonal ambition throws some light on the moment of measure (mutual disempowerment or limitation) in the *Übertragung* of the evil into the good Eris. Ambition is an egoistic, potentially destructive affect which, in agonal contestation, becomes a creative force of the good Eris. Let's suppose that it represents a transposition of the 'tiger-like rage for destruction' of the 'evil Eris', (mentioned in the above note (16[18], KSA 7): what, then, is their relation? Not one of denial, negation in the name of love (Christian culture) or 'the human' (humanism); it is rather an affirmative transformation of the rage for destruction *by way of communal goals*. Agonal ambition exploits and harnesses this destructive, egoistic force by subjecting it to a new goal, in line with an aesthetic *techne*, described by Nietzsche as '[t]he application of what is damaging for useful ends [*Die Verwendung des Schädlichen zum Nützlichen*]' idealised in Heraclitus' worldview:

I. **Problem** : *how is the will, the terrifying* [will],
purified and reformed, that is, transposed [*umgesetzt*]
and transformed [*verwandelt*] into nobler drives?
    Through a change in the world of representations, through the
great distance of its goal, so that it must ennoble itself in
excessive extension [*Ausspannen*].
    Influence of art on *the purification of the will.*
    The *contest* [*Wettkampf*] emerges from war? As an
artistic play and imitation?
    The presupposition of the contest. (16[26], KSA 7.403)

The 'distance' of this goal, the representational 'extension' of ambition, allowing it to moderate or measure individual rage, lies in its communal reference to the good of the city:

> When the delusion [*Wahnvorstellung*] is dissolved as such, the will must create a *new* one – *if* it wants our continued existence. *Formation* [cultivation, education: Bildung] is a continuous substitution of delusions in the direction of nobler ones; that is, our "motives" in thinking become ever more spiritual [*geistigere*], belonging ever more to a greater generality [commonalty: *Allgemeinheit*]. The goal of "humankind" is the outermost that the will can offer us as a phantom [...] Formation lies in thinking of the well-being of greater organisms than is the individual. (5[91], KSA 7)

The transposition (*Übertragung*) of destructive into culture-creative affects – the formation (*Bildung*) or 'spiritualization' (*Vergeistigung*) of passion (GD Moral als Widernatur) – works through the ennobling or 'becoming-spiritual' of their goals. Here, 'spiritualization' is explained with reference to the Schopenhauerian-Wagnerian term *Wahnvorstellung*. This term stems from a paradox of power in Schopenhauer's system: although the World-Will is sovereign and omnipotent, it depends on our co-operation, since conscious goals or 'motives', egoistic by nature, are the sovereign movers of individual action. If, therefore, individuals are to be mobilised for the Will's 'spiritual', i.e. *trans-individual* ends, they must be deluded, so that these ends *appear* as egoistic.[33] In time, Nietzsche will jettison this cumbersome metaphysical baggage, but he does retain Schopenhauer's insight into our heteronomy (vis-à-vis the passions, affects and drives). It is central to aphorism 214 of MA, which describes transposition – the ennobling or 'spiritualization of passion' – as the 'art of idealization':

> *Ennobling of actuality.*– Because humans saw a deity in the aphrodisiac drive and felt it acting in them with reverent gratitude, that affect has in the course of time been laced with higher representations and actually become greatly ennobled. Thus have certain peoples, through this art of idealization, created great instruments [*Hülfsmächte*] of culture out of illnesses: the Greeks for example, who in earlier centuries suffered great nervous epidemics (in the manner of epilepsy and the St. Vitus dance) and out of them formed the splendid type of the Bacchant. – For the Greeks possessed nothing less than a burly health; – their secret was to worship [revere: *verehren*] even illness as a god, if only it had *power*. (MA 214)

The 'art of idealization', integrating (*Einordnen*) the orgiastic ways (16[18], KSA 7) of the aphrodisiac drive within the confines of dionysian festivals (16[18], KSA 7; cf. 5[146], KSA 8), is grounded in a deep doxa or collective belief in fate: a reverential acknowledgement of heteronomy, a celebration of passion, a thanksgiving for its

---

[33] For a discussion of Schopenhauer's *Wahn* theory and its reception by Hartmann and Nietzsche, see Gerratana 1988. I would like to take this opportunity to pay tribute to the late Federico Gerratana as an outstanding Nietzsche scholar and a hard, but deeply sympathetic, critic of my work.

power through deification.[34] This affirmative motif, essential for the agonal dynamic of mutual empowerment, can be traced to both *Homer's Wettkampf* and to *Moral als Widernatur*. The former speaks of the deification of envy 'as the effect of a *beneficent deity*' (HW, KSA 1.787); the latter describes 'naturalism in morality' as being 'mastered by an instinct of life' and the fulfilment of 'some commandment of life' (GD Moral 4). As for fate, Nietzsche here writes:

> Even when the moralist just turns to the individual and says to him: "*You* ought to be thus and thus" he does not cease to make himself ridiculous. The individual is, in its future and its past, a piece of fate, one law more, one necessity more for all that is and all that will be. To say to him "change yourself" means to demand that everything should change, even in the past... (GD Moral 6, KSA 6.87)

Nietzsche's agonal confrontations, too, demand that we change – from moralists to immoralists. They are, however, less ridiculous for a number of reasons. In the first place, they are grounded in an affirmative acknowledgement that the individual is commanded by instincts of life, a belief in 'fate' qua unconscious, affective forces. In the second place, the demand is not formulated as a law addressed to the individual; instead it is somatic, a specific form of practice, regulated by mores, pitched at the level of affects, instincts – a collective configuration of wills. Finally, there is no desire for finality, no pretence at conclusive change; Nietzsche's agons are rather open-ended, eternally recurring festivals dedicated to the overcoming of our collective past.

---

[34] See 14[127], KSA 13.309 on the cultic origins of tragedy:
'Noch eine Form der Religion. Der Gott wählt aus, der Gott wird Mensch, oder Gott wohnt mit Menschen zusammen und hinterläßt große Wohlthaten, die Ortslegende, als "Drama" ewig dargestellt [...]
   – ehedem glaubte man sich zu ehren, wenn man für die höchsten Dinge, die man that, sich nicht verantwortlich wußte, sondern – Gott –
   die *Unfreiheit des Willens* galt als das, was einer Handlung einen höheren Werth verlieh: damals war ein Gott zu ihrem Urheber gemacht...'

Chapter 4
The First Transvaluation of All Values: Nietzsche's Agon with Socrates in *The Birth of Tragedy*

In *Götzen-Dämmerung*, Nietzsche refers to *Die Geburt der Tragödie* as his 'first transvaluation of all values' (GD Alten 5). He goes on in *Ecce Homo* to describe his project of transvaluation as 'my formula for an act of supreme self-examination on the part of humanity become flesh and genius in me' (EH Schicksal 1). While a good deal has been written about Nietzsche's relation to Socrates,[1] not enough attention has been given to the complexity, precision and penetration of Nietzsche's engagement with Socrates in GT as an articulation of his 'first transvaluation of all values'. This chapter is an attempt to make good this deficit.[2]

---

[1] To mention only a few: Dannhauser 1974; Kofmann 1991; Schmidt 1969 Acampora 2013, 77–109.
[2] An exception in this regard is Christa Acampora in chapter 3 of her book *Contesting Nietzsche* (2013), which uses the contest with Socrates in GT to introduce some fundamental and enduring themes in Nietzsche's thought: life-affirmation, naturalism and non-teleological development, the concept of *Schein*, and the plural, agonistic soul. Her argument, like mine in this chapter, is that Nietzsche attempts to develop a better alternative to the Socratic dialectic he criticises. Her emphasis is on the substantive legacies for Nietzsche's thought that can be derived from his early engagement with Socrates, which she places under the rubric of 'artful naturalism'. In this chapter, I emphasise Nietzsche's *critical* thought: his critique of Socrates' claim to critical thought in GT, and its legacy for forms of critique in Nietzsche's later thought.
  Regarding Nietzsche's critique of Socratic dialectic, Acampora (2013, 82–83) proposes an ingenious thesis. Socrates is accused by Nietzsche of 'shifting the agon inward to become a psychic contest', in which 'he contends with parts of himself, including his so-called animal nature'. Linking this move with virtue and knowledge, she argues, has been 'particularly destructive, he thinks' – despite the textual evidence to the contrary: GT 15, where Socrates is elevated into the 'turning point' of world history for having saved the world from wars of annihilation driven by egoism by channelling an 'incalculable sum of energy' in the service of knowledge instead. Acampora takes this passage to be, not about the destructive consequences of egoism (à la Schopenhauer), but about 'the same agonistic impulses that were at the root of the Greeks' accomplishments' (also called 'destructive desires' by her) being turned inward by Socrates. On this account, Socrates sounds more like the priest of GM ('the *direction-changer* of *Ressentiment*': GM III 15) and his machinations with 'bad conscience' (the turning backwards of destructive instincts: GM II 16) than the Socrates of GT and the salutary effects of his cognitive optimism. He is certainly much closer to the Socrates of JGB 212 and GD Das Problem des Sokrates, who, like Acampora's Socrates, recognised 'the nascent decadence of his own culture' (GD Sokrates 3, KSA 6.84). The (later) concept of décadence plays no part in GT, nor do the Greeks' 'agonistic impulses' driving their cultural achievements, which are read back into GT from HW and GD.
  In this chapter, the 'psychic contest' introduced by Socrates is thematised as the theoretical closure against life and linked to the problem of discursive closure (Blondel) and the closure of the intellect against the body (Plato's *Phaedo*). But closure in these senses does not involve an agon or 'psychic contest'. As argued in chapter 2, it is Nietzsche who advances an agonal ontology of human nature (Acampora's 'psychic conflict'). In line with Nietzsche's governing distinction in HW, it

I Overcoming Socrates: *The Birth of Tragedy* as Nietzsche's first Transvaluation

At stake in GT, as always in transvaluative texts, is the question of overcoming: what would be the overcoming of Socrates and Socratism, conceived broadly as theoretical discourse and culture? This question breaks down into two. On the negative or critical side: what is required to pose a radical challenge to theoretical discourse and culture? What kind of confrontation is *open* to us? And on the positive side: what would a counter-position look like, a manner of thinking beyond theory, a culture beyond Socratism?

For preliminary orientation on these questions, I shall draw on Nietzsche's famous claim, in the 1886 *Versuch einer Selbstkritik*, that he dared '*to see Wissenschaft through the optic of the artist, but art through that of life*' (GT Versuch 2).[3] The broad terms of Nietzsche's transvaluative contest with Socrates and Socratism are, then, theoretical knowledge and discourse (*Wissenschaft*), art and life. How exactly are we to understand the two-fold optic on theoretical discourse Nietzsche claims for himself?

The contours of Nietzsche's 'optic of life' are, without doubt, shaped by Schopenhauer, not Socrates, and the more intimate contest with his thought. As a *philosopher of life*, Nietzsche's tasks are defined against Schopenhauer in two ways. Schopenhauer's fundamental questions are a questioning of life: what is existence (*Dasein*) worth? Why live (*Wozu leben*) (see FW 357, KSA 3.600)? These questions represent a *theoretical* (metaphysical and moral) interrogation of life, its value and meaning. They are informed by the assumption that the negativity of life – the preponderance of pain, suffering, violence – constitute an argument *against* life: they ought not to be (*sollen nicht sein*). Whence the practical negation of life: the claim that the world ought not to be.[4] Nietzsche attempts to invert and transvaluate this line of thought. His move is to put himself on the side of life and existence in order to evaluate theory; that is, to substitute the theoretical evaluation of life for a perspective whose standard of evaluation is determined by life, in order to evaluate the value of theoretical discourse (*Wissenschaft*, as embracing scientific, metaphysical and moral interpreta-

---

must be clearly distinguished from the *Vernichtungskampf* against the passions advanced by Christian morality and humanism. In these terms the Socratic life would, I think, also be a *Vernichtungskampf*, a practice or preparation oriented to the *Vernichtung* of the body and the release of the soul (*Phaedo*). This distinction is not clearly made by Acampora (2013, 109), who in the end re-casts Socrates' psychic agon into the non-agonal domination of reason.

3 '[...] die Wissenschaft unter der Optik des Künstlers zu sehn, die Kunst aber unter der des Lebens....' (KSA 1.14).

4 See especially *The World as Will and Representation*, vol. II chapter 17: *On the Metaphysical Need of Man*, chapters 41, 46 and 48. See also Nietzsche's critique of this line of thought in GT Versuch 5. Also note 1[161], KSA 12: '[...] Whoever feels that suffering is an argument against life counts as superficial in my books, including our pessimists [...]'.

tions of life). In the context of GT, this takes the form of a critical interrogation of Socratism from a perspective in life. Against the main charge that Socrates initiated a fateful strategy of theoretical denial or closure against life, Nietzsche claims to *open theory up to life*, to *bring discourse back to life* by making his text be the *saying and yes-saying* of life. But what does it mean to take 'the side of life' against theory? What kind of discourse is it that deploys a standard of evaluation determined by life against the claims of theory? How is it to be constructed and organised? Or to sharpen the problem with a little Nietzschean suspicion: what is to say that, under the guise of an anti-theoretical standpoint in life, he does not actually offer just another theoretical discourse, another metaphysics that again denies the life it claims to embrace?

This is, of course, the charge that Nietzsche will level against his earlier notion of 'metaphysical consolation' in the *Versuch einer Selbstkritik*.[5] But is he right? If, as I maintain, GT avoids the trap of replicating what it is contesting, then one thing is clear: it cannot do so *as a theoretical discourse*, a conceptual discourse of metaphysics or science; a purely theoretical discourse cannot of its own accord overcome the closure of discourse against life, so as to become the saying and affirmation of life against the claims of theory.[6] This is *not* to deny that Nietzsche engages in discourse: he clearly does conceptualise life as the highest value and deploy it against Socratic discourse. On pain of self-destruction, however, Nietzsche's discourse needs to be transgressed and *supplemented* by a *performative* challenge that *enacts* the concept of life raised against the claims of theory. Here, the 'optic of the artist' enters into his transvaluative contest.

Nietzsche's two-fold optic in the *Versuch* suggests an opposition between theory on one side, and life and art on the other: against the claims of theoretical discourse, Nietzsche's text opposes art as the saying of life. This reading certainly conforms to a dominant reading of Nietzsche as a romantic advocate of art as the Other of reason.[7] On this view, the 'artist's optic' names an impulse to abandon theory on the wings of art, a totalization of the aesthetic as the way to a total, unreflective submersion in life. In another well-known line from the *Versuch*, Nietzsche expresses the regret that in practice he betrayed this impulse: 'it should have *sung*, this 'new soul' – not spoken! What a shame that I did not dare to say what I had to say then as a poet' (GT Versuch 3). But is he right to regret that he spoke instead of singing? Perhaps not, for art can only exacerbate the problem of discourse. Against theoretical discourse, as we saw, Nietzsche faces the problem of making his text be the saying

---

5 See GT Versuch 7. The underlying problem – first worked out against Socrates in GT – is that metaphysics, according to Nietzsche, denies the reality it claims to embrace ('denies' in both the epistemic sense of 'falsifies' and the ethical sense of 'negates') in the name of a fictional realm of static being, responding to our wishes. It is just such a wishful falsification that Nietzsche attacks in the notion of 'metaphysical consolation', used to articulate the affirmation of life offered by tragedy in GT 7.
6 See Introduction, p. 11 f.
7 Habermas 1987, 83 ff. (chapter IV).

and yes-saying of life without getting trapped in the very discourse it would supplant. Art or song may well offer an alternative to metaphysical or scientific discourse: but does it offer any more than a mute limit on the perimeter of discursive thought? To displace theory with art would certainly rob Nietzsche of the means to make any truth claims; for art is, in the Platonic terms that still dominate our thinking, no more than an illusion.

Nietzsche is, it seems, faced with two equally unattractive options. If, in opposing theory with life and art, he remains trapped in a metaphysical discourse of life, then the radicality of his challenge is undermined. If, on the other hand, he seeks to avoid this trap through an artistic challenge to theory, then he banishes himself to the realm of illusion, robbing himself of the means to pose a powerful challenge. The value of Nietzsche's 'first transvaluation' hinges on whether he can avoid the horns of this dilemma. The key to Nietzsche's contest with Socrates, I shall argue, lies less in a flight from theory to art, than in a holding together of disparate powers, the kind of synthesis without reconciliation ascribed by Nietzsche to the dionysian artist or the tragic philosopher.[8] GT, I shall argue, combines theoretical discourse and art in a way that avoids the pitfalls of either on its own. Ultimately, it occupies an undecidable, ambivalent space between theory/discourse and art. This 'duplicitous'[9] position inscribes a different kind of Romanticism in Nietzsche's text, in which art is not a substitute for theory, but its *necessary correlative* and *supplement*, the medium through which to overcome or make good the failure of theory to meet *its own demands*.

---

[8] The tragic philosopher 'seeks to let the total sound of the world resound within himself and to re-project it in concepts: while he is contemplative like the plastic artist, compassionate like the religious, in search of purposes and causalities like the man of science, while he feels himself swelling out into the macrocosm, he all the while retains the composure to view himself coldly as the mirror of the world: that composure which the dramatic artist possesses when he transforms himself into other bodies, speaks out of them and yet knows how to project this transformation outwards in written verses.' (PHG 3 (1872), KSA 1.817). In a similar vein, Acampora (2013, 77, 84–86) reads the figure of the music-practising Socrates in GT as an attempt to unify the 'agon or contest between art and science' in a manner close to the pre-Platonic philosophers, and best embodied by Nietzsche's figure of Zarathustra. This unification of art and science is then elaborated by Acampora into what she calls 'artful naturalism', developed by Nietzsche as an alternative to Socratic dialectic and culminating in his notion of gay science. In her account, however, the tension between art and knowledge is rather lost by her attempts to diffuse the tension between the will to truth and the 'good will to semblance' (FW 107), and the underlying tension between truth and life (where error is the condition for life) as the highest values, which is already at the heart of Nietzsche's contest with Socrates in GT and endures across his work.

[9] This term is borrowed from 'the duplicity [*Duplicität*] of the Apollinian and the Dionysian' in the opening lines of GT (GT 1, KSA 1.25), which names anything but a stable opposition. See also GT 15, KSA 1.99, where Nietzsche refers the 1778 text 'Eine Duplik' (without naming it) by Lessing, in which he argues that the search for truth, and the honesty with which one does so, are more important than the claim to have the truth (Lessing 1993 vol. 9, 510).

I Overcoming Socrates: *The Birth of Tragedy* as Nietzsche's first Transvaluation

The claim I will advance in this chapter is that Nietzsche's two-fold 'optic' assigns a two-fold role to art: i) art *enacts* the concept of life raised against Socratism, through a *performative* challenge that *supplements* Nietzsche's discursive confrontation with theory from a perspective in life; and ii) art exposes, and then makes good, the failure of Socratism to meet its own demands, as its necessary *correlative* and *supplement* through which alone the claims of theory can be realised. The claim here is that art is the privileged optic, not just for the affirmation of life, but also for the critique of theory. If, as Nietzsche writes in the *Versuch*, 'the problem of *Wissenschaft* cannot be recognised [*erkannt*] on the ground of *Wissenschaft*' (GT Versuch 2, KSA 1.13), then Nietzsche seems to promise, but a few lines later, that it *can* be recognised if we 'see *Wissenschaft* through the optic of the artist' (GT Versuch 2, 1.14). What exactly are we to make of the privilege given to art as an optic for the critique of theory?

In her account of the Nietzsche's contest with Socrates in GT, Acampora (2013, 77 f.) writes of an 'opposition', 'agon or contest between art and science'. There is certainly a contest or 'ancient quarrel between philosophy and poetry' (*Rep.* X 607b) in Plato. And with Jähnig (1972, 30), we can say that Plato grounded philosophy by displacing the poets from their position of authority on truth. But none of these remarks captures the contours or dynamic form of Nietzsche's engagement with Socrates as a *narrative* contest in GT. In this book, the 'antipodal relation' between Socratism and art (GT 14, KSA 1.96) is *transformed* by a narrative contest, in which Nietzsche effectively rewrites Plato's *Phaedo*. Nietzsche's narrative does not suggest that philosophy be displaced by art. Rather, the narrative unfolds *within* 'the monstrous driving wheel [*Triebrad*] of logical Socratism' and recounts the necessity (1) of Socratic philosophy: the need to practice the demand to limit knowledge. But Nietzsche also recounts how this practice runs up against its limits, and the necessity (2) for art, *not* to supplant philosophy or critical reason, but as its *necessary correlative* and *supplement*. One way to put this is that the rebirth of tragedy is placed by Nietzsche, not under the sign of Aeschylus instead of Socrates, but under the sign of the music-practising Socrates (GT 17, KSA 1.111; GT 16, KSA 1.102).

As the *correlative* and *supplement* of theory, art bears both an external challenge to theory from a perspective in life, and an internal challenge from a perspective in theory. These functions come together in what I call 'the art of listening'. As I will try to show, this posture or practice can be ascribed to Nietzsche's authorship of GT. But it is also thematised in the text itself at the end of chapter 14 under the sign of the 'music-practising Socrates'. This figure is drawn from Plato's *Phaedo*, and it is in Nietzsche's depiction of this figure that his narrative contest with Plato is concentrated. Unravelling this contest will yield a preliminary formulation of the relation between art, theory and life in Nietzschean transvaluation, as an *inversion* of Platonic determinations. The first step is, then, a brief examination of the *Phaedo*.

II Plato's Socrates: Art, Philosophy and the Practice of Dying in the *Phaedo*

At issue in the *Phaedo*, as always for Plato, is the question of the best human life. As in the *Republic*, he will advocate philosophy as the life devoted to wisdom, eschewing, as far as possible, the claims of the body and the passions. One passion in particular is central to the dialogue: our fear of death. And in the figure of Socrates, Plato presents philosophical activity as 'charming away the fear of death'.[10] With his usual cheerfulness, Socrates devotes his full attention to the arguments, after which he drinks the cup of poison, meeting his death with perfect composure. He thereby demonstrates the philosophical detachment of the intellect from the body for which he argues as the best life.

Yet, in the opening exchanges, this is far from clear. Socrates appears to hesitate, hanging a question mark over his life-long dedication to philosophy. What is more, the threat comes from poetry, condemned in the *Republic* for nourishing the passions (*Rep.* 606). The occasion is some poetry which, for the first time in his life, he writes while awaiting execution. When questioned, Socrates explains:

> I did it in the attempt to discover the meaning of certain dreams, and to clear my conscience, in case this was the art which I had been told to practice. It is like this, you see. In the course of my life, I have often had the same dream, appearing in different forms at different times, but always saying the same thing, "Socrates, practice and cultivate the arts [*mousiken poiei kai ergazou*]". In the past I used to think that it was impelling and exhorting me to do what I was actually doing; I mean that the dream, like a spectator encouraging a runner in a race, was urging me on to do what I was doing already, that is, practicing the arts, because philosophy is the greatest of the arts, and I was practicing it. But ever since the trial [...] I have felt that perhaps it might be this popular form of art that the dream intended me to practice, in which case I ought to practice it and not disobey. I thought it would be safer not to take my departure before I had cleared my conscience by writing poetry and so obeying the dream. I began with some verses in honour whose festival it was. When I had finished the hymn, I reflected that a poet, if he is to be worthy of the name, ought to work on imaginative themes, not descriptive ones, and I was not good at inventing stories. So I availed myself of Aesop's fables which were ready to hand and familiar to me, and I versified the first of them that suggested themselves to me. (*Ph.* 60e–61b)

How is Socrates' recourse to art or *mousike* to be taken? Is there a question concerning the philosophical life, a genuine hesitation provoked by – his fear of death? Answering these questions requires an understanding of the relation of philosophy to art developed across the dialogue.

---

10 The *Beschwörung der Todesfurcht*, as Nietzsche translates it in his lecture on the *Phaedo* in his *Einleitung in das Studium der platonischen Dialoge* (1871–2, KGW II/4.85). Nietzsche continues: 'Death was called the real inspiring genius of philosophy or the muse of philosophy: according to Plato, philosophy is really *thanatou melete*.' See also GT 15, KSA 1.99 and note 6[14], KSA 7. All of this refers to *Phaedo* 77e–78, where Socrates speaks of casting 'a magic spell over him' who is afraid of death, and of 'charming his fears away'.

The main body of the *Phaedo* is concerned with proofs of the immortality of the soul. These are crucial to Socrates' chief purpose: to advocate the philosophical pursuit of wisdom through a progressive detachment of the soul from the body. Certain knowledge, he argues, comes only when the realm of invisible, constant entities is apprehended through intellectual activity, untainted by sensory receptivity or other distractions of the body (*Ph.* 65a-c; 66b). In our lives, we should therefore cultivate a distance from our bodies, closing ourselves off in pure intellectual activity against the body and the other receptive areas of personality (emotions, desires) and directing our attention towards the soul instead (*Ph.* 64d-e). But it is death alone that promises the fulfilment of wisdom: by releasing the soul from the 'shackles of the body', death gives it passage to a place which is, 'like itself, invisible, divine, immortal and wise' (*Ph.* 66e) – provided, of course, it *is* immortal. The life of philosophy is only viable if it can be proved that personal identity is contained in an immortal, intellectual soul, which unites with the forms after death. In this sense, Socrates claims that 'those who really apply themselves in the right way to philosophy are directly and of their own accord preparing themselves for dying and death' (*Ph.* 64a). Hence Nietzsche's equation of the theoretical with '*the dying Socrates*', as the new 'ideal of noble Greek youth' – including Plato (GT 13, KSA 1.91); for he is the 'first who could not only live, guided by the instinct of science, but also – and this is far more – die that way'. As 'the human being whom knowledge and reasons have liberated from the fear of death' he becomes the 'emblem' of science (GT 15, KSA 1.99).

Yet the 'practice of dying' is more than a theoretical ethos. The language of redemption – from 'contamination', the 'prison' of the body, from 'uncertainty and folly, from fears and uncontrolled desires, and all other human evils' (*Ph.* 81) – betrays a deeper religious interest, a hatred of embodied existence animating the theoretical life. Philosophical wisdom is 'a sort of purification' akin to religious initiation.[11] Accordingly, as Nietzsche writes in GD, Socrates demands the ritual sacrifice to Asclepius for convalescence from the protracted illness of his life, for his 'return to "virtue", to "health", to happiness' through death: '"living – that means to be a long time ill: I owe a cock to Asclepius the healer."' (GD Sokrates 1, 11).

This is how Nietzsche spins out Socrates' last words in GD. But he does so in a way that is true to the pessimistic, religious animus of the *Phaedo*. And it is in the same spirit that Plato's Socrates writes his hymn to Apollo, or at least interprets it,

---

[11] 'You know how the initiation practicioners say, "Many bear the emblems, but the devotees are few"? Well, in my opinion these devotees are simply those who have lived the philosophical life in the right way – a company which, all through my life, I have done my best in every way to join, leaving nothing undone which I could do to attain this end.' (*Ph.* 69d). A paraphrase of this passage occurs in *Das griechische Musikdrama* (KSA 1.522) but it is referred to the devotees of Dionysos in the proto-tragic cult. As we shall see, this prefigures the twist given to philosophy in GT: from an initiation in death, to an initiation in art.

after the event. With clear reference to his own music, he reinterprets the swan's lament as a celebration:

> I believe that the swans, belonging as they do to Apollo, have prophetic powers and sing because they know the good things that await them in the unseen world, and that they are happier on that day than they have ever been before. Now I consider that I am in the same service as the swans, and dedicated to the same god, and that I am no worse endowed with prophetic powers by my master than they are, and no more disconsolate at leaving this life. (Ph. 85b)

Socrates' artistic swan-song is thus subsumed under philosophy as preparation for death. It joins the philosophical initiation in death as its joyful celebration. There is nothing, therefore, in Socrates words to suggest that through his music he laments or falters in the ascetic life he advocates, and he goes with serene confidence to his death. But what about his disciples – and us? Can philosophy cast a spell over the child in us and charm away his fear of death (Ph. 77 f)? There is a marked contrast between Socrates' composed self-sufficiency, and the dependence of his devastated disciples: '"But Socrates", said Simmias, "where shall we find a magician who understands these spells now that you – are leaving us?"' (Ph. 77 f). In the repeatability of Socrates' performance lies the real test for the life of philosophy; and in this space, art re-enters Plato's conception of the best human life in the form of mythology.

After advising his disciples to seek out the magician by their 'own united efforts' (Ph. 77 f), Socrates offers another proof of the soul's immortality, and then another. With trepidation, Cebes and Simmias then raise objections to Socrates' arguments, and after these are countered, both declare themselves satisfied with the truth of his arguments. 'All the same,' Simmias continues in true Socratic style, 'the subject is so vast, and I have such a poor opinion of our weak human nature, that I can't help feeling misgivings.' (Ph. 107 f). 'Quite right' Socrates replies and, after telling them to re-examine the assumptions, he launches into a lengthy and detailed myth recounting the transcendent rewards awaiting the souls of those who philosophise, and the punishments awaiting those souls that neglect philosophy for bodily pleasures and adornments. Upon concluding, Socrates remarks:

> Of course, no reasonable man ought to insist that the facts are exactly as I have described them. But that either this or something very like it is a true account of our souls and their future habitations – since we have clear evidence that our souls are immortal – this I think is a reasonable contention and a belief worth risking, for the risk is a noble one. *We should use such accounts to inspire ourselves with confidence*, and that is why I have drawn out my tale so long. (Ph. 107d; emphasis added).

Once again, it is clear that Socrates' poetry in no way threatens or challenges the claims of his philosophical activity; it serves, rather, to support the philosophical evidence for the immortality of the soul. In this subordinate role, art has a positive meaning for the man of reason: by prefiguring truths to which reason alone can lay absolute and exclusive claim, it guides his soul towards theoretical enquiry. Art, Plato suggests, is a useful *ancilla* to the best human life, the life of philosophy.

Or is he suggesting a little more – that art can also do something philosophy cannot? Socrates himself performs the ideal of courage described in the *Republic:* altogether self-sufficient in his pure contemplative activity, he is in need of no-one and nothing from without to complete the value, happiness and goodness of his life.[12] Having overcome the fear of death, art is for him not only ancillary; it is superfluous. Not so for his disciples, as he clearly appreciates. For them, one, two or more philosophical proofs of the immortality of the soul are *insufficient* to overcome the fear of death, and mythology *must* be adduced to 'inspire [...] confidence' in the philosophical life. What is more, there seem to be good *philosophical* reasons for their misgivings: practically quoting from Socrates' defence, Simmias invokes the worthlessness of human wisdom, the knowledge of ignorance which Socrates claims to practise, in order to point out the inconclusiveness, the limits of philosophical enquiry.[13] Who is to say that, on the day after Socrates' death, someone will not come up with a devastating proof of the soul's mortality? In the gap dividing Socrates from the rest of us, Plato deploys mythology as a *necessary supplement* of reason in the philosophical life. At the very least, art leaves a dent – a lingering doubt – in the ideal of self-containment, the capsule of pure intellectual activity promoted by Socrates in Plato's middle dialogues.

III Nietzsche's Socrates: the Practice of Music in *The Birth of Tragedy*

It is evidently to Socrates' myth at the end of the *Phaedo* that Nietzsche refers when invoking 'the dying Socrates', as

> the emblem that above the entrance gate of science, reminds all of its mission – namely, to make existence appear comprehensible and thus justified, and if reasons do not suffice, *myth* must also at the end serve – myth which I just designated as the necessary consequence [*Consequenz*], indeed as the purpose [*Absicht*], of science. (GT 15, KSA 1.99)

---

[12] See the description of courage in *Republic* Book III, culminating in the claim that the good man 'is most of all men sufficient unto himself for a good life and is distinguished from other men in having least need of anybody else.' (*Rep.* 386e). See also Nussbaum 1986, chapter 5 (& 7) on the ideal of self-sufficiency through pure contemplative activity in Plato's middle works.

[13] As quoted above, Simmias says 'the subject is so vast, and I have such a poor opinion of our weak human nature, that I can't help feeling misgivings'. Cf. the *Apology*, where Socrates' account of his divine, peripatetic mission, culminating in his negative claim to wisdom as ignorance (21d), is presented as a form of human wisdom: 'I have gained this reputation, gentlemen, from nothing more or less than a kind of wisdom. What kind of wisdom do I mean? Human wisdom, I suppose. It seems that I really am wise in this limited sense' (20e). The narrative concludes with the claim that 'real wisdom is the property of God, and this oracle is his way of telling us that human wisdom has little or no value. It seems to me that he is not literally referring to Socrates, but has merely taken my name as an example, as if he would say to us, The wisest of you men is he who has realised, like Socrates, that in respect of wisdom he is really worthless' (23b).

This passage resonates with Plato's view of myth as a *necessary supplement* to the *insufficiency* of theory, casting doubt on its capacity to inspire confidence. But for a precise grasp of Nietzsche's view of myth as the 'necessary consequence' of theory, we need to examine *his* version of Socrates' death in GT 14.

Nietzsche begins with a seemingly accurate report of Socrates' explanation of his poetry in the *Phaedo:* how a recurrent dream urging him to practice music provoked, for the first time, a hesitation concerning his contempt for art and his life-long conviction that philosophy is the highest art of the muses. Only, Socrates' sense of 'duty' or 'conscience' (*Ph.* 60e, cited above) regarding the dream becomes, in Nietzsche's telling, 'the feeling of a gap, a void, a half-reproach' (GT 14, KSA 1.96). Then the dream itself becomes a 'dream apparition' (*Traumerscheinung*) and, likened to Socrates' renowned 'daemonic warning voice', is cast as a daemonic voice of conscience throwing his philosophical practice and identity into question. Socrates is made to see that

> like a barbarian king he did not understand [*nicht verstehen*] a noble divine image and was in danger of sinning against a deity – through his not-understanding [lit. understanding-nothing: *Nichtsverstehen*]. (GT 14, KSA 1.96)

In this mythological scenario of hubris, Socrates' philosophical vocation of not-knowing or understanding nothing (*Nichtsverstehen*) is portrayed as a sin. The account concludes with Nietzsche's interpolation of Socrates' thoughts:

> These words of the Socratic dream apparition are the only sign of a misgiving concerning the limits of logical nature: perhaps – so he must have asked himself – what is incomprehensible to me [*mir Nichtverständliche*] is not as such without comprehension [*Unverständige*] after all? Perhaps there is a realm of wisdom from which the logician is banned? Perhaps art is even a necessary correlative and supplement to theory [*ein nothwendiges Correlativum und Supplement der Wissenschaft*]?' (GT 14, KSA 1.96)

There is no question here of art confirming Socrates' philosophical practice. Predicated on a unique, daemonic hesitation concerning the limits of his 'logical nature' and understanding, it signifies a dramatic switch of practice, a reversal or *peripeteia*. In GT, the switch from dialectical to musical practice takes on a meaning radically at odds with the *Phaedo*. In the first instance, Socrates' hesitation signifies an intervention in philosophical practice. As a response to the daemon of music, Socrates' music marks a unique transformation of his *hearing:* for the first time, he allows a 'gap', a 'void' to disrupt his lifelong dialectical practice, a moment of receptivity to override his intellectual activity. And in listening beyond the capsule of his intellect, he hears the 'limits of logic', the limitations of pure intellectual activity, suspending his conviction that philosophy is the highest art of the muses: he learns for the first time the *art of listening.*[14]

---

14 Cf. PHG 3 (cited above) on the tragic (pre-Socratic) philosopher who lets 'the total sound of the

In putting the limitations of Socrates' theoretical practice to his own ears, Nietzsche is subjecting him to doubts like those surrounding Plato's treatment of myth at the end of the *Phaedo*. But whatever doubts Plato may have had about the form and feasibility of the Socratic life are radicalised by Nietzsche: in Socrates' ears the very *meaning* of the philosophical life is put into question. Socrates' musical practice becomes the moment when the true significance of his philosophical practice recoils upon him and he discovers his real philosophical identity – as the music-practising Socrates.[15] By radicalising Plato's mythological hesitation and writing it into Socrates' speech, Nietzsche twists the relation between art and theory/philosophy in the *Phaedo*. Art is transformed from a useful *ancilla* of the philosophical life into a threat that challenges its form and value as the best life, confounding Socrates' philosophical identity. The music-practising Socrates, far from celebrating the practice of dying, is turned against his philosophical counterpart, the dying Socrates, confronting him with new questions concerning the limits and meaning of his enterprise. In short, GT revises the *Phaedo*, casting Nietzsche into confrontation with theoretical Socratism.

The precise contours of Nietzsche's confrontation can be determined with reference to the words he puts into Socrates' mouth:

Is art perhaps 'a necessary correlative' (GT 14, KSA 1.96), that is, the 'necessary consequence' (GT 15, KSA 1.99) or *conclusion* of philosophical practice?

Here, the words of Nietzsche's Socrates elevate art from the handmaiden (*ancilla*) of philosophy into its true goal or ultimate meaning; philosophical practice, conversely, is humbled, diminished from the telos of art into its handmaiden, a preparation for artistic practice. As Socrates' philosophical life recoils upon him in its true significance, it appears as something that points beyond itself, guiding his soul towards art. What, then, becomes of the telos of philosophical practice: wisdom-in-death?

Is art perhaps 'a necessary [...] supplement' (GT 14, KSA 1.96) to the philosophical life?

Since the notion of 'supplement' implies a lack, philosophy here is *grounded*, not in the lack of wisdom-in-death, but *in the lack of art*, in a 'neediness of art' (*Kunstbedürftigkeit:* GT 15, KSA 1.102). Art forms the conclusion of Socrates' life as the fulfil-

---

world resound within himself'. Also note 6[15], KSA 8: '*Comparison* of the older philosophy with the post-Socratic [...] it is *not* the negation of the *other* life [*des* andern *Lebens*], but grew out of it as a rare blossom [...]'.

15 The contention here is that, in transcribing Socrates' speech, Nietzsche *mythologises* it into a tragic drama: 'It is only when the drama is over that actions take on their true significance and agents, through what they in reality accomplished without realizing it, discover their true identity.' (Vernant 1990, 45). Nietzsche transforms the meaning of this episode not simply by distorting it, but by giving it the structure of tragic action, of which Vernant writes 'that it is not so much the agent who explains the action but rather the action that, revealing its true significance after the event, recoils upon the agent and discloses what he is and he has really unwittingly done' (Vernant 1990, 32).

ment of his desire for wisdom, the hidden telos of his lack of wisdom, finally exposed through the 'feeling of a gap' by the daemon of music – a voice of remembrance. Thus wisdom-in-death is displaced by wisdom-in-art, or the art of listening, as the end of philosophical desire.

For Plato, the love of wisdom or *philosophia*, as a form of eros, desires what it lacks; arising out of lack, its satisfaction spells the end of desire. In line with this negative concept of desire, the art of listening inscribed in Nietzsche's text terminates philosophical desire in satisfying it. As Diotima points out in the *Symposium*, 'None of the gods philosophise, nor do they desire to become wise – they are; nor if anybody else is wise does he philosophise' (*Symp.* 204a). But does the art of listening in Nietzsche's text spell the end of *all* desire – of desiring life – in death, like Socratic wisdom? Or does Nietzsche's Socrates, through the art of listening, come to hear a new, positive sense of desire in *excess*, rather than lack?[16] The recurrent conjugation of 'excess' with the task of 'aesthetic justification' throughout GT indicates what figures as the object of desire in the text: *art-as-life*, or *life-as-art* drowns the siren voice of death as the new 'inspiring genius', the 'muse' or daemon of philosophical thought. Like Plato's mythological supplement, it comes to 'inspire [...] confidence' in the philosophical life, even in its final moments. But for Nietzsche's Socrates, it celebrates an initiation (*Einweihung*) into life, not death.

We are now in a position to settle the precise terms of Nietzsche's first transvaluation. The contest of narratives enacts a confrontation between two positions:

For Plato (Plato's Socrates): *art (as ancilla) serves philosophy (theory) as a preparation for wisdom-in-death.*

For Nietzsche (Nietzsche's Socrates): *philosophy or theory (as ancilla) serves art-as-life or life-as-art.*

Thus, philosophy or theory prepares *not* for death, but for a new kind of life: *the art of listening.* In these terms, GT performs a *re-determination* of the relation between art and theory (philosophy) in Platonic/Socratic thought. It challenges the subordination of art to theoretical truth as the highest value, and its subordination to theoretical practice as the best human life.

But is this just an *inversion* of Platonic-Socratism? Plato's Socrates grounds art in the lack of theory: As an *ancilla* of theory, an indeterminate yearning, a preparation, a prefiguration of theoretical insight, art derives its meaning and value from theoretical contemplation as its end and true purpose. Does Nietzsche merely invert the terms of this definition, maintaining the theoretical logic of opposition and subordination controlling them? Does GT offer no more than a theoretical inversion of Platonic/Socratic values, a mere theoretical opposition to theory?

---

[16] On the difference between Plato's negative concept of desire as lack and Nietzsche's dionysian concept of desire as excess, see Rethy 1988, 26–31. A clear measure of this difference and the gap dividing Nietzsche from Plato's concept of philosophy is the supposition in JGB 294 'that gods also philosophise'.

IV The Problem of Inversion and Nietzsche's Duplicitous Optic in Art

The question of mere inversion returns us to the opening problem of discourse. In this section, I will try to sketch a response to this question by way of the duplicitous optic of art claimed by Nietzsche in the *Versuch*. For it is the artistry of Nietzsche's contest with the *Phaedo*, its form *as narrative*, if anything, that that promises to take his confrontation beyond mere inversion. And yet, as argued earlier, a purely artistic challenge does not resolves the problem of discourse. The first step, then, will be to argue that, at one level, Nietzsche's narrative 'encodes' an internal, epistemic critique of Socrates' epistemic practice. I will then argue that Nietzsche's narrative is organised by an *artistic cultural practice*, the *agon*, which enacts the concept of life-as-excess limned by the musical Socrates in GT 14. In this way I hope to flesh out the initial thesis that Nietzsche adopts a duplicitous optic in art as a *supplement* to theory, bearing both an external challenge from a perspective in life, and an internal, theoretical challenge. Guiding both readings is the question of Nietzsche's standpoint as narrator and specifically, as narrator of the 'necessary' switch from Socratic theory to art. In what sense *must* theoretical practice turn into art, as its 'necessary' conclusion and supplement?

IV.1 The Epistemic Reading

The co-ordinates for my first reading are: a) the discussion of the Socratic daemon and the monstrous deformation of Socrates' instincts in GT 13 (KSA 1.90); and b) the discussion of his daemonic hesitation in GT 14 (KSA 1.96). In the latter passage, as we saw, the target of divine repulsion is Socrates' hubristic Nichtsverstehen. More than just a 'lack of understanding', this term refers to the active, critical programme of 'knowing-nothing' through which Socrates sought to establish the limits of human understanding:

> The sharpest words for that new and unprecedented glorification of knowing [*Wissen*] and [conscious] insight were spoken by Socrates when he found himself to be the only one who would admit to himself that *he knew nothing* [nichts zu wissen] (GT 13, KSA 1.89)

These lines, from GT 13, already indicate that something is amiss. Concealed in Socrates' critical programme is a critical deficit, an unquestioned, positive belief or 'instinctive wisdom' rooted in his 'abnormal', 'logical nature': while 'excessively developed', it is also a 'monstrous defect' (GT 13, KSA 1.90). The key to this paradox lies in Socrates' 'daemon'. In their 'unbridled flooding', his critical instincts were turned on the claims of others; yet, as Nietzsche emphasises, his 'logical drives were completely incapable of turning against themselves' (GT 13, KSA 1.90 f.).

Turning, with this remark in mind, to Socrates' death-bed, we find him attending to 'something similar to the daemonic warning voice' (GT 14, KSA 1.96). Yet the difference is critical: for the daemon of music *does* enable the 'logical drives' to turn against themselves, provoking Socrates' hesitation. For the first time he has 'misgivings about the limits of the logical nature'. For once, his logical nature throws itself in question: 'perhaps there is a realm of wisdom from which the logician is banished?' (GT 14, KSA 1.96). Taken together, these passages indicate that Nietzsche's story of daemons and instincts intends or encodes an *epistemic* critique of Socratic practice from an *internal* Socratic standpoint: Socrates' dialectic fails to realise his own promise of critique, his own demand to limit knowledge. While critical of others' claims, it is incapable of being self-critical – until disrupted by an entirely different exercise, the art of listening. It is, then, by realizing the promise of critique that Socrates' music forms the 'necessary' conclusion and supplement of his theoretical practice.

The root necessity here is a *Sollen*, an intellectual imperative: if the demand to limit knowledge is to be realised in full, then active critique of others *must (soll)* turn into the art of listening; for only then will critique turn against the critic as well. Nietzsche's critique of the critical deficit in Socrates' method of questioning is expressed with great precision in the unpublished text, *Sokrates und die Tragödie* (1870), where he writes:

> Never did a doubt occur to him concerning the correctness of the entire form of questioning [*Fragestellung*]. "Wisdom consists in knowing [*Wissen*]", and "one knows nothing as long as one cannot express it and convince others of it." (KSA 1.541).

By taking issue with Socrates' form of questioning, Nietzsche is contesting the entire ontology implied by the question: 'What is...?' For, as Deleuze points out, 'the opposition of essence and appearance, of being and becoming, depends primarily on a mode of questioning, a form of question' (Deleuze 1983, 76). And with this ontology goes the standard of knowledge deployed by dialectical critique: whatever cannot be conceptualised and expressed articulately in dialectical exchange, namely 'the continuity of concrete objects taken in their becoming' (Deleuze 1983, 76), is worth nothing. The claims of sensuous particularity, articulated best in narratives like Nietzsche's, are excluded from wisdom. Nietzsche's critical point in these lines is that Socrates' form of question and his standard of knowledge are both removed from critical questioning by the dialectic.[17] Active contention of others' claims goes half-

---

[17] Compare Acampora (2013, 83) on Nietzsche's critique of the dialectic: '[H]e regards it as fundamentally destructive because no one wins a Socratic dialectical contest by being better; instead, the character Socrates always bests his opponents, and he does so by tearing them down, not by offering his own superior views. Nietzsche's Socrates debilitates and incapacitates what he contests.' At the same time, she sees Nietzsche as crediting Socrates with a special insight ('If only he could have such insight *and* practice music, he would then wield the most tremendous creative power', Acam-

way to meeting the demand to limit knowledge. In order to be met in full, it must *(soll)* recoil upon the critic's standard of critique, throwing his form of questioning into question. How, then, is the art of listening, as the moment of self-critique, supposed to supplement the dialectical contest and meet these conditions? It is, I want to suggest, as a breach of practice, a momentary stillness that exposes theoretical discourse to its Other.

With Deleuze's remark in mind, we can return to the question raised at the outset concerning the privilege Nietzsche ascribes to art, not just as an optic for life-affirmation, but as an optic for the critique of theory. The strength of Nietzsche's critique, as I have set it out above, is that it is an immanent critique: Socratic dialectic fails to realise Socrates' own demand to limit knowledge, in failing to put its own form of questioning into question. Yet in GT, this critique does not take the discursive form of a Socratic critique of Socratic method. How could it, if dialectical questioning is blind to the presuppositions in its very form of questioning? Instead, it takes the artistic form of a narrative contest with Plato's *Phaedo*, which revises the story of Socrates' life and final hours in a way that completely reconfigures the meaning of the Socratic philosophy, and its relation to art and life. The real strength of Nietzsche's critique is, then, that it 'encodes' his immanent critique in a narrative that captures this complex operation in a way that theoretical discourse cannot: in the simple form of 'the continuity of a concrete person taken in his becoming', to paraphrase Deleuze. The claims of sensuous particularity can be described in theoretical terms, but they can only be made, i.e. performed, through art. And Nietzsche's narrative tells us something else about the critical power of art: that critique can only be realised if the active contention of others' claims is combined with the art of listening: a moment of stillness and receptivity that punctures the capsule of purified intellectual activity and the closure of theoretical discourse against the life of the body.

IV.2 The Agonal Reading

The successive combination of active contention and receptive retraction does describe not just Socrates' trajectory in GT. In *Homer's Wettkampf*, written shortly after GT, it appears in dynamic terms as the signature practice or institution of pre-Socratic culture: the agon. Here Nietzsche describes the agon as a 'play of forces' (*Wettspiel der Kräfte*): a dynamic interplay of mutual affirmation and negation, em-

---

pora 2013, 86) and overlooks Nietzsche's criticism of the Socratic reduction of knowledge to whatever can be articulated and defended verbally, and his criticism of Socrates' form of questioning. By dismissing whatever cannot be defended verbally as worth-less ('Nur aus Instinkt!'), Socratic dialectic instantiates a 'war of annihilation' (*Vernichtungskampf*) at the level of discourse, in sharp contrast to the practice of *limited* negation in Nietzsche's agonal discourse (qua *Wettkampf*) described in chapter 1.

powerment/disempowerment, among a plurality of forces or 'geniuses who rouse (or stimulate: *reizen*) one another to action, as they also hold one another within the bounds of measure' (HW, KSA 1.789). This text thematises in a generalised form the dynamic conditions for self-critique limned in GT. But in GT the agonal dynamic already inform Nietzsche's authorship, which exceeds the internal, Socratic critique of Socratism outlined above. At a performative level, his critique of Socrates enacts an *agonal confrontation* with the dialectic. Nietzsche does not simply oppose theory or (Platonic) Socratism within theoretical discourse; he contests it from within an *artistic cultural practice*, the agon, which sustains and organises his discourse. Agonal discourse occupies that duplicitous space between theoretical discourse and art proposed as Nietzsche's response to the problem of discourse. As an artistic practice, it plays the two-fold role for art claimed by Nietzsche in the *Versuch*. On the one hand, it enables him to raise life against theoretical discourse without falling into the trap of discursive closure – mere opposition. Nietzsche's agon is a *performative* challenge that *supplements* his discursive confrontation by *enacting* the concept of life-as-art raised against the claims of theory. Nietzsche's text becomes the saying and yes-saying of life, less by offering a series or system of designating signifieds, than through its movement, the very process of *signifying*, which replicates, feigns, or enacts the dynamic and mobile character of life or becoming.[18] On the other hand, agonal discourse is also a performative response to the problem of self-critique: the agonal dynamic of empowerment/disempowerment engages Nietzsche in a process of signification, but also a retraction of signifieds, a process of saying and unsaying, an unstable discourse that also undoes its own discursivity, exposing itself to the Other of discourse.

In order to elucidate this thesis, I shall draw out certain aspects or moments of Nietzsche's critique of Socrates which, on a discursive reading, are incoherent, but in agonal terms begin to make sense. After Socrates' death-scene, GT 15 opens by reiterating his dying question: 'whether art is not a necessary correlative and supplement to theory?' (GT 14, KSA 1.96). Only here, it is no longer a question, but a futural 'guarantee', an extravagant, mythological claim concerning Socrates' endless influence on 'all futurity' and how it 'always again necessitates the recreation of art [...] in the metaphysical and broadest sense' (GT 15, KSA 1.97). If this is not strange enough, the chapter ends by reiterating this claim, or rather reopening it as an anxious question:

> Will that 'turning' [of theory into art – HS] lead to ever new configurations of genius and indeed of the *music-practising Socrates?* Will the net of art [*Netz der Kunst*] spread over existence, whether under the name of religion or theory [*Wissenschaft*], be woven ever tighter and more delicately, or is it destined to tear into shreds in the restless barbaric whirl of activity that goes by the name of "the present"? (GT 15, KSA 1.102)

---

18 See the Introduction, II, p. 9ff. on Blondel's account of saying and unsaying.

IV The Problem of Inversion and Nietzsche's Duplicitous Optic in Art — 105

At issue, as these lines show, is the question of closure. The Socratic belief in the possibility of a completely closed and coherent interpretation or discourse of life[19] is contested by a bold claim on the future that would determine or enclose it within the necessity for theory to turn into dionysian art. Why, then, retract this contention? Why should Nietzsche reopen a fate which he initially presented as sealed? Why end the chapter by calling the necessary recreation of dionysian art, announced at the start, into question? It is tempting to dismiss these contradictions as examples of an uncontrolled, '*impossible* book' (GT Versuch 2, KSA 1.13).

Alternatively, the logic of this move can be approached from two angles:

1) First, we can ask: what is required to mount an effective critique of closure? Clearly, a direct counter-claim asserting the impossibility of closure would itself presuppose closure, building defeat into the challenge. Nietzsche's opening move in chapter 15, as we have seen, is to contest the claim to closure with a powerful counter-claim that would bind or en-close the future within the necessary failure of closure, turning theory into art; a move which, however, remains trapped within the circle of opposition or inversion. He therefore goes on to reopen his own attempt at closure, throwing his own counter-claim into question at the end of GT chapter 15. In this light, Nietzsche's question enacts the moment of self-critique found lacking in the dialectic, whereby the demand to limit knowledge recoils upon the critic, putting his critical standard and his form of questioning into question. In the frayed or fractured form of GT 15, we can glimpse what Nietzsche means by the art of listening, as a breach of critical practice where critique is sharpened into self-critique and the active contention of another's claim is disrupted by a retraction of one's own counter-claim, an unsaying of what is said.

2) From a second angle, this response to the problem of closure can be placed within a fuller, positive account of Nietzsche's critical practice, as one side of an agonal confrontation with the dialectic. This reading takes off from the affirmation or empowerment of Socrates into 'the one turning point and vortex of [...] world history' (GT 15, KSA 1.100). In GT 15, the theoretical Socrates is affirmed as the symbol and 'progenitor of the theoretical human', who deflected an 'incalculable sum of energy' from destructive, egoistic conflict towards the pursuit of truth. Yet, at the very turning point, the transition to the theoretical age, Socrates negates or disempowers himself as philosopher, turning into a musician. On the verge of being transported into im-

---

[19] At times, Nietzsche deploys the metaphorics of depth and height to describe 'the pyramid' of knowledge and Socrates' cognitive optimism or 'metaphysical delusion': 'the unshakable belief that thought, under guidance of causality, can reach into the deepest abysses of being' ('unerschütterliche Glaube, dass das Denken, an dem Leitfaden der Causalität, bis in die tiefsten Abgründe des Seins reiche') (GT 15, KSA 1.99). But there is also a marked use of a 'horizontal' metaphorics of a net or network, suggesting a problematic of closure (rather than adequatio of thought to the abyss of being). Apart from the above quote, there is talk of 'a common net of thought' stretched over the entire globe' ('ein gemeinsames Netz des Gedankens über den gesammten Erdball [...] gespannt') and the desire to 'spin the net impenetrably tight ('das Netz undurchdringbar fest zu spinnen') (GT 15, KSA 1.100).

mortality as 'the dying Socrates' (GT 13, KSA 1.91), he senses danger: transfixed by the envious eye of a god resting upon him and bowing in a vertiginous fear of victory to the divine envy, he makes his offering of music. But Socrates' undoing is, at the same time, Nietzsche's own empowerment into the mythologist who binds or encloses the future within the necessity – 'always again' (GT 15, KSA 1.97) – for theory to turn into art. In other words, Nietzsche aligns himself with the music-practising Socrates, as a mythological figure for the necessity of dionysian art, so as to overcome the philosophical Socrates and his hold over the present. And yet, within the agonal play of forces, this victory must also be contained, Nietzsche too must reach a limit, where his own claim to closure is undone or opened to question. Nietzsche's question at the end of GT 15 thus inscribes the limits of his victory over Socrates into the text.

Conclusion: Agonal Critique

The logic of this confrontation is agonal through and through: a dynamic of mutual affirmation or empowerment drives each to a limit where it negates itself and limits its victory over the other. Agonal critique can be summarised as an open-ended to-and-fro of two moments:

    1) the active contention of the opponent's claim, in response to the demand to limit knowledge (suspicion): can we really suppose that theoretical closure is possible? As an act of contention it is also a positing (*Setzen*). Like dialectic, it posits a standard of critique, but the agonal critic is roused and empowered by his opponent to go further, to op-pose (*Gegen-setzen)* the opponent's claim with a counter-claim (the impossibility of closure). Insofar as this counter-claim itself presupposes closure, it is strictly speaking self-defeating. Agonal critique does not, however, rest here. Instead, it is followed by:

    2) the recoil of critique, whereby the demand for critique folds back upon the agonal critic and his standard of critique. A retraction to disrupt the critic's active contention, creating a moment of stillness that enables him to question his form of questioning, to reopen his attempt at closure and check his limitless desire for power over the antagonist. It is this moment of limitation in agonal critique that provides the best measure of the gap dividing it from dialectical critique. In the first place, it fulfils the demand to limit knowledge where dialectical critique fails – by putting its own form of questioning and opposition into question. In the second place, the moment of limitation gives agonal critique the open-ended, inconclusive repeatability of all play, in sharp contrast with the will-to-closure animating the dialectic. If, as Nietzsche claims, 'the Socratism of our times is the belief in being finished' (1[8], KSA 7), then agonal critique opens and re-opens the horizon of the future as an invitation to contest Socratism under the sign of endless repeatability.

I would like to mark some points on this horizon and use them to instantiate and flesh out the model of agonal critique sketched above. Three texts from Nietzsche's later work will be considered, with a focus on some of the moves and moments from the agonal model *oduction*.

Beyond Good and Evil 12 (JGB 12, KSA 5.27)
In this aphorism, Nietzsche declares war – 'a ruthless war to the bitter end' – on what he calls 'atomism of the soul': 'the belief', taught 'best and longest' by Christianity (but also, we might add, by Plato), 'that the soul is something indestructible, eternal, indivisible, that it is a monad, an *atomon*'. I take this to be the *position* he will subject to agonal critique or 'warfare', in response to the Socratic demand to limit knowledge, which here he calls 'a new suspicion'. Nietzsche begins by contesting this position in the strongest possible terms: '*this* belief must be thrown out of science!', and if we ask 'why?' it can only be because the soul is *not* indestructible, *not* eternal, *not* indivisible, *not* a monad or *atomon*. This is the counter-claim or *op-position*, implied (but not declared) by Nietzsche's suspicion. But does this mean that 'atomism of the soul' is utterly worthless, that this and all soul-talk should be 'thrown out of science', as 'naturalists' would have it? This would be the consequence of the *absolute negation* or op-position to soul atomism implied by Nietzsche's suspicion. But he immediately *limits* his negation:

> Between you and me, there is absolutely no need to give up "the soul" itself, and relinquish one of the oldest and most venerable hypotheses – as often happens with naturalists: given their clumsiness, they barely need to touch "the soul" to lose it.

Here, it is clear that Nietzsche distances himself from the absolute negation of the soul hypothesis that he ascribes to scientific naturalists, and he goes on to offer a sequence of *limited affirmations* of the position under critique:

> But the path lies open for new versions and sophistications of the soul hypothesis – and concepts like the "mortal soul" and the "soul as subject-multiplicity" and the "soul as a society constructed out of drives and affects" want henceforth to have civil rights [*Bürgerrecht*] in science.

Despite the tentative and plural nature of these anti-metaphysical reinterpretations of the soul, we cannot but suspect that the suspicion driving Nietzsche's opposition to the metaphysics of the soul will result in absolute claims to truth or closure, akin to those of scientific naturalists he opposes. For 'Bürgerrecht' could just mean 'citizenship', but it could also mean 'civil rights', and it is the business of rights to secure and justify inviolable claims. In response to this worry, aroused by *suspicion turning against itself*, at the end of the aphorism Nietzsche puts such claims into question, equivocating between fiction and truth, between *Erfinden* and *Finden*, 'invention' and 'discovery':

> [...] in the end, [the new psychologist] knows by this very token that he is condemned to *invention* – and, who knows? perhaps to *discovery*.

Beyond Good and Evil 22 (JGB 22, KSA 5.37)

In this aphorism, the *position* that Nietzsche is contesting is that laws of nature exist, and that nature has a 'necessary' and 'calculable' course because laws of nature rule (*herrschen*). Nietzsche opens with a philological critique of 'laws of nature' as a conflation of interpretation and text:

> [T]his "lawfulness of nature," which you physicists are so proud of [...] exists only because of your interpretation and bad "philology". It is not a matter of fact, not a "text" [...]

The position under critique is subjected to the philological operation of interpretation – that is, interpreted *as* an interpretation. In effect, Nietzsche's philological critique collapses the ontological claim made on behalf of laws of nature: they *do* exist, but only on the plane of interpretation (*limited affirmation*). The genealogical question then arises: What kind of interpretation is it? What human, all too human needs and desires does it answer to?

> It is not a matter of fact, not a "text," but instead only a naive humanitarian correction and a distortion of meaning that you use in order to comfortably accommodate the democratic instincts of the modern soul! "Everywhere, equality before the law, – in this respect, nature is no different and no better off than we are" [...]

With this nicely hidden motive (*artiger Hintergedanke*), we can see that ontologising laws of nature answers to the *moral* needs of modern democrats – to give vent to their 'plebeian antagonism against all privilege' and have everything equal before the law. Nietzsche then redirects the philological operation of interpretation from the position under critique to the phenomena it interprets, and moves into *op-position* by invoking 'somebody with an opposite intention and mode of interpretation', someone who could come along and declare: 'laws are totally *absent*'. On this opposed interpretation,

> somebody [...] could read from the same nature, and with reference to the same set of appearances, a tyrannically ruthless and pitiless execution of power claims. This sort of interpreter would show the unequivocal and unconditional nature of all "will to power" [...]

This 'somebody' stands for the *absolute negation* of laws of nature through a counter-interpretation of the same phenomena, a *counter-claim to closure*. But his absolute negation of laws of nature immediately undergoes a modification *that affirms in part* the position under critique:

> This interpreter might nevertheless end up claiming the same thing about this world as you, namely that it follows a "necessary" and "calculable" course [...]

The opposition and counter-claim to closure are nevertheless sustained, for the '"necessary"' and '"calculable"' course of nature is 'not because laws rule in it, but rather because laws are totally *absent*, and every power draws its final consequence at every moment'. But in the final move of the aphorism, Nietzsche's counter-claim concerning will to power is *re-opened* in an act of *limited negation*, which results in an equivocation, or aporia:

> Granted, this is only an interpretation too – and you will be eager enough to make this objection? – well then, so much the better.

On the one hand, this negation puts Nietzsche's counter-claim in question; on the other hand, it affirms the counter-claim by drawing 'the final consequence' from the 'will to power': that interpretation is will to power.

Twilight of the Idols: Morality as Anti-nature §§ 4 and 6 (GD Moral, KSA 6.85 – 87)
As the title of this section of GD indicates, the *position* or praxis being contested is the 'war' waged by the anti-natural morality of the church against the passions, a war of annihilation (*Vernichtungskampf*) that would '*destroy* [vernichten] the passions and desires' (GD Moral 1, KSA 6.82). As an assault on the 'roots of the passions', it is a 'praxis' that is '*hostile to life*' (lebensfeindlich) (KSA 6.83), and Nietzsche contests it in the name of life and life-affirmation. His form of confrontation is agonal critique, or what he here calls 'our spiritualization of *enmity*' (GD Moral 3, KSA 6.84). It comes to a head in § 4, where he opposes 'morality as anti-nature' with a *counter-claim*, a 'principle' that he calls 'naturalism in morality'. '[G]overned [beherrscht] by an instinct of life' – 'a command [Gebot] of life [...] with a specific canon of "ought" and "ought not"' – it is placed in *op-position* to the moral praxis of turning '*against* the instincts of life' through their '*condemnation*'. Nietzsche's 'naturalism in morality' therefore stands for the *absolute negation* of the moral praxis under critique, as a counter-claim to morality.

In the course of § 6, however, this negation undergoes a *limitation* as Nietzsche's counter-claim cracks at the seams. For does his 'naturalism in morality' not remain a morality, a 'reversed' ('umgekehrt': GD Moral 4, KSA 6.85) morality, which nonetheless retains the moral gestures of 'command', 'canon' and '"ought" and "ought not"'? To the extent that 'our spiritualization of *enmity*' is what drives this confrontation, it cannot but arouse our suspicion that it just repeats the problem of morality, thereby turning against itself and putting itself in question. We can almost hear Nietzsche laughing at himself as his critique recoils upon him in the lines:

> But even when the moralist just addresses the individual [*Einzelne*] and says to him: "*you* ought to be thus and thus!" he does not cease to make himself laughable.

The absurdity of the moral demand '"change yourself"' in the name of virtue (or even, we suspect, in the name of moral naturalism) is then grounded in the claim that the individual (*Einzelne*) is indissolubly connected with everything that is, will be and has been – 'a piece of fatum, forwards and backwards'. The command to change yourself therefore implies that everything change – 'even backwards'! And this amounts to a total negation of the world, at least among consistent moralists.

We seem, then, to have arrived back at the starting point with the claim that the *position* or 'praxis' under critique is *'hostile to life'*. Only this time, it is unclear whether Nietzsche's agonal critique is really capable of contesting it in the name of life and life-affirmation, or whether the 'naturalistic' *op-position* in which it issues is complicit in life-negation. In response to this suspicion, Nietzsche tries in the closing lines to reassert his – or 'our' – affirmative credentials: 'We do not negate lightly, we seek our honour in being *Yes-sayers* [Bejahende].' This time, however, his *op-position* as Yes-sayer to the *position* of life-negating morality is immediately followed by an *affirmation* of his opponents. This is, after all, what is required of a Yes-sayer; only it is a *limited affirmation* that concedes the necessity of his opponents for him – or us? – to oppose their hostility to life with an open heart that affirms life:

> We have increasingly opened our eyes to that economy that needs and knows how to make use of everything rejected by the holy madness of the priest, by the *diseased* reason in the priest, that economy in the law of life that reaps benefit from even the disgusting species of idiot, the priest, the virtuous one, – *what* benefit? – But we ourselves, we immoralists, are the answer to this ...

But even with this admission, the question remains whether the priest is the opposition needed for the formulation of a naturalistic morality of life-affirmation, or as the genealogical forbear of an open heart that cannot twist free from the strictures of morality.

Chapter 5
Agonal Configurations in the *Unzeitgemässe Betrachtungen:* The Problem of Origins, Originality and Mimesis in Genius and Culture (Nietzsche and Kant)

Introduction

Without doubt, Nietzsche's *Unzeitgemässe Betrachtungen* (UB) offer one of the classic articulations of the problem of modernity in the philosophical literature. Among the various statements of the problem Nietzsche offers, two stand out: the demand for an origin of German culture in UB I, and the demand for radically individual self-legislation in UB III. At stake in both is a problem of origins, of unprecedented birth and formation (*Bildung*).

In the first case, the problem is not just that German culture is in need of reform. The UB offer a bewildering variety of critical perspectives on contemporary culture, from the quasi-aesthetic critique of 'lack of style' (*Stillosigkeit*), to the quasi-scientific critique of 'atomistic chaos' and the quasi-medical diagnosis of historical sickness. But for Nietzsche, the crisis of German culture runs deeper than these medical, scientific or aesthetic discourses suggest: it is *not* that German culture exists, living in a chaotic and unhealthy state that needs to be 'cured' or reformed around a new unifying principle. The problem is one of absence: absence of a German style, absence of a 'foundation' for German culture, indeed the absence or *non-being* of the German: 'You have no culture, not just a bad or degenerate culture, for even it would still have unity of style', Nietzsche writes in a preparatory note. Or again:

> The German must first form itself: Formation not on a national basis, but rather *formation of the German*. The German must be formed: that does not yet exist.[1]

Given the non-existence or absence of the German qua culture (and qua people or *Volk*[2]), the problem is one of origins, of giving birth or being to an original German culture and people.[3]

---

[1] 27[66] (1873), KSA 7.607: 'Ihr habt keine Kultur, nicht etwa eine schlechte oder entartete, sondern auch die würde noch Einheit des Stils haben.' 19[284], KSA 7.508: 'Das Deutsche muss sich erst bilden: Bildung nicht auf nationaler Grundlage, sondern *Bildung des Deutschen*. Das Deutsche muss gebildet werden: das noch nicht existiert.' Cf. 27[65], 19[298], KSA 7.511. Also UB II, KSA 1.328 on the 'Nothwahrheit: dass der Deutsche keine Cultur hat'.

[2] As the note quoted above (19[284], KSA 7.508) indicates, according to Nietzsche, a real 'nationale Grundlage' for German *Bildung*—what he calls a 'Volk' as a 'living unity' (UB II, KSA 1.274f.) – does not yet exist. See also UB II, KSA 1.302: 'Schafft euch den Begriff eines "Volkes": den könnt ihr nie

In the second case, the demand for self-legislation is Nietzsche's response to the problem he shares with Schiller, the young Hegel and early German Romanticism – the pervasive and radical sense of disorientation brought on by the collapse of traditional authorities, and the demand that modernity find ways to orient and guide itself in its own terms. In the absence of credible rules or models from the past, we are thrown back on ourselves for the norms that could guide and ground our actions and judgements.[4] In Nietzsche's words, modernity represents the 'low tide of all moral powers' and is incapable of generating values. Instead we live on a dwindling capital of inherited morality:

> What has become of any reflection on questions of morality [*sittliche Fragen*], questions that have at all times occupied every more highly civilised society? (SE 2, KSA 1.344)

Any shared values or mores that could give orientation to modern humans elude us; they are not even discussed. We are therefore thrown back on ourselves and 'have to answer to ourselves for our existence':

> our wondrous existence, just in this moment, gives us the strongest incentive to live according to our own measure and law [*nach eignem Maass und Gesetz*] (SE 1, KSA 1.339)

Nietzsche's 'particularist' orientation is established at the very start of SE, where the cause of 'every human being' as 'Unicum' is taken up against the forces of conformity and convention. It is, he argues, the artists alone who reveal the mystery

> that every human is a unique miracle, they dare to show us the human being just as it is, uniquely itself down to every last movement of its muscles, more, that in being thus strictly consistent in its singularity [*Einzigkeit*], it is beautiful and worthy of contemplation [*betrachtenswerth*], new and unbelievable like every work of nature, and not at all tedious. (SE 1, KSA 1.337f.)

But the artist just confronts us with the problem. For what is to be the 'measure' and 'law' for us in the absence of traditional norms? And what are to be its sources, given the bankruptcy of mores 'in this now'? At stake in Nietzsche's concept of radically individual self-legislation is, once again, the problem of origins: of original norms and standards of evaluation.

Both cases – the problem of original German culture and original values or norms – are very much a problem of originality in the sense developed by Kant in his reflections on genius in the *Kritik der Urteilskraft* (KU). In this chapter, I argue that Nietzsche's way of addressing his problems in the UB is best understood as

---

edel und hoch genug denken.' The existing 'nationale Grundlage' for German identity, militarist statism, is of course dismissed at the very start of the UB (UB I, KSA 1.159f.).
3 For this ontological reading of Nietzsche's diagnosis, see Lacoue-Labarthe 1990, 223.
4 On the problem of modernity see Habermas 1987, 1–19.

an engagement with Kant's account of genius. In the first case, it is because Nietzsche thinks original German culture on the model of the original work of art. Drawing on categories for the work of art (unity, necessary relation between form and content, adequation between 'inside' and 'outside'),[5] Nietzsche translates the problem of birth and formation into the *problem of the work*.[6] In the second case, Nietzsche thinks self-legislation as a transaction between one (would-be) genius and another, who serves him as an exemplar of human perfection. Schopenhauer is cast in shape of Kantian genius as a natural disposition 'that makes itself into the law' (SE 2, KSA 1.346), and the problem of normativity is treated by Nietzsche as the question of the rule or law of taste in a relation of succession (*Nachfolge*) between one (would-be) genius and another.

In both cases, Kant is important because Nietzsche thinks the problem of origins or originality in the light of our inescapable historicity, the central theme of UB II. Kant first tackles this problem in §32 of KU, where he tries to reconcile originality with the existence of classical precedent and historical continuity or tradition. What Nietzsche calls 'das Klassische' in a preparatory note to UB II refers to culture ('der Grundgedanke der Kultur'): the questions of greatness (*Grösse*), of continuity and precedent. But in the first instance it refers to the '"historische" Urphänomen' of human memory.[7] For Schopenhauer, time involves the progressive destruction (*Vernichtung*) of each moment by the next.[8] For Nietzsche, time remains conflictual and problematic, but a conflictual interpenetration of past, present, and future is determining for the human condition.[9] Historicity, i.e. the openness of the present to the past, is embedded in basic human drives and elementary processes of concept-formation by way of memory. Coming to the problem of the work of art from very different angles, both thinkers come under the same pressure of demanding origins / originality under the seemingly impossible conditions imposed by their com-

---

5 Lacoue-Labarthe 1990, 217.
6 See 19[278], KSA 7.506; 19[298], KSA 7.511; 19[309], KSA 7.513.
7 'All remembering is comparing, that is, establishing an equivalence. Every concept tells us that; it is the "historical" primal phenomenon. Life, then, requires establishing equivalences between present and past; so that a certain violence and distortion is tied to the act of comparing. I designate this drive as the drive to the classical and exemplary: the past serves the present as model or exemplar.' (29[29], KSA 7.636f.) ('Alles Erinnern ist Vergleichen d.h. Gleichsetzen. Jeder Begriff sagt uns das; es ist das "historische" Urphänomen. Das Leben erfordert also das Gleichsetzen des Gegenwärtigen mit dem Vergangnen; so dass immer eine gewisse Gewaltsamkeit und Entstellung mit dem Vergleichen verbunden ist. Diesen Trieb bezeichne ich als den Trieb nach dem Klassischen und Mustergültigen: die Vergangenheit dient der Gegenwart als Urbild.'). This passage relates to the discussion of memory introducing UB II, and the concept of monumental history developed further on (UB II, KSA 1.249f.; UB II, KSA 1.258f.). It is, in fact, one of a series of notes (see also 29[24], KSA 7.635; 29[31], KSA 7.637f.; 29[38], KSA 7.640f.; 29[97], KSA 7.676; 29[101], KSA 7.678; 29[102], KSA 7.679) where the contrast between monumental and antiquarian history is first worked out in rather undifferentiated forms. On this see Salaquarda 1984, esp. 15–30.
8 See PHG, KSA 1.823; CV 3, KSA 1.768.
9 29[29], KSA 7.636f., and UB II, KSA 1.293ff.

mitment to historicity or tradition: our inescapable openness in the present towards the past and precedent.

In Kant, the notion of genius and the problem which it foregrounds, namely, the historicity of art, shifts the question of originality (original sense or meaning) towards the questions of imitation and succession (*Nachahmung / Nachfolge*). Of particular significance for Nietzsche's *Betrachtungen* is the key distinction Kant makes between passive imitation (*Nachahmung*), which *precludes* creative originality, and creative succession (*Nachfolge*), which *allows for* creative originality. For Nietzsche, I shall argue, the birth of German culture is a matter of replacing a *passive imitation* of French culture with a relation of *creative succession* to Greek culture. Both here and in the question of original norms or values, Nietzsche is drawn by the *radical freedom* in Kant's notion of original genius. But he also seeks to break Kant's opposition between creative freedom or originality on one side and passive mimesis on the other, through a concept of antagonistic or *agonal mimesis* between one genius and another, one culture and another. In elaborating this moment of antagonism, I shall argue, Nietzsche is more successful than Kant in thinking creative originality and precedent or tradition together.

To begin, I will indicate how Kantian genius plays into Nietzsche's portrait of Schopenhauer in UB III and transforms the problem of normativity into the question of the rule or law of genius (§I). I will then focus on Kant's account of genius and the problem of originality, imitation and succession (§II), before turning to Nietzsche's model of overcoming-through-imitation as a conflictual form of succession that addresses the problem raised by Kantian succession (§III-IV). Thereafter (§ V-IX), I will turn to the problem of original German culture as a problem of transposition or *Übertragung* and examine Nietzsche's notion agonal mimesis as a response to 'the old question, whether an alien culture can be transposed at all [*sich überhaupt übertragen lasse*]' (UB IV 4, KSA 1.446).

I Schopenhauer as Kantian Genius

In the low tide of moral forces in modernity, the task of orientation is inscribed by Nietzsche in a one-to-one relation with (his representation of) his educator, Schopenhauer, whom he casts as a creator of morality on the model of Kantian genius, in response to the question:

> Where are we all, learned and unlearned, high placed and low, to find our moral exemplars [*Vorbilder*] and models among our contemporaries, the visible embodiments [*Inbegriff*] of creative morality in this time? (SE 2, KSA 1.344)

For Kant, the genius is a legislator, the creator of a new rule for art or standard of taste, embodied in original works (KU §46). When Nietzsche begins his account of Schopenhauer as a moral educator, legislation is equally prominent. As an author,

Schopenhauer has no truck with social conventions or established rule of rhetoric; in conversation 'with himself', he writes 'for himself' and 'to himself' (SE 2, KSA 1.346, 350), as a 'philosopher, who even makes himself into the law' (SE 2, KSA 1.346). Now according to Kant, genius does not actually plan or think through his creative legislation; it is rather 'nature' in him – his 'talent' or 'innate disposition' (*Gemütsanlage, ingenium*) – that gives the rule to art (KU §46, esp. 307).[10] For Nietzsche likewise, Schopenhauer's law or standard of style is not in any way contrived; it is, Nietzsche writes, an inner 'law of gravity' which, like any law of nature, he is compelled to follow (SE 2, KSA 1.350). The language of nature is used with remarkable insistence throughout this passage, where Schopenhauer is portrayed as both a legislator and an 'unhampered natural being' (*ungehemmtes Naturwesen*) or 'natural growth' (*Naturgewächs*) (SE 2, KSA 1.349f.). Indeed, the thematic focus on style and writing allows Nietzsche to capture the dual emphasis on law and nature in Kant's account of taste, and to cast Schopenhauer in the image of Kantian genius as a *disposition of nature that makes itself into the law* (*Natürlichkeit, die sich zum Gesetz macht*):

> The speaker's powerful well-being embraces us immediately with the first sounds of his voice; we feel as we do entering the high forest, we take a deep breath and feel the same sense of well-being ourselves. Here is a steady, bracing wind, we feel; here is a certain inimitable unaffectedness and naturalness, such as those have who are within themselves masters of their house, and a very rich house at that. (SE 2, KSA 1.347)

At stake in Nietzsche's language of nature is the question inherited from the Greeks at the end of the UB II; namely, the nature and constitution of a 'moral nature' (*sittliche Natur*) such as theirs in the context of modernity. And it is because the question of creative moral legislation is posed by Nietzsche at the level of nature that he draws on Kantian genius. At the same time, however, Nietzsche's interest in SE lies principally in the *moral* resources harboured by Kantian genius. What Kant calls the 'attunement of the faculties' in genius (*Stimmung der Vermögen*: KU §46 307) can be heard in the 'attuned, self-contained and self-moving, unconstrained and unhampered natural being' (*einstimmiges, in eignen Angeln hängendes und bewegtes, unbefangenes und ungemmtes Naturwesen*) ascribed to Schopenhauer in SE (SE 2,

---

[10] Following the tradition, Kant conceives genius as male. The same goes for Nietzsche up to a point. By the time of JGB at the latest, however, it is clear that *das Weibliche* is no longer simply external to *Genie* for him; at times they are even identified (FW 24, KSA 3.399; NL 5[1]11, KSA 10.188; NL 25[202], KSA 11.67; NL 14[119], KSA 13.298). At issue in this shift for Nietzsche is the problem of creativity: Does genius create essentially from within, or does it require in the first instance exceptional receptivity (*Empfängniskraft*)? This question informs Nietzsche's differentiation of *Genie* into male / generative (*zeugende*) and female / child-bearing (*gebärende*) types (JGB 206, KSA 5.133f; JGB 248, KSA 5.191). In these reflections two of Nietzsche's interlocutors are influential: Wagner's notion of genial receptivity (*Empfängniskraft*) and his distinction between the 'weibliche Element des Kunst' (*absolute Kunst*) and the 'männliche, zeugungsfähige Richtung der Kunst' (*dichterische Kunst*) (MF 217); and J. Paul's distinction (in 'Vorschule der Ästhetik') between *weibliches/ empfangendes / passives Genie* (§10) and (*aktives*) *Genie* (§11ff.).

KSA 1.350).¹¹ But for Nietzsche, this is a specifically *moral* quality: the 'virtue of honesty' (*Ehrlichkeit*) required of a 'moral educator'. In choosing the thematics of style and writing to portray Schopenhauer's genius, Nietzsche is not concerned with laws or rules of taste in the narrow, non-moral sense used by Kant. Rather, the question of style is used by Nietzsche to subvert the categorial separation of art from morality, with the purpose of rethinking the moral law and legislation on the model of taste and the rule of art. It allows him to treat the problem of normativity as a question of moral education, focussed on the rule or law of taste in a transaction between one (would-be) genius and another, his model or 'exemplar'. The question is how an original law of taste can be thought together with the process of learning, a question very much on Kant's mind in his account of genius.

II The Problem of Originality and Precedent in Kant's Account of Genius

When Kant introduces the notion of genius as the source of fine art in KU §46, he names, as 'its first property', originality (*Originalität*); that is, the capacity to make original sense (as distinct from original nonsense or *Unsinn*: KU A180, 308).¹² But in its proper radicality as absolute novelty and unprecedented birth, originality creates serious difficulties for Kant; for it needs to be reconciled with a certain *regularity* in art and with the existence of *precedent, tradition or continuity*, all of which are essential for a rich, progressive concept of culture (cf. KU §32). Ultimately, Kant tries to resolve these difficulties by distinguishing two kinds of relation in art: passive imitation ('Nachahmung'), identified with mere learning; and creative succession ('Nachfolge'), an inspired exemplarity that allows for both continuity and originality. These efforts have a direct bearing on Nietzsche's problem of original self-legislation, as well as the problem of original German culture, since he thinks of culture on the model of the art work, and 'expects the Germans [...] to succeed to the heritage of Greek genius'.¹³ Before turning to Nietzsche, we need to ask why Kant should insist on a notion as problematic as originality.

The notion of genius goes back to Kant's fundamental interest in the groundlessness or indeterminacy of the work of (fine) art; that is, the absence of a 'concept of the way in which it is possible' (ground of possibility) or a 'determinate rule' for the production of the work of art (KU, 307–308). This requirement, in turn, must be understood from two perspectives. On the one hand, Kant's attempt to construe fine art as the sensory presentation (*Darstellung*) of the idea of freedom; on the other, his at-

---

11 Cf. also the 'Einhelligkeit zwischen Leben, Denken, Scheinen und Wollen' (UB II 10, KSA 1.334) of ancient Greek culture born of their 'moral nature'.
12 References to KU follow section number (§) and/or paragraph number (A##) and/or page number in the Akademie Ausgabe volume 5. Page numbers are preceded by a comma.
13 Lacoue-Labarthe 1990, 224.

tempt to show that judgements of taste are autonomous. The former involves showing that art is produced through freedom (KU §43) and manifests that freedom through the absence of determinate antecedents;[14] the latter requires showing that judgements of taste have their source a priori in the faculty of Reason, without there being any rule or concept as the determining ground of judgement. For both ends, it is essential that the production of art be radically indeterminate or groundless; for otherwise it would embody a rule or concept – not radical freedom – which could then serve as the rule for judgement.

The work of 'originality' is, then, to place the production of fine art beyond any explanation in terms of determinate antecedents. In doing so, however, it creates two problems. For one, it is unclear how we can speak of any precedent or continuity amongst things whose antecedents are, by definition, unavailable; originality seems rather to constitute the history of art as permanent revolution.[15] Kant addresses this difficulty for the first time in §32. But when he introduces genius in §46, he faces the more urgent problem of showing that originality is compatible with the very existence of artworks. As human, intentional products or products of *techne*, works of art must in some sense be rule-governed (KU A184, A180; 310, 307). Thus, the declared aim of §46, to prove that fine art is necessarily the art of genius, is also an attempt to show that genius or originality is compatible with rules (rule-boundedness, to be precise).

In order to establish the radical indeterminacy or groundlessness of the work of fine art, namely that 'fine art cannot itself think through the rule, according to which it should bring its product into being' (A180, 307), Kant recurs to *nature:* 'talent (nature's gift)' or the 'inborn productive capacity of the artist (that) belongs to nature' is defined precisely as 'that for which no determinate rule can be given', and distinguished from 'competence [*Geschicklichkeitsanlage*] towards what can be learned following a rule' (A180, 307). Clearly, the point of appealing to nature here is that it is inscrutable, opaque enough to founder any attempt to determine the creative antecedents or rules for fine art. But how, then, can nature be the source of fine art which is, by definition, rule-bound? Kant's solution is to make nature the source of art's rules:

> Since [...] a product can never be called art unless it is preceded by a rule, it must be nature in the subject (and through the attunement of his powers [*Stimmung der Vermögen*]) that gives the rule to art [...] (A180, 307)

Upon this point rests Kant's proof that art is necessarily the work of genius. Yet it lacks conviction. It is unclear how nature, opaque and impenetrable as it is here,

---

14 In their purely inner finality without external ends (*zweckmässig ohne Zweck:* KU §44, 306), works of fine art are produced of actions done purely for their own sake and manifest the freedom presupposed by such actions. For a brilliant discussion of this issue, see Bernstein 1992, 91 ff.
15 On this point, see Bernstein 1992, 94.

can be the source of rules, or indeed anything intelligible at all; and art is, for Kant, required to make original sense. It seems that he has gone too far in burying the antecedents of art in this notion of nature. The rules of art are not just inexplicable; they are *external* to the work. As if in response to this worry, Kant returns to rules with the second feature of genius: its products must be

> models, i.e., they must be *exemplary [exemplarisch]*; hence, though they do not themselves arise through imitation [*Nachahmung*], still they must serve others for this, i.e. as a standard or rule by which to judge. (A180, 307)

Here, Kant tries to recuperate the intentional origins of art, which were lost in the opacity of nature, after the event, as it were, in the 'rule for judgement' that is derived from the work.[16] But he seems to have swung from one extreme – obscure origins – to another – public effect – that remains equally external to the work itself: to use 'exemplarity', i.e. the occurrence of imitation, as the measure of a work of art's rule-bound sense is to rely on something utterly contingent, which depends on many factors outside the work itself. Moreover, the notion of imitation itself is deeply problematic, as Kant indicates by pointedly excluding it from the origins of fine art (in the above quote). For Kant, imitation involves the application of a determinate rule, undermining originality and the autonomy of judgements of taste; it involves subjection to a rule, undermining freedom in producing art. How, then, to define proper succession that is inclusive of originality? How can precedent be understood in a way that allows for freedom? In the succeeding sections of KU, Kant tries to correct his reliance on imitation in §46, especially through the opposition of imitation (*Nachahmung*) to genius in §47 and to inspired succession (*Nachfolge*) in §49. I shall begin with the question of precedence, discussed earlier in §32, where the distinction *Nachahmung* / *Nachfolge* is first made.

KU §32
§32 addresses the Nietzschean problem of reconciling originality with historicity and tradition, or in more Kantian terms, radical freedom with binding 'classical' precedents. As his starting point, Kant takes the autonomy of judgements of taste: they must have their source a priori in Reason without, however, having a conceptual ground or rule to follow. The subject must, above all, 'judge for himself and not as imitation, (say) on the grounds that a thing is liked universally' ('für sich [...] urteilen [...] nicht [...] als Nachahmung, weil ein Ding etwa allgemein gefällt'); for 'to make others' judgements into the determining ground of one's own would be heteronomy ('[f]remde Urteile sich zum Bestimmungsgrund des seinigen zu machen, wäre Heteronomie': A135–6, 282f.). But this is the very threat posed by the work of the

---

16 See also KU §47 (A18, 309) on the primacy of the deed (*Tat*) over the rule (*Regel*) that must be abstracted from it.

ancients as exemplary classics: like the noble class they were named after (by Aulus Gellius) they seem 'through their precedent to give laws: seem to reveal a posteriori sources of taste and to refute its autonomy in every subject' (KU A137, 282 f.). Kant's task is to neutralise this threat, to show that obeying the laws set by precedent does not preclude the autonomy of judgement. His strategy will be (a) to argue for the ineluctable historicity of our rational powers ((*Vernunft–*)*Kräfte*) and their a priori application, and (b) to privilege non-conceptual 'examples' (*Beispiele*) over 'general prescriptions' as the medium of instruction and continuity.

a) Kant's response is first to show, by analogy with mathematics, that following precedent does not preclude autonomy (KU A137, 282). Modern mathematicians demonstrate that following an ancient model (*Muster*) does not condemn one to a mere 'imitative Reason' (*nachahmende Vernunft*). Obeying the 'a posteriori' laws of precedent is compatible with the (autonomous) use of Reason 'from within oneself' (*aus sich selbst*) with 'sources a priori'. Indeed, the core of the argument is that *there is no ahistorical use of our 'powers'(Kräfte), including Reason*: whoever tried to begin from the 'crude predisposition given him by nature' (*rohen Anlage seines Naturells*) would inevitably fail; precedent is *constitutive of* the autonomous employment of our powers. In order to explain this sense of necessary or binding precedent that preserves creative autonomy and originality, Kant distinguishes 'succession that relates to a precedent' (*Nachfolge, die sich auf einen Vorgang bezieht*) from 'imitation' (*Nachahmung*) as a mere 'mechanism' (A138, 283), i.e. application of rules. Classical precedents, Kant argues, serve

> not to make successors into mere imitators, but rather through their procedure to put others on the track of *searching within themselves* for the principles and thereby to take their *own better path*. (A137, ?12. HS)

Kant, like Nietzsche, thinks cultural continuity, not in static terms, nor as mere repetition (passive mimesis), but *dynamically*, as a process of intensification, surpassing the precedent you follow in search of a new, original principle or law, a new 'greatness' (*Grösse*).[17] But in §32, the discontinuities required by originality and autonomy prove too much for Kant, and he looks for a ground of identity to stabilise the 'progress of culture' (*Fortgange der Kultur*: KU A138, 283).

b) Kant's second move to reconcile precedent and autonomy is to privilege 'examples' over 'general prescriptions' as the source of tradition and regularity. Examples are particulars, not concepts, and so do not threaten the autonomy of judgements of taste. Moral exemplars, by analogy, are more effective than abstract (conceptual) rules as teachers of virtue, but they do not impinge on personal responsibility or the personal ('a priori', 'from within oneself') quest for virtue (KU A138, 283). By now, however, Kant's law of precedent is so crossed by difference, autonomy and contingency that it is hard to see any continuity or necessity in it. This is a law

---

[17] Nietzsche's *Grundgedanke der Kultur*: see p. 122 f. below.

with (1) contingent, empirical – not transcendental – origins in a particular (*Vorgang, Beispiel*); a law that (2) culminates in another particular, which (3) deviates from the original, exceeds and outbids it in search of its own, better path (*besseren Gang*). How can such a law be in any way necessary or binding on the present? At this point the radical historicity of nature (*unsere Kräfte*) and Reason proves unsustainable. In the name of continuity and identity, Kant tries to ground this law *outside* historicity and appeals, once again, to nature as an original plenitude, an inscrutable reserve of identity and regularity: 'Succeeding' means

> drawing on *the same sources* [*aus denselben Quellen*] from which [the exemplary creator] himself drew, and to learn from one's predecessor only the way to proceed. (KU A138, 283 HS)

In other words, continuity between one genius and the next is secured by the transhistorical identity of the very same (*Vernunft–)Kräfte* they draw on (*denselben Quellen*); originality (*aus sich selbst schöpfen*) is the same as following precedent (*aus einer fremden Quelle schöpfen*). As for technique, or the application of these powers, continuity is ensured by *repetition* through taught rules (*ablernen*). In seeking to conjugate continuity with originality, Kant negates historicity, our openness to the past, in a gesture of closure. But he seems dissatisfied with his solution in §32, and after introducing genius in §46, he returns in subsequent sections to the question of succession and offers a different account of continuity.

KU §47

One of Kant's priorities in §47 (and §49), as mentioned, is to correct his reliance in §46 on imitation (*Nachahmung*) as the measure of an artwork's original sense and regularity. He therefore begins §47 by opposing genius to the spirit of imitation (*Nachahmungsgeiste*) A181, 308), or rather, to *learning:*

> Now since learning is nothing but imitating, the greatest competence, quickness (capacity) to learn, as a capacity to learn, can still not count as genius.

Kant's argument against learning as genius is, in two ways, the negative counterpart to the analogy drawn in §32 between autonomy in art (and aesthetic judgement) and mathematics. In the first place (i) he emphasises the qualitative difference ('spezifisch unterschieden') or *dis*analogy between the artistic genius (e.g. Homer, Wieland) and even 'the greatest discoverer' in science (e.g. Newton). A Newton is denied genius, in part, because his procedures are too close to *Nachahmung:* his discovery could have been learned; since it lies 'on the natural path of research and thinking according to rules' ('auf dem natürlichen Weg des Forschens und Nachdenkens nach Regeln'), it is distinguished from mere learning *only by degree* ('nur dem Grade nach' A182, 309). More importantly, Newton was a good teacher, able to present (*vormachen, vortragen*) all his steps for others 'completely intuitively and enabling others to follow' ('ganz anschaulich und zur Nachfolge bestimmt': A182, 309). Artistic genius, by contrast, is devoid of *techne* for Kant, as it is for Plato: a Homer cannot explain the provenance of his ideas 'just because does not know it and cannot therefore teach it to others' (A182, 309). This point is underscored further on, where Kant recurs again to the immediacy of nature: '[s]uch a skill [of artistic genius – HS] cannot be communicated but must be conferred directly on each person by the hand of nature' (A182, 309) – only to die with him.

The second disanalogy between art and science (ii) follows from the first, and reverses the emphasis in §32 on dynamic intensification and 'progress' (*Besserma-chen*) in artistic culture. Precisely because Newton was such a good teacher, he made a decisive contribution to 'the progressive, ever greater completion of knowledge', knowledge which, moreover, is useful (*Nutzen*). The progressive character of science is then denied to art: because artistic genius is divorced from learning (without *techne*, without knowledge of the antecedents of art, unable to communicate its ability), because it is buried in an opaque and inarticulate nature, art becomes static. For the genius,

> art comes to a standstill at one point or other, because a limit is set for it beyond which it cannot go and which has probably long since been reached and cannot be extended any further. (A182, 309)

At this juncture, Kant's account reaches crisis point. It is a crisis of continuity, as in §32, only worse. He has gone so far in divorcing and distancing art from imitation, in the name of originality and autonomy, that any sense of tradition – i.e. transmission, communication, learning – breaks down. We have: the inability to teach (lack of *techne* and thus of teachable rules), incommunicable ability; we have stasis, finitude, the hand of nature that gives and takes – death and rupture, but no continuity. Kant's immediate response to the death of genius in his text is weak: we must wait

> till nature one day endows someone else who needs nothing but an example in order to put the talent of which he is conscious to work in a similar way. (A182, 309)

In order to clarify this statement, Kant goes on to specify the kind of rule (*Regel*) which nature (in genius) gives to art. A rule that could be formulated as a prescription or 'Vorschrift' would undermine creative originality and autonomy of judgement. It must therefore be post hoc:

> the rule must be abstracted from the deed, i.e. from the product, against which others may test their own talent, letting it serve them as a model, not to be imitated [*Nachmachung*. Read: *Nachahmung*] but to be followed [*Nachahmung*. Read: *Nachfolgen*]. How that is possible is hard to explain. The artist's idea provokes similar ideas in his apprentice if nature has provided the latter with a similar proportion of mental powers. That is why the models of fine art are the only means of transmitting these ideas to posterity. Mere descriptions could not accomplish this. (KU §47 A184, 309)

There are, I suggest, two ways to read this passage as a solution to the problem of continuity.

1) The reaffirmation of (particular) examples/models (*Muster*) over (conceptual) prescriptions or descriptions (*Vorschriften, Beschreibungen*), in line with originality and autonomy, forces an admission of defeat from Kant: the possibility of *Nachfolge* is 'hard to explain'. This admission is mitigated by an appeal to the notion of similarity (*Ähnlichkeit*): the bond or continuity between exemplar and *Nachfolger* derives from 'similar ideas' and similar natures ('proportion of mental powers', 'attunement of faculties'). Here, Kant is but one step away from the transhistorical reserve of identity proposed in §32: in following precedent the genius draws on 'the same sources' as his precedent. It is a significant step, since, unlike identity, similarity implies difference as well, and so allows for a dynamic concept of tradition. Yet, it remains unexplained and obscure – Or does it?

2) A second reading – one that I will trace in Nietzsche – places the accents elsewhere in the passage, and finds a clue to continuity or similarity (i.e. identity *and* difference) *in a relation of provocation and contestation:* the exemplar *provokes* (*erreg[t]*) ideas in the *Nachfolger*, who *tests* (*prüf[t]*) his own powers (talent) against the former's work by treating it as a model to be *surpassed* through the creation of a *new rule for art*. This *agonal* moment was implicit in §32, when Kant referred to the *Nachfolger's* 'quest' (*Suchen*) for new principles, for his 'own, better path' (*eigenen, besseren Gang*).[18] Integrating both passages we can say: the exemplar *provokes* the *Nachfolger* to *search* for new principles of his own; the *Nachfolger tests* his own powers against the former's work by treating it as a model to be *surpassed* through the creation of a new rule for art.

Intermezzo: Nietzsche's Programme of Aesthetic Perfectionism

In what follows, I argue that in the period of UB, Nietzsche explores this antagonistic or agonal moment in Kantian *Nachfolge* as the *clue* to a dynamic understanding of cultural history that allows for both precedent *and* freedom, continuity *and* originality. Just how important this connection between continuity and contestation is for Nietzsche can be seen in what he calls 'the foundational thought of culture' (*der Grundgedanke der Kultur*):

> That which was *once* there to plant forth the concept "human" more beautifully, that must also be eternally at hand. That the great moments form a chain, that they, as a mountain range con-

---

[18] It becomes most explicit and most extreme in §49, when he describes the *Nachfolger* as
'ein anderes Genie, welches dadurch [durch die Nachfolge eines Beispiels – HS] zum Gefühl seiner eigenen Originalität aufgeweckt wird, Zwangsfreiheit von Regeln so in der Kunst auszuüben, dass diese dadurch selbst eine neue Regel bekommt, wodurch das Talent sich als musterhaft zeigt.' (§49 A198, 318).
Here, the dynamic of provocation-contestation has been radicalised into one of destruction-creation: *Nachfolgen* means to be provoked (*aufgeweckt*) by the exemplar to break and transgress all existing rules and create a new rule.

nect humanity across millenia, that what is greatest from a time past is also great for me and that the belief in the **desire for fame** should fulfil itself, that is the foundational thought of *culture* [...] The demand that what is great ought to be eternal ignites the fearful struggle of culture [...] Who would suspect among them [mortal beings – HS] that demanding **competitive torch race**, through which alone that which is great lives on [...] The boldest **knights among these fame-seekers**, who believe they can see their coat of arms hanging among the stars, these must sought among the *philosophers*. (CV 1, KSA 1.757, **HS**)[19]

If, as I maintain, Kant fails to conjugate originality and continuity in his conception of culture, it is because *Nachfolge* excludes any concept of *mimetic reception* between one genius and the next. In Nietzsche's UB, I will argue, Kantian *Nachfolge* is displaced by an ideal of *overcoming-through-mimesis* or *emancipatory reception*, comprising at least four moments:

1) an *antagonistic* moment of emancipation or overcoming;
2) a *mimetic* moment, both receptive and creative;
3) an *affirmative* moment of gratitude that attenuates the antagonism with genius by acknowledging it as an origin and a necessary opponent; and
4) an *energetic* moment that turns the oppressive tyranny of genius into a source of power, a stimulant to self-legislation.

Nietzsche's agonal dynamic of overcoming-through-imitation *corrects* the polarization of active autonomous creation (originality in genius) against passive imitation and learning that leads Kant to swing between permanent revolution, stasis and ahistorical identity in his account of *Nachfolge*. Rather than exclude learning from succession, Nietzsche develops a notion of *active antagonistic imitation*: 'Nachahmen' *as* 'Bessermachen' (UB II 2, KSA 1.258). Agonal contestation becomes the organising principle of a new concept of succession aimed at surpassing (*überwinden*) the precedent you need to follow in search of greatness or 'Grösse'.

This thesis will be advanced by drawing on two key passages from UB IV and HW in the following sections. To begin with, I turn to some retrospective notes from the

---

19 Cf. 'der Grundgedanke im Glauben an die Humanität':

'Zumeist winkt ihm kein Lohn, wenn nicht der **Ruhm, das heisst die Anwartschaft auf einen Ehrenplatz im Tempel der Historie** [...] Denn sein Gebot lautet: das was einmal vermochte, den Begriff "Mensch" weiter auszuspannen und schöner zu erfüllen, das muss auch ewig vorhanden sein, um dies ewig zu vermögen. **Dass die grossen Momente im Kampfe der Einzelnen eine Kette bilden, dass in ihnen ein Höhenzug der Menschheit durch Jahrtausende hin sich verbinde** [...] Wer möchte bei ihnen jenen schwierigen **Fackel-Wettlauf** der monumentalen Historie vermuthen, durch den allein das Grosse weiterlebt [...] [die] Forderung, dass das Grosse **ewig** sein solle In dieser verklärtesten Form ist der **Ruhm** doch etwas mehr als der köstlichste Bissen unserer Eigenliebe, wie ihn Schopenhauer genannt hat, es ist der Glaube an **die Zusammengehörigkeit und Continuität des Grossen aller Zeiten, es ist ein Protest gegen den Wechsel der Geschlechter und die Vergänglichkeit**.' (UB II 2, KSA 1.259 f.; **HS**). In this passage we see continuity (*Kette*) in the assertion of being (*ewige*) against becoming (*Vergänglichkeit*), mediated by an agon of geniuses at both metaphorical (*Kampf des Einzelnen, Fackelwettlauf*) and affective (*Ruhm*, i.e. *Ehrgeiz*) levels.

Nachlass of the 1880s, which situate (the first three moments of) Nietzsche's model of overcoming-through-imitation in the context of his philosophical programme in the UB. The UB belong to what he calls in one note the 'the first stage' on his 'path to wisdom':

> *The path to wisdom.*
> Pointers towards the overcoming of morality.
> *The first stage.* To learn how to honour (and obey and
> *learn*) better than anyone. To gather all things worthy of honour
> in oneself and allow them to fight it out. To bear all that is heavy.
> Asceticism of the spirit – courage period of community [...]
> (26[47] (1884), KSA 11.159 f.)[20]

What exactly this means is spelled out in another note, which describes Nietzsche's programme of 'aesthetic' perfectionism:

> To win *for myself* the *immorality* of the artist with regard to my material (humankind): this has been my work in recent years.
> To win for myself the *spiritual freedom* and *joy* of being able to create and not to be tyrannised by alien ideals. (At bottom it matters little *what* I had to liberate myself from: my favourite form of *liberation* was the artistic form: that is, I cast an *image* of that which had hitherto bound me: thus Schopenhauer, Wagner, the Greeks (genius, the saint, metaphysics, all ideals until now, the highest morality) – but also a *tribute of gratitude*. (16[10] (1883), KSA 10.501)[21]

Aesthetic perfectionism: The first lines ('To win ... recent years') inscribe Nietzsche's philosophical work within his enduring commitment to the species-concept 'human' or 'humankind' (his 'material') and its open-ended perfectibility – what he elsewhere calls the extension (*Vergrösserung*), elevation (*Erhöhung*) or intensification (*Steigerung*) of human life towards new possibilities. But they do so in *aesthetic* terms,

---

20 Cf. 26[48], KSA 11.160: 'Die Überwindung der bösen kleinlichen Neigungen. Das umfänglishe Herz, man erobert nur mit Liebe [...]'.
21 '*Mir* die ganze *Immoralität* des Künstlers in Hinsicht
 auf meinen Stoff (Menschheit) zu erobern: dies war die
 Arbeit meiner letzten Jahre.
  Die geistige *Freiheit* und *Freudigkeit* mir zu
 erobern, um schaffen zu können und nicht durch fremde Ideale
 tyrannisirt zu werden. (Im Grunde kommt wenig darauf an,
 wovon ich mich loszumachen hatte: meine Lieblings-Form
 der *Losmachung* aber war die künstlerische: d. h. ich
 entwarf ein *Bild* dessen, was mich bis dahin gefesselt hatte: so
 Schopenhauer, Wagner, die Griechen (Genie, der Heilige, die
 Metaphysik, alle bisherigen Ideale, die höchste Moralität) —
 zugleich ein *Tribut der Dankbarkeit*.'
 Cf. 16[14] (1883), KSA 10.503:
 'An Stelle des Genies setzte ich den Menschen, der über sich selber *den Menschen hinausschafft* (neuer Begriff der Kunst (gegen die Kunst der Kunstwerke).'

on the model of the 'artist' or genius. This connection between the genius and the philosopher's perfectionist labour is made in another note from the same notebook, where Nietzsche writes with and against Kant:

> In the place of the genius I posited the human being who *creates the human being* over and above itself (new concept of art against the art of artworks) (16[14] (1883), KSA 10.503).

For Kant, as we saw, the genius is the creator of a new rule for art, a new standard of taste.[22] The genius is thus uniquely suited for the work of perfectionism, conceived by Nietzsche as *creative legislation*. Since Nietzsche poses the question of human perfectibility in a genuinely open way, without prepared answers, the figure of the philosopher cannot work to any inherited or pre-determined standard or telos of human perfection. His task is rather to *re-create* the concept 'human', so as to *expand* the range of human powers and possibilities; in short, to *redefine* the horizon of human perfectibility. But as the creator of a new rule or standard for evaluating human life, Nietzsche's philosopher also transgresses the boundaries of the aesthetic, where Kant sought to confine genius. In Nietzsche's new aesthetic, the concept of the artwork is rejected in favour of a dynamic and open-ended process of creative overcoming (*über sich hinausschaffen*) centered on human existence. We can therefore say: the perfectionist work of philosophy is modelled on a *displaced* version of Kantian genius in a gesture that would overcome the isolation and alienation of the aesthetic in modernity.

Emancipation from tyranny: The subsequent lines ('To win for myself... alien ideals') place the question of freedom or emancipation (*Losmachung*) at the centre of Nietzsche's perfectionist work. They do so by setting out the problem-background to this task in a *prior condition of radical heteronomy:* bondage or subjection to tyrannical, 'alien ideals'. Nietzsche's interest in genius as a model for the work of perfectionism is thus clearly an interest in the *radical freedom* of Kantian genius. Yet the Nietzschean problem of heteronomy raises the stakes dramatically.[23] For the problem for philosophy is now: *How to free ourselves from the tyranny of alien ideals? – How to turn heteronomy into autonomous legislation in the name of human perfectibility beyond good and evil?*

Freedom as creative mimesis: Nietzsche's answer, given in the closing lines of the text ('I cast an *image* ... gratitude'), is to identify emancipatory agency or freedom with *active reception* – the creative mimesis of tyrannical ideals – in a move that focuses on the purely formal, or rather *performative* character of emancipatory reception. It matters little which particular ideal or law we break with – the Greeks, Schopenhauer, Wagner, and their ideals of the saint and the genius... What matters

---

22 Genius is the talent or 'innate mental disposition (ingenium) *through which* nature gives the rule to art' (KU §46 A180, 307).
23 Cf. 6[78], KSA 9.215: 'Geht die edle Unabhängigkeit verloren, so werden alle Talente *matt* – ob es unter der Tyrannei Napoleon's oder des Altruismus ist: Ende der Genies!'

is not the *content* of this or that system, teaching or ideal, and its replacement by another content. Rather, it is the tyranny of an alien law over us, and our emancipation from it by way of creative mimesis or appropriation.

The emphasis on form or performance over content in Nietzsche's aesthetic model takes up an important strand in Kant's account of *Nachfolge* and radicalises it: the particular, a posteriori sources of Kant's law of genius in 'examples', 'precedents' and 'models', rather than 'general precepts' or conceptual 'descriptions', intended to safeguard the *Nachfolger*'s autonomy. This can be traced to Nietzsche's portrait of Schopenhauer in SE, where the primacy of form or performance is thematised as exemplarity. Schopenhauer is an 'example' or 'model' (*Beispiel, Vorbild*), whose value lies, not in created works of any kind (including books and systems), but in the 'visible life' of genius, whose very speech and writing are dismissed in favour of his mores or customs (*Sitten*), habits and attitudes (SE 3, KSA 1.350).[24] In other words, the concept of 'genius' is emptied of determinate normative content, and concentrated on the performative aspect of his life. As a 'Beispiel', the philosopher's task is to enact or perform emancipation; he is to offer a 'practical proof' of radical freedom in the sense of 'creative self-restraint':

> Very gradually our bodies are emancipating themselves, long after our minds seem to be free; and yet it is only a delusion that a mind can be free and independent if this sovereignty [*Unumschränktheit*] – which is at bottom creative self-restraint – is not proven anew from morning till night through every glance and move. (SE 3, KSA 1.350 f.)

In Nietzsche's case, as we have seen, the stakes are raised by his prior condition of heteronomy and the question how subjection to an alien law can be turned into the radical freedom needed to create a new law for humankind. In response, Nietzsche's model once again takes up and radicalises a key moment in Kantian *Nachfolge*, the adversarial relation between geniuses.[25] But Nietzsche also brings to it two further

---

24 For Schopenhauer as 'Beispiel' and 'Vorbild' see: SE 3, KSA 1.351, 359, 360 ('das Vorbildliche und Erzieherische in Schopenhauers Natur'); SE 6, KSA 1.403. See also 30[9], KSA 8.524 and 34[8], KSA 7.794 f.
25 If Nietzsche radicalises the negative moment of (ant)agonism in Kant's account of *Nachfolge* between one (would-be) genius and its precedent, Harold Bloom, in *Agon: Towards a Theory of Revisionism* (1982), radicalises the Nietzschean moment of negativity in his 'agonistic' account of poetic creativity and tradition, based on the later Freud: '[O]ur instinctual life is agonistic and ultimately self-destructive [...] our most authentic moments tend to be those of negation, contraction and repression. Is it so unlikely that our creative drives are deeply contaminated by our instinctual origins?' (Bloom 1982, 98). He goes on to insist that 'the creative or Sublime "moment" is a negative moment' and 'that this moment tends to rise out of an encounter with someone else's prior moment of negation, which in turn goes back to an anterior moment, and so on.' (Bloom 1982, 98). This is a complex theory that combines several Freudian motifs – repetition-compulsion, repression, anxiety, the death instinct – in order to locate the creative moment in an (ant)agonistic relation of poet-creator to his precursor (and his precursor etc.), as does Nietzsche. Yet, one can wonder whether Bloom's theory is not altogether *too* negative. Where is the productive moment of stimulation or provocation in agonal confron-

moments that completely transform it. According to these retrospective notes, Nietzsche's philosophical programme in UB involves a confrontation (*Auseinandersetzung*) with his ideals that combines (1) an *antagonistic* moment of emancipation and overcoming with (2) a *mimetic* moment of creative reception and learning (excluded by Kant) and (3) an *affirmative* moment of gratitude or reverence (*Dankbarkeit, Verehrung*), absent in Kant. This description will now be brought to bear on Nietzsche's actual practice in the UB. Focusing on a key passage in Nietzsche's engagement with Wagner from UB IV, I will argue that this relation is best understood as an engagement between one (would-be) genius and another that takes up, but also corrects and supplements Kant's account of *Nachfolge*.

III Nietzsche's Engagement with Wagner: Daemonic Transmissability or Agonal *Betrachten*

There is a real paradox in the suggestion that the best way to break free from a tyrant is to imitate or cast an image of him: as an image *of him*, it implies mimetic dependence. Clearly Nietzsche has more in mind than the passive mimesis condemned by Plato and Kant. Aristotle's more active conception of mimesis as the creation of 'plausible yet fictional structures of possible (rather than actual) events'[26] certainly fits better with Nietzsche's actual portraiture of Schopenhauer and Wagner in the UB. In these essays, the mixture of creative activity and mimetic reception, of overcoming and thanks-giving described in the retrospective notes, can be seen at work in Nietzsche's portraiture.

In §7 of *Richard Wagner in Bayreuth*, the consideration (*Betrachtung*) or image cast of Wagner instantiates or *performs* the act of emancipation through portraiture described in the retrospective note. As described in the note, Nietzsche approaches freedom from the perspective of reception and bondage: the *Betrachtende* begins with a sense of 'smallness and frailty', of self-alienation or non-identity, in the

---

tation when he proposes, for example, that 'the drive towards poetic expression originates in an agonistic repression, where the agon or contest is set against the pattern of the precursor's initial fixation upon an anterior figure.' (Bloom 1982, 111)? And why does creativity have to involve the revenge against time, as when he writes: '"Creativity" is thus always a mode of repetition *and* of memory and also of what Nietzsche called the will's revenge against time and against time's statement of: "It was."' (Bloom 1982, 98)? Nor is it always clear why Bloom uses the concept of the agon for what seem to be different kinds of conflict: What makes our instinctual life 'agonistic' if it is 'ultimately self-destructive'? Is it not more appropriate to call it a 'civil war in the psyche' (Bloom 1982, 99) or a 'psychomachia' (Bloom 1982, 96)? And when he writes of 'greatness or strength conceived agonistically, which is to say against all possible competition' (Bloom 1982 101), is this not precisely non-agonistic?

26 See Halliwell 1987, 74. See also Lacoue-Labarthe 1990, 221 ff. on Nietzsche's active concept of mimesis, and my critical rejoinder in Siemens 2001b.

face of Wagner's overwhelming force. But *Betrachten* is also the medium of emancipation and empowerment. In this portrait of Wagner, freedom (from Wagner) is portrayed as a transference (*Übertragung*) of energy or power from the tyrannical force to its subject *by way of an intensified reception:* the active reception or mimesis of Wagner's own capacity for active reception or mimesis (*Empfängniskraft*), what Nietzsche calls his 'daemonic transmissibility' (*dämonische Uebertragbarkeit*). In a sense, self-alienation is not just the problem:

> for with this feeling one partakes of the mightiest expression, the central point of his power, that daemonic *transmissability* and self-relinquishment of his nature, which is able to communicate itself to others just as it communicates other beings to itself and has its greatness in giving and taking. In succumbing apparently to Wagner's out- and over-flowing nature, the *Betrachtende* has himself partaken of its energy [*Kraft*] and has become powerful *through and against him*, so to speak; and everyone who examines himself closely knows that a mysterious antagonism [*Gegnerschaft*] belongs even to *Betrachten*, that of looking over [*Entgegenschauen*]. (RWB 7, KSA 1.466)[27]

In line with the retrospective note, freedom is approached here by emptying action of all determinate / normative content in favour of *performative* qualities. The figure of genius is stripped of any determinate form or content (subjectivity) by the concept of 'daemonic *transmissibility*' and focused instead on the performance of 'giving and taking' in the sphere of communication ('to communicate itself to others just as it communicates other beings to itself'). Freedom works through the active reception of genius, itself conceived in purely performative terms, as the power of active reception: through the active reception of genius, understood as a power of active reception, the *Betrachtende* is empowered '*through and against him*'. The act of emancipation through portraiture constitutes itself through a *performative doubling* of the purely performative actions of genius.

The dynamic of *overcoming-through-imitation* in Nietzsche's concept of contemplation or 'Betrachten' is best understood as a reworking of Kantian *Nachfolge*. In §47 of the KU, as we saw, Kant concedes his difficulty in explaining any real sense of continuity or transmission between genius and genius. But he does hint at a solution in the form of a relation of similarity (*Ähnlichkeit*) born of a dynamic of provocation and antagonism between the two: the exemplar *provokes* (*erregt*) similar ideas in his successor, who in turn *tests* (*prüft*) his powers against the former's

---

27 'Denn gerade mit diesem Gefühle nimmt er Theil an der gewaltigsten Lebensäusserung Wagner's, dem Mittelpuncte seiner Kraft, jener dämonischen *Uebertragbarkeit* und Selbstentäusserung seiner Natur, welche sich Anderen ebenso mittheilen kann, als sie andere Wesen sich selber mittheilt und im Hingeben und Annehmen ihre Grösse hat. Indem der Betrachtende scheinbar der aus- und überströmenden Natur Wagner's unterliegt, hat er an ihrer Kraft selber Antheil genommen und ist so gleichsam *durch ihn gegen ihn* mächtig geworden; und Jeder, der sich genau prüft, weiss, dass selbst zum Bètrachten eine geheimnissvolle Gegnerschaft, die des Entgegenschauens, gehört.' 'Entgegenschauen' is untranslatable, but seems to combine the concept of regarding, viewing, considering with a sense of opposition or antagonism.

work, treating it as a model to be *surpassed* through the creation of an original work and a new rule for art. In Nietzsche's idiom, we can say: the contemplator or *Betrachtende* is empowered and emancipated *through and against* genius, such that the rule of genius acts, not as a constraint on his creative freedom, but as a *provocation or stimulant*, a source of energy and a *model* to be overcome or *surpassed* through the creation of a new rule or law.

Nietzsche's dynamic of antagonistic emancipation works through a mimetic practice of *Betrachten*, the very thing that Kant excludes from genius. And in this sense, he turns Kantian *Nachfolge* on its head. Kant's difficulty in explaining succession comes from the absence of any concept for a receptive relation between genius and genius as a consequence of his overly sharp distinction between creative originality and freedom on one side, and passive conceptions of mimesis (*Nachahmung*) and learning on the other. *Nachfolge* between one genius and the next is therefore defined against the *Nachahmung* that would compromise the latter's freedom. For Nietzsche, by contrast, it is only through an intensified or 'daemonic' mimesis of genius that full creative autonomy is to be won against the rule of genius. With his concept of *Betrachten*, he *corrects* the polarization of freedom and passive mimesis in Kant, and *supplements* Kantian *Nachfolge* with a concept of *active antagonistic mimesis* (*Nachahmung*) or reception. In agonal contemplation or *Betrachten*, emancipation is achieved through the *active reception (Empfangen) or appropriation* (not of any rule or given content, but) of *the very power of active reception or appropriation* at the core of genius; for the contemplator 'partakes of' (*nimmt Theil an*) the 'daemonic *transmissability* and self-relinquishment of [Wagner's] nature, which is able to communicate itself to others just as it communicates other beings to itself and has its greatness in giving and taking' (RWB 7, KSA 1.466).

With Nietzsche's concept of *Betrachten*, the exemplarity of genius is effectively stripped of any determinate content and becomes purely performative. Here again, there is an engagement 'with and against' Kant: whereas for Kant, it is the *work of art* that, produced through freedom (KU §43), manifests the freedom of genius, Nietzsche locates the manifestation (*Darstellung*) of freedom, not in created works or any determinate content whatsoever, but in the visible life of genius and its *performative* qualities. Nietzsche effects this shift by displacing Kant's conception of genius with Wagner's, for whom art is the need (*Bedürfnis*) 'to *give* and to *receive*, such that each penetrates and conditions the other through multiple relations', and who describes the 'performing, artistic human' as one 'who communicates himself according to the highest plenitude of his capacities in active reception [*Empfängniskraft*]'.[28] In 'Eine Mitteilung an meine Freunde' (1851), Wagner concentrates his views on art in a (re)definition of genius around what he calls 'power of active receiving' (*die Kraft des Empfängnisvermögens*: Wagner 1983, 217): through his heightened power of reception, the genius is filled 'with impressions to the point of ecstatic ex-

---

28 'Das Kunstwerk der Zukunft' §IV (1849), in Wagner 1983 vol. VI, 128, 133, 137.

cess', giving rise to the 'need [*Bedürfnis*] to give back the seething mass of impressions [*überwuchernde Empfängnis*] from himself through communication' (Wagner 1983, 217; cf. 218–219). But Nietzsche's appropriation of Wagnerian genius is not just mimetic; it is also antagonistic. The active reception of the active receptivity of Wagnerian genius serves Nietzsche not only to describe the 'mysterious antagonism' of contemplation, but also to perform it in relation to Wagner. For, in effect, he is deploying Wagner's own ideal of receptive genius against the tyrannical genius[29] that Wagner himself became.

IV Agonal Jealousy: Originality and Mimesis

In KU, I have argued, Kant fails to think the originality and freedom of genius together with the continuity needed for a progressive concept of culture. In his account of *Nachfolge*, he swings between an account of culture as permanent revolution and as stasis (with the death of genius), while helping himself to an ahistorical concept of nature as a reserve of identity that guarantees the continuity between one genius and the next. Kant's failure is a consequence of the polar opposition between active freedom and passive mimesis or learning, which Nietzsche corrects with his concept of active antagonistic mimesis (*Nachahmung*) or *Betrachtung*. Nietzsche's concept of agonal *Betrachtung* points forwards the overcoming of genius altogether, which is engaged in MA and described most succinctly in VM 407:

> What is genius worth if it does not communicate such freedom and heights of feeling to its contemplator [*Betrachter*] and venerator that he no longer has need of the genius! *To make oneself superfluous* – that is the distinction of those who are great.
> (VM 407, KSA 2.533; cf. 29[19] (1878), KSA 8.515)

This may well be the telos of the 'mysterious antagonism' described in RWB 7, where the emancipation from genius is indeed rather 'mysterious', an instance of wishful thinking perhaps, rather than an intelligible concept. It is far from clear how agonal *Betrachtung* can account for the relation of continuity or similarity between one genius and the next in a way that allows for radical freedom or originality.

In this section, I turn to a passage from *Homer's Wettkampf* where, in thinking through the moment of antagonism, Nietzsche offers what I believe is his best response to this problem. The passage in question concerns the notion of agonal envy or jealousy (*Eifersucht*), in which Nietzsche focuses on the moment of transition, when the rule of one genius is wrested by another. Agonal jealousy is described in a way that gives genius the *freedom* to create a new rule for art, but also the op-

---

[29] On Wagner as a tyrannical force see e.g. 32[32] (1874), KSA 7.764f. (cf. MA 577); 32[34] (1874), KSA 7.765; 32[61] (1874), KSA 7.775.

portunity *receive and learn* from his antecedent. The jealous attacks on Homer by, say, Xenophanes or Plato, he writes, need to be grasped in their true strength, as the

> monstrous desire [...] to take the place of the fallen poet themselves and to inherit his fame. Every great Hellene passes on the torch of the contest; every great virtue ignites a new greatness. (HW, KSA 1.788)[30]

In these terms, jealousy is (a.) not a desire to belittle, degrade or destroy Homer, but rather to 'take his place' as a better poet, and so to 'inherit his fame' and authority. Jealousy forges an affirmative, genealogical bond of inheritance with the antecedent: the new poet does not seek to undermine fallen poet's fame and authority; rather, he acknowledges and affirms it, while seeking to appropriate it for himself. But jealousy is also (b.) a source of rupture and originality insofar as it is the desire not just to surpass what is valuable in precedent, but to create an entirely new standard or rule of evaluation: Homer's 'great virtue' provokes, not an even greater virtue (according to the same standard of 'greatness'), but the creation of 'a new greatness'; that is, a new standard or rule of virtue.

What Nietzsche means here is then exemplified by Plato's relation to the poets and sophists. On the one hand, he strove to surpass them at their own game: to be a better poet, a better dramatist, a better speaker, so as to 'take their place', 'inherit their fame' and appropriate their authority. Plato, then, sought to outperform his opponents according their *own* standards of greatness (a. above). At the same time, however, he sought to establish an entirely new standard of greatness. While incorporating unsurpassed tracts of poetry and rhetoric in his work, he also rejected the poets and sophists, and tried, in those same works, to establish a new standard or rule for education (b. above), namely dialectical philosophy:

> That which is of particular artistic significance in Plato's dialogues, for instance, is mostly the result of a contest with the art of the speakers, the sophists, the dramatists of his time, devised with the purpose of being able to say: "Look, I can also do what my great rivals can; what is more, I can do it better than them. No Protagoras ever created as beautiful myths as I, no dramatist ever composed a living and gripping whole like the Symposium, nor any rhetorician speeches like mine in the Gorgias – and now I reject it all together and condemn all mimetic art! Only the contest made me into a poet, a sophist, and rhetorician!" What a problem opens itself to us when we question the relation of the agon to the conception of the work of art! (HW, KSA 1.790f.)[31]

---

30 'Wir verstehen diesen Angriff auf den nationalen Heros der Dichtkunst nicht in seiner Stärke, wenn wir nicht, wie später auch bei Plato, die ungeheure Begierde als Wurzel dieses Angriffs uns denken, selbst an die Stelle des gestürzten Dichters zu treten und dessen Ruhm zu erben. Jeder große Hellene giebt die Fackel des Wettkampfes weiter; an jeder großen Tugend entzündet sich eine neue Größe.'
31 'Das, was z. B. bei Plato von besonderer künstlerischer Bedeutung an seinen Dialogen ist, ist meistens das Resultat eines Wetteifers mit der Kunst der Redner, der Sophisten, der Dramatiker seiner Zeit, zu dem Zweck erfunden, daß er zuletzt sagen konnte: "Seht, ich kann das auch, was meine großen

Nietzsche's account of agonal jealousy can be reconstructed around three key moments:
1. The new poet or second genius (e.g. Plato) *incorporates* in his works and deeds the standard or rule created by the fallen poet or first genius (e.g. Homer).
2. The new poet *surpasses* his precedent in the realization of that standard or rule. These two moments make for a creative reception or appropriation of the Other in its particularity. In this sense, the new poet takes, or takes up, the perspective of the first poet. At the same time, however,
3. the new poet or second genius incorporates the rule of his antecedent and surpasses his achievements in a way that establishes an *entirely new standard or rule of greatness*, one that exceeds his precedent (e.g. dialectical philosophy vs. poetry).

Under the rubric of jealousy, then, Nietzsche tries to combine or conjugate the demand for originality and freedom of creation and judgement, with the need to receive, imitate or appropriate the rules and works of others. As such, this text is a mimetic reworking of Kantian succession or *Nachfolge* at an affective level. It is a reworking that takes up Kant's clue that antagonism is the key to understanding the relation of continuity and rupture between one genius and the next, and develops it beyond Kantian Nachfolge, using the affect of jealousy to describe a relation in which one genius *incorporates* the rule of another, *surpasses* the first genius in the realization of that rule, but does so in a way that establishes an entirely *new rule or standard of greatness*.

In this passage on Plato's agon with Homer, we find an intelligible account of the four moments in Nietzsche's aesthetic model of *mimetic overcoming* first described in a somewhat mystifying form in RWB – the *mimetic* moment, both receptive and creative; the *antagonistic* moment of emancipation or overcoming; the *affirmative* moment of honouring that attenuates the antagonism with genius by acknowledging it as an origin; and the *energetic* moment that turns the oppressive tyranny of genius into a source of power, a stimulant to (self-)legislation. The importance of Nietzsche's account of agonal jealousy lies in the precision and intelligibility it brings to these moments by connecting them in a double-movement that *affirms and incorporates the standard or rule of the other and at the same time limits by containing it within an attempt to set an entirely new standard or rule.*

Nebenbuhler können; ja, ich kann es besser als sie. Kein Protagoras hat so schöne Mythen gedichtet wie ich, kein Dramatiker ein so belebtes und fesselndes Ganze, wie das Symposium, kein Redner solche Rede verfaßt, wie ich sie im Gorgias hinstelle – und nun verwerfe ich das alles zusammen und verurtheile alle nachbildende Kunst! Nur der Wettkampf machte mich zum Dichter, zum Sophisten, zum Redner!" Welches Problem erschließt sich uns da, wenn wir nach dem Verhältniß des Wettkampfes zur Conception des Kunstwerkes fragen! –'.

V The Problem of German Culture and the Actuality of the Greeks

Having considered the relation of creative succession between one (would-be) genius and another as a relation of agonal *Betrachtung*, I return now to the problem of original German culture with which I opened the chapter. As Lacoue-Labarthe has shown, the question of the origin or birth of German culture is addressed by Nietzsche on the model of the *original work of art* with questions like: How to effect the passage from absence to presence (*poiesis*) for German culture? How is German culture to 'set itself to work', to form itself into a work? And whence the 'formative power' for this task? For the problem of origin is inextricably linked to the problem of formation or *Bildung*, as Nietzsche makes clear when he writes: 'The German must be formed [*gebildet werden*]: that does not yet exist' (19[284] 7.508, cited on p. 111). For Nietzsche existence or being is not static. To be means to live, where life is thought as dynamis – power, intensity – and as growth, continual self-unfolding and self-formation.[32] And as a problem of *self*-formation or forming yourself, the problem of being is also inseparable from the question of proper being or identity; in short, of being-German.

Nietzsche poses the question of original German culture, like that of the original work of art and its creator, in the light of our inescapable historicity, shifting the question of originality towards the questions of imitation and succession (*Nachahmung / Nachfolge*). For Nietzsche, I shall argue, the birth of German culture is a matter of replacing a *passive imitation* of French culture with a relation of active imitation or *creative succession* to Greek culture.[33] In the style of 'agonal *Betrachtung*' – the term used above to name Nietzsche's style of thought and portraiture in the UB – he proposes a form of antagonistic or *agonal mimesis* between German and archaic Greek culture, analogous to that between one genius and another. By analogy with the latter, the agonal mimesis of cultures is designed to conjugate creative freedom and originality with receptivity and an openness to what is alien (*das Fremde*), in what can be called the *art of fruitful learning*.

We can begin with the *locus classicus* for agonal *Betrachtung*, §7 of *Richard Wagner in Bayreuth*, (see p. 127 f.), and three moments in particular:
1. The *insight into non-identity* (self-alienation) or extreme depropriation as the key to the problem of identity or proper being. At stake here is an openness or receptivity to alien or foreign (*fremde*) sources at all levels: sensory, affective, theoretical and practical.

---

[32] Lacoue-Labarthe 1990, 211, 219. Sections V, VI and IX draw on the article "Nietzsche's '*Agonale Betrachtungen*': On the Actuality of the Greeks in the *Unzeitgemässe Betrachtungen*", in *Rethinking the Nietzschean Concept of 'Untimely'*, ed. A. Caputo (Mimesis International, 2018), pp. 23–39.

[33] Or as Lacoue-Labarthe (1990, 224) puts it, he 'expects the Germans [...] to succeed to the heritage of Greek genius'.

2. A *mimetic capacity of transposition or transmission*, as the key to self-formation in the face of alien forces: what Nietzsche usually calls *Übertragung*, or in Wagner's case a 'dämonische Uebertragbarkeit' that can 'communicate itself to others, just as it communicates other beings to itself'.³⁴
3. The *antagonistic character* of this communicative exchange. As a strategy of empowerment and self-formation *through and against* alien forces, it appropriates what is best in them in order to do better than them, to surpass or overcome their achievements, while acknowledging them as an origin and necessary opponent in a gesture of gratitude.

These three moments, I shall argue, can be made out in Nietzsche's response to the crisis of German culture in the UB: he appeals to the Greeks in a move that combines the mimetic appropriation *and* overcoming of Greek culture for the sake of a better future.

The expression 'agonal *Betrachtung*' comes from a letter to Rohde from 1872, in which Nietzsche refers to *Homer's Wettkampf* as the latest in his tireless efforts at 'agonale[.] Betrachtungen'.³⁵ As this expression indicates, the agon lies at the epicentre³⁶ of Nietzsche's engagement with Greeks – and not just in *Homer's Wettkampf*. But the qualification 'agonal' also indicates that Nietzsche's ambition is to *perform*, in his manner of engagement or 'Betrachtung', what he thematises as the epicentre of Greek culture. This interplay between thematic and performative dimensions of Nietzsche's writing is emblematic of his engagement with the Greeks in the UB: as a complex, reciprocal interplay of affirmation and negation, the Greek agon shares with Nietzschean *Betrachten* the antagonism of acknowledgement and overcoming, of empowerment through and against the antagonist. Indeed, if the ancient Greek agon is the *source* and inspiration for Nietzsche's (ant)agonistic style of *Betrachten*, as I shall argue, his treatment of ancient Greek culture can be seen as a mimetic doubling of the ancient Greek agon. Paradoxically, but also with logical necessity, it culminates in an overcoming of ancient Greek culture, inaugurating Nietzsche's turn to modernity in *Human, All Too Human*.

The *Unzeitgemässe Betrachtungen* are of course very much about the present, the present as a crisis; but the Greeks are never far from Nietzsche's mind. Their place on the horizon of Nietzsche's *Betrachtungen* is marked by recurrent references and analogies throughout the texts; also by his plans, notes and texts for another *Unzeitge-*

---

34 'welche sich Anderen ebenso mittheilen kann, als sie andere Wesen sich selber mittheilt' (UB IV, KSA 1.466).
35 'Ich habe einen Entwurf zur nächsten Schrift unter den Händen, genannt "Homers Wettkampf". Du magst nur immer lachen über die Unermüdlichkeit meiner agonale Betrachtungen; diesmal kommt etwas heraus. –' (Nietzsche to Rohde, 25 July 1872, KSB 4.35).
36 I borrow this term from earth science to indicate the place that has the highest level of an activity *without* implying that it works as an 'essence' or unitary ground in Nietzsche's text, as would the term 'centre'.

mässe Betrachtung called *Wir Philologen*;[37] and, of course, by the well-known lines from the preface to UB II. It is, he claims, only as a 'pupil of older times, especially the Greek' that he has come to 'such untimely experiences' of himself as a 'child of the present time'. The only sense he can make of his profession as a classical philologist in the present is to act in an untimely manner—that is, counter to our time, thereby acting upon our time and hopefully for the benefit of a time to come (UB II Vorwort, KSA 1.247).[38] What these lines articulate is the hallmark, the signature 'duplicity', of Nietzsche's thought throughout the early 1870s: *critique of the present*, and *engagement with archaic Greek culture* as a *standard of critique*, are two sides of the same programme to place antiquity into antagonistic confrontation with modernity for the sake of cultural reform. This is nowhere more apparent than in the thematic duplicity of *Die Geburt der Tragödie*, Nietzsche's curiously de-centered *Erstlingsschrift*.[39] If in texts like *Die Geburt der Tragödie* and *Die Philosophie im tragischen Zeitalter der Griechen*, the Greek side is in the forefront of Nietzsche's thought, the *Unzeitgemässe Betrachtungen* are marked by a decided *Zeitbezogenheit*. To examine Nietzsche's relation to the Greeks in the *Unzeitgemässe Betrachtungen* is thus to examine the reverse side of the texts, the indispensable *background* to the critique of the present that Nietzsche *foregrounds*.

Nietzsche's allusion to classical philology in the preface to UB II, raises two obvious sets of questions:

1. Why should archaic Greek culture be *binding* on the present? What does Nietzsche hope to find in them that is *classical* or *exemplary*, given his interest in overcoming the present? And
2. *How* are they to be engaged for the sake of a better future? What does it mean to be a pupil (*Zögling*) of the ancient Greeks, to be educated or formed by them (*erzogen, gebildet*), as 'classical', as 'exemplars'?

---

[37] See: *Nachlass* 1875 and 1876/77, KSA 8, sources 2–7, 18, 19, (20). Actually planned as the fourth *Unzeitgemässe Betrachtung*, but interrupted *by Richard Wagner in Bayreuth*, and never completed. The title page—'Notizen zu Wir Philologen' (3[1] (1875), KSA 8)—was written by Gersdorff in March 1875, although Nietzsche planned to use already-available material and have it complete by 1877, the 'Geburtstag der Philologie' (3[2], KSA 8). RWB was written between summer 1875 and spring 1876 and published in July on time for the opening of the *Baythreuther Festspiele*. On this and reasons for why *Wir Philologen* was not completed, see Cancik 1994. Cancik refers it not to the interruption by *Richard Wagner in Bayreuth*, but to Nietzsche's discovery of a new form—the aphorism—and his unwillingness to bring his material 'in die guten alten Formen von Einleitungswissenschaft, Streitschrift, Programmrede oder Essay' (Cancik 1994, 87).
[38] 'in ihr unzeitgemäss—das heisst gegen die Zeit und dadurch auf die Zeit und hoffentlich zu Gunsten einer kommenden Zeit—zu wirken.'
[39] On the thematic duplicity of GT as theory of Greek tragedy and critique of modernity at once, see Jähnig 1972, 32ff. See also the notes to *Wir Philologen*, and most succinctly: MA 616, KSA 2.349.

VI Succeeding to (*Nachfolgen*) the Greeks

The non-existence of the German means that the fundamental problem in Nietzsche's eyes is a problem of origin and self-formation or *Bildung*.[40] How to give birth (being) to the German (culture, people)? How best to grow, to form oneself as 'properly' German—if not on a 'national basis'?

In the first two *Unzeitgemässe Betrachtungen*, we first meet with *negative* answers to these questions.

1. Giving birth to German culture is *not* a matter of imitation, of borrowed fashions. Imitating 'the forms, colours, products and curiosities of all times and places' (UB I, KSA1.163), especially of French culture, has led only to a 'chaotic tangle [*Durcheinander*] of all styles' and dependency [*Abhängigkeit*], not to the unified style required for an 'original German culture' (UB I, KSA1.163). The opposition between 'original' and imitated (*nachgeahmt / nachgemacht*) is a key theme in UB I.[41] In UB II, this critique of mimesis is generalised as a critique of historical knowledge – 'memory opens all its gates', 'the alien [*das Fremde*] and incoherent forces itself', leading to an 'huge amount of indigestible stones of knowledge [*Wissenssteinen*]' – and the breach between inner and outer. Modern German *Bildung* is therefore nothing living (*nichts Lebendiges*), but 'an indifferent convention, a pitiful imitation [*Nachahmung*] or even a crude caricature' (UB II, KSA 1.272–3). This critique culminates in a denunciation of cosmetic concept of 'culture as decoration'. Instead, each of us

> must organise the chaos within him by thinking back to his authentic needs. His honesty, the strength and truthfulness of his character must at some time or other rebel against a state of things in which he only repeats, re-learns, imitates [*immer nur nachgesprochen, nachgelernt, nachgeahmt werde*]; he will then begin to grasp that culture can be something other than a decoration of life, that is to say at bottom no more than dissimulation and disguise; for all adornment conceals that which is adorned. (UB II, KSA 1.333 f.)[42]

---

40 Lacoue-Labarthe 1990, 223, 211, 219.
41 E.g. 'Hätten wir wirklich aufgehört, sie nachzuahmen, so würden wir damit noch nicht über sie gesiegt, sondern uns nur von ihnen befreit haben: erst dann, wenn wir ihnen eine originale deutsche Kultur aufgezwungen hätten, dürfte auch von einem Triumphe der deutschen Kultur die Rede sein. Inzwischen beachten wir, dass wir von Paris nach wie vor in allen Angelegenheiten der Form abhängen—und abhängen müssen: denn bis jetzt giebt es keine deutsche originale Kultur' (UB I, KSA 1.163). Also: 'Freilich wird die Philister-Kultur in Deutschland entrüstet sein, wenn man von bemalten Götzenbildern spricht, wo sie einen lebendigen Gott sieht [...] sie selbst [haben] verlernt [...], zwischen lebendig und todt, ächt und unächt, original und nachgemacht, Gott und Götze zu unterscheiden' (UB I, KSA 1.241).
42 'muss das Chaos in sich organisiren, dadurch dass er sich auf seine ächten Bedürfnisse zurückbesinnt. Seine Ehrlichkeit, sein tüchtiger und wahrhaftiger Charakter muss sich irgendwann einmal dagegen sträuben, dass immer nur nachgesprochen, nachgelernt, nachgeahmt werde; er beginnt dann zu begreifen, dass Cultur noch etwas Andres sein kann als Dekoration des Lebens, das heisst

In both UB I and II, then, the aesthetic concept of mimesis or imitation (*Nachahmung*) stands for de-formation, chaotic growth and self-alienation.

2. The alternative to imitation is not, however, to engage in a process of 'purification', of closure against 'das Fremde', so as to concentrate upon the properly German. This isolationism is precisely the attitude of the *Bildungsphilister*, the philistine denounced in UB I as a negative or negating being[43] who prides himself on German culture:

> We have our culture, he says, for we have our "classics"; not only is the foundation there, no, even the edifice itself stands already grounded upon it —we ourselves are this edifice.[44]

For Nietzsche, there is an ontological fallacy here: the belief that German culture exists. And his response is to redefine or reverse (*umkehren*)[45] the German '"classics"' from the 'finders' (*Findende*) or 'foundation' of German culture into 'searchers': *Suchende*, who 'sought with such perseverance precisely that which the *Bildungsphilister* imagines he possesses: authentic, originary German culture'.[46] It is *as searchers*, Nietzsche claims, that the classics[47] are exemplary and essential: honouring them (*ehren*) means 'that one continues [*fortfährt*] to search in their spirit and with their courage, and not to grow weary in doing so' (UB II, KSA 1.168). In this connection, Nietzsche also speaks of 'nachfolgen': following, imitating, or succeeding to them.

Behind the critique of the *Bildungsphilister* there looms once again the problem of imitation. In place of the passive imitation of French culture, the philistine substitutes the passive imitation of the German classics, 'die epigonenhafte Nachah-

---

im Grunde doch immer nur Verstellung und Verhüllung; denn aller Schmuck versteckt das Geschmückte.'

43 The philistine 'only wards off, negates, closes off, stops his ears, averts his eyes, he is a negative being, even in his hatred and his enmity' (UB I, KSA 1.166). The result is 'a cohesive group of such negations, a system of non-culture [*Nicht-Kultur*]', a poor approximation to a genuine 'unity of style' (UB I, KSA 1.166).

44 'Wir haben ja unsere Kultur —denn wir haben ja unsere "Klassiker", das Fundament ist nicht nur da, nein auch der Bau steht schon auf ihm gegründet—wir selbst sind dieser Bau. Dabei greift der Philister an die eigene Stirn.' (UB I, KSA 1.167).

45 See Politycki 1989, 227f. Also: Politycki 1981, 64f.

46 UB I, KSA 1.167: 'eben das inbrünstig und mit ernster Beharrlichkeit suchten, was der Bildungsphilister zu besitzen wähnt: die ächte ursprüngliche deutsche Kultur'. Cf. 27[65] (1873), KSA 7. The 'Suchen' of the German Classics has a special reference to ancient Greece for Nietzsche: see BA, KSA 1.691.

47 See Nietzsche's remarks on the 'klassisches exemplum' as 'Vermittler zwischen uns und der Idee' (1[50] (1869), KSA 7. In *Der Wanderer und sein Schatten* 125 (KSA 2.607) Nietzsche famously denies the epithet 'classisch' to German authors *because* they were *Suchende* or 'Anpflanzer', returning to the traditional notion of Klassiker as 'Vollender' or Findende. On this, see Politycki 1989, 227.

mung',⁴⁸ and dreams, like Strauss, of his 'waxworks cabinet', where the classics stand 'delicately imitated [*nachgemacht*] in wax and pearls' (UB I 4, KSA 1.181). Closure or purification cannot be the alternative to imitation, since the 'original', the foundations of being-German, are absent, searching for a German style. The philistine's gesture of purification is hollow; his mistake is to conflate and reject all kinds of 'searching' together with the wrong kind of searching: passive, chaotic *mimesis*.

Nietzschean imitation or *Nachfolgen* will clearly need to be different from both hollow philistine *mimesis* and chaotic, historical *mimesis*. It will need to be *active*, rather than passive; and it will need to be *organised* rather than chaotic. In what follows, I argue that Nietzschean imitation is a *techne* of organised growth (*Einordnung*), through *active* (transformative) *assimilation* of what is 'past and alien', archaic Greek culture in particular. But first we need to attend to the mimetic exigency in these texts: Nietzsche's insistence on *imitation* in response to the problem of origins.

The mimetic exigency derives from two key presuppositions of the UB. The first is existential, and concerns the finitude of human existence as a 'never to be completed imperfect tense' (UB II 1, KSA 1.249); that is, the historicity of human existence and culture, our ineluctable openness in the present via memory to what is past and alien. This 'historische Urphänomen', our historicity, is embedded in basic human drives and memory, as we saw, and is conceived by Nietzsche as a conflictual interpenetration of past, present and future (p. 113). The same applies to human culture, due to the idiosyncratic (actually: Emersonian)⁴⁹ linkage made between individual memory and history as a cultural phenomenon. Nietzsche cannot, therefore, argue for the annihilation of history – however problematic it is – without advocating the annihilation of the human. This is why he argues instead for the transformation, restriction (*Bändigung*) or moderation (*Maass*) of history; and it is also why the problem of an original German culture is, from the very start, a matter of mimesis. The problem of origins cannot even be formulated without regard for the fact of human memory, and that means: an abysmal openness of the German to what is past and alien.

For Nietzsche, as we saw, the 'historische Urphänomen' of historicity is also the 'drive to the classical and exemplary' (*Trieb nach dem Klassischen und Mustergültigen*), prompting the question:

---

48 Or 'Nachahmung der Wirklichkeit bis zum Aeffischen' (UB I 2, KSA 1.171), i.e. realism. Nietzsche also speaks of 'freie Copien der anerkanntesten und berühmsten Werke der Klassiker' (UB I 2, KSA 1.171), and 'nachmalen' (UB I 2, KSA 1.169).
49 See Stack 1992, 110.

But what use is the drive to the classical to the present? It indicates that what was once the case was in any case once *possible* and should therefore also be possible again [...] (29[29]) (1873), KSA 7.637)[50]

In these lines, a futural reference to the open-ended perfection of the human ('den Begriff "Mensch" weiter auszuspannen und schöner zu erfüllen', UB II 2, KSA 1.259) is tied to a reference to the ancient Greeks, for the modality of 'the possible' is a privileged term of reference for the ancient Greeks in Nietzsche's vocabulary at this time: the Romans, he argues, are needed to show how things became as they are, but 'in order to show how completely other it can be [*wie ganz anders es sein kann*], one can show, e.g. the Greeks' (5[46] (1875), KSA 8). With this compact formulation, Nietzsche articulates, under the sign of the possible (*sein kann*), the radical otherness (*ganz anders*) of the ancient Greeks, and their instrumental value for the purposes of formation (*Erziehung, Bildung*). In these notes, then, we receive a first response to the question of the ancient Greeks: within a *Bildungs*-programme aimed at perfecting the 'human', Greek culture is uniquely valuable as a sign of the possible that is radically Other to the present.

This is of course but half an answer and leaves us asking: But why the Greeks? Why should they be 'classical', given Nietzsche's properly German problem? These questions lead directly to Nietzsche's second, 'epigonal' presupposition in the early 1870s. At times, Nietzsche speaks in the tradition of a certain classical philology, of a mysterious 'bond' (*Band*) tying the 'inner German being'(*innersten deutschen Wesen*) with the 'Greek genius'.[51] At other times he views modern culture as ineluctably epigonal, so that in UB II (KSA 1.306) he can write 'that we Germans [...] must always be mere "descendants" [or "latecomers"; *Nachkommen*], because we can be only this', and, quoting the philologist Wilhelm Wackernagel: '"We Germans"' are but '"followers [*Nachfolger*] of the ancient world"', fated to breathe '"the immortal spirit of classical culture"' next to the spirit of Christianity: 'were someone to succeed in excising [...] these two elements from his life-breath, there would not be much left over on which to continue nourishing a spiritual life'

---

50 'Wodurch nützt aber der Trieb zum Klassischen der Gegenwart? Er deutet an, dass, was einmal war, jedenfalls einmal möglich war und deshalb wohl auch wieder möglich sein wird [...].' Cf. UB II, KSA 1.260. See also 'der Grundgedanke im Glauben an die Humanität' (UB II, KSA 1.259), and 'der Grundgedanke der Kultur' (CV 1, KSA 1.756). For a comparative reading of these passages focused on the question of 'Empfindung', see Geijsen 1997, chapter 5 : Vom Tempel des Ruhms.
51 See e.g. Welcker's *Über die Bedeutung der Philologie*, quoted in Orsucci 1996, 17. In *Ueber die Zukunft unserer Bildungsanstalten*, Nietzsche names the German classics (Goethe, Schiller, Lessing, Winckelmann) the 'Führer und Mystagogen der klassischen Bildung, an deren Hand allein der richtige Weg, der zum Alterthum führt, gefunden werden kann' (BA, KSA 1.685). The argument turns on language and form: only through the disciplined practice of one's 'Muttersprache' via the classics of that language can students develop the 'Sinn für die Form' that offers access to Greek antiquity, as the 'einzige[.] Bildungsheimat' (BA, KSA 1.685). See also: BA, KSA 1.691 on 'das Band'; further on he speaks of their 'innig verwandten Geistes' (BA, KSA 1.747).

(KSA 1.306).⁵² Thus, for Nietzsche the relation to the ancient Greeks is *constitutional* (an 'innermost dependency': GT 15, KSA 1.97), so that excising them from the German will only hollow out the German. Accordingly, Nietzsche goes on to distinguish two kinds of *mimesis* or succession: to remain eternal 'students [*Zöglinge*] of declining antiquity' – i.e. 'Alexandrian-Roman culture' – or the 'mightier task' of 'striving to get behind and beyond this Alexandrian world and boldly to seek our models [*Vorbilder*] in the originary ancient Greek world of the great, the natural and the human' (UB II, KSA 1.306 f.). Under inescapable, epigonal conditions, then, German culture can only be born of a transformed relation to antiquity, an overcoming of Alexandrian-Roman culture in favour of the archaic world. So what is it in archaic Greek culture that can redeem our epigonal condition, and how are we to engage with it in a way that can give birth to German culture?

The simplest answer lies in Nietzsche's appeal to the '*essentially unhistorical formation* [unhistorische Bildung]' of the ancient Greeks, when he writes that in the archaic

> primal world of the great, the natural and the human [...] *we find the reality of an essentially unhistorical formation* [unhistorische Bildung] *and one that is nonetheless, or rather on that account an inexpressibly rich and living* [lebensvolle] *formation.*⁵³

One might speak in this vein with of 'a non-historical relation to the being, itself unhistorical, of the Greeks'.⁵⁴ By way of the Greeks, as natural humans unburdened by history, origins can be found in a natural power of auto-creation and -formation; it is, then, a matter of appropriating Greek power and self-sufficiency for the German cause. But if this is Nietzsche's only response, we can say that it fails on his own terms. For is this anything but the philistine gesture of closure projected onto the Greeks, a 'Finding' that *negates* the historicity of human existence, a closure of memory, an escape from the endless mediation of pasts in the immediacy of nature?

Without doubt, there is a longing for closure in the *Unzeitgemässe Betrachtungen*, a temptation on Nietzsche's part to sidestep the problem of history by appealing to the natural immediacy of feeling, or a notion of *being* that gives respite from *becoming*, what Nietzsche called 'metaphysical consolation' in *Die Geburt der Tragödie*. Consider his appeals to the German youth, as bearers of the future without a past, to their 'heightened vital feelings [*Lebensgefühle*]' and 'ownmost experience [*eigensten Erfahrung*]' (UB II 10, KSA 1.330 ff.). Then there is the total repudiation of becoming in UB III 4 ('In becoming everything is hollow, deceptive, shallow and worthy of our

---

52 'gelänge es Einem, aus der Lebensluft [...] diese zwei Elemente auszuscheiden, so würde nicht viel übrig bleiben, um noch ein geistiges Leben damit zu fristen.'
53 'in der altgriechischen Urwelt des Grossen, Natürlichen und Menschlichen [...] *finden wir auch die Wirklichkeit einer wesentlich unhistorischen Bildung und einer trotzdem oder vielmehr deswegen unsäglich reichen und lebensvollen Bildung.*'
54 Lacoue-Labarthe 1990, 223.

contempt': KSA 1.374f.), and the advice 'to destroy all that is becoming [*alles Werdende zu zerstören*]' in the name of *being*-something that is only problematically alive. It would be wrong, however, to dwell only on this metaphysical longing. Emblematic of the *Unzeitgemässe Betrachtungen* is the tension between this longing and Nietzsche's insight that the problem of history can only be resolved through an entwinement, a conjugation of *being* and *becoming* and a richer, historicised conception of life and nature. Nietzsche's view of the Greeks may also be implicated in this tension and figure, at times, as a way out of the labyrinth of pasts (like German youth), as Lacoue-Labarthe suggests. But there is also a line of thought far more compelling and fruitful, an approach to the Greeks in which history – or rather ἱστορία[55] – is at the epicentre of their supposedly 'unhistorical *Bildung*'. Towards the end of UB II, Nietzsche writes: the ancient Greeks

> never lived in proud immaculacy: their "formation" was rather, for a long time, a chaos of foreign, Semitic, Babylonian, Lydian Egyptian forms and concepts and their religion a true struggle of the gods from the entire Orient; somewhat as "German formation" and religion is now a chaotic struggle amongst all foreign [cultures], all past ages. (UB II, KSA 1.333)[56]

Any simple sense of closure or natural immediacy is dissolved by these lines. Within a thoroughly historicised picture of human existence, Nietzsche draws before our eyes an uncanny doubling of the German predicament in the epigonal condition of the ancient Greeks. In this context, what is 'classical' in the ancient Greeks is not their 'unhistorical' being (Lacoue-Labarthe 1990, 223), but their capacity to deal with the historicity of human existence: it is their ability to assimilate and transform what is past and alien (non-Greek, barbarian), to *organise this chaos*, which is at once unique and binding on the Germans: they offer a *model (Muster) of searching and learning*.

With the focus on learning, the question of succeeding to (*Nachfolgen*) what is 'classical' in the ancient Greeks undergoes a subtle, but decisive change: for what *distinguishes* the ancient Greeks from barbarians – that is, their 'classical' ability to learn – is now inseparable from their alien sources, and the effort to 'place the

---

[55] 'Nicht in der Studirstube wuchsen sie; es sind weitgereiste Männer, die zu hören und zu sehen und zu fragen verstanden und ihr ganzes Leben hindurch sich im Erzählen und im Erzählen-hören geübt haben. Das ist eben ἱστορία.' GGL I, KGW II/5.230. ('They grew not in the study-room; these are well-travelled men who knew how to hear [listen], to see and to ask, and throughout their whole lives practised telling [narrating] and listening to tales. Precisely that is ἱστορία.' GGL I, KGW II/5.230.). See also note 82 below.

[56] 'Niemals haben sie [die Griechen —HS] in stolzer Unberührbarkeit gelebt: ihre "Bildung" war vielmehr lange Zeit ein Chaos von ausländischen, semitischen, babylonischen, lydischen aegyptischen Formen und Begriffen und ihre Religion ein wahrer Götterkampf des ganzen Orients: ähnlich etwa wie jetzt die "deutsche Bildung" und Religion ein in sich kämpfendes Chaos des gesammten Auslandes, der gesammten Vorzeit ist.'

life of civilised peoples in connection with that of the savages and barbarians'.[57] It is this approach to ancient Greek religion that Nietzsche will develop in his *Gottesdienst* lectures of 1875. As Andrea Orsucci has shown, Nietzsche draws on various unorthodox sources to undermine the classicist dogmas of Greek isolation and national unity,[58] and to relativise their unique, classical value for German culture.[59] By 1878, Nietzsche can thus write:

> *National* is the after-effect of a past culture in a completely changed culture resting on different basis. Thus, the logical contradictoriness in the life of a people. (30[70] (1878), KSA 8)[60]

– And in this sense:

> *To be a good German means [demands] to de-Germanify oneself* [...]. (VM 323, KSA 2.511)[61]

But this approach is already at work in *Unzeitgemässe Betrachtungen*. At the very beginning of the second essay, Nietzsche speaks of the 'plastic power of a human being, a people, a culture' as 'a power to grow out of oneself in one's own way, to transform and incorporate what past and alien, to heal wounds, replace what has been lost, to re-create broken forms out of oneself' (UB II 1, KSA 1.251).[62] There is clearly nothing unhistorical about proper being or identity for Nietzsche here; auto-formation (*aus sich heraus eigenartig wachsen*) and identity can only be understood in connection with what is past and alien, by way of self-alienation, to return to the idiom of Nietzsche's agonal *Betrachtung* of Wagner. In what follows, I will argue that this insight into non-identity, self-alienation or depropriation as the answer to the question of identity (see p. 127 f.) derives from his engagement with the ancient Greeks as classical models of learning. To paraphrase Nietzsche on Wagner: it is only *through and against* what was past and alien that ancient Greek culture was born and formed. And it is only *through and against* the Greeks, *as past and alien*, that German culture can be born:

> Thus the Germans may yet achieve what the Greeks achieved in relation to the Orient – coming only then to find what "German" is. (29[191] (1873), KSA 7)[63]

---

57 From E. B. Tyler's definition of anthropology, quoted by Orsucci 1996, 48.
58 E.g. Preller, H.D. Müller.
59 Orsucci 1996, 28 f., 42 f.
60 '*National* ist das Nachwirken einer vergangenen Cultur in einer ganz veränderten, auf anderen Grundlagen gestützten Cultur. Also das logisch Widerspruchsvolle im Leben eines Volkes.'
61 '*Gut deutsch sein heisst sich entdeutschen* [...]'.
62 'die plastische Kraft eines Menschen, eines Volkes, einer Cultur [...] jene Kraft, aus sich heraus eigenartig zu wachsen, Vergangenes und Fremdes umzubilden und einzuverleiben, Wunden auszuheilen, Verlorenes zu ersetzen, zerbrochene Formen aus sich nachzuformen [...]'.
63 'So gelingt vielleicht den Deutschen noch, was den Griechen in Betreff des Orients gelang—und so das, was "deutsch" ist, erst zu finden.'

The questions of origin and identity, I shall argue, devolve into a matter of antagonistic exchange or 'agonal mimesis' with a past and alien culture. At stake is the concept of transposition or *Übertragung*, as the key to the fundamental problem of culture, as Nietzsche puts it in UB IV: 'whether an alien culture can at all be transposed' (UB IV, KSA 1.446).⁶⁴

VII Learning from the Greeks and the *Übertragung* of Alien Cultures

As a capacity to absorb and transform, *Übertragung* is very much a 'historical sense':

> The stronger the roots of a human being's innermost nature, the more readily will he be able to appropriate or assimilate things of the past; and were one to think of the most powerful and tremendous nature, it would be characterised by the fact that there would be **absolutely no limit to the historical sense** [*gar keine Grenze des historischen Sinnes*], at which it [the historical sense –HS] would begin to have overwhelming and damaging effects; everything past, its own and that most alien to it [*eigenes und fremdestes*], would be drawn to itself, drawn into itself and transformed into blood, as it were. (UB II, KSA 1.251. **HS**)⁶⁵

Nietzsche's interest in the historical sense of the ancient Greeks does not begin with the *Unzeitgemässe Betrachtungen*. It cuts right across the early 1870s, as evinced by two early *Nachlass* texts from 1870, where Nietzsche's own evaluations are easy to gauge. In the lecture *Sokrates und die Tragödie*, he writes:

> In Socrates that one side of the Hellenic was embodied, that Apollinian clarity **without any alien admixture,** appearing like a pure transparent ray of light, as the harbinger and herald of science, that was also to be born in Greece (ST, KSA 1.545. **HS**)⁶⁶

If Socrates and *Wissenschaft* embody, for Nietzsche, all that went wrong with ancient Greek and European culture in general, it is to the Homeric age that he looks for sources of inspiration. In a note on the audience of Homeric poetry, he writes:

> The audience was still unreflective: as children hear fairy tales, they estimated the singers according to the best material. But the singer stepped completely into the background for them:

---

64 'ob eine fremde Cultur sich überhaupt übertragen lasse'.
65 'Je stärkere Wurzeln die innerste Natur eines Menschen hat, um so mehr wird er auch von der Vergangenheit sich aneignen oder anzwingen; und dächte man sich die mächtigste und ungeheuerste Natur, so wäre sie daran zu erkennen, dass es für sie gar keine Grenze des historischen Sinnes geben würde, an der er überwuchernd und schädlich zu wirken vermöchte; alles Vergangene, eigenes und fremdestes, würde sie an sich heran, in sich hineinziehen und gleichsam zu Blut umschaffen.'
66 'In Sokrates hat sich jene eine Seite des Hellenischen, jene apollinische Klarheit, ohne jede fremdartige Beimischung, verkörpert, wie ein reiner durchsichtiger Lichtstrahl erscheint er, als Vorbote und Herold der Wissenschaft, die ebenfalls in Griechenland geboren werden sollte.'

the material is what they desire. **The proper and the alien *[Eigenthum und Fremdthum]* are not yet differentiated with the poets of these times.** (2[24] (1869/70), KSA 7, **HS**)

The ancient Greeks' ability to assimilate and transform 'das Fremde' rests, according to Nietzsche, on three factors above all:
1) The imagination (Imagination, Phantasie), as an active metaphorical power, i.e. a creative power to forge analogies, sustained by:
2) A sensitivity to similarities (Ähnlichkeiten),[67] i.e. a passive or receptive openness to alien or external stimuli (Reiz).
Together these constitute a synthetic faculty of as-similation, which, however, depends upon:
3) What could, in a pointed manner, be called self-alienation: a free and unconstrained intercourse with their own past, a highly supple form of memory.

In this light, Nietzsche insists that the Greeks 'in no way deny what comes from without and is non-originary', in a note which begins with the remark:

> The Greeks as the only *genial* people of world history; this they are also as learners, they understand this the best and know how not just to decorate and dress up with what they borrow: as the Romans do.
> The constitution of the *polis* is a Phoenician invention: even this the Hellenes imitated [*nachgemacht*]. For a long time they learned from everything around them as happy dilettantes, just as Aphrodite is Phoenician. Nor do they in any way deny what comes from abroad and is the non-originary. (5[65] (1875), KSA 8)[68]

These remarks are from the notes to *Wir Philologen*, Nietzsche's planned (but unwritten) fifth *Unzeitgemässe Betrachtung*. They can, however, be traced back to a series of reflections from 1872–3 (19[226]–19[228] (1872/73), KSA 7), in which Nietzsche contrasts culture as *Übertragung* with conceptual knowledge on a *physiological* level:

---

67 This capacity has a pre-history in philosophy and rhetoric under the rubric of 'Witz' and 'ingenium' See e.g. Baumgarten's Metaphysik §426: 'Der Witz (ingenium strictus dictum) ist die Fertigkeit die Übereinstimmungen der Dinge zu bemerken [...]' (Baumgarten 2004 [1783], 130).
68 'Die Griechen als das einzig *geniale* Volk der Weltgeschichte; auch als Lernende sind sie dies, sie verstehen dies am besten und wissen nicht bloß zu schmücken und zu putzen mit dem Entlehnten: wie es die Römer thun.
  Die Constitution der Polis ist eine phönizische Erfindung: selbst dies haben die Hellenen nachgemacht. Sie haben lange Zeit wie freudige Dilettanten an allem herum gelernt; wie auch die Aphrodite phönizisch ist. Sie leugnen auch gar nicht das Eingewanderte und Nicht-Ursprüngliche ab.' The archetype of the 'Fremde' or 'Eingewanderte' is, of course, Dionysos: 'ein fremder Gott' (GGL I, KGW II/5.81. On the ancient Greeks as *dilettanti*, see GGL III, KGW II/5.341 f. ; cf. GGL I, KGW II/5.142 f.

> *Imitation* [*Das* Nachahmen] is the means of all culture, the instinct is thereby gradually engendered. *All comparing (primal thinking) is an imitating.* Types [or classes: Arten] are built in this way, that intensely imitate the first, merely similar [*ähnliche*] exemplars [...]. (19[226], KSA 7)[69]

Primitive thought, viewed as the instrument of culture *par excellence*, is understood as a form of *mimesis*, and Nietzsche goes on to interrogate the presuppositions of this mimetic capacity in terms of the three factors needed to transform 'das Fremde': a receiving or taking in ('ein Aufnehmen': second moment of reception) 'and then a repeated transposing [*Übertragen*] of the received image in a thousand metaphors, all acting' (first active metaphorical moment). In the next note, these moments are clarified in relation to the third moment, the Greeks' supple form of memory:

> Stimulus – memory image tied together through metaphor (analogical inference)
> Result: similarities [*Ähnlichkeiten*] are discovered and re-vitalised.
> The *repeated* stimulus occurs once again in a memory image. (19[227], KSA 7)[70]

This process is then multiplied through a highly flexible intercourse between alien impressions and memory images:

> *Stimulus perceived* – now *repeated* in many metaphors, related images come flocking from diverse rubrics. Every perception attains a manifold imitation of the stimulus, yet with transpositions [*Übertragung*] to diverse areas. (19[227], KSA 7)[71]

In a more familiar idiom, Nietzsche also writes of 'the freely poeticising way in which the Greeks treated their gods' (19[40], KSA 7) and the absence of a normative theology in Greek religion.[72] This unconstrained and creative relation to one's own heritage (past) allows for *an agonal play of perspectives*, and is the key condition for learning from alien peoples[73] and for the *Übertragung* of alien cultures. For Nietzsche, it stands in sharp contrast with the rigidity of modern empirical methods, on one side, where concepts serve to isolate impressions and block the processes of *Übertragung*;[74] while on the other side, it contrasts with the rigidity of one-sided per-

---

[69] 'Das *Nachahmen* ist das Mittel aller Kultur, dadurch wird allmählich der Instinkt erzeugt. *Alles Vergleichen (Urdenken) ist ein Nachahmen.* So bilden sich *Arten*, daß die ersten nur ähnliche Exemplare stark nachahmen [...]'.
[70] 'Reiz—Erinnerungsbild durch Metapher (Analogieschluß) verbunden.
   Resultat: es werden Ähnlichkeiten entdeckt und neu belebt.
   An einem Erinnerungsbilde spielt sich der *wiederholte* Reiz noch einmal ab.'
[71] '*Reiz percipirt*—jetzt *wiederholt*, in vielen Metaphern, verwandte Bilder, aus den verschiedenen Rubriken, herbeiströmen. Jede Perception erzielt eine vielfache Nachahmung des Reizes, doch mit Übertragung auf verschiedene Gebiete.'
[72] 'Die alten Griechen ohne normative Theologie. Jeder hat das Recht zu dichten und zu glauben, was er will' (VPP, KGW II/4.215, footnote 5).
[73] Orsucci 1996, 125.
[74] 19[228] (1872/73), KSA 7: 'Das *Nachahmen* ist darin der Gegensatz des *Erkennens*, daß das Erkennen eben keine Übertragung gelten lassen will, sondern ohne Metapher den Eindruck festhalten will

spectives that comes from close bonds to a 'proper', unified tradition – as desired, for instance, by the modern German *Bildungsphilister*. The condition for proper being or identity, as we know from Nietzsche's agonal *Betrachtung* of Wagner, is *self-alienation*, now understood on the level of cultures as this supremely supple and creative form of memory evinced by the Greeks. On this basis, we can now say: according to Nietzsche, *self-alienation* is the condition for the forging of cultural identity through the integration or *Übertragung* of *alien* cultures. So how exactly are the ancient Greeks to be engaged as classical models of learning, so as to give being to the German?

Die Philosophie im tragischen Zeitalter der Griechen gives us our first clue as to how to succeed to the Greek model of learning:

> Nothing is more foolish than to ascribe to the Greeks an autochthonous formation [*Bildung*]; on the contrary, they all absorbed the living culture of other peoples. The reason they got so far is precisely that they understood how to pick up and throw the spear further from the point where others left it. They are worthy of admiration [*bewunderungswürdig*] in the art of fruitful learning: and we ought [*sollen*], just like them, to learn from our neighbours, for the sake of life and not learned knowledge, using everything learnt as a support for swinging high and higher than the neighbour. (PHG, KSA 1.806)[75]

Nietzsche here declares how, as author of the text, he proposes to engage the Greek philosophers: by aligning himself with their 'art of fruitful learning', their will 'to live what they learned, at once' (PHG, KSA 1.807), *against* modern *Wissenschaft*. In this polemical move, two moments stand out: a) a mimetic moment, and b) the adversarial moment of swinging 'higher than the neighbour'. In the first mimetic moment (a) Nietzsche appeals to the binding classical status of ancient Greeks in the imperative form: we ought (*sollen*), like them, to learn from our neighbours for the sake of life (*zum Leben*). No doubt, Nietzsche is thinking of the Germans and their neighbours (French culture?) here. But he also has a *problem of method* in mind. To the question, 'how best to learn from the Greeks?' he responds with a *doubling-back* of Greek exemplarity on the very method we use to understand them: our method and the discoveries we make should fertilise each other; whatever is valuable in the Greeks

---

und ohne Consequenzen. Zu diesem Behufe wird er petrificirt: der Eindruck durch Begriffe eingefangen und abgegränzt, dann getödtet, gehäutet und als Begriff mumisirt und aufbewahrt.'

75 Cf. 19[196] (1872/73), KSA 7: 'Wir sollen so lernen, wie die Griechen von ihren Vergangenheiten und Nachbarn lernten—zum *Leben*, also mit größter Auswahl und alles Erlernte sofort als Stütze benutzend, auf der man sich hoch und höher als alle Nachbarn schwingt. Also nicht gelehrtenhaft! Was nicht zum Leben taugt, ist keine wahre Historie.' See also *Die vorplatonischen Philosophen* (KGW II/4.212), where Nietzsche responds to the view that Greek philosophy was 'nur [...] ein importirtes Gewächs' not through denial, but by stressing their 'Erfindsamkeit' in creating 'Philosophentypen': 'Die Erfindsamkeit hierin zeichnet die Griechen vor allen Völkern aus.'

ought to be used to form and inform our very engagement with them.⁷⁶ As a method, this mimetic imperative is clarified by Nietzsche in a note to *Wir Philologen*:

> The *measure* for study lies here: *only that which provokes imitation* [zur Nachahmung reizt], *that which* is grasped with love [*Liebe*] and demands continued begetting [*fortzuzeugen*], ought to be studied. That would be *the most correct:* an *advancing* canon of the *exemplary* [...] (5[171] (1875), KSA 8.89 f.)⁷⁷

Greek exemplarity acts as a constraint, a demand (*Verlangen*), but also as a *Liebe*, a seduction, and a *Reiz*, a provocation or stimulus to creative overcoming (*fort-zeugen, fort-schreiten*). Mimesis is hereby complicated, and any simple sense of identification, of passive or epigonal mimicry (*nach-äffen*), is removed by the creative impulse that brings difference and distance to our engagement with the ancient Greeks. We might, with Lacoue-Labarthe, speak of *creative mimesis*; or, combining the mimetic (*nach-*) and creative (*schaffen*) moments, use Nietzsche's own idiom of *nach-schaffen*. In the preamble to PHG, he writes:

> [...] it is a beginning towards the recovery and re-creation [*nachschaffen*] of those natures by way of comparison, so that the polyphony of the Greek nature may at long last resound once more: the task is to bring to light what we must always love and honour, and what no subsequent knowledge can steal: the great human being. (PHG, KSA 1.801 f.)⁷⁸

---

76 Thus in *Die Philosophie im tragischen Zeitalter der Griechen*, Nietzsche demands that in studying the pre-Socratic philosophers we apply the very restraint (*Bändigung des Wissenstriebs*) that distinguishes them from contemporary *Wissenschaften* (PHG, KSA 1.806 f.). In Nietzsche's text, the methodological imperative of restraint takes the form of a philosophical portraiture (see note 78): his account restricts itself to the interface between the pre-Socratics' personalities and their teachings. This contrasts with the unrestrained attempts by some of his contemporaries to trace Greek philosophy back as far as possible, via 'the more original' Persian and Egyptian philosophies, to its very beginnings. For Nietzsche, however, this leads only to 'barbarism'; for 'the beginnings are always raw, unformed, empty and ugly' (PHG, KSA 1.806 f.).
77 'Das *Maaß* des Studiums liegt darin: *nur was zur Nachahmung reizt*, was mit Liebe ergriffen wird und fortzuzeugen verlangt, soll studirt werden. Da wäre das *Richtigste:* ein fortschreitender Kanon des *Vorbildlichen* [...]'.
78 For *Nachschaffen* see also 6[48] (1875), KSA 8: 'Wer diese Möglichkeiten des Lebens wieder entdecken könnte! Dichter und Historiker sollten über diese Aufgabe brüten: denn solche Menschen sind zu selten, dass man sie laufen lassen könnte. Vielmehr sollte man sich gar nicht eher Ruhe geben bis man ihre Bilder nachgeschaffen und sie hundertfach an die Wand gemalt hat—und ist man so weit,—dann freilich wird man sich erst recht nicht Ruhe geben.' Also: 6[10] (1875), KSA 8: 'Hinter solchen Menschen muss man her sein, bis sie wieder von einem Dichter nachgeschaffen sind: die ergänzende Phantasie Vieler muss hier arbeiten.' And VPP (KGW II/4.214.): 'Jetzt müssen wir wesentlich die Bilder jener Ph. und ihrer Lehren nachschaffend ergänzen...' The other, imitative component of Nietzschean 'nachschaffen' is brought out in the *Vorstufe* to 6[48] (KSA 8) above, where the pre-Socratics are described as 'nachahmungswürdig': worthy of imitation (KSA 14.566). Cf. also 21[6] (1872/73), KSA 7 on 'lebendig nachempfinden'. Although the word 'Nachschaffen' was not coined by Nietzsche, nor unique to him (it is to be found in, e.g., Sanders 1878), its use was much less common than 'Nachahmen'. Nietzsche's repetitive use of 'Nachschaffen' instead of 'Nachahmen'

But the creative moment (*-schaffen*) is also an *adversarial* moment (b) in Nietzsche's alliance with the art of fruitful learning: it is, Nietzsche says, 'for the sake of life' (*zum Leben*) that we should, like the Greeks, learn from our neighbours, 'using everything learnt in order to swing high and higher than' them (PHG, KSA 1.806). No doubt, Nietzsche has the 'Grundgedanke der Kultur' in mind, as the ultimate value served by creative mimesis: the demand that 'that which was once there in order to propagate the concept "human" more beautifully, that must also be eternally present' (CV 1, KSA 1.756; cf. note 50). As the preamble to PHG (above) suggests, it is for the sake of *human* life, its elevation or perfection, evinced by 'the great human being' (*der grosse Mensch*), that we ought to recover and re-create ancient Greek learning. But how exactly are we to understand this adversarial-creative moment on Nietzsche's path to human greatness?

In the next section, I will draw on Nietzsche's understanding of the ancient Greek agon in order to explicate the Greeks' 'art of fruitful learning', adversarial and creative at once, and to distinguish it from the kind of antagonism that would break the perfectionist horizon of creative mimesis: exclusive self-assertion against the other.[79]

VIII The Greek Agon

Three features of the agon are of particular importance for the ancient Greeks' 'art of fruitful learning'. The first is that it is not destructive or exclusive of the antagonist; it is a *creative* and *inclusive* form of antagonism. As we saw in chapter 2 (p. 50 ff.), this goes first of all for the relation or entwinement (*verwachsen*) of 'the so-called "human"' and '"natural"' or base impulses in Nietzsche's polemic against their separation (*Abscheidung*) by humanism at the beginning of Homer's Wettkampf (HW 1.783). Base, destructive drives were not condemned and suppressed; they were *acknowledged* (*anerkannt*) as a source of power, a stimulus (*Reiz*), to be *overcome* (*überwunden*) through measured, creative discharge in the contests that regulated all aspects of life, from religion and art to education, sports and politics. 'Nature as it shows itself is not denied, but integrated [*eingeordnet*], restricted to specific cults and days' (5[146], KSA 8). We can therefore say that destruction was *excluded* from social life by *including* or integrating (*Einordnen*) antagonistic impulses like envy and ambition into social life.

---

in relation to the ancient Greeks, as shown in the above texts, is therefore unusual, and it supports the claim that 'Nachschaffen' serves him to name his own, unique conception of mimesis.
79 For a strong statement of negativity and division against neighbours as the condition for the ancient Greeks' 'Pfad der Grösse' and for the life of a 'Volk' in general, see Z I Ziele, KSA 4.74 f.

This transformative inclusion – or *Übertragung* – of 'natural', destructive drives is traced by Nietzsche back to the poets. It is from the poets that the Greek law-givers learned, and of Homer, the architect of Greek culture, he writes:

> The poet overcomes the struggle for existence by idealising it into a free contest. Existence, which must still be fought for, is here sung in praise, in fame.
> The poet *educates:* he knows how to transfer [*übertragen*] the tiger-like, destructive drives of the Greeks into the good Eris. (16[15] (1871/72), KSA 7)[80]

At the same time, the *creative* and *inclusive* qualities of the agon also hold for the relations *between* contestants. For the Greeks, who believed that '[e]very gift must unfold through antagonism' (HW, KSA 1.789), the *agon* was first and foremost the great creative *stimulant* for human and cultural achievement. The poet who envies his predecessor is *provoked* by that very envy to *outbid* his achievements, to set a new standard for poetry and so to inherit the other's fame and authority. This is the second important feature of the agon: as *creative stimulant*.

The third important feature for the 'art of fruitful learning' concerns the form taken by the inclusive nature of agonal antagonism. Nowhere does Nietzsche describe this more clearly or more graphically than in the case of Plato's jealousy of Homer, analysed in §IV of this chapter. Rather than reject or degrade Homer, Plato's texts *incorporate* tracts of poetry that would surpass Homer by his own standards – while advancing dialectical philosophy as an entirely new standard for education and ethics. By including poetry in his dialogues, Plato certainly *limits* Homer's achievement in seeking to surpass it, but in doing so he acknowledges and includes the standard of Homeric poetry in his work, even if it is limited by the new standard of philosophy. In advancing this new standard of evaluation to supplant poetry, Platonic dialogues again *limit* the poets' achievements, but they do not *exclude* them or *annul* their value. As this example shows, the other is valued in the agon, as the stimulant for one's deeds, but also as a relative equal whose works are acknowledged as a 'great virtue' and preserved, albeit within the overarching attempt to establish an entirely new standard or 'greatness'. In short, the agonal logic of overcoming does not trade on *degrading, deforming or impoverishing* the opponent.[81]

In the context of the Greek agon, then, we can once again speak in the idiom of Nietzschean *Betrachten* of a logic of *acknowledgement* and *overcoming*. It is this very

---

80 'Der Dichter überwindet den Kampf um's Dasein, indem er ihn zu einem freien Wettkampf idealisirt. Hier ist das Dasein, um das noch gekämpft wird, das Dasein im Lobe, im Nachruhm.
  Der Dichter *erzieht:* die tigerartigen Zerfleischungstriebe der Griechen weiss er zu übertragen in die gute Eris.' (Cf. 16[18], KSA 7).
81 This is most clearly expressed in *Der Wanderer und sein Schatten* 29 (KSA 2.562), where Hesiod's evil Eris is identified with the kind of envy (*Neid*) that would 'put down' (*herabdrücken*) an outstanding individual to 'the common measure' (*das gemeinsame Maass*), while the good Eris is identified with a 'nobler' envy that would 'raise' (*erheben*) the envious individual to the level of the outstanding one.

logic of acknowledgement and overcoming that informs the ancient Greek model of learning from other cultures. As learners – philosophers, wanderers, discoverers, historians, geographers[82] – the ancient Greeks were not out to diminish, exclude or subjugate other peoples. When Nietzsche speaks of them as 'conquerors of nature' or 'overcomers of barbaric conditions', he is thinking of their 'monstrous power to assimilate', to take up and re-order, to transpose (*Übertragen*) the elements of the other; that is, 'to make use of [*benutzen*] what they learn' so as to 'fulfil, to intensify, to elevate' Greek life (PHG, KSA 1.807), *not* to impoverish the other. It is, Nietzsche reminds us, from the poets and their love of particulars of every kind, that the Greek law-givers learned, not a narrow priestly caste (5[146], KSA 8). And it is the poets who taught them to 'overcome the struggle for existence by idealising it into a free contest', to 'transpose [*übertragen*]' the evil Eris into the good Eris of the agon (16[15], KSA 7). As a feature of *agonal* culture, then, the antagonistic or adversarial element of ancient Greek learning ('to swing [...] higher than the neighbour') signifies *not* a divisive logic of exclusion, but a *techne* of appropriation through contention, premised on two or more active forces: they learn *through and against* the other, by acknowledging and assimilating its achievement, while *using it as a stimulus to enrich and elevate Greek culture, to create their own gods, types, world-views, and values.*

---

[82] 'Die griechische Aufklärung: durch Reisen. Herodot: wie viel hat er gesehen! Reconstruktion des ihm zeitgenössischen Dramas und Lebens aus seinen Vergleichungen.' (3[69] (1869/70), KSA 7). ('The Greek Enlightenment: through journeys. Herodotus: how much he saw! Reconstruction of the drama and life of his time from his comparisons.') Cf. 3[73] (1869/70), KSA 7 under the heading:
   '*Staatslehre, Gesetze, Volksbildung* [...] Herodot über das Ausland. Das Wandern. Die hellenischen Wahnvorstellungen. Rache und Recht. Die Griechen als Eroberer und Überwinder barbarischer Zustände (Dionysoskult). Das erwachte Individuum.' ('*Doctrine of the state, laws, popular education [formation]* [...] Herodotus on foreign countries. The wandering. The Hellenic delusions. Revenge and right. The Greeks as conquerors and overcomers of barbaric conditions (Dionysos cult). The awakened individual.') Also: 19[42] (1872/73), KSA 7: 'Die Griechen als Entdecker und Reisende und Kolonisatoren. Sie verstehen zu lernen: ungeheure Aneignungskraft. Unsre Zeit soll nicht glauben, in ihrem Wissenstrieb so viel höher zu stehen: nur wurde bei den Griechen alles Leben! Bei uns bleibt es Erkenntniß!' ('The Greeks as discoverers and travellers and colonisers. They understand how to learn: monstrous power of assimilation. Our time should not believe that in its drive to knowledge it stands so much higher: only, with the Greeks everything became life! With us it remains knowledge!'). And 16[25] (1871/72), KSA 7:
   '2. Die *wandernden Hellenen.* Sie sind Eroberer von Natur.'
   (*2. The wandering Hellenes.* They are conquerors of nature.)
   See also GGL I, KGW II/5.230 on 'ἱστορία.' (quoted in note 55 above).

IX Overcoming the Greeks

If it is as agonal learners that the Greeks are exemplary, then they are to be engaged through a doubling-back of that very agonal *techne* of learning on our method for engaging them. This mimetic-agonal doubling has two important implications:

1. It evacuates any sense of origin or identity from the concept of *mimesis*, replacing any stable point of reference with a differential dynamic of surpassing or overcoming. To duplicate the 'art of fruitful learning' in our very relation to the Greeks means *to learn from them, as a past and alien culture, how to learn from cultures past and alien*. In this formulation, the concept of learning that is to provide the point of reference for *mimesis*, is itself referred to what is alien or other, twice-over: it is because their style of learning is *alien* to ours that the ancient Greeks are worth imitating; and what we should imitate in turn is their capacity to learn *from what is alien*. There can therefore be no question of isolating Greek culture as a self-sufficient good, an originary plenitude or a natural talent. This brings us to the second implication:

2. Since learning cannot be divorced from its sources, following ancient Greek precedent means following them as wanderers into alien, 'barbaric' cultures and assimilators of them. It is therefore *with full consequence:* as a consequence of succeeding to the Greeks as learners, that Nietzsche goes beyond ancient Greek culture to investigate its sources, and comes to *relativise* their value as classical models:

> A culture that runs after Greek culture can create nothing. The creator can certainly **borrow from everywhere** so as to nourish himself. Thus we will, as creators alone, also be able to have something from the Greeks. (7[1] (1875), KSA 8, **HS**)[83]

At this point in Nietzsche's engagement with the ancient Greeks, following them as assimilators has spilled over into a generalised programme of assimilation (*überall her entlehnen und sich nähren*) in which the Greeks are but one player. For a 'very precise thinking-back [*Zurückdenken*] leads to the insight that we are a multiplication of many pasts' (3[69] (1875), KSA 8). Thus, to *acknowledge* the Greeks as classical models of learning leads inevitably to an *overcoming* of the Greeks as a unique and incomparable source of Western civilization.

We see, then, how Nietzsche's antagonistic or *agonal* style of engagement leads him to advocate the overcoming of the Greeks as a *consequence*, not a rejection, of Greek classicity. This consequence is drawn in the notes to *Wir Philologen* and marks the end point of Nietzsche's *Unzeitgemässe Betrachtungen* at the interface with *Menschliches, Allzumenschliches*.

---

[83] 'Eine Kultur, welche der griechischen nachläuft, kann nichts erzeugen. Wohl kann der Schaffende überall her entlehnen und sich nähren. Und so werden wir auch nur als Schaffende etwas von den Griechen haben können.'

> To *overcome* Greece in deeds would be the task. But for that, one must first be familiar with it [...] One *ought* even to know no more of a subject than what one could also create. Furthermore, the only means to gain true *knowledge* of something is when one tries to *do* it. Just try to live in the manner of the ancients – one comes immediately a hundred miles closer to the ancients than with all learning [...]
> Study as **contestation** [*Wetteifer*] (Renaissance, Goethe) and study as **despair!** (5[167] (1875), KSA 8)[84]

For the ancient Greeks, we have seen, assimilation was inseparable from contestation: to learn from the other means turning that other into an antagonist, provoking a contending claim or creation that draws on the other in order to surpass it. In this process, the other is not degraded or impoverished, but *acknowledged* and 'honoured'[85] as a source (or origin) and a necessary opponent within an overall practice of *overcoming* (*überwinden*). Doubling this agonal *techne* of learning brings a *dynamic of overcoming* right next to *the bond of acknowledgement* and honour, at the epicentre of Nietzsche's agonal engagement with the Greeks as classical. Difference and creative originality are implicit from the very start in Nietzsche's bid to turn an *epigonal* relation to the ancient Greeks into an *agonal* relation *inter pares*, to turn an *inescapable precedent* into a *necessary opponent*, whose value is affirmed but limited. All of this makes for a paradoxical solution to the non-existence or non-identity of German culture: origins through precedent, auto-formation through assimilation, identity through difference. The first task, however, is to learn from the Greeks how to learn in the spirit of the agon:

> To make the individual *uneasy:* my task!
> Stimulus towards liberation of the single individual in contestation [or struggle]!
> Spiritual eminence has its *time* in history, inherited energy belongs to it. In the ideal state it is over. (5[178] (1875), KSA 8)[86]

---

84 'Das Griechenthum durch die That zu *überwinden* wäre die Aufgabe. Aber dazu müßte man es erst kennen! [...] Man *sollte* sogar nicht mehr von einer Sache wissen, als man auch schaffen könnte. Überdies ist es selbst das einzige Mittel, etwas wahrhaft zu *erkennen*, wenn man versucht es zu *machen*. Man versuche alterthümlich zu leben—man kommt sofort hundert Meilen den alten näher als mit aller Gelehrsamkeit [...] *Studium des Wetteifers* (Renaissance, Goethe) und *Studium der Verzweiflung!*' (Cf. 5[172] and 6[2] (1875), KSA 8).
85 See 5[146] (1875), KSA 8, cited above on the 'freedom of mind [*Freisinnigkeit*] in antiquity'. See also Nissen, an important source for Nietzsche's *Gottesdienst* lectures, on 'der Ehrfurcht vor dem unbekannten Gotte' (in Orsucci 1996, 137. See also 256f. on Aidos).
86 'Das Individuum *unbehaglich* zu machen: meine Aufgabe! / Reiz der Befreiung des Einzelnen im Kampfe! / Die geistige Höhe hat ihre *Zeit* in der Geschichte, vererbte Energie gehört dazu. Im idealen Staat ist es damit vorbei.'

Chapter 6
Of (Self-)Legislation, Life and Love

Introduction

The concept of (self–)legislation or (*Selbst–)Gesetzgebung* is well-known as a central category in both Nietzsche's philosophy of power and his affirmative ethics. But in the research literature, the articulations of this category with Nietzsche's concept of life have not received sufficient attention. This chapter aims to make good this deficit by examining the concept of (self–)legislation in its multiple intersections with Nietzsche's dynamic, pluralistic and conflictual conception of life.

Law contra Life
The concepts of law and (self–)legislation have a central, but profoundly ambivalent place in Nietzsche's 'ontology' of life. They are central because for Nietzsche life is becoming (*Werden*), and the character of becoming is to be an incessant and radically plural *Fest-setzen*, a dynamic and multiple fixing (*Feststellen*) or positing (*Setzen*) of being across power-differentials.[1] In Nietzsche's vocabulary, *Gesetz* (law) is consistently associated with *das Feste* (that which is fixed, fast, firm) *das Gesetzte* (the posited), understood as the result of processes *Festsetzen* (fixing, making fast, establishing) and *Gesetzgeben* (legislation).[2] And yet, where *Gesetz* and *Gesetzgebung* signify the positing of the (moral) law as immutable and universal, they are radically life-negating. As becoming, occurring (*Geschehen*), and self-overcoming, life is dynamic and fluid in character. Traditional concepts of law, by contrast, are static, rigid and eternal[3] in character, and according to Nietzsche, they are often the result of human efforts to 'petrify', to 'eternalise', to arrest or fix the flow of things through an act of legislation or making-fast: *Fest-setzen*.[4] This is clearly expressed in the concept of immutable, eternal laws common to natural science, religion and morality, but also more subtly in the conventions, traditions, habits, and the status quo in which we acquiesce.[5] There is, then, a conflict or contradiction between the dynamism of

---

1 E. g. 9[91], KSA 12.385: 'Alles Geschehen, alle Bewegung, alles Werden als ein Feststellen von Grad- und Kraftverhältnissen, als ein *Kampf* ...'. See also: 34[88] and [89], KSA 11.449; 26[359], KSA 11.244; 39[13], KSA 11.623; 2[139] , KSA 12.135 f.; UB III 3, KSA 1.360; FW 370, KSA 3.622; AC 58, KSA 6.245.
2 See e. g. FW 76, KSA 3.431; 26[359], KSA 11.244; 34[88], KSA 11.449; 39[13], KSA 11.623; JGB 188, KSA 5.108 f.
3 For *das Starre, Statische, Feste, Ewige*: 3[15], KSA 7.63; MA 34, KSA 2.55; 15[29], KSA 10.486; AC 32, KSA 6.204 with reference to Jesus; cf. 11[368], KSA 13.164.
4 SE 3, KSA 1.360; 34[88], [89], KSA 11.449; 26[359], KSA 11.244; 39[13], KSA 11.623; 2[139], KSA 12.135; FW 370, KSA 3.622; AC 58.
5 All of these have strong associations with law for Nietzsche. See e. g. JGB 21; WS 140; SE 6, KSA 1.386; RWB 4, KSA 1.451; MA 34, 96; AC 57; 23[9], KSA 8.406; 4[67], KSA 9.115; 7[209], KSA 9.360 f.; 11[126], KSA 9.486.

life and the rigidity of law, as when Nietzsche writes: 'Every thought, like flowing lava, builds a bulwark around itself and suffocates itself with "laws"', or more simply: 'where life becomes rigid, the law towers up'.[6] For Nietzsche, life is also radically plural in character, identified with difference and diversity, particularity, even disorder and chaos.[7] Once again, this conflicts with legislation and law, which have the function of creating unity and order. Law is also universal in scope and claims universal validity (as opposed to particularity and nuance), claims that Nietzsche links with gestures of subjection, coercion and tyranny (*Unterwerfung, Zwang, Tyrannei*).[8]

Life as the Ground of Law
For Nietzsche, then, the unifying, universalising, and eternalising functions of traditional concepts of law and (self–)legislation in Christian-Platonic civilization are radically life-negating or hostile to life. On the other hand, Nietzsche cannot simply take the side of life against law. The problem of law and (self–)legislation is complicated by his (negatively derived) one-world hypothesis and the impulse inherited from Heraclitus to overcome the self-understanding of morality as transcendent and sovereign by rethinking law in radically *immanent* terms.[9] It is life itself, as multiple and incessant *Fest-Setzen*, that constantly produces its opposite, projecting a fixed image of itself that is its counterpart and negation (being). From a radically immanent standpoint in Nietzsche's concept of life, then, legislation and law must be understood and acknowledged as a necessary feature of life as *Fest-Setzen*, as a contradiction or tension *intrinsic* to life. Insofar as they negate life, however, they cannot simply be affirmed in the name of life. The task is, then, to rethink law and legislation in ways that express and enhance the dynamic and pluralistic qualities of life – against

---

6 15[29], KSA 10.486 (cf. 20[127], KSA 12); 20[128], KSA 13.570.
7 See e.g. FW 109; FW 322; 11[157], KSA 9.502; 11[225], KSA 9.528; 11[311], KSA 9.560; 4[5], KSA 10.110; 9[106], KSA 12.396; 11[74], KSA 13.37. See also the seminal account of the will to power: Müller-Lauter 1971. Also: Deleuze 1983. On chaos, see Busch 1989, esp. 226 ff.
8 See: 11[311], KSA 9.560; 25[409], KSA 11.119; FW 76; FW 117; FW 290; FW 291; FW 335; 7[7], KSA 12.290; 7[23], KSA 10.248; JGB 21; 5[1].124, KSA 10.201; 43[2], KSA 11.702; 14[79], KSA 13.257 f.; 7[209], KSA 9.360 f.; WS 140; 34[88], KSA 11.449; 15[88], KSA 13.458; MA 261; 16[29], KSA 13.490; 26[360], KSA 11.245; 4[221], KSA 9.156; 37[14], KSA 11.589.
9 This is clearly expressed in the following *Nachlass* note, where Nietzsche rejects the opposition of law and life in favour of the absolute fulfilment of law and necessity:
 'Heraclitus: the world an absolute lawfulness: how could it be a world of injustice! – so, a *moral* judgement "the fulfilment of the law" is absolute; the opposition [of law and life or the world – HS] is a deception; even bad people do not alter this, the absolute *lawfulness* is fulfilled in them, just as they are. Here necessity is glorified and *felt* in a moral sense.'
 ('Heraclit: die Welt eine absolute Gesetzlichkeit: wie könnte sie eine Welt der Ungerechtigkeit sein! – also eine *moralische* Beurtheilung "die Erfüllung des Gesetzes" ist absolut; der Gegensatz ist eine Täuschung; auch die schlechten Menschen ändern nichts daran, so wie sie sind, erfüllt sich an ihnen die absolute *Gesetzlichkeit*. Die Nothwendigkeit wird hier moralisch verherrlicht und *gefühlt*.': 26[67], KSA 11.166: 1884. Cf. 19[116], KSA 7.457: 'Ethische Anthropomorphism[us]'). On Nietzsche and Heraclitus, see chapter 7 note 4.

the rigidity and homogenizing universalism of the moral law. What would be an affirmative law of life, where life depends upon its own negation qua *Festsetzen?* What form of legislation affirms and enhances life in negating it, working not just *against* life, but *with and against* it? We see Nietzsche engaging this task in his repeated attempts to formulate models of legislation that are life-affirmative and life-enhancing.

Legislation is an important theme in Nietzsche's thought from his early engagement with the pre-Socratics, the *Kulturphilosophie* of the UB, the natural histories of morality from MA onwards (especially the phase of the 'Sittlichkeit der Sitten or 'morality of mores'), through to Zarathustra's 'Old and New Tables', and the question of the transvaluation of all values dominating his later writings. Equally constant is Nietzsche's view that legislation has its sources in the individual and is to be understood as a function of individuated power. In this respect, Nietzsche's thought conforms to the psychologization of power in the 19th century.[10] Because Nietzsche sees legislation as a function of individuated power, his attention is directed towards the legislator as a *type*, or rather: towards a variety of different legislator– types and their exemplifications, including: the Greeks (in the early 1870s); Schopenhauer and Wagner as legislative types in cultural crisis of the present (1874–1875); Zarathustra (1883), and finally, the legislators of the future, the 'legislators of the future' or *Gesetzgeber der Zukunft* (1884–1886). The problematic of legislation is therefore best studied by tracing the sequence of legislator-types across Nietzsche's writings and reconstructing the systematic relations between them. In this chapter, Nietzsche's ambivalent relation to legislation will be examined by way of some key moments in this diachronic typology of the legislator: Schopenhauer, Wagner and Zarathustra. I will examine these legislator-types, and their temporal articulations, as efforts to solve the problem of life-affirmative / –enhancing legislation, attempts (*Versuche*) that are successively problematised and superseded by the next type. These attempts culminate in the agon of legislation explored in the *Nachlass* to *Zarathustra* Part III. Thereafter, the task of legislation is deferred by Nietzsche to the future.

To begin with, it is worth noting a number of constants that cut across the different legislator-types generated by the Nietzschean thought process of attempt, self-critique and renewed attempt (*Versuch-Selbstkritik-Versuch*). In the first place, it is characteristic of all these contexts that the thematics of legislation and self-legislation are hard to separate. This is not just sloppy thinking, but a consequence of Nietzsche's conviction that true legislators must at the same time be self-legislators (e. g. 2[57], KSA 12.87 f.). Secondly, what emerges clearly from all these contexts is that the creative and evaluative moments of legislation are central for Nietzsche. And thirdly, that the forms of legislation affirmed or sought by him combine both the descriptive / theoretical meaning and the prescriptive / evaluative meaning of the term 'law', so that Nietzsche's affirmative notion of legislation can be seen as an attempt

---

10 See e. g. 6[40], KSA 8.113; cf. 5[170], KSA 8.89 (Männer); 1[68], KSA 9.20; 34[88], KSA 11.449. See also Gerhardt 1996, 76–78.

to overcome the categorial separation of 'is' from 'ought' in modern philosophy, to synthesise the theoretical and the moral domains. This, I would suggest, goes emphatically for Nietzsche's own performative instantiations of philosophical legislation (as in e.g. the formulation 'Gesetzt... ').[11]

Throughout the chapter, attention will be paid to *Gesetzgebung* or 'legislation' as a *word* in Nietzsche's vocabulary, not just as a concept. Despite Nietzsche's unrelenting criticisms of the moral connotations of traditional and existing conceptions of law and legislation, and his concern that they may be indissolubly bound up with the very signifiers 'Gesetz' and 'Gesetzgebung', he does not usually call for their excision from our (moral) vocabulary, or their replacement with alternative words. Instead, we see him attempting repeatedly to invest the words with new meanings and values. In this regard, the topic of legislation presents a rich case-study in Nietzsche's sense of *linguistic finitude*. Just as the moral law can only be overcome from within, through an effort to re-think the concept of law in the context of its genealogy – what Nietzsche calls the 'self-sublation of morality' (*Selbstaufhebung der Moral:* M Vorrede 4, KSA 3.16) – so too our only recourse against the word 'law' is the effort to invest it with new meanings that affirm the dynamic, pluralistic and conflictual character of life. In this chapter, I propose to shed light on some of ways in which Nietzsche engages in this task.

I The Problem of Legislation: Sources and Features

I take my initial bearings from the thesis advanced by Volker Gerhardt[12] that Nietzsche tries to articulate *a radically individual morality*. In this section it will be reconstructed as a project of *radically individual self-legislation* around five features of that project. As my point of entry, I will take a number of texts from Nietzsche's middle phase onwards that tell us about the sources of his concept of legislation. From the middle phase on, self-legislation is consistently opposed by Nietzsche to two phenomena: on the one hand to the (1) *heteronomy of self-subjection*; and on the other, to (2) *moral universalism*, especially the Kantian morality of the universal law. Both objections are often combined by Nietzsche, as in the following examples:

> The virtues are as dangerous as the vices insofar as one allows them to rule from the outside as authority and law and one does not first engender them from oneself, as is right, as the most personal self-defence and need, as the condition for just *our* existence and well-being, which

---

11 Following normal usage, this term is taken by readers and translators in a hypothetical sense as 'Supposing...' But the association of *Gesetz* with *das Gesetzte* and the ontology of *Festsetzen* in Nietzsche's usage also suggests a different, legislative sense.
12 Gerhardt 1992.

we know and acknowledge, regardless of whether others grow with us under the same or under different conditions. (7[6], KSA 12.278)[13]

What? You admire the categorical imperative within you? This "firmness" of your so-called moral judgement? This "absoluteness" [*Unbedingtheit*] of the feeling, "here everyone must judge as I do"? Rather admire your *self-centeredness* here! And the blindness, pettiness, and simplicity of your self-centeredness! For it is self-centered to consider *one's* own judgement a universal law, and this selfishness is blind, petty, and simple because it shows that you haven't yet discovered yourself or created for yourself an ideal of your very own – for this could never be someone else's, let alone everyone's, everyone's! ! – – (FW 335, KSA 3.562)[14]

This two-fold opposition gives us important clues to Nietzsche's understanding of (self–) legislation. Insofar as it is opposed to (1) the heteronomy of self-subjection, Nietzschean self-legislation must involve, not just obedience, but also a *sovereign act of commanding* (*Befehlen*). Insofar as it is opposed to (2) moral universalism, it must be radically individual or particular, a *radically individual law*; what Gerhardt, borrowing a phrase from Simmel, calls 'das individuelle Gesetz'.[15] Nietzsche's moral particularism, in turn, is to be understood as part of the project to (re–)*naturalise morality*, formulated with increasing clarity in his later thought,[16] and is grounded in two features of that project: his pluralistic 'ontology' of diverse life-forms, the uniqueness of each and its particular life-conditions (*Lebens–* or *Existenz-Bedingun-*

---

13 'Die Tugenden sind so gefährlich als die Laster, insofern man sie von außen her als Autorität und Gesetz herrschen läßt und sie nicht aus sich selbst erst erzeugt, wie es das Rechte ist, als Persönlichste Nothwehr und Nothdurft, als Bedingung gerade unseres Daseins und Wohlthuns, die wir erkennen und anerkennen, gleichgültig ob Andere mit uns unter gleicher oder verschiedener Bedingung wachsen.'
14 '– Wie? Du bewunderst den kategorischen Imperativ in dir? Diese "Festigkeit" deines sogenannten moralischen Urtheils? Diese "Unbedingtheit des Gefühls" "so wie ich, müssen hierin Alle urtheilen"? Bewundere vielmehr deine *Selbstsucht* darin! Und die Blindheit, Kleinlichkeit und Anspruchslosigkeit deiner Selbstsucht! Selbstsucht nämlich ist es, *sein* Urtheil als Allgemeingesetz zu empfinden; und eine blinde, kleinliche und anspruchslose Selbstsucht hinwiederum, weil sie verräth, dass du dich selber noch nicht entdeckt, dir selber noch kein eigenes, eigenstes Ideal geschaffen hast: – diess nämlich könnte niemals das eines Anderen sein, geschweige denn Aller, Aller! – –'. See also: 7[6], KSA 12.275; M 108, KSA 3.96; 3[159], KSA 9.98; AC 11, KSA 6.177.
15 Gerhardt 1992, 41. See Simmel 1968. The expression 'das individuelle Gesetz' also occurs in a note of Nietzsche's where it is opposed to the 'ewiges Sittengesetz': see 11[182], KSA 9.512.
16 On the (re–)naturalization of morality, see: 9[86], KSA 12.380: 'meine Aufgabe ist, die scheinbar emancipirten und *naturlos* gewordenen Moralwerthe in ihre Natur zurückzuübersetzen– d.h. in ihre natürliche "Immoralität"'; or, more bluntly: 'Grundsatz: wie die Natur sein' (25[309], KSA 11.91). On the physiology of morality, see: 23[87], KSA 8.434; M 174, KSA 3.154f.; 4[90], KSA 10.140 ; 7[76], KSA 10.268 ('In Wahrheit folgen wir unseren Trieben, und die Moral ist nur eine Zeichensprache unsrer Triebe?'); 25[460], KSA 11.135 (cf. FW 162, KSA 3.498; also 26[38], KSA 11.158); 10[157], KSA 12.545f.; 14[105], KSA 13.282f.; 14[158], KSA 13.343; see also 4[67], KSA 9.115; JGB 188 5.108. On legislation from the perspective of the body, see 7[126], KSA 10.285; 7[150], KSA 10.291f.

gen); and his naturalised concept of values as means for a given life-form to meet its life-conditions.[17]

The project to naturalise morality does not, of course, emerge *ex nihilo* in Nietzsche's middle works; it has a long pre-history in his critique of morality's self-understanding as transcendent and sovereign, a critique developed in later years under the rubrics of genealogy, morality as anti-nature, and nihilism. It is Nietzsche's increasing concentration on (3) *contemporary nihilism* in later years that often provokes his call for (self–)legislation: with the death of God, all transcendent grounds for the law crumble, throwing the individual back on itself as the source of law. This thought is expressed with extraordinary clarity in two notes from 1884:

> [...] in the founders of religion, their "Thou Shalt" has reached them as a commandment of God. As in the case of Muhamed, their legislation of values was for them "inspiration" ["*Eingebung*"], and that they executed it, an act of obedience. –
>
> Now as soon as those ideas have collapsed 1) that of God 2) that of eternal values: then the task of the legislator of values is raised in terrible greatness. (26[407], KSA 11.259; cf. 38[13], KSA 11.612)
>
> Morality *is* destroyed: present this factum! What is left over: "*I will*" [or *want*] (26[353], KSA 11.243)[18]

The question is: What *do* I want? And how do I know what I want? Because, with the nihilistic demise of transcendence, the individual is thrown back on itself for the sources of law, (4) *the question of self-knowledge* becomes central to the exercise of self-legislation.

In this respect, there is a striking parallel between Nietzschean self-legislation and the concept of self-realization at the centre of Charles Taylor's 'exercise-concept' of freedom. In his well-known paper 'What is Wrong with negative Liberty?' (1985), Taylor argues that exercising freedom requires an ordering of our capacities and motives for the sake of true self-realization. We need to work out what is essential and what is non-essential to our self; we need to work out which goods are genuine goods for us and which are dispensable (Taylor 1985, 215). In short, we need genuine self-knowledge. The necessity, but also the profound difficulty, of self-knowledge is acknowledged by Taylor at the end of the paper, where the exercise of freedom is virtually assimilated to the exercise of self-knowledge with the words: 'I must be actual-

---

17 See: 11[118], KSA 13.56; 14[158], KSA 13.343.
18 '[...] bei den Religionsstiftern, ist ihr "Du sollst" ihnen als Befehl ihres Gottes zugekommen: wie im Falle Muhameds, ihre Gesetzgebung der Werthe galt ihnen als eine "Eingebung", und daß sie sie ausführten, als ein Akt des Gehorsams.—

Sobald nun jene Vorstellungen dahingefallen sind 1) die von Gott 2) die von ewigen Werthen: entsteht die Aufgabe des Gesetzgebers der Werthe in furchtbarer Größe.'

'Moral *ist* vernichtet: factum darstellen! Es bleibt übrig: "*ich will*" [...]'

ly exercising self-understanding in order to be truly free' (Taylor 1985, 229). The difficulty involved can be put as the question: What is to be my standard for evaluating what is essential and non-essential? What is a genuine, and what a dispensable good for the purpose of self-realization?

For Nietzsche, too, the profound difficulty and necessity of self-knowledge are at the core of free or sovereign self-legislation, and he gives a great deal of attention to the question of self-understanding as the precondition for a radically individual morality.[19] But in Nietzsche's case, the question of the standard for evaluating what I genuinely want is aggravated by two factors without any parallel in Taylor's thought. The first is that the demand for self-legislation is predicated on a radical rejection of morality thus far (recall: 'Moral *ist* vernichtet: factum darstellen!'). The second factor goes back to Nietzsche's insistence on the radical particularity of self-legislation. This makes it hard to imagine any public or inter-subjective reference for my standard of evaluation, raising the spectre of self-delusion in place of self-knowledge.

One clue to Nietzsche's thought on the standard or measure of evaluation is given by his use of the word 'Gesetz' or law. Nietzsche associates this term not just with radically individual morality, but equally with radically individual self-knowledge or 'die individuelle Wissenschaft' (4[118], KSA 9.130) that it requires. Thus, in the context of self-knowledge he writes of 'das Grundgesetz deines eigentlichen Selbst' ('the fundamental law of your real self': SE 1, KSA 1.340f.), 'das Gesetz seiner höheren Mechanik' ('the law of one's higher mechanics': SE 2, KSA 1.343), and, on a physiological level, of 'Kenntniß seiner Kräfte, Gesetz ihrer Ordnung und Auslösung' ('knowledge of one's powers, the law of their order and discharge': 4[118], KSA 9.130), and of the profound difficulty, if not impossibility, of knowing one's drives (*Triebe*): 'die Gesetze ihrer *Ernährung* bleiben ihm ganz unbekannt' ('the laws of their *nourishment* remain entirely unknown to him': M 119, KSA 3.111; cf. M 108, KSA 3.95).

This use of 'Gesetz', for both moral self-legislation and the self-knowledge it requires, is an example of how Nietzsche's affirmative use of the term cuts across the prescriptive and the descriptive domains. But in the context of self-knowledge, 'Gesetz' sometimes takes on a further, quite specific meaning: it points towards a sense of necessity and constraint ('Notwendigkeit und Zwang'), described variously as a necessity of nature, an inner law of mechanics, a radically individual fate that is fixed ('Granit', 'Unbildbares') and absolutely binding on each 'self'. The claim embodied in this use of 'Gesetz' is that there is a necessity, a *Müssen*, which is an irresistible and binding source of obligation (*Sollen*). As the standard for evaluating what I truly want, it serves as the ground of self-legislation, and it is the business of self-knowledge to lay bare this necessity. To the extent that it succeeds, (5) *the exercise of freedom through self-legislation makes contact with necessity.*

---

19 See: SE 1, KSA 1.340f.; SE 2, KSA 1.343; 4[118], KSA 9.130; M 108, KSA 3.95; M 119, KSA 3.111; FW 335, KSA 3.562f.

II Schopenhauer and Wagner as Legislators

The middle and later writings, then, give us five co-ordinates for understanding the problematic of Nietzschean legislation and its sources. They are:
1) that (self–)legislation is opposed to the *heteronomy of self-subjection*, is *sovereign (self–)commanding*;
2) that (self–)legislation, in opposition to *moral universalism*, is radically individual or particular, an articulation of Nietzsche's *moral particularism*;
3) that the demand for (self–)legislation is a response to *contemporary nihilism*, the bankruptcy of transcendent ideals;
4) that, under these conditions, the individual is thrown back on itself for the sources of law, raising in an acute form the problem of *self-knowledge* as the key to exercising self-legislation; and
5) that as the key to self-knowledge, Nietzsche points to a sense of necessity, a fixed and binding constraint or *Müssen* as the ground of the *Sollen* of legislation.

From Nietzsche's middle phase on, this constraint or *Müssen* is increasingly located at the physiological level. It is the business of self-knowledge to lay bare the workings of our physis, to understand its demands and the constraints it exercises on our self-legislation, if our law is to meet our radically individual life-conditions.[20] In this context, Nietzsche uses the word 'Gesetz' with reference to the drives ('Triebe'), and especially to their 'tempo' or rhythm and their 'relations of power with one another' ('Machtverhältnisse miteinander').[21] In Nietzsche's early thought, however, the sense of this constraint or *Müssen* is less clear. In order to examine it in the context of his early account of legislation, I now turn to the *Unzeitgemässe Betrachtungen* and the two legislator-types they present: Schopenhauer (as philosophical legislator) and Wagner (as artistic legislator).

II.1 *Schopenhauer als Erzieher* (SE/UB III)

SE is Nietzsche's first-published text in which legislation / self-legislation are absolutely central. Despite its complex, transitional character, this text is of fundamental importance for understanding the nature and sources of Nietzsche's demand for leg-

---

[20] Thus, in FW 335, KSA 3.561, Nietzsche writes that in order to become self-legislators we must first become 'die besten Lerner und Entdecker alles Gesetzlichen und Nothwendingen in der Welt'. In the context of self-knowledge, this means attending to the prehistory (*Vorgeschichte*) of your moral judgements 'in your drives, inclinations, aversions, experiences and non-experiences' (*deinen Trieben, Neigungen, Abneigungen, Erfahrungen und Nicht-erfahrungen*).
[21] M 119, KSA 3.111; cf. FW 1, KSA 3.372 on the 'neue Gesetz der Ebbe und Fluth' and1[58], KSA 12.25 on the 'Entwicklungsgesetz' of drives (*Triebe*). On 'Naturgesetze' as a 'Feststellung von Machtverhältnissen', see: 39[13], KSA 11.623; 40[55], KSA 11.655; 2[139], KSA 12.135f.

islation throughout his work. As we shall see, the five co-ordinates for understanding legislation in the middle / later works receive their first expression in this work. Yet in this, its first appearance, the concept of legislation becomes enmeshed in an aporia of time that Nietzsche is unable to resolve. RWB is the first of several subsequent attempts to come to grips with the temporal aporia of legislation.

The demand for self-legislation appears in the very first section of the text. This opening section reads as a manifesto of radical individualism against conformism with prevailing tastes and fashions:

> At bottom, every human knows perfectly well that he is only once in this world, as an unicum, and that no such rarity of chance will throw together for a second time such a wonderfully motley plurality into the oneness that he is: he knows it, but he hides it from himself like a terrible conscience – Why? Out of fear for the neighbour who demands convention and cloaks himself with it. But what is it that compels the singular individual [den Einzelnen] to fear his neighbour, to think and act in a herd-like fashion and not to take joy in himself? Shame, perhaps, in a few rare cases. In most, it is complacency [Bequemlichkeit], inertia, in short, that tendency towards laziness [...] (SE 1, KSA 1.337)[22]

Nietzsche goes on to describe artists as the non-conformists *par excellence:*

> Only the artists hate this casual complicity in borrowed manners and adopted opinions and who reveal the mystery, the bad conscience of everyone, the proposition that every human is a unique miracle, they dare to show us the human being just as it is, uniquely itself down to every last movement of its muscles, more, that in being thus strictly consistent in its singularity [Einzigkeit], it is beautiful and worthy of contemplation [betrachtenswerth], new and unbelievable like every work of nature, and not at all tedious. (SE 1, KSA 1.337f.)[23]

Value is located in the (potential) uniqueness of each of us, or more precisely: in the unique convergence of multiplicity, chance and necessity that makes each of us what we are, but is buried or suppressed in oblivion by the ease of conformism. As a way to free ourselves from conformity towards our own, unique existence, Nietzsche goes on to propose radically individual self-legislation. Our measure of happiness can

---

[22] 'Im Grunde weiss jeder Mensch recht wohl, dass er nur einmal, als ein Unicum, auf der Welt ist und dass kein noch so seltsamer Zufall zum zweiten Mal ein so wunderlich buntes Mancherlei zum Einerlei, wie er es ist, zusammenschütteln wird: er weiss es, aber verbirgt es wie ein böses Gewissen – weshalb? Aus Furcht vor dem Nachbar, welcher die Convention fordert und sich selbst mit ihr verhüllt. Aber was ist es, was den Einzelnen zwingt, den Nachbar zu fürchten, heerdenmässig zu denken und zu handeln und seiner selbst nicht froh zu sein? Schamhaftigkeit vielleicht bei Einigen und Seltnen. Bei den Allermeisten ist es Bequemlichkeit, Trägheit, kurz jener Hang zur Faulheit [...]'.
[23] 'Die Künstler allein hassen dieses lässige Einhergehen in erborgten Manieren und übergehängten Meinungen und enthüllen das Geheimniss, das böse Gewissen von Jedermann, den Satz, dass jeder Mensch ein einmaliges Wunder ist, sie wagen es, uns den Menschen zu zeigen, wie er bis in jede Muskel-bewegung er selbst, er allein ist, noch mehr, dass er in dieser strengen Consequenz seiner Einzigkeit schön und betrachtenswerth ist, neu und unglaublich wie jedes Werk der Natur und durchaus nicht langweilig.'

only be attained by exercising freedom; that is, by gaining control over our lives and taking responsibility for our own existence, so that we exhibit what its meaning is. We must, in short, find a way to 'live according to our own law and measure' (SE 1, KSA 1.339: 'nach eignem Maass und Gesetz zu leben').[24]

In this account of (self–)legislation, two moments from Nietzsche's later concept stand out: radically individual legislation as the expression of *moral particularism* (2), and its opposition to the *heteronomy of self-subjection* (1). In SE, they are given a peculiar twist under the influence of Emerson. Moral particularism is combined with *a positive perfectionist* impulse to extend one's present attainments and enrich the range of human possibilities. As Cavell (1990), Conant (2001)[25] and others have shown, Nietzsche's Emersonian perfectionism is fuelled by an aversion to heteronomy, to our-self-subjection to prevailing norms and conventions; or, in Emerson's English, to the complacent, conformist acceptance of who we are. Nietzsche's opposition to heteronomy takes the form of a practice of aversion, driven by a positive perfectionist impulse.

In SE, then, self-legislation is a response to twin moral impulses of *particularism* and *perfectionism*. These impulses do not simply stand on their own. They constitute an affirmation of what Nietzsche will come to describe as the pluralistic character of life as will to power and its intrinsic dynamic of self-overcoming and intensification. In the context of SE itself, Nietzsche's particularist and perfectionist ethic is a response to the critical diagnosis of the present generated by his practise of aversion. It is a diagnosis that bears striking similarities with the account of *contemporary nihilism* (3) that fuels Nietzsche's demand for self-legislation in later years. It is also related to the problem of modernity, as perceived by Schiller, the young Hegel and others of his generation – the pervasive and radical sense of disorientation brought on by the collapse of traditional authorities at the hands of modern, Enlightenment critique.[26] In the absence of credible rules or models from the past, modernity is thrown back on itself and must find ways to orient and guide itself in its own terms. In SE, the need for self-legislation stems from the moral bankruptcy of the present, denounced as a 'low tide of all moral powers', incapable of generating values; we live instead on a dwindling capital of inherited morality.[27]

---

24 '[…] unser wunderliches Dasein gerade in diesem Jetzt ermuthigt uns am stärksten, nach eignem Maass und Gesetz zu leben: jene Unerklärlichkeit, dass wir gerade heute leben und doch die unendliche Zeit hatten zu entstehen, dass wir nichts als ein spannenlanges Heute besitzen und in ihm zeigen sollen, warum und wozu wir gerade jetzt entstanden. Wir haben uns über unser Dasein vor uns selbst zu verantworten; folglich wollen wir auch die wirklichen Steuermänner dieses Daseins abgeben und nicht zulassen, dass unsre Existenz einer gedankenlosen Zufälligkeit gleiche.'
25 Cavell 1990; Conant 2001. See also Conway 1997, esp. 52–56.
26 See chapter 5, p. 111 f.
27 '[S]o frage man ihn endlich: wo sind eigentlich für uns Alle, Gelehrte und Ungelehrte, Vornehme und Geringe, unsre sittlichen Vorbilder und Berühmtheiten unter unsern Zeitgenossen, der sichtbare Inbegriff aller schöpferischen Moral in dieser Zeit? Wo ist eigentlich alles Nachdenken über sittliche Fragen hingekommen, mit welchen sich doch jede edler entwickelte Geselligkeit zu allen Zeiten be-

The line from here to Nietzsche's later account of nihilism, as a bankruptcy of transcendence, is obvious. The same goes for another feature of Nietzsche's *Zeitdiagnose* in SE: the pervasive conflict (*Vernichtungskrieg*)[28] of forces and values, resulting in a condition of diremption, atomistic disgregation and alienation (see SE 4, KSA 1.367f.). For Hegel, this is the second major problem of modernity, stemming from the loss of the unifying powers of religious belief and worship brought on by Enlightenment critique. Modernity must, then, find ways both to *unify* and *orient* itself, and for Nietzsche, self-legislation is to be both the source of orientation and a unifying power. And yet, at crucial junctures in the text, a profound ambiguity enters into Nietzsche's concept of legislation. It is unclear whether self-legislation serves to overcome *the times* by provoking the actualization of better selves in a perfectionist dynamic of intensification; or whether it serves the overcoming or transcendence of *time itself* in a metaphysics of being. I will briefly indicate three moments in which this ambiguity comes to light.

a) The first intimation comes in Nietzsche's account of self-knowledge in SE 1. As in his later writings, Nietzsche's thought moves from the demand for self-legislation to the need for self-knowledge (point 4 in the problem of legislation). In §1, he describes an indirect, Emersonian route to self-knowledge by way of others – the objects of our love and reverence, who serve to reveal (not who are, but) a higher, unattained but attainable self.[29] The telos of self-knowledge is described by Nietzsche as 'the fundamental law of your real [or authentic] self' ('das Grundgesetz deines eigentlichen Selbst'), but also as something 'utterly beyond education or formation' ('durchaus Unerziehbares und Unbildbares'). Here, as in Nietzsche's later writings, the term 'Gesetz' serves to connect and synthesise moral legislation and self-knowledge, a self-knowledge that points to something fixed and binding, a sense of necessity or *Müssen* as the ground of the *Sollen* of legislation (point 5). But is this 'something fixed' and the constraint it exercises any more than a name for being?

b) This temporal ambiguity resurfaces in a passage from §4 where, under the sign of the 'Schopenhauerian human', Nietzsche describes his own practice of critical aversion and its sources in a perfectionist longing to extend human life. The specific question addressed in this passage is: What is to be the standard of critique for the aversive practice of the Schopenhauerian(–Emersonian) human?

---

schäftigt hat? Es giebt keine Berühmtheiten und kein Nachdenken jener Art mehr; man zehrt thatsächlich an dem ererbten Capital von Sittlichkeit, welches unsre Vorfahren aufhäuften und welches wir nicht zu mehren, sondern nur zu verschwenden verstehen.' (SE 2, KSA 1.344).

[28] For the resemblance between Nietzsche's early texts and later texts on nihilism as a pervasive conflict of forces, compare 30[8], KSA 7 (1873–4): '[...]Jetzt fehlt das, was alle partiellen Kräfte bindet: und so sehen wir alles feindselig gegen einander und alle edlen Kräfte in gegenseitigem aufreibendem Vernichtungskrieg' and 9[35], KSA 12.351: '[...] daß die Synthesis der Werthe und Ziele (auf der jede stärke Cultur beruht) sich löst, so daß die einzelnen Werthe sich Krieg machen: *Zersetzung*'.

[29] See SE 1, KSA 1.340 on the problem of self-knowledge.

> But there is a way of negating and destroying which is the discharge of that mighty longing for sanctification and salvation, and as the first teacher of which Schopenhauer came among us secularised [*entheiligte*] and truly this-worldly humans. All existence that can be negated deserves to be so negated; and being truthful means believing in an existence which could never be negated and is itself true and without lie. That is why the truthful one [*Wahrhaftige*] feels his activity to be a metaphysical one, explicable from laws of another higher life, and one that is affirmative in the profoundest sense: however much all that he does appears to be a destroying and shattering of the laws of this life. (SE 4, KSA 1.372)[30]

But what exactly is the status of this 'other and higher life' and 'the laws' or standard of critique that it offers? Is it transcendent and unattainable, a vision of pure being (*Sein*) like Plato's Sun? A metaphysical ground or standard of judgement that distends the untimely (*unzeitgemässe*) critique of the present into a total negation of becoming? Or is it immanent, the vision of a possible form of life, whose law or standard makes possible a *transformative* critique of the present in favour of a better life,[31] a 'transfigured physis'?

c) The ambiguity of legislation takes its most virulent form in §3 of the text, where Nietzsche first presents Schopenhauer as the philosophical legislator-type:

> Let us think of the eye of the philosopher resting upon existence : he wants to establish its worth [*Werth*] anew. That has been the proper work of all great thinkers, to be legislators [*Gesetzgeber*] for the measure, coinage and weight of things. (SE 3, KSA 1.360)[32]

But Nietzsche does not go on to offer a faithful account of Schopenhauer. Instead, the passage involves a reflection on, and *correction* of Schopenhauer's problem: What is the value of life? What is life worth? Nietzsche takes up the question of the value of life, but then corrects it by asking the prior question: What are conditions for a 'fair or just judgement' of the value of life (*ein gerechtes Urteil*)?

The argument developed in the passage can be put as follows. With Schopenhauer, Nietzsche agrees that life *as it is* cannot be affirmed. He does not, however, draw Schopenhauer's practical conclusion: that life therefore *ought not to be*. In-

---

30 'Aber es giebt eine Art zu verneinen und zu zerstören, welche gerade der Ausfluss jener mächtigen Sehnsucht nach Heiligung und Errettung ist, als deren erster philosophischer Lehrer Schopenhauer unter uns entheiligte und recht eigentlich verweltlichte Menschen trat. Alles Dasein, welches verneint werden kann, verdient es auch, verneint zu werden; und wahrhaftig sein heisst an ein Dasein glauben, welches überhaupt nicht verneint werden könnte und welches selber wahr und ohne Lüge ist. Deshalb empfindet der Wahrhaftige den Sinn seiner Thätigkeit als einen metaphysischen, aus Gesetzen eines andern und höhern Lebens erklärbaren und im tiefsten Verstande bejahenden: so sehr auch alles, was er thut, als ein Zerstören und Zerbrechen der Gesetze dieses Lebens erscheint.'
31 Barbera has argued persuasively for the influence of the young Schopenhauer (before *Die Welt als Wille und Vorstellung*), and especially his notion of the 'besseres Bewusstsein' on SE. See Barbera 1994, 229 f.
32 'Denken wir uns das Auge des Philosophen auf dem Dasein ruhend: er will dessen Werth neu festsetzen. Denn das ist die eigenthümlicheArbeit aller grossen Denker gewesen, Gesetzgeber für Maass, Münze und Gewicht der Dinge zu sein.'

stead, he questions the standpoint of this judgement of life, and argues that a 'gerechtes Urteil', a just judgement, requires first a *transformation* of life into something better. The problem is, the transformation of life brings practical and aesthetic resources into play, which compromise the philosopher-legislator's truthfulness ('Wahrhaftigkeit'). The philosopher gets torn between 'the reformer of life and the philosopher, that is: the judge of life' ('Reformator des Lebens', 'Richter des Lebens'). He gets caught in 'the discord between the wish for freedom, beauty and greatness of life, and the drive for truth which asks only: what is existence worth?'[33] The worry expressed in these lines is whether the legislator can be truthful ('wahrhaftig') like Schopenhauer and still affirm existence, or whether *illusion* is necessary to affirm existence. There is, in other words, a tension for Nietzsche between the truthfulness of the philosopher and the possibility of life-affirmation.

The background to this tension in SE is a conflict of loyalties in Nietzsche's mind, between Schopenhauer and Wagner and specifically: between their respective concepts of genius. For Schopenhauer, the genius is primarily a theoretical figure, a thinker devoted to truth, dwelling on the margins of culture; his exceptional insights culminate in the realization that life is worthless. For Wagner, by contrast, the self-modelled genius is an ecstatic, affirmative figure at the very heart of culture; he is a primarily practical figure, who devotes himself to the creation of life-serving illusions ('lebensdienliche Täuschungen', 'Wahnbilder'). What troubles Nietzsche is the Wagnerian linkage between illusion and affirmation: Is illusion necessary for life-affirmation? And if so, what is an affirmation of life worth, if it is based on an illusory vision of life?

It is not until MA that Nietzsche will break with this equation decisively and shake off the Wagnerian figure of genius in favour of the 'free spirit'. In SE, Nietzsche is genuinely torn between Wagner and Schopenhauer. His equivocation is laid bare by a telling slippage in his portrait of Schopenhauer, one that culminates in an ambiguity in his use of the word 'Zeit'. The slippage is between Schopenhauer's rejection *of the timely* (*das Zeitgemässe*) and his rejection *of time itself* as a 'false, vain, unworthy mother'. The slippage trades on the ambiguity of Nietzsche's use of the word 'Zeit' when he speaks *first* of Schopenhauer's struggle against 'die Zeit' (meaning: the times, the present), and *then* of Schopenhauer's struggle against 'Zeit' (meaning: time, temporal existence, becoming).

Consider the following three lines from closing passage:

'endlich erweist sich das angebliche Kind der Zeit nur als
Stiefkind derselben'

Here 'die Zeit' means the times, the present:

'in the end the supposed child of the times proves to be only its stepchild'

---

[33] This analysis draws on SE 3, KSA 1.360f.

> 'So strebte Schopenhauer, schon von früher Jugend an, jener falschen, eiteln und unwürdigen Mutter, der Zeit, entgegen'

Again: 'die Zeit' probably means the times, the present:

> 'Thus Schopenhauer strove, already from early youth on, against that false, vain and unworthy mother, the times'

But then come the lines:

> 'sobald er die Zeit in sich besiegt hatte, musste er auch, mit erstauntem Auge, den Genius in sich erblicken. Das Geheimniss seines Wesens war ihm jetzt enthüllt, die Absicht **jener Stiefmutter Zeit,** ihm diesen Genius zu verbergen, vereitelt, das Reich der verklärten Physis war entdeckt.' (**HS**)

> 'as soon as he had conquered the times [or time] in himself, he had to behold with astonished eye the genius in him. The mystery of his being was now revealed to him, the intention of **that stepmother time,** to conceal this genius from him was thwarted, the realm of transfigured physis uncovered.'(**HS**)

Here 'jene[.] Stiefmutter Zeit' (without the definite article 'die') can only mean: time itself. If this is correct, and Schopenhauer's struggle against the times becomes a struggle against time itself – that is, against becoming in name of being – then we have to ask: Does the affirmation of being (against becoming) constitute an affirmation or a negation of life? Can one possibly negate becoming and affirm life? In what sense is being alive? In his effort to escape the Wagnerian equation of life-affirmation and illusion, Nietzsche lurches back into Schopenhauerian metaphysics. For in this passage, there is an unmistakable alignment of philosophical legislation ('Wahrhaftigkeit') with being *against* becoming.

II.2 *Richard Wagner in Bayreuth* (UB IV/RWB)

RWB represents an effort to rethink genius, and specifically: the legislation of genius in its temporal character, its articulations with being and becoming. In the figure of Wagner, self-legislation is once again identified with emancipation from the present, and in this text, the word 'Gesetz' denotes the latter: the 'evil' external power of society and convention (Jacob Burckhardt's 'böse Macht': see Gerhardt 1996, 71–76, 104–112). Nietzsche speaks of 'power, law, ancestry, contract and the whole order of things' and their 'apparently unconquerable necessity' or 'ἀνάγκη' ('Macht, Gesetz, Herkommen, Vertrag und ganze Ordnungen der Dinge' and their 'scheinbar unbezwingliche Nothwendigkeit': RWB 4, KSA 1.451; 11[20], KSA 8.206). But 'Gesetz' is also used for the 'good' power of the individual cultural warrior or *Kulturkämpfer* and his striving for freedom. As Gerhardt (1996, 99f.) points out, Wagner's life-story is dramatised between these two poles of power, from conformity to convention in his early ambitions for 'honour and power', through to a Wotan-like renunciation of external power, in which he gives himself over to his free creative force. In RWB, Nietzsche looks for a standpoint or ground of legislation that is sufficiently removed or distant from 'power, law, ancestry, contract and the whole order of things' to allow for radically individual legislation; yet one that also resists the transcendence of becoming / temporality towards being that we saw in SE. Thus, Wagner is portrayed as caught in a 'crossroads of feeling' (*Kreuzung der Empfindung*) – between hatred and rejection of the present and a yearning need for love and community with his contemporaries.[34]

Nietzsche's quest for a ground of legislation that is removed from, yet immanent to, becoming – or at least, too indeterminate to signify being – culminates in a kind of 'homelessness', *a legislation from nowhere*, as when he writes of

> that uncanny-arrogant estrangement and wonder at the world, coupled with the yearning impulse to come close to the same world as its lover. (RWB 7, KSA 1. 471)
>
> (*jene unheimlich-übermüthige Befremdung und Verwunderung über die Welt mit dem sehnsüchtigen Drange paart, derselben Welt als Liebender zu nahen.*)

Or again:

> For it is certainly a life full of manifold torment and shame, to be unsettled and homeless in a world [*in einer Welt unstät und unheimisch zu sein*] and still to speak to it, to have to make demands on it, to despise it and yet be unable to dispense with that which is despised, – it is the real neediness of the artist of the future. (RWB 10, KSA 1.500)[35]

But on its own, this displacement is evidently unsatisfactory for Nietzsche, and he looks to characterise Wagner's actual insertion in the present in positive terms. What he wants is to describe the real necessity for Wagnerian art in modernity, a necessity that is opposed to the 'seemingly unconquerable necessity' (*scheinbar unbezwingliche Nothwendigkeit*) of convention opposed by genius. He does so in the language of 'Gesetz', describing 'true music' (*wahre Musik*) as 'a piece of fate and primordial law' (*ein Stück Fatum und Urgesetz*), which speaks through the mysterious 'primordially determined nature'(*ur-bestimmte Natur*) (RWB 6, KSA 1.464–5). This mysterious necessity, linking Wagner's art to the present, is explained in §9:

---

34 RWB 7, KSA 1.470. For 'Kreuzung der Empfindung' see RWB 7, KSA 1.471.
35 See also RWB 10, KSA 1.504 on saving 'diese heimathlose Kunst' for the future.

> His appearance in the history of the arts resembles a volcanic eruption of collective, undivided, artistic capacities of nature itself, after humanity had got used to the spectacle of the separation of the arts as a rule. (RWB 9, KSA 1.485; cf. RWB 7, KSA 1.468)[36]

Here, Wagnerian art is cast as an organising force that brings together and synthesises the chaotic multiplicity of individual arts in its works. What Nietzsche here says of art is part of the broader explanation offered for the real necessity of Wagner and Wagnerian legislation in the present: namely as a unifying, organising force able to bind the centripetal, atomising forces of modernity. As Gerhardt argues, Wagner's later self-realization as a free, (self–)legislative genius, described in RWB 9, is to be understood above all as a 'new form of exercising power': as the organizational genius with his 'sovereign disposal over conflicting forces' (Gerhardt 1996, 100 f.). Here, legislation is thought as inseparable from freedom or emancipation (RWB 9, KSA 1.494 f.), as a unifying instance that binds and holds together the most disparate elements. This goes for the personal domain (the forces within Wagner), for the domain of art, for the particular arts and elements of his dramatic works, but also – what Nietzsche especially values – for the political domain, for the 'connection between state, society and art'.[37]

Wagner's organizational legislation is made possible by his eye for 'relations' or 'large-scale connections'. And it is often presented in Heraclitean terms as 'unity in diversity' (*Einheit im Verschiedenen*: 32[12], KSA 7.757; 33[7], KSA 7.789), or as the 'unity of justice and enmity' (*Einheit von Gerechtigkeit und Feindschaft*: RWB 9, KSA 1.493 f.). This applies in particular to Wagner's dramas, which Nietzsche describes as the realization of the 'inner lawfulness' of his life-story; namely, of his 'One will' and the 'strictly individuated passion' that enforces itself over 'a plurality of passions' and the 'confusing multiplicity of claims and desires' (RWB 9, KSA 1.493 f.; cf. RWB 2, KSA 1.435). What these expressions reveal, however, is not a genuine Heraclitean balance between the One and the Many (*Einheit im Verschiedenen*), but a preponderance of the One over the Many. Nor do they express a Heraclitean affirmation of conflict, but a desire for peace. This can be seen from the following series of expressions from RWB 9 (KSA 1.493 f.):

> '[...] the compelling force of a personal will [...]'
> (*die zwingende Gewalt eines persönlichen Willens*)

> '[...] an overpowering symphonic understanding, which gives birth continuously to concord out of war [...]'
> (*ein übermächtiger symphonischer Verstand, welcher aus dem Kriege fortwährend die Eintracht gebiert*)

---

36 '[S]ein Auftreten in der Geschichte der Künste gleicht einem vulcanischen Ausbruche des gesammten ungetheilten Kunstvermögens der Natur selber, nachdem die Menschheit sich an den Anblick der Vereinzelung der Künste wie an eine Regel gewöhnt hatte.'
37 'die Verbindung von Staat, Gesellschaft und Kunst': 33[7], KSA 7.789. Cf. 11[51], KSA 8.241; 33[4], KSA 7.788 f; 32[10], KSA 7.756.

'[...] that we have before us particular currents going against each other, but also, in force over all of them, a stream with One mighty direction [...]'
(*dass wir widerstrebende einzelne Strömungen, aber auch über alle mächtig, einen Strom mit Einer gewaltigen Richtung vor uns haben*)

'[...] to assert One will across a confusing multiplicity of claims and desires – [...]'
(*durch eine verwirrende Mannichfaltigkeit von Ansprüchen und Begehrungen, Einen Willen durchführen –*)

These distortions of Heraclitus for Wagner's sake unwittingly exhibit Nietzsche's insight into the tyrannical absolutization of power as Wagner's true tendency. Nietzsche's worries about the egocentric absolutization of power into the tyrannical in Wagner are strongly attested in the *Nachlass*, even before the writing of RWB.[38] With time, this perception gains the upper hand, as can be seen in the later critique of Wagner under the sign of décadence, as a tyrannical absolutization of bad taste.[39]

III Zarathustra as Legislator-Type: Nietzsche's Agonal Model of Self-Legislation

The Wagnerian model of legislation may or may not avoid the metaphysical pitfalls of Schopenhauer's model, but it certainly fails the test of pluralism required for a life-affirming form of legislation. It is in response to this problem that Nietzsche elaborates the third type of legislator I shall examine. At stake here is a *pluralistic, egalitarian* and *dynamic* model of legislation inspired by the signature institution of archaic Greek culture: the agon or contest. Already in *Homer's Wettkampf*, written three years before RWB (1872) Nietzsche's abhorrence of Wagner's absolutization of power is not hard to read in his description of 'the Hellenic notion of the contest: it abhors the rule of one [*Alleinherrschaft*] and fears its dangers; it desires, as a *protection* against genius – a second genius.'[40] This same sentiment is expressed 11 years later in the Zarathustra *Nachlass* of 1883 with even greater clarity:

---

38 See 32[32], KSA 7: 'Die "falsche Allmacht" entwickelt etwas "Tyrannisches" in Wagner. Das Gefühl ohne *Erben* zu sein – deshalb sucht er seiner Reformidee die möglichste Breite zu geben und sich gleichsam durch Adoption fortzupflanzen. Streben nach Legitimität. Der Tyrann lässt keine andre Individualität gelten als die seinige und die seiner Vertrauten. Die Gefahr für Wagner ist gross, wenn er Brahms usw. nicht gelten lässt: oder die Juden.' (cf. MA 577). Also 32[34], KSA 7: 'Der Tyrannensinn für das Colossale. Es kommt ihm gar keine Pietät entgegen, der ächte Musiker betrachtet ihn als einen Eindringling, als illegitim.' And 32 [61], KSA 7: 'Hier liegt Wagner's Bedeutung: er versucht die Tyrannis mit Hülfe der Theatermassen.'
39 15[88], KSA 13.458; cf. 4[221], KSA 9.156.
40 (*Homer's Wettkampf*, KSA 1.789) – a line that needs to be read together with Kelterborn's remark that Nietzsche honoured Wagner as 'a *fellow fighter next to him* (not above him) in the struggle for a higher German culture' (quoted in chapter 2 note 45).

> To rule? dreadful! I do not want to enforce *my* type.
> My joy is *diversity*!
> Problem!
>
> Herrschen? gräßlich! Ich will nicht *meinen* Typus
> aufnöthigen. Mein Glück ist die *Vielheit*!
> Problem!
> (15[21], KSA 10.485; cf. 16[86], KSA 10.529)[41]

It is to this period, and the pluralistic model of self-legislation developed in a series of notes from 1883 (KSA 10: notebooks 15 and 16), that I now turn. In these notes, as will become clear, the first three moments of Nietzsche's problematic of legislation, as set out in §1 above, are very prominent; that is, his opposition to the *heteronomy of self-subjection* (1) and to *moral universalism* (2) in the context of the necessity to respond to *contemporary nihilism* (3). What is distinctive about these notes is how the claims of moral particularity are articulated in a pluralistic context of collective self-legislation. This implies a shift towards a more political concept of legislation, and suggests that Gerhardt's thesis concerning Nietzsche's radically individual morality needs to be modified in the direction of moral laws that bind collectively across particular communities.[42]

The task of self-legislation in these notes is primarily to overcome morality. The problem-background for this task is, of course, nihilism and specifically: the loss of authority of traditional morality under nihilistic conditions. It is worth looking at the way in which Nietzsche formulates the problem in three notes from the same period:

> The dissolution of morality leads in its practical consequences
> to the atomistic individual and then further to the partition of
> the individual into pluralities – absolute flux.
>   That is why now more than ever there is the need for a goal and love, a
> new love.
>
> Die Auflösung der Moral führt in der praktischen Consequenz
> zum atomistischen Individuum und dann noch zur Zerteilung
> des Individuums in Mehrheiten – absoluter Fluß.
>   Deshalb ist jetzt mehr als je ein Ziel nöthig und Liebe, eine
> neue Liebe.
> (4[83], KSA 10.138)

This note reiterates the problems of disorientation and atomistic disgregation in modernity motivating Nietzsche's call for self-legislation in SE. But it does so in a way that indicates why a radically individual morality is insufficient. The problem

---

[41] The excerpts from the *Nachlass* notes used in this section are rendered in broader or full citations of the notes, together with my translations, in the order in which they appear in KSA, in the Appendix to this chapter.
[42] As argued by Daniel Conway (1997 29 f.). See also chapter 8, on Conway in the context of community.

of 'atomistic chaos' (SE 4, KSA 1.363) from SE is now radicalised into a boundless 'war of annihilation' (*Vernichtungskrieg*) of forces and values that threatens not just relations between 'atomistic individuals', but the very constitution of the individual. In line with this heightened perception of the threat, Nietzsche's demand for a source of orientation, a new 'goal', is coupled with the call for a unifying counter-force that cannot be met by individual self-legislation: for 'a *new love*'. This is taken further in a subsequent note, where the demands for orientation and unification are formulated as the question of 'the morality of the higher men':

> *Of the morality of the higher men*
> All that is otherwise morality has here become love.
> But now a new "Thou shalt" begins – knowledge
> of the free spirit – the question of the highest *goals*.
>
> *Von der Moral der höheren Menschen.*
> Alles, was sonst Moral ist, ist hier Liebe geworden.
> Aber nun beginnt ein neues "Du sollst" – die Erkenntniß
> des Freigeistes – die Frage nach den höchsten *Zielen*.
> (4[89], KSA 10.140)

The suggestion here is that traditional morality can – in the hands of 'higher men' – be dissolved and replaced by love. And yet, it is clear to Nietzsche that on its own, love will be insufficient: the problem of orientation persists, and the question of 'goals' (now *pluralised*) is referred explicitly to the demand for legislation: 'a new "Thou Shalt"'. The problem of legislation can therefore be formulated as the question: How to conjugate legislation, or rather a pluralistic form of legislation able to generate new 'goals', with the cohesive powers of 'a *new love*'? As we will see, Nietzsche addresses this task by recurring to the line of thought first developed 10 years earlier in *Homer's Wettkampf*. There Nietzsche argued that, in the face of the pervasive 'war of annihilation' (*Vernichtungskampf*) of nature and world-history, the Greeks sought not to condemn, negate or suppress destructive, antagonistic drives and affects (see 5[146], KSA 8.79), but to transform them into constructive cultural forces via the institution of the agon (*Wettkampf*), as a regime of limited antagonism. In the notes of 1883, where Nietzsche's problem concerns the possibility of life-affirmative legislation under nihilistic conditions, he recurs to the *Wettkampf* in the form of an *agonal model of self-legislation* capable of generating a plurality of 'new goals'. On this model of legislation, the demand for cohesion cannot be derived from a concept of love that precludes antagonism; instead, Nietzsche looks to derive it from 'a *new love*', that is, a new concept of love that works through resistance (*Widerstreben*). But before turning to Nietzsche's account of legislation, there is a further note in this sequence that deserves attention. It is important because in it Nietzsche underscores the need for legislation, a new '"Thou Shalt"', in spite of the hollowing-out of existing morality and religion under modern, nihilistic conditions:

> Just as we no longer need morality, so – we no longer need religion.
> The "I love God" – the only ancient form of religion – is transposed into the love of *an ideal* – has become creative – only god-men.
> Morality is needed: by what standard will we act, given that we must act? And what we have done, we must *assess* it – by what standard?
> To show an error in the genesis [of morality] is not an argument against morality. Morality is a life-condition. "Thou shalt"
>
> So wie wir die Moral nicht mehr nöthig haben, so – auch
> nicht mehr die Religion. Das "ich liebe Gott" – die einzige alte
> Form des Religiösen – ist in die Liebe *eines Ideals*
> umgesetzt – ist schöpferisch geworden – lauter Gott-Menschen.
> Moral ist nöthig: wonach werden wir handeln, da wir doch
> handeln müssen? Und was wir gehandelt haben, müssen wir
> *schätzen* – wonach?
> Irrthum in der Genesis nachweisen ist kein Argument gegen
> die Moral. Moral ist eine Lebensbedingung. "Du sollst"
> (4[90], KSA10.140)

As Gerhardt (1992) has made clear, the critique of morality and religion, which began in MA and will culminate in JGB and GM around three years after this note, does not make morality or legislation dispensable. Of particular interest here is how the need for legislation is referred not just to the nihilistic demise of traditional morality and religion, but to life itself: "'Du sollst'" is a 'condition for life'. It is in response to the pluralistic and dynamic character of life, above all else, that Nietzsche formulates his agonal model of legislation.

In these notes, the task of legislation and new goals is not taken on by Nietzsche himself; nor is it given to Zarathustra as such. Instead the task is pluralised around the figure of Zarathustra, who serves as the legislator for further legislators (not subjects). In response to the question: 'What *sense* does it have to give laws?' Nietzsche writes:

> the general type of the law-giver, who is the *herald* of **many** law-givers.
> *Chief teaching:* to bring to completeness and a **sense of well-being**
> on every level – *not* to jump!
>
> Welchen *Sinn* hat es Gesetze zu geben?
>
> der allgemeine Typus des G<esetzgebers>, der **vielen** Gesetz–
> gebern der *Herold* ist.
> *Hauptlehre:* auf jeder Stufe es zur Vollkommenheit
> und zum **Wohlgefühl** bringen – *nicht* springen!
> (15[10], KSA 10.481f.)

According to this lapidary response, law or law-giving must meet two basic demands, if it is to have any sense: *first*, the law must be counter-final and provisional, not the law to end all laws; *secondly*, the law must be responsive to diversity, a law *for* many, not a law that subjects the many to One. In these terms, it is clear that Nietzsche's concept of law is radically opposed to the moral law in its traditional claims to *eternity* and *universal validity.*

But Nietzsche's underlying motives are positive, not negative: the counter-final, pluralistic qualities of Nietzsche's law are intended to *take the side of life* against the moral law within the Nietzschean project to naturalise morality. This is clearly expressed in two subsequent notes. In note 15[19], he writes:

> Zarathustra offers the model for **how** one has to behave
> towards the law, insofar as he *supersedes* the law of
> laws, morality, through higher [ones]
>
> Zarathustra giebt das Muster **wie** man sich zum Gesetze zu
> verhalten hat, indem er das Gesetz der Gesetze die Moral
> *aufhebt* durch höhere (15[19], KSA 10.484)

It is as an expression of the *dynamic character of life* that Zarathustra's attitude to the law becomes exemplary: like him, we are to engage in the dynamic of destruction and creation, in the processes of self-overcoming and intensification intrinsic to life.[43]

In the second note (cited earlier), it is the joy Zarathustra takes in the plurality of life forms, in 'the spectacle of many *others*' that first brings him face to face with the problem of legislation:

> To rule? dreadful! I do not want to enforce *my* type.
> My joy is *diversity!*
>   Problem!
>
> Herrschen? gräßlich! Ich will nicht *meinen* Typus
> aufnöthigen. Mein Glück ist die *Vielheit!*
>   Problem!
> (15[21], KSA 10.485; cf. 16[86], KSA 10.529)

The problem is, then, whether law and law-giving can be re-thought in a way that reflects and enhances the *dynamic* and *pluralistic* qualities of life against the rigidity and universalism of the moral law. Nietzsche's solution, adumbrated in the next line, is to rethink law and law-giving on the model of the agon or 'contest for power':

> To call for the agon! Precisely those, who would dearly like to hide
> themselves, the *still ones*, the *pious ones*, – competition for mastery!
>
> Zum agon aufrufen! gerade die, welche sich gern verstecken
> möchten, die *Stillen, Frommen*, – Bewerbung um Herrschaft!
> (15[21], KSA 10.485; cf. 16[86], KSA 10.529)

---

43 See also note 16[84], KSA 10.528, where the '"law-giver"' is literally placed in between the destruction of existing laws and the clarion call for new laws: 'Das Zerbrechen der Tafeln. Der idealische "Gesetzgeber". Heroldsruf.'

In order to reconstruct Nietzsche's agonal solution, we must return to note 15[10], KSA 10, and Nietzsche's demand that law-giving be counter-final and pluralistic, if it is to have any sense. In order to meet this demand, Nietzsche indicates three lines of thought:

1. It is to be a 'law for law-givers', not for passive subjects or 'supplicants':

> Law for law-givers
> From supplicants we must become those who bless!
>
> Gesetz für Gesetzgeber
> Aus *Betenden müssen wir Segnende* werden! (15[58], KSA 10.494)

2. It is to be productive and pluralistic, the creative source of many ideals and not a subjection of many to the ideal or law of One:

> Not One ideal of the wise one, but a hundred *ideals of the fool*
> is what I want to establish!
>
> Nicht Ein Ideal des Weisen, sondern hundert *Ideale des Thoren* will ich aufstellen! (16[86], KSA 10.530)

3. It is to be law or law-giving that blesses, completes and fulfils 'on every level', not a leveller that demands or pleads that we all 'jump' to One level (see 15[10], KSA 10).

The first two points are best understood by way of the third. What Nietzsche means here is explicated in the note 15[19], KSA 10 (cited above) on Zarathustra's exemplary, destructive-creative attitude to the law, which continues:

> the *fulfillability greater* than before (accessible to
> the individual's interpretation)
>   NB. it ***must*** be ***fulfillable*** and from the fulfilment a
> higher ideal and its law ***must*** grow!
>
> die *Erfüllbarkeit größer* als vorher (dem Indivi-
> duum die Deutung zugänglich)
>   NB. es ***muß erfüllbar*** sein und aus der Erfüllung ***muß*** ein
> höheres Ideal und dessen Gesetz wachsen!
> (15[19], KSA 10.484)

In these lines, Zarathustra figures as the counterpart or counter-exemplar to Saint Paul and his tortured relation the law that *cannot be fulfilled* (see M 68, KSA 3.65 f.). But again, Nietzsche's thought must be grasped from a positive perspective in his concept of life: the demand for fulfillable laws, in the sense of laws that are accessible to individual interpretation, addresses the claims of *particularism*, understood as the ethical articulation of the radical plurality and diversity of life forms. This demand, in turn, is presented as the key to the development of further, higher laws; that is, to a dynamic sense of law-giving that replicates the self-overcoming and

III Zarathustra as Legislator-Type: Nietzsche's Agonal Model of Self-Legislation

intensification intrinsic to life. But how exactly are we to understand the 'fulfilment' of Zarathustra's law through individual interpretations? And how is a higher law to 'grow' from this process? These thoughts are filled out in note 16[86], KSA 10.530, which takes up the demand for fulfillable laws:

> [...] *Demand:* the new law must be *fulfillable* –
> and from the fulfilment the overcoming and the higher
> law must grow. Zarathustra gives the attitude towards the law,
> insofar as he *supersedes* the "law of laws", morality.
>   Laws as a backbone.
>   to work on them and create, insofar as one carries them out.
> Hitherto slavishness *before* the law! [...]

> [...] *Forderung:* das neue Gesetz muß *erfüllbar* sein –
> und aus der Erfüllung muß die Überwindung und das höhere
> Gesetz wachsen. Zarathustra giebt die Stellung zum Gesetz,
> indem er das "Gesetz der Gesetze", die Moral *aufhebt*.
>   Gesetze als Rückgrat.
>   an ihnen arbeiten und schaffen, indem man sie vollzieht.
> Bisheriger Sklavensinn *vor* dem Gesetze! [...]
> (16[86], KSA 10.530)

With the image of laws as a 'backbone', Nietzsche returns us to the notion of a 'law for law-givers'. Laws that are subject to individual interpretation and fulfilment break, for the first time, our slavish subjection to eternal, immutable laws, what Nietzsche elsewhere calls our 'fear of commanding':

> [...] one would rather obey an available law than *create* a law for oneself, than command oneself and others. The fear of commanding – Rather subject oneself than react [...]

> [...] man gehorcht lieber einem vorhandenen Gesetz als daß man sich ein Gesetz *schafft*, als daß man sich und Anderen befiehlt. Die Furcht vor dem Befehlen – Lieber sich unterwerfen als reagiren. [...] (7[6], KSA 12.275)

At the centre of Nietzsche's dynamic conception of laws is the notion of creativity: where laws are subject to interpretation and fulfilment, on the model of a 'backbone' or provisional framework, individuals are placed in a position to work and re-work them so as to create new and better laws of their own. Indeed, Nietzsche's point seems to be that self-legislation just *is* the creative reinterpretation of the preceding law in response to one's particular life-needs. With this notion of a 'law for law-givers', we come up against the central paradox for Nietzsche's re-interpretation of law: How our 'slavishness before the law' (16[86], KSA 10) can be overcome through an act of law-giving? How to legislate active self-legislation, rather than passive obedience or prostration? Under what conditions does law-giving cease to be coercive and become instead productive – a stimulant of individual self-emancipation and autonomy in the sense of radically individual self-legislation?

These questions go to the heart of Nietzsche's problematic relation to the law. For with them, the challenge is posed: Can the gestures of tyranny, coercion, subjection, and making-fast be overcome? Can the concept of law be divorced from the functions of unity and universal validity so closely wedded to it? Or must we abandon the concept of law altogether in the name of life? It is these questions that Nietzsche's agonal model of the law is designed to address. Nietzsche's agon does not attempt to reinvent the concept of law from scratch, as if this were possible. Rather, it exploits the traditional meanings and functions of law – coercion/subjection, rigidity/eternity and universality – in order to transform the meanings and functions of law. By situating the traditional concept of law within a unique constellation of forces, Nietzsche effectively turns it against itself, so as to generate a dynamic, pluralistic and emancipatory sense of law.

Nietzsche's concept of the agon turns on a re-interpretation and re-evaluation of *resistance* in the context of conflicting or competing powers. The resistance offered by an opponent need not be experienced as a negative, inhibiting force, as pain, loss or a diminution of power to be avoided at all costs. It can also be a stimulant that one seeks out, an obstacle that provokes one to exercise, extend and measure one's own resources in the effort to achieve mastery.[44] When placed in the context of a 'contest for power', 'law' takes on precisely this meaning, as an obstacle or stimulus that provokes others to resist and surpass it with their own, better laws:

> The rights that I have conquered for myself I will
> not *give* to the other: rather, he ought to *rob* them for himself! like
> me – and [he] may appropriate them and wrest them from me! To
> this extent there must be a law which emanates from me, as if it wanted
> to make all into my likeness: so that the singular individual discovers and strengthens
> itself in contradiction with it [...]
>
> Whoever *appropriates* a right will not *give* this right to the
> other – but will be an opponent to him *insofar as he appropriates
> it for himself*: the love of the father who clashes with his son.
>
> The great educator, like nature: he must pile up *obstacles*,
> so that they are *overcome*. [...]
>
> Die Rechte, die ich mir erobert habe, werde ich dem
> Anderen nicht *geben:* sondern er soll sie sich *rauben!* gleich
> mir – und mag sie nehmen und mir *abzwingen!* Insofern
> muß ein Gesetz da sein, welches von mir ausgeht, als ob es Alle zu
> meinem Ebenbilde machen wolle: damit der Einzelne sich im
> Widerspruch mit ihm entdecke und stärke [...]
>
> Wer ein Recht sich *nimmt*, wird dies Recht dem Anderen
> nicht *geben* – sondern ihm Gegner sein, *indem er es
> sich nimmt:* die Liebe des Vaters, der dem Sohn
> widerstrebt.

---

44 See HW, KSA 1.789; EH weise 7 6.274; cf. 14[173], KSA 13 and 14[174], KSA 13.

> Der große Erzieher wie die Natur: er muß *Hindernisse*
> thürmen, damit sie *überwunden* werden.
> (16[88], KSA 10.531)

On one level, these lines leave the traditional, problematic meanings of the word 'Gesetz' untouched. Indeed, they *exploit* these meanings in order to undo them. For *only* if Zarathustra legislates *as if* he wanted to coerce others and make a claim on all, only then will he evoke their resistance, provoking each single one (*der Einzelne*) to extend itself by appropriating Zarathustra's law and reinterpreting it in singular terms, thereby destroying its universal claim in a plethora of self-legislation.

On another level, however, traditional meanings of the law do undergo significant re-interpretation. Most importantly, the relation of law to rights is reversed. The traditional (liberal) concept of legislation as a *giving* of (equal) rights to others and safeguarding of those rights is rejected in favour of a symmetrical regime of power, in which rights are claimed, conquered, or usurped by dint of one's deeds, not given.[45] This is fully in line with Nietzsche's exercise-concept of freedom in GD Streifzüge 38, as the *struggle for* rights – which turns into unfreedom once those rights are established, granted and protected by liberal institutions.

On this model, ‚the problem of law is: How to stimulate others to conquer and exercise their own rights? Nietzsche's agonal solution is to raise one's own law as if (*als ob*) it were universally binding, thereby usurping all rights and forcing others oppose one, to discover and assert their own capacities in re-claiming their rights – like the love of a father who intentionally clashes with his son. Even here, where the relation of laws to rights is reversed, the coercive character of law remains the key to re-thinking law in non-coercive terms.

Whether Nietzsche's agonal solution works is questionable. What, after all, is to distinguish 'as if' universal claims designed to provoke conflict and self-legislation from those that simply passify and subject? What separates the father who clashes with his son out of love, from tyrannical, overbearing fathers like Kafka's? The agonal regime of power presupposes conditions – creative resources and a resilience on the part of many – which, on Nietzsche's own diagnosis, are hard to imagine in the present.[46] As far as I can tell, Nietzsche does not go on to ask what, for contemporary democratic sentiments, are the most urgent questions: Under what conditions does law-giving cease to be coercive and become instead productive – a stimulant towards individual self-emancipation?[47] And how can these conditions be promoted and ex-

---

45 Cf. *My Concept of Freedom* (GD Streifzüge 38, KSA 6.139 f.) where Nietzsche argues that the safeguarding of liberal values under liberal institutions has had the effect of producing unfreedom: they turn *Gleichheit* into *Gleichmachung*. Against this, Nietzsche defines his concept of freedom as the *struggle for* rights, that is, in the exercise of illiberal – agonal – capacities in struggle for liberal institutions.
46 On this 'energetic' question and the agon, see chapter 8.
47 In note 24[9], KSA 10.647, Nietzsche does seem to recognise that resistance does not always work as a stimulant, when he writes that a feeling of power arises (only) when we perceive an obstacle to

tended across social life? Such questions seem rather to arouse his suspicion,[48] and these notes issue in a very different line of thought: the *deferral of legislation to the future*.[49]

The next phase of Nietzsche's thought on law sees the agon migrate to particular communities, to a class or caste of 'legislators of the future' charged with the task of transvaluation.[50] Nonetheless, these notes are valuable as a record of Nietzsche's effort to retain the language of law, while reinvesting it with naturalistic meanings that undo the problematic, life-negating features of the traditional concept of law. Moreover, the agonal model of power they deploy brings with it two insights of fundamental importance to the problematic of law and legislation: first, that legislation is irreducibly *relational* and *public* in character; solitude is at best a 'means of education' (15[21], KSA 10), at worst an evasion of responsibility. Building on the relational character of law, the second insight is that, under agonal conditions, radically individual self-legislation is exercised through the appropriation and creative reinterpretation of the prevailing law in terms of one's own needs as a unique form of life. Only in this way, can the coercive law of One be pluralised into 'fulfillable' laws that affirm and bless the life of each; for to treat to Zarathustra as an exemplar means to replicate his overcoming of morality by overcoming his law. The implication of these insights is that moral particularism, and its realization in radically individual legislation, is unthinkable without relations of action – resistance – attraction to concrete others, a '*new love*' that includes the tension and antagonism legislation and counter-legislation. A radically individual morality cannot, in other words, be achieved in isolation, but is inseparable from the task of founding the kind of ethical community that makes it possible. In the next chapter, I turn to the question of community and ask what kind of ethical community and what kind of ethical law are invoked by Nietzsche's agonal confrontations.

---

which we believe we are equal: 'If we do something, a feeling of power [strength] arises, often before the deed, with the representation of what is to be done (as in the sight of an enemy, an obstacle, to which we believe we are equal): always accompanying.' ('Wenn wir etwas thun, so entsteht ein Kraftgefühl, oft schon vor dem Thun, bei der Vorstellung des zu Thuenden (wie beim Anblick eines Feindes, eines Hemmnisses, dem wir uns gewachsen glauben): immer begleitend.')

48 See e.g. JGB 259 5.207: 'Mutually refraining from injury, violence, and exploitation, positing [*setzen*] your will as equal to the other's: in a certain, crude sense, this can become a good custom [*Sitte*] between individuals when the conditions for it are given (namely, that the individuals actually have similar amounts of force and standards of value, and belong together within a single body). But as soon as one wanted [*wolllte*] to take this principle further, and maybe even to take it as the *fundamental principle of society*, it would immediately show itself for what it is: as the will to *negate* life, the principle of disintegration and decay.'

49 See: 26[407], KSA 11.258; 34[33], KSA 11.430; 34[199], KSA 11.488; 34[207], KSA 11; 34[212], KSA 11.493; 35[9], KSA 11.512; 35[39], KSA 11.528; 35[45], KSA 11.531f.; 35[47], KSA 11.533; 37[14], KSA 11.589; 2[57], KSA 12.87.

50 On the legislators of the future and their relation to democratic or aristocratic political conditions, see Siemens 2008b.

Appendix
Zarathustra as Legislator-Type: The Texts

4[83], KSA 10.138

    The dissolution of morality leads in its practical consequences to the atomistic individual and then further to the partition of the individual into pluralities – absolute flux.
    That is why now more than ever there is the need for a goal and love, a *new love*.

    Die Auflösung der Moral führt in der praktischen Consequenz zum atomistischen Individuum und dann noch zur Zerteilung des Individuums in Mehrheiten – absoluter Fluß.
    Deshalb ist jetzt mehr als je ein Ziel nöthig und Liebe, eine *neue Liebe*. (4[83], KSA 10.138)

4[89], KSA 10.140

    Of the morality of the higher men.

    All that is otherwise morality has here become love.

    But now a new "Thou shalt" begins – knowledge of the free spirit – the question of the highest *goals*.

    Von der Moral der höheren Menschen.

    Alles, was sonst Moral ist, ist hier Liebe geworden.

    Aber nun beginnt ein neues "Du sollst" – die Erkenntniß des Freigeistes – die Frage nach den höchsten *Zielen*.

4[90], KSA 10.140 (excerpt)

    Just as we no longer need morality, so – we no longer need religion. The "I love God" – the only ancient form of religion – is transposed into the love of *an ideal* – has become creative – only god-men.
    Morality is needed: by what standard will we act, given that we must act? And what he have done, we must assess it – by what standard?
    To show an error in the genesis [of morality] is not an argument against morality. Morality is a life-condition. "Thou shalt"

    So wie wir die Moral nicht mehr nöthig haben, so – auch nicht mehr die Religion. Das "ich liebe Gott" – die einzige alte Form des Religiösen – ist in die Liebe *eines Ideals* umgesetzt – ist schöpferisch geworden – lauter Gott-Menschen.
    Moral ist nöthig: wonach werden wir handeln, da wir doch handeln müssen? Und was wir gehandelt haben, müssen wir *schätzen* – wonach?

Irrthum in der Genesis nachweisen ist kein Argument gegen
die Moral. Moral ist eine Lebensbedingung. "Du sollst" [...]

15[10], KSA 10.481 f. (excerpt)

The legislator as type.
His development and his sufferings.
What *sense* does it have to give laws?
the general type for the law-giver, who is the *herald* of **many** law-givers
Chief teaching: to bring to completeness
and a **sense of well-being** on every level – *not* to jump!

Typus der Gesetzgebers.
Seine Entwicklung und seine Leiden.
Welchen *Sinn* hat es Gesetze zu geben?
der allgemeine Typus des G<esetzgebers>, der **vielen** Gesetzgebern der *Herold* ist.
Hauptlehre: auf jeder Stufe es zur Vollkommenheit
und zum **Wohlgefühl** bringen – *nicht* springen!

15[19], KSA 10.483 f.

Laws as a *backbone* – working on them and continuing to create them
Zarathustra offers the model for **how** one has to behave towards the law, insofar as he supersedes [aufhebt] the law of laws, morality, through higher [ones]
the *fulfillability greater* than before (accessible to the individual's interpretation)
NB. it must be **fulfillable** and from the fulfilment a higher ideal and its law **must** grow!

Gesetze als *Rückgrat* – an ihnen arbeitend und fortschaffend
Zarathustra giebt das Muster **wie** man sich zum Gesetze zu
verhalten hat, indem er das Gesetz der Gesetze die Moral
aufhebt durch höhere
die *Erfüllbarkeit größer* als vorher (dem Individuum die Deutung zugänglich)
NB. **es muß erfüllbar** sein und aus der Erfüllung **muß** ein
höheres Ideal und dessen Gesetz wachsen! (15[19], KSA 10.484)

15[21], KSA 10.485 (excerpt; cf. 16[86], KSA 10.529)

To rule? Dreadful! I do not *want* to enforce
my type. My felicity is *plurality!*
Problem!

To call for the agon! Precisely those who would dearly like to hide themselves, the *still ones*,
the *pious ones*, – to competition for mastery!
Solitude only a means of education!

Against those who merely *take pleasure!*
Solitude also falls under this point of view!

***Self-overcoming** and all virtue* has no sense at all apart
from as a means to mould the *ruling strength* [or *power*].

Herrschen? gräßlich! Ich *will* nicht *meinen* Typus
aufnöthigen. Mein Glück ist die *Vielheit!*
Problem!

Zum agon aufrufen! gerade die, welche sich gern verstecken
möchten, die *Stillen, Frommen,* – Bewerbung
um Herrschaft!
Einsamkeit nur Mittel der Erziehung!

gegen alle bloß *Genießenden!*
Auch die Einsamkeit fällt unter diesen Gesichtspunkt!
Selbstüberwindung und alle *Tugend* hat gar keinen
Sinn außer als Mittel zur Ausbildung der *herrschenden*
Kraft.

15[58], KSA 10.494

Law for law-givers
From supplicants we must become *those who bless!*

Gesetz für Gesetzgeber
Aus Betenden müssen wir Segnende werden!

16[86], KSA 10.529 f.

To rule? To enforce *my* type? Dreadful! Is my
happiness not exactly the beholding of many *others?*
Problem.

To call just those who to the contest for power, who
like to hide and would like to live for themselves – also the wise,
the pious, the still one in the land! Contempt for their *self-indulgent*
solitude!

All *creative* natures struggle for influence, even when
they live alone – "Fame after death" is but a false expression
for what they want.

The tremendous task of the ruler, who educates himself –
the kind of humans and people over whom he rules, must be *pre-formed*
in him: here is where he must first have become ruler!

All virtue and *self-overcoming* only has sense
as a preparation of the *one ruling!*

Against all who **merely** indulge themselves! Also solitude as pleasure
in oneself, even that of the self-torturer. [...]

Demand: the new law must be *fulfillable* –
and from the fulfilment the overcoming and the higher
law must grow. Zarathustra gives the attitude towards the law,
insofar as he *supersedes* [*aufhebt*] the "law of laws", morality.

Laws as a backbone.

working on them and creating, insofar as one carries them out.
Hitherto slavishness *before* the law!
　　Zarathustra has himself become the wise one, who takes joy in his folly and the poor one who takes joy in his richness. [...]
　　Not One ideal of the wise one, but a hunderd *ideals of the fool* is what I want to establish! Zarathustra 4
　　Against the grumpy histrionic stoic magnificence of the "wise one".
　　The legislator as type, his development and
his sufferings.
　　What sense does it have at all to give laws?
　　Zarathustra is the herald who calls upon many law-givers.

Cf. 7[6] 12.275 (excerpt)

[...] one would rather obey an available law than *create* a law for oneself, than command oneself and others. The fear of commanding –
Rather subject oneself than react [...]

16[86], KSA 10.529 f. (excerpts)

　　Herrschen? Meinen Typus Andern aufnöthigen? Gräßlich! Ist
mein Glück nicht gerade das Anschauen vieler *Anderer*?
Problem.
　　Gerade jene zum Wettkampfe um Macht aufrufen, welche
sich gerne verstecken und für sich leben möchten – auch die
Weisen, Frommen, Stillen im Lande! Hohn über ihre *genießende*
Einsamkeit!
　　Alle *schöpferischen* Naturen ringen um Einfluß,
auch wenn sie allein leben – "*Nachruhm*" ist nur ein
falscher Ausdruck für das, was sie wollen.
　　Die ungeheure Aufgabe des Herrschenden, der sich selber
erzieht – die Art Menschen und Volk, über welche er herrschen
will, muß in ihm *vorgebildet* sein: *da* muß er erst Herr
geworden sein!
　　Alle Tugend und *Selbstüberwindung* hat nur
Sinn als Vorbereitung des *Herrschenden!*
　　Gegen alle **bloß** Genießenden! Auch die Einsamkeit
als Selbstgenuß, selbst die des Selbstquälers.[...]
　　Forderung: das neue Gesetz muß *erfüllbar* sein –
und aus der Erfüllung muß die Überwindung und das höhere
Gesetz wachsen. Zarathustra giebt die Stellung zum Gesetz,
indem er das "Gesetz der Gesetze", die Moral *aufhebt*.
　　Gesetze als Rückgrat.
　　an ihnen arbeiten und schaffen, indem man sie vollzieht.
Bisheriger Sklavensinn *vor* dem Gesetze! [...]
　　Nicht Ein Ideal des Weisen, sondern *hundert Ideale des
Thoren* will ich aufstellen! Zarathustra 4.
　　Gegen die bärbeißige schauspielerische stoische Herrlichkeit
des "Weisen".

Typus des Gesetzgebers, seine Entwicklung und
sein Leiden.
Welchen Sinn hat es überhaupt, Gesetze zu geben?
Zarathustra ist der Herold, der viele Gesetzgeber aufruft.

Cf. 7[6] 12.275 (excerpt)

[...] man gehorcht lieber einem vorhandenen Gesetz als daß man sich ein Gesetz *schafft*, als daß man sich und Anderen befiehlt. Die Furcht vor dem Befehlen – Lieber sich unterwerfen als reagiren.

16[88], KSA 10.531 (excerpt)

The rights that I have conquered *for myself* I will not *give* to the other: rather, he ought to *rob* them for himself! like me – and [he] may appropriate them and *wrest* them from me! To this extent there must be a law which emanates from me, as if it wanted to make all into my likeness: so that the individual [*Einzelne*] discovers and strengthens itself in contradiction with it [...]
Scorn at the slavish *subjection* in
morality (under the old law of one or other human being)
To form a long-lasting individual (a people) in order to translate one's thoughts into flesh blood and will

Whoever *appropriates* a right will not *give* this right to the other – but will be an opponent to him *insofar as he appropriates it for himself:* the love of the father who clashes with his son.
The great educator, like nature: he must pile up *obstacles*, so that they are *overcome*.

Die Rechte, die ich *mir* erobert habe, werde ich dem
Anderen nicht *geben:* sondern er soll sie sich *rauben!* gleich
mir – und mag sie nehmen und mir *abzwingen*! Insofern
muß ein Gesetz da sein, welches von mir ausgeht, als ob es Alle zu
meinem Ebenbilde machen wolle: damit der Einzelne sich im
Widerspruch mit ihm entdecke und stärke [...]
Hohn gegen die sklavenhafte *Unterwerfung* in der
Moral (unter das alte Gesetz irgend eines Menschen)
Ein langdauerndes Individuum bilden (ein Volk), um
seine Gedanken in Fleisch Blut und Wille zu übersetzen

Wer ein Recht sich *nimmt*, wird dies Recht dem Anderen
nicht *geben* – sondern ihm Gegner sein, *indem er es
sich nimmt:* die Liebe des Vaters, der dem Sohn
widerstrebt.
Der große Erzieher wie die Natur: er muß *Hindernisse*
thürmen, damit sie *überwunden* werden.

Chapter 7
Law and Community in the Agon: Agonal Communities of Taste and Lawfulness without a Law

Introduction

As argued in chapter 3, agonal texts do not consist simply of dyadic confrontations with Nietzsche's chosen representatives of the values under critique. The ancient Greek agon, Nietzsche's model for critique, was deeply embedded in communal life, mores and institutions, and artists were dependent on 'the right public' for adjudicating performances and outcomes (16[21], KSA 7.402). But what *is* the '*right* public' (*das* rechte *Publikum*)? From what standpoint is it right (*recht*) – and by what standard of judgement or justice (*Gerechtigkeit*)? At stake here is the question of judgement or adjudication in the agon, of the law or standard of adjudication, or of justice. As readers of Nietzsche's texts, the agon also implicates us as a public, together with his chosen adversaries in his critical confrontations. We can speak of an agonal law of production regulating his transvaluative texts *only if* production is inseparable from the question of interpretation: how to understand and adjudicate his agonal confrontations? What does it mean to respond to them and interpret them *in agonal terms*? And for Nietzsche's readership, too, the question of 'the *right* public' needs to be raised. What is an *agonal community of readers* today? And by what standard or law can this community be convoked and constituted as the *right* readership? These questions, first raised in chapter 3, will now be pursued from a perspective in law by asking: What is the nature and status of law in an 'agonal community'?[1] In what sense can we speak of justice (*Gerechtigkeit, Dike*) as a standard of adjudication binding the public with agonal contestants, us readers, with Nietzsche's critical confrontations?

Given Nietzsche's focus on values and the project of transvaluating all values, we also need to ask whether there is an *ethical* dimension to the question of law in the

---

[1] Interesting work has been done by political theorists and legal scholars on agonism as a contender to liberal theories of law, which brings social and political struggles to our understanding of the nature and role of legal and political institutions in contemporary democracies. Minkkinen (2020) provides an overview, somewhat flawed by reducing disagreements in democracy to conflicting interests and interest groups; agonistic democracy is not about interest group politics. An excellent collection of papers is to be found in *Law and Agonistic Politics* (2009), edited by Andrew Schaap. One author, above all, deserves mention in this connection: Hans Lindahl (2008, 2009). In my view, however, these questions should be preceded and informed by an investigation into the nature and status of law in the agon, and specifically, Nietzsche's concept of the agon, which has been inspirational for most agonistic democratic theories. This chapter is an attempt to make good this deficit.

agon, something like an 'agonal ethos' (as many contemporary scholars and agonistic theorists believe) or ethical law binding participants and public.[2] It is clear that the *Wettkampf* involves a degree of measure entirely lacking in the *Vernichtungskampf:* a 'reciprocal holding within the bounds of measure'. In what sense, if at all, can we speak of an ethical law regulating and measuring agonal forms of engagement and interaction?

As the principle regulating the production-interpretation of Nietzsche's transvaluative texts, the agon can also be expected to house an *epistemic* dimension. Indeed, in the absence thereof, agonal readings would be easy prey to critics like Habermas, according to whom Nietzsche's total critique of reason leads him to *abandon the claims of reason* altogether and capitulate to the Other of reason in the name of aesthetic and archaic values such as the 'Tragic', the 'Dionysian', the 'Noble' (Habermas) or – we might add – the 'Agonal'. So in what sense (if at all) can we identify an agonal episteme, one that does not appeal to the Other of reason, but could sustain the claims of Nietzsche's total critique of values as a viable *philosophical* project? And what would be the normative status of such an episteme in relation to the claims of modern science underwritten by Kant and much post-Kantian thought?

In response to these questions, I will argue in this chapter that the concept of taste (*Geschmack*) best encapsulates the nature and status of law in Nietzsche's concept of the agon, for which I draw on the Kantian expression *Gesetzmässigkeit ohne Gesetz* or 'lawfulness without law'. But the concept of taste in question is not so much Kantian as pre-Kantian. In the western philosophical tradition prior to Kant, social, ethical and epistemic qualities have been ascribed to taste, and various moments from this tradition can be traced to Nietzsche's texts, invoking a sense of community with substantive ethical and epistemic dimensions: an 'agonal community of taste'.

For Nietzsche, as we saw in the introduction to chapter 6, traditional and prevailing notions of law are problematic because they are life-negating. On the other hand, Nietzsche's one-world hypothesis means that law can only be internal to life in its character as a multiple and incessant *Fest-setzen* of being; that life is inescapably, immanently law-bound. In response to this double-bind, Nietzsche cannot possibly reject law in the name of life, and his thought gravitates instead around the task of *differential evaluation:* to discriminate between different meanings of the word, between different kinds or forms of law, and to interrogate them from a standpoint in life; that is, in terms of the value or *quality of life* they exhibit or make possible.[3]

---

[2] See the Introduction, note 8 on agonistic respect. See also note 14 below on the 'fundamental immunity to the normative rule making so dear to ethics' in competitive sports, both ancient and modern.

[3] See e.g. 1[63], KSA 10: 'Wer nach Größe strebt, hat Gründe in der Quantität seine Vollendung und Befriedigung zu haben. *Die Menschen der Qualität streben nach Kleinheit.*'; 26[224], KSA 11: 'Daß mit der Einsicht in die *Entstehung* der moralischen Werthurtheile noch nicht eine Kritik und Werthbestimmung derselben gegeben ist – ebenso wenig eine Qualität durch Kenntniß der quantitativen Bedin-

Nietzsche's genealogical questioning concerns the forms of life, the dispositions, attitudes or types that flourish under the rule of law: What form of life is conditioned, preserved or fostered by (this or that kind of) law, and what quality of life does it exhibit? At stake in these reflections is the philosophical task of determining the value, worth or quality of diverse forms of human life. The problem here is to find the right form or measure (*Maass*) of law, so that law works not just *against* life, but *with and against* it. My contention in this chapter is that Nietzsche locates the right measure of law in an agonal community of taste, which represents or pre-figures the highest form of life in his eyes.

The argument begins (I) with an examination of the concept of 'immanent lawfulness' (*immanente Gesetzmässigkeit*), which, Nietzsche claims, Heraclitus drew from the agon. This section serves to advance the *medial sense of law and justice*, elaborated in the rest of the chapter under the sign of 'taste'. The bulk of the chapter concerns Nietzsche's sense of community and its relation to law. By drawing on the notion of taste, I reconstruct an agonal sense of community around the pre-Socratic notion of wisdom presented by Nietzsche in PHG as an *episteme of taste*, which is legislative but indemonstrable (II.1). I then turn to the question of *ethical law*, focusing first on Nietzsche's perfectionist ideal, which I interpret as a radically indeterminate norm embodied in the 'agonal communities of taste' invoked by transvaluative texts (II.2). The argument works by drawing a key figure in the history of taste, the seventeenth century Jesuit philosopher Baltasar Gracián, and a number of analogies between his social ideal of taste or 'gusto' and the agon, both of which imply a *medial sense of justice* (II.3). In the last part of the chapter (III), I revisit the agonal concept of measure, in order to propose two analogies with Nietzsche's medial sense of law, both of which incorporate a medial sense of measure. The first concerns Homer's *Iliad*, understood as a pre-moral text, which nonetheless houses a sense of justice embodied in Zeus' 'equilibrium of sympathy'; the second analogy concerns the notion of freedom developed by Hannah Arendt through an analysis of action in relation to what she (following Montesquieu) calls 'principles'.

---

gungen, unter denen sie entsteht, erklärt ist.'; 27[5], KSA 11: 'Wer die Bedingungen eingesehn hat, unter denen eine moral‹ische› Schätzung entstanden ist, hat ihren Werth damit noch nicht berührt: es sind viele nützliche Dinge, und ebenso wichtige Einsichten auf fehlerhafte und unmethodische Weise gefunden worden; und jede Qualität ist noch unbekannt, auch wenn man begriffen hat, unter welchen Bedingungen sie entsteht.'; also 2[76], KSA 12: '"Mechanistische Auffassung": will nichts als Quantitäten: aber die Kraft steckt in der Qualität: die Mechanistik kann also nur Vorgänge beschreiben, nicht erklären.'

I Immanent DIKE

For preliminary orientation on the nature and status of law in the agon, I turn to the young Nietzsche's engagement with Heraclitus in his lectures on 'The Pre-Platonic Philosophers' (*Die vorplatonische Philosophen:* VPP) and in the unpublished text 'Philosophy in the Tragic Age of the Greeks' (*Philosophie im tragischen Zeitalter der Griechen:* PHG).[4] These texts are an important source for Nietzsche's one-world hypothesis and the demand to rethink law in radically immanent terms. But they are also important because, in his interpretation of the Heraclitean identity of justice and war, *Dike* and *Polemos*, Nietzsche formulates the concept of 'immanent lawfulness' (*immanente Gesetzmässigkeit*)[5] by analogy with the agon:

> [C]onflict as the continuous effectivity [*Wirken*] of a unitary lawful rational Δίκη, an idea drawn from the deepest fundaments of Greek existence. It is Hesiod's good Eris made into the world-principle. The Greeks are distinguished by the contest, above all by the immanent lawfulness in the deciding of the contest. Every single being [*Einzelne*] fights as if it alone were in the right: but an infinitely sure measure of adjudicating judgement decides where victory is leaning. H. had come to know this type of πόλεμος from the gymnasia, from the musical agons, from the life of the state. The thought of πόλεμος – δίκη is the first specifically *Hellenic* thought in philosophy, which is not to say that it is not of universal, but only national validity: rather: only a Greek was in the position such a sublime thought of cosmodicy. (VPP 10, KGW II/4.272)[6]

---

4 On Nietzsche and Heraclitus, see Herschbell and Nimis 1979; Busch 1989, 271 ff.; and Hölscher 1977.
5 See also: 'Δίκη is not supposed to punish: it is the immanent lawfulness' ('Die Δίκη soll nicht strafen: sie ist die immanente Gesetzmäßigkeit': VPP 10, KGW II/4.281). Also, on the Heraclitean world-child: 'The child then throws the toy away: but soon it starts all over again in innocent caprice. But as soon as it builds, it connects, joins and forms in a lawful manner and according to inner orders' ('Das Kind wirft einmal das Spielzeug weg: bald aber fängt es wieder an, in unschuldiger Laune. Sobald es [das Kind] aber baut, knüpft und fügt und formt es gesetzmäßig und nach inneren Ordnungen': PHG 7, KSA 1.831; cf. PHG 19, KSA 1.872: 'zwecklos'; VPP 10, KGW II/4.278). Nietzsche goes on to compare Heraclitus' world-view with the aesthetic human's, who sees in the creation of the art-work 'how the conflict of the multiplicity can nonetheless bear law and right within it […] how necessity and play, discord and harmony must couple for the (pro)creation of the art-work' ('wie der Streit der Vielheit doch in sich Gesetz und Recht tragen kann […] wie Nothwendigkeit und Spiel, Widerstreit und Harmonie sich zur Zeugung des Kunstwerkes paaren müssen'). For immanent or absolute lawfulness in Heraclitus, see also 19[114], KSA 7.456; 21[9], KSA 7.525; 23[35], KSA 7.555; 6[21], KSA 8.106; PHG 19, KSA 1.869 for Nietzsche's Heraclitean interpretation of Anaxagoras. Also 38[12], KSA 11.611 for a late Heraclitean vision.
6 '[D]er Streit als das fortwährende Wirken einer einheitlichen gesetzmäßigen vernünftigen Δίκη, eine Vorstellung, die aus dem tiefsten Fundament des griechischen Wesens geschöpft ist. Es ist die gute Eris Hesiods, zum Weltprinzip gemacht. Die Griechen unterscheidet der Wettkampf, vor allem aber die immanente Gesetzmäßigkeit im Entscheiden des Wettkampfes. Jedes Einzelne kämpft als ob es allein berechtigt sei: aber ein unendlich sicheres Maß des richterl. Urtheils entscheidet, wohin der Sieg sich lenkt. Aus den Gymnasien, aus den musikal. Agonen, aus dem Staatsleben hatte H. das Typische dieses πόλεμος kennen gelernt. Der Gedanke von πόλεμος – δίκη ist der erste spezifisch *hellenische* Gedanke in der Philosophie, womit nicht gesagt ist, daß er nicht universal, sondern nur national gültig sei: sondern vielmehr: nur ein Grieche war im Stande, einen so erhabe-

In both VPP and PHG Nietzsche places tremendous emphasis on Heraclitus' conception of unity (his 'ungeheure Einheitsvorstellung'), embodied above all in 'the unitary lawfulness of the world' ('die einheitliche Gesetzmäßigkeit der Welt': VPP 10, KGW II/4.266) or what he here calls 'unitary, lawful rational Δίκη'. At issue in this unitary concept of justice, as the closing reference to cosmodicy in the above passage indicates, is the affirmation or justification of the cosmos in its character as becoming – what, for Nietzsche, will become the problem of life-affirmation at the centre of his project of transvaluation. For Nietzsche's Heraclitus the justification of becoming is pitted against Anaximander's (and Schopenhauer's!) identification of becoming and multiplicity with injustice (ἀδικία) and its atonement in death and the passing away (φθορά) of all things (VPP 10, KGW II/4.271). Nietzsche's argument is that the negation of becoming as injustice and punishment is the consequence of an incoherent dualism in Anaximander (and Parmenides), so that life-affirmation requires breaking the opposition between the One, as a static world of indeterminacy (ἄπειρον), and the physical world of determinate qualities in continual becoming: 'But if becoming and passing away are the effects of one δίκη, then there is no such dualism between a world of ἄπειρον and [one] of the qualities' (VPP 10, KGW II/4.271).[7] Hence, the emphasis of Nietzsche's Heraclitus on unity, one world, and the One qua Δίκη and lawfulness ('Gesetzmäßigkeit') as *immanent* to multiplicity and becoming.

We see Nietzsche struggling to make sense of this thought, when he writes (above) of becoming and passing away as 'effects' (*Wirkungen*) of 'one δίκη', or as the 'continuous revelation of existence [*Existenzoffenbarung*] of the One', or of multiplicity as 'the garment [*Gewand*], form of appearance [*Erscheinungsform*] of the One' (VPP, KGW II/4.270 – 1).[8] Perhaps most telling for the difficulty here is the criticism of Anaximander's dualism as incoherent in VPP, and the alternative put forward by Nietzsche's Heraclitus:

> "All that is furnished with qualities comes to be and passes away: hence there must be a being without qualities" was Anaximander's teaching [...] But how can that which bears qualities, that which is becoming, come out of the ἄπειρον? And how can a world with eternal lawfulness in its entirety like this be a world of nothing but particular ἀδικίαι? (VPP, KGW II/4.271)[9]

---

nen Gedanken der Cosmodicee zu finden.' See also the corresponding passage in PHG 5, KSA 1.825, cited in note 11 below.

7 'Wenn aber Werden u. Vergessen Wirkungen einer δίκη sind, so giebt es auch keinen solchen Dualismus zwischen einer Welt des ἄπειρον u. der Qualitäten.' 'Vergessen' should presumably be 'Vergehen': 'passing away', not 'forgetting'.

8 'Alle Qualitäten der Dinge, alle Gesetze, alles Entstehen [und] Vergehen, ist [die] fortwährende Existenzoffenbarung des Einen: die Vielheit [...] ist für Heraclit das Gewand, die Erscheinungsform des Einen, keineswegs eine Täuschung: anders überhaupt erscheint das Eine nicht.'

9 '"Alles mit Qualitäten Versehene entsteht u. vergeht: also muß es ein qualitätsloses Sein geben" war Anaximander's Lehre. [...] Aber wie kann aus dem ἄπειρον das mit Qualitäten Behaftete, das Werdende werden? Und wie kann eine Welt mit solcher ewigen Gesetzmäßigkeit im Ganzen eine Welt lauter einzelner ἀδικίαι sein?' Already in 1867, in the critical notes known as 'Zu Schopenhauer',

To which Nietzsche's Heraclitus responds:

> [T]he qualities are, after all, instruments of coming to be and passing away, hence instruments of Δίκη. The ἀρχή, the One in coming to be and passing away, must therefore rather be in the right even in its qualities: in opposition to Anaximander, it must consequently have all the predicates, all the qualities, because they all bear witness to δίκη. (VPP, KGW II/4.271)[10]

But if the One has all the predicates and qualities, it is hard to see how it can be thought as One. It seems that, in the effort to think the One as immanent to multiplicity, Nietzsche's Heraclitus has instead assimilated the many into the One, leaving its oneness in tatters.

Nietzsche's awareness of this problem can be seen in his subsequent appeal to the agon as a source of unity. Becoming and the multiplicity of qualities are referred by Heraclitus to the never-ending conflict (*Streit, Kampf, Krieg*) of opposed qualities, and this conflict, in turn, is referred back to unitary lawfulness: the 'continual effectivity of a unitary, lawful rational Δίκη' ('das fortwährende Wirken einer einheitlichen gesetzmäßigen vernünftigen Δίκη'), a 'specifically Hellenic' thought that Nietzsche claims was born of the good Eris of the agon. Or, as Nietzsche puts it in PHG:

> It is a wonderful idea, drawn from the purest springs of Hellenism, the view of strife as the continual exercise of a unitary justice, bound to everlasting laws [...] it is the contest-idea [*Wettkampfgedanke*] of the Greek individual and the Greek state, taken from the gymnasium and the palaestra, from the artists' agons, from the contest between political parties and between cities – all transferred into the most universal realm [*in's Allgemeinste übertragen*] so that now the wheels of the cosmos turn on it. Just as the Greek individual fights as though he alone were right, and an infinitely sure measure of adjudicating judgement determines where victory is leaning in every moment, so the qualities wrestle with one another, in accordance with inviolable laws and standards [measures] that are immanent to the struggle. (PHG, KSA 1.825 f.)[11]

Nietzsche had already denounced the dualism of Schopenhauer's philosophy as incoherent in a similar fashion. See *Zu Schopenhauer*, dated Oktober 1867 – April 1868, in KGW I/4.421 ff.; also in: BAW III 352–370 (452–3 for *Nachbericht*).

10 '[D]ie Qualitäten sind ja Werkzeuge des Entstehens u. Vergehens, also Werkzeuge der Δίκη. Vielmehr muß die ἀρχή, das Eine im Entstehen u. Vergehen, also auch in seinen Qualitäten im Recht sein: im Gegensatz zu Anaximander muß es demnach alle Prädikate, alle Qualitäten haben, weil alle Zeugniß von δίκη ablegen.'

11 'Es ist eine wundervolle, aus dem reinsten Borne des Hellenischen geschöpfte Vorstellung, welche den Streit als das fortwährende Walten einer einheitlichen, strengen, an ewige Gesetze gebundenen Gerechtigkeit betrachtet [...] es ist die gute Eris Hesiods, zum Weltprincip verklärt, es ist der Wettkampfgedanke des einzelnen Griechen und des griechischen Staates, aus den Gymnasien und Palästren, aus den künstlerischen Agonen, aus dem Ringen der politischen Parteien und der Städte mit einander, in's Allgemeinste übertragen, so daß jetzt das Räderwerk des Kosmos in ihm sich dreht. Wie jeder Grieche kämpft als ob er allein im Recht sei, und ein unendlich sicheres Maaß des richterlichen Urtheils in jedem Augenblick bestimmt, wohin der Sieg sich neigt, so ringen die Qualitäten mit einander, nach unverbrüchlichen, dem Kampfe immanenten Gesetzen und Maaßen.'

Both here and in the corresponding passage from VPP (see p. 187), the agon is proposed as a metaphor or analogy (*Übertragung*) for the oneness in multiplicity of Heraclitus' immanent justice. For the agon, we are told, is bound to the eternal laws of unitary justice. Yet, on its own, this claim does nothing to explain how the agonal conflict that gives rise to becoming and multiplicity can be thought as the 'effectivity' or 'exercise' (*Wirken, Walten*) of a unitary, lawful justice. What kind of oneness is it that characterises agonal strife?

In a remarkable note from the *Nachlass* to *Homer's Wettkampf* Nietzsche answers just this question:

> 2. *Wonderful* process, how the generalised conflict [*Kampf*] of all Greeks gradually comes to acknowledge one δίκη in all areas: where does this come from?
> The contest unleashes the individual: and at the same time, it restrains [or measures: *bändigt*] the individual according to eternal laws.
> The gods in feud. The *wars of the Titans* know *nothing* as yet about the *contest*.
> The most ancient Greece exhibits the most brutal unleashing of Eris.
> 2. The Panhellenic festivals: unity of the Greeks in the
> Norms of the contest.
> 2. *Struggle before a tribunal*. (16[22], KSA 7.402)[12]

As this note makes clear, the agon among city-states did not *presuppose* a unitary concept of justice. On the contrary, Nietzsche appeals to the socialising, unifying powers of the agon to explain the '[w]*onderful process*' through which all the Greeks came to acknowledge a common sense of justice. As Nietzsche's colleague, Jacob Burckhardt, describes it, the Panhellenic festivals were decisive in breaking down the enmity between tribes and mutually hostile poleis: 'It was the agon alone which united the whole nation as both participants and spectators', so that during the truces that held for the duration of the festivals, citizens of warring poleis could not only compete peacefully but also mingle with each other.[13] But how exactly

---

12 '2. *Wunderbarer* Prozeß, wie der allgemeine Kampf
aller Griechen allmählich auf allen Gebieten eine δίκη
anerkennt: wo kommt diese her? Der Wettkampf entfesselt das
Individuum: und zugleich bändigt er dasselbe nach ewigen
Gesetzen.
 Die Götter in Fehde. Die *Titanenkämpfe* wissen noch
nichts vom *Wettkampf*.
 Das älteste Griechenland zeigt die roheste Entfesselung der
Eris.
 2. Die panhellenischen Feste: Einheit der Griechen in den
Normen des Wettkampfes.
 2. *Kampf vor einem Tribunal*'

13 See Pearson (2019, 49), who quotes Burckhardt (1998, 168–9): 'The establishment of these Panhellenic sites [...] was uniquely decisive in breaking down enmity between tribes, and remained the most powerful obstacle to fragmentation into mutually-hostile *poleis*. It was the agon alone which united the whole nation as both participants and spectators [...]. The extraordinary thing is

are we to understand the emergence of a shared concept of justice from the socialising powers of the agon?

In this note, Nietzsche draws on the distinction, familiar from HW, between the lawless and unmeasured 'war of annihilation' or *Vernichtungskampf* – associated here with the Titans and the most ancient Greeks – and the contest or *Wettkampf*, in order to underline the sense of *measure* that made agonal conflict productive rather than destructive, and unified the Greek nation during the festival. Unlike HW, however, this note does not inscribe measure in agonal relations – 'reciprocal provocation and reciprocal holding within the bounds of measure' (HW, KSA 1.789) – but ascribes it instead to the 'everlasting laws' and 'norms of the contest' that unified the Greeks. Yet, these laws are emphatically plural in Nietzsche's text, and it is unclear how they relate the unitary sense of justice that he also emphasizes. The simplest explanation for the emergence a common sense of justice is that it came out of a process of negotiation and agreement on the norms of the agon that competitors and judges brought with them from their various tribes and poleis. But how exactly are we to understand these 'everlasting laws' or 'norms' of measure in the agon? How, in particular, can they be seen as 'everlasting' or 'eternal' (*ewig*)?

It is tempting to think of the agonal 'norms' of measure along the lines of contemporary sports, as explicit and impartial rules of fair play that are fixed in advance and external to the course of each contest.[14] But this would be wrong for several rea-

---

that different sections of the nation not only competed together at these famous sites but also mingled with each other, so that during the truce that reigned for their duration even the citizens of warring *poleis* could meet in peace. About Olympia in particular there was a special sacredness for the whole nation, and the games there, which had been largely Peloponnesian at the start, slowly became the unique revelation of Greek unity [*Einheit*] in the true sense of the word, whether of those living in the motherland or in the colonies.' See also Fisher (2009, 256), quoted in Tuncel 2009, 157 f. on the interstate games having 'great value in creating cohesion of spirit and co-operation inside Greek communities, and building ideals of Panhellenic unity across the Greek world, however often these tendencies towards consensus were threatened or destroyed by wars and civil conflicts.' See Tuncel 2009 for further contemporary literature on this topic.

14 As mentioned in chapter 2 (note 12) Tuncel's remarks on fair play and justice in the archaic Greek agon concern only athletic contests. The question is: what do we learn from contemporary sports / athletics about the archaic Greek agon and/or Nietzsche's concept of the agon? For Tuncel (2016), athletic competition serves as a model for Nietzsche's agon, and the agon offers a 'hermeneutic key' to sports. Yet, there are salient differences between them that cannot be overlooked: the micro-quantification of achievement in modern sports, the technological-pharmacological micro-management of the body, the use of performance drugs, among others. And where, despite these differences, sports historians do see a similarity, it is precisely in the problematic relation between performance and rules for athletes. Performance requires the 'removal of virtually all restraints on the development of athletic powers' (Hoberman 1997, 294 f.), a kind of unmeasured ambition, and rule-following inhibits the spontaneity and flexibility needed for an athlete's maximal performance. Hoberman refers to the sports historian Gebauer, who emphasises 'the competitor's search for almost any kind of advantage over his rival and his mobilization of both physical and mental capabilities in the pursuit of victory. The "spirit" or "essence" of the game that corresponds to this agon cannot appropriately be gov-

sons. In the first place, as mentioned in chapter 2 (p. 45f.), the idea of fair play was an invention of British public schools of the 18th and 19th centuries; as Nietzsche and Burckhardt were well aware, it is totally alien to the agonal Greeks, who were inveterate cheats. Secondly, the strongest formulations of the unitary lawfulness of the agon are to be found in Nietzsche's account of Heraclitus, and even here they are described not as explicit rules, but as 'unwritten laws':

> For this one world which he retained – bounded by eternal unwritten laws, flowing upward and downward in brazen rhythmic beat – nowhere shows an enduring, an indestructibility, a bulwark in the stream. (PHG 5, KSA 1.823)[15]

The context is Heraclitus' negation of being (*Sein*) in favour of the one world of becoming (*Werden*), where everything is in a kind of rhythmic flux; it would be odd, if not self-defeating, for Nietzsche's Heraclitus to posit fixed, enduring, indestructible laws in the very same context.[16] On the contrary, the emphasis throughout both PHG and VPP is on the *immanent lawfulness* ('immanente Gesetzmäßigkeit': VPP 10, KGW II/4.272, cited above) of the agon and, by analogy, of Heraclitus' unitary justice; that is, immanent to the one world of becoming in upward and downward flux. And yet, as Nietzsche's Heraclitus also insists, the laws of the agon are also eternal or everlasting: *ewig*.

Perhaps a clue to these unwritten laws, immanent to agonal struggle and yet eternal, lies in the *festival character* of the Panhellenic agon, mentioned in note 16[22] ('Die panhellenischen Feste: Einheit der Griechen in den Normen des Wettkampfes'). As laws of the agonal festival they would have been considered eternal, part of the founding of the festival and the legend of the festival site.[17] At the

---

erned by the "rules" of a game, since the proscriptions inherent in such regulations will damage the scope and spontaneity of the creative agon.' (Hoberman 1997, 294f.). According to Gebauer, the tension between maximal performance and rule-following means that competitive sports, both ancient and modern, exhibit a 'fundamental immunity to the normative rule making so dear to ethics'. (Gebauer 1990, 468, in: Hoberman 1997, 295). In this chapter, overly-regularian interpretations of Nietzsche's concept of the agon are also problematised.

15 'Denn diese eine Welt, die er übrig behielt – umschirmt von ewigen ungeschriebenen Gesetzen, auf- und niederfluthend im ehernen Schlage des Rhythmus – zeigt nirgends ein Verharren, eine Unzerstörbarkeit, ein Bollwerk im Strome.'

16 This is my disagreement with James Pearson (2019, 46f.), who does not seem to see a problem with the notion of eternal, fixed laws being immanent to flux and struggle, even if it makes Nietzsche's account of the Heraclitean cosmos incoherent ('while this law is immanent to the universal flux of becoming, it is not itself subject to the change and fluctuation over which it legislates') and claims that Nietzsche interprets Heraclitus' eternal law as 'something akin to natural-scientific law', even though Nietzsche writes of 'unwritten laws'.

17 See Nietzsche's anti-Aristotelian interpretation of the word 'drama':

'Das Wort Drama ist dorischer Herkunft: und nach dorischem Sprachgebrauch bedeutet es "Ereigniss," "Geschichte," beide Worte in hieratischem Sinne. Das älteste Drama stellte die Ortslegende dar, die "heilige Geschichte," auf der die Gründung des Cultus ruhte (– also kein Thun,

same time, it was only during the periodic celebration of the festival that they were actually in force, fully present and 'immanent' to the agonal contests being performed each time. Indeed, with Gadamer and Kerenyi,[18] we can go one step further and say: the eternal laws of the festival have their being (*Sein*) and identity only in being celebrated periodically, since it lies in the character of festivals, in their origin or founding, that they should be regularly celebrated. Yet each festival is different from others insofar as it is celebrated in specific circumstances, with these contestants and these spectators at this historical juncture. It is therefore part of the original meaning and identity of the festival that it is always different. We can, then, say of the festival – and by analogy the lawfulness of the agon – that it is something that has its identity of being (*Sein*) only in becoming and recurring (*Werden, Wiederkehren*): it *is* only insofar as it is always different.

The festival character of the agon gives a radically temporal structure (always different) and open-endedness to the eternal laws of the agon, but also an identity of meaning over time (eternal): namely, as unitary justice or (for Nietzsche's Heraclitus) as the immanent justification of reality as becoming. It is, in other words, fully in line with Heraclitus' dynamic yet regulated world of becoming. For the laws are not to be thought as having an original being or meaning at the foundation of the festival, as fixed and explicit rules for every contest; and thereafter being celebrated in this way, then in that way in always-different repetitions. Rather, the identity and meaning of the rules of the agon, their being (*Sein*), is constituted in being celebrated in always different ways (*Werden*).[19] If the laws of the agon have a unitary identity and meaning over time, but also a certain open-endedness, it is because they are not external to the agon, as fixed rules governing all contests, but immanent to the course taken by each and therefore open to the next contest.

It is the open-endedness of the rules or norms of the agon that allowed for negotiations among competitors and judges, leading to the gradual emergence of a

---

sondern ein Geschehen: δρᾶν heisst im Dorischen gar nicht "thun").' (WA 9, KSA 6.32). Also 14[127], KSA 13.309: 'Der Gott wählt aus, der Gott wird Mensch, oder Gott wohnt mit Menschen zusammen und hinterläßt große Wohlthaten, die Ortslegende, als "Drama" ewig dargestellt. And 14[14], KSA 13.224 f.: 'der Ursprung der Tragödie und Komödie als ein *Gegenwärtig-sehen* eines göttlichen Typus im Zustand einer Gesammt-Verzückung, als ein Miterleben der Ortslegende, des Besuchs, Wunders, Stiftungsakts, des "Dramas" –'. See also note 19 below on 2[120], KSA 12.121.

18 Gadamer 1996, 103–104. Gadamer refers to the work of Walter Otto and Karl Kerenyi: *Vom Wesen des Festes* (1938). On the archaic agon as festival, see Tuncel 2009 151–157; and Tuncel 2016, 353–355.

19 For Nietzsche, the ancient Greek cults celebrated a one-off (*einmalig*) event, the coming to presence of a god, but they did so by fixing (*fest-stellen*) this event and its sense (*Sinn*) through repetition (*immer wieder*):

'Alle Culte stellen ein *einmaliges* Erlebniß, das
Zusammenkommen mit einem Gotte, einen Heils-Akt in irgend
einem Sinne, fest, und führen es immer wieder vor. Die
Ortslegende als Ursprung eines Dramas: wo die Poesie den Gott
spielt.' (2[120], KSA 12.121)

common sense of justice among the Greeks through the Panhellenic festivals. Indeed, this process exemplifies the more general thesis advanced by Nietzsche in MA that law and justice derive from *an approximate equilibrium among more-or-less equal powers*.[20] It is important to recall Burckhardt's point concerning the suspension of hostilities between the tribes and poleis during the festivals. This allowed competitors to encounter and engage one another *as equals* in the agon, unleashing its unifying forces.[21] We can therefore say: the suspension of political hostilities for the duration of the agonal festival allows for *an equilibrium among more-or-less equal powers*, a *Gleichgewicht der Mächte*. Since this is a key condition for the agon (as argued in chapter 3), Nietzsche's thesis in note 16[22] would be: it was the agon among a plurality of more-or-less equal powers that led to a gradual recognition of a common sense of justice among Greeks. But according to MA, the *Gleichgewicht der Mächte* is also the origin of law and in social life überhaupt. We can therefore say: the festival character of the agon is such that, in suspending existing socio-political power relations and establishing an equilibrium among more-or-less equal forces, it *enacts and re-enacts the foundation of law and justice at the origin of social life*.

For a good illustration of what these formulations mean in practice, we can return to MA 170 and two related features of the agon that it brings to light (see chapter 2 p. 75ff.). The first concerns the *scope* of contestation. In other, familiar competitive games, the rules for winning and losing are fixed and codified in advance of any particular bout. In the agon, as an open-ended contestation of excellence, these rules are open to contestation and the standard or measure of victory is determined *immanently* to the dynamic course of each contest. Contestants strive to win by determining anew what counts as winning; theirs is not just a contest of excellence in speech, works or deeds, but also of judgements: judgements of excellence, or a contestation of justice – of the very standard or measure of excellence and victory. It is distinctive of the agon as a form of play that it puts *both the question of adjudication and the standard or law of adjudication into play*.

As Nietzsche describes it in MA 170, the great tragedians did not work according to prevailing taste or standards; instead, each of them effectively reinvented tragedy by striving for victory 'in their own eyes', 'before their own seat of judgement'. Like Kant's genius, they created not just original works, but a new standard or rule for art; they were 'artistic legislators'. But at the same time, Nietzsche tells us, they were dependent on the public for victory. This is the second feature of the agon I would like to recall, and it means that agonal artists work according to their own 'artistic standard' *with and against* others. While free to follow their own law or judgement of excellence *against* prevailing taste, they are also constrained to win the con-

---

20 See MA 92, 93; WS 22, 26, 28, 29, 33, 39, 57 and Gerhardt (1983).
21 In GT, Nietzsche describes tragedy as a 'festival of reconciliation' (*Versöhnungsfest*) and goes so far as to say that 'now the slave is a free man': 'Jetzt ist der Sclave freier Mann, jetzt zerbrechen alle die starren, feindseligen Abgrenzungen, die Noth, Willkür oder "freche Mode" zwischen den Menschen festgesetzt haben.' (GT 1, KSA 1.29).

sent of others. And where this consent is wanting, they need to 'educate' the public to be receptive to their new standard, so as to receive in turn external consent (*Zustimmung von Aussen her*), confirmation (*Bestätigung*) of their judgement of excellence. As noted in chapter 3, this account confounds the opposition between artist and public[22] by drawing the public into the agon of judgements, while the contestants, in contesting the judgement and standard of excellence, are at the same time also part of the public.[23] In subverting this opposition, MA 170 in effect triangulates the agon as a contest of adjudication among the contestants and the public,[24] thereby displacing the locus of judgement. For it tells us that the standard of judgement resides neither with the public (prevailing opinion), nor simply with the artists, who

---

[22] See note 16[6], KSA 7.395 from the period of HW:
'7. Der Künstler und der Nichtkünstler. Was ist
Kunsturtheil? Dies das allgemeine Problem.
   Der Dichter nur möglich unter einem Publikum von
Dichtern. (Wirkung der Nibelungen Wagners.) Ein phantasiereiches
Publikum. Dies ist gleichsam sein Stoff, den er formt. Das
Dichten selbst nur eine Reizung und Leitung der Phantasie. Der
eigentliche Genuß das Produziren von Bildern, an der Hand
des Dichters. Also Dichter und Kritiker ein unsinniger
Gegensatz – sondern Bildhauer und Marmor, *Dichter* und
Stoff.
   Die Entscheidung im ἀγών ist nur das Geständniß: der und
der macht uns mehr zum Dichter: dem folgen wir, da schaffen
wir die Bilder schneller. Also ein künstlerisches Urtheil, aus
einer Erregung der künstlerischen Fähigkeit gewonnen. Nicht
aus *Begriffen*.
   So lebt der Mythus fort, indem der Dichter seinen Traum
überträgt. Alle Kunstgesetze beziehn sich auf das
Übertragen.
   Aesthetik hat nur Sinn als Naturwissenschaft: wie das
Apollinische und das Dionysische.'

[23] In the *Philologica*, it must be said, Nietzsche is quite dismissive of the public, emphasising the ancient Greeks' incapacity for aesthetic judgement. See e.g. GGL III, KGW II/5.323f., 329. Also: 9[9], KSA 7.274

[24] Note 16[22] ends by raising the question of adjudication under the heading : '2. Kampf vor einem Tribunal.' This question is then taken up in the subsequent note with a hypothesis concerning the etymology of the word 'agon' in 'scales' :
   'ἀγών vielleicht das "Wägen".
   Der Wagen und die Wage ist doch wohl von gleichem Stamme?' (16[23], KSA 7.402).
'Tribunal' means court of justice or judicial assembly, and originally had egalitarian connotations deriving from the latin 'tribunus' meaning 'magistrate', an officer appointed to protect the rights and interests of the plebeians against the patricians. Since there were originally three (tri–) magistrates, Nietzsche may be playing on this etymology to highlight the triangulation of adjudication among contestants and public in the agon. Another possible reference is to the official judges of athletic games, the *hellenodikai*, who were split into groups of three to preside over the games (Tuncel 2009, 170).

must win the public over in order to win, but somewhere in between them. Nietzsche makes this point with great precision in VPP, when he writes:

> The Greeks are distinguished by the contest, above all by the immanent lawfulness in deciding the contest. Every single being [*Einzelne*] fights as if it alone were in the right: but an infinitely sure measure of adjudicating judgement decides where victory is leaning. (VPP 10, KGW II/4.272)[25]
>
> ('Die Griechen unterscheidet der Wettkampf, vor allem aber die immanente Gesetzmäßigkeit im Entscheiden des Wettkampfes. Jedes Einzelne kämpft als ob es allein berechtigt sei: aber ein unendlich sicheres Maß des richterl. Urtheils entscheidet, wohin der Sieg sich lenkt.')

Here the 'immanent lawfulness' of the agon, is referred to the de-cision (*Ent-scheiden*) or judgement (*Ur-theil*) concerning victory and defeat. This judgement, Nietzsche writes, is determined by an 'infinitely sure measure (*Maß*) of adjudicating judgement', which 'decides where victory is leaning' in every moment. The standard or measure of judgement is therefore situated in the present regarding a victory yet to be won; that is, squarely *within* an ongoing contest, not in advance. This is not, however, to identify it with any of the contestants. The immanent measure of judgement is clearly set off (by the word 'but'[26]) and distinguished from the standpoint of the antagonists: it is because each antagonist 'struggles as if *he alone* were in the right' (*HS*), but they cannot both be, that a measure or standard of judgement is needed to adjudicate between them.[27] What, then, *is* this standard (*Maß*) of judgement? Who is the judge (*Richter*), and what is the standpoint of immanent adjudication? These questions are taken up in the opening lines of the subsequent section of PHG:

> While Heraclitus' imagination gauged the restlessly moving cosmos, "actuality", with the eye of a blissful spectator, who sees numberless pairs of contestants joyfully sparring under the super-

---

25 Cf. the corresponding passage in PHG:
   'Just as the Greek individual fights as though he alone were right and an infinitely sure measure of judicial opinion determines where victory is leaning in every moment, so the qualities wrestle with one another, in accordance with inviolable laws and standards that are immanent in the struggle.'
('Wie jeder Grieche kämpft als ob er allein im Recht sei, und ein unendlich sicheres Maaß des richterlichen Urtheils in jedem Augenblick bestimmt, wohin der Sieg sich neigt, so ringen die Qualitäten mit einander, nach unverbrüchlichen, dem Kampfe immanenten Gesetzen und Maaßen.': PHG 5, KSA 1.825).
26 The corresponding passage from PHG (cited in the above note) has the word 'and' in this place instead of 'but'. This is rather imprecise, since it suggests that the standpoint of adjudication is continuous with the contestants' standpoints, which cannot be the case, since each contestant fights 'as though he alone were right'.
27 This point eludes Tuncel, who ascribes a sense of fairness or justice to the contestants: the Greek 'agon relied on the sense of justice of the contestants' (Tuncel 2009, 169, note 55); 'the agonal Greeks agreed to uphold fair game' (Tuncel 2009, 171 note 63); also Tuncel 2016, 357 on the agonist who 'remains just and upholds the "norms of the contest" despite all personal injuries'.

vision of strict judges, a still greater intuition overtook him. He could no longer see the contesting pairs and their judges as separate from each other; the judges themselves seemed to be struggling in the contest and the contestants themselves seemed to be judging. Indeed, perceiving at bottom only the everlastingly ruling one justice, he dared proclaim: the struggle of the many is itself the one justice! And all in all: the one is the many. (PHG 6, KSA 1.826 f.)[28]

Nietzsche here draws on the two features of the agon described in MA 170 to pinpoint the standpoint of agonal adjudication. If the agon is an *inconclusive, open-ended contestation of justice or the standard of victory*, and if the public is implicated in the agon as a contestation of judgements or justice, then it is clear: the standpoint of adjudication cannot be separated from the contestants as external to their contestation. Yet we already know that it cannot be collapsed into the standpoint of any contestant or the public. The only alternative is that the standard or measure (*Mass*) of judgement is determined from a *medial position* in the *agonal relations between the contestants and the public*. This *medial sense of justice* will be taken up in the examination of Nietzsche's sense of community and its relation to ethical law.

II Agonal Communities of Taste

Nietzsche's thoughts on the nature and status of law and justice in the Greek agon will help us to understand the sense of community informing his transvaluative agons. The question here concerns the 'right' kind of readership – the kind of readership that would save him from philosophical exile. What is an *agonal community of readers*?

Nietzsche is commonly taken to be *autarkic individualist* (Stern, MacIntyre), philosophically insensitive to the sphere of social relations and deaf to the ethical claims of community. He is often thought to *abandon the claims of reason* altogether as a consequence of a totalizing critique of reason (Habermas), and to entrust our destiny to a *mighty act of will* on the part of superhuman redeemers (the *Übermensch*, Dionysos) who are yet to come: 'let will replace reason and let us make ourselves autonomous moral subjects by some gigantic and heroic act of the will…' (MacIntyre 1984, 114). In his book *Nietzsche and the Political*, Daniel Conway (1997) has offered a helpful corrective to this standard reading, focused on the character of ethical law in Nietzsche's thought. As the 'ethical core of Nietzsche's political thought' he identifies a commitment to the open-ended enhancement or perfection of human existence

---

[28] 'Während die Imagination Heraklit's das rastlos bewegte Weltall, die "Wirklichkeit" mit dem Auge des beglückten Zuschauers maß, der zahllose Paare, im freudigen Kampfspiele, unter der Obhut strenger Kampfrichter ringen sieht, überkam ihn eine noch höhere Ahnung; er konnte die ringenden Paare und die Richter nicht mehr getrennt von einander betrachten, die Richter selbst schienen zu kämpfen, die Kämpfer selbst schienen sich zu richten – ja, da er im Grunde nur die ewig waltende eine Gerechtigkeit wahrnam, so wagte er auszurufen: der Streit des Vielen selbst ist die eine Gerechtigkeit! Und überhaupt: das Eine ist das Viele.'

that is as absolute as it is indeterminate. This captures well the orientation towards the 'highest and noblest capacities' of the ancient Greeks in Nietzsche's concept of the agon, as well as the concern with life-enhancement driving his project of critical transvaluation. Nietzsche's perfectionist demand for self-transformation, far from being a solipsistic glorification of power, is inseparable from the creation of ethical communities. Exceptional individuals, Conway argues, are valued by Nietzsche for enhancing the life of particular ethical communities that spring up around them (1997, 24, 30 ff., 47 ff., 93 f.). Nietzsche's sense of community is encapsulated in a relation to ethical laws that bind collectively, but only across a limited group of people – particular communities.

This is a valuable suggestion that steers the only viable course between two extremes strongly criticised by Nietzsche: moral universalism (a relation to universal laws) on one side, and libertarian individualism or 'misarchism' (hatred of rule: JGB 188; GM II 12) on the other. It also serves to dismiss the accusation of an irrational, solipsistic glorification of power from Nietzsche's thought, for whom it is *only in relation to a concrete ethical community* that the exceptional individual (the genius, the *Übermensch*) stands a chance of extending and perfecting the concept 'human'.

However, Conway's actual account of community falls short of these insights. Nietzschean communities are said to consist only of aesthetic-affective bonds between self-sufficient beings who associate around an *Übermensch*-figure at their centre. As accidental associations between self-sufficient beings with a 'similar capacity for affective engagement and expression' (Conway 1997, 93), such communities lack any genuine sense of reciprocity and interdependence. The emphasis on a central figure also forfeits any genuine pluralism and the kind of polycentric, egalitarian relations it would require. Moreover, the aesthetic-affective bonds Conway describes are devoid of any moral or epistemic-rational significance. It remains unclear what place morality or ethical laws could possibly have in these communities; they also seem to exclude rational principles altogether, opening the door to those for whom Nietzsche capitulates to the Other of reason. In short, Conway's insight into the status of law in Nietzsche's thought is short-changed by reducing aesthetic interaction to irrational, affective bonds.

But it is precisely in a community of taste (*Geschmack*), for Kant, that reason loses its moorings and the rift with sensibility is crossed or crossed out. His key notions – genius (nature gives the law, originality as a new rule for art); aesthetic ideas (defying articulation and conceptualization); reflective judgement (non-subsumptive thought); and especially lawfulness without a law (law-like behaviour without coercion, harmonization both within and between subjects): all of these served Kant to exploit the traditional social characteristics of taste in order to shore up the fragmentation of reason. His systematic interest in a strict separation of beauty (aesthetic judgement), truth (cognition), and goodness (morality) as three autonomous discourses did, however, entail a loss and, as Gadamer has argued, an impoverishment of earlier concepts of taste and the community of taste.²⁹ A far richer, genuinely pluralistic sense of community can be located in Nietzsche's thought if we attend to the social, ethical and epistemic qualities ascribed to taste in the philosophical tradition prior to Kant. By tracing various moments from this tradition to Nietzsche's text, I shall draw out a sense of community with substantive ethical and epistemic dimensions. Situating these features of taste within Nietzsche's conception of the agon, as an equilibrium among more-or-less equal forces, will allow for a more egalitarian sense of community marked by an *ethics of measure* and an *episteme of wisdom*, understood as a necessary *correlative* and *supplement* of science (*Wissenschaft*).³⁰

II.1 Wisdom as Taste

Looking with the help of Gadamer and Schümmer³¹ at the concept of taste in its long history before Kant, we find that it was not exclusively, nor even primarily, an aesthetic category. Although used as an aesthetic term for speech and conduct by the likes of Quintilian, Petronius and Cicero (Schümmer 1955, 121 f.), it was as an epistemic and moral concept that taste was taken up in the 17th century with such enthusiasm that it became known as 'das Zeitalter der Geschmackskultur' (Schümmer 1955, 124). Tracing the *epistemic* meaning of taste as a particular way of knowing (*Erkenntnisweise*) to Nietzsche's text will serve to dismiss any charges of simple irrationalism from Nietzsche's community of taste. It also provides a first clue to the nature and status of law therein.

Four moments above all go to make up the epistemic qualities of taste. In the first instance, 'taste' names an immediate, animal sense bound up with pleasure and pain. But as a pleasurable reception or painful rejection of items that present themselves to our senses, it already implies a *mental capacity to discriminate* (*geistige Unterscheidungsvermögen:* 1). For Baltasar Gracián, it represents a 'spiritualization of our animality' and holds an anomalous place as a middle term linking sensory drives on one side and freedom of the mind on the other: having taste requires a capacity to *distance oneself from mere drives, impulses, preferences* (*Abstand nehmen von blossen Trieben und privaten Vorlieben:* 2), so as to attain the freedom to consciously discriminate, choose and judge. Indeed, taste acts as a *corrective* against private preferences and prejudices in the name of a more general point of view, a collective that it intends and represents (Gadamer 1986, 33). This social reference in taste is evident in the peculiar *normative power* invested in its judgements: the acceptance or rejection expressed with such certainty in a judgement of taste goes hand-in-hand with its *claim to general validity* (*Normkraft, allgemeine Geltungsanspruch:* 3). The normative,

---

29 See Gadamer 1972, 31 ff., esp. 37 f., 40 f.
30 These terms are taken from the end of GT Ch14, as discussed in chapter 4 (pp. 92 f., 98 ff., 104 ff.).
31 Gadamer 1972; Schümmer 1955.

law-like power of judgements of taste is, however, peculiar insofar as they are ungrounded: despite their certainty and decisiveness, such judgements are indefensible, indemonstrable (*unbeweisbar*): *universally binding conceptual standards of judgement* (*begrifflich allgemeine Massstäbe:* 4) are neither given nor sought. Hence the old refrain: 'de gustibus non est disputandum' and Kant's remark that matters of taste allow for conflict (*Streit*) but not for disputation (Gadamer 1986, 33).

Taste, then, names a peculiar episteme which is normative or law-like, without there being any actual laws or norms that could serve to ground or demonstrate its judgements. The epistemic moment of certainty is articulated, not through recourse to a universal standard of judgement, but through the exclusion of bad taste: 'Certainty of taste is certainty in the face of the tasteless. [*Sicherheit des Geschmacks ist also Sicherheit vor dem Geschmacklosen*]' (Gadamer 1986, 33). It is, in fact, this negative, exclusive gesture that we usually encounter in Nietzsche's early use of the term *Geschmack:* in his polemics against David Strauss and other *Bildungsphilister* (UB I), against the judges and connoisseurs of art (UB II 2, KSA 1.263 f.), against the 'grey-beards' of historical sense (UB II 9, KSA 1.322 f.) and others, he is concerned, above all, to show that those who lay claim to taste are in fact tasteless.

There are, however, also some positive uses of the term. One in particular carries strong epistemic traces from the tradition. In his account of pre-Socratic *Philosophy in the Tragic Age of the Greeks*, Nietzsche remarks:

> The Greek word which designates the "wise one" belongs etymologically to sapio, I taste, sapiens, he who tastes, sisyphos, the man with the keenest taste; a keen singling out and identifying, a significant discriminating [*Unterscheiden*] makes up the peculiar art of the philosopher, in the eyes of the people.
>
> Das griechische Wort, welches den "Weisen" bezeichnet, gehört etymologisch zu sapio ich schmecke, sapiens der Schmeckende, sisyphos der Mann des schärfsten Geschmacks; ein scharfes Herausmerken und –erkennen, ein bedeutendes Unterscheiden macht also, nach dem Bewußtsein des Volkes, die eigenthümliche Kunst des Philosophen aus. (PHG 3, KSA 1.816)

Isidorus' etymology 'sapientia a sapore' (Schümmer 1955, 124) serves Nietzsche to connect taste with the activity of thought, inscribing the first epistemic moment of *mental discrimination*. The second moment of *distance from mere drives* takes an idiosyncratic form in Nietzsche's text. Drawing on Aristotle, he defines philosophical discrimination as a 'selecting and marking out [*Auswählen und Ausscheiden*] of what is unusual, astonishing, difficult, divine [*des Ungewöhnlichen Erstaunlichen Schwierigen Göttlichen*]', and continues:

> Science [*Wissenschaft*] throws itself without this selectivity, without this refinement of taste, upon everything that can be known in the blind desire to know everything at any cost; philosophical thinking, by contrast, is always on the scent of those things that are most worth knowing [*wissenswürdig*], the great and important insights.
>
> Die Wissenschaft stürzt sich, ohne solches Auswählen, ohne solchen Feingeschmack, auf alles Wißbare, in der blinden Begierde, alles um jeden Preis erkennen zu wollen; das philosophische

Denken dagegen ist immer auf der Fährte der wissenswürdigsten Dinge, der großen und wichtigen Erkenntnisse. (PHG 3, KSA 1.816)

It is not, then, so much from private impulses or preferences, as from the signature drive of modern theoretical culture – the unrestrained desire for knowledge at any cost – that philosophical taste takes distance. And it does so through a controlling act of legislation that embodies the third epistemic moment of taste – a self-certain judgement that lays claim to general validity:

> Philosophy, then, begins with a legislation of greatness, a name-giving is bound up with it. "That is great", it says, and thereby raises human beings above the blind, unrestrained greed of their knowledge-drive. It restrains this drive through the concept of greatness: and it does so mostly by considering the greatest knowledge, that of the essence and core of things, as within reach and as reached.
>
> [S]o beginnt die Philosophie mit einer Gesetzgebung der Größe, ein Namengeben ist mit ihr verbunden. "Das ist groß" sagt sie und damit erhebt sie den Menschen über das blinde ungebändigte Begehren seines Erkenntnißtriebes. Durch den Begriff der Größe bändigt sie diesen Trieb: und am meisten dadurch, daß sie die größte Erkenntniß, vom Wesen und Kern der Dinge, als erreichbar und als erreicht betrachtet. (PHG 3, KSA 1.816 f.)

Philosophical legislation is an act of evaluation and judgement. It involves the discrimination and selection (*Auswählen*) of *what is most worth knowing* (*wissenswürdig*). As such, it presupposes a standard of evaluation, a rule through which it forms and grounds its judgements. But nowhere is such a standard or rule given, or even sought in Nietzsche's text. In the absence of a universally binding conceptual standard – the fourth epistemic moment of taste – philosophical judgement operates instead *under the rule of taste* and rehearses the gesture of certainty through exclusion characteristic of judgements of taste:

> When Thales says: "All is water", humans are stung out of the worm-like probing and crawling around of the separate sciences, he intuits [*ahnt*] the last resolution of things and through this intuition, overcomes the common [or vulgar: *gemein*] confinement of the lower grades of knowledge.
>
> Wenn Thales sagt "Alles ist Wasser", so zuckt der Mensch empor aus dem wurmartigen Betasten und Herumkriechen der einzelnen Wissenschaften, er ahnt die letzte Lösung der Dinge und überwindet, durch diese Ahnung, die gemeine Befangenheit der niederen Erkenntnißgrade. (PHG 3, KSA 1.817)

This is, as Nietzsche's says elsewhere, a case of 'indemonstrable philosophising' (*unbeweisbare Philosophiren:* PHG 3, KSA 1.814), a law-like thinking without any actual law; in short, an episteme of taste.

The relation of distance between wisdom (*Weisheit*) and science (*Wissenschaft*) is clearly crucial to understanding Nietzsche's epistemic conception of taste. Here again, several moments from the history of taste play into his text in a way that precludes any simple irrationalism. We are reminded, for one, of Leibniz and the opposition between 'monkish scholarship' (*Mönchsgelehrsamkeit*) and the 'taste of science' (*Geschmack der Wissenschaft*) to be cultivated outside the cloisters in the vulgar tongue (Schümmer 1955, 135). More importantly, Nietzsche's text re-activates a medieval use of taste against its later contraction to mere feeling in the 18th century: Master Eckhart's 'taste of God' (*gesmecken gotes*) and Lyly's 'taste of heauenly things' both name a thoughtful relation to the highest, worthiest objects of thought, contents that cannot be adequately grasped through the power of ratio (Schümmer 1955, 122–124). From this perspective, Nietzsche's concept of philosophical taste is no mere flight from reason: it signifies an *empowerment* of thought beyond the limitations imposed by ratiocination.

For Nietzsche, the inadequacy of ratio is bound up with the tools and methods of *Wissenschaft*, what he calls the 'calculating Understanding' (*rechnende Verstand*) and its 'thinking in measures' (*abmessende Denken*: PHG 3, KSA 1.814). In wisdom, by contrast, thinking disposes over sensory and anomalous media, such as: 'Phantasie', 'geniales Vorgefühl', 'blitzartiges Erfassen und Beleuchten', 'Ahnung', 'philosophische Intuition'.[32] These and similar terms were already associated with taste by 18th century thinkers, such as Johan Ulrich König, who were concerned with articulating a form of immediate sensory knowledge (*alsfortige sinnliche Erkenntnis*: Schümmer 1955, 138f.). In this light Nietzsche, like König, is part of the movement, associated with Baumgarten's 'sensate knowledge' or 'cognitio sensitiva', to re-evaluate the senses and to rethink sensory faculties (*Sinnlichkeit*) as a distinct medium of thought. Far from being the unreliable witness that misleads thought, a 'cognitio confusa', or Leibniz's 'dumpfes Denken', the senses elevate philosophy into the 'more divine consort' (*göttlichere Gefährte*) of the cripple 'Understanding' (*Verstand*: PHG 3, KSA 1.814), reaching, in thought, what *Wissenschaft* cannot think in its own medium. This is not, however, to dismiss *Wissenschaft* or annul its results. If König insisted that the immediate judgements of taste need not contradict judgements of the Understanding, Nietzsche himself insists that Thales 'made use of *Wissenschaft* und the demonstrable (*das Beweisbare*: PHG 3, KSA 1.816), before springing beyond them. There is, in short, no question of wisdom simply *replacing Wissenschaft*. Next to binding (*Bändigen*) and guiding the indiscriminate impulses of *Wissenschaft*, next to using its results, wisdom is to make good the shortcomings of ratio *for the sake of thought*. It names not the 'Other' of reason, but its *necessary correlative* and *supplement*.

---

[32] 'phantasy'/ 'imagination', 'genial presentiment', 'lightning-fast grasping and illuminating', 'intimation', 'philosophical intuition' (PHG 3, KSA 1.814, 816).

II.2 The Normativity of Taste

The peculiar normativity of wisdom-as-taste is key to the nature of ethical law in Nietzsche's agonal sense of community: the so-called 'eternal laws' of measure, the commitment to life-affirmation, and the commitment to life-enhancement – what Conway calls the perfectionist core of his thought. If taste names an episteme which is normative or law-like, without there being any actual laws or norms that could be used to ground or demonstrate its judgements, what then is the ground or source of its normativity? Whence the normative power of taste, the authority of its claims over others? In the absence of explicit, conceptual norms it cannot be authorised or grounded by reason. The answer given by the tradition revolves instead around common sense (*Gemeinsinn*) or sensus communis, that is, the social reference of taste.

Taste does not, however, derive its authority from any given or empirical communities; rather, it is the characteristic of fashion (*Mode*) to be determined with reference to what others actually do, to *conform* to common or general habits or customs. The freedom of judgement that is essential to taste, by contrast, takes it normative bearings from an *ideal community* and the certainty of its consensus (*Zustimmung, Einhelligkeit*) (Gadamer 1986, 34 f.). In the *Kritik der Urteilskraft* §22, Kant even plays with idea that 'taste' does not name an *actual* ability, but 'only the idea of an ability yet to be acquired'.[33] Common sense, he argues, denotes 'an indeterminate norm', 'a merely ideal norm' with 'subjective-universal' validity, which I presuppose in making a judgement of taste, such that my judgement serves as an example of its judgement. Yet, the question remains open as to whether my judgement exemplifies common sense as an actual, constitutive principle of experience, or whether it serves 'to bring forth in us [...] a common sense in the first place' (KU §22, A67/B68), that is, to form or give form to (*hervorbringen*) a community of taste that would assent to my judgement.

These thoughts resonate unmistakably with the agonal relation between the tragic poets and their public described by Nietzsche in MA 170. While free to follow their own law or judgement of excellence *against* the prevailing taste (read: fashion), they were also constrained to win the consent of the public (*Zustimmung von Aussen her*) and if necessary, to 'educate' them; that is, to form (*hervorbringen*) a community of taste that would assent to their judgement (For Kant: a public of whose judgement their own would be an example). Kant's thoughts on the ideal community that would authorise my judgement of taste also resonate with Nietzsche's fictive community of free spirits in the late Preface to MA (see p. 69 ff.), created, he tells us, in order to accelerate (*beschleunigen*) the advent of actual communities responsive to the

---

[33] Sensus communis is crucial for Kant's account of taste in grounding its normative claims. As Gadamer has argued, however, Kant works with an impoverished, negatively derived understanding of sensus communis as that which abstracts from personal or private preferences.

project of critical transvaluation and life-affirmation; that is, to cultivate or form them.

But the problem here runs far deeper for Nietzsche than for Kant. For Nietzsche, it concerns the crisis of normative authority brought on by the death of God, compelling Zarathustra to 'go down' to actual communities who would authorise his life-affirmative discourse, – but who cannot, since they have no ears for his teaching (p. 69). Like Zarathustra, Nietzsche is dependent on an absent community, a readership yet to come, to authorise his discourse. At stake in Nietzsche's episteme of taste is not the question of beauty per se, as with Kant, but the fundamental question of *what is most worth knowing*, indeed the entire philosophical project of critical transvaluation in the name of life and life-enhancement, and the question of community or the 'right' readership needed to authorise and give sense to this project. As Conway points out, the perfectionist concern with the enhancement of human existence at the core of Nietzsche's project is genuinely open-ended, without prepared answers. His perfectionist ideal is therefore of necessity radically indeterminate – like the 'ideal norm' of Kant's sensus communis. And like Kant's 'indeterminate norm', it claims 'subjective-universal' validity if, with Arendt,[34] we interpret this as a law that binds collectively, but only across particular communities.

But what sense are we to make of this merely ideal, radically indeterminate ethical law and its normative power? A first indication can be gleaned from UB III, when Nietzsche writes:

> All that exists that can be negated deserves to be negated; and being truthful means to believe in an existence that could in no way be negated and which is itself true and without mendacity. That is why the truthful man feels that the meaning of his activity is metaphysical, explicable from the laws of another and higher life, and in the profoundest sense affirmative: however much all that he does may appears to be destroying and breaking the laws of this life. (UB III 4, KSA 1.372)[35]

No doubt, these lines reflect the pressure Nietzsche is under in the UB to side with Schopenhauer's truthfulness (*Wahrhaftigkeit*) and the metaphysics of being against Wagner's invocation of life-redeeming delusions (*Wahn*).[36] Yet, in linking his critical labour together with 'laws of another and higher life' that can only be affirmed,

---

34 '[J]udgment, to be valid, depends on the presence of others. Hence judgment is endowed with a certain specific validity, but is never universally valid. Its claim can never extend further than the others in whose place the judging person has put himself for his considerations.' (Arendt 1993, 221: 'The Crisis in Culture').
35 'Alles Dasein, welches verneint werden kann, verdient es auch, verneint zu werden; und wahrhaftig sein heisst an ein Dasein glauben, welches überhaupt nicht verneint werden könnte und welches selber wahr und ohne Lüge ist. Deshalb empfindet der Wahrhaftige den Sinn seiner Thätigkeit als einen metaphysischen, aus Gesetzen eines andern und höhern Lebens erklärbaren und im tiefsten Verstande bejahenden: so sehr auch alles, was er thut, als ein Zerstören und Zerbrechen der Gesetze dieses Lebens erscheint.'
36 See chapter 6 II.2, p. 164 ff. See also chapter 3, p. 87.

Nietzsche also points towards a normative claim which derives from an *affirmative bond with a form of life yet to come*. In what follows, I will interpret this as a claim to the normativity of taste embodied in an ideal futural community. The thesis is that Nietzsche articulates his futural ideal of humanity in a community of taste, inspired by the Greek agon, as an anti-humanist ideal of humanity in the service of human perfection: an agonal community of taste. The argument begins with a key figure in the history of taste: Baltasar Gracián.

II.3 Taste as Lawfulness without a Law

It is Gracián who first identified, as features of taste, the key epistemic powers of Nietzsche's concept of wisdom, the capacities to discriminate and to distance oneself from mere impulses and preferences. But taste or 'gusto' names only one pole of Gracián's thought, which turns on the relation between 'gusto' or 'genio' (and associated terms like 'cor', 'naturaleza') on one side, and 'razon' (reason) or 'ingenio' (mind) (and associated terms like 'entendimiento', 'arte') on the other. These two poles are related in way that resonates in Nietzsche's conception of wisdom and *Wissenschaft:* they are opposed yet inseparable, correlates that derive their meaning in relation to each other. 'There is', Gracián says, 'an education [or formation: *cultura*] of taste [*gusto*], as well as the mind [*ingenio*]' (Gracián Oráculo 65, quoted in Schümmer 1955, 125). With this formulation, Gracián gives us new co-ordinates for interpreting Nietzsche's conception of taste. For it indicates that Gracián's *gusto* figures not within a strictly epistemic problematic, but rather, within a pedagogic or *Bildungs*-problematic oriented towards a new moral ideal, what can be called 'an ideal of authentic humanity' (Gadamer 1986, 32) or the 'art of living' (*Lebenskunst:* Schümmer 1955, 124).[37] Gracián, then, conceives *gusto (taste) as the correlative and supplement of ratio within a Bildungs-programme geared towards a new ideal of humanity (or: the 'art of living')*.

Gracián's essentially *moral* concept of taste uncovers an underlying pedagogic-moral or *Bildungs*-problematic behind Nietzsche's concept of wisdom. By drawing on the history of taste for his concept of wisdom or *sapientia*, Nietzsche effectively over-rules the separation of epistemic, moral and aesthetic value in Kant and cultural modernity. For the concept of greatness (*Grösse*), through which wisdom discriminates and legislates what is most worth knowing, is not just an epistemic category according to Nietzsche, but is 'changeable in both the moral and in the aesthetic

---

[37] On the art of living, see Oráculo 90: 'The spirit's integrity is passed on to the body, and a good life is held to be a long life not only through its intensity but through its very extension.' See also Oráculo 134. The translation used here is by Jeremy Robbins in Gracián 2011. Nietzsche will have known the translation into German by Schopenhauer: *Das Handorakel und Kunst der Weltklugheit von Baltasar Gracian in der Übertragung von Schopenhauer.* It was in his personal library (see Campioni et al 2003, 265).

realms' (PHG 3, KSA 1.816). It was 'in consideration of life, through an ideal life-need [*Lebensbedürfniß*]' that the pre-Socratic philosophers legislated against their 'insatiable knowledge-drive [*Wissenstrieb*]', and it was as 'men of culture and with the goals of culture' that they philosophised (PHG 1, KSA 1.807). Drawing inspiration from them, Nietzsche conceives *sapientia (taste) as the correlative and supplement of ratio (Wissenschaft) within a Bildungs-programme geared towards a new, life-affirmative ideal of culture.* Once again, Gracián's account of *gusto* gives us a way into Nietzsche's thought.

Gracián's man of taste is conceived as member of a social ideal, what Gadamer (1986, 32) calls a 'Bildungsgesellschaft' that is beyond differences of class. Similarly, when Nietzsche describes his ideal of cultivation, the 'Gebildeten', he insists: 'He is to be found in all classes [*Ständen*], with all levels of education [*Unterrichtetheit*]' (34[26], 1874, KSA 7). By cultivating his taste, Gracián's *Gebildete* wins the inner and outer distance that enables him to discriminate, choose and judge freely and consciously.[38] But the man of taste is a social being,[39] and when Gracián comes to characterise con-genial taste, his account is markedly pluralistic and conflictual; it is, in fact, an agonal community of taste.[40] Among the plurality of *gustos*, one

---

38 See e.g. Oráculo 33: 'Don't so belong to others that you don't belong to yourself. Even friends should not be abused; you shouldn't want more from them than they're willing to concede. Any extreme is a vice, and especially in dealings with others. Sensible moderation is the best way to maintain goodwill and respect because ever-precious dignity won't be worn away. Be free in spirit, passionate about all that's fine, and never sin against your own good taste.' Also Oráculo 43: 'Thought is free; it cannot and should not be coerced.' But also 147: 'Someone who refuses to listen is an incurable fool. The most independent person must still accept the need for friendly advice; even a monarch must be willing to be taught [...] The most self-sufficient person must leave a door open to friendship, from where all help will come. You need a friend of sufficient influence over you to be able to advise and admonish you freely.'
39 'Taste is acquired through interaction with others and secured through continual use: it's a real stroke of luck to come into contact with someone with perfect taste. But you shouldn't make a habit of disliking everything. This is to take things to a stupid extreme, and is more detestable when due to affectation than to natural disposition. Some want God to create another world and other perfections to satisfy their extravagant imagination.' (Oráculo 65). Also 108: '*A short cut to being a true person:* know how to rub shoulders with others. Interaction is very effective: custom and taste can be learnt, character and even ingenuity can rub off on you without your knowing.' And 93: '*A universal person.* Having every perfection, such an individual is worth many others put together and makes life a complete joy, passing this on to their friends. Variety joined with perfection makes life a delight. It is a great art knowing how to enjoy all that's good. And since, given their pre-eminence, nature made humans the compendium of the natural world, let art make each a universe through the exercise and cultivation of taste and understanding.'
40 On rivalry in taste, see Oráculo 75: '*Choose a heroic model*, more to emulate than to imitate. There are examples of greatness, living texts of renown. Select the best in your own area, not so much to follow as to surpass. Alexander wept, not for Achilles in his tomb, but for himself, not yet risen to universal fame. Nothing so incites ambition within the spirit as the trumpeting of another's fame: it demolishes envy and inspires noble actions.' Also Oráculo 84: 'Enemies are of more use to the wise man than friends are to the fool. Ill will usually levels mountains of difficulty which goodwill

gusto can completely contradict another, to the point of annulling its judgement; and yet, Gracián insists, each is thoroughly right and complete. Conflict is not a shortcoming in this community, a problem to be resolved through disputation. On the contrary, 'de gustibus disputare' would be a problem: to argue about taste, erecting an explicit, collectively binding rule or standard of judgement by which differences could be settled once and for all – that would in effect be to dissolve taste. For Gracián, the variety and conflict (*Gegeneinander*) of *gustos* is the essence of taste (Schümmer 1955, 129).[41]

Gracián's social ideal of *gusto* exhibits some striking affinities with the dynamic form of the Greek agon, as Nietzsche describes it in *Homer's Wettkampf*. Four co-ordinates or points of comparison stand out:

1) If the variety and conflict of *gustos* designates the essence of taste, then taste is what it is by virtue of a conflict between different positions or judgements; to have taste *means* to be embroiled in (a potential) conflict of taste with other judgements. This points towards the social ontology of agonal interaction presupposed by Greek pedagogy in HW. If '[e]very gift or capacity [*Begabung*] must unfold through antagonism' (HW, KSA 1.789), it is because *each particular gift or capacity can only become what it is through antagonistic striving against others*. The same goes for *gusto* and the capacities it requires, which can only unfold in (potential) conflict with others, and cannot therefore be understood from the subject-position alone. Like the agon, taste is a *social* phenomenon, a *clash* of judgements, and it needs to be grasped from an *intersubjective* or *medial* position in the dynamics of this particular kind of conflict; what Nietzsche, in the

---

would balk at tackling. The greatness of many has been fashioned thanks to malicious enemies. Flattery is more harmful than hatred, for the latter is an effective remedy for the flaws that the former conceals. Sensible people fashion a mirror from spite, more truthful than that of affection, and reduce or correct their defects, for great caution is needed when living on the frontier of envy and ill will.' On the danger of envy: 'Envy has its own form of ostracism, the more popular, the more criminal. It accuses something truly perfect of sinning in not sinning and condemns it completely for being completely perfect.' (Oráculo 83).

41 On the agonal plurality of *gustos:* 'What one pursues, another flees. Whoever wants to make their own opinion the measure of all things is an insufferable fool. Perfection doesn't depend on one person's approval: tastes are as plentiful as faces, and as varied. There's not a single failing without its advocate. Nor should we lose heart if something doesn't please someone, for there'll always be someone else it does. But their applause shouldn't go to our heads, for others will condemn such praise. The measure of true satisfaction is the approval of reputable men who are experts in the relevant field. Life doesn't depend on any one opinion, any one custom, or any one century.' (Oráculo 101). Also Oráculo 108: 'Let the impulsive get together with those who are restrained, and similarly other opposite temperaments. In this way, a proper balance will be effortlessly achieved. To know how to accommodate is a great skill. The alternation of opposites beautifies and sustains creation, and if it creates harmony in the natural world, even more so in the moral sphere. Make use of this politic advice when choosing friends and helpers, for from such communication between extremes, a discreet balance will be achieved.'

case of agonal conflict, calls a dynamic of 'reciprocal provocation to deeds, as also a reciprocal holding within the bounds of measure' (HW, KSA 1.789).

2) The dynamics of conflict in the community of *gustos* are determined, first and foremost, by the absence of any explicit, collectively binding rules or laws for adjudicating right and wrong: there is no standard of judgement that could serve to resolve and settle the various conflicts that arise. Similarly, Nietzsche's agonal community is characterised by the absence of any codified rules or standards that could be used to adjudicate victory and defeat for all the contests that take place. A contest begins by throwing any prevailing standards in question, and antagonists strive not just to win, but to determine what counts as winning; it is not just victory, but the very standard or rule of victory that is at stake in each contest.

3) To erect an explicit and binding rule, by which all conflicts and differences of taste could be resolved once and for all, would be to destroy or dissolve the possibility of taste. Taste can only thrive where conflict is radically inconclusive or open-ended. Similarly, to erect a standard of victory that is beyond contention is to destroy or dissolve the agon. Like taste, the agon names a radically inconclusive form of conflict; in the narratology of HW, it was the conclusive victory of Alexander over all other contestants that put an end to the Greek agon.[42]

4) Within the conflictual plurality of *gustos*, each position or judgement is right and complete. With this formulation, Gracián touches on a paradox of justice (*Gerechtigkeit*). For how can two contradictory judgements both be right? For both judgements to be 'right', some form of adjudication or justice must be in play; the conflict of *gustos* is not simply law-less. Yet, it does preclude any actual, explicit code of laws. We can therefore speak, with Kant, of a *lawfulness without a law* (*Gesetzmässigkeit ohne Gesetz*).[43] The paradox of justice is, moreover, resolutely impartial, giving right to each judgement; it cannot therefore be identified with the subject-position; for a judgement of taste secures its certainty by excluding conflicting judgements (as 'tasteless' or 'bad taste'). The paradox of justice can therefore only be situated in the *medial position*, at the interspace of conflict, as function of its particular dynamic.

In the agon, too, we must speak of lawfulness without a law. There is no law or standard that could adjudicate victory for all contests, apart from the course taken by each; any such law, if established beyond contention, dissolves the agon. It is not, however, law-less. In the first place, the agon is a social phenomenon, and for Nietzsche, social life is inseparable from the establishment of law.[44] In HC, Nietzsche makes this point by delimiting the contest or *Wettkampf* against the *Vernichtung-*

---

42 HW, KSA 1.792. See also KSA 1.788f. on ostracism, and KSA 7: 3[73], 16[16], 16[43], 38[7].
43 Kant KU A69/B70 (Allgemeine Anmerkung zum ersten Abschnitt der Analytik).
44 See Gerhardt 1983.

skampf, the pervasive and lawless struggle for annihilation. With reference to Heraclitus, as we saw, Nietzsche identifies the agon as the continuous articulation (*Wirken*) of an immanent Δίκη or 'immanent lawfulness in deciding the contest [*immanente Gesetzmässigkeit im Entscheiden des Wettkampfes*]' (VPP 10, KGW II/4.272). Justice, or the standard of victory, is immanent to the course of each contest, yet it cannot be collapsed into the standpoint of the contestants, for 'every single being [*Einzelne*] fights as if it alone were in the right [*berechtigt sei*]'. The 'absolutely certain measure of adjudicating judgement [Mass des richterl. Urtheils]' for deciding victory can therefore only be located in the relations *between* contestants. As in the conflict of *gustos*, justice is determined from the medial position, as a function of the agonal play of forces (*Wettspiel der Kräfte*).

We can now ask what consequences this account of the *agonal rule of taste* has for Nietzsche's transvaluative discourse. An agonal community of taste is a community of (self–)legislators engaged in a radically inconclusive conflict of *gustos* or judgements of taste. At issue in such a community, if we take our cue from the account of wisdom in PHG, is a 'legislation of greatness'; that is, judgements that discriminate and select what is most worth knowing (*wissenswürdig*), uttered by the first philosophers under the rule of taste, as an ungrounded law or norm that fuses epistemic, aesthetic and moral values in a concept of greatness (PHG 3, KSA 1.816). As judgements of taste, they are radically individual, self-certain judgements, which nonetheless make a normative claim on others, without grounding that claim. As such, they instantiate what Kant calls *reflective judgements* – radically individual judgements or acts of self-legislation, which nonetheless make an ungrounded claim on others: not a universal claim, but a claim on a particular community of those who – in Nietzsche's case – respond to the call for the transvaluation of values. The authority of this claim is therefore of the order of taste: an ungrounded, indeterminate normativity, or lawfulness without a law, elicited by the agonal form of Nietzsche's critical confrontations, the ideal communities invoked in his texts, and the readership they convocate. Under the agonal rule of taste, Nietzsche's transvaluative discourse (like the tragedies in MA 170) depends for its authority on the consensus (*Zustimmung*) of his readership. At the same time, as we saw in chapter 6 (p. 176f.), any act of legislation under agonal conditions will provoke or stimulate acts of counter-legislation by his readers, counter-claims, whose authority also depends on the response of others – the only possible source of authority under nihilistic conditions.

As is well known, Kant's notion of reflective judgement stands for the problem of thinking in the absence of a concept, a thinking that attends first and foremost to the concrete singularity of an event or object we perceive and then looks to create a concept for it. This describes well Nietzsche's understanding of pre-Socratic philosophy as a 'legislation of greatness': judgements of taste, through which every philosopher redefined or recreated what is 'great' and worth knowing. For Nietzsche, as we saw above, it is around life – 'in consideration of life, through an ideal life-need' (PHG 1, KSA 1.807) – that the pre-Socratic legislation of what is most worth knowing gravitated. In Nietzsche's case, too, the project of transvaluation responds to an 'ideal life-need': it is in the name of life, its affirmation and (indeterminate) perfection, that he looks to transvaluate and overcome the life-negating values of Christian-Platonic culture. The difficulty here, as in Kant's notion of reflective judgement, is how to think in the absence of a concept; for it is the absence of (a concept of) life-affirmation and the contraction (*Verkleinerung*) of human life, not its perfection or 'greatness', that Nietzsche's genealogy of European values uncovers. In this regard, the notion of reflective judgement captures the profound difficulty of formulating a life-affirmative discourse and a concept of human perfection in which the project of transvaluation is to issue. In Nietzsche's case, the singularity from which reflective judgement takes off is that of the legislator and the legislator's body, the unique multiplicity of its existence as a living being, to which the practice of self-legislation must respond if it is to be radically individual. Nietzsche's affirmative impulse is, then, to be understood as so many attempts to formulate affirmative concepts for the singularity of his existence as a form of life, through processes of analogical thinking which, in contrast to subsumptive thought, do not erase the singularity of lived experience.[45] This is perhaps the best way to understand Nietzsche's turn to physiology in the early 1880s and then to the will to power: as conceptual lexica that offer the best analogies for the singularity of embodied existence, the affirmative impulse and the perfectionist dynamic of intensification (*Steigerung*) endemic to all forms of life.

III Agonal Measure or the 'Measure of Judgement'

Nietzsche's talk of the 'the measure [*Maß*] of adjudicating judgement' invokes the 'eternal laws' of measure by which the agonal individual is limited (16[22], KSA 7). If ethical law takes the form of an indeterminate, perfectionist ideal in agonal communities of taste, then measure is integral to the workings of this law. And if the measure (*Maß*) of judgement is determined from a *medial standpoint in the antagonistic relations between the contestants*, then agonal measure, too, is medial. The case for the medial sense of measure in Nietzsche's agon was first made in chapter 3. In concluding this chapter, I revisit this claim from a perspective in law by proposing two analogies to Nietzsche's medial sense of law, both of which incorporate a medial sense of measure.

III.1 Justice and Measure in Nietzsche's Agon and Homer's *Iliad*

The first analogy takes it cue from the title of Nietzsche's essay on the agon, *Homer's Wettkampf*, and concerns the historical conjuncture of his conception of the ancient

---

45 See Terra Polanco 2019, esp. chapter 3.3 and 3.5.

Greek agon and Homer's *Iliad*. As argued in chapter 2, Nietzsche proposes an antihumanist ideal of humanity as an agon between so-called 'human' and 'inhuman' impulses, between measure and excess (*Maass* and *Übermaass*) in every antagonist (see p. 63f.). In this regard, Hartmut Schröter writes of the ambivalence of agonal culture towards tyrannical impulses and the temptation to hubris and *Übermaass*, an enduring fascination with the world of heroes and heroic excesses at a historical juncture where the Greeks were already aware of the need for measure and restraint (Schröter 1982, 114). The agon and agonal measure are hereby identified with an important moment of human self-awareness, what can be called the *transition from the heroic-superhuman to the problematic-human.*[46]

At issue is the step from the hero's unconditional passion to something more complex, a diremption and conflict of the psyche that is clearly visible in the ambivalent attitude to *envy* amongst agonal Greeks. On one side, Nietzsche writes, envy was praised and valued as the 'effect of a beneficent deity', the good Eris who stirs men to new deeds; on the other side, it was feared in the fear of divine envy reminding victors of 'the transitoriness of every human lot [*das Vergängliche jedes Menschenlooses*]' (HW, KSA 1.787). Clearly, it is this experience of human finitude which gives rise to the call for measure and restraint. But it is important see that fear of divine envy was only one side of an ambivalent attitude, and inseparable from a celebration of human envy. Together they express an experience of human existence in *new, untold possibilities,* as well as its limits.

It is these two poles of the possible and its limits that are activated and combined in the agonal dynamic of reciprocal provocation and reciprocal limitation within the bounds of measure. There is, in short, a clear connection between the dynamic character of the agonal play forces and the moment of human self-awareness described by Schröter: they are isomorphic. If the experience of human finitude is bound up with the experience of human possibilities, *it is because they are a product of agonal interaction,* not solitary reflection.[47] By embedding agonal measure in this experience of the human, Schröter's perspective thus moves from the subject-position to a medial position in the *intersubjective* dynamics of agonal conflict. This allows for the tyrannical impulses emphasised by Nietzsche, and brings us much closer to the unique character of agonal measure that fascinated him, as the product of an equilibrium of tyrannical forces.

The transition from the heroic-superhuman to the problematic-human, from unconditional pathos to the conflictual diremption of the human soul, is usually identified with the age of tragedy. These are, however, the words used by Karl Reinhardt to describe the very first work of Greek literature: Homer's *Iliad*. The *Iliad* is usually read as *the* heroic text of western civilization, a poem about Achilles' wrath that em-

---

[46] Reinhardt 1948 [1938], 36 (quoted in Schadewaldt 1944, 199).
[47] According to Schröter (1982, 113), it is the experience of the human in its possibilities ands limits that 'grounds their belonging together, the sphere of society'. This expresses well the generative social powers of agon.

bodies the heroic values of honour, courage, loyalty and the immortality of fame. It is also common to see the *Iliad* as a national poem; according to Hegel, it asserts and justifies the world of the ancient Greeks as absolute by pitting them against a foreign nation in a way 'that leaves nothing over for those defeated'.[48] But these views have been discredited due largely to the work the philologists Karl Reinhardt and Wolfgang Schadewaldt.[49] They have argued that, next to the wrath of Achilles, the *Iliad* sings his *death* in a way that portrays his absolute self-assertion as an act of hubris. Indeed, for Reinhardt, the entire Iliad is a 'poem of death' or *Todesdichtung*, with its battles for the fallen and its finale in the contrasting fates of two corpses: 'In the lamentation over the dead, the human [*das Menschliche*] seems to free itself for the first time, to become the purest of songs' (Reinhardt 1962, 16). Schadewaldt (1944, 198) too speaks of the 'conciliatory humanness [*versöhnende Menschlichkeit*]' at the close of the *Iliad*. It is the reconciliation between Achilles and Priam over Hector's corpse that shows most clearly the distance separating the *Iliad* from the heroic age. The victory of the Greeks is not celebrated here; it *problematised* in a way that curbs their unconditional, unmeasured will-to-victory. Far from justifying the ancient Greek nation as absolute (à la Hegel), this conciliatory scene places limits on the heroic pathos of victory in favour of an agonal acknowledgement of their opponents (Schröter 1982, 78).

On this reading, then, the *Iliad* marks the transition from the *Vernichtungskampf* to the *Wettkampf*, from the heroic pathos of absolute victory to the transient, questionable victory of agonal humanity. But how is this transition managed? How is the agonal moment of measure inscribed in the *Iliad* such that the pathos of unconditional victory gives way to an acknowledgement of both victors and losers? Pursuing these questions opens a new perspective on agonal measure.

The sense of measure in the *Iliad* cannot be understood from the subject-position in its heroes. Subjects with self-identity and developmental continuity centred in an inner will are wanting in Homer's world. What Nietzsche praises as the ethical qualities of the agonal Greeks, their 'openness' (*Offenheit*), 'freedom of mind' (*Freisinnigkeit*) and 'the visibility of the soul in action'[50] are clearly evinced by in Homer's heroes. The great deeds of the *Iliad* do not emerge from a private, inner process of deliberation, as the result of unified acts of the will. As Bruno Snell and others have shown, Homer's heroes are transparent and highly pervious to their surroundings; they are more like open fields of forces, in which conflicting impulses or qualities, with the help of the gods and mortals, alternate or combine to yield their actions.[51] Nor can we speak of self-restraint in any sustained sense on the part of individual characters, whose actions bear all the marks of unmeasured, wilful her-

---

48 Hegel 1965 Bd. II, 423.
49 See esp. Schadewaldt 1944, 199 (note 2) and Reinhardt 1962, 7–18.
50 'Sichtbarkeit der Seele im Handeln' 3[49], KSA 8.27 See also chapter 2 (p. 54 f.).
51 Snell 1982, chapter 1: 'Homer's View of Man'; Auerbach 1991, chapter 1: 'Odysseus' Scar'; also Hatab 1990.

oes. As Reinhardt points out, they are crossed by sharp oppositions and typically illuminated from their sudden turning points: from the cruel to the human (Achilles), from narrow-mindedness to conciliatory openness (Agamemnon) (Reinhardt 1962, 15, 17).

It would be equally inappropriate to appeal to a transcendent concept of justice as the source of measure. Explicit laws, imperatives or ideals that would govern or even adjudicate human actions are absent from the *Iliad*. As Hegel rightly notes, the poem pre-dates the stage of morality, since there is no reflexive self-determination with reference to a universal standard. What, then, takes the place of morality as the source of measure? According to Reinhardt, a 'diremption' or 'equilibrium of sympathy' (*Spaltung, Gleichgewicht der Sympathie*) is the 'foundation' of the *Iliad*, its 'Grundgesetz', applied in different variations throughout the text (Reinhardt 1962, 11, 13). It is, however, a curiously inarticulate law, felt rather than stated. No victor celebrates for long before others, losers, appear to compete for our sympathy; no figures are so bad or worthless as to be utterly god-forsaken. There is, in Nietzsche's words, a lack of distinction between black and white (5[146], KSA 8). The equilibrium of sympathy can be seen in the gods, especially Zeus, whose sympathies become so divided as to approach weakness (Reinhardt 1962, 13). As the highest god, he is also the one closest to the human problematic, fighting out the conflicts within himself until he pronounces judgement. The more impartial he is, the more diremot and tragic he becomes. That the highest god should be the most indecisive: this, for Reinhardt, is Homer's 'most sublime thought' (Reinhardt 1962, 13).

The predicament of Zeus is symbolised by the scales (*Waage*) that he holds, a word that Nietzsche connects etymologically with the word 'agon' (16[23], KSA 7). This connection is particularly apposite if, as I suggest, Zeus' predicament describes the status of law in the agon, as the source of agonal measure. The 'equilibrium of sympathy' in Homer's Zeus is the counterpart of the equilibrium of forces in Nietzsche's agon. Both Homer and Nietzsche allow for tyrannical forces and heroic excesses in their diversity and particularity. Adjudication and measure cannot therefore be identified with, or reduced to, the deeds of individual antagonists. They must, however, be immanent: in the absence of explicit, pre-established universal laws or standards of judgement covering every conflict that arises, adjudication and measure must be responsive to particular conflicts, formed in response to the particular claims or deeds that arise on both sides. They must, in short, be human; or as human as can be without falling prey to particular interests on one side or the other. It is this third position between human particularity and the rigid universality of law that Zeus, as the most 'spellbound spectator' (*hingerissene Zuschauer*), occupies – a place that best describes the 'lawfulness without a law' that is the source of agonal measure. As a figure of law and justice, Zeus is not as reassuring as we would wish: a reminder of the fragility of measure, not its guarantor. But as a figure of indecision, he does guarantee that the question of justice is opened and re-opened through the agon of judgements amongst us mortals.

III.2 Agonal Measure and Hannah Arendt on Freedom under Laws or 'Principles'

The second analogy with Nietzsche's medial sense of law and measure concerns Hannah Arendt's performative concept of political action. As is well known, Arendt reads the history of western philosophy as the suppression of the political. In the essay 'What is Freedom?' (WF, 1993), she concentrates on the concept of freedom, arguing that the philosophical tradition has divorced freedom from the political realm, transposing it inwards as an attribute of will and thought. Freedom, in the sense of free will (*liberum arbitrium*) or sovereignty, gives precedence to the intellect, which chooses what is right and calls upon the will to command its execution; action is thus guided by a future aim, chosen independently of others (Arendt 1993, 151 f., 163). From Plato on, she contends, *poiesis* has served as a model for action in general, and especially political action, in a sustained effort by philosophy to assert control over action by subordinating it to ends or works selected by the intellect and realised by the will. Against this 'distortion', Arendt proposes to recuperate the pre-philosophical, *political* concept of freedom as an attribute of doing or acting itself, understood as *praxis*. In WF, she appeals primarily to the ancient Greek experience in order to develop an aesthetic, performative concept of action,[52] in which freedom becomes a kind of virtuosity. On this model, action is self-contained and intrinsically valuable (its own end) insofar as its meaning and value derive from the doing or performance itself (– not from an end-product or work, as in *poiesis*). This account exhibits significant affinities with Nietzsche's agonal model of action.

For Arendt, virtuosity is inimical to order, or at least to too much order. Like Nietzsche, she sees spontaneity, unruliness and excess as essential for action to be genuinely free and great. But she also rejects the radical instability of pure lawlessness, what Nietzsche calls the *Vernichtungskampf*, which pervades all areas of life – with the exception of the agonal polis (*Wettkampf*). For both, then, freedom turns on a *non-coercive concept of the law*, one that provides a measure of stability, a fragile measure, without ruling out action's unruliness. Nietzsche's agon, like Arendt's virtuosity, requires a tension between the unruliness of action and a measure of law, between the temptation to hubris and the warning of measure, or what humanism calls the 'inhuman' and the 'human', according to the opening paragraph of *Homer's Wettkampf*.[53] In this vein, Nietzsche, like Burckhardt, maintains that 'every Greek, in his secret wishes was a tyrant; and everyone who could be, was in fact a tyrant' (6[7], KSA 8; cf. MA 261). 'The hardness, the arrogance [*Übermut*], the tyrannical' in the blood of ancient Greek philosophers (6[7], KSA 8; 23[1], KSA 7) was by no means restricted to them since, for Nietzsche, following Plato's Gorgias, '[a]ll Greeks (fr. Gorgias in Plato) believed the possession of power as tyrant to be

---

52 See Villa 1992 and my criticism in Siemens 2005.
53 This interpretation of Arendt's position is indebted to Honig 1993a, esp. chapters 3 and 4, and Honig 1993b.

the most enviable happiness' (4[301] KSA 9; see also chapter 2, p. 59f.). This same note goes on to connect the achievement of moderation or measure in the polis with the principle of equality or isonomia: 'The equality of citizens is the means for avoiding tyranny, their reciprocal invigilation and constraint' (*Die Gleichheit der Bürger ist das Mittel zur Verhinderung der Tyrannei, ihre gegenseitige Bewachung und Niederhaltung*). In the agon, tyranny is curbed by an approximate equality (*Gleichheit*) of tyrannical forces in equilibrium, (*Gleichgewicht*); it is, in other words, not from the subject-position of the would-be tyrannical antagonists, but from a medial position in the 'agonal play of forces' (*Wettspiel der Kräfte*), that measure is achieved. It is Nietzsche's medial concept of law and measure in the agon that exhibits the most striking affinities with Arendt's thought on free action and law.

In WF, Arendt (1993, 152f.), addresses the problem of the relation of free action to the law in a crucial and densely argued passage, where she presents her performative concept of action in relation to what she (following Montesquieu) calls 'principles'.[54] As examples of principles, Arendt (again following Montesquieu) cites honour, glory, love of equality, distinction, excellence, but also fear, distrust or hatred. For Montesquieu, 'principles' name the passions or springs that animate political forms, and they are distributed across his three-fold typology of political forms: Monarchy (animated by honour, glory, distinction), Republic (animated by love of equality or excellence; Montesquieu also mentions moderation in aristocratic republics), and Despotism (animated by fear, distrust, hatred).[55] It is unclear how close Arendt's use of 'principles' is to Montesquieu's, but her thought in WF seems to be working on a level that precedes typologies, on the level of political being or the political, with the question: What are the conditions for bringing political spaces into being? In this regard, her thought is close to Nietzsche's when he cites the principle of Greek popular pedagogy: 'Every gift must unfold through antagonism' (*Jede Begabung muss sich kämpfend entfalten*: HW, KSA 1.789). For this implies not only a necessary, antagonistic relation of individual capacities to others, but also a necessary relation (*muss*) of individual capacities to the public sphere (*sich entfalten*), what Nietzsche also calls the 'visibility of soul in action' (3[49], KSA 8). If, as Nietzsche claims, this pedagogic principle is realised through the institution of the agon, this suggests that Arendt has an agonal conception of action in mind when arguing that free action, animated by principles, is what brings political spaces into being. And it reminds us, conversely, that at stake in agonal action for Nietzsche is freedom, and that free action is political: the *Offenheit*, *Leidenschaft* and *Sichtbarkeit* (openness, passion and visibility) he so values in the agon are valuable because they open political spaces.

---

54 My account of Arendt's notion of principles owes much to an anonymous reviewer for *Constellations*.
55 See Montesquieu 1989, 21–30 (Part I Book 3), 8.

Nietzsche's agon may also be close to Arendt's conception of 'principles' in her indifference to, or refusal of, Montesquieu's typology. One might expect Arendt to single out Montesquieu's republican principles of 'love of equality' or 'excellence' for her conception of free action. Nietzsche also associates these principles with the agon,[56] but it is probably Montesquieu's aristocratic principle of moderation or measure (*Maass*) that has the greatest affinity with his conception of agonal action.[57] Yet, both thinkers seem to be more interested in the entire range of principles or passions than in singling out any specific principle(s) or passion(s) for their conceptions of action. And perhaps this is because for Arendt, no less than for Nietzsche, agonal action, in its unruliness and unpredictability, can draw on the entire range of principles named by Montesquieu: honour, glory, love of equality, distinction, excellence, as well as fear, distrust or hatred – not to mention (in Nietzsche's case): cruelty, vindictiveness, wrath, deceit. (HW, KSA 1.783–785), guile, revenge, slander, and at the very least – envy, jealousy and ambition. In HW, these are schematically distributed between Hesiod's 'good Eris' of jealousy, wrath, envy, which rouse men to great deeds and works, and the 'evil Eris' of 'cruelty, hatred, vindictiveness, lust and deceit', which drive men to the lawless, unmeasured struggle for annihilation (*Vernichtungskampf*). However, like the so-called 'human' and 'inhuman' impulses separated and opposed by humanism, Nietzsche's claim is that they are 'inseparably entwined' in agonal deeds and works. As noted in chapter 2 (p. 44), Nietzsche's conception of agonal agency spans the entire semantic range characteristic of the word 'agon' in Greek usage, from murder and the 'tiger-like rage for destruction' (HW, KSA 1.783) to play and creative contestation.

The affinities between agonal agency in Nietzsche and Arendt's performative concept of agency turn on five features of her account of political action in relation to principles (1993, 152f.):

1. Principles are the source or springs of free action. Action needs the intellect and the will, but must transcend their determination through principles, if it is to be free. Unlike motives or the ends chosen by the intellect, principles do not operate from within; rather 'they inspire, as it were, from without'. We can therefore speak of *external sources of free action*.
2. Although principles can serve to judge a particular aim once the action is initiated, they cannot prescribe a particular aim in advance; they are 'too general' or *indeterminate* to be formulated as a precept or prescription.
3. Unlike the operations of the intellect and the will, principles do not guide or dictate action in advance; on the contrary, they are *post hoc* or *derivative* of actions, and they become fully manifest only through and in the performing act itself.

---

[56] See e.g. 16[19], KSA 7.400: 'Am Meister lernen, am Gegner sich erkennen!'; also EH weise 7 and JGB 259 on equality; MA 170 on excellence and WS 29 on the 'nobler brother' of envy.
[57] On the relation of Nietzsche's agon to democracy and the aristocratic character of Greek democracy, see Siemens 2001c.

4. Since their appearance is bound to the performing act, principles remain 'as long as the action lasts, but no longer'; their appearance is *provisional*.
5. The power of principles is *not*, however, bound to specific acts. Unlike the commanding will, which exhausts itself in the course of the act that it executes, principles are inexhaustible and *indefinitely repeatable*.

All of these features have analogues in Nietzsche's agon. In HW, as we know, the agonal play of forces presupposes a plurality of forces or geniuses 'who stimulate each other reciprocally to deeds, as they also hold each other reciprocally within the bounds of measure' (HW, KSA 1.789). That is to say, the agon *begins* with reciprocal stimulation, where affects such as ambition, envy or love of excellence (or...) set in motion a dynamic of reciprocal provocation, arousal, inspiration or empowerment. Within this dynamic, as with Arendt's 'inspiring principles', each antagonist is moved less from within than *from without*, in response to the other's deed or word (see 1. above). This is not, however, to identify the other antagonist as the external source of agonal action; rather, it is *by way of* the other antagonist *in the relations of antagonism or tension* themselves that action has its sources. These relations, I have argued (see esp. p. 61ff.), are best understood as an *approximate equilibrium (Gleichgewicht) among more-or-less equal forces*, where equilibrium is not a subjective aim or achievement, but rather a contingent outcome of the *relations of tension between* forces, each striving for supremacy – 'to be the best.' It is, then, from an *external, medial* position in the relations of tension between antagonists that agonal equilibrium is determined and action takes off.⁵⁸

For Arendt, principles of performative action are too *indeterminate* to act as prescriptions that precede and guide action (2. above); they are *derivative*, appearing only in and through the performing act itself (3. above). For Nietzsche, the dynamic character of the 'agonal play of forces' derives from the *absence of determinate rules* or laws for adjudicating victory and defeat for all the contests that take place. On the contrary, a contest begins by throwing prevailing standards in question, and ends only with a deed or work which brings a new standard or rule for victory or excellence into force. For the antagonists strive not just to win, but to determine what counts as winning; their ambition, as we have seen from MA 170, is 'attain the highest excellence *in their own eyes*', 'before their own seat of judgement' and to win the assent (*Zustimmung*) of the public. Thus, the rule for victory or excellence does not *precede* the contest or dictate the actions of those involved; it does not stand above the contest, but is strictly immanent to each one and *derivative* of the dynamic course it takes.

Conversely, to erect an absolute and conclusive rule for victory, a standard that is beyond contention, is to destroy the agon. This, Nietzsche claims, was the original

---

58 Cf. Gerhardt (1983, 115): 'Die Kräftrelation – nicht die einzelne Kraft! – wird als die Quelle der Gerechtigkeit an gesehen.'

sense of ostracism in the Greek polis: to remove the 'towering individual' *(den überragenden Einzelnen)* to whom none are equal, so that, by restoring equilibrium, the agon might go on. And it was the hegemony *(Alleinherrschaft)* of Alexander the Great over all other contestants that put an end to the agon and with it, the polis.⁵⁹ This account suggests two further affinities with Arendt's principles of performative action. For it implies, first, that the agon admits only provisional, intermittent victors – the Olympic champion or winner of the poetic contest *this year.* Like Arendt's principles, the rule or law of victory expressed in their performance is *provisional* (4. above): it is bound to that performance and remains in force only until challenged in the next contest. Nietzsche's exclusion of absolute, conclusive victory implies, secondly, that the agonal play of forces is intrinsically *inconclusive* or *open-ended* and can be defined as the *inconclusive contestation of victory, or rather, of the very law or rule for victory* (see p. 75f.). As the actual issue of contention in every agon, the law or rule for victory is, like Arendt's principles, *inexhaustible*. Contestants may aim to fix the law of victory once and for all through their performance, but the contest to determine that rule or law *is endlessly repeatable*. The 'agonal play of forces' involves the endless repeatability characteristic of all play in the medial sense, in stark contrast to the particular aims, strategies and acts of will of the players involved (see p. 60f.).

These affinities are perhaps best understood in the light of the festival character of the agon (see p. 192ff.). Arendt's (1993, 152) central claim (3. above) is that principles do not precede or guide performative actions in the manner of the intellect and will, but appear belatedly, as it were, in the performative act itself, and (4. above) remain in force provisionally – 'as long as the action lasts, but no longer'. This is not to say that they appear ex nihilo. For Arendt, a principle like courage is certainly there prior to any political act of courage, but it only becomes part of the world and politically significant in and through that act – and for no longer than that act. If Arendt's point is that principles only gain normative force through political enactment, then principles have the same temporal structure as the laws of the agonal festival: while considered to be 'eternal' (co-eval with the festival) they actually come into force and are fully present only when enacted in (as immanent to) actual contests. While having an identity of meaning over time ('eternal'), as acts of political courage, their actual enactment is always different and unique: their identity of meaning is constituted through always different acts of courage (see p. 193). There is also a sense in which the suspension of political hostilities during the agonal festivals, in allowing competitors to meet and compete as equals, unified the Greek city-states by opening up a political space of isonomia, in which a shared concept of justice could be negotiated and 'founded' (see p. 190f.). In this regard, Nietzsche's thoughts on the origin of ancient Greek justice in the Panhellenic agonal festivals answers to Arendt's question concerning the origins of political being. For Arendt, it is

---

59 HW, KSA 1.792. See also KSA 1.788f. on ostracism, and KSA 7: 3[73], 16[16], 16[43], 38[7].

not just the performance of an act, but the way in which it engages others that establishes political relations and opens political spaces animated by the principle(s) in question. And as Dana Villa and others have noted, it is the reception of the act by others, their judgments and re-actions, that secure the measure of law needed for political life, without neutralising the unruliness of political action. Again, this is close to Nietzsche's reflections on the '[w]onderful process' by which a shared concept of justice was negotiated among competitors and spectator-judges, as to the way he draws the public into the agon (pace Villa[60]) and triangulates it as a contest of adjudication among contestants and public (see p. 195; also p. 77).

Drawing on the medial sense of the agon, I have argued in this chapter that Nietzsche locates (the sources of) laws or rules of the agon in an anomalous *third* position, somewhere between the contestants and spectators, between determinate, external laws governing all contests, on one side, and the particular claims and interests of the contestants themselves, on the other. In the context of Heraclitus' concept of 'immanent lawfulness', I drew on the Kantian expression: *lawfulness without a law (Gesetzmässigkeit ohne Gesetz)* to describe this anomalous status of agonal laws. At stake in this displacement of law, as argued in the comparative analysis with Arendt's notion of free action animated by principles, is the problem of thinking the radical freedom of action together with the constraints of law. It is this problem that connects Nietzsche with Arendt and underlies the affinities I have sought to establish between agonal action and Arendt's performative, political action. The central thought for both thinkers is that *free action precedes its principle or law, which only comes to light and gains normative force in and through the performing act itself*. In this light, the concept of law acquires a *precarious* character; it is situation-bound, derivative and as a consequence, radically contingent. But it also acquires a pluralistic and anti-subjectivistic character. Arendt's principles serve to enmesh free action in a pluralistic order or 'web of interests' and conflicting claims, which are its external sources (1. above). In their performative quality (3. above), they displace the meaning of free action from the subjective domain of intellectual deliberation and willing: 'principles' name the *relational, interactional* sources of law needed for action to be free. For Nietzsche, the laws or rules of the agon have their sources in the medial domain of a contingent equilibrium between more-or-less equal forces. Like Arendt's principles, the concept of equilibrium serves to de-subjectivise the concept of law and to cut off the significance of virtuosic, agonal action from the subjective intentions of the antagonists. For both thinkers, action can only be free where the law has its sources, not in the agent, but in the relations of reciprocal inspiration, resistance and adjudication among a plurality of forces.

---

60 See Siemens 2005.

Chapter 8
Nietzsche's Agon with *Ressentiment:* Towards a Therapeutic Reading of Critical Transvaluation (Nietzsche and Freud)

> 'That humankind be redeemed from revenge: that is the bridge to the highest hope for me and a rainbow after lengthy bad weather' (Z II Taranteln).

> Every art, every philosophy may be viewed as a cure [*Heilmittel*] and an aid in the service of growing and struggling [*kämpfenden*] life [...] (FW 370)

Introduction: The Problematic of Sickness, Health and Redemption

In Nietzsche's life-project of critical transvaluation (*Umwertung*), the prevailing values of European (Christian-Platonic) culture – whether religious, metaphysical or moral – are contested in the name of life as the highest value. It is his critical diagnosis of modernity that motivates his call for a transvaluation of all values, giving it direction and urgency, and from the period of *Die fröhliche Wissenschaft* and *Zarathustra* onwards, Nietzsche's diagnosis is often expressed as a problematic of revenge and *ressentiment*, uncovered by his genealogical critique of modern values and their sources.[1] In this chapter, I examine the practical implications of Nietzschean transvaluation through the lens of therapy and redemption. What practical consequences does Nietzsche draw from his diagnosis of *ressentiment* as our malady and the source of our malaise? Does he have a *cure* to offer, a way to heal the wound of *ressentiment*? Does he offer us a way out, a *redemption* from *ressentiment*? These questions raise in an acute form two of the fundamental problems afflicting Nietzsche's critical thought. The first is an *energetic* problem: if, as Nietzsche argues, 2,000 years of re-

---

[1] Nietzsche has a long-standing interest in revenge and its complexity ('Rache sehr complicirt!', 42[26], KSA 8.600). Already in GT 18 the revolutionary movements of the present are diagnosed as *Rache*. The association with the Jewish and/or Christian religion begins in 1875 (5[166], KSA 8.88). See also: 18[34], KSA 8; VM 52; M 68 (Paul); M 71; M 323. The exposure of feelings of revenge underlying moral sentiments and values also begins in the mid–1870s. See e.g. WS 57, M 133, M 138; 3[69], KSA 9, 7[284], KSA 9. His most extensive and detailed analysis of revenge is probably in WS 33. Nietzsche first came across the concept of *ressentiment* in Dühring's *Der Werth des Lebens* (1865) in 1867–68 (Janz 1981, I, 196), excerpted long sections and commented them in the summer of 1875 (9[1], KSA 8; see Gerhardt 1983, 118–121). It then disappears until the *Nachlass* of 1885 and GM. But many of the themes in GM and the later works were already being developed in the earlier analyses of 'Rache' and related terms in the context of religion and morality. From FW and Z on, revenge, and then (from GM on) *ressentiment*, acquire greater importance and become a key structural element in his pathogenesis of the present.

OpenAccess. © 2021 Herman Siemens, published by De Gruyter. This work is licensed under the Creative Commons Attribution-NonCommercial-NoDerivatives 4.0 International License.
https://doi.org/10.1515/9783110722291-013

ssentiment have progressively depleted our volitional resources, how *can* we do anything about it? Where are we to find sources of energy for tackling *ressentiment?* The second problem concerns the critic's auto-implication in his total critique. As we shall see, therapeutic or redemptive impulses on Nietzsche's part risk implicating his own project in the very *ressentiment* they would overcome.

There are good reasons for supposing redemptive and therapeutic impulses to issue from the project of transvaluation. In different ways, they seem to articulate one and the same desire to overcome the legacy of *ressentiment*. Typically, Nietzsche's texts combine a critical philosophical discourse on values with a psychological/physiological discourse purporting to uncover and evaluate the instinctual economy that sustains them. The critique of modern 'slave' values in opposition to 'noble' values has led many to read transvaluation as a programme to redeem modernity by annihilating slave values and reversing them into a noble morality.[2] At the same time, the bad conscience and *ressentiment* sustaining prevailing values are diagnosed by Nietzsche as 'sickness' or 'décadence', leading to vociferous appeals of concern for the 'health' and 'future' of humankind.[3] It is hard *not* to read therapeutic interests into such contexts and to begin asking: what would Nietzschean psychotherapy look like?

However, there are also good reasons for resisting such readings. In the *Genealogie der Moral* (GM III 13) the ascetic ideal is cast as the 'healing instinct of a degenerating life', and much of the third essay (sections 13–21) is devoted to criticising the various forms of priestly medication for aggravating the problem of *ressentiment*.[4] Zarathustra, to the contrary, is cast as the opposite of a 'holy man' and a 'world-redeemer'. He tells his disciples to lose and deny him that he may return to them, and he declines to heal the blind, the cripples and the hunchback so that the people may come to believe in his teaching.[5] If Zarathustra refuses the mantle of the analyst alongside that of the priest, Nietzsche's counter-therapeutic impulse has its deepest and most interesting reasons in the questions 'of whether we could *dispense* with our illness in the development of our virtue', and 'whether the will to health alone is not a prejudice, a cowardice' (FW 120). The ambiguities of these questions unfold in the self-referential dimension of Nietzschean critique and his profession of interest in

---

[2] The closing sections of GM I on 'Rome versus Judea' could be read in this vein. See also GM I 12, where Nietzsche appeals for a 'redeeeming case of human existence [*erlösenden Glücksfall des Menschen*]'.

[3] E.g. EH Vorwort 2 identifies 'ideals' with 'the worship of the *reverse* values from those with which the flourishing, the future, the high *right* to the future would be guaranteed'. In AC 3, Nietzsche defines his problem as follows: 'what type of human one ought to *breed*, ought to *will*, as more valuable, more worthy of life, more certain of the future.'

[4] E.g. through the moralization of *ressentiment* as sin. For Nietzsche this is typical of priestly therapy, as 'a mere affect-medication, not at all a real *healing* for the sick in the physiological sense' (GM III 16).

[5] See EH Vorwort 4; Z II Erlösung. Or again: 'I am a railing by the torrent: let those who can, grasp me! Your crutch, however, I am not' (Z I Verbrecher).

bad conscience as 'tension' and 'hope', as a sickness that is 'pregnant' with a future (GM I 6; GM II 16, 19). If Nietzsche affirms the will to health, he also appears to value sickness or a will to sickness; if he asks 'why weakness is not contested [*bekämpft*], but only justified' by morality (14[66], KSA 13), he also writes:

> *Decline, decay, refuse* is not something to be condemned in itself: it is a necessary consequence of life, of growth in life. The appearance of décadence is as necessary as any upward and forward movement of life: one does not have it in hand to *put an end* to it. Reason requires quite the reverse [*umgekehrt*]: that *it [décadence – HS] receives its right*... (14[75], KSA 13)

The reversal of rights, or transvaluation of sickness in these lines goes hand-in-hand with a reinterpretation or reconceptualization of health. In questioning whether we can dispense with our illness (FW 120), Nietzsche also complicates the notion of 'health in itself', a normative or 'normal health', proposing instead that we multiply health into polymorphous, 'countless healths of the body'.

How, then, are we to reconcile Nietzsche's counter-therapeutic remarks with the therapeutic and redemptive implications that seem to issue from his critical labour? How exactly are sickness and health, the will to health and the will to sickness, related in his thought? Can the conflicting impulses running through his texts be thought together – as a counter-therapeutic therapy that would contest sickness, while giving sickness 'its right'?

I Dreams of Annihilation: the Problem of Repetition

An important clue to these questions can be found in the well-known line from aphorism 370 of *Die fröhliche Wissenschaft*, that 'every art, every philosophy may be viewed as a cure and an aid in the service of growing and struggling [*kämpfende*] life'. The connection between healing and struggle (*Kampf*) as an agon is central to the therapeutic reading of Nietzsche's philosophy to be advanced in §II of this chapter. But as it stands, this line makes a global statement ('every...') and says nothing specific about *Nietzsche's* philosophy. The point of the aphorism, as a full reading shows, is to distinguish two kinds of philosophy or art – romantic, and classical or dionysian – and to align Nietzsche's thought with the latter against the former. This distinction complicates the question of therapy, since it implies a distinction between 'good' and 'bad' therapy and the forms they can take at the level of philosophical discourse. As a consequence, the identification of therapeutic with redemptive impulses will have to be revised, for as an instance of 'bad' therapy, redemptive impulses come into conflict with Nietzsche's therapeutic interests.

Nietzsche's argument in FW 370 turns on an irresolvable conflict of interests between two forms of life:

> Every art, every philosophy may be viewed as a cure and an aid in the service of growing and struggling life: they always presuppose suffering and suffering beings. But there are two sorts of suffering beings: first, those suffering from the *excess [Ueberfülle] of life*, who want a dionysian art, and with it, a tragic view of life, a tragic insight, – and then those suffering from the *impoverishment [Verarmung] of life*, who seek peace, stillness, calm seas, redemption from themselves through art and knowledge, or intoxication, spasms, numbing, madness. (FW 370)[6]

The difference between impoverishment or lack and excess serves Nietzsche to distinguish the Romantic from the Classical. Those suffering from impoverishment seek redemption or respite from their suffering. These interests are served by Romanticism in various ways, Nietzsche tells us. Typically, it offers 'closure in optimistic horizons', sabbatical visions governed by goodness, gods or logic ('for logic soothes'), visions that would resolve what is most frightening and senseless in existence. Alternatively, it employs the physiological means of affective discharge – the intoxicating rush or spasms of passion. But the semiotics of suffering are complex, and Nietzsche warns that romantic therapy can take unexpected, even opposed forms: not just the projection of personal suffering into a binding universal law (Schopenhauer's 'revenge' on all things), but also destructive misarchism, the anarchists' hatred of the law. What they all share is a non-acceptance of personal pain and the impulse to soothe or numb it, usually through visions that resolve or destroy its perceived sources in negativity. These sources include struggle and conflict (*Kampf*), and for Nietzsche this is crucial: to reject them is to reject the very 'growing, struggling [*kämpfende*] life', in which even impoverished, romantic types take part. This, for Nietzsche, is bad therapy; not because it does not relieve pain, but because it negates and falsifies life in its character of conflict. Good therapy, by contrast, is centred on the productive aspects of conflict. Optimistic closure is eschewed in favour of an openness towards pain and suffering, perceived as necessary for growth and production. It is this interpretation of pain – the 'tragic insight' – that serves the interests of life as excess, whether in destructive dionysian visions expressing 'the overfull force, pregnant with the future', or in classical visions that express a 'gratitude and love' of life without falsifying its tragic reality. Good therapy is able to affirm life as it is.

It is plain from Nietzsche's language – such as the identification of the 'Classical' with the 'Dionysian' – where he would have us situate his thought along the axis of 'good' and 'bad' therapy. Yet, serious obstacles to a 'good' therapeutic reading of his work arise from the opposition, or conflict of interests, between ascending forms of life (excess) and declining forms of life (lack). The first concerns the redemptive impulses in Nietzsche's thought. These can no longer be assumed to converge with a sound therapeutic interest in overcoming *ressentiment*, for the above text is quite clear: redemptive impulses serve the interests of declining forms of life *against* the

---

[6] Cf. NW Antipoden, where this passage occurs with slight modifications and the further connection with revenge: 'The revenge against life itself – the most voluptuous kind of intoxication [*Rausch*] for those so impoverished.' (KSA 6.425). The connection between weakness, revenge and narcosis is discussed below.

interests of ascending life in growth, struggle and fertility. From this perspective, any desire on Nietzsche's part to redeem modernity from *ressentiment* not only undermines his therapeutic interests; it threatens to co-opt them into the service of declining life. A second, related difficulty comes from Nietzsche's treatment of closure. If 'closure in optimistic horizons' also serves the interests declining life, then any attempt to enclose the horizon of the future becomes suspect – including redemptive visions of health free from *ressentiment*. More seriously, it threatens any directive or teleological orientation towards health, any attempt to determine the passage from present sickness to future health with reference to a governing telos or goal. It is not enough for Nietzsche's will-to-health is to remain open to sickness, conflict and suffering (the tragic insight); in the interests of ascending life, it must take a form that is resolutely anti-teleological and open-ended.

At the root of these 'impossible' demands is the fundamental problem posed by aphorism 370: that sound therapy presupposes an excess of life. Nietzsche is quite clear that it is 'the one richest in the fullness of life, the dionysian god or human' who can afford exposure to negativity and tragic insight. He is also quite clear that he was wrong in Die Geburt der Tragödie to ascribe excess to contemporary philosophy and music (Schopenhauer, Wagner). Indeed, the closing lines of the aphorism seem to rule out tragic pessimism from Nietzsche's present altogether, in a gesture that defers by renaming it a 'pessimism of the future'. And is this gesture not correct? Tragedy and pre-Socratic philosophy may have been predicated on excess, and Nietzsche can lay claim to this insight as his very own 'intimation and vision'. But Nietzsche's philosophy cannot lay claim to excess: his own diagnosis of the pervasive debilitation of life in modernity implicates him, no less than 'us', the potential beneficiaries of a Nietzschean therapy, robbing his thought of any therapeutic force in the present. On Nietzsche's own terms, then, the depleted volitional resources of modernity confront his therapeutic interests with an *energetic deficit*. The semiotics of lack and impoverishment are certainly not hard to discern in Zarathustra's hope: '*That humankind be redeemed from revenge:* that is the bridge to the highest hope for me and a rainbow after lengthy bad weather' (Z II Taranteln, KSA 4.128). The ambiguity of Nietzsche's project announces itself in these lines, where the vengeful impulses condemned by him reappear as the redemptive hope and sabbatical desire inspiring Zarathustra – or do they? To what extent *are* Nietzsche's practical interests 'infected' by the very disease he sought to combat? A straightforward redemptive reading of the problem of revenge, as suggested by Zarathustra's words, raises an acute problem for Nietzsche, whose entire project is vitiated if it merely *repeats* those impulses subjected to critique. For a 'good' therapeutic reading, on the other hand, resources must be found that would turn the energetic deficit of modernity into the surplus of ascending life.

The suspicions we have raised can be taken further if we turn to the *Genealogie der Moral*. Here the redemptive impulses discerned in Romanticism are given a closer analysis in the context of what Nietzsche calls the 'slave-revolt of morality' (GM I 7 f.). At the same time, he brings a new, external dimension to his analysis, situating the redemptive urges of slave morality in a socio-political context of power-relations. The analogy with Nietzsche's own philosophical situation is so strong as to suggest that redemptive impulses are rooted deep in the conditions governing the project of transvaluation, locking his thought into a hopeless repetition of the logic of revenge. The *Genealogie* identifies two kinds of impulse behind redemptive hopes and sabbatical desires. First, there is narcosis:

> "happiness" on the level of the impotent, the oppressed, those festering with poisonous and inimical feelings [...] appears essentially as narcosis, numbing [*Betäubung*], rest, peace, "sabbath", emotional relaxation and limb-stretching [...] (GM I 10, KSA 5.272; cf. FW 370 above).

Then there is revenge:

> These weak ones – sometime *they* too want to be the strong ones for once, there is no doubt, sometime *their* "kingdom" too will come – "The Kingdom of God" it is called amongst them [...] (GM I 15, KSA 5.183)

Later on, in the third Essay, the intimate connection of revenge to narcosis is explained in the context of *ressentiment*:

> It is here alone, I would suggest, that the real physiological causality of *ressentiment*, revenge and related [impulses] is actually to be found: in a demand for the *numbing* [*Betäubung*] *of pain through affects.* (GM III 15, KSA 5.374)

The presupposition of this analysis is pain.[7] The pain of weakness, impoverishment or lack, familiar from Romanticism, is given a more concrete turn in these passages. The slave suffers not for existential or metaphysical reasons; he suffers from 'weakness' *vis-à-vis a class of masters*; from a 'lack' of power *in relation to overpowering forces*; from the secret, slow-burning pain of actual 'impotence' that cannot reverse its suffering and dare not even reveal it. In the *Genealogie*, redemptive hopes arise in the face of oppression, under conditions of antagonism, as a destructive reaction to being-overpowered. In the context of this power differential, the romantic strategies of narcosis (Wagner) and revenge (Schopenhauer) form a single dynamic, for the slave's redemptive hopes relieve the feeling of impotence by means both physiological *and* spiritual: a narcotic 'rush' tied to the promise of release, of peace – an end to the pain of antagonism. But the narcotic effect of this promise depends on desires and impulses that are far from peaceful. A central claim of the *Genealogie* is that vengeful wishes and destructive phantasies nest and fester in our most 'harmless' sabbatical longings. To eliminate the source of the pain, the antagonist, would bring instantaneous and lasting relief; since actual impotence rules this out, destructive impulses feed instead on dreams of annihilation.

---

7 The non-acceptance of pain and suffering is connected with revenge in several texts, e.g. M 133; M 214; 6[5], KSA 9; 6[280], KSA 9; 6[300], KSA 9; FW 290. Also 9[1], KSA 8.150 (Dühring).

It is such dreams that threaten Nietzsche's own thought, not for personal reasons, but because his project is subject to the same conditions under which they flourish. Impotence, the feeling of being-overpowered, are built into the scene of transvaluation as its initial conditions. It is important to see that an interest in growth and conflict does not place the critic in a position of strength. On the contrary, it is weak and impoverished forms of life, under the hegemonial values spawned in their interest, that constitute the *force majeure* of Western civilization. The historical meaning of the 'slave-revolt of morality' is to have reversed political weakness into power, bondage into victory, as a result of reversing 'good' into 'evil'. Thus, the project of transvaluation is predicated on the reversal of weakness and bondage into power, casting the one who would resist them into a position of weakness.[8] From this position, nothing could be more tempting than the slavish desire to destroy the legacy of our Christian-Platonic past once and for all, and redeem us from *ressentiment*. Yet, to succumb to this temptation would be to play into the hands of the opponent, for it is declining forms of life that crave annihilation (*Vernichtung*) of antagonistic forces[9] – for the sake of peace. Once again, it is Zarathustra who intimates Nietzsche's implication in his own critique, this time with the voice of impotent rage:

> The Now and the Then on earth – Oh my friends – that is *for me* the most unendurable: and I would not know how to live, if I were not still a seer of what must come.
> A seer, a willer, a creator, a future itself and a bridge to the future – and oh, still a cripple on this bridge, as it were: all this Zarathustra is. (Z II Erlösung, KSA 4.179)

It is hard, on Zarathustra's own admission, to disentangle these lines from the crippling revenge against time and time's '"it was"'. The impulse to destroy the legacy of our Christian-Platonic past and redeem us from *ressentiment* does seem to make of Nietzsche the 'evil spectator' condemned by Zarathustra: 'Impotent against that which has been done – he is an evil spectator of all that is past' (Z II Erlösung).

The self-referential dimension of Nietzschean critique has rightly come under increasing scrutiny in the literature. Daniel Conway, for instance, has argued that the *Anti-Christ(ian)* replicates the priestly *ressentiment* of St. Paul which it so vehemently condemns.[10] More than that, Conway proposes a general theoretical framework for the self-referential dimension of Nietzschean critique bearing on the *whole* of his project. Nietzsche, Conway claims, recognises but two modes of evaluation: the ac-

---

[8] On this point see Müller-Lauter 1971, 55, 78, 121.
[9] Cf. Ottmann 1987, 223: 'A radical will to annihilate [*Vernichtungswille*] attests to weakness, not strength.' This view, central to Nietzsche's philosophy of power from the late 1870s on, is traced by Ottmann back to his early reception of Thucydides, whose 'dialectical turn against total power' leads Nietzsche to advocate a certain equilibrium and reciprocity of power. An analogous turn towards agonal relations of power will be traced in §II of this chapter.
[10] Conway 1997b, esp. 191–200. Nietzsche's 'unwitting' complicity with St. Paul is a theme repeated throughout this book, which strangely casts him as blind and impotent in the face of the self-referential implications of his critique of morality.

tive creation of values *ex nihilo*, and the reactive transvaluation of existing values thematised as the 'slave-revolt of morality' (GM I 7). Nietzsche's self-confessed décadence disqualifies him from the former, for spontaneous value-creation is reserved for healthy peoples and ages. His transvaluation of values must therefore be situated 'squarely' within the tradition of reactive evaluation with its foundational gestures of slave-revolt (revenge) and the promise of redemption (Conway 1997b, 183; cf. 109). It is no accident, then, that Nietzsche's texts betray a *ressentiment* against *ressentiment*. The vengeful eye on the spirit of revenge, the hope of redemption from our redemptive desires: on Nietzsche's own theoretical presuppositions, such 'slavish' attitudes are *bound* to infect any attempt to transvaluate prevailing values from a position of weakness.

But are we really to suppose that Nietzsche was blind to these self-referential consequences? And if not, that he knowingly acquiesced in a hopeless repetition of the attitudes he criticised? Nietzsche's insight and resilience should make us think twice about redemptive readings *because* of their consequences. We should perhaps pause to ask whether there is another way to take the self-referential dimension of Nietzsche's critique seriously. Is there a way for him to contest prevailing values that does not simply replicate the foundational gestures of slave-revolt (revenge) and the promise of redemption? A way to react against them that does not remain locked in a reactive mode of evaluation? There is a good deal of textual evidence that Nietzsche repeats the logic of revenge in reacting against Christian-Platonic values. My argument does not deny this; rather, it denies that in repeating these motions, Nietzsche remains locked in a reactive mode of evaluation. Transformation through repetition: this is the paradox I shall try to think through. The argument turns on the concept of 'agonal transvaluation'.

II Agonal Transvaluation as Therapy

Let me begin by reviewing some key elements of the agon, considered as a model for Nietzsche's transvaluative discourse; they will then serve as the basis for an agonal concept of therapy.

As I have argued throughout this book, Nietzsche's textual confrontations draw us into a critical contestation of dominant values, whose dynamic form is modelled on the pre-Socratic 'agonal' community presented in the early essay *Homer's Wettkampf* (1872). The agon involves a specific *organization of power*, a dynamic tension or equilibrium (*Gleichgewicht*) between a plurality of more-or-less equal, active forces contesting one another. Agonal contestation engages the antagonists in a complex interplay of mutual affirmation and mutual negation, an agonal 'play of forces' (*Wettspiel der Kräfte*) that stimulates or provokes each contestant to deeds that would surpass the other, while containing both within the limits of measure. The productive relation of mutual empowerment-disempowerment creates a dynamic of *limited aggression* that precludes destruction (death or total negation) on one side, and absolute, conclusive victory (total affirmation) for any single contestant on the other. Agonal victory is provisional, and like all forms of play, the agon is inconclusive: repeatable and open-ended.

As a productive conflict of active forces, agonal culture embodies Nietzsche's therapeutic interest in 'growing and struggling life' as fertility from FW 370. In Homer's *Wettkampf*, the agon serves to explain the extraordinary productivity 'in deeds and works' of archaic Greek culture: through mutual provocation and empowerment, it propitiates the elevation (*Steigerung*) or growth of life and the cultivation of greatness (*Grösse*). It should not, however, be thought that horror, despair and sickness are simply absent from this picture. Health is not a given; it is an *achievement* of agonal culture, which is unthinkable in the absence of terrifying and destructive affective forces (of the *Vernichtungskampf*).[11] Like tragedy,[12] the agon effects a *practical transformation* of 'inhuman' into human, culture-building forces in conjunction with an *affirmative interpretation* of life, radically opposed to Christian morality as 'Anti-Nature' (GD Moral). In Nietzsche's account, aggressive, thanatos drives dominate: as a regime of *limited aggression* the agon transforms and assimilates them into a productive and affirmative practice of life.

From this brief sketch, it can be seen that the agon combines in a quite striking way various elements which Nietzsche associates, at one time or another, with health.[13]

---

11   'How *Greek nature knows how to make use of all terrifying qualities:*
the tiger-like rage for destruction (of the tribes etc.) in the agon
the unnatural drives (in the education of the youth by the man)
the Asiatic *orgiastic* ways (in the Dionysian)
the hostile isolation of the individual (Erga) in the Apollinian.
The application of the harmful towards useful [ends] is idealised in the world-view of *Heraclitus*.
7. Finale: Dithyramb to *art and the artist* : because they first create [*herausschaffen*] the human and transpose [*übertragen*] all its drives into culture.' (16[18], KSA 7).

The poet overcomes the struggle for existence by idealising it into a free agon [contest]. Here is the existence, for which there is still a struggle, existence in praise, in undying fame.
The poet *educates:* he knows how to transpose [*übertragen*] the Greeks' tiger-like drives to ravaging devastation into the good Eris.' (16[15], KSA 7).

12   Note 5[146], KSA 8 (see chapter 2, p. 53 f.) on Greek mores, speaks not only of agonal affects like revenge and envy, but of intoxication and licentiousness: thoroughly dionysian affects, and their measured integration into Greek life: a reference to dionysian cults and tragedy. ('The pleasure of *intoxication*, the pleasure of *guile*, of *revenge*, of *envy*, of *slander*, of *licentiousness* [*Unzüchtigkeit*] – all of this was *acknowledged* [*anerkannt*] by the Greeks as human, and on that basis integrated into [*eingeordnet*] the edifice of society and mores.') See also 16[16] and 16[18], KSA 7 (quoted in full in note 11 above), where parallels are also drawn between agon and love and the Dionysian:

The means [*Mittel*] against the unmeasured egoism of the individual.
The instinct for the homeland
the public domain
the contest
love φιλία.' (16[16] 7.398)
('*Die Mittel gegen die maßlose Selbstsucht des Individuums.*

Equilibrium (*Gleichgewicht*) and measure (*Maass*) (e.g. FW 113; see Pasley 1978, 148) are of paramount importance in the agon. Then there is innocence (*Unschuld*) in the sense of an extra-moral attitude, a non-judgemental liberality (*Freisinnigkeit*), open to instincts and passions (5[146], KSA 8). For the question of therapy, the next two features are crucial: the dynamic, energetic conception of health (as in FW 370), of abundant strength and vitality, able to thrive on obstacles as challenges in a dynamic of productive self-overcoming (Pasley 1978, 124 f.); and then the more radical picture of a 'health in the teeth of sickness' (Pasley 1978, 154), or what Nietzsche calls 'great health', which thrives on sickness 'as its eternally stimulating and eternally re-forming antagonist' (Pasley 1978, 149), turning damaging forces into stimulants, to its advantage. 'For the Greeks possessed nothing less than a burly health; – their secret was to worship [honour: *verehren*] even sickness as a god, if only it had *power*.'[14]

II.1 Agonal Hermeneutics and Beyond: the Problem of Energy

The case for the therapeutic potential of Nietzsche's critical confrontations turns on the affirmative transformation of pathological, destructive impulses through agonal contestation. The argument takes off from the thesis that agonal culture regulates Nietzsche's transvaluative discourse as its *productive and organising principle*, as a model that organises his critical confrontations (see chapter 3). Again, the discussion will be confined to those points that bear directly on the question of therapy.

In the first place, the agon involves a *symmetrical* organization or economy of power, presupposing a plurality of more-or-less equal, antagonistic forces. Agonal discourse is therefore contingent on the participation of a plurality of forces in a sym-

---

    Der Heimatsinstinkt
    die Öffentlichkeit
    der Wettkampf
    die Liebe φιλία.')

And:
    '*How Greek nature knows how to make use [benutzen] of all terrifying qualities:*
    the tiger-like rage for destruction (of the tribes etc.) in the agon [...]
    the Asiatic orgiastic ways (in the Dionysian) [...]' (16[18], KSA 7.399 f.)
    ('*Wie die griechische Natur alle furchtbaren*
    Eigenschaften zu benutzen weiß:
    die tigerartige Vernichtungswuth (der Stämme usw.) im
    Wettkampf [...]
    das asiatische Orgienwesen (im Dionysischen) [...]')

13 For an overview of different conceptions of health in Nietzsche's thought, see Pasley 1978, 123–158. The chronological emphasis in Pasley's account is useful, but rather too stark. Conceptions that he separates into different phases often occur in one and the same text.

14 In note 7[75] (KSA 9) the affirmative praise of drives includes reference to such agonal affects as envy and hatred; significantly, Nietzsche's thoughts are directed towards the future ('A hint for the future?? NB').

metrical contestation of values: transvaluation only occurs where 'we' are drawn into critical contests, as an 'agonal community' of readers (see chapter 7). Under these conditions, deference to Nietzsche or any single force is ruled out. Nietzsche's judgements do, of course, claim authority, but not the incontrovertible authority of truth-claims delivered by a great master, healer or priest. They serve rather to 'open play', to provoke dispute and draw us into controversy; like Zarathustra, Nietzsche would sooner have hated friends than command belief (EH Vorwort 4, KSA 6.260). Agonal authorship throws its own authority in the balance, to be won by the assent (*Zustimmung*) of its readership (see p. 76 ff.): judgements and counter-values, together with the very standards of evaluation or judgement, are opened to contestation by a collective readership which would respond to the challenge it issues. In this regard, agonal hermeneutics can accommodate at least one of Nietzsche's counter-therapeutic impulses: the rejection of *asymmetrical* (saviour/priest-sinner; master-disciple) relationships voiced by Zarathustra.

Conclusive victory for any antagonist spells the death of the agon: since the agon precludes both conclusive defeat (destruction) and conclusive victory, it is repeatable and *inconclusive* in its very mode of being. As a consequence, the agon gives an *open-ended, inconclusive* orientation to transvaluative discourse. Nietzschean critique is not out to destroy its opponents (life-negating values or attitudes – like *ressentiment*) and assert a single-handed victory (conclusive counter-values) over them. Instead, it serves to *open and re-open* the question of victory: What would constitute the overcoming of life-negating values? What would be an affirmative practice beyond *ressentiment*? In this regard, agonal hermeneutics addresses the most serious threat to a therapeutic reading: the redemptive desire to destroy Christian-Platonic values. If it is declining forms of life that dream of annihilating (*Vernichtung*) opponents for the sake of peace, then the interests of ascending life, by contrast, require the *empowerment* of the antagonist for the sake of continued conflict and growth. Under this constraint, Nietzsche's philosophy must resist the lure of finality and the expedient of destroying its opponents, while *practising conflict or struggle* in a form that (a) *empowers* its opponents, and (b) remains *open-ended or inconclusive*. That is, it must practice *agonal* conflict.

If understood correctly, the open-ended, dynamic qualities of the agon also address the problem of closure at its most intractable: the demand that therapeutic discourse be non-directional or anti-teleological, in the interests of ascending life. At issue here is repeatability as a feature *intrinsic to* the agon as a dynamic ordering of forces, a feature we have identified with the agon as a *festival* and a form of *play*. As Gadamer has argued, play in its original, 'medial sense'[15] acquires a structure of repetition that is radically impersonal and anti-teleological. In the medial sense, the real subject of play is the play itself, which holds the player in thrall (Gadamer 2004, 106), so that the dynamics of play are freed from the players' intentions,

---

15 See chapter 2 III.2, esp. p. 60 and chapter 7, p. 192 ff.

goals and efforts: 'the movement which is play, has no goal which brings it to an end; rather it renews itself in constant repetition' (Gadamer 2004, 103). Equally, repetition or return is *intrinsic* to festivals – including agonal festivals – in their character as *celebration*.[16] Since it belongs to the establishment of a festival, at its very origin, that it should be regularly celebrated, the festival is something that 'only is insofar as it is always different'; it has its 'being only in becoming and recurring' (Gadamer 2004, 121; see p. 193).

In this light, the open-ended repeatability of agonal discourse is not contingent on the self-restraint of antagonists who are able to hold back from destroying the other in order to achieve absolute victory. Contestants cannot be relied on to avoid excess in the agon, which, by its very nature, allows the temptation of hubris to compete with the warning of self-restraint – with uncertain results. This goes for Nietzsche as well, whose authorship is notoriously unrestrained at times. According to Gadamer, however, the antagonists must be clearly distinguished from the agon itself, as the 'subject' of play in the medial sense. Whatever their attitudes or intentions, they are, as agonal players, subject to the to-and-fro dynamics of empowerment-disempowerment, an inconclusive, repeatable movement detached from any telos. If the agon gives the temporal character of play and celebration to Nietzsche's textual confrontations, then we can say that agonal discourse is a radically impersonal, non-directional and repeatable medium of thought; something that only *is* insofar as it is becoming. Individual goals and desires are embedded in the anti-teleological medium of agonal exchange to which they give themselves; any bids for power, any attempts at closure are checked or undone by the vicissitudes of empowerment-disempowerment to which they are subject. Agonal hermeneutics thus ensures that Nietzsche's therapeutic interests remain non-directional and open-ended, in line with the interests of ascending life, despite the temptations to closure that haunt his project.

There is an obvious objection to this line of thought. For it is hard to see how agonal discourse, if non-directional, can promote the interests of ascending life. How can a non-directional medium be in any sense orientated towards health? In response, it is important to consider the feint of writing, that is, the emphatically fictive style of Nietzsche's agonal confrontations. As noted above, the agon epitomises the notion of ascending life advocated in FW 370, and agonal discourse is best understood as *enacting* the highest form of life for Nietzsche: growth, fertility, conflict, excess – and health. The agonal dynamic regulating his discourse *supplements* the discursive critique of pathological, life-negating regimes with a *performative* challenge that anticipates or *pre-figures* the therapeutic telos of health – a productive and affirmative form of life.

The notion of fiction is important for two reasons. First, because it involves a *particular* vision, a *possible* form of life or health amongst others, not a normative con-

---

16 See chapter 7, p. 192f.

cept of health enjoined upon all as a binding, universal norm or telos. The distance between teleology and fiction is measured by the difference between enclosing the horizon of the future, and playing with an open horizon. The agonal feint thus orients transvaluation towards health without subsuming it under norms, goals or directives that would in fact promote the interests of declining life: the anti-teleology of fiction joins the anti-teleology of play. Fiction is also important in its *performative* dimension as the *agonal dynamic of mutual empowerment-disempowerment enacted in Nietzsche's texts*. This agonal dynamic not only throws valuable light on certain features of Nietzsche's thinking that resist discursive understanding; it also opens up an *energetic dimension* in Nietzsche's texts essential to their therapeutic potential.

With regard to what Blondel calls the 'enigma' of Nietzsche's texts,[17] I have argued that the agonal dynamic captures the movement of 'saying and unsaying' through which Nietzsche's texts contain yet exceed philosophical discourse (see esp. p. 10 f.). The agon allows us to see this movement of critique as a coherent practice of limited aggression in a way that escapes purely discursive readings. At the same time, the agonal dynamic also brings out the energetic dimension Nietzsche's 'enigmatic' texts, of cardinal importance for the problem of therapy. In a way, Nietzsche's texts present a conundrum similar to Freud's. In *Freud and Philosophy* (1970)[18], Ricoeur argues that a hermeneutic reading of psychoanalytic discourse falls short; for at crucial junctures, hermeneutics, as an interrogation of meaning in the medium of language, must be supplemented by an economics that addresses the dynamic, energetic dimension of Freud's thought. In Nietzsche's case too, hermeneutics is insufficient; even a broad hermeneutics embracing not just discursive sequences, but the other strands – narrative, metaphorical etc. – woven into them, must be supplemented by an energetic point of view that makes sense of the dynamic, performative dimension of Nietzsche's texts. There is, in other words, more to Nietzsche's texts than a critical discourse on values; next to the *thematic* dimension of his writing, we need to attend to 'what inside Nietzsche's text remains outside discourse':[19] a *performative* dimension that continuously irrupts on the surface of the text, moving, forming and deforming Nietzsche's discourse in ways that exceed discursive readings It is this 'enigmatic' surplus, the forces that disrupt and distort discursive order which, for the most part, carry its affective charge: the pathos *and* pathology animating Nietzsche's project. Any insight into the pathology of transvaluation, let alone its therapeutic transformation, is therefore barred until we find ways of linking what Nietzsche says to what he does not say, but enacts.

The agonal model is a way to do this, for it brings a 'vertical' or energetic dimension to our readings. The dynamics of empowerment-disempowerment regulating Nietzsche's philosophical discourse at the surface of the text are but part of a larger

---

[17] Blondel 1991, Introduction. See pp. 9f., 68 above.
[18] Ricoeur 1970, esp. Book II Part I: 65 ff.; and 390 ff. on psychoanalysis and phenomenology
[19] Blondel 1991, 7.

organization or economy of energy, grounded in embodied, affective engagement. From this perspective, Nietzsche's discourse means what it says, but it also works as a code (*Zeichensprache*) for a body in action. In fact, it becomes a *metaphor of the body* in extreme, violent agitation, the *transference of an affective engagement* bound by an agonal economy of energy. Agonal discourse, I shall argue, is both a commentary on the *ressentiment* animating it and the site for its therapeutic transformation into the productive aggression of critical transvaluation. To see why this is so, we need to probe the vertical axis of agonal culture.

II. 2 Agonal Transference (*Übertragung*) as Therapy

We have come across the term 'Übertragung' several times, a key term for the young Nietzsche deployed with various, context-specific meanings depending on the specific problem under consideration.[20] Of relevance in the present context are the transformative and metaphorical meanings discussed in chapter 3, where we saw Nietzsche describe the agon as an aesthetic *techne* for excluding destructive conflict from social life through the transference or *Übertragung* of the 'evil' Eris (goddess of war and hatred) into the 'good' Eris (goddess of envy and ambition). Agonal *Übertragung* signifies the affirmative transformation of aggressive, destructive affects into constructive cultural forces (HW 1.787; cf. pp. 25, 73 ff., 148 f.). As such, it falls within Nietzsche's broad concept of culture as *metaphor* or 'vita femina' (FW 339) – the transference or repressive displacement of embodied, instinctual forces towards the conscious surface of thought and language (expression). Meta-phorical culture results from the primal, i.e. constitutive act of bad conscience: the scission of human life into conscious and unconscious, very close to Freud's conception of primary or primal repression, as Blondel has argued.[21] As a result of the primal split, 'the sequence of phenomena that are really connected takes place on a *subconscious* level; the apparent series and successions of feelings, thoughts etc. are *symptoms* of the real sequences' (1[61], KSA 12). Thus, cultural phenomena become 'symptomatic and displaced metaphorical manifestations' (Blondel 1985, 167) of desire; even thought is 'but another sign language which expresses a compromise between the powers [*Machtausgleich*] of different affects' (1[28], KSA 12), what Nietzsche elsewhere calls 'a more or less fantastic commentary upon an unknown [or: unconscious], perhaps unknowable, but felt text' (M 119). As cultural artefacts, Nietzsche's agonal texts are subject to the same vicissitude: his critical discourse means what it says, but it also means more than it says; it too performs a metaphorical commentary upon an unconscious text. But which unconscious text? What kind of 'compromise

---

20 See chapter 3 III, esp. p. 84; chapter 5, pp. 128, 134 f. and sections VII-VIII.
21 Blondel 1985, 153.

[is held] between the powers of different affects' in *agonal* culture? And what is the *agonal* rule of transference or displacement?

Agonal culture is not so much distinguished by the *kinds* of affect that animate it as by their organization, the peculiar 'compromise' between powers it makes possible. Hate, cruelty, lust, deceitfulness, vindictiveness, all those affects symbolised by Hesiod's 'evil Eris', are the 'fertile ground' of agonal deeds. These form the latent meaning of the Homeric dream world, according to Nietzsche; but then they also form the latent meaning of Aquinas and the Apocalypse of St. John, the disciple of love (see GM I 15–16). The agon draws on affective powers no different from those which, although repressed, fill the subterranean workshops of Christian-Platonic values. The difference lies in the direction (goal, object) given to these affective powers and their configuration with other powers. They are not repressed or internalised in the agon, but externalised or discharged in deeds of mutual antagonism, governed by codes of *disempowerment* that limit the pathos of aggression. They are not condemned, but openly acknowledged as stimulants, provoking and *empowering* each antagonist to contest the other. The agonal dynamic of mutual empowerment-disempowerment controls and limits powerful, destructive affects for the purposes of *exploitation*; it is about 'using' these 'great sources of power, the wildwater of the soul, often so dangerous, overwhelming, explosive, and *economising* them' (14[163], KSA 13).

In Nietzsche's texts, we also find, as their 'fertile ground' or 'source of power', those vengeful and deceitful desires animating agonal contestation. These, then, form of the 'unconscious text' upon which the discourse of limited aggression performs a metaphorical commentary. At the same time, they also feed the sickness which the 'conscious text' of critical transvaluation discovers behind Christian-Platonic values. But the agonal dynamic of Nietzsche's discourse is no mere commentary on the hatred animating it; much less does it justify hatred or moralise it in the guise of Johannine love (14[65], KSA 13). Rather, it draws on hatred as a 'source of power', within an *economy* that serves to *transform* it.

Within an agonal economy of energy, *Übertragung* means both the metaphorical transference of destructive affects and their affirmative transformation into constructive, culture-building impulses. Accordingly, Nietzsche's textual confrontations economise destructive, vengeful affects for the purposes of value-contestation and -creation. With this transformative impulse, a *therapeutic* perspective on Nietzschean transvaluation is opened. One could say: Nietzschean transvaluation performs an *unconscious therapy on the unconscious text of its own explosive sickness*. Insofar as we participate in the contestation of values inaugurated by Nietzsche's text, we too perform an unconscious therapy on our own sickness. The therapeutic perspective is made up of four claims:

1. The agonal contestation of values is suited to transforming our condition as moderns because it draws on just those affects which, although repressed, are constitutive of our modern sickness: the unconfessed spirit of revenge and hatred animating our modern ideals.

2. Agonal transvaluation allows for a transformative will to health, while acknowledging and affirming the value of illness. In line with the age-old war of annihilation against the passions ('il faut tuer les passions': GD Moral 1), Christian and post-Christian, humanist morality outwardly condemns the aggressive impulses that covertly animate them in attitudes of *ressentiment*. At the same time, they would rather justify (by falsifying) hatred as love than transform it. In agonal culture, by contrast, the transformation of destructive affects goes hand-in-hand with an affirmative attitude of acknowledgement, gratitude, reverence. As an agonal economy of power, transvaluation can therefore accommodate the most serious of Nietzsche's counter-therapeutic impulses: not just his rejection of asymmetrical relationships, but his affirmative remarks concerning sickness, its indispensability and its 'right' (14[75], KSA 13). Agonal transvaluation precludes the total negation of illness, a war of annihilation (*Vernichtungskampf*) that would extirpate pathological forces for the sake of 'normal health'; instead, it inaugurates an open-ended *contest (Wettkampf) with illness*, an *affirmative transformation* that repeats and affirms pathological, destructive forces, while transforming them into critical and constructive philosophical impulses.

3. To replace the negation of hatred with acknowledgement, the repression of aggression with its expression in agonal deeds of envy and ambition, is also to *release new sources of power or energy*. The affirmative moment of agonal culture has an *economic* consequence of vital importance, given the energetic deficit obstructing a viable therapeutic reading. From an economic point of view, agonal transvaluation dissolves inherited systems of solitary *debilitation* through a collective regime of mutual *empowerment*: it is what Nietzsche calls a 'systeme fortifiant' or fortifying system, in opposition to the debilitation or weakening promoted by moral systems:

> *Debilitation* as **task:** debilitation of desires, of feelings of pleasure and unpleasure, of will to power, to pride, to having and wanting-to-have-more; debilitation as humility; debilitation as faith; *debilitation* as aversion and shame in all that is natural, as the negation of life, as sickness and habitual weakness...
>
> *Debilitation* as renunciation of revenge, of resistance, of enmity and wrath.
> the *blunder* in treatment: one does not want to contest sickness through a systeme *fortifiant*, but through a kind of justification and *moralization:* that is, through an *interpretation...* (14[65], KSA 13.251)

Agonal transvaluation, by contrast, *would contest our inherited sickness through a 'systeme fortifiant'*. Through the non-repressive transference of revenge and wrath, energy is released for a therapeutic contestation of sickness in the interests of ascending life. We are familiar with *ressentiment* as sickness and as the slow-burning agent of debilitation and self-contempt (EH weise 6). The agonal perspective reminds us that it is also explosive, a tremendous reserve of affective resources, housing a potential excess of expendable energy – if only it can be harnessed in productive deeds.²² The agonal dynamic of empowerment-disempowerment is a prime instance of that 'propitious gathering and intensification of forces and tasks' needed for us to 'grasp with one look all that could still be cultivated out of the human being' (JGB 230). It reminds us 'how the human being is still not exhausted for the greatest possibilities', despite the ravages of our 'natural history of morality' documented in Part 5 of *Jenseits von Gut und Böse*.

4. The question of therapeutic transformation turns on the *re-organization of the active forces of human existence*. As Nietzsche insists in the *Genealogie der Moral*, reactive affects and postures of internalised aggression are animated by forces that are *active*, i.e. actively engaged in affirming and empowering themselves in their given configuration or life-form.²³ This means that active forces which are bent into reactive attitudes can be released towards novel forms of self-affirmation by changing their direction (externalization) and their configuration with other forces. In agonal transvaluation, reactive postures of internalised aggression are externalised into active deeds of mutual critical antagonism; the unconfessed spirit of revenge animating our modern ideals is openly acknowledged in deeds of envy and ambition that express *and* limit these affects at once. Meanwhile, their source in a feeling of impotence is gradually eroded by a regime of symmetrical power-relations geared towards mutual limitation *on the basis of mutual empowerment* (provocation, stimulation, arousal, inspiration, but also recognition, gratitude).

Finally, it is important to recall and re-affirm the fictive or figurative character of agonal transvaluation. The therapeutic mechanisms of affirmation (2), empowerment (3) and externalization (4) can only operate under the sign of fiction. This does not, however, undermine their therapeutic value. As a fictive anticipation of health regulating Nietzsche's discourse, the agon enacts a *possible* form of health, orienting transvaluation towards health without subsuming it under a telos of health imposed upon all alike. In this way, it avoids both forms of romantic sickness: Schopenhauer's binding universal law and the anarchist hatred of the law. For Nietzsche's agonal feint of health enacts a *possible formation of the law of health:* the law or rule of agonal engagement that binds collectively across *particular* communities (as argued in chapter

---

22 See Conway 1997a, 94 ff. for a compelling exposition of this insight.
23 See e.g. GM III 13 where the ascetic ideal is derived from the 'protective and curative instinct of a degenerating form of life', as a 'means' (*Mittel*) to preserve that form of life; or more precisely, as a means whereby active forces, 'the instincts of life that are deepest and have remained intact', combat a 'partial physiological inhibition and exhaustion'. Despite its apparent complicity with other-worldly wishes of sick and exhausted forms of life, the ascetic ideal is exposed as a 'ruse for the *preservation of life*' in the hands of the ascetic priest, the 'incarnate wish for a being-other, a being-elsewhere': 'but the very *power* of his wishing is the fetter that binds him here, and through it he becomes the instrument which must work at creating more favourable conditions for being-here and being-human [...] this apparent enemy of life, this *negator*, – precisely he belongs to the greatest of the *conserving* and *Yes-creating* forces of life...'.

7). Rather than prescribe a 'normal' or normative health in the present, Nietzsche *plays at health* in the company of imaginary agonal communities to come. We are reminded once again of Nietzsche's strategy of *acceleration* when he writes of his imagined 'free spirits':

> [...] and perhaps I shall do something to accelerate their coming if I describe in advance under what vicissitudes I *see* them arising, upon what paths I *see* them coming? – – (MA I Vorrede 2)

Pitched between prescription (law) and *laissez faire* (anarchism), between prophetic vision and fatalistic waiting, agonal discourse serves to stimulate and guide actual readers in the collective construction of new forms of health.

III Nietzsche and Freud: Agonal and Analytic Transference

Reading Nietzsche through the optics of the agon affords a way to think through some of the major difficulties confronting a therapeutic interpretation of his thought.[24] Against the prohibitive deficit of energy in modernity, the agonal regime uncovers and harnesses the enormous affective resources bound up with *ressentiment*. At the same time, there is the playful/ pre-figurative orientation of thought towards health without recourse to directives, goals that would promote the interests of declining life. Then there is the paradox of transformation *and* repetition: the agon opens a transformative perspective on the project of transvaluation without denying the self-referential implications of Nietzschean critique or the overwhelming textual

---

24 Attempts to think psychotherapy in agonal terms tend to focus on psychic conflict in Freud (and Nietzsche), nicely summed up by Lungstrum (1997, 18): 'The unconscious versus the preconscious, the pleasure principle versus the reality principle, Eros versus the death instinct, civilization versus aggression – through Freud's work runs a concatenation of dualities. This is Freud's version of the agon: the notion of a clash between two antithetical entities, and the insight that this clash is a powerful explanatory key.' But what exactly makes these 'dualities' or clashes 'agonistic' remains rather unclear, as does the explanatory power of this epithet. Gay (1997, 125) writes of Freud's view in *Analysis Terminable and Interminable* that by 'giving up the urge to secure wholeness and cessation of conflict' we can achieve a 'peaceful recognition of our essential nature as self-conscious creatures whose struggles are unending'. Yet, Freud refers not to *agon* or *eris*, but to Empedocles' concepts of strife *(nexos)* and love *(philia)*. Marten (1997, 132ff.) traces Freud's trajectory from the 1890s, in which psychic conflict was seen as pathological, to *The Interpretation of Dreams* (1900), where the split in consciousness is seen as 'a fundamental feature of every healthy psyche'. Freud's early view is aligned with Nietzsche's concept of the 'horizon', as the condition for health qua wholeness (NNHL), and its rupture by the malady of history. But she fails to see an analogous trajectory in Nietzsche's understanding of health and sickness, declaring that 'Freud's decisive innovation' over and against Schopenhauer and Nietzsche 'is his insistence on *conflict* as the basis of life' (Marten 1997, 148). The present chapter takes an entirely different approach to the relation between Nietzsche and Freud, focussing on the agon between (the will to) health and (the will to) sickness enacted by Nietzsche's discursive agons, and on analogies with Freud's concepts of transference, repetition compulsion and sublimation.

evidence that it repeats vengeful attitudes. Finally, the conflicting impulses towards health and sickness in Nietzsche's thought are accommodated and conjugated by the agon, which allows for the *therapeutic transformation of forbidden, pathological desires through their affirmative, repetitive re-enactment.*

With this formula we have not only the key to a viable therapeutic perspective on Nietzsche's philosophical practice; we also have the alpha and omega of Freud's psychoanalytic practice – repetition compulsion in its manifestation as transference.[25] Freud maintains that the individual entering psychoanalysis is invariably compelled to relive fixed experience patterns. According to the theory of neurosis, intolerable thought contents, repressed into unconsciousness, return to consciousness in the distorted form of neurotic symptoms, which, as metaphoric re-enactments of the repressed thought, offer substitutive expression and gratification. The compulsive-repetitive return of the repressed is displayed most clearly in the phenomenon of transference: here analysands transfer episodes from their affective life onto their relation with the analyst without realising that the seemingly novel interactions are but new editions of old, unconscious experience patterns. Because transference maintains the symptoms and the substitutive satisfactions they afford, Freud saw it as one of the strongest 'weapons of resistance' (*The Dynamics of Transference*, SE 12.104).[26] But he was also prepared to admit repetition compulsion 'into the transference as a playground in which it is allowed to expand in almost complete freedom and in which it is expected to display to us everything in the way of pathogenic instincts that is hidden in the patient's mind.' (*Remembering, Repeating, and Working Through*, SE 12.150). Because it 'makes the patients hidden and forgotten love impulses actual and manifest' (*The Dynamics of Transference*, SE 12.108; SA Erg.214), transference is also the key to treatment.

For Freud, treatment works, first of all, through a paradox of *remembering through forgetful re-enactment* performed in transference: a repressed thought content is re-enacted in an oblique, displaced manner, without the patient's conscious awareness of what it enacts:

> [T]he patient does not *remember* anything of what he has forgotten and repressed, but *enacts* it [*agierte*]. He reproduces it not as a memory but as an action [*Tat*]; he *repeats* it, without, of course, knowing that he is repeating it. (*Remembering, Repeating, and Working Through*, SE 12.150; SA Erg.209–10)

---

[25] The phrase 'alpha and omega' is from Chapelle 1993. As will become evident, this illuminating account of the dynamics of transference therapy and its bearing on Nietzsche's thought has been a valuable source of information and inspiration for the argument in this chapter.

[26] References to Freud's writings include the English name of the text and its location in the *Standard Edition of the Complete Psychological Works of Sigmund Freud* (J. Strachey ed., Hogarth Press, London 1953), as follows: SE 12.104 = *Standard Edition* vol. 12, page 104. Where appropriate, references to the German text are included, as follows: SA 12.104 = *Freud-Studienausgabe* (Hrsg. A. Mitscherlich, A. Richards, J. Strachey, Fischer Vlg., Frankfurt-a-M, 1975), vol. 12, 104. There are a number of references to the *Ergänzungsband (Schriften zur Behandlungstechnik)*, denoted as Erg.

To the analyst, the repetition compulsion offers a displaced, metaphorical commentary on the unconscious text of forgotten, repressed thoughts. To the extent that he can decypher this text and show the patient that his contemporary experience belongs to a forgotten past, the analyst can transform the compulsion to repeat along the paths of remembering.

But there is more to psychoanalytic treatment than the intellectual task of remembering. The work of 'becoming conscious' certainly involves understanding, remembering, recognising the past and oneself in the past, but it also involves an *economic* problem that goes beyond the replacement of ignorance with understanding:

> The pathological factor is not his [the patient's] ignorance in itself, but the root of this ignorance in his *inner resistances*; it was they that first called this ignorance into being, and they still maintain it now. The task of the treatment lies in combating these resistances. (*Wild Psychoanalysis*, SE 11.225)

The liquidation of resistances requires two things; in both, transference proves again to be crucial. First, there is the strictly economic problem of finding new sources of energy for the work of overcoming resistances. Freud regarded transference as supplying that additional energy when he wrote that treatment 'only deserves the name if the intensity of the transference has been utilised for the overcoming of resistances.' (*On Beginning the Treatment*, SE 12.143). In the second place, resistances need to be recognised and mapped. Accordingly, the technique of transference therapy focuses less on the thought content repressed than on the ongoing process of repression as manifested in transference phenomena. The patient's task of saying all that comes to mind, precisely because it fails, ultimately reveals, through a shadow play of sorts, the sources of resistance feeding the repressions.[27]

In the book *Nietzsche and Psychoanalysis* (1993, 5), Daniel Chapelle argues that the therapeutic effect of transference analysis comes from a readjustment to the past and the passage of time on the patient's part. The process of abandoning defences, accompanied by an increasing sense of vulnerability and loss, involves not an intellectual correction of a failure to remember, but 'an affective revaluation of what is forgotten' (Chapelle 1993, 165). The initial problem or sickness lies in a resentment against time and becoming, a resentment of the kind that brought metaphysics into being; for the compulsive repetition of fixed experience patterns betrays 'an attempt to cling to the past in spite of evidence that nothing and nobody lasts' (Chapelle 1993, 168). The abandonment of defences in analysis, on the other hand, 'amounts to an affective "revaluation" of the value judgement placed on the experience of the past' (Chapelle 1993, 163), leading to an 'affirmation of the passage of time and of the impermanence it bestows on everything' (Chapelle 1993, 168). On this basis, Chapelle argues that transference therapy shares with Nietzsche's thought

---

[27] See Chapelle 1993, 165–167.

of eternal return the goal of redeeming the past, and the formula of compulsive repetition for achieving this goal. Psychoanalysis, like the thought of eternal return,

> is preoccupied with resentment over impermanence and [...] it aims at overcoming this resentment. The self-imposed task of psychoanalysis is the same as that of eternal return: to redeem the past, with past defined as the process of passing rather than as content past. Nietzsche and Freud both prescribe the formula of compulsive repetition to achieve their goal. (Chapelle 1993, 5)

III.1 Analytic and Agonal Transference Therapy: Affinities and Differences

In what follows, Chapelle's thesis will be adapted to Nietzsche's textual practice of critical transvaluation and the problem of *ressentiment*. We have already asked whether Nietzsche's text merely repeats the vengeful impulses it seeks to overcome; and more generally, whether *any* attempt to react against inherited values inevitably locks itself into a reactive *ressentiment* against the past. My thesis is that *critical transvaluation, when viewed from an agonal perspective, performs an unconscious therapy on its constitutive ressentiment along the lines of compulsive repetition in transference analysis*. Agonal transvaluation enacts a *compulsive-repetitive contestation of sickness*. It does not simply accept or justify the sickness of *ressentiment*; nor would it redeem us from this sickness by extirpating it once and for all. Rather, the agonal transference of vengeful, destructive impulses releases energy for an open-ended contestation of sickness that would empower us to *master* it; as such, it serves to inaugurate a therapeutic transformation of sickness.

Underpinning my thesis are certain striking similarities between the agonal transference (*Übertragung*) at play in Nietzschean transvaluation and the analytic manifestations of transference:

1) The first concerns their *open-ended, repetitive character*, which Chapelle rightly identifies with the thought of eternal recurrence. In the performative context of transvaluation, this temporal structure points towards a deeper affinity with transference therapy: both can be viewed from a *ludic* perspective as *games*. Agonal transvaluation, like the original Greek contests, is a festive game held periodically. As such, it is temporal in a radical sense: it is, in its originary meaning, such that it is always different. For, as Gadamer points out, the festival or game 'has its being [*sein Sein*] only in becoming and recurring'.[28] We can therefore say that agonal transvaluation enacts or plays out the thought of eternal recurrence as its mode of being.

2) Nietzschean and Freudian transference are both marked by a powerful compulsion to *metaphor*. In both we can speak of displaced, metaphorical re-enactments of old, unconscious experience patterns in a conscious discourse which itself re-

---

[28] Gadamer 1986, 107–139, esp. 128.

mains curiously detached and oblivious to what it is enacting. In Nietzsche's texts, the unconscious patterns are not Oedipal (cf. *Beyond the Pleasure Principle*, SE 18.7–64), but involve an embodied *ressentiment* against the legacy of *ressentiment*, the impotent rage of one wishing to put an end to a past which he rejects. Agonal transference offers these vengeful, destructive desires a substitutive expression and gratification in the critical discourse at the conscious surface of Nietzsche's text. Nietzsche's discourse establishes a value-critique in relation to an Other, often leading to a diagnosis of pathology. But at the same time, the strategies, moves and dynamics of Nietzschean critique perform or enact (*agieren*) a shadow play of these forgotten, hidden impulses, an oblique, metaphorical commentary that makes them manifest. Thus Nietzsche's text, like the analysand's discourse, works along two distinct axes, the conscious and the unconscious, the thematic and the performative; and in both, the transference of repetitive, affective patterns connects the two axes. The agon serves, in Freud's words, as a 'playground' in which repetitive compulsive patterns are given expressive 'freedom' so that they may display 'pathogenic instincts'.

3) Both Nietzsche and Freud value sickness as a source of instruction.[29] But the agonal, like the analytic game, is governed by *therapeutic* interests that demand more than instruction: they demand *energy*. And in both, the transference of pathological impulses serves to harness energy for therapeutic, transformative purposes. But difficult questions arise regarding the precise mechanisms, dynamics and goals of therapy in each case. Transference therapy and the agonal contestation of values are patently different procedures; yet, the similarities broached above already indicate that they may have more in common than meets the eye. Without wishing to assimilate them, I shall argue in what follows that there are deep, underlying affinities between the two as therapeutic procedures. To begin with, I shall focus on the goals of therapy.

III.2 The Goals of Therapy: Affinities and Differences between Nietzsche and Freud

These present particular difficulties, not least because of Freud's vacillations and ambiguities. Already two similarities are evident from Chapelle's thesis. The common goal of psychoanalysis and the eternal return, he argues, is to overcome the resentment against time and redeem becoming. The same goes for agonal transvaluation, understood as a festive 'war-game' of the spirit that enacts the eternal recurrence. In

---

29 For Nietzsche, see e.g. MA I Vorrede, 4, KSA 2.17 f.; FW Vorrede 3, KSA 3.349 f. As for Freud, he declared: 'We can catch the unconscious only in pathological material' (from Salomé 1965, 64). The particular value of transference neuroses is often emphasised by Freud. See e.g. *The Dynamics of Transference* (SE 12.108) and *Introductory Lectures*, 27 (SE 16.444), where transference is called the 'best tool' of treatment.

the second place, Chapelle connects the redemption of becoming with Nietzsche's peculiar ethos of resignation: *amor fati*. In personal terms, a growing sense of vulnerability and mortality accompanies the analytic revaluation of impermanence, which culminates in 'an affective affirmation of the task of tragic destiny whose plot requires the discovery and acceptance of one's own impermanence' (Chapelle 1993, 168). Tragic heroism must, however, overcome the resistances against the ego's original and repressed discovery of its fear of dying. Quoting Ricoeur, Chapelle writes that 'the goal of psychoanalysis is the 'victory over my narcissism, over my fear of dying, over the resurgence in me of childhood consolations' (Ricoeur 1970, 328). 'There is', Chapelle (1993, 168) adds, 'an echo of Dionysus and Dionysian *amor fati* in Ricoeur's statement.' Certainly, Nietzsche's *amor fati* also aims to overcome false consolations, the childish consolations of moral metaphysics that would deny reality to the advantage of human desires and wishes. If for Nietzsche sickness means to confuse the projections of human desires with the characters that make up reality, then therapy aims at submitting desire to the alterity and disorder of becoming. In Freudian terms, the common goal of *amor fati* sets up a struggle or contest between the *reality principle* and the *pleasure principle* that controls the ongoing process of repression. The ego, Freud writes,

> seeks to avoid the unpleasure which would be produced by the liberation of the repressed. *Our efforts, on the other hand, are directed towards procuring the toleration of that unpleasure by an appeal to the reality principle*. (*Beyond the Pleasure Principle*, SE 18.20. Cf. Ricoeur 1970, 411).

The connection with Nietzsche's *amor fati* is perhaps best put by Blondel, who writes that

> [the task of] psychoanalysis consists is forcing the *ananke* on the libido without repressing it, by substituting resignation (the reality principle) for the neurotic defence mechanisms (the pleasure principle); in the same way, in Nietzsche, the will to power must be positively affirmed and the *amor fati* substituted for the consoling illusions of the ideal. (Blondel 1991, 47 f.)

Despite these similarities, agonal therapy also seems to pursue goals radically different from analysis. At stake is, first of all, the *healing power* Freud attributes to *ego-centered consciousness*. According to one formulation, the task of psychoanalytic treatment is anamnesis, or to make 'the unconscious accessible to consciousness [...] by overcoming resistances' (*Psycho-analytic Procedure*, SE 7.253). We have already seen that transference therapy does not involve a purely intellectual process of remembering: as a *forgetful* re-enactment of repressed thoughts, transference offers a playground for unconscious, polymorphously perverse processes to express themselves – *while protecting the conscious ego from awareness of them*. Yet, analysis does aim to break down the ego's resistances and the neurotic cycle of repetition compulsion by inducing a remembrance of traumatic episodes *as belonging to the past* (Cf. *Beyond the Pleasure Principle*, SE 18.18 f.). Behind this goal lies a reliance on the power of consciousness to heal or dissipate the pathological force of traumatic episodes.

For Nietzsche, by contrast, consciousness is our 'weakest and most fallible organ',[30] and it is our increased reliance on consciousness that has bred the *sickness* of bad conscience. While the *Genealogie der Moral* affirms the *futural* memory of the 'animal that can promise' bred by culture (GM II 1, KSA 5.291), Nietzsche also places positive value on the active power of forgetting in a way that does not seem to register in analytic therapy. For Nietzsche, forgetting is an organising power: it serves to maintain 'psychic order' throughout the process of experience, so that the horizon of consciousness can remain open to new experiences. Significantly, in GM the process of 'forgetful' experience or in-psychation (*Einverseelung*) is connected with *somatic* processes of incorporation (*Einverleibung*), rather than any conscious processes: it is dark and complex, like 'digestion', the 'thousand-fold process in which our physiological nourishment, the so-called incorporation [*Einverleibung*], plays itself out' (GM II 1, KSA 5.291; cf. 14[142], KSA 13.326) without our awareness. And the second *Unzeitgemäße Betrachtung* actually locates *healing* power in a capacity to 'incorporate' (*Einverleibung*) experiences, when Nietzsche writes of a 'plastic power to [...] transform and incorporate [*Einverleibung*] what is past and alien, to heal wounds, to replace what is lost, to recreate broken forms out of itself' (NNHL I, KSA 1.251). Rather than bringing things to consciousness, Nietzsche seems to advocate *bringing consciousness back to the body*. This is confirmed in *Die fröhliche Wissenschaft*, which derides our 'ridiculous overestimation and misrecognition of consciousness' and proposes a new task:

> *to incorporate knowledge in oneself* and make it instinctive, – a task which is only seen by those who have grasped that hitherto only our *errors* were incorporated in us and that all our consciousness relates to errors! (FW 11, KSA 3.383. Cf. AC 57, KSA 6.242; 14[216], KSA 13.392; 14[111], KSA 13.288)

In line with this task, agonal transvaluation relies on an unconscious *play of forces*, rather than consciousness, to heal the wounds of our *ressentiment*. If our metaphysical and moral errors are sustained by a bodily diet of *ressentiment* inherited from the past, then it is not enough 'to confront our inherited and hereditary nature with our *knowledge* of it'; for 'if we condemn those errors and consider ourselves above them, this does not remove the fact that we stem from them' (NNHL 3, KSA 1.270). Knowledge of our inherited patterns of *ressentiment* must also be *incorporated* through a 'fortifying diet' that empowers us to 'transform [...] what is past and alien'. The agonal play of forces regulating our critical discourse is just such a diet: an unconscious therapy that operates at the level of forces and their configurations. Or, in the language of Nietzsche's second *Unzeitgemäße Betrachtung* on history, it is a 'strict discipline' with which 'to combat our inborn, inculcated heritage and implant in our-

---

[30] GM II 16, KSA 5.322. Cf. AC 14.

selves a new habit, a new instinct, a second nature, so that our first nature withers away' (NNHL 3, KSA 1.270).

More light is shed on the Nietzschean task of incorporation by considering a second, related sticking point in relation to Freudian therapy. This concerns the goal of *ego-development* expressed in Freud's famous formula '*Wo Es war, soll Ich werden*' (Where it/Id was, there I/Ego ought to become) (*New Introductory Lectures*, SE 22.80). The exact meaning of this formula is disputed. For Castoriadis (1994), it signifies the elimination of the Id, a reclaiming of the marshes of the unconscious for the dry land of conscious control – a goal so monstrous that Freud's formula must be supplemented with: Where I/ego am (is), it (id) ought to emerge (*Wo ich bin, soll auch Es auftauchen*) (Castoriadis 1994, 4). Like James Hillman, Castoriadis reads an imperialism of the Ego in Freud's formula and modifies it with the goal of an *altered relation between ego and id*. For Hillman (1992, 26 f.), Freud is complicit in the civilising process of ego-domination, which has branded two different *styles of consciousness* – the centre and the periphery – as conscious and unconscious (qua psychopathological) respectively. According to Hillman the true goal of psychotherapy is betrayed by Otto Fenichel, Freud's follower, when he writes: 'The common denominator of all neurotic phenomena is the insufficiency of the normal control apparatus' (quoted in Hillman 1992, 26 f.). Against the ideal of integrated control, Hillman argues that 'consciousness must be reapportioned', without reduction, to its 'polycentric roots' (Hillman 1992, 26 f.).

Both of these anti-Freudian therapies or counter-therapies have deep affinities with agonal transvaluation. Castoriadis disavows 'saintliness' – Nietzsche's ascetic ideal – or any 'ethics based on the condemnation of desire and therefore on guilt' (Castoriadis, 1994, 4). The pathos of aggression animating Nietzsche's agonal critique is echoed with remarkable precision in the phrase used by Castoriadis to illustrate his anti-ascetic prescription: '*I want to kill you – or rape you – but I will not*' (Castoriadis 1994, 4). He also rejects 'the elimination of psychical conflict' in favour of a reflexive subjectivity that recognises unconscious contents, controls and chooses between them (Castoriadis 1994, 4). This Enlightened ideal of autonomy approximates the agonal goal of 'mastery', as we shall see; but it will also need to be relativised to the telos of *multiplication* or *pluralization* emphasised by Hillman:

> Instead of trying to cure pathological fragmentation wherever it appears, we would let the content of this fantasy cure consciousness of its obsession with unity. By absorbing the plural viewpoint of 'splinter psyches' into our consciousness, there would be *a new connection with multiplicity* and we would no longer need to call it disconnected schizoid fragmentation. Consciousness, and our notion of consciousness, would reflect a *world view that is diverse and unsettled*.' (Hillman 1992, 42)

This can be compared to what Nietzsche writes (against Spinoza) of the necessity of conflict:

> A fundamental error is to believe in concord [*Eintracht*] and the absence of conflict – that would actually be death! [...] Diversity [*Verschiedenheit*] reigns in the smallest things, spermatozoa eggs – equality [or sameness: *Gleichheit*] is a great delusion [...] – Whether reason, with its phantasy of knowing everything, of knowing the body first-hand [*kennen*], of "willing", has hitherto preserved overall more than it destroyed – ? Centralization is far from being perfect – and reason's phantasy to be this centre is certainly the gravest defect of this perfection. (11[132], KSA 9.490; cf. Blondel 1991, 232)

The agonal conflict or contest of forces brings to our intersubjective critical practice '*a new connection with multiplicity*', close to Hillman's psychic fragmentation. But in Nietzsche's case, this is a matter of incorporation or *Einverleibung*. Agonal transvaluation is an attempt to enact Nietzsche's *physiological* insight that 'struggle is expressed even in the swapping around of commandment and obedience' and that 'a forever floating delimitation of power [*fließendes Machtgrenzen-bestimmen*] belongs to life.'[31] As a 'forever floating delimitation of power', the agonal play of forces establishes a new, non-repressive relation between the relative unity of discourse and the relative multiplicity of the body. By opening discourse up to the plurality of drives or affects, agonal transvaluation opens a space or field of tension between the ideal of mastery – integrated, autonomous control – on one side, and the absolute disorder of multiplicity on the other. In this sense Nietzsche's agon would also 'reapportion' consciousness – by rediscovering the multiple, sensuous consciousness of the body. The agon is 'a collective game [*Zusammenspiel*] as subtly intelligent as, for example, the digestive process. It is the collective game of a *great number of intellects!*'[32] Moreover, like the ludic plurality of the body, the agonal play of forces reflects a '*world view that is diverse and unsettled*' (Hillman, 1992, 42). 'If affects interpret,' Blondel (1991, 206f.) remarks, 'they institute a certain simplicity only in order to pluralise it, the affects constituting the unstable points of view of a game in which they exist only in the plural.' According to Blondel, Nietzsche's image of the body as a *collective game (Zusammenspiel) of intelligences in conflict* serves to re-conceive physiology in a way that defies the univocal regulation of conscious voluntarism on one side, and the lawful regulation of mechanism on the other. The agonal play of forces regulating Nietzsche's transvaluative discourse is a performative transposition of his physiological indeterminism:[33] as such, it allows for the spontaneous autonomy of affects within the collective order it institutes, bringing instability, fragility and danger to the game of transvaluation.

---

31 40[21], KSA 11.638, quoted in Blondel 1991, 232; translation amended.
32 12[37], KSA 10.407, quoted in Blondel 1991, 231; translation amended.
33 See 9[91], KSA 12 for Nietzsche's critique of determinism. See Siemens 2014 for the overcoming of the opposition: free will – determinism through Nietzsche's concept of facticity.

III.3 Sublimation, Play and the Mastery over *Ressentiment*

Besides the critical interpretations we have considered, there are also more sympathetic interpretations of Freudian ego-development that are compatible with Nietzschean agonal therapy. In this closing section, I explore the affinities between agonal therapy and the interpretation offered by Haslinger in his book *Nietzsche und die Anfaenge der Tiefenpsychologie* (1993). Haslinger interprets the analytic task of ego-development in the light of Freud's remarks on the 'binding' or 'taming' *(Bändigung)* of the drives. He quotes Freud's explanation of his desideratum that 'a drive's demand be finished off [or settled: *Erledigung*]': it

> certainly does not mean that it is made to disappear, so that it never makes itself heard again. In general, that is impossible and would not be desirable anyway. No, [it means] rather something else which one could approximately designate as the "binding" [or "taming": *Bändigung*] of the drive: this means that the drive is wholly taken up in the harmony of the I, that it is accessible to all influences through the other tendencies in the I and no longer pursues its own way to gratification.
> (*Analysis Terminable and Interminable:* SE 23.224–5; SA Erg.365. Cf. Haslinger 1993, 242)

According to Haslinger, Freudian ego-development serves the Enlightened goal of a 'binding association' *(bändigender Umgang)* with the demands made by our drives: these are not to be silenced, nor 'blindly acted out, but rather subordinated to the free autonomy of the I' (Haslinger 1993, 242); hence Freud's insistence on the need for a powerful ego. This interpretation comes close to the therapeutic goal advocated by Castoriadis,[34] but the context for Haslinger's discussion is the concept of *sublimation*, which, he claims, is 'at the core of Nietzsche's as of Freud's educational (therapeutic) concern' (Haslinger 1993, 241). This goal can be brought to bear on agonal transvaluation with the claim that *the conscious and unconscious axes of Nietzsche's text are related through an economy of sublimation*. In other words, Nietzsche's transvaluative discourse emerges through sublimation of embodied ressentiment, the compulsive repetitive sickness animating it. Ricoeur has remarked that sublimation is as much a problem as a solution in Freud's thought (Ricoeur 1970, 175). Nonetheless, a number of characteristics can be used to illuminate the goal of agonal therapy in a *binding mastery (bändigende Herrschaft) over ressentiment*.

Although a rather protean concept in Freud's writing, sublimation is used by most authors today to describe the vicissitude of an instinct under three conditions:
i) the instinct is deflected from its original *aim*;
ii) the instinct is deflected from its original *object*; and

---

[34] Castoriadis explicitly allows for psychic conflict, in contrast with Freud's emphasis on the harmony of the I. His picture of conflict does, however, seem rather too tame and manageable.

iii) the instinct is gratified by (non-instinctual) means that find moral/cultural acceptance.³⁵

Under these conditions, sublimation names a non-pathological, qualitative transformation of instinctual into spiritual energies of enormous cultural value. With this goes an important *dynamic* feature of sublimation: since impulses are reorganised or channelled, rather than blocked, their energy or intensity is more-or-less sustained.³⁶ In both respects, transformative and dynamic, sublimation runs counter to any radical discontinuity or opposition between desire and spirit – a tendency already familiar from Nietzsche's conception of agonal culture. And with this, we have a clue to the *healing power* of sublimation. As a way by which the organic and the super-organic can be bridged or bound together in human activity, it heals the wound constitutive of cultural development: the primal split of bad conscience or, in Freud's terms, the primal repression.

In his *Five Lectures on Psycho-Analysis*, Freud makes the same point in a different way: essential to sublimation is its sharp differentiation from repression. After rejecting 'extirpation of the infantile wishful impulses' as the 'ideal aim of development', he continues:

> Owing to their repressions, neurotics have sacrificed many sources of mental energy whose contributions would have been of great value in the formation of their character and in their activity in life. We know of a far more expedient process of development, called "*sublimation*," in which the energy of the infantile wishful impulses is not cut off but remains ready for use [*verwertbar*] – the unserviceable aim of the various impulses being replaced by one that is higher, and perhaps no longer sexual. (SE 11.53–4)

Sublimation is not anti-instinctual like repression, a force of exclusion that impoverishes the ego. Instead, it makes *use* of instinctual forces, encompassing them within the ego-organization by channelling and re-organising them around 'remote and socially valuable aims' (SE 11.53–4).³⁷ 'Sublimation,' Freud writes in *On Narcissism*, 'is a way out, a way by which the claims of the ego can be met *without* involving repression' (SE 14.95). This means that reality ceases to be a source of frustration demanding the sacrifice of pleasure; by deflecting drives from their original (sexual) objects and goals, sublimation makes it possible for them to derive pleasure *from* reality along the paths of intellectual or artistic activity. Crucial to this transformation is the mediating role of the ego, which does not seek to quash our passions or sensuality through pressure, but on the contrary allows them to unfold by '*adapting* them to reality through *binding* [Bändigung], through *mastery* [Herrschaft] over the Id' (Ha-

---

35 Deri 1939, 325–334. See also Laplanche, J. & Pontalis 1967, 465–467. The best discussion I know of is Loewald 1988.
36 See e.g. *"Civilised" Sexual Morality and Modern Nervous Illness*, SE 9.187. Also *Five Lectures on Psycho-Analysis*, SE 11.53–4, cited below.
37 The relation between sublimation and ego-organization is central to Loewald's (1988) chapter 2.

slinger 1993, 241). Here, a first approximation to the goal of Nietzsche's agonal project in the *binding mastery* over *ressentiment* can be ventured by way of analogy: Could it be that Nietzsche's critical discourse serves to *adapt* resentful desires to destroy inherited values to a *reality* that frustrates their satisfaction?

As Kaufmann has argued at length,[38] the opposition between sublimation and ascetic practices of denial, rejection, extirpation and repression is also central to Nietzsche's thought on culture and his critique of morality:

> The affect, the great desire, the passions of power, love, revenge, possession –: the moralists want to extinguish them, tear them out, "cleanse" the soul of them [...]
> The great sources of power [*Kraftquellen*], that wildwater of the soul, often so dangerous, overwhelming, explosive: these the most short-sighted and pernicious mode of thought, the moral mode of thought, wants to *dry up*, instead of making use [*in Dienst zu nehmen*] of their power and *economising* it. (14[163], KSA 13)

The moment of *utility* or *exploitation*, familiar from Freud's *Five Lectures* and central to the agonal economy of energy or power, is again prominent in other notes where Nietzsche develops his alternative to a culture based on ascetic repression:

> All that is fearsome to be *made use of* [in Dienst nehmen], one by one, step by step, experimentally: this is what the task of culture demands; but until it is *strong enough* for that, it must combat [the fearsome], moderate it, veil it, even curse it ... [39]

And when Nietzsche comes to summarise his goal of cultural development, the moment of mastery comes to the fore:

> *Summa:* the mastery over the passions, *not* their weakening or elimination! The greater the will's power of mastery [*Herren-Kraft des Willens*], the more freedom can be given to the passions.
> "great human beings" are great through the space for free play [*Freiheits-Spielraum*] of their desires and through the still greater power which knows how to make use of [*in Dienst nehmen*] these splendid beasts. (9[139], KSA 12)

This passage comes unmistakably close to psychoanalytic telos of mastery as a 'binding association' with our desires: ego-development serves, not to silence desires, but

---

38 Kaufmann 2015, chapters 7 and 8.
39 'Alles Furchtbare *in Dienst nehmen*, einzeln, schrittweise, versuchsweise: so will es die Aufgabe der Cultur; aber bis sie *stark genug* dazu ist, muss sie es bekampfen, mäßigen, verschleiern, selbst verfluchen...' (9[138], KSA 12). This note suggests systematic connections between Nietzsche's ideal of culture and his practice: apart from the moment of *utility*, the moments of *particularization* ('einzeln') and *experimentation* ('versuchsweise') are also integral to agonal transvaluation: the breaking down of 'all that is fearful' into 'particulars' to be used 'one by one' has been discussed under the rubric of digestion or *Einverleiben*, in the relation to Hillman's 'psychic fragmentation' (see p. 244 f.). The notion of 'step-by-step experimentation' describes well the agonal dynamic of contention-retraction characterising Nietzsche's style of interpretation (see pp. 12, 74, 103–106).

to dispose over them freely. Even more striking is the resonance of this passage with the dynamics of repetition compulsion in transference therapy, when Freud writes:

> We render [the compulsion] harmless, and indeed useful [*nutzbar*], by giving it the right [i.e. freedom – HS] to assert itself in a determinate field [*bestimmten Gebiete*]. We admit it into the transference as a playground [*Tummelplatz*] in which it is allowed to expand in almost complete freedom [...] [40]

The Nietzschean 'task of culture', like that of transference therapy, is *to make use of fearsome, harmful compulsions as invaluable sources of energy, while at the same time breaking their destructive edge, rendering them harmless*. This task is engaged through a paradoxical dynamic at play in both: 'great' culture, like transference therapy, offers a '*space for free play*' (*Freiheits-Spielraum*) or '*playground*' (*Tummelplatz*) in which harmful compulsions can assert themselves 'in a determinate field' and are 'allowed to expand in almost complete freedom'. But the terms 'almost' (*fast*) and 'determinate' (*bestimmt*) or limited are decisive, for in both cases, these harmful compulsion are also *bound* or *limited*,[41] so as to make them harmless. To free destructive human energies *and* bind them, to conjugate their affirmation *and* limitation: this describes the *dynamic* task of *sublimation as mastery* for both Nietzsche and Freud.

---

40 *Remembering, Repeating, Working Through*, SE 12.154. The proximity of these two texts is best seen in the German:
  'Wir machen ihn [den Wiederholungszwang] unschädlich, ja vielmehr nutzbar, indem wir ihm sein Recht einräumen, ihn auf einem bestimmten Gebiete gewären lassen. Wir eröffnen ihm die Übertragung als den Tummelplatz, auf dem ihm gestattet wird, sich in fast völliger Freiheit zu entfalten...' (SA Erg.214).

  '*Summa*: die Herrschaft über die Leidenschaften, *nicht* deren Schwächung oder Ausrottung! je grösser die Herren-Kraft des Willens ist, um so viel mehr Freiheit darf den Leidenschaften gegeben werden
  der "grosse Mensch" is gross durch den Freiheits-Spielraum seiner Begierden und durch die noch grössere Macht, welche diese prachtvollen Unthiere in Dienst zu nehmen weiss.[..]' (9[139], KSA 12)

41 In the line preceding the above-cited passage from *Remembering, Repeating, Working Through* (SE 12.154), Freud describes 'the proper management [*Handhabung*] of transference' as the 'chief means for binding [*bändigen*] the patient's compulsion to repeat and transforming it into a motive for remembering'. He also writes earlier (SA Erg.213), in a very Nietzschean vein, of 'putting the leash of transference on wild drives' (*den wilden Trieben den Zügel der Übertragung an[.]legen*). Loewald locates sublimation at play *in* transference and writes of its moderating influence with reference to Freud's postscript to Dora's case: 'There, likening some transferences to facsimiles and others to new editions of earlier impulses or phantasies, he explained that the content of new editions 'has been subjected to a moderating influence – to '*sublimation*' as I call it' (1905, p. 116 [= SE 7.116]; Freud's emphasis). He explains that these transferences are 'revisions' (*Neubearbeitungen*), not mere 'reprints' (*Neudrucke*)' (Loewald 1988, 12).

We are confronted, once again, with the question: How are affirmation and limitation to be combined in this way? How is the dynamic of mastery achieved? Nietzsche's talk of '"great human beings"' and their power to 'make use of these splendid beasts' sheds no more light on the cultural and institutional underpinnings of mastery than does Haslinger's talk of 'subordinating' our drives to the 'free autonomy of the I' in Freud; indeed, both suggest that mastery is a solitary achievement of self-control. Yet therapy and culture are both *intersubjective* or *collective* affairs. According to Nietzsche, as we have seen, the ancient Greeks' freedom of mind or *Freisinnigkeit* meant that 'a measured discharge was sought for the forces of nature, not their annihilation or negation'; excessive, destructive affects were 'acknowledged as human', not condemned, and integrated (*eingeordnet*) or transferred into cultural life through agonal institutions, which offered them a space for free play (*Freiheits-Spielraum*), but one 'restricted to determinate cults and days'.[42] Elsewhere, Nietzsche writes of the agon as an 'artistic play [*Spiel*] and imitation [*Nachahmung*]' of war (16[26] 7.404), which suggests that *play* – the 'playground' (*Tummelplatz*) given to compulsions in transference therapy, and the 'space for free play' (*Freiheits-Spielraum*) that Nietzsche's '"great human beings"' give their desires – is the key to the intersubjective dynamic of affirmation and limitation sustaining sublimation as mastery, the telos shared by Nietzsche and Freud. Pursuing the notion of play in Freud will unlock the third and decisive meaning of *mastery* for agonal transvaluation.

According to Ricoeur, the notion of sublimation represents Freud's indirect approach to a problem raised by his perspective on art and culture in general. Dreams loom large in Freud's theory of culture, acting as the privileged exemplar or model for the cultural production of meaning and its exegesis from the unitary viewpoint of an economics of instincts:

> [P]sychoanalysis offers to the interpretation of culture the submodel of wish-fulfilment [...] it knows cultural phenomena only as analogues of the wish-fulfilment illustrated by dreams. (Ricoeur 1970, 155)

As the 'royal road to psychoanalysis', dreams reveal

> all that is nocturnal in man [...] Man is a being capable of realizing his desires and wishes in the mode of disguise, regression and stereotyped symbolization. In and through man desires advance masked. (Ricoeur 1970, 162).

But the structural analogy of dream-work to artistic work is also problematic, since it seems to elide the transient sterility of dreams with the durable creativity of art, regressive symbols of our unresolved sexual conflicts with the prospective promotion

---

[42] '*auf bestimmte Culte und Tage beschränkt*' (5[146] 8.79; see p. 53 f.). Cf. Freud's '*bestimmten Gebiete*', the determinate or circumscribed fields in which the compulsion to repeat is given the freedom to expand (*Remembering, Repeating, Working Through*, SE 12.154).

of new meanings. The concept of sublimation, as a distinct vicissitude of our instincts, represents Freud's attempt to address this difference in value. But we can also look to the notion of *play*, linked to art and to dreams in the chain of oneiric analogies set out in the 1908 paper *Creative Writers and Daydreaming*. The creative writer, like the child at play,

> creates a world of fantasy which he takes seriously – that is, which he invests with large amounts of emotion – while separating it sharply from reality. (SE 9.144; in Ricoeur 1993, 165)

Thus play, like day-dreaming, novel-writing and poetry, partakes of the fantastic, whose motive force, Freud writes, is unsatisfied wishes: 'every fantasy is the fulfilment of a wish, a correction of unsatisfying reality' (SE 9.146). Is play, then, no more than a dream, a false consolation like the illusions of religion, metaphysics and morality scorned by both Freud and Nietzsche? What exactly is the difference between sublimation and self-delusion? According to Ricoeur, play is more than just a link in a chain of fantastic analogies; it 'implies a *mastery over absence* [...] of a different nature than the mere hallucinatory fulfilment of desires' (Ricoeur 1970, 166). To see why, we need to look at Freud's interpretation of play in *Beyond the Pleasure Principle*.

But first, one more link must be added to Freud's chain of fantastic analogues in *Creative Writers and Daydreaming*. Nietzschean transvaluation, a critical and creative form of writing, also has unsatisfied wishes as its motive force and subtext. In Nietzsche's case, these are aggressive, destructive wishes born of his critical experience, not the infantile sexual desires of Freud's personae; and instead of sexual conflicts, an acute conflict of *ressentiment* threatens to vitiate his project with the prospect that his writing will merely replicate what it wishes to destroy. Granted these differences, what could be more *fantastic* than an attempt to re-enact agonal contestation, the ideal of a 'great' culture long gone, in one's style of critical writing? What could be more *oneiric* in Freud's sense of wish-fulfilment than the 'attempt to give oneself, *a posteriori* as it were, a past from which **one would like to stem** in opposition to that from which one stems' (NNHL 3, KSA 1.270; **HS**)?[43] But agonal transvaluation is not just a 'strict discipline' (NNHL 3, KSA 1.270); it is also a festive *game*, a *playing-at-war*, and as such, it too implies a form of *mastery* distinct from hallucinatory wish-fulfilment.

Play has entered psychoanalytic lore by way of Freud's one-and-a–half year old grandson and his famous '*Fort-Da*' game discussed in *Beyond the Pleasure Principle* II.[44] We are presented with a good boy who obeys his parents, lets them sleep and

---

[43] From the passage on critical history used in chapter 1 to characterise Nietzsche's agonal project as a 'strict discipline' which would 'combat our inborn, inculcated heritage and implant in ourselves a new habit, a new instinct, a second nature. It is an attempt to give oneself, *a posteriori* as it were, a past from which one would like to stem in opposition to that from which one stems [...]'

[44] SE 18.12–17. Henceforth BPP.

above all, never cries when his mother leaves him. He plays at making a wooden reel disappear and reappear by throwing it away and then pulling it by a piece of string, shouting first '*Fort*' (gone) and then '*Da*' (there). What does the game mean?

> The interpretation of the game then became obvious. It was related to the child's great cultural achievement – the instinctual renunciation (that is, the renunciation of instinctual satisfaction) which he had made in allowing his mother to go away without protesting. He compensated himself for this, as it were, by himself staging the disappearance and return of the objects within his reach. (BPP, SE 18.15)

As the reference to cultural achievement indicates, the game enacts a *sublimation* of instinctual into cultural activity. The satisfaction of instinctual needs by instinctual means is renounced for the substitute satisfaction offered by cultural activity: the creation of symbols. Within the performative boundaries of the game, the reality of the mother's absence ceases to be a source of unpleasure; reality, when repeated with tangible reels and strings, becomes instead a source of pleasure. But what is the exact nature of the cultural activity performed in the game? Freud's interpretation, although inconclusive, highlights some features of sublimation with important implications for the cultural activity at play in agonal transvaluation.

1) In the first place, the child cannot literally *repeat* the mother's disappearance-reappearance; his game re-enacts or re-presents it with wooden figures that substitute for the mother, as imaginative symbols or metaphors. 'The compulsion to repeat', Chapelle (1993, 114 f.) observes, 'is at the same time a compulsion into metaphor'; entry into cultural life is an 'entry into metaphoric existence that establishes identities where none exist'. The wooden reel and the other small objects of his world are

> effigies. They are [...] objects endowed with a suprasensuous meaning [...] objects that place the child in the role of the high priest performing an exacting ceremony, repeating the same performance again and again. (Chapelle 1993, 114 f.)

It is impossible to read these lines without thinking of priestly *ressentiment* and the imaginary revenge at the origin of slave values from the *Genealogie*.[45] These affinities have serious implications for Nietzsche's own transvaluative discourse and its metaphorical re-enactment of *ressentiment*. The motif of revenge is also taken up by Freud, who suggests that

---

[45] GM I 10 speaks of slavish *ressentiment* as a process of falsification 'through which the internalised hatred, the revenge of an impotent being will assault its opponent – in effigy, of course' (KSA 5.271). GM I 13 goes on to identify this effigy with the suprasensuous 'subject' or 'soul' who stands 'behind' actions who is free to choose them and can therefore be held responsible for them (KSA 5.279–280). The slave-type does not *invent* the belief in an 'indifferent, freely choosing "subject"'; rather, it stands at his disposal as a function of language, and the 'affects of revenge and hatred exploit it for themselves'.

> Throwing away the object so that it was 'gone' might satisfy an impulse of the child's, which was suppressed in his actual life, to revenge himself on his mother for going away from him. (BPP, SE 18.16)

And again, further on, he discusses a child who, having just been to the doctor, 'hands on the disagreeable experience to one of his playmates and in this way revenges himself on a substitute' (BPP, SE 18.17). We could, by analogy, suggest that Nietzsche's transvaluative discourse, as the metaphorical shadow-play of a *suppressed ressentiment* against the overpowering legacy of *ressentiment*, merely repeats the metaphorical act of revenge that gave birth to slave values from a position of impotence; or alternatively, that his discourse is a futile stratagem by which the *ressentiment* he has inherited would be *handed on* to his antagonist – whether it be the priest, Socrates, Rousseau – on whom, as a *substitute* or *effigy* of his own *ressentiment*, Nietzsche takes revenge. Clearly, such readings would lock agonal transvaluation in the reactive mode of evaluation it aspires to overcome.

2) There is, however, a second prominent feature of Freud's interpretation that undercuts these readings:

> At the outset he [the little boy – HS] was in a *passive* situation – he was overpowered by the experience; but by repeating it, unpleasurable though it was, as a game, he took on an *active* part. (BPP, SE 18.16)

Through playful repetition, a *passive* experience of *impotence* is transformed into an *active* game; something that must be *suffered* or *undergone* in real life, a great overpowering impression, is transformed into something that is *actively made to occur* (cf. Chapelle 1993, 115). In this transformative power of play lies the key that promises to unlock Nietzschean transvaluation from a sterile repetition of *ressentiment*. Nietzsche's text bears the signature of impotence twice over: once in the *ressentiment* it inherits from the past, born, as GM recounts, of a slave caste being overpowered by a violent master caste; twice, in the impotent rage of one who feels alone in challenging the 'victorious' heritage of slave values.⁴⁶ As a festive *game* of the spirit, however, Nietzsche's transvaluative agon *empowers* this subtext of *ressentiment passively* suffered, *transforming* it into the *active force of aggression* needed for a total critique of slave morality. To this analogy, a further link can be added, suggested by Chapelle's reading of the Fort-Da game. In its symbolic or metaphorical power, he argues, the game stands as a paradigm for the *creation of meaning* understood as a product of cultural activity, not something given to us (Chapelle 1993, 115f.). Transposed to the metaphorical game of transvaluation, this implies that agonal contestation transforms the creation of meaning and values from the *reactive* mode of revenge against life-negating values, into an *active* mode born of mutual affirmation and negation

---

46 See pp. 33–37, 226, 241, 253 above, and GM I 7–13. The slave revolt is called 'victorious' in GM I 7, KSA 5.268.

among a plurality in a competitive play of forces (*Wettspiel der Kräfte*). From this perspective, then, it is the *ludic* character of agonal transvaluation that explains how repetition might transform a *reactive* mode of evaluation, based on *ressentiment*, into an *active* form of value creation that draws on *ressentiment* as its 'fertile ground'.

3) To conclude, I shall return to the agonal ideal of *mastering ressentiment* from a third perspective on the Fort-Da game. The transformation of *sterile* repetition into *creative* play is twice referred by Freud to an 'instinct for mastery'. In first instance, it is the *unpleasure* suffered in the mother's absence that the boy masters by staging her disappearance-reappearance with symbolic figures in things within his reach. But Freud goes on to disengage the notion of mastery from pleasure/unpleasure, suggesting that 'an instinct for mastery' might be acting 'independently of whether the memory was in itself pleasurable or not' (BPP, SE 18.16). In this light, he writes that

> in their play children repeat everything that has made a great impression on them in their real life, and in doing so they abreact the strength of that impression and, as one might put it, make themselves master of the situation (BPP, SE 18.17)

In the end, however, Freud remains undecided as to whether the impulse to master powerful impressions through their playful repetition is a primary impulse *beyond* the pleasure principle or not. As such, it is unclear why he discussed play at all in this text. Ricoeur (1970, 286) has suggested that 'he saw, mixed up with the motives of domination and revenge, the manifestation of a more essential tendency, driving one to the repetition of unpleasure in the form of symbolism and play.' Departing from Freud's own development of the death instinct, Ricoeur sees in play a 'nonpathological aspect of the death instinct' consisting in a 'mastery over the negative, over absence and loss, implied in one's recourse to symbols and play' (Ricoeur 1970, 286). In closing, I would like to suggest, by analogy, that Nietzsche's agonal games manifest not a sterile, oneiric fulfilment of destructive wishes, but a creative 'nonpathological aspect of the death instinct', as repetitive attempts to *master* the negative of *ressentiment* and frustrated revenge, through recourse to transvaluative discourse.

Chapter 9
Umwertung: Nietzsche's 'War-Praxis' and the Problem of Yes-Saying and No-Saying in *Ecce Homo*

Dedicated to Gerd Schank
† 12.11.2007

Introduction

Ecce Homo is a book of excesses, a book bursting to the point of incoherence. The text is saturated with the hyper-identity of an I inflated to world-historical, not to say cosmic proportions; yet One whose parts, whose claims collide or clash like a jigsaw puzzle that keeps going wrong. A self who is 'wise' and 'healthy' enough to have 'always chosen [*wählte*] the *right* means' of defence under bad conditions and the right company (books, people, landscapes) (EH weise 2, KSA 6.266 f.); but also a self who proclaims *amor fati*, that is: 'not wanting anything otherwise' ('dass man Nichts anders haben will', EH klug 10, KSA 6.297) and accordingly 'stuck to virtually intolerable situations, places, lodgings, company once I had chanced upon them' (EH weise 6, KSA 6.273). These difficulties are exacerbated by the narrative structure of the book, which invites a continuous reading as the story of a life, yet continually disrupts such a reading with contradictions, discrepancies, incongruities and distortions that make us throw up our arms and exclaim, 'How absurd!' How absurd that Nietzsche should claim that the 'no-saying, no-doing part' of his task began with JGB (EH (JGB) 1, KSA 6.350). How absurd that he should invoke 'the greatest of all tasks, the cultivation of higher humanity' (EH Schicksal 4, KSA 6.313), but also claim that he has no memory of '"striving"' or '"struggling"', that '"willing"' or '"wishing"' anything at all are alien to him (EH klug 9, KSA 6.294 f.). Perhaps the most glaring discrepancies are those between Nietzsche's self-descriptions in the book and what we know of his actual life. Yet, EH forces us to question the authority of biographical narratives, to recognise that however often the narratives intersect with what we know of Nietzsche's life, this book is not about Herr Nietzsche: 'What do we care about Herr Nietzsche?' (to paraphrase FW Vorrede 2). Rather, we have to do with the construction of a fictional world, or more to the point: with fictional worlds, populated by fictional selves, and narrated from various positions.

In this chapter, I will engage the feint of Nietzsche's writing in EH by concentrating on some of the discrepancies and incongruities that are strictly internal to the book. They concern the term 'Umwertung', and the expression 'Umwertung Aller Werte,' which, while not unique to EH, do belong to it in a special way. As good Nietzsche scholars, we all think we know what this means. But if we consult EH, we are likely to come away more confused than confirmed in our conviction. For a start, it used not just for Nietzsche's own project, but also for the birth of the moral or idealist age out of the tragic age ('Die Umwertung Aller Werte ins Lebensfeindliche', EH Schicksal 7, KSA 6.373). With reference to Nietzsche's own work, it is used a number of times to refer to AC (EH, Motto, KSA 6.263; also KSA 6.355, 364). But then it is also used to refer to the 'historical insights [*Erkenntnisse*]' gained in MA (EH (MA) 6, KSA 6.328). Then again with reference to M, where Nietzsche emphasises the affirmative character of the *Umwertungs*-project, insisting that 'there is not a negative word to be found, no attack' (EH (M) 1, KSA 6.329). In the context of JGB, it is quite the contrary. For in this text, 'Umwertung' is said to launch the no-saying, no-doing part of his task:

> die neinsagende, *neinthuende* Hälfte derselben [...]: die Umwerthung der bisherigen Werthe selbst, der grosse Krieg, – (EH (JGB) 1, KSA 6.350)
>
> the no-saying, *no-doing* half of it [...]: the transvaluation itself of values hitherto, the great war, –

As my guiding thread through Nietzsche's text, I will take this notion of war, his war-talk, and concentrate on two moments in particular: Nietzsche's 'war-praxis' (*Kriegspraxis*), presented under the sign of 'wisdom' (EH weise 7, KSA 6.274f.), and the 'great politics' (*grosse Politik*) that is his 'destiny' (EH Schicksal 1, KSA 6.365f.). In the first, limits, measure, generosity, gratitude and the affirmation of the opponent predominate; the second aligns *Umwertung* instead with radical, explosive destruction. Is there a way to account for these conflicting descriptions in a coherent notion of *Umwertung* – or do we have to give up and consign this text to creeping onset of madness?

I On War

A central concern of EH, bound up with the project of *Umwertung*, is to show the feasibility of combining radical no-saying with radical yes-saying. This task is most clearly formulated as the 'psychological problem' of the Zarathustra type:

> Das psychologische Problem im Typus des Zarathustra ist, wie der, welcher in einem unerhörten Grade Nein sagt, Nein *thut*, zu Allem, wozu man bisher Ja sagte, trotzdem der Gegensatz eines neinsagenden Geistes sein kann [...] (EH (Z) 6, KSA 6.344f.)
>
> The psychological problem in the Zarathustra type is how someone who to an unprecedented degree says no, *does* no, to everything everyone has said yes to so far, – how somebody like this can nevertheless be the opposite of a no-saying spirit [...]

What Nietzsche means by 'the opposite of a no-saying spirit' is explained further on as Zarathustra's aspiration

> das ewige Ja zu allen Dingen *selbst zu sein*, "das ungeheure unbegrenzte Ja- und Amen-sagen" ... (EH (Z) 6, KSA 6.344f.)
>
> *to be* the eternal yes to all things itself, "the tremendous, boundless yes-saying, amen-saying"....

At the most abstract level, the problem is how this unconditional and total affirmation of life – identified variously with the concept of Dionysos, *amor fati* and the Eternal Return – can be thought together with the negative practice of total critique in a coherent way. In what sense, if any, are total affirmation and total negation not flatly contradictory and incompossible? While the critique of life-negating values seems to be indispensable for a total affirmation of life, to affirm the practice of critique must surely mean to negate with it the object of critique. Conversely, to affirm the object of critique must be to affirm life-negating practices, thereby negating and invalidating the practice of critique. Clearly both fall short of total affirmation.

One of several things wrong with this formulation of the problem is that negativity, negation and destruction (*Verneinung, Vernichtung*) are intrinsic, indeed central to Nietzsche's dionysian concept of life, so that life-affirmation is perfectly compatible with the critical destruction of life-negating values and practices. Hence the places where Nietzsche writes of 'dionysian philosophy' as 'the yes-saying to opposition [*Gegensatz*] and war' (EH (GT) 3, KSA 6.313), or simply: 'in yes-saying negating *and destroying* are conditions [*Verneinen* und Vernichten *Bedingung*]' (EH Schicksal 4, KSA 6.368). But this solution, logically defensible as it is, misses a difficulty that is captured by the initial, more abstract formulation of the problem, and is best explained in the idiom of warfare.

It is, as Nietzsche writes with reference to Zarathustra, a 'psychological problem', and we need to enter into the perspective of the critic or no-sayer. As a warrior or antagonist (*Krieger, Kämpfer*), the critic can only engage life-negating values and ideals by adopting an '*aggressive* pathos' (EH weise 7, KSA 6.274) of contention (*Ringen*), what Nietzsche calls a 'Sich-im-Kampf-fühlen' (AC 29), a feeling-oneself-in-struggle. It is, in short, only by asserting oneself *against* the other antagonist, by adopting a posture of opposition driven by a desire for victory, that one can engage in struggle or warfare of any kind. This attitude of opposition, of self-assertion *against the other*, is what resists assimilation to the standpoint or attitude of unconditional and total affirmation, which is one of openness and love.

These standpoints are not, of course, presented in abstraction in EH, where the problem of yes– and no-saying is attached to the life-story that it recounts. In the beautiful text of the Motto 'On this perfect day...'(*An diesem vollkommnen Tage...*), the author inserts himself in the narrative he recounts of one who has undergone or performed the '*Umwerthung Aller Werthe*', and as a consequence can turn around and look back from a new vantage point of total affirmation and 'give thanks to my whole life' (EH Motto, KSA 6.263). In spite of the multiple disruptions of linear time in EH, the standpoint of total affirmation claimed by the author comes *after* the *Umwertungs*-project; it is a standpoint first made possible by that project, but one that is radically different from the *Umwertungs*-project with its constitutive no-saying.

Under no-saying, we need to understand Nietzsche's critical project of contesting the Christian-Platonic values that wind up as modern nihilism, and proposing a new set of values beyond the death of God and nihilism.[1] As Blondel (1991 65f.) points out, this is a *moralist* project in the sense that it responds to the state of things by demanding that it be transformed. We should not forget that this transformative project informs Nietzsche's writing right up to the end: in GD, with its 'prescriptive paths for culture' (*vorzuschreibende Wege der Kultur*)(EH (GD) 2, KSA 6.355; cf. GD Deutschen 6, KSA 6.108 ff.); in AC with its declaration of 'war', its 'law' or 'Moral-Codex' (EH Bücher 5, KSA 6.307) against the Christian vice of anti-nature; and in EH with its evangelium of hope (EH Schicksal 1, KSA 6.366), its invocation of 'the greatest of all tasks', the 'cultivation of higher humanity' (*Höherzüchtung der Menschheit*), and its 'promise of a tragic age' (EH (GT) 4, KSA 6.313). None of this is easily reconciled with the *refusal* of transformative impulses or the rejection of free will that are so marked in the affirmative attitude of *amor fati*:

> *amor fati:* dass man Nichts anders haben will, vorwärts nicht, rückwärts nicht, in alle Ewigkeit nicht. Das Nothwendige nicht bloss ertragen, noch weniger verhehlen – aller Idealismus ist Verlogenheit vor dem Nothwendigen –, sondern es *lieben*... (EH klug 10, KSA 6.297)

> *amor fati:* that one does not want anything to be different, not forwards, not backwards, not for all eternity. Not just to endure necessity, still less to conceal it –, all idealism is mendacity towards necessity –, but to *love* it...

Or again, what Nietzsche describes as his 'fatalism without revolt':

> – Sich selbst wie ein Fatum nehmen, nicht sich "anders" wollen – das ist in solchen Zuständen die *grosse Vernunft* selbst. (EH weise 6, KSA 6.273)

> – To take oneself as a fatum, not to want oneself to be "otherwise" – that is in these states *great reason* itself.

It is perhaps in the light of these irreconcilable tensions that we should read the baffling series of denials:

> Es fehlt in meiner Erinnerung, dass ich mich je bemüht hätte, – es ist kein Zug von Ringen in meinem Leben nachweisbar, ich bin der Gegensatz einer heroischen Natur. Etwas "wollen", nach Etwas "streben", einen "Zweck", einen "Wunsch" im Auge haben – das kenne ich Alles nicht aus Erfahrung. (EH klug 9, KSA 6.294 f.)

> I miss in my memory ever having made an effort, – not a trace of struggle is demonstrable in my life, I am the opposite of a heroic nature. To "will" anything, to "strive" after anything, to have a "goal", a "wish" in mind – I know none of this from experience.

Is denial the only recourse, or is there a way to accommodate the project of critical transformation from an affirmative standpoint that goes beyond the desire to trans-

---

[1] Blondel 1991, 23.

form reality so as to embrace necessity? To affirm the lion from the perspective of the child?

If the problem of yes- and no-saying revolves around two incommensurable standpoints, it is profoundly complicated if we consider Nietzsche's critical project in relation to the object of his critique more closely. The complication concerns the possible *complicity* of Nietzschean critique in what it criticises, and here again, the language of war helps to describe the problem. In EH (weise 6) Nietzsche locates the centre of gravity of his philosophy in the

> *Struggle* against vengeful and lingering feelings, as far as the doctrine of "free will" – the *struggle* against Christianity is just a single instance of this –
>
> *Kampf* mit den Rach- und Nachgefühlen bis in die Lehre vom "freien Willen" hinein [...] – der *Kampf* mit dem Christenthum ist nur ein Einzelfall daraus – (EH weise 6, KSA 6.273)

What exactly do 'Rach- und Nachgefühlen' and '"freien Willen"' refer to, given that they are broader than Christianity? And what is the nature of Nietzsche's philosophical struggle?

Preliminary orientation can be gained from the account of GT further on in EH, where Nietzsche writes:

> – Ich sah zuerst den eigentlichen Gegensatz: – den *entartenden* Instinkt, der sich gegen das Leben mit unterirdischer Rachsucht wendet (– Christenthum, die Philosophie Schopenhauers, in gewissem Sinne schon die Philosophie Platos, der ganze Idealismus als typische Formen) und eine aus der Fülle, der Überfülle geborene Formel der *höchsten Bejahung*, ein Jasagen ohne Vorbehalt, zum Leiden selbst, zur Schuld selbst, zu allem Fragwürdigen und Fremden des Daseins selbst... (EH (GT) 2, KSA 6.311)
>
> – I was the first to see the real opposition: – the *degenerating* instinct that turns against life with subterranean vengefulness (– Christianity, Schopenhauer's philosophy, in a certain sense even Plato's philosophy, the whole of idealism as typical forms) and a formula of the *highest affirmation* born out of fullness, out of overfullness, a yes-saying without reservation even to suffering, even to guilt, even to everything questionable and strange in existence...

From this passage, it is clear that with the 'feelings of revenge', Nietzsche is referring not just to Christianity, but to idealism in general.[2] Nietzsche's philosophy is, then, a struggle against idealism. But what kind of a struggle? What is described in the context of GT from a distance as an opposition or *Gegensatz* – the opposition between unconditional, tragic-dionysian affirmation and idealism – is appropriated in the preceding passage, or rather *incorporated* ('in mir Fleisch geworden', EH Schicksal 1, KSA 6.365) as the struggle of his philosophy with idealism, his philosophical struggle or war against idealism from a standpoint in tragic-dionysian affirmation. If so,

---

[2] Both Salaquarda and Willers focus too narrowly on St. Paul and his distortion of Jesus as the target of Nietzsche's attacks in EH. See Salaquarda 1980, 288–322 and Willers 1988. On this point (and many others in this paper) I concur with Gerd Schank's (1993) broader interpretation of Nietzsche's target as 'Idealismus'.

the claim is not just that the standpoint of unconditional and total affirmation can *accommodate* Nietzsche's life-long project of critical warfare, but that the attitude of affirmation *involves* engaging in warfare or struggle.

If this is hard to reconcile with love or *amor fati*, the problem becomes even more virulent when we consider that what Nietzsche is warring against – namely idealism – is itself understood as warfare. In relation to MA, for instance, Nietzsche describes his critical project to expose the '*underworld*' of idealism as follows:

> [...] mit einer schneidenden Helle wird in diese *Unterwelt* des Ideals hineingeleuchtet. Es ist der Krieg, aber der Krieg ohne Pulver und Dampf, ohne kriegerische Attitüden, ohne Pathos und verrenkte Gliedmaassen – dies Alles selbst wäre noch "Idealismus". Ein Irrthum nach dem andern wird gelassen aufs Eis gelegt, das Ideal wird nicht widerlegt – *es erfriert...* (EH (MA) 1, KSA 6.323)
>
> [...] with a searing clarity, this *underworld* of the ideal is illuminated. It is war, but a war without powder or smoke, without belligerent attitudes, without pathos and contorted limbs – all this would still be "idealism". One error after another is calmly put on ice, the ideal is not refuted, *it freezes...*

In contrasting his 'cold' philosophical war against idealism with the 'hot' war of gunpowder, smoke and twisted limbs, we can see that Nietzsche is fully aware of the problem raised by his appropriation of warfare, namely: How to avoid repeating the warfare of idealism in his own war against idealism? How can Nietzsche's philosophical war or struggle against idealism avoid replicating the logic of revenge that drives the war waged by idealism?

In order to gauge Nietzsche's response to this problem, we need to determine more precisely the nature of idealism's warfare. For this we can do no better than turn to AC. The first few occurrences of the term 'war' (*Krieg*) give us the co-ordinates needed to understand the problem at hand. 'War' first occurs in AC 2 as one in the list of anti-Christian counter-values grounded in the will to power:

> *Nicht* Zufriedenheit, sondern mehr Macht; *nicht* Friede überhaupt, sondern Krieg; *nicht* Tugend, sondern Tüchtigkeit (Tugend im Renaissance-Stile, virtù, moralinfreie Tugend) (AC 2)
>
> *Not* contentment, but more power; *not* peace at all, but war; *not* virtue, but prowess (virtue in the Renaissance-style, *virtù*, moraline-free virtue)

In line with this immoral or extra-moral 'imperative', in the course of the book Nietzsche goes on to declare war, or identify with those who waged war, against various aspects of Christianity: in AC 9 he declares war against the 'theological instinct' ('Diesem Theologen-Instinkte mache ich den Krieg'); in AC 13 '*free spirits*' are convoked and reminded that they or we 'are already a '"transvaluation of all values", *an embodied declaration of war and victory* on all old concepts of "true" and "untrue"',[3] a gesture repeated in AC 36, where 'we *liberated spirits*' are ascribed the hon-

---

3 'Unterschätzen wir dies nicht: *wir selbst*, wir freien Geister, sind bereits eine "Umwerthung aller

esty (*Rechtschaffenheit*) needed to 'make war on the "holy lie", even more than every other lie';[4] in AC 58 he identifies with Epicurus' 'struggle' against the guilt-ridden soul of Christianity,[5] in AC 61 with the Renaissance, understood as the '*transvaluation* [Umwerthung] *of Christian values*', the one and only 'great war' that sought to bring noble counter-values 'to victory'.[6] This pattern is repeated in EH, where almost every book that he wrote – GT, UB, MA, M, Z, JGB – is identified with war, struggle or destruction.[7] One wonders what the final 'Declaration of war' (*Kriegserklärung*), listed then struck from table of contents for EH (KSA 6.262) would have looked like. In AC, the series of war-postures does of course culminate in an open declaration of war, the notorious 'Law against Christianity', subtitled '*war to the death against vice*'.[8] But the word used here, 'Todkrieg', points directly to the problem of repetition or replication raised by Nietzsche's war-mongering. For it is the very term used near the beginning of AC to describe Christianity. After Nietzsche's immoral or extra-moral 'imperative': '*nicht* Friede überhaupt, sondern Krieg', 'war' next occurs in AC 5 to describe Christianity as 'waging a *war to the death* [Todkrieg]' against the '*higher* type of human being'.[9] So what is to distinguish Nietzsche's 'Todkrieg' against Christian Anti-nature from the Christian 'Todkrieg' against higher types – apart from their

---

Werthe", eine *leibhafte* Kriegs –und Siegs-Erklärung an alle alten Begriffe von "wahr" und "unwahr".' (AC 13, KSA 6.179).

4 '— Erst wir, wir *freigewordenen* Geister, haben die Voraussetzung dafür, Etwas zu verstehn, das neunzehn Jahrhunderte missverstanden haben, – jene Instinkt und Leidenschaft gewordene Rechtschaffenheit, welche der "heiligen Lüge" noch mehr als jeder andren Lüge den Krieg macht ...' (AC 36, KSA 6.208).

5 '[...] *was* Epicur bekämpft hat, *nicht* das Heidenthum, sondern "das Christenthum", will sagen die Verderbniss der Seelen durch den Schuld–, durch den Straf- und Unsterblichkeits-Begriff. – Er bekämpfte die *unterirdischen* Culte, das ganze latente Christenthum [...]' (AC 58, KSA 6.2467).

6 'Versteht man endlich, *will* man verstehn, *was* die Renaissance war? Die *Umwerthung der christlichen Werthe*, der Versuch, mit allen Mitteln, mit allen Instinkten, mit allem Genie unternommen, die *Gegen*-Werthe, die vornehmen Werthe zum Sieg zu bringen ... Es gab bisher nur *diesen* grossen Krieg, es gab bisher keine entscheidendere Fragestellung als die der Renaissance, – *meine* Frage ist ihre Frage —' (AC 61, KSA 6.250).

7 EH Bücher 5, KSA 6.306; EH (GT) 3, KSA 6.312; cf. 2[110] 12.115; 14[14] 12.224 f.; 4[24] 12.229; EH (Z) 1, KSA 6.300; EH (UB) 1, KSA 6.316; EH (UB) 2, KSA 6.319; EH (MA) 1, KSA 6.232; EH (M) 2, KSA 6.332; EH (JGB) 1, KSA 6.350.

8 'Gesetz wider das Christenthum. / Gegeben am Tage des Heils, am ersten Tage des Jahres Eins (– am 30. September 1888 der falschen Zeitrechnung) / Todkrieg gegen das Laster: das Laster ist das Christenthum.' (AC Gesetz, KSA 6.254).

9 In 11[408], KSA 13.188 Christianity's 'Todkrieg gegen den starken Typus Mensch' is explicitly linked with idealism: 'es hat ein Ideal aus dem Widerspruch gegen die Erhaltungs-Instinkte des starken Lebens gemacht...'.

chosen antagonists? Does the very act of war not undermine itself by repeating the gesture it seeks to displace?[10]

To begin with, we need to ask what exactly Nietzsche means by Christianity's or idealism's war to the death against the '*higher* type of human being'. In AC 5, Nietzsche unpacks this formulation by writing that Christianity 'made an ideal out of *contradicting* the survival-instinct of the strong life' ('es hat ein Ideal aus dem *Widerspruch* gegen die Erhaltungs-Instinkte des starken Lebens gemacht'). The genesis of Christian values or ideals is *reactive*; they are born out of contradiction with the conditions of existence, that is, the *values* of a strong life-form, which they are to destroy and replace. In this regard, they are the very opposite of Buddhism, which demands no conflict: 'keinen Kampf gegen Andersdenkende'(AC 20). For Nietzsche, Buddhism's opposition to struggle or war is best understood as a physiological defence-mechanism against the debilitating feelings of revenge and *ressentiment*, and this gives us our second clue to the warfare of idealism. Not only is it born as a reaction against other forms of life and thought, its reaction is born in the hidden recesses of bad instincts:

> das Christenthum hat jedem Ehrfurchts- und Distanz-Gefühl zwischen Mensch und Mensch, das heisst der Voraussetzung zu jeder Erhöhung, zu jedem Wachsthum der Cultur einen *Todkrieg* aus den heimlichsten Winkeln schlechter Instinkte gemacht, – es hat aus dem Ressentiment der Massen sich seine Hauptwaffe geschmiedet gegen uns, gegen alles Vornehme, Frohe, Hochherzige auf Erden, gegen unser Glück auf Erden... (AC 43)
>
> Christianity has waged a *war to the death* on every feeling of reverence and distance between people, which is to say the presupposition of every elevation, of every growth of culture, – it has forged from the *ressentiment* of the masses as its main weapon against us, against everything on earth that is noble, joyful, magnanimous, against our happiness on earth...

Combining both moments, we can say that idealism originates in feelings of *ressentiment* and revenge against other forms of life and thought, and reacts against them by positing values that are meant to exclude or destroy counter-values. This dynamic can be traced to the bivalent, oppositional structure of idealist thought, as Gerd Schank has shown in his study of the terms 'gegen' and 'Gegensatz' in EH:

> In the case of "idealist oppositions" an "idealist war" is in play: Any given plus value aims at the elimination or "usurpation" of the minus value: the "evil ones" ought to disappear, the "good ones" alone ought to remain. The intention is, then, the quasi-amputation of the opposed pair: only the plus part ought to be left over, whereby of course the opposition as such is completely removed: in favour of the plus halves that alone remain. (Schank 1993, 145)[11]

---

[10] The same question arises in GD Moral, where 'Krieg' is used to describe Christianity's attitude to the passions and to its enemies, followed in section 3 by (what seems to be) a paean to war: 'Man hat auf das grosse Leben verzichtet, wenn man auf den Krieg verzichtet...'.

[11] 'Bei den "idealistischen Gegensätzen" spielt sich ein "idealistischer Krieg" ab: der jeweilige Pluswert zielt ab auf die Abschaffung bzw. völlige "Vereinnahmung" des Minuswertes: die "Bösen" sollen verschwinden, die "Guten" sollen allein bleiben. Intendiert ist also quasi die Amputation des Gegen-

Idealism's 'Todkrieg' names a form of bivalent (*zweiwertig*), oppositional thinking that intends a total and exclusive claim for its positive values (*Absolut-setzen*) by
(1) eliminating the negatively-valued terms ('evil');[12] but also
(2) by eliminating opposition or war altogether, in favour of – 'peace'.

It is in this light that Nietzsche's imperative, '*nicht* Friede überhaupt, sondern Krieg', needs to be understood: as an act of defiance against the total hegemony or tyranny (*Alleinherrschaft, Tyrannei*) of idealist values. Already we can see that if Nietzsche's kind of warfare is to avoid repeating this logic and offer a genuine alternative, it *cannot* be a kind of warfare bent on the destruction of its opponents or counter-values and of opposition altogether. It must be a war-praxis that preserves opposition, struggle or war, precisely by *not* destroying its opponents: by *limiting* its negation of counter-values.

The logic of idealism's 'Todkrieg' can be taken one step further by considering a few notes from the *Nachlass* from late 1887. At issue in these notes are the eminently modern forms of idealism embodied in the autonomous ideals of '"*morality for morality's sake*"', '"*art for art's sake*"', and knowledge for knowledge's sake (cf. EH Bücher 4, KSA 6.304 f.). Each of these, Nietzsche argues, constitutes an important stage in the 'de-naturalization' (*Entnaturalisierung*) of morality, art and knowledge; each looks to 'slander reality' (*Realitäts-Verleumdung*) by reading a 'false opposition into things' (*falschen Gegensatz*), which allows an 'ideal to be separated from the actual' (*ein Ideal ablöst vom Wirklichen*).[13] To separate the ideal and place it in opposition to

---

satzpaares: nur die Plushälfte soll übrig bleiben, womit natürlich der Gegensatz als solcher überhaupt beseitigt wäre: zugunsten der allein verbleibenden Plushälften.'

12 11[138] 13.64: '[…] das *widernatürliche Ideal* / – man negirt, man *vernichtet* –'.

13 "*Die Moral um der Moral willen!*" – eine wichtige Stufe in ihrer Entnaturalisirung: sie erscheint selbst als letzter Werth. In dieser Phase hat sie die Religion mit sich durchdrungen: im Judenthum z.B. Und ebenso giebt es eine Phase, wo sie die Religion wieder *von sich abtrennt*, und wo ihr kein Gott "moralisch" genug ist: dann zieht sie das unpersönliche Ideal vor… Das ist jetzt der Fall.
"*Die Kunst um der Kunst willen*"- das ist ein gleichgefährliches Princip: damit bringt man einen falschen Gegensatz in die Dinge, – es läuft auf eine Realitäts-Verleumdung ("Idealisirung" ins *Häßliche*) hinaus. Wenn man ein Ideal ablöst vom Wirklichen, so stößt man das Wirkliche hinab, man verarmt es, man verleumdet es. "*Das Schöne um des Schönen willen*", "*das Wahre um des Wahren willen*", "*das Gute um des Guten willen*" – das sind drei Formen des *bösen Blicks* für das Wirkliche. (10[194], KSA 12.572f.)

"*Morality for morality's sake*" – an important stage in its denaturalization: it appears as the ultimate value itself. In this phase it has permeated religion: e.g. in Judaism. There is also a phase when it *severs itself from* religion again, and no God is "moral" enough for it: then it prefers the impersonal ideal . . . That is the case today.
"*Art for art's sake*" – this is an equally dangerous principle: it brings a false opposition into things – it amounts to slandering reality ("idealization"*into the ugly*). When one separates an ideal from what's real, one casts down the real, impoverishes it, slanders it. "*Beauty for*

life is to impoverish (*verarmt*) life and make it ugly ("Idealisirung" *ins Häßliche*), instead of recognising art, knowledge and morality as ways to intensify and propel life towards new possibilities.[14] Nietzsche then takes these false oppositions and situates them on the plane of immanence with the claim that the separation they effect in the domain of values serves idealist warfare as a means to separate and secure idealist power-complexes from their adversaries.

> – "*beautiful* and *ugly*", "*true* and *false*", "*good* and *evil*" – these *separations* and *antagonisms* betray conditions of existence and enhancement, not of man in general, but of various fixed and lasting complexes which sever their adversaries from themselves. The *war* thus produced is what is essential: as a means of *separating* that *strengthens* the isolation...
>
> – „*schön* und *häßlich*", „*wahr* und *falsch*", „*gut* und *böse*" – diese *Scheidungen* und *Antagonismen* verrathen Daseins– und Steigerungs-Bedingungen, nicht vom Menschen überhaupt, sondern von irgendwelchen festen und dauerhaften Complexen, welche ihre Widersacher von sich abtrennen. Der *Krieg*, der damit geschaffen wird, ist das Wesentliche daran: als Mittel der *Absonderung*, die die Isolation *verstärkt*... (10[194], KSA 12.572f.)

By *separating* positive from negative values through false value-oppositions, the idealist power-complex seeks to *separate* itself from antagonistic complexes (*Widersacher*) and strengthen itself in isolation. For, as Nietzsche writes in the subsequent note, idealist war works by identifying oneself with the positive value ("'the good cause'", 'reason, taste, virtue') and turning the opponent into one's opposite (*seinen Gegner zu seinem Gegensatz umbilden*) by identifying it with the negative value as evil, irrational, ugly, false etc.[15]

---

beauty's sake", "Truth for truth's sake", "Good for the sake of the good" – these are three forms of the *evil eye* for the real.

14   – *Kunst, Erkenntniß, Moral* sind **Mittel:** statt die Absicht auf Steigerung des Lebens in ihnen zu erkennen, hat man sie zu einem *Gegensatz des Lebens* in Bezug gebracht [...] (10[194], KSA 12.572f.)

– *Art, knowledge, morality* are *means*: instead of recognising in them the purpose to enhance life, one has placed them in *opposition to life* [...]

15   (289) **Consequenz des Kampfes:** der Kämpfende sucht seinen
Gegner zu seinem *Gegensatz* umzubilden, – in der
Vorstellung natürlich
– er sucht an sich bis zu dem Grade zu glauben, daß
er den Muth der "guten Sache" haben kann (als ob er die
gute Sache sei): wie als ob die Vernunft, der
Geschmack, die Tugend von seinem Gegner bekämpft
werde...
– der Glaube, den er nöthig hat, als stärkstes
Defensiv- und Aggressiv-Mittel ist ein *Glaube an sich*,
der sich aber als Glaube an Gott zu mißverstehen weiß
– sich nie die Vortheile und Nützlichkeiten des Siegs
vorstellen, sondern immer nur den Sieg um des Siegs willen,

Isolation and separation are also prominent in EH, where idealism is introduced under the sign of separation (*Trennung*) or (self-)alienation in the context of Nietzsche's youth. He writes of idealism as the unreason ('Grund-Unvernunft meines Lebens – den "Idealismus"': EH klug 2, KSA 6.283) that separated him from the 'realities', as the ignorance of physiology ('Unwissenheit in physiologicis': EH klug 2, KSA 6.283) that sidetracked him from his life–'task', alienating him from his 'lowermost self' ('unterste Selbst': EH (MA) 4, KSA 6.326), and most importantly, from his own 'instinct' ('Gesammt-Abirrung meines Instinkts', EH (MA) 3, KSA 6.324; cf. Schank 1993, 110, 114, 100 f.). It takes the protest of Nietzsche's instincts, sickness and the 'cold' philosophical war against idealism in MA to overcome these separations of the ideal from the real, of the soul from the body, and bring him back to himself.

What, then, must Nietzsche's war against idealism look like, if it is to avoid repeating the warfare of idealism? Two essential features of the warfare waged by idealist or oppositional thought have been identified above as *isolation / separation* and *destruction*. Idealist or oppositional thinking seeks

1. to *separate* and *isolate* positively from negatively-valued terms, in order
2. to eliminate or *destroy* the negatively-valued terms and with them,
3. to eliminate opposition or war altogether, so as to make an absolute and exclusive claim for its positive values ('peace').

---

als "Sieg Gottes" –
– Jede kleine im Kampf befindliche Gemeinschaft (selbst
Einzelne) sucht sich zu überreden: "*wir haben den
guten Geschmack, das gute Urtheil und die Tugend für uns*"... Der Kampf zwingt zu
einer solchen *Übertreibung* der *Selbstschätzung*... (10[195] 12.573)

Consequence of struggle: the one struggling seeks to
transform its opponent into its *opposite*, – in
representation naturally
– it seeks to believe in itself to the degree that
it can have the courage of the "good cause" (as if it
were the *good cause*): as if reason, taste, virtue is being fought by its opponent...
– the belief that it needs, as the strongest
means of defence and aggression is a *belief in itself*,
which is capable of misunderstanding itself as belief in God
– never to think of the advantages and uses of victory,
but only ever victory for the sake of victory,
as "God's victory" –
– Every small community that finds itself in struggle (even
individuals) seeks to persuade itself: "*we have
good taste, good judgement and virtue for us*"... Struggle forces this kind
Of *exaggeration* in *self-assessment* ...

In these terms Nietzschean warfare must
1. *bind together* (*Verbinden*) opposed terms, instead of separating (*Trennen*) them, and
2. *preserve its opponents* or counter-values, instead of destroying them, and so as to
3. preserve the very dynamic or *necessity* of opposition, struggle or war.

These constraints give us the key co-ordinates for understanding Nietzsche's account of his own war-praxis in EH, Warum ich so weise bin 7.

II Nietzsche's War-Praxis (EH Warum ich so weise bin 7)

In this text, as argued in the opening chapter (pp. 33, 36 ff.), Nietzsche presents his philosophical war-praxis on the model of the Greek agon as a form of critique governed by *a dynamic of reciprocal affirmation or empowerment, and reciprocal limitation or disempowerment*. As Nietzsche presents it in EH weise 7, agonal critique involves a form of critical, oppositional thinking in which two strategic moments are emphasised: the effort to *limit* the negation of counter-values and the effort to *forge bonds* with them. In the light of the preceding analysis, this model can be understood as a response to the constraints under which Nietzschean warfare must operate if it is to avoid undermining itself by repeating the warfare of idealism it is contesting. As Nietzsche describes in EH, his war-praxis offers effective resistance to the absolute claims or tyranny of idealist values without, however, destroying them. By *limiting* its negation of counter-values and *forging bonds* with them, it looks to *preserve* opposition, struggle or war between counter-values, as the greatest stimulus towards the creation of new values beyond idealism and beyond good and evil.

Nietzsche removes his critical warfare from the *absolute negativity* of destruction in three stages, each of which inscribes a *limit in the negation of counter-values* (see chapter 1, p. 33 ff.). The first concerns the goal of his war-praxis in *mastery* (*Herr werden, Herrschaft*) over a worthwhile resistance, not its destruction. Driven by an interest in 'strength' or 'growth', the critic seeks out cultural forces that are 'victorious' with the intention, not of annihilating them, but of placing a limit or measure on their tyranny, so as to make place for competing ideals.[16] This implies the second

---

16 See 10[117] 12.523:
'I have declared war on the anaemic Christian ideal (including what is closely related to it), not with the intention of annihilating [*vernichten*] it, but only of putting an end to its *tyranny* and making place for new ideals, more *robust* ideals... The *continued existence* of the Christian ideal belongs to the most desirable things that there are: and just for the sake of the ideals that wish to assert themselves next to it and perhaps over it – they must have opponents, *strong* opponents in order to become *strong*. – Thus we immoralists need the *power of morality*: our drive for self-preservation wills that our *opponents* retain their strength – wills only to become master over them [Herr über sie].'

limit in the negation of counter-values: Mastery requires the *preservation* of what it masters, as the kind of opposition that forces the agonal critic to *exercise* its strength to the full, to deploy its full range of capabilities, thereby acting as a standard or measure (*Maass*) of its strength. The third limit comes with the fourth rule of Nietzsche's war-praxis, where the interest in preserving the opponent is intensified in affirmative gestures of 'good will', 'gratitude', 'honour' and 'distinction', expressed in the *binding of names* between critic and issue or person under attack (EH weise 7, KSA 6.275).

Dynamic reciprocity is the mark of agonal interaction, and the affirmative gesture towards the opponent is reciprocated by the opponent, who acts as a standard or measure (*Maass*) for the critic to exercise and affirm its own strength against it. In this way, agonal critique takes the dynamic form of *reciprocal affirmation or empowerment*. But the term 'Maass' means 'measure' not just in the sense of 'standard' or 'gauge', but also as an actual limit, so that the opponent, qua *Maass* of the critic's strength, is also what limits the critic's negation to *mastery*; that is, to contesting but preserving the opponent or counter-value, rather than destroying it. Given that mastery means placing a limit or measure on the tyranny of prevailing ('victorious') values, the critic finds itself limited to limiting the tyranny of the ideals it seeks, in a *dynamic of reciprocal limitation or disempowerment*. Combining affirmative and negative moments, we can therefore say that Nietzsche's war-praxis in EH involves a dynamic of *reciprocal affirmation or empowerment and reciprocal limitation or disempowerment*.

III Nietzsche's War-Praxis and the Standpoint of Total Affirmation

The dynamic of *reciprocal affirmation (empowerment) and reciprocal limitation (disempowerment)* of Nietzsche's declared war-praxis instantiates the dynamic principle of the agon described in HW as a 'reciprocal stimulation to deeds' and reciprocal 'holding within the bounds of measure'.[17] The affinities between Nietzsche's war-praxis in EH and the Greek agon extend to several other structural moments common to both: the presupposition of equality in the face of the enemy;[18] the antagonism

---

17 '[…] daß, in einer natürlichen Ordnung der Dinge, es immer *mehrere* Genies giebt, die sich gegenseitig zur That reizen, wie sie sich auch gegenseitig in der Grenze des Maaßes halten.' (HW, KSA 1.789).
18 The task is to become master [*Herr werden*], *not* over any resistances, but over those against which one has bring one's entire strength, suppleness and mastery of weapons to bear, – over equal opponents… Equality in the face of the enemy – first presupposition of an honest duel. (EH weise 7, KSA 6.274).

towards tyranny, the exclusive 'rule of one' (*Alleinherrschaft*)¹⁹ or the 'victorious forces' singled out for attack in EH; and the prospect of mastery or provisional victory between the contests, rather than the absolute victory of annihilation.²⁰ Of particular importance for the problem of affirmation are the two constraints under which Nietzschean *Umwertung* must operate if it is to avoid repeating idealist warfare, with its gestures of *destruction* and *separation*, in contesting it – namely: to *limit* its negation of counter-values, and to *forge bonds* with them. Under these constraints, Nietzsche contends, effective and productive resistance can be offered to idealist, oppositional thinking, opening and re-opening the question of the *overcoming* of idealist, life-negating values. The question now is whether this model can address the problematic of radical affirmation and critical negation at the centre of *Ecce Homo*. Does Nietzsche's agonal war-praxis offer a coherent, practicable model for combining unconditional, total affirmation and total critique?

Let me start by asking the more basic question of whether the agonal account of *Umwertung* offers a coherent model for warfare at all. The cue for this question lies in certain 'remainders' in Nietzsche's text that cast doubt on the agonal model. These difficulties, I will argue, force us to ask whether *any* single model of warfare can address the problem of combining total affirmation and total critique. The approach I propose to this problem abandons the prospect of accounting for Nietzschean *Umwertung* by way of any model of warfare and identifies instead the demand *to overcome any single standpoint*, as the key of the *Umwertungs*-project.

There are at least three features of Nietzsche's text on war-praxis that exceed the agonal account offered above and compromise the coherence of Nietzschean war-praxis.

1. Nietzsche's third rule of warfare states that the causes of war are cultural, *impersonal* problems, persons (such as Wagner) serving only as 'a strong magnifying glass with which one can make visible a general, but evasive and barely tangible state of need' (décadence) (EH weise 7, KSA 6.274 f.; cf. Schank 1993, 87–96).²¹ But in the next line he goes on – the fourth rule of warfare – to claim that he

---

19 'Das ist der Kern der hellenischen Wettkampf-Vorstellung: sie verabscheut die Alleinherrschaft und fürchtet ihre Gefahren, sie begehrt, als *Schutzmittel* gegen das Genie – ein zweites Genie.' (HW, KSA 1.789).
20 At the same time, there are also features of Nietzsche's war-praxis in EH which instantiate the will to power and thereby distance it from his early concept of the Greek agon: the principal interest in 'growth', a shorthand for the expansionist dynamic of will to power, is not shared by the Greek agon. The seeking out of resistances, the search for powerful opponents, as the means for expansion through incorporation, is repeatedly emphasised in the context of will to power, but absent from the Greek agon. In this regard, the war-praxis text in EH can be viewed as an attempt to overcome the tensions between agon and will to power through a model of conflict, which, while based on the will to power, incorporates elements of the agon.
21 In the effort to make sense of what Nietzsche writes about 'persons', Tuncel (2009, 165) suggests that we distinguish persons from individuals, and private from public individuals, so as to associate only the latter with the agon. This would leave the person qua private individual out of agonal war-

> attack[s] only those things where all personal disagreement [*Personen-Differenz*] is ruled out, where a background of bad experiences is lacking. (EH weise 7, KSA 6.275)

With regard to Wagner, this statement can be taken as false, as a lie, as a distortion of what we know was the case, etc. But it can also be seen as a distortion that comes from an affirmative excess, an expansive affirmation of the Other that spills over into a curious denial of difference (*Differenz*).

2. This gesture is then repeated further on when, in relation to his emphatically *impersonal* war on Christianity, he goes on to insist that

> I have never experienced any fatalities or hindrances from this side, – the most earnest Christians have always been well disposed towards me. (EH weise 7, KSA 6.275)

Again, Nietzsche seems to overplay his hand in an affirmative embrace of the antagonistic Other that leads him to falsify and deny his own bitter complaints about his pious mother and sister (EH weise 3, KSA 6.268).[22] In this case, it is clear that the affirmative excess stems from the *forging of bonds* with (*Verbinden*) opposed values – the very gesture through which Nietzschean warfare is to overcome the separations (*Trennungen*) of idealism.

3. These gestures come to a head in the moment when Nietzsche seems to lose sight of warfare altogether.

> To attack in my case is a proof of good-will, under circumstances, of gratitude. I do honour, I confer distinction insofar as I bind my name with that of an issue, a person: for or against – in this respect that counts as the same for me. (EH weise 7, KSA 6.275)

Here, the affirmative embrace of the Other through the binding of names not only overrules critical negation, it *neutralises* it. All difference slides into indifference when Nietzsche says that negation and affirmation, pro and contra, count as the

---

fare, so that Nietzsche can write 'I never attack persons' and can exclude 'personal disagreements' from his attacks. This does not make etymological sense, since 'Person' derives from latin 'persona' meaning mask, coming to mean 'role', then 'outward appearance' in German (Paul 1981[8], 482): all *public* aspects of an individual. We can assume that Nietzsche was aware of this. Nor do these distinctions strike me as helpful for understanding the passage in question: if Nietzsche uses 'persons' as magnifying glasses for broad cultural problems and goes on to 'bind' his name with 'that of an issue, a person' (EH weise 7, KSA 6.275), he cannot mean a private individual, but a public or publically-recognizable persona. At times, Nietzsche does use 'Person' / 'Personal–' with a specific meaning: to denote an exceptional form of human life whose value is *sui generis* and who confers this personal value on its actions – whereas most actions reflect external influences on the agent, not personal qualities (see e.g. 10[59], KSA 12.491f.). This does not seem relevant to the passage on warfare, however.

22 See also AC 8 KSA 6.174 on theologians: 'Man muss das Verhängniss aus der Nähe gesehn haben, noch besser, man muss es an sich erlebt, man muss an ihm fast zu Grunde gegangen sein, um hier keinen Spaass mehr zu verstehn [...]'.

same. Agonal mastery, as the impulse (not to destroy but) to place a limit on the tyranny of idealist ideals, can account for the limits on negation in Nietzschean warfare and its productive orientation – to make room for other ideals. But mastery remains a critical, evaluative engagement with the Other, and so falls short of the declared indifference in Nietzsche's text: for or against 'counts as the same'.

How *can* we account for the slippage from difference to indifference, provoked by the affirmative excess of Nietzsche's text? And what can we learn from it about the standpoint of affirmation? To my mind, there is only one way to make sense of the moment of indifference in Nietzsche's text: as a pronouncement from a standpoint that breaks with, or overcomes the perspective of the antagonist-critic engaged in warfare (perspective of *difference*), and occupies instead an 'impossible' standpoint *in the relations of antagonism between* the critic and his counter-values (perspective of *indifference*).

On this interpretation, the distortions that rob Nietzsche's war-praxis of its coherence as a practicable model of warfare are the manifestations or surface-effects of a slippage of the standpoint of narration: from the *subject-position of the antagonist* to the *relations of antagonism or opposition between the antagonist and his counter-values* (indifference). But what is it that motivates this shift? Is it just a slip of the pen, the sign of an increasingly unstable authorial hand – or is there a way to make sense of it? We should remember that the slippage of the narrative standpoint is driven by an affirmative excess in Nietzsche's text, as expressed in the forging of bonds with counter-values. If the impulse or demand to affirm the other motivates this shift of perspective, it is – I suggest – because for Nietzsche the demand to *affirm reality as antagonism, war and opposition* against the absolute rule or 'peace' of idealism requires *an overcoming of all antagonistic standpoints* – the subject-position – *towards an 'impossible' standpoint in the relations of antagonism*.

This claim opens up a new approach to the problem of combining radical affirmation and negation. The problem here, as we saw, revolves around the incommensurability of two standpoints: 1. the aggressive pathos, the attitude of op-position, of self-assertion *against the Other* required for 'no-saying' (*Neinsagen*), and specifically, the critical negation of idealism qua life-negation; and 2. the openness and love required for unconditional and total affirmation. These two positions are incompatible and cannot be combined in a practicable manner on the grounds that affirmation involves the affirmation of *all* antagonistic positions and op-positions, while 'no-saying' involves the self-assertion *against* the Other. But what if 'yes-saying' and 'no-saying' do not simply name two philosophical standpoints that can be occupied at will by us as subjects? Perhaps the practical force of the logical contradiction between these positions is to confront us with the question: Does 'yes-saying' represent a practicable philosophical 'standpoint' or 'position' *at all* – or does it represent instead the requirement *to break with the subject-position altogether, to overcome all antagonistic positions* for the sake of total affirmation? If so, the *logical* paradox of claiming to occupy two incompatible positions is made fruitful by Nietzsche for the *practical* or *existential* task of conjugating total affirmation and total critique.²³

The move from subject-position to the relations between subjects can be tracked by attending to the narrative standpoints or perspectives Nietzsche adopts. No-saying is narrated from the perspective of the antagonist or warrior (*Krieger, Kämpfer*) and exhibits *the intentional state of negation* required for warfare: the pathos of contention (*Sich-im-Kampf-fühlen*) or critical op-position to the other, driven by the impulse to transform the status quo and prevail. Yes-saying, on the other hand, cannot exhibit any such intentional states if it is to affirm *all* antagonistic positions. It is therefore narrated by Nietzsche from a standpoint that abstracts from this or any subject-position within the struggle, a standpoint in the relations of struggle *between* subjects. It is this move alone that makes it possible to embrace all differential positions from a position of indifference, as part and parcel of reality understood as a conflictual multiplicity. On this reading, the problem is not that Nietzsche looks to combine two standpoints or attitudes that contradict one another; rather, it is that affirmation is narrated from a standpoint that cannot be occupied by *any subject*, a strictly impossible or fictional 'standpoint', predicated on the overcoming of all positions.

The relational standpoint, even if impossible or fictional, represents not a flight of fancy or the touch of madness, but *the most immanent* standpoint in reality, given Nietzsche's understanding of the 'relational character of all occurrence' (*Relations-Charakter Alles Geschehens*: 26[36], KSA 11.157; cf. 14[93], KSA 13.270). By the same token, it represents *the most affirmative* standpoint in reality, the standpoint of *amor fati*, as expressed in Zarathustra's aspiration not just to say Yes, but '*to be* the eternal Yes to all things' (EH (Z) 6, KSA 6,344 f.). For if Nietzsche's critique of substance-ontology reconfigures reality around relations of power between 'things' without substance, affirmation seems to require our dislocation from the 'subject'–position towards these relations: '*to be* the eternal Yes to all things' can only mean to occupy a standpoint, not in 'things' without substance, but in the antagonistic relations that institute, transform, dislocate and destitute them. It is this requirement, necessary and impossible at once, that is embodied by the fictional qualities of *Ecce Homo* and its narrator's all-pervading feint of affirmation.

This suggestion can be tested against Nietzsche's own accounts of affirmation, where the incommensurability of standpoints receives its strongest expression. I have in mind Nietzsche's formulations of his dionysian concept of reality, where, as pointed out earlier (p. 257), negativity and destruction have an integral, privileged place in relation to affirmation, as the following examples illustrate:

---

23 The claim that Nietzsche makes logical contradictions fruitful for practical or existential purposes has been developed more extensively by Werner Stegmaier. In the context of the same problem in EH, he distinguishes between logical and existential contradictions or oppositions, arguing that Nietzsche makes the former productive for the latter (Stegmaier 2008, 62–114, esp. 105 f., 110 f.). On Nietzsche's attitude to paradoxes, see Stegmaier 2004.

> Für eine *dionysische* Aufgabe gehört die Härte des Hammers, die *Lust selbst am Vernichten* in entscheidender Weise zu den Vorbedingungen. (EH (Z) 8, KSA 6.349)
>
> For a *dionysian* task, a decisive precondition is the hardness of the hammer, the *pleasure even in destroying*.

Or again:

> Die Bejahung des Vergehens *und Vernichtens*, das Entscheidende in einer dionysischen Philosophie, das Jasagen zu Gegensatz und Krieg, das *Werden*, mit radikaler Ablehnung auch selbst des Begriffs "Sein" [...] (EH (GT) 3, KSA 6.313)[24]
>
> The affirmation of passing away *and destroying*, which is decisive in a dionysian philosophy, the yes-saying to opposition and war, *becoming* along with a radical rejection of the very concept of "being" [...]

There is no question of mastery in these passages: of *limiting* one's negation of the other, let alone affirming it. If anything, the opponent figures as an obstacle to be overcome by destroying it – with 'pleasure'. This insistence on destruction brings the problem of affirmation and negation to a head. For one cannot affirm life or reality as 'opposition and war' and at the same time affirm destruction. To destroy the antagonist is to eliminate the resistance it offered and so put an end to opposition and war; to affirm opposition and war, on the other hand, implies the necessity of resistance and obstacles, ruling out destruction as the end of war.

However, the problem can be averted if we distinguish the relational standpoint of affirmation from the subject-position of the antagonist, as I have proposed. Here, the line of thought can be rendered as follows:

- To affirm life or reality in dionysian terms is to affirm opposition and war.
- To affirm opposition or war, in turn, requires affirming the necessary conditions for warfare, and that includes the subjective or psychological conditions for waging war.
- One can only engage effectively in war if driven by the desire to win, that is, to bring an end to war through a decisive victory, and if one takes pleasure in destroying all obstacles to one's victory; anything short of this will weaken one's position and be self-defeating.
- Whether the war *ends* in the actual destruction of the opponent, or in mastery over it, depends on the opponent (one chooses) and the resistance it offers; but warfare can only *begin* with the will to vanquish the other.
- While it is a necessary condition for affirming warfare and opposition, this psychology precludes the affirmation of opposition and war, precisely because it wills the decisive victory that spells the end of war.

---

24 For *Vernichten*, see also EH Bücher 1, KSA 6.300 (Zarathustra as '*Vernichter*[.] der Moral'); EH (GT) 3, KSA 6.313; EH (JGB) 1, KSA 6.350; EH Schicksal 1–2, KSA 6.366; EH Schicksal 4, KSA 6.368; EH Schicksal 8, KSA 6.373.

- To affirm reality as warfare and opposition requires that one affirm or acknowledge *all* antagonistic positions as *necessary* for warfare. This can only be achieved by breaking with or overcoming the subject-position of all antagonists involved, for whom their opponents are not *necessary*, but obstacles to be overcome for the sake of victory.

On this interpretation, the affirmation of reality as opposition and war includes the affirmation of destruction, but only as what Nietzsche calls a 'precondition' for the dionysian task of total affirmation: as the 'pleasure in destruction', which is to say, as the *subjective or psychological* condition for waging war (EH (Z) 8, KSA 6.349). To affirm reality as opposition and war necessitates that one affirm the psychological conditions for warfare and occupy this standpoint, but also that one breaks with this or any standpoint, for the sake of affirming *all* antagonistic positions, as the necessary condition for affirming reality as war. From this impossible or paradoxical 'standpoint' in the relations of antagonism, destruction is necessarily affirmed, but indirectly, at one remove, from a radically different perspective.

This analysis can be extended to Nietzsche's declaration of the *'Umwerthung Aller Werthe'* under the sign of 'great politics' or *grosse Politik* in EH, Warum ich ein Schicksal bin 1. Here, the problem of affirmation and negation is broached with the claim:

> Ich widerspreche, wie nie widersprochen worden ist und bin trotzdem der Gegensatz eines neinsagenden Geistes. (EH Schicksal 1, KSA 6.366)

> I contradict as has never been contradicted and am nonetheless the opposite of a no-saying spirit.

Here again, destruction plays a pivotal role in Nietzsche's self-description, not only implicitly, as the 'dynamite' that explodes linear time and breaks the history of humanity in two,[25] but also explicitly in the follow-up section of the text:

> Ich kenne die Lust am *Vernichten* in einem Grade, die meiner *Kraft* zum Vernichten gemäss ist, – in Beidem gehorche ich meiner dionysischen Natur, welche das Neinthun nicht vom Jasagen zu trennen weiss. Ich bin der erste *Immoralist:* damit bin ich der *Vernichter* par excellence. – (EH Schicksal 2, KSA 6.366)

> I know the pleasure in *destroying* to a degree that matches my *power* to destroy, – in both I obey my dionysian nature, which knows not how to separate no-doing from yes-saying. I am the first *immoralist:* that way I am the destroyer par excellence. –

---

25 See EH Schicksal 8, KSA 6.373:
'Wer über sie [die christliche Moral – HS] aufklärt, ist eine force majeure, ein Schicksal, – er bricht die Geschichte der Menschheit in zwei Stücke. Man lebt *vor* ihm, man lebt *nach* ihm ... Der Blitz der Wahrheit traf gerade das, was bisher am Höchsten stand: wer begreift, *was* da vernichtet wurde, mag zusehn, ob er überhaupt noch Etwas in den Händen hat.'

One can hardly miss the emphatically subjective perspective of Nietzsche's self-description as destroyer in these lines. One need only add that this falls short of the total affirmation of reality as conflict, which must affirm not just Nietzsche's 'pleasure in destruction' but also that which it seeks to annihilate.

This point can, I suggest, be generalised across *Ecce Homo* as a whole as a way of making sense of many of the contradictions and discrepancies that seem to sabotage a philosophical engagement with the book. The proposal is that *all* the passages, like that on 'grosse Politik', which describe the task of *Umwertung* as a *transformative* philosophical project are narrated by Nietzsche from the standpoint of the subject of *Umwertung*, and his self-understanding as a free, intentional agent. This goes for the grand gestures – the 'Moral-Codex' against the Christian anti-nature described with reference to AC (EH Bücher 5, KSA 6.307), the invocation of the 'cultivation of higher humanity' as 'the greatest of all tasks', and the 'promise of a tragic age' (EH (GT) 4, KSA 6.313) – but also for the passages on 'Why I am so Wise' and 'Why I am so Clever' that proffer advice on how to survive sickness and the decadent age by describing Nietzsche's micro-management of his environment and the choices that enabled him to remain open to everything through a controlled distance from everything. All of this forms part of Nietzsche's philosophy of affirmation, as the necessary (subjective) condition (1) for affirming reality as conflict and opposition. But it should not simply be identified with the possibility of affirmation, which requires that we break with any antagonistic subject-position, its aspirations (such as transforming the status quo) and presuppositions (choice, free will). This is the necessary (relational) condition (2) for affirming *all* antagonistic positions, that is, reality as conflictual multiplicity. This requirement is met through Nietzsche's claims to have achieved affirmation or *amor fati*, claims that are narrated through the feint of a standpoint that cannot actually be occupied, a fictional standpoint in the relations between antagonistic subject-positions. What makes EH so perplexing and frustrating for philosophical engagements is the way Nietzsche slides seamlessly between the subjective and relational standpoints of narration, even mixing the perspectives they afford, as if a perspective of difference were the same as a perspective of indifference, as if one can engage in, and repudiate, transformative thinking in one breath. On the interpretation advanced in this chapter, no-saying and yes-saying cannot simply be identified, but they do form a *differentiated* unity in the demand that we (1) occupy a range of antagonistic subject-positions, and (2) break with each and every position, if we are to affirm reality as antagonism, struggle and opposition.

In these terms, the total dionysian affirmation of life can accommodate Nietzsche's critique of idealism qua life-negation, as a standpoint that must be occupied but also surpassed. Yet, the same would seem to apply to idealism, as a standpoint to be occupied and then surpassed, if dionysian affirmation means to affirm or acknowledge *all* antagonistic positions as necessary for warfare. What, then, we may ask, is to stop the relational standpoint of indifference from sliding into a bland relativism or an incoherent negation-and-affirmation of idealism or any standpoint? In response, we do well to bear in mind that dionysian affirmation cannot be a final or fixed state that affirms irreconcilable standpoints, but must be grasped as a becoming, a process that makes for a particular trajectory with its own story. In EH, as we saw, Nietzsche recounts his youthful idealism (EH klug 2, KSA 6.283), how it side-tracked him from his 'task' and alienated him from himself until his 'cold' philosophical war against idealism in MA. By enabling him to overcome the separation of the ideal from the real, to break with the negation of reality (*Realitäts-Verleumdung*) from a standpoint in the ideal, it brought him back to himself (see p. 265 above). What this narrative illustrates is made explicit in the late *Vorrede* to MA I, where Nietzsche recounts his critical emancipation from his youthful ideals as a convoluted, counter-final trajectory from sickness, through convalescence (with relapses), to health (which cannot do without sickness) or 'countless healths of the body' (FW 120). Here it becomes clear that the critique of values and ideals cannot be performed from a safe distance outside them, but only as a 'circumnavigator of that inner world called "human being"',[26] who occupies each and every standpoint under critique, overcoming each in turn so as to attain as the most ample and inclusive perspective possible. It is this standpoint, won through the adoption and overcoming of moral standpoints in sequence, that I have identified as the relational standpoint of affirmation: both necessary and impossible. In the later *Vorrede* Nietzsche describes it as a 'median' or 'medial' state, as 'something third':

> Es giebt einen mittleren Zustand darin, dessen ein Mensch solchen Schicksals später nicht ohne Rührung eingedenk ist: ein blasses feines Licht und Sonnenglück ist ihm zu eigen, ein Gefühl von Vogel-Freiheit, Vogel-Umblick, Vogel-Uebermuth, etwas Drittes, in dem sich Neugierde und zarte Verachtung gebunden haben. [...] Man lebt, nicht mehr in den Fesseln von Liebe und Hass, ohne Ja, ohne Nein, freiwillig nahe, freiwillig ferne, am liebsten entschlüpfend, ausweichend, fortflatternd, wieder weg, wieder empor fliegend; man ist verwöhnt, wie jeder, der einmal ein ungeheures Vielerlei *unter* sich gesehn hat [...] (MA I Vorrede 4, KSA 2.18)[27]

---

26 '[...] als Abenteurer und Weltumsegler jener inneren Welt, die "Mensch" heisst, als Ausmesser jedes "Höher" und "Uebereinander", das gleichfalls "Mensch" heisst – überallhin dringend, fast ohne Furcht, nichts verschmähend, nichts verlierend, alles auskostend, alles vom Zufälligen reinigend und gleichsam aussiebend [...]' (MA I Vorrede 7, KSA 2.21).

'[...] as adventurers and circumnavigators of that inner world called "human", as surveyors and measurers of what is "higher" and "one above the other" that is likewise called "human" – penetrating everywhere, almost without fear, disdaining nothing, losing nothing, tasting everything, cleansing everything of what is accidental in it and as it were sifting it [...]'.

27 See also the description of 'great health' as:
'[...] Selbstbeherrschung und Zucht des Herzens [...] die Wege zu vielen und entgegengesetzten Denkweisen erlaubt –, bis zu jener inneren Umfänglichkeit und Verwöhnung des Ueberreichthums, welche die Gefahr ausschliesst, dass der Geist sich etwa selbst in die eignen Wege verlöre und verliebte und in irgend einem Winkel berauscht sitzen bliebe, bis zu jenem Ueberschuss an plastischen, ausheilenden, nachbildenden und wiederherstellenden Kräften, welcher eben das Zeichen der *grossen* Gesundheit ist, jener Ueberschuss, der dem freien Geiste das gefährliche Vorrecht giebt, *auf den Versuch* hin leben und sich dem Abenteuer anbieten zu dürfen: das Meisterschafts-Vorrecht des freien Geistes!'

> There is a median condition, which a man of such a destiny cannot later recall without emotion: it is characterised by a pale, fine light and sunny happiness, a feeling of bird-like freedom, bird's eye overview, bird-like haughtiness, something third in which curiosity is united with a tender contempt. [...] One no longer lives in the fetters of love and hatred, without yes, without no, freely near or freely far, preferably slipping away, evading, fluttering off, gone again, again flying aloft; one is spoiled, as everyone is who has at some time seen a tremendous multiplicity of things *beneath* him [...]

Just as the adoption of specific standpoints – whether critical or affirmative, no-saying or yes- saying, hating or loving – cannot be separated from the overcoming ('flying aloft') of each and every standpoint for the sake of total affirmation, so too the relational standpoint of total affirmation, which is no standpoint at all, but 'something third' – a 'bird's eye view', a 'slipping away', a 'fluttering off' – is inseparable from a specific trajectory, and can only be presented as a narrative or life-story without an end– or stand-point.

IV Consequences for *Umwertung:* the Question of 'gegen'

By way of conclusion, I would like to consider some implications of the medial position for the question of *Umwertung*. In doing so, I will build on the results of Gerd Schank's study of the word 'gegen' in EH in the context of 19th century usage of this term in his book *Dionysos gegen den Gekreuzigten. Eine philologische und philosophische Studie zu Nietzsches 'Ecce Homo'*. Taking his bearings from the climactic finale of EH, he argues that the problematic of *Umwertung* receives its most condensed expression in the words:

> – Hat man mich verstanden? – *Dionysos gegen den Gekreuzigten...* (EH Schicksal 9, KSA 6.374)
>
> – Have I been understood? – *Dionysos against the Crucified...*

Understanding Nietzschean *Umwertung* turns on how we decypher this formulation, and in particular the word 'gegen'. In line with the interpretation presented in this chapter, the '*Crucified*' is taken to refer to Idealism (not just Christianity or St. Paul) and '*Dionysos*' to the unconditional affirmation of reality as a conflictual multi-

---

> '[...] self-mastery and discipline of the heart that permits access to many and contradictory modes of thought –, to that inner capaciousness and indulgence of superabundance which excludes the danger that the spirit may even perhaps lose itself on its own paths and become infatuated and remain seated intoxicated in some corner or other, to that surplus of plastic, healing, moulding and restorative forces which is precisely the sign of *great* health, that surplus which grants to the free spirit the dangerous privilege of living *by trial* and of being permitted to offer itself to adventure: the master's privilege of the free spirit!'

plicity (*gegenstreitige Vielheit*).²⁸ How, then, are we to take the 'gegen' in this formula, understood as a semiotic for the *Umwertung* of idealism into unconditional, dionysian affirmation?

The least convincing candidate, according to Schank, is the 'idealist' sense of 'gegen'; that is, the *separation* of positively– from negatively-valued terms, serving to *destroy* the latter and to *eliminate* opposition altogether for the sake of an absolute and exclusive claim for its positive values (see p. 265 above). According to Schank, 'gegen' does not function as an indicator or call for war-like activities at all (Schank 1993, 124). Rather than separate, isolate and attack idealism, the function of 'gegen' is to place idealism and dionysian affirmation *in relation to* one another (*In-Beziehungsetzen*). But what kind of relation or bond does it forge? Unlike current German, where 'gegen' simply means 'contra', Schank points out that in the 19ᵗʰ century, it was frequently used to mean 'instead of' (*anstatt*) or 'over and against' (*gegenüber*) in comparative contexts. In this vein, he argues for a *comparative* interpretation of the closing formula:

"Dionysos against the Crucified" in the sense: "Dionysos *as measured* against the Crucified"

Or in German:

"Dionysos gegen den Gekreuzigten" in the sense: "Dionysos gegen den Gekreuzigten *gehalten*" (– a formulation used by Nietzsche elsewhere in EH, e.g.: "Dante, gegen Zarathustra gehalten" (EH (Z) 6, KSA 6.343)

In these terms, Schank offers the following gloss of the closing formula:

"Meine Leser, habt ihr mich verstanden? Vergleicht einmal Dionysos mit dem erfrierenden 'Ideal'"[...]'²⁹

"My readers, have you understood me? Compare Dionysos with the freezing 'ideal'" [...]'

The comparative meaning of 'gegen' displaces the idealist and war-like meanings, but it should not be taken to eliminate opposition (*Gegensatz*) altogether,³⁰ and Schank goes on to situate the function of comparison, of measuring oneself against the other, within an agonal process of *Umwertung*, based on Nietzsche's declared war-praxis in EH weise 7. He calls this a dionysian 'gegen' that preserves and affirms the conflictual multiplicity of reality by excluding destruction. In this regard, the agonal model of *Umwertung* presented in section II above could stand as a working-out of this interpretation of 'gegen' / *Umwertung*, in which

---

28 Schank actually offers a more accurate, differentiated account of the dionysian perspective in the table on p. 150.
29 Schank 1993, 102. 'Ihr' is mistakenly printed as 'ich' in Schank's book, and 'Ideal' as 'ideal'.
30 This is clear from 14[89], KSA 13.265 ff.

1. opposed terms are *bound together* / placed in relation (rather than separated), such that
2. the opposed terms / counter-values are *preserved* (rather than destroyed) as a *limit* (*Maass*) that force one to deploy one's full strength, and as a *measure* (*Maass*) of what one can do, allowing
3. the dynamic or necessity of opposition or struggle to be preserved and affirmed (cf. schema on p. 266 above)

I concur to a large extent with this account of *Umwertung*, but it raises at least two questions that call for correctives:
1. If *Umwertung* is to be understood as a comparative procedure whereby two opposed terms are measured against each other, what is the standpoint of comparison? What standpoint can Nietzsche occupy as the narrator of *Umwertung*, understood as a reciprocal measuring of Idealism 'against' dionysian affirmation?
2. How can an agonal interpretation of *Umwertung* account for the moment of destruction (*Vernichtung*) that is present in (at least some of) Nietzsche's accounts of *Umwertung* considered above (e.g. *grosse Politik*) and is emphatically present in his accounts of dionysian affirmation?

Each of these questions points to a *deficit* in the agonal model of *Umwertung*. To begin with the second question: if the dionysian affirmation of reality as a conflictual multiplicity requires the affirmation of *all* antagonistic positions, it precludes (the) destruction (of any). Yet, destruction is emphatically present in affirmative and (some) *Umwertungs*-contexts of EH. The only way to make sense of this, I have argued, is to take Nietzsche's pointedly subjectivistic accounts of the 'pleasure in destruction' as a reference to the psychological conditions for conflict that must be affirmed if we are to affirm conflict as a feature of reality. This destructive intentionality must not, however, be identified with the standpoint of affirmation, if the latter is to affirm all antagonistic positions. The only way to affirm reality from an *immanent* standpoint – 'to be the eternal Yes to all things' – is from a standpoint *in the relations of antagonism* that constitute reality. As long as the standpoint of *Umwertung* is located in the antagonistic relations between idealism and dionysian affirmation, it can accommodate the subjective moment of destructiveness without collapsing into it.

An agonal model of *Umwertung* has difficulty coping not just with the excessive *negativity* of destruction in Nietzsche's text, but also with its *affirmative* excesses. As we saw, Nietzsche's account of his war-praxis exhibits an affirmative impulse that exceeds the agonal model, cancelling not only destructive negation, but even the limited negation of agonal mastery in a declaration of *indifference:* 'for or against [...] counts as the same' (EH weise 7, KSA 6.275). This is hard to make of sense of from a subjective perspective, which is always a perspective of difference, and can only be narrated from a 'standpoint' *in the relations of difference between them*, or so I argued. Furthermore, this seems to be the only standpoint from which to narrate *Um-*

wertung, if *Umwertung* is to be a *genuinely agonal* process of comparison; that is, a measuring of idealism 'against' dionysian affirmation that is genuinely *reciprocal*. If the agon begins by throwing prevailing standards of judgement into question – what constitutes the standard of victory? – then the response comes not from one or other antagonist, but from a third place in the relations of antagonism, a place that Nietzsche calls 'immanent justice':

> Jedes Einzelne kämpft als ob es allein berechtigt sei: aber ein unendlich sicheres Maß des richterl. Urtheils entscheidet, wohin der Sieg sich lenkt. (VPP 9, KGW II/4.272; cf. PHG 5 1.825)
>
> Every single being fights as if it alone were in the right: but an infinitely sure measure of adjudicating judgement decides where victory is leaning.

In this chapter, I have traversed the arc that began, in the first chapter, with the promise of opening up new agonal perspectives on Nietzsche's life-project of critical transvaluation, and ends here by inscribing the limits of the agonal model. This is my attempt at an 'attempt at self-criticism'.

Agon-Related Publications by the Author

Books

Siemens, H.W., / Roodt, V. (eds.) (2008a): *Nietzsche, Power and Politics. Rethinking Nietzsche's Legacy for Political Thought*. Berlin / New York: de Gruyter.

Siemens, H.W. / Pearson, J.S. (eds.) (2019): *Conflict and Contest in Nietzsche's Philosophy*. New York and London: Bloomsbury.

Chapters/Articles

Siemens, H.W. (1998): "Nietzsche's Hammer: Philosophy, Destruction, or The Art of Limited Warfare". In: *Tijdschrift voor Filosofie* 60/2, 321–347.

Siemens, H.W. (2001a): "Nietzsche's Agon with Ressentiment: Towards a Therapeutic Reading of Critical Transvaluation". In: *Continental Philosophy Review* (formerly *Man & World*) 34/1, 69–93.

Siemens, H.W. (2001b): "Agonal Configurations in the *Unzeitgemässe Betrachtungen*: Identity, Mimesis and the *Übertragung* of cultures in Nietzsche's early thought". In: *Nietzsche-Studien* 30, 80–106.

Siemens, H.W. (2001c): "Nietzsche's Political Philosophy. A Review of Recent Literature". In: *Nietzsche-Studien* 30, 509–526.

Siemens, H.W. (2002): "Agonal Communities of Taste: Law and Community in Nietzsche's Philosophy of Transvaluation". In: *Journal of Nietzsche Studies* 24 Special Issue on Nietzsche and the Agon, 83–112. (reprinted in: Francis Mootz III / Peter Goodrich (eds.): *Nietzsche and Law*, (Series: Philosophers and the Law). Aldershot, Ashgate, 309–338.)

Siemens, H.W. (2005): "Action, Performance and Freedom in Hannah Arendt and Fr. Nietzsche". In *International Studies in Philosophy* 37:3, 107–126.

Siemens, H.W. (2006): "Nietzsche contra Liberalism on Freedom". In: Keith Ansell-Pearson (ed.): *A Companion to Nietzsche*. Oxford and Malden MA: Basil Blackwell, 437–454.

Siemens, H.W. (2007): "The first Transvaluation of all Values: Nietzsche's *Agon* with Socrates in *The Birth of Tragedy*". In: Gudrun von Tevenar (ed.): *Nietzsche and Ethics*. Bern: Peter Lang, 171–196.

Siemens, H.W. (2008b): "Nietzsche's equivocations on the relation between democracy and 'grosse Politik'". In: Herman W. Siemens / Vasti Roodt (ed.s): *Nietzsche, Power and Politics. Rethinking Nietzsche's Legacy for Political Thought*. Berlin / New York: de Gruyter, 231–268.

Siemens, H.W., (2008c): "Nietzsche and the Temporality of self-Legislation". In: Manuel Dries (ed.): *Nietzsche on Time and History*. Berlin / New York: de Gruyter, 191–210.

Siemens, H.W. (2009a): "(Self–)legislation, Life and Love in Nietzsche's Philosophy". In Isabelle Wienand (ed.): *Neue Beiträge zu Nietzsches Moral–, Politik– und Kulturphilosophie*. Fribourg: Press Academic Fribourg, 67–90.

Siemens, H.W. (2009b): "Nietzsche's Critique of Democracy". In: *Journal of Nietzsche Studies* 38, Fall 2009, 20–37.

Siemens, H.W. (2009c): "Umwertung: Nietzsche's 'war-praxis' and the problem of Yes-Saying and No-Saying in *Ecce Homo*". In: *Nietzsche-Studien* 38, pp.182–206.

Siemens, H.W. (2009d) : Review of D. Conway: *Nietzsche and the Political*. In: *Journal of Nietzsche Studies*, 36, 207–216.

Siemens, H.W. (2012a): "The Rise of Political Agonism and its Relation to Deconstruction". In: A. Martinengo (ed.): *Beyond Deconstruction: Rethinking Myth, Reconstructing Reason*. Berlin / New York: de Gruyter, 213–223.

Siemens, H. W. (2012b): "Nietzsche's 'post-Nietzschean' political 'Wirkung': The Rise of Agonistic Democratic Theory". In: Renate Reschke / Marco Brusotti (eds.) : *"Einige werden posthum geboren": Friedrich Nietzsches Wirkungen*. Berlin / New York: de Gruyter, 393–406.

Siemens, H. W. (2013): "Reassessing Radical Democratic Theory in the light of Nietzsche's Ontology of Conflict". In: Keith Ansell-Pearson (ed.): *Nietzsche and Political Thought*. London: Bloomsbury, 83–106.

Siemens, H. W. (2014): "Nietzsche's Concept of 'Necessity'and its Relation to Laws of Nature". In: Vanessa Lemm (ed.): *Nietzsche and The Becoming of Life*. New York: Fordham University Press, 82–102.

Siemens, H. W. (2015a): "Nietzsche's Socio-Physiology of the Self". In: Joao Constâncio / Maria Joao Branco / Bartholomew Ryan (eds.): *Nietzsche and the Problem of Subjectivity*. Berlin / New York: de Gruyter, 629–653.

Siemens, H.W. (2015b): "Nietzsche sobre el conflicto y el Pluralismo de los Ordenes Legales" (Nietzsche On Conflict and the Pluralism of Legal Orders). In: *Estudios Nietzsche* 15, Special Issue on Nietzsche and Politics, 113–125.

Siemens, H.W. (2015c): "Agonal Writing: Towards an Agonal Model for Critical Transvaluation". In: *Logoi.ph – Journal of Philosophy* I/3 – Playing and Thinking, 1–29.

Siemens, H.W. (2015d): "Nietzsche's Philosophy of Hatred". In: *Tijdschrift voor Filosofie* 77/4, Special Issue on Anger & Hatred, 747–784.

Siemens, H.W. (2015e): "Contesting Nietzsche's Agon. On Christa Davis Acampora's 'Contesting Nietzsche'. Discussion paper". In: *Nietzsche-Studien* 44, 446–461.

Siemens, H.W. (2016a): "Nietzsches Sozio-Physiologie des Selbst und das Problem der Souveräntität". In: Helmut Heit / Sigridur Thorgeirsdottir (eds.): *Nietzsche: Denker der Kritik und der Transformation*. Berlin / New York: de Gruyter, 167–182.

Siemens, H.W.(2016b): "Nietzsche e a sociofisiologia do eu". In: *Cadernos Nietzsche* 37/1, 185–218.

Siemens, H.W. (2017): "Nietzsche contra Kant on Genius, Originality and Agonal Succession". In: Marco Brussotti / Herman Siemens / Joao Constancio / Tom Bailey (eds.): *Nietzsche's Engagements with Kant and the Kantian Legacy*, vol. III: *Aesthetics, Anthropology and History*, Maria Joao Branco / Katia Hay (eds.), 15–42.

Siemens, H.W. (2018a): "Nietzsche's Agon". In: Paul Katsafanas (ed.): *The Nietzschean Mind (The Routledge Philosophy Minds* series). New York / Oxford: Routledge, 314–333.

Siemens, H.W.(2018b): "Nietzsche's *'Agonale Betrachtungen'*: On the Actuality of the Greeks in the *Unzeitgemässe Betrachtung*". In: Analisa Caputo (ed.): *Rethinking the Nietzschean Concept of 'Untimely'*, Milan: Mimesis International, 23–39.

Bibliography

Acampora, Christa (2013): *Contesting Nietzsche*. Chicago: Chicago University Press.
Adkins, A.W.D. (1960): *Merit and Responsibility*. Oxford: Oxford University Press.
Adorno, Theodor / Horkheimer, Max (1969): *Dialektik der Aufklärung*, Frankfurt am Main: Fischer.
Allison, David B. (1985): "Nietzsche Knows No Noumenon". In: *Why Nietzsche now?* D. O'Hara (ed.). Bloomington: Indiana University Press.
Andreas-Salomé, Lou (1965): *The Freud Journal*. London: Hogarth.
Ansell-Pearson, Keith (1990): "Nietzsche: A Radical Challenge To Political Theory?". In: *Radical Philosophy* 54, 10–18.
Auerbach, Eric (1991): *Mimesis*. W. Trask (tr.). Princeton, New Jersey: Princeton University Press.
Baeumler, Alfred (1931): *Nietzsche der Philosoph und Politiker*, Leipzig: Reclam.
Barbera, Sandro (1994): "Ein Sinn und unzählige Hieroglyphen". In: *'Centauren-Geburten' Wissenschaft, Kunst und Philosophie beim jungen Nietzsche*. Tilman Borsche / Federico Gerratana / Aldo Venturelli (eds.), Berlin / New York: De Gruyter, 217–233.
Baumgarten, Alexander G. (2004 [1783]): *Metaphysik*. G. F. Meier (tr.). Jena: Scheglmann.
Benjamin, Walter (1977): "Das Glück des antiken Menschen". In: *Gesammelte Schriften*, R. Tiedemann / H. Schweppenhäuser (eds.), Frankfurt am Main: Suhrkamp, vol. II.1, 126–129.
Berlin, Isaiah (1965): "Herder and the Enlightenment". In: Earl R. Wasserman (ed.): *Aspects of the Eighteenth Century*. Baltimore: The Johns Hopkins Press, 47–105.
Bernstein, Jay M. (1992): *The Fate of Art: Aesthetic Alienation from Kant to Derrida and Adorno*. London: Polity Press.
Billeter, Gustav (1911): *Die Anschauungen vom Wesen des Griechentums*. Leipzig and Berlin: Teubner Verlag.
Blondel, Eric (1985): "Nietzsche: Life as Metaphor". In: *The New Nietzsche*, David B. Allison (ed.), Cambridge Mass.: MIT Press, 150–175.
Blondel, Eric (1991): *Nietzsche: The Body and Culture*. Sean Hand (tr.), London: Athlone Press.
Bloom, Harold (1982): *Agon: Towards a Theory of Revisionism*. New York: Oxford University Press.
Bloom, Harold (1994): *The Western Canon: The Books and School of the Ages*. New York: Riverhead Books.
Borsche, Tilman / Gerratana, Federico / Venturelli, Aldo (eds.) (1994): *'Centauren-Geburten': Wissenschaft, Kunst und Philosophie beim jungen Nietzsche*. Berlin / New York: De Gruyter.
Bullock, Marcus Paul (1997): "Walter Benjamin: The Prophet's War against Prophecy". In: Janet Lungstrum / Elizabeth Sauer: *Agonistics: Arenas of Creative Contest*. Albany: SUNY Press, 92–108.
Burckhardt, Leonhard (1999): "Vom Agon zur 'Nullsummenkonkurrenz'". In: *Nikephoros* 12, 71–93.
Burckhardt, Jacob (1929–34), *Gesamtausgabe*. Therein: "Griechische Kulturgeschichte", (vol. 8–11). F. Stähelin / S. Merian (eds.), Stuttgart, Leipzig and Berlin: Deutsche Verlags-Anstalt.
Burckhardt, Jacob (1950): "Der griechische Mensch". In: Griechische Kulturgeschichte, vol. III. Leipzig: Kröner.
Burckhardt, Jacob (1998): *The Greeks and Greek Civilization*. S. Stern (tr.), New York: Saint Martin's Griffin.
Busch, Thomas (1989): *Die Affirmation des Chaos. Zur Überwindung des Nihilismus in der Metaphysik Friedrich Nietzsches*. St. Ottilien: EOS Verlag.
Campioni, Giuliano / Müller-Buck, Renate et al (2003): *Nietzsches persönliche Bibliothek*, Supplementa Nietzscheana, vol. 6. Berlin / New York : De Gruyter.
Cancik, Hubert (1994): "'Philologie als Beruf'. Zu Formengeschichte, Thema und Tradition der unvollendeten vierten Unzeitgemässen Friedrich Nietzsches". In: Tilman Borsche / Federico

Gerratana / Aldo Venturelli (eds.): *'Centauren-Geburten': Wissenschaft, Kunst und Philosophie beim jungen Nietzsche*. Berlin / New York: De Gruyter, 81–98.
Castoriadis, Cornelius (1994): "Psychoanalysis and Politics". In: Sonu Shamdasani / Michael Münchow (eds.): *Speculations after Freud*. London: Routledge, 2–12.
Cavell, Stanley (1990): "Aversive Thinking: Emersonian Representations in Heidegger and Nietzsche". In: *Conditions Handsome and Unhandsome: The Constitution of Emersonian Perfectionism*. Chicago / London: University of Chicago Press, 33–63.
Chapelle, Daniel (1993): *Nietzsche and Psychoanalysis*. Albany N.Y.: SUNY Press.
Conant, James (2001): "Nietzsche's Perfectionism: A Reading of Schopenhauer as Educator". In: Richard Schacht (ed.), *Nietzsche's Postmoralism*, Cambridge: Cambridge University Press, 181–257.
Connolly, William (1991): *Identity/Difference*. Ithaca: Cornell University Press.
Conway, Daniel W. (1988): "Solving the Problem of Socrates. Nietzsche's *Zarathustra* as Political Irony". In: *Political Theory*, 16/2, 257–280.
Conway, Daniel W. (1997a): *Nietzsche and the Political*, London: Routledge.
Conway, Daniel W. (1997b): *Nietzsche's Dangerous Game*. Cambridge: Cambridge University Press.
Curtius, Ernst (1877): "Der Wettkampf". In: *Alterthum und Gegenwart. Gesammelte Reden und Vorträge*. Berlin.
Dannhauser, Werner (1974): *Nietzsche's View of Socrates*. Ithaca / London: Cornell University Press.
Deleuze, Gilles (1983): *Nietzsche and Philosophy*. Hugh Tomlinson (tr.), London: Athlone.
Deri, F. (1939): "On Sublimation". In: *Psychoanalytic Quarterly* 8, 325–334.
Diels, H. (1960^9): *Die Fragmente der Vorsokratiker*. W. Kranz (ed.). Berlin: Weidmann.
Ellsworth, J. D. (1981): "The Meaning of 'agon' in Epic Diction". In: *Emerita*, 49, 97–104.
Ellsworth, J. D. (1976): "Agamemnon's Intentions, 'Agon', and the Growth of an Error". In: *Glotta* 54, 228–235.
Finley, Moses I. (1982^4): *The World of Odysseus*. New York: Viking Penguin.
Fisher Nick (2009): "The Culture of Competition". In: Kurt A. Raaaflaub / Hans van Wees (eds.): *A Companion to Archaic Greece*. Malden / Oxford / Chichester: Wiley-Blackwell, 524–541.
Freud, Sigmund (1953ff.): *Standard Edition of the Complete Psychological Works of Sigmund Freud*. James Strachey (ed.), Hogarth Press, London. References include the English name of the text and its location in the *Standard Edition*, as follows: SE12:104 = *Standard Edition* vol. 12, page 104. Where appropriate, references to the German text are included, as follows: SA 12:104 = *Freud-Studienausgabe* (1975): A. Mitscherlich, A. Richards, J. Strachey (eds.), Frankfurt am Main: Fischer Verlag., vol. 12, page 104. There are a number of references to the *Ergänzungsband (Schriften zur Behandlungstechnik)*, denoted as Erg.
Gadamer, Hans-Georg (1996^2): *Truth and Method*. J. Weinsheimer and D. G. Marshall (tr.), New York: Continuum.
Gadamer, Hans-Georg (1986): "Wahrheit und Methode". In: *Gesammelte Werke*. Tübingen: Mohr, vol. 1.
Gay, Volney (1997): "Interpretation Interminable: Agonistics in Psychoanalysis". In: Janet Lungstrum & Elizabeth Sauer: *Agonistics: Arenas of Creative Contest*. Albany: SUNY Press, 111–128.
Gebauer, Gunter (1991): "Citius—Altius—Fortius and the Problem of Sport Ethics: a Philosopher's Viewpoint". In: Fernand Landry / Marc Landry / Magdeleine Yerlès (eds.): *Sport, the Third Millennium: Proceedings of the International Symposium, Quebec City, Canada, May 21–25, 1990*. SainteFoy: Les presses de l'Université Laval, 467–473.
Geijsen, Ludwig (1997): *Geschichte und Gerechtigkeit: Grundzüge einer Philosophie der Mitte im Frühwerk Nietzsches*. Berlin / New York: De Gruyter.
Gerhardt, Volker (1983): "Das 'Prinzip des Gleichgewichts'". In: *Nietzsche-Studien* 12, 111–133.

Gerhardt, Volker (1992): "Selbstbegründung. Nietzsche's Moral der Individualität". In: *Nietzsche-Studien* 21, 28–49.
Gerhardt, Volker (1996): *Vom Willen zur Macht. Anthropologie und Metaphysik der Macht am exemplarischen Fall Friedrich Nietzsches*. Berlin / New York: De Gruyter.
Gerratana, Federico (1988): "Der Wahn jenseits des Menschen". In: *Nietzsche-Studien* 17, 391–433.
Gould, T. (1982): "The Audience of Originality". In: *Essays in Kant's Aesthetics*, Paul Guyer / Ted Cohen (eds.). Chicago / London: University of Chicago Press.
Gouldner, Alvin (1965): *Enter Plato: Classical Greece and the Origins of Social Theory*. New York: Basic Books.
Gracián, Baltasar (2011 [1647]): *The Pocket Oracle and Art of Prudence* [Oráculo manual y art de prudencia]. Jeremy Robbins (tr.). London: Penguin Classics.
Gschwendt, L. (1999): *Nietzsche und die Kriminalwissenschaft*. Zürich: Schulthess Polygraphischer Verlag.
Habermas, Jürgen (1987): *The Philosophical Discourse of Modernity: Twelve Lectures*, F. Lawrence (tr.), Cambridge, MA: MIT Press.
Halliwell, Stephen (1987) (tr. and commentary): *The Poetics of Aristotle*. London: Duckworth.
Haslinger, R. (1993): *Nietzsche und die Anfaenge der Tiefenpsychologie*. Regensburg: Roderer Verlag.
Hatab, Lawrence J. (1990): *Myth and Philosophy: A Contest of Truths*. La Salle, Ill.: Open Court.
Hatab, Lawrence (1995): *A Nietzschean Defense of Democracy*. Chicago: Open Court.
Hatab, Lawrence: (2002): "Prospects for a Democratic Agon: Why we can still be Nietzscheans". In: *Journal of Nietzsche Studies* 24 (2002), 132–147.
Hatab, Lawrence (2008): "Breaking the Contract Theory: The Individual and the Law in Nietzsche's *Genealogy*". In: Herman W. Siemens / Vasti Roodt (eds,): Nietzsche, Power and Politics. Rethinking Nietzsche's Legacy for Political Thought. Berlin / New York: De Gruyter, 169–188.
Hegel, Georg W. F. (1965): *Aesthetik*, 2 vols. Fr. Bassenge (ed.). Berlin / Weimar.
Heidegger, Martin (1961): "Der Wille Zur Macht al Kunst". In: *Nietzsche*. Pfullingen: Neske, vol. I, 11–254.
Heller, Peter (1972): *"Von den ersten und letzten Dingen"; Studien und Kommentar zu einer Aphorismenreihe von Friedrich Nietzsche*. Berlin / New York: De Gruyter.
Herschbell, J.P. & Nimis, S.A. (1979): "Nietzsche and Heraclitus". In: *Nietzsche-Studien* 8, 22–26.
Hesiod (2018): *Works and Days*. (Ἔργα καὶ Ἡμέραι), Stallings, A. E. (tr.). London: Penguin.
Hillman, James (1992): *Re-Visioning Psychology*. New York: HarperPerennial.
Hoberman, John (1997): "The Sportive Agon in Ancient and Modern Times": In: Janet Lungstrum / Elizabeth Sauer: *Agonistics: Arenas of Creative Contest*. Albany: SUNY Press, 293–304.
Hölscher, U. (1977): "Nietzsche's debt to Heraclitus." In: R. Bolgar (ed.): *Classical Influences on European Culture Vol III: 1650–1870*. Cambridge: Cambridge University Press, 339–348.
Honig, Bonnie (1993a): *Political Theory and the Displacement of Politics*. Ithaca: Cornell University Press.
Honig, Bonnie (1993b): "The Politics of Agonism". In: *Political Theory* 21/3, 528–533.
Huizinga, Johan (1939, 1940^3), *Homo Ludens*. Amsterdam: Pantheon Verlag.
Jackson, Michael (1989): *Paths Towards a Clearing; Radical Empiricism and Ethnographic Inquiry*. Bloomington: Indiana University Press.
Jähnig, Dieter: "Nietzsche's Kunstbegriff (erläutert an der 'Geburt der Tragödie')". In: Helmut Koopman, Adolf Schmoll, (eds.): *Beiträge zur Theorie der Künste im 19. Jahrhundert*, vol. II. Frankfurt am Main: Klostermann, 29–68.
Janz, Kurt-Paul (1981): *Friedrich Nietzsche Biographie*, 3 vol.s. Munich: DTV.
Jean Paul, (1923): "Vorschule der ästhetik: nebst einigen Vorlesungen in Leipzig über die Parteien der Zeit". Leipzig: F. Meiner.
Kant, Immanuel (1987): *Critique of Judgement*. W. Pluhar (tr.), Indianapolis/Cambridge: Hackett.

Kant, Immanuel (1902–): "Kritik der Urteilskraft". In: *Gesammelte Schriften* (= AA). Königlich-Preussischen Akademie der Wissenschaften zu Berlin (ed.), vol. 7.

Kaufmann, Walter (1974⁴): *Nietzsche. Philosopher, Psychologist, and Antichrist.* . Princeton, New Jersey: Princeton University Press.

Kerényi, Karl (938): "Vom Wesen Des Festes. Antike Religion und Ethnologische Religionsforschung." In: *Paideuma* 1/2, 59–74.

Kofmann, Sarah (1991): "Nietzsche's Socrates: 'Who' is Socrates?". In: *Graduate Faculty Philosophy Journal* 15/2, 7–30.

Krause, J. H. (1841): *Die Gymnastik und Agonistik der Hellenen*. Leipzig: Barth.

Kuenzli, R. E. (1983): "The Nazi Appropriation of Nietzsche". In: *Nietzsche-Studien* 12, 428–435.

Lacoue-Labarthe, Philippe (1990), "History and Mimesis". In: Rickels, Laurence (ed.) *Looking after Nietzsche*. Albany: State University of New York Press, 209–231.

Laplanche, J. / Pontalis, J. B. (1967): *Vocabulaire de la Psychoanalyse*. Paris: P.U.F.

Lessing, Gotthold Ephraim (1993): "Eine Duplik". In: *Werke und Briefe*. Wilfried Barner (i.a.) (ed.), vol. 9: Werke 1774–1778. Frankfurt am Main: Deutscher Klassiker Verlag, 510–585.

Lindahl, Hans (2008): "Law's 'Uncanniness': A phenomenology of legal decisions". In: *Nederlands Tijdschrift voor Rechtsfilosofie en Rechtstheorie* 38, 137–150.

Lindahl, Hans (2009): "The Opening: Alegality and Political Agonism, in Law and Agonistic Politics". In Andrew Schaap (ed.): *Law and Agonistic Politics*. London: Routledge, 57–70.

Lloyd, G. / Sivin, N. (2002): *The Way and the Word: Science and Medicine in early China and Greece*. New Haven: Yale University Press.

Lloyd-Jones, Hugh (1979): "Nietzsche and the Study of the Ancient World". In: J.C. O'Flaherty / T. F. Sellner / R.M. Helm (eds.): *Studies in Nietzsche and the Classical Tradition*. Chapel Hill, N. Carolina: University of North Carolina Press.

Loewald, H.W. (1988): *Sublimation: Inquiries into Theoretical Psychoanalysis*. New Haven & London: Yale University Press.

Lungstrum, Janet / Sauer, Elizabeth (1997): *Agonistics: Arenas of Creative Contest*. Albany: SUNY Press.

Marcuse, Herbert (1937): "Über den affirmativen Charakter der Kultur". In: *Zeitschrift für Sozialforschung* VI/1, 54–94.

MacIntyre, Alasdair (1984): *After Virtue*. Notre Dame: Notre Dame University Press.

Martens, Lorna (1997): "The Institutionalization of Conflict as an Interpretative Strategy in Freud's The Interpretation of Dreams". In: Janet Lungstrum / Elizabeth Sauer: *Agonistics: Arenas of Creative Contest*. Albany: SUNY Press, 129–151.

Martin, Alfred von (1945): *Nietzsche und Burckhardt. Zwei geistige Welten im Dialog*. Basel: E. Reinhardt Verlag.

Martin, Nicholas (1996): *Nietzsche and Schiller: Untimely Aesthetics*. Oxford: Oxford University Press.

Minkkinen, P. (2020): "Agonism, Democracy, and Law". In: S. Stern / M. Del Mar / B. Meyler (eds.): *The Oxford Handbook of Law and the Humanities*. Oxford: Oxford University Press, 427–442.

Mouffe, Chantal (2005): *On the Political*. London: Routledge.

Müller-Lauter, Wolfgang (1971): *Nietzsche: Seine Philosophie der Gegensätze und die Gegensätze seiner Philosophie*. Berlin / New York: De Gruyter.

Müller-Lauter, Wolfgang (1978): "Der Organismus als innerer Kampf. Der Einfluss von Wilhelm Roux aud Fr. Nietzsche". In: *Nietzsche-Studien* 7, 189–223.

Nussbaum, Martha (1986): *The Fragility of Goodness*. Cambridge: Cambridge University Press.

Orsucci, Andrea (1996): *Orient – Occident. Nietzsche's Versuch einer Loslösung vom Europäischen Weltbild*. Berlin / New York: De Gruyter.

Otto, Walter (1962): "Ursprung der Tragödie". In: K. von Fritz (ed.), *Das Wort der Antike, Band 1 von Nachgelass. Schriften [Teils.] / Otto, Walter F.* Stuttgart: Klett.
Owen, David (1995): *Nietzsche, Politics & Modernity*. London: Sage.
Paul, Hermann (1981[8]): *Deutsches Wörterbuch*. Tübingen: Max Niemeyer Verlag.
Pearson, James (2018): *Nietzsche's Philosophy of Conflict and the Logic of Organisational Struggle*. PhD dissertation, Leiden University.
Pearson, James (2019): "Unity in Strife: Nietzsche, Heraclitus and Schopenhauer". In: Herman Siemens / James Pearson (eds.): *Conflict and Contest in Nietzsche's Philosophy*. London: Bloomsbury, 44–69.
Pippin, Robert B. (1983): "Nietzsche and the Origin of the Idea of Modernism". In: *Inquiry* 26, 151–180.
Pippin, Robert B. (1988): "Irony and Affirmation in Nietzsche's *Thus Spoke Zarathustra*". In: M. A. Gillespie / T. B. Strong (eds.): *Nietzsche's New Seas*. Chicago & London: University of Chicago Press, 45–71.
Plato (1980): *Phaedo*. In: Huntington Cairns / Edith Hamilton (eds.), Hugh Tredennick (tr.): *The Collected Works of Plato*. Princeton, New Jersey: Princeton University Press, 41–67.
Plato (1980): *Republic*. In: Huntington Cairns / Edith Hamilton (eds.), Paul Shorey (tr.): *The Collected Works of Plato*. Princeton, New Jersey: Princeton University Press, 575–844.
Politycki, Matthias (1981): *Der frühe Nietzsche und die deutsche Klassik*. München: Münchener Hochschulschriften.
Politycki, Matthias (1989): *Umwertung aller Werte? Deutsche Literatur im Urteil Nietzsches*. Berlin / New York: De Gruyter.
Reinhardt, Karl (1948): "Das Parisurteil" (1938): In: *Von Werken und Formen*. Godesberg: Verlag Helmut Küpper, 11–36.
Reinhardt, Karl (1949): *Aischylos als Regisseur und Theologe*. Bern: Francke.
Reinhardt, Karl (1962): "Tradition und Geist im Homerischen Epos". In: *Die Krise des Helden*. München: dtv, 7–18.
Renson, R. (2009), "Fair Play: Its Origins and Meanings in Sport and Society". In: *Kinesiology* 41/1, 5–18.
Rethy, Robert (1988): "The Tragic Affirmation of the *Birth of Tragedy*". In: *Nietzsche-Studien* 17, 1–44.
Ricoeur, Paul (1970): *Freud and Philosophy: An Essay in Interpretation*. D. Savage (tr.), New Haven & London: Yale University Press.
Salaquarda, Jörg (1980): "'Dionysos gegen den Gekeuzigten'. Nietzsches Verständnis des Apostels Paulus". In: Jörg Salaquarda (ed.): *Nietzsche*. Darmstadt: Wissenschaftliche Buchgesellschaft, 288–322.
Salaquarda, Jörg (1984): "Studien zur Zweiten Unzeitgemässen Betrachtung". In: *Nietzsche-Studien* 13, 1–45.
Salin, Edgar (1938): *Jacob Burckhardt und Nietzsche*. Basel: Verlag der Universität.
Salin, Edgar. (1959): *Vom deutschen Verhängnis. Gespräch an der Zeitenwende: Burckhardt – Nietzsche*. Hamburg: Rohwolt.
Sanders, D. (1878): *Handwörterbuch der deutschen Sprache*. Leipzig: Wiegand.
Sax, Benjamin (1997): "Cultural Agonistics: Nietzsche, the Greeks, Eternal Recurrence". In: Janet Lungstrum / Elizabeth Sauer: *Agonistics: Arenas of Creative Contest*. Albany: SUNY Press, 46–69.
Schaap, Andrew (2009): *Law and Agonistic Politics*. London: Routledge.
Schadewaldt, Wolfgang (1944): *Von Homers Welt und Werk. Aufsätze und Auslegungen zur Homerische Frage*. Stuttgart: Koehler Verlag.
Schank, Gerd (1993): *Dionysos gegen den Gekreuzigten. Eine philologische und philosophische Studie zu Nietzsches 'Ecce Homo'*. Wien: Europäische Hochschulschriften.

Schopenhauer, Arthur (1966): *The World as Will and Representation*, E.F.J. Payne (tr.), 2 vols. London: Dover.
Schopenhauer, Arthur (1977): "Die Welt als Wille und Vorstellung". In: *Werke in zehn Bänden* vol. 1–4 (Zürcher Ausgabe). Zürich: Diogenes,.
Schmidt, H.-J. (1969): *Nietzsche und Sokrates – Philosophische Untersuchungen zu Nietzsches Sokratesbild*. Meisenheim an Glan: Hain Verlag.
Schrift, Alan (1999): "Respect for the Agon and Agonistic Respect: a Response to Hatab and Olkowski". In: *New Nietzsche Studies* 3/1&2, 129–144.
Schrift, Alan (2000): "Nietzsche For Democracy?". In: *Nietzsche-Studien* 29, 220–233.
Schröter, Hartmut (1982), *Historische Theorie und Geschichtliches Handeln*, Mittenwald: Mäander.
Schümmer, Fr. (1955): "Die Entwicklung des Geschmacksbegriffs in der Philosophie des 17. und 18. Jahrhunderts". In: *Archiv für Begriffsgeschichte* I, 120–141.
Seitter, W. (1970): "Franz Grillparzer und Friedrich Nietzsche; ihre Stellung zueinander". In: *Jahrbuch der Grillparzer-Gesellschaft* III/8, 87–109.
Siemens, H.W.: *See separate bibliography: Agon-related publications by the author.*
Simmel, Georg (1920): *Schopenhauer und Nietzsche. Ein Vortragszyklus*. München & Leipzig: von Duncker & Humblot.
Simmel, Georg (1964): *Conflict and the Web of Group Affiliations*. Kurt Wolff / R. Bendix (tr.). New York: Collier-Macmillan.
Simmel, Georg (1968): "Das individuelle Gesetz. Ein Versuch über das Prinzip der Ethik" (1913). In: Michael Landmann (ed.), *Das individuelle Gesetz. Philosophische Exkurse*, Frankfurt: Suhrkamp, 174–230.
Snell, Bruno (1982): *The Discovery of Mind in Greek Philosophy and Literature*. T. Rosenmeyer (tr.). New York: Dover.
Stack, George (1992): *Nietzsche and Emerson. An Elective Affinity*. Athens, Ohio: Ohio University Press.
Staten, Henry (1990): *Nietzsche's Voice*. Ithaca, N.Y.: Cornell University Press.
Stegmaier, Werner (2004): "'Philosophischer Idealismus' und die 'Musik des Lebens'. Zu Nietzsches Umgang mit Paradoxien. Eine kontextuelle Interpretation des Aphorismus Nr. 372 der Fröhlichen Wissenschaft". In: *Nietzsche-Studien* 33, 90–128.
Stegmaier, Werner (2008): "Schicksal Nietzsche? Zu Nietzsches Selbsteinschätzung als Schicksal der Philosophie und der Menschheit (Ecce Homo, Warum ich ein Schicksal bin 1)". In: *Nietzsche-Studien* 37, 62–114.
Strong, Tracy B. (1988): "Nietzsche's Political Aesthetics". In: M.A. Gillespie / T.B. Strong (eds.): *Nietzsche's New Seas*. Chicago & London: Chicago University Press, 153–174.
Taylor, Charles (1975): *Hegel*. Cambridge: Cambridge University Press.
Taylor, Charles (1985): "What is Wrong with negative Liberty?". In: *Philosophical Papers*, Cambridge: Cambridge University Press, vol. 2, 211–229.
Terra Polanco, Maria. C. (2019): *Analogy, Technical Reason, and Living Beings: The Role of Analogy for Enabling Kant's Concept of Naturzweck*. PhD dissertation, Leiden University.
Tongeren, Paul van (1988): *Die Moral von Nietzsches Moralkritik*. Bonn: Bouvier.
Tuncel, Yunus (2009): "Agon Symbolism in Nietzsche": In: *Nikephoros* 22, 145–185.
Tuncel, Yunus (2013a) *Agon in Nietzsche*, Milwaukee: Marquette University Press.
Tuncel, Yunus (2013b): "Nietzsche's Agonistic Rhetoric and its Therapeutic Affects". In: H. Hutter / E. Friedland (eds.): *Nietzsche's Therapeutic Teaching*. New York: Bloomsbury, 81–96.
Tuncel, Yunus (2016): "Nietzsche, Sport, and Contemporary Culture". In: *Sport, Ethics and Philosophy* 10/4, 349–363.
Turner, Brandon. "The Thrill of Victory, the Agony of Defeat: The Nietzschean Vision of Contest." Annual meeting of the American political science association. vol. 31. 2006 at https://sites01.

lsu.edu/faculty/voegelin/wp-content/uploads/sites/80/2015/09/Brandon-Turner.pdf (last access 23.04.2021)

Vernant, Jean-Pierre (1982): *The Origins of Greek Thought*. Ithaca / New York.

Vernant, Jean-Pierre / Vidal-Naquet, Pierre (1988): *Myth and Tragedy in Ancient Greece*. New York: Zone Books.

Vogt, E. (1962), "Nietzsche und der Wettkampf Homers". In: *Antike und Abendand* 11, 103–113.

Wagner, Richard (1983 [1849]): "Das Kunstwerk der Zukunft". In: Dieter Borchmeyer (ed.): *Dichtungen und Schriften. Jubiläumsausgabe in zehn Bänden*. Frankfurt am Main: Insel Verlag, vol. VI, 9–157.

Wagner, Richard. (1983 [1851]), "Eine Mitteilung an meine Freunde" (= MF). In: Dieter Borchmeyer (ed.), *Dichtungen und Schriften. Jubiläumsausgabe in zehn Bänden*, Frankfurt am Main: Insel Verlag. vol. VI, 199–325.

Warren, Mark (1988): *Nietzsche and Political Thought*. Cambridge Mass.: MIT Press.

Weiler, Ingomar (1969): *Agonales in Wettkämpfen der griechischen Mythologie*. Innsbruck: Publikation-stelle der Universität.

Weiler, Ingomar (1974): *Der Agon im Mythos. Zur Einstellung der Griechen zum Wettkampf*. Darmstadt: Wissenschaftliche Buchgesellschaft.

Weiler, Ingomar (1975): "AIEN APICTEYEIN: ideologiekritische Bemerkungen zu einem vielzitierten Homerwort". In: *Stadion* I/2, 199–227.

Weiler, Ingomar (1991): "Regel und Regelbruch bei den antiken Olympischen Spielen". In: R. Renson et al (eds.): *The Olympic Games through the ages: Greek antiquity and its impact on modern sport*. Athens: Hellenic Sports Research Institute, 55–64.

Willers, Ulrich (1988): *Friedrich Nietzsches antichristliche Christologie*. Innsbruck / Wien: Tyrolia.

Name Index

Achilles 80, 206, 211–13
Aeschylus / Aischylos 29–30, 75–77, 93
Agamemnon 29, 213
Alcibiades 80
Alexander 37, 38, 74, 80, 140, 206, 208, 218
Anaxagoras 187
Arendt, Hannah 20, 186, 204, 214–19
Aristotle 39, 127, 200
Auerbach, Eric 212
Baumgarten, Alexander 144, 202
Baumgartner, Adolf 43
Billeter, Gustav 44, 45
Bloom, Harold 1, 47, 126, 127
Burckhardt, Jacob 1, 6, 25, 43–48, 51, 55, 59, 166, 190, 192, 194, 214
Calderón, Pedro 52
Cavell, Stanley 162, 283
Cicero 199
Clytaemnestra 29
Curtius, Ernst 43–45
Diotima 100
Dühring, Eugen 25, 220, 225
Eckhart. Meister 202
Emerson, Ralph W. 17, 138, 162, 163
Empedocles 237
Euripides 75–77
Freud, Sigmund 1, 4, 20, 21, 34, 126, 220, 232, 233, 237–42, 244, 246–54
Gadamer, Hans-Georg 60, 80, 193, 198–200, 203, 205, 206, 230, 231, 240
Gersdorff, Carl v. 43, 135
Gracián, Baltasar 19, 186, 199, 205–8
Habermas, Jürgen 91, 112, 185, 197
Hegel, Georg W. F. 51, 82, 112, 162, 163, 212, 213
Heidegger, Martin 67
Herder, Johann v. 51
Heraclitus 1, 2, 4, 5, 18, 25, 26, 46, 52, 86, 154, 168, 169, 186–90, 192, 193, 196, 197, 209, 219, 228
Herodotus 47, 150
Hesiod 20, 25, 37, 38, 48, 49, 52, 75, 149, 187, 189, 216, 234
Homer 25, 39, 40, 42, 47, 49, 51, 52, 54, 83, 120, 131, 132, 143, 149, 186, 210–13, 234
Huizinga, Johan 44, 57
Humboldt, Alexander v. 50
Iphigeneia 29
Kafka, Franz 177
Kant, Immanuel 4, 5, 7, 16, 18, 19, 111–23, 125–30, 132, 156, 185, 194, 198–200, 203–5, 208–10, 219
Kelterborn, Louis 43, 57, 169
Kerenyi, Carl 193
Leibniz, Gottfried 201, 202
Lessing, Gotthold W. 20, 186, 215, 216
Napoleon 125
Newton, Isaac 120, 121
Overbeck, Franz 43
St. Paul 34, 174, 220, 226, 259, 276
Philoctetes 68
Pindar 6, 45
Plato, Platonic, Platonism 13, 15, 30, 34, 39, 40, 47, 59, 67, 71, 89, 92–100, 103, 104, 107, 120, 127, 131, 132, 149, 164, 214, 259, 284, 286
Rohde, Erwin 1, 43, 44, 134
Schopenhauer, Arthur 2, 10, 16, 17, 51–53, 56, 87, 89, 90, 113–16, 123–27, 155, 160, 163–66, 169, 188, 189, 204, 205, 223–25, 236, 237, 259
Socrates, Socratism 4, 11, 15, 16, 64, 65, 76, 80, 83, 89–107, 143, 253
Thales 201, 202
Thucydides 47, 226
Sophists 47, 131, 132
Sophocles 30, 52
Spinoza, Baruch 244
Stendahl 51
Wagner, Richard 2, 16–18, 34, 56, 57, 82, 115, 124, 125, 127–30, 134, 135, 142, 146, 155, 160, 165–69, 195, 204, 224, 225, 268, 269
Xenophanes 39, 131

Subject Index

Absolutsetzung – Nicht-Absolutsetzung 12, 74, 263
accelerate (*beschleunigen*) 70, 77, 204, 237
acknowledgement (*Anerkennung*) 3, 14, 16, 52, 53, 80, 85, 87, 88, 123, 131, 132, 134, 148–52, 154, 157, 190, 212, 228, 234–36, 250, 273, 274
active, *aktiv* 3, 6, 16–18, 20, 24, 25, 31, 40, 68, 95, 97, 98, 101–3, 105, 106, 115,123, 125, 127–30, 133, 138, 144, 145, 150, 164, 175, 200, 227, 228, 236, 243, 253, 254
   See also agieren, reactive
adequatio 105
adversary 6, 13, 44, 68, 76, 126, 146, 148, 150, 184, 264
aesthetic 10, 15, 47, 66, 68, 72, 73, 76, 84, 86, 91, 100, 111, 120, 122, 124–26, 132, 137, 165, 185, 187, 195, 198, 199, 205, 209, 214, 233
affirmation *See* life-affirmation, yes-saying
AGEIN 42, 43
agency 2, 5, 7, 13, 14, 20, 34, 42, 44, 54, 58, 59, 77, 82, 99, 125, 216, 219, 269, 274
agieren 238, 241
agonism, political 1–3, 5, 6, 44, 89, 127, 184, 185, 237
Alleinherrschaft (one-man rule, hegemony) 37, 57, 74, 169, 218, 263, 268
amen-saying (*Amen-sagen*) 257
   See also life-affirmation, yes-saying
amor fati 242, 255, 257, 258, 260, 271, 274
amoral 54, 63–65, 71, 83, 84
ancilla 15, 96, 97, 99, 100
annihilation (*Vernichtung*) 4, 11, 14, 25, 26, 35, 38–40, 48, 49, 52–54, 63, 64, 79, 83, 85, 89, 103, 109, 138, 171, 191, 209, 216, 221, 222, 225, 226, 230, 235, 250, 266, 268, 274
anti-natural 85, 109
anti-nature (*Widernatur*) 15, 66, 109, 158, 258, 261, 274
anti-teleological 60, 224, 230–32
   See also counter-final, open-ended
appropriation 16, 17, 39, 40, 58, 78, 85, 126, 129–32, 134, 140, 143, 150, 176–78, 183, 259

approximate (equality, equilibrium) 4, 6, 14, 65, 194, 215, 217
archaic 25, 32, 46, 49, 54, 59, 133, 135, 138, 140, 169, 185, 191, 193, 228
aristocratic 45, 47, 48, 61, 82, 178, 215, 216
art (artist, artistry, artwork) 10, 13, 15, 25, 26, 67, 68, 72, 75, 84, 86, 90–94, 96, 99, 101, 103, 104, 112, 117, 118, 120, 121, 124, 125, 129, 131, 160, 161, 167, 168, 184, 187, 189, 194, 195, 228, 247, 250, 263
   See also Kunst
ascetic 61, 72, 73, 85, 96, 124, 221, 236, 244, 248
Asia 48
Asiatic 44, 86, 228, 229
assimilate 138, 141, 143, 144, 150–52, 228, 257
Athens 46, 58, 80
athletics 43, 46, 191, 195
attack 23, 33–37, 39, 64, 78, 131, 256, 267–69, 277
attempt 32, 41, 53, 54, 60, 67, 68, 77, 78, 89, 92, 94, 105, 106, 116, 117, 132, 149, 155, 176, 184, 224, 227, 239, 240, 245, 251, 268, 279
   See also Versuch
attraction 178
attraction-repulsion 77
attunement (*Stimmung*) 70, 115, 117, 122
audience 44, 54, 69, 143
   See also public
Aufgabe 182, 248, 272

backbone, law as 175, 180, 182
balance 168, 207, 230
barbarian 98, 141
battle(s) 51, 64, 212
becoming 11, 18, 19, 21, 31, 68, 102–4, 123, 140, 141, 153, 164–67, 188–90, 192, 193, 231, 240–42, 272, 275
Befehlen 157, 158, 175, 183
   See also command
Begabung 60, 207, 215
   See also talent
being 17–20, 31, 32, 50, 55, 60, 91, 111, 123, 133, 136–42, 146, 153, 154, 163, 164, 167,

185, 188, 192, 193, 215, 218, 230, 231, 240, 272
beschleunigen See accelerate
Bildung 16, 55, 70, 87, 111, 133, 135–36, 137, 139–41, 146, 183, 200, 205, 206
See also cultivation
bird-like (perspective) 276
bless 174, 178, 181
body 2, 9, 11, 12, 14, 15, 21, 34, 63, 67, 71, 89, 90, 94, 95, 103, 157, 178, 191, 205, 210, 222, 233, 243, 245, 265, 275
bond (genealogical) 35, 41, 122, 131, 139, 152, 198, 205, 266, 268–70, 277
bondage 125, 127, 226

caricature 80, 136
caste 25, 83, 150, 178, 253
castratism 54, 64
celebration 19, 51, 87, 96, 193, 211, 213, 231
Certamen 49, 52
challenge 5, 11, 12, 15, 33, 39, 45, 61, 67, 68, 71, 74, 90–93, 96, 99–101, 104, 105, 218, 229–31, 253
chaos 65, 111, 136–38, 141, 154, 168, 171
cheating 46, 192
check (in the sense of limit) 40, 47, 58, 59, 80, 106, 231
Christianity 10, 23, 25, 26, 33–36, 54, 63, 64, 79, 81, 85, 86, 90, 107, 139, 220, 228, 235, 258–62, 266, 269, 273, 274, 276
Christian-Platonic 3, 7, 9, 11, 67, 74, 154, 210, 220, 226, 227, 230, 234, 258
church 15, 63–66, 79, 81, 109
citizen(s) 49, 59, 107, 190, 191, 215
classical 1, 4, 16, 48, 51, 113, 118, 119, 138, 139, 141, 142, 146, 151, 152, 222, 223
classics, German 119, 137–39
closure 4, 11, 12, 14–16, 67, 68, 89, 91, 103–9, 120, 137, 138, 140, 141, 223, 224, 230, 231
code 10, 12, 13, 32, 54, 84, 85, 194, 208, 233, 234
coercion 61, 154, 175–78, 198
collective 8, 13, 15, 34, 38, 40, 53, 66, 68, 70, 71, 77, 83, 87, 88, 168, 170, 198, 199, 204, 207, 208, 230, 235–37, 245, 250
command 4, 6, 79, 85, 88, 109, 110, 157, 158, 175, 182, 214, 217, 245
See also *Befehlen*
communication 62, 121, 128–30, 134, 207

community 1, 4, 15, 18, 19, 38, 55–60, 63, 66, 68–71, 73, 75, 77, 79–83, 85–87, 124, 167, 170, 178, 184–86, 191, 197–99, 203–10, 227, 230, 236, 237, 265
compulsion 250, 252
See also repetition
conclusive victory 1, 2, 37, 38, 74, 88, 208, 217, 218, 228, 230
Concurrenz 24
condemn 28–31, 51, 53, 68, 119, 131, 171, 207, 243
conflict 1–4, 7, 11, 14, 19, 24, 25, 27, 42, 48, 49, 51–53, 57, 61, 72, 73, 80, 84, 90, 105, 127, 153, 154, 163, 165, 168, 176, 177, 184, 187, 189–91, 200, 207–9, 211–13, 219, 222–24, 226, 228, 230, 231, 233, 237, 238, 244–46, 250, 251, 256, 262, 268, 274, 278
conformism 112, 161, 162, 167, 203
confrontation 1, 3, 10, 13, 15, 16, 18, 20, 21, 24, 26, 30, 39, 43, 54, 60, 63, 66, 68, 73, 74, 76, 78, 80, 81, 88, 90, 93, 99–101, 104–6, 109, 127, 135, 178, 184, 209, 227, 229, 231, 234
conscience (bad, good) 61, 64, 72, 73, 78, 81, 85, 89, 94, 98, 161, 221, 222, 233, 243, 247
consciousness 14, 21, 54, 60, 62, 63, 65, 71, 87, 101, 121, 233, 234, 237–46
consensus 75, 77, 195, 203, 209
See also *Zustimmung*
consolation 30, 91, 140, 242, 251
constructive 14, 15, 20, 25, 53, 63, 65, 73, 83, 85, 171, 233–35
contention 12, 13, 16, 17, 40, 61, 74, 78, 102, 103, 105, 106, 150, 208, 217, 218, 248, 257, 271
correlative 92, 93, 98, 99, 104, 199, 202, 205, 206
See also supplement
counter-final 74, 172–74, 275
See also anti-teleological, open-ended
counter-ideal 14, 63, 64, 83
counterpart 99, 120, 154, 174, 213
counter-position 14, 65, 90
counter-values 21, 74, 77, 86, 230, 260–63, 266–68, 270, 278
courage 8, 26, 97, 124, 137, 212, 218, 265
crisis: of modernity, of authority 9, 14, 17, 34, 66, 69, 76, 111, 134, 155, 204

critique (critical, criticism, critic)   3, 4, 7–9, 11–13, 15, 16, 20, 21, 24, 26–36, 38–42, 44, 51, 54, 61, 63, 64, 66, 68, 70, 72, 74, 75, 77–80, 82, 87, 89–91, 93, 101–11, 127, 135–37, 156, 158, 162–64, 169, 172, 184, 185, 188, 197, 198, 204, 209, 220–22, 224, 226, 227, 229–37, 240, 241, 243–46, 248, 251, 253, 257–60, 266–71, 274–76, 279
cruelty (*Grausamkeit*)   14, 28, 38, 44, 48, 49, 51–53, 213, 216, 234
cultivation (*Bildung*)   70, 87, 206, 228, 255, 258, 274
culture   1–7, 9, 12–18, 25–28, 31–35, 37–39, 43, 44, 48–50, 55–57, 59, 63–69, 71–73, 76–78, 83–87, 89, 90, 101, 103, 104, 111–14, 116, 119, 121–23, 130, 133–46, 149–52, 155, 163, 165, 166, 169, 171, 201, 204–6, 210, 211, 220, 228, 229, 233–35, 243, 247–53, 258, 262, 266, 268, 269
custom (more)   34, 53, 54, 56, 77, 83, 88, 112, 126, 155, 178, 184, 203, 206, 207, 228
  See also *Sitte*

daemon, daemonic (*Dämon*)   98, 100–102, 127–29, 134
Dankbarkeit   16, 73, 124, 127
  See also gratitude
destruction   2, 6, 13–15, 20–31, 33–36, 38–41, 44, 48, 49, 51–54, 58, 63, 65, 73, 74, 79–81, 83–87, 89, 102, 105, 109, 113, 131, 141, 148, 149, 158, 164, 171, 173, 177, 191, 204, 208, 216, 217, 223, 225–31, 233–35, 240, 241, 245, 248–51, 254, 256, 257, 261–63, 265–68, 270–74, 277, 278
  See also *Vernichtung*
destruction-creation   122, 174
Deutsch   111, 136, 137, 139, 141, 142, 258
  See also German
diagnosis (of modernity)   8, 9, 14, 66, 68, 111, 112, 162, 177, 220, 221, 224, 241
dialectic, Socratic   1, 73, 89, 92, 98, 102–6, 131, 132, 149
Dichter, Dichtung, Dichtkust   69, 75, 76, 83, 84, 115, 131, 132, 145, 147, 149, 195
  See also poet
Dionysian   22, 44, 51, 64, 65, 86, 87, 92, 95, 100, 105, 106, 144, 150, 185, 195, 197, 222–24, 228, 229, 242, 257, 271–74, 276–79
discipline   28, 32, 44, 46, 64, 243, 251, 276
discourse   7, 9–15, 19–21, 63, 66–71, 74, 76, 77, 80–82, 89–93, 101, 103–5, 111, 198, 204, 209, 210, 221, 222, 227, 229–34, 236, 237, 240, 241, 243, 245, 246, 248, 252–54
dispute   200, 207, 230
disrespect   6
distance   86, 87, 95, 147, 199–201, 205, 206, 262, 274, 275
diversity   4, 55, 61, 145, 154, 157, 168, 170, 172–74, 186, 213, 244, 245
drama, dramatist   29, 30, 46, 57, 88, 92, 99, 131, 132, 167, 168, 192, 193
dream   94, 98, 222, 225, 226, 230, 234, 237, 250, 251
drive(s)   1, 3, 9, 20, 34, 36, 38, 40, 44, 47, 48, 52, 53, 58, 59, 63, 65, 67, 73, 78–80, 82–87, 101, 102, 106, 107, 109, 113, 126, 127, 138, 139, 148–50, 159, 160, 165, 171, 199–201, 216, 228, 229, 245–47, 249, 250, 260, 266
  See also *Trieb*
dualism   1, 64, 68, 188, 189, 237
duel   33, 37, 267
dying, (practice of, Socrates)   15, 64, 94, 95, 97, 99, 104, 106
dynamic   1–7, 11–19, 21, 24–26, 35, 36, 38, 42, 56–62, 65, 66, 68, 73–76, 78, 80, 83, 85, 88, 93, 103, 104, 106, 119, 121–23, 125, 128, 129, 151–54, 156, 162, 163, 169, 172–76, 193, 194, 207, 208, 210, 211, 217, 225, 227, 229–32, 234, 236, 238, 241, 247–50, 262, 266–68, 278

economy (of body, drives)   34, 77, 81, 110, 129, 165, 221, 229, 232–35, 239, 246, 248, 250
education   25, 39, 55, 58, 77, 85–87, 116, 131, 148–50, 163, 178, 180, 195, 203, 205, 206, 228, 246
educator   52, 58, 60, 73, 75, 84, 114, 116, 135, 149, 176, 181, 183, 228
  See also *Erzieher*
ego   169, 242, 244, 246, 247
ego-development   21, 244, 246, 248
egoism   54, 56, 58, 59, 80, 86, 87, 89, 105, 228
Ehrgeiz (ambition)   58, 75, 78, 123

Eifersucht (jealousy) 39, 58, 78, 130
Einheit 111, 168, 187–92
  See also unification
Einordnen, integrate 53, 54, 85, 87, 138, 148, 228, 250
Einverleibung 21, 142, 243, 245, 248
  See also incorporation
Einverseelung 21, 243
emancipation 1, 16, 30, 56, 123, 125–30, 132, 157, 166, 168, 176, 275
Empfängniskraft 115, 128–30
  See also reception, openness, listening
empowerment 20, 34–38, 40, 74, 79, 80, 85, 88, 104–6, 128, 129, 134, 202, 217, 228, 230, 234–36, 240, 243, 253, 266, 267
empowerment-disempowerment 13, 16, 38, 73, 74, 227, 231, 232, 234, 236
enactment (performative) 11, 12, 15, 19, 20, 67, 68, 73, 81, 91, 93, 100, 101, 104, 105, 126, 194, 218, 231, 232, 236–38, 240, 241, 245, 252
English 162, 238
enigma 9, 10, 68, 232
Entfesselung 44, 55, 56, 190
Entgegenschauen 128
Entladung 53, 55, 84
envy 3, 13, 14, 19, 39–41, 48, 53–55, 58–60, 65, 73, 78, 79, 81, 83, 85, 86, 88, 106, 130, 148, 149, 206, 207, 211, 215–17, 228, 229, 233, 235, 236
  See also Neid
epistemic 18, 19, 91, 101, 102, 185, 186, 198–201, 203–5, 209
equality 4–6, 33, 37, 45, 59, 61, 62, 74, 108, 194, 215, 216, 218, 245, 267
  See also Gleichheit
equilibrium 2, 14, 19, 61, 62, 65, 74, 186, 194, 199, 211, 213, 215, 217–19, 226, 227, 229
  See also Gleichgewicht
Erga 48, 86, 228
Erhöhung 124, 262
Eris 6, 15, 20, 37, 38, 48, 49, 52–54, 73, 75, 83, 84, 86, 149, 150, 187, 189, 190, 211, 216, 228, 233, 234, 237
Erkenntnis, erkennen 27, 77, 82, 93, 143, 145, 150, 152, 157, 171, 179, 199–202, 216, 256, 264
eros 1, 100, 237
error 28–31, 72, 92, 172, 179, 243, 245, 260

Erzieher 52, 73, 76, 84, 126, 135, 139, 149, 160, 177, 181–83
  See also educator
ethical 13, 18, 19, 42, 53, 54, 63, 64, 91, 174, 178, 184–86, 197–99, 203, 204, 210, 212
European 3, 7, 8, 25, 66, 68, 76, 143, 210, 220
evaluation 8, 26, 28, 34, 35, 39, 41, 49, 62, 63, 67, 70, 71, 76, 77, 79, 90, 91, 112, 125, 131, 143, 149, 155, 159, 185, 201, 221, 226, 227, 230, 253, 254, 270
evil 6, 15, 20, 26, 28, 38, 41, 48, 52–54, 58, 64, 66, 70, 71, 73, 74, 76, 83, 84, 86, 107, 108, 125, 149, 150, 166, 216, 226, 233, 234, 262–64, 266
excellence 6, 38, 40, 46–48, 55, 72, 75–77, 145, 161, 194, 195, 203, 215–17, 273
excess 14, 15, 21, 22, 33, 39, 46, 56, 63, 65, 85, 86, 100, 211, 213, 214, 223, 224, 231, 235, 250, 255, 269, 270, 278
exemplarity 16, 32, 44, 113, 114, 116, 118–20, 122, 126, 128, 129, 135, 137, 138, 145–47, 151, 173, 174, 178, 250
existence (human, struggle for) 1, 10, 26–28, 31, 36, 49, 51–53, 84, 87, 90, 95, 97, 104, 108, 111–13, 122, 125, 133, 137, 138, 140, 141, 149, 150, 156, 157, 161, 162, 164, 165, 171, 173, 187, 188, 194, 197, 204, 210, 211, 221, 223, 225, 227, 228, 236, 252, 259, 262, 264, 266, 271
experiment 27, 55, 74, 81, 248
exploitation 79, 84–86, 176–78, 198, 234, 248, 252
extramoral 71, 229, 260, 261

fame 6, 39–41, 45, 52, 58, 59, 78, 80, 84, 123, 131, 149, 181, 206, 212, 228
fantasy 244, 251
fatalism, fatality (*Verhängniss*) 29, 30, 33, 70, 237, 258, 269
fatum 110, 167, 258
  See also amor fati
festival 19, 20, 87, 88, 94, 135, 190–94, 218, 230, 231, 240, 241, 251, 253
Festsetzen See fix
fiction 11, 15, 21, 22, 25, 32, 45, 66, 68–71, 73, 91, 107, 127, 203, 231, 232, 236, 255, 271, 274
feint 15, 68, 71, 83, 104, 231, 232, 236, 255, 271, 274

fight   63, 73, 187, 189, 196, 209, 279
finality   88, 117, 230
fix (in the sense of *Festsetzen*)   10–12, 19, 153, 154, 159, 160, 163, 192–94, 218, 239, 264, 274
Festsetzen   153–56, 160, 164, 185, 193
flesh   13, 27, 31, 39, 89, 101, 107, 183
flux, fluid   153, 170, 179, 192
force   1, 2, 13–15, 21, 24, 25, 29, 35, 37, 38, 40, 44, 51, 53, 55–57, 60–63, 65, 73–75, 77, 83, 85, 86, 88, 103, 104, 106, 128, 130, 134, 150, 163, 167–69, 171, 176, 178, 194, 199, 209, 211–13, 215, 217, 218, 223, 225–30, 232, 233, 235, 236, 245, 247, 250, 251, 253, 265–67, 278
   See also *Kraft*
forgetting   20, 21, 238, 239, 241–43
formative   70, 77, 133
Fort-Da game   251–54
foundation   72, 111, 137, 193, 194, 213
freedom (exercise concept of, of mind, creative), *frei*   3, 14, 16, 17, 36, 42, 45, 53–55, 57, 63–65, 72, 82, 83, 114, 116–18, 122, 124–30, 132, 133, 145, 149, 152, 158, 159, 162, 165, 166, 168, 171, 177, 179, 186, 194, 199, 203, 206, 212, 214, 215, 219, 229, 238, 241, 248–50, 252, 259–61, 275, 276
free spirit   75, 165, 171,179, 203, 237, 260, 276
   See also *freie Geist*
Friede   260, 261, 263
friendship   70, 79, 206, 207, 226, 230
fulfillable, law as   45, 85, 88, 95, 106, 154, 174, 175, 178, 180, 181

gathering (agon as)   42, 236
gegen   22, 128, 135, 163, 261, 262, 268, 276, 277
Gegenbewegung   67
Gegensatz   1, 24, 81, 106, 195, 257–59, 262–64, 272, 273, 277
   See also oppose
Geist   9, 14, 36, 63, 65, 72, 86, 87, 124, 140, 152, 199, 275
freie Geist   72, 139, 256, 260, 261, 273, 275
genealogical, genealogy   11, 29, 34, 35, 41, 46, 48, 54, 72, 108, 110, 131, 156, 158, 186, 210, 220, 221, 224, 225, 236, 243, 252
genius   4, 16–18, 25, 37, 38, 47, 52, 55–57, 61, 73–75, 77, 82, 89, 94, 100, 104, 111–18, 120–30, 132, 133, 139, 144, 165–69, 194, 198, 202, 205, 217, 261, 267, 268
Gerechtigkeit   18, 68, 76, 164, 165, 168, 184, 189, 197, 208, 217
   See also justice
German   4, 16, 17, 43–45, 57, 70, 111–14, 116, 133, 134, 136–42, 146, 152, 169, 205, 238, 249, 269, 277
   See also *Deutsch*
Gesetz, Gesetzgeber, Gesetzmässigkeit   17, 18, 112, 115, 150, 153–60, 162–64, 166, 167, 172–77, 180–83, 185–90, 192, 196, 201, 204, 208, 209, 219, 261
   See also law, legislation
Gewalt   82, 113, 128, 168, 169
   See also violence
Gleichgewicht   14, 61, 62, 65, 194, 213, 215, 217, 227, 229
   See also equilibrium
Gleichheit   59, 61, 177, 215, 245
   See also *Gleichheit*
goal   5, 9, 13, 20, 21, 26, 33, 34, 45, 58, 60, 62, 69, 72, 79–81, 86, 87, 99, 170–72, 179, 206, 224, 231, 232, 234, 237, 240–42, 244, 246–48, 258, 266
   See also *Ziel*
god, goddess, *Gott, göttlich*   4, 5, 9, 15, 17, 27, 29, 38–40, 45, 47–49, 54, 58, 60, 69, 72, 73, 78, 83, 87–88, 96–97, 100, 106, 136, 141, 144–45, 150, 152, 158, 172, 179, 190, 193, 200, 202, 204, 206, 212, 213, 223–25, 229, 233, 258, 263–65
gratitude   16, 33, 35, 73, 87, 123–25, 127, 134, 223, 235, 236, 256, 267, 269
   See also *Dankbarkeit*
greatness. *Grösse*   6, 8, 39–41, 75, 78, 79, 81, 86, 113, 119, 123, 127–29, 131, 132, 148, 149, 158, 165, 185, 201, 205–7, 209, 210, 228
Greece, Greek, *Griechen(thum)*   1–4, 6, 13, 14, 17, 19, 25–29, 32–34, 36–40, 43–61, 63, 64, 67, 68, 70, 72, 73, 75, 77, 78, 80, 83–85, 87, 89, 95, 114–16, 124, 125, 133–52, 155, 169, 171, 184, 187, 189–98, 200, 205, 207, 208, 211, 212, 214–16, 218, 228, 229, 240, 250, 266–68
   See also Hellene
Grenze   37, 57, 65, 73, 143, 267
   See also limit, *Maass*

growth 33, 34, 40, 51, 55, 79, 80, 115, 133, 137, 138, 222–24, 226, 228, 230, 231, 262, 266, 268
  See also Wachsthum
gusto 19, 186, 205–9
  See also taste

happiness 39, 59, 78, 81, 95–97, 161, 181, 215, 225, 262, 276
hardness 24, 59, 214, 272
harmony 38, 187, 198, 207, 246
Häßlichkeit 82, 263, 264
hate, hatred, *Hass* 25, 38, 48, 51, 53, 65, 73, 83, 95, 137, 161, 167, 198, 207, 215, 216, 223, 229, 230, 233–36, 252, 275, 276
heal, healer, healing power 21, 23, 27, 95, 142, 220–22, 230, 242, 243, 247, 276
health 27, 68, 87, 95, 220–22, 224, 227–29, 231, 232, 235–38, 255, 275, 276
Hellene, Hellas, *hellenisch* 19, 37, 39, 43, 44, 47, 48, 52, 54, 57–60, 65, 80, 83, 84, 131, 143, 144, 150, 169, 187, 189, 268
hero, *Heros* 4, 5, 19, 29, 45, 54, 65, 131, 197, 206, 211–13, 242, 258
Herrschaft 8, 21, 36, 73, 79, 108, 157, 170, 173, 181, 182, 246–49, 266, 267
  See also mastery
heteronomy 87, 118, 125, 126, 156, 157, 160, 162, 170
hierarchy 4–6, 24
  See also Rangordnung
history, historical, *Historie* 4, 13, 16, 22, 25, 27–32, 34, 35, 40, 43–45, 47, 49, 52, 54, 59, 66, 69, 70, 77, 89, 105, 111, 113, 114, 117–20, 122, 123, 133, 136, 138, 140, 141, 143, 144, 146, 147, 150, 152, 155, 168, 186, 191, 193, 199–201, 205, 210, 211, 214, 226, 236, 237, 243, 251, 256, 273
honour 6, 16, 33, 35, 39, 45, 47, 54, 57, 58, 75, 110, 124, 132, 137, 147, 152, 167, 169, 212, 215, 216, 229, 267, 269
hostility 26, 27, 31, 47, 53, 64, 72, 74, 76, 85, 86, 109, 110, 154, 190, 194, 218, 228
hubris 27, 45, 46, 51, 63, 65, 98, 101, 211, 212, 214, 231
humanism, neo-humanism 4, 14, 15, 42, 50, 51, 53–55, 59, 61, 63, 64, 66, 83–86, 90, 148, 214, 216, 235
humanity 4, 13, 14, 19, 50, 51, 55, 63–65, 67, 83, 87, 89, 123, 124, 126, 139, 168, 205, 211, 212, 220, 221, 224, 255, 258, 273, 274
  See also Menschheit

ideal 3, 8, 19, 34–36, 44–48, 51, 52, 56, 61, 63, 65, 67, 69, 70, 72, 74, 77, 79, 84, 86, 87, 95, 97, 123–27, 130, 149, 150, 152, 157, 160, 172–74, 179, 180, 182, 186, 191, 203–7, 209–11, 213, 221, 228, 234, 236, 242, 244, 245, 247, 248, 251, 254, 257, 260–67, 270, 275, 277
idealism 21, 256, 258–66, 268–70, 274–79
identity 17, 19, 20, 52, 58, 61, 70, 82, 95, 98, 99, 112, 119, 120, 122, 123, 130, 133, 142, 143, 146, 151, 152, 187, 193, 218
image 13, 16, 23, 24, 26, 70, 74, 98, 115, 124, 125, 127, 145, 154, 175, 245
imagination 144, 196, 197, 202, 206
  See also Phantasie
imitation 16, 46, 84, 86, 114, 116, 118–21, 123, 127, 132, 133, 136–38, 144, 145, 147, 151, 206, 250
  See also Nachahmung
immanence 8, 14, 15, 18, 19, 62, 64, 75, 76, 103, 154, 164, 167, 185–90, 192–94, 196, 209, 213, 217–19, 264, 271, 278, 279
inconclusive 15, 25, 38, 74, 76, 77, 97, 106, 197, 208, 209, 218, 228, 230, 231, 252
  See also anti-teleological, open-ended, counter-final
incorporation 21, 131, 243–45, 268
  See also Einverleibung
indeterminate 19, 100, 116, 117, 167, 186, 188, 198, 203, 204, 209, 210, 216, 217
individual 8, 14, 16–18, 26, 33, 34, 37, 38, 42, 45, 47, 48, 51, 53–59, 62, 63, 65, 74, 77, 78, 80–83, 86–88, 109, 111, 112, 138, 149, 150, 152, 155–62, 166–71, 174–80, 183, 189, 190, 196–98, 206, 209, 210, 212, 213, 215, 218, 228, 231, 238, 265, 268, 269
inhuman 13, 14, 50, 51, 53, 54, 63, 64, 83, 211, 214, 216, 228
instinct 11, 14, 20, 21, 23, 28, 32, 33, 65, 71–73, 85, 88, 89, 95, 101–3, 108, 109, 126, 127, 145, 221, 228, 229, 233, 236–38, 241, 243, 244, 246, 247, 250–52, 254, 259–62, 265
intoxication 53, 223, 228, 276
  See also Rausch

judge   4, 5, 31, 46, 58, 62, 75, 118, 165, 191, 193, 195–97, 199, 206, 216
   See also Richter
judgement (aesthetic, reflective, morality of, in agon)   5, 19, 28–32, 40, 42, 46, 47, 54, 55, 62–64, 68, 75–77, 85, 117–21, 132, 154, 157, 160, 164, 165, 184, 187, 189, 194–204, 207–10, 213, 217, 219, 230, 265, 279
justice   2, 6, 18, 19, 25, 30, 42, 46, 53, 62, 68, 76, 168, 184, 186–97, 208–10, 213, 218, 219, 279
   See also Gerchtigkeit

Kampf   21, 24, 25, 30, 34, 36, 49, 52, 60, 73, 123, 141, 149, 152, 153, 187, 189, 190, 195–97, 215, 220, 222, 223, 257, 259, 262, 264, 265, 271, 279
Kampfrichter   46, 197
Klassiker   137, 138
klassisch   113, 138, 139
knowledge   8, 15, 16, 27, 28, 31, 32, 50, 52, 73, 84, 85, 89, 90, 92, 93, 95, 97, 101–3, 105–7, 121, 136, 144, 146, 147, 149, 150, 152, 159, 171, 179, 199–202, 204, 205, 209, 223, 228, 229, 243, 245, 248, 263, 264
Kraft   13, 14, 25, 36–38, 44, 50, 56, 57, 60, 62, 63, 65, 74, 75, 80, 103, 119, 120, 128, 129, 142, 153, 159, 163, 178, 181, 186, 209, 215, 217, 227, 248, 253, 273, 275
   See also force
Krieg   21, 24, 36, 46, 163, 168, 189, 256, 257, 260–64, 271, 272
   See also war
Kritik   8, 185, 195
Kultur   25, 43, 57, 111, 113, 119, 122, 136, 137, 139, 145, 148, 151, 155, 166, 258
Kunst   25–27, 46, 68, 75, 76, 90, 99, 104, 115, 122, 124, 129, 131, 132, 167, 168, 187, 189, 195, 200, 205, 263, 264
   See also art
Künstler   68, 75, 90, 124, 161, 195

law   1, 4, 6, 16–20, 42, 44, 47, 55, 56, 59, 61, 62, 65, 70, 81, 83, 88, 108–10, 112–16, 119, 120, 125, 126, 129, 150, 153–60, 162–64, 166–68, 170, 172–78, 180–94, 196–201, 203–5, 208–10, 213–19, 223, 236, 237, 245, 258, 261
   See also Gesetz
legislation   3, 4, 17, 18, 114–16, 125, 153–58, 160–64, 166–73, 175, 177, 178, 192, 201, 205, 206, 209
   See also Gesetz
legislator, law-giver   17, 18, 114, 115, 149, 150, 155, 158, 160, 164, 165, 169, 172–75, 177–82, 194, 210
   See also Gesetz
liberal   2, 59, 82, 83, 177, 184
liberality (*Freisinnigkeit*)   54, 55, 229
Liebe   27, 124, 147, 167, 170–72, 176, 179, 183, 229, 258, 275
   See also love
life   2–4, 7–15, 17, 18, 21, 25–32, 34, 40, 42–45, 48, 49, 51–57, 59, 64, 66–74, 76, 78, 79, 81, 84, 85, 88–97, 99–101, 103–5, 109–11, 113, 124–27, 129, 133, 136, 139–42, 146, 148, 150, 153–58, 160, 162–67, 172–76, 178, 179, 184–87, 194, 198, 204–10, 214, 219–24, 226, 228, 230–33, 235–38, 245, 247, 250, 252–55, 257–59, 262, 264, 265, 269, 272, 274, 276
Leben   10, 27, 55, 73, 82, 90, 99, 109, 113, 116, 128, 136, 140–42, 146–48, 150, 152, 157, 162, 164, 165, 172, 180, 182, 195, 204–6, 220, 256, 258, 259, 261, 262, 264, 265, 273, 275
life-affirmation   3, 11, 12, 14, 15, 17, 18, 41, 52–54, 63, 67, 69–71, 89, 103, 109, 110, 155, 165, 166, 169, 171, 188, 203, 204, 206, 210, 257
life-as-art   13, 15, 67, 100, 104
life-enhancement   155, 198, 203, 204
life-negation   9, 11, 14, 17, 21, 64, 66, 73, 74, 81, 110, 153, 154, 178, 185, 210, 230, 231, 253, 257, 268, 270, 274
   See also Verneinung
limit   4, 7, 13–16, 19–21, 23, 25, 27, 28, 30–41, 55–59, 61–63, 65, 73, 74, 78–81, 83, 85, 86, 92, 93, 97–99, 101–3, 105–10, 121, 132, 143, 149, 152, 171, 198, 210–12, 227, 228, 232, 234, 236, 249, 250, 256, 263, 266–68, 270, 272, 278–79
   See also Grenze
listening, art of   93, 98, 100, 102, 103, 105, 141
   See also reception, receptivity

love   26, 56, 86, 100, 147, 150, 153, 163, 167, 170–72, 176–79, 183, 215–17, 223, 228, 234, 235, 237, 238, 248, 257, 258, 260, 270, 276
   See also Liebe
lust   38, 51, 53, 73, 83, 216, 234, 272, 273

Maass, maaßlos   8, 14, 18, 33, 35, 37, 42, 45, 46, 53, 55–57, 64, 65, 73, 82–84, 112, 138, 147, 149, 162, 164, 186, 187, 189, 196, 197, 209–11, 216, 228, 229, 248, 267, 278, 279
   See also measure
Macht, mächtig   36, 128, 143, 160, 164, 166, 169, 182, 194, 233, 245, 249, 260
   See also power
making-fast   153, 176
   See also Festsetzen
master   33–37, 79, 88, 115, 225, 240, 253, 254, 266, 267, 276
mastery   13, 21, 25, 27, 33–41, 73, 79, 84, 173, 176, 180, 244–51, 254, 266–68, 270, 272, 278
   See also Herrschaft
measure (as standard, as moderation)   2, 3, 5, 6, 14, 15, 18–20, 26, 29, 33, 35–38, 41, 42, 45, 48, 49, 51, 53–57, 59, 61–63, 65–67, 71, 73, 75, 76, 79, 80, 83–87, 100, 104, 106, 112, 118, 120, 138, 147–49, 159, 161, 162, 164, 176, 185–87, 189–91, 194, 196, 197, 199, 202, 203, 206–17, 219, 227–29, 232, 248–50, 256, 266, 267, 277–79
medial   5, 14, 19, 20, 42, 59–63, 65, 80, 186, 197, 207–11, 214, 215, 217–19, 230, 231, 275, 276
memory   40, 78, 113, 127, 136, 138, 140, 144–46, 238, 243, 254, 255, 258
Mensch   8, 29, 40, 43, 50, 51, 76, 82, 84, 88, 123, 124, 139, 142, 143, 147, 148, 154, 161, 164, 171, 179, 182, 183, 185, 193, 194, 201, 221, 249, 261, 262, 264, 275
Menschheit   9, 123, 124, 168, 258, 273
   See also humanity
menschlich   50, 53, 140, 151, 212
metaphor   12, 13, 20, 71–73, 84, 105, 123, 144, 145, 190, 232–34, 238–41, 252, 253
   See also Übertragung
metaphysics   1, 7, 11–13, 18, 31, 66–68, 76, 87, 90–92, 104, 105, 107, 124, 140, 141, 144, 163, 164, 166, 169, 204, 220, 225, 239, 242, 243, 251
mimesis   16, 17, 25, 111, 114, 119, 123, 125–34, 136–38, 140, 143, 145–48, 151
   See also Nachahmung
modernity   3, 8, 16–18, 25, 34, 51, 82, 111, 112, 114, 115, 125, 134, 135, 162, 163, 167, 168, 170, 205, 220, 221, 224, 234, 237
monumental (history)   31, 113, 123
   See also history
moral, *Moral, Moralität, moralisch*   7–9, 11, 12, 14, 17, 18, 36, 55, 59, 63, 65, 67, 71, 73, 76, 79, 82, 83, 85, 90, 91, 108, 112, 114–16, 119, 124, 153–60, 162, 163, 170–73, 175, 178–80, 182, 183, 185, 186, 197–99, 205, 207, 209, 220, 242, 247, 248, 256, 258, 263, 272–75
moralise   88, 109, 110, 221, 234, 235, 248, 258
morality   2–4, 8, 13, 15, 18, 19, 25, 36, 54, 55, 61, 63, 64, 66–68, 71, 73, 79, 82, 84, 85, 88, 90, 109, 110, 112, 114, 116, 124, 153–59, 162, 170–73, 175, 178–81, 183, 198, 213, 220–22, 224–28, 235, 236, 247, 248, 251, 253, 263, 264, 266
mores   *See* custom
multiplicity   7, 17–19, 21, 40, 75, 129, 151, 153, 154, 161, 168, 169, 185, 187–90, 210, 244, 245, 271, 274, 276–78
music   9, 43, 46, 57, 96–102, 105, 106, 167, 169, 187, 224,
music-practising Socrates   15, 92, 93, 99, 104, 106
mutual   36–39, 58, 80, 82, 83, 85, 86, 88, 103, 106, 178, 190, 227, 228, 232, 234–36, 253
   See also reciprocity
myth   30, 56, 96–100, 104, 106, 131, 132, 195

Nachahmung   16, 25, 46, 84, 114, 116, 118–21, 123, 129, 130, 133, 136–38, 145, 147, 250
   See also imitation
Nachfolge   16, 113, 114, 116, 118–23, 126–30, 132, 133, 136–39, 141
   See also succession
Nachschaffen   147, 148
narcosis   223, 225
national   111, 112, 131, 136, 142, 187, 212

naturalise   2, 17, 51, 85, 88, 89, 92, 107, 109, 110, 157, 158, 173, 178
necessity, *Nothwendigkeit*   93, 98, 102, 105, 106, 110, 119, 134, 154, 158–61, 163, 166–68, 170, 187, 204, 244, 258, 259, 266, 272, 278
negation, negativity, negative   1, 4, 13, 15, 16, 21, 23, 27, 28, 30–36, 38, 39, 51–54, 63, 64, 67, 73, 74, 79, 83, 85, 86, 90, 91, 99, 103, 105–10, 120, 126, 134, 137, 140, 148, 154, 155, 164, 166, 171, 176, 178, 188, 192, 200, 204, 223, 224, 227, 235, 236, 250, 253, 254, 256, 257, 263, 264, 266–75, 278
See also Verneinung, no-saying
Neid   39, 53, 58, 78, 149
See also envy
neurosis, neurotic   1, 20, 238, 241, 242, 244, 247
nihilism   9, 14, 66, 69, 76, 77, 80, 158, 160, 162, 163, 170–72, 209, 258
noble   45, 46, 48–51, 72, 86, 87, 95, 96, 98, 119, 149, 185, 198, 206, 216, 221, 261, 262
no-doing, *Neinthun*   255, 256, 273
normativity, normative, norm(s)   4, 16, 19, 20, 34, 50, 51, 55, 112–14, 116, 126, 128, 145, 162, 185, 190–93, 196, 199, 200, 203–5, 209, 218, 219, 222, 231, 232, 237
no-saying, *Neinsagen*   21, 255–59, 270, 271, 273, 274, 276

obedience   4, 6, 119, 124, 157, 158, 175, 182, 245, 251, 273
occurrence   29, 118, 271
one-man rule   37, 57
See also Alleinherrschaft
open-ended   11, 15, 20, 38, 40, 70, 74–78, 88, 106, 124, 125, 139, 193, 194, 197, 204, 208, 218, 224, 228, 230, 231, 235, 240
See also anti-teleological, counter-final, inconclusive
openness   17, 42, 55, 64, 113, 114, 120, 133, 138, 144, 212, 213, 215, 223, 257, 270
See also reception, receptivity
opponent   21, 33–37, 39–41, 48, 58, 60, 64, 73, 74, 79–81, 102, 106, 110, 123, 131, 149, 152, 176, 183, 212, 226, 230, 252, 256, 263–68, 272, 273
oppose (an opponent)   12, 13, 21, 33, 35, 36, 50, 51, 53, 63, 67, 71–73, 79, 80–81, 91, 92–3, 104, 106–10, 120, 128, 154, 156, 157, 160, 167, 173, 177, 189, 205, 207, 216, 223, 228, 257, 262, 265–7, 269, 270, 271–4, 277–8
See also Gegensatz
opposition (in thought)   1, 14–16, 28, 32, 48, 49, 54, 63, 66, 68, 74, 91, 92, 100, 102, 104–9, 114, 118, 130, 136, 154, 157, 160, 162, 170, 188, 195, 201, 213, 221, 235, 245, 247, 248, 251, 259, 264, 268, 278
organization, organising power   9, 18, 69, 136, 138, 141, 168, 227, 229, 233, 234, 243
origin   2, 3, 11, 16, 17, 25, 42, 45, 47, 61–63, 66, 67, 84, 88, 111–13, 118, 120, 123, 126, 127, 132–34, 136–38, 140, 143, 151, 152, 193, 194, 218, 231, 240, 252, 262
original   4, 16, 17, 29, 37, 56, 111–14, 116–23, 129–33, 136, 138, 147, 152, 193, 194, 198, 217, 230, 242, 246, 247
otherness   54, 64, 65, 84, 139
overcome, overcoming   3, 4, 7, 9, 15–18, 20, 21, 27, 29, 30, 52, 66–71, 74, 76, 77, 79, 81, 84, 88, 90–92, 97, 106, 114, 123–25, 127–30, 132, 134, 135, 140, 147–52, 154, 156, 163, 170, 175, 176, 178, 181, 183, 201, 210, 221, 223, 228, 230, 239–42, 245, 253, 265, 268–73, 275, 276

Panhellenic festivals   19, 190–92, 194, 218
paradox   11, 19, 57, 59, 87, 101, 127, 134, 152, 175, 208, 227, 237, 238, 249, 270, 271, 273
particularity   20, 42, 55, 57, 61, 83, 102, 103, 112, 119, 132, 150, 154, 157, 159, 160, 162, 170, 174, 178, 213, 248
passion(s), *Leidenschaft*   1, 9, 14, 15, 20, 28, 40, 42, 45, 54, 55, 63–66, 83–87, 90, 94, 109, 168, 211, 215, 216, 223, 229, 235, 247, 248, 262
passive   16, 25, 114, 116, 119, 123, 127, 129, 130, 133, 137, 138, 144, 147, 174, 175, 253
pathological   9, 20, 21, 78, 229, 231, 232, 235, 237–39, 241, 243, 244
pathos   13, 23, 29, 33, 34, 48, 49, 63, 65, 78, 211, 212, 232, 234, 244, 257, 260, 270, 271
people(s), (in the sense of *Volk*)   40, 43, 45, 51, 87, 111, 136, 142, 144–46, 150, 183, 200, 221, 227
See also Volk
performance   11, 66, 68, 96, 103, 126, 128, 129, 184, 191–93, 214, 216–19, 238, 252, 257, 275

Subject Index — 299

performative   2, 10–12, 14, 15, 20, 42, 45, 67, 68, 73, 78, 81, 83, 91, 93, 97, 100, 104, 125–30, 134, 156, 214–19, 231–34, 240, 241, 245, 252
perspective   4, 13, 18, 20, 34, 71, 79, 90, 91, 93, 101, 111, 127, 132, 145, 157, 174, 184, 210, 212, 234, 235, 237, 238, 240, 254, 257, 259, 270, 271, 273–75, 277–79
Phantasie   144, 147, 195, 202
philosophy   1–4, 7, 9–11, 14, 15, 17, 18, 20, 23–32, 34, 42, 44, 47, 49, 53, 66–68, 74, 78, 79, 84, 93–100, 103, 106, 111, 124, 125, 127, 131, 132, 144, 146, 147, 149, 153, 156, 160, 164, 166, 185–87, 189, 197, 199–202, 204, 206, 209, 214, 220–26, 230, 235, 238, 257, 259, 260, 265, 266, 270, 272, 274–76
physiological   2, 69, 82, 84, 144, 157, 159, 160, 210, 221, 223, 225, 236, 243, 245, 262, 265
play   25, 45, 46, 60, 80, 84, 85, 151, 218, 230–32, 237, 238, 240–43, 249–54
   See also *Spiel*
plurality, pluralism   1, 13–15, 17, 18, 25, 38, 40, 42, 55–57, 60, 61, 63, 67, 73–75, 77, 78, 104, 153, 154, 156, 157, 161, 162, 168–74, 176, 178–80, 194, 198, 199, 206–8, 217, 219, 227, 229, 244, 245, 253
poet   4, 15, 39, 46, 52, 54, 66, 73, 76, 83, 84, 91, 93, 94, 126, 127, 131, 132, 144, 149, 150, 193, 203, 211–13, 218, 228
   See also *Dichter*
polemic   14, 23, 50, 53, 59, 63, 66, 146, 148, 200
polemos   19, 187
polis   47, 49, 53, 55, 80, 83, 144, 190, 191, 194, 214, 215, 218
political   2, 3, 6, 14, 20, 26, 38, 47, 55, 56, 73, 82, 84, 168, 170, 178, 184, 189, 194, 197, 214–16, 218, 219, 226
politics   2, 25, 69, 82, 148, 184, 256, 273, 274, 278
portraiture   114, 116, 126–28, 133, 147, 165
power   2, 4–6, 9, 13, 17, 19, 25, 28, 33, 34, 36, 38, 44, 55, 57–59, 61, 62, 69, 79, 80, 87, 88, 92, 102, 104, 106, 108, 115, 119, 120, 123, 125, 128, 129, 132, 133, 140, 142–44, 148, 150, 153, 155, 159, 160, 163, 166–69, 171, 173, 176–78, 191, 194, 198, 211, 214, 225–27, 229, 231, 233–36, 243, 245, 246, 248, 250, 253, 264, 266, 271, 273
   See also *Macht*
prefiguration   13, 19, 67, 95, 96, 100, 186, 231, 237
priest   4, 64, 65, 72, 73, 76, 81, 83, 84, 89, 110, 150, 221, 226, 230, 236, 252, 253
primus inter pares   5
production   41, 65, 75, 86, 116, 117, 184, 223, 250
productive   2, 3, 9, 27, 38, 68, 69, 72–74, 79, 117, 126, 174, 175, 177, 191, 223, 227–29, 231, 233, 236, 268, 270, 271
provocation-contestation   14, 18, 19, 29, 38–40, 56–58, 61, 65, 71, 73, 77, 78, 83, 85, 121, 122, 126, 128, 129, 131, 147, 149, 152, 158, 176, 177, 191, 208, 209, 211, 217, 227, 228, 230, 234, 236
   See also *Reiz*, stimulant
psychoanalysis   20, 232, 238–42, 247, 248, 250, 251
public   18, 40, 44–47, 54, 55, 68, 73–78, 118, 159, 178, 184, 185, 192, 194–97, 203, 215, 217, 219, 228, 268, 269
   See also audience

quality (of life-forms)   4, 5, 8, 9, 61, 185, 186

rage   44, 85–87, 216, 226, 228, 229, 241, 253
Rangordnung   4–6, 67
   See also hierarchy
Rausch   53, 68, 223
   See also intoxication
reactive   20, 25, 225, 227, 236, 240, 253, 254, 262
   See also active
readership   6, 9, 13, 15, 18, 63, 66, 68–71, 73, 75, 77, 78, 80–83, 184, 197, 204–209, 230, 237
reality   7, 11, 21, 29, 31, 46, 49, 54, 76, 83, 91, 193, 223, 237, 242, 247, 248, 251, 252, 259, 263, 270–78
reason   55, 63, 82, 90, 91, 93, 96, 97, 110, 117–20, 185, 197, 198, 202, 203, 205, 222, 245, 258, 264, 265
reception, receptivity   16, 17, 95, 98, 103, 115, 123, 125, 127–30, 132, 133, 144, 145, 195, 199, 219
   See also openness, listening, *Empfängniskraft*

reciprocity   4, 14, 15, 19, 29, 35, 36, 38, 56–60, 65, 73, 77, 134, 185, 191, 198, 208, 211, 215, 217, 219, 226, 266, 267, 278, 279
   See also mutual
recurrence (eternal)   12, 19, 88, 193, 231, 240, 241
redemption   38, 69, 70, 81, 95, 220–25, 227, 230, 242
Reiz   14, 37, 38, 57, 61, 65, 72, 73, 104, 144, 145, 147, 148, 152, 195, 267
   See also provocation, stimulant
relational   4, 18, 22, 60, 62, 63, 83, 178, 219, 271, 272, 274–76
religion   7, 8, 11, 13, 31, 44, 66, 67, 76, 81, 84, 88, 92, 95, 104, 141, 142, 145, 148, 153, 158, 163, 171, 172, 179, 220, 251, 263
repeatability   2, 38, 74, 96, 106, 217, 218, 228, 230, 231
repetition (-compulsion)   20, 30, 60, 119, 126, 127, 193, 222, 225, 227, 230, 231, 237–42, 246, 249, 253, 254, 261
repression   1, 11, 20, 64, 65, 71, 73, 85, 126, 127, 233–35, 238, 239, 242, 247, 248
resistance (power)   3, 6, 14, 28, 34, 36, 39, 47, 56, 60, 61, 65, 69, 70, 80, 171, 176–78, 219, 226, 235, 238, 239, 266, 268, 272
resistances (psychological)   20, 23, 33, 34, 37, 40, 239, 242, 267, 268
respect   5, 6, 46, 185, 206
ressentiment   4, 20, 25, 89, 220, 221, 223–27, 230, 233, 235, 237, 239–41, 243, 246, 248, 251–54, 262
revenge   20, 21, 25, 29, 30, 53, 64, 65, 69, 85, 127, 150, 216, 220, 223–28, 234–36, 248, 252–54, 259, 260, 262
Rache   53, 150, 220, 259
reverence, Verehrung   31, 87, 127, 163, 235, 262
Richter, Richterthum   68, 76, 165, 187, 189, 196, 197, 209, 279
   See also judge
rights   61, 107, 176, 177, 183, 195, 222
Ringen   26, 182, 189, 196, 197, 257, 258
rivalry   24, 25, 37, 75, 131, 191, 206
Romanticism   91, 92, 112, 222–25, 236
rule(s), rule-bound, law   16, 19, 35, 40, 46, 75, 77, 78, 112–22, 125, 129–32, 162, 168, 185, 191–94, 201, 207–9, 217–19, 234, 236, 267

sabbatical (happiness)   223–25
sacrifice   39, 40, 58, 78, 95
saying and unsaying   11–13, 74, 232
saying and yes-saying   11, 91, 92, 104
Schaffen   47, 111, 124, 147, 148, 151, 152, 175, 182, 183, 195
Schein   See semblance
Schicksal   7, 89, 255–59, 272, 273, 275, 276
schön   76, 132, 161, 263, 264
Schöpfen   56, 120, 162, 172, 179, 182
science   1, 2, 19, 25, 34, 44, 91–93, 95, 97, 107, 111, 120, 121, 143, 153, 185, 199–202
   See also Wissenschaft
self-alienation   127, 128, 133, 137, 142, 144, 146
self-assertion   148, 212, 257, 270
self-critique   21, 102–5, 155, 279
self-destruction   13, 27, 31, 32, 38, 39, 72, 85, 91, 126, 127
self-knowledge   158–60, 163
self-legislation   4, 16–18, 111–13, 116, 123, 155–63, 166, 169–71, 175, 177, 178, 209, 210
self-overcoming   72, 153, 162, 173, 174, 181, 182, 229
self-preservation   36, 70, 71, 79, 266
self-referential   13, 20, 27, 221, 226, 227, 237
self-restraint, -contrrol   5, 19, 56, 126, 212, 231, 250
semblance, Schein   72, 73, 89, 92, 116
sensus communis   19, 203, 204
separation   14, 21, 50, 64, 116, 148, 156, 168, 198, 205, 216, 263–66, 268, 269, 275, 277
Sieg   45, 47, 75, 76, 187, 189, 196, 261, 264, 265, 279
   See also victory
singularity   5, 112, 161, 176, 177, 209, 210
Sitte   53, 55, 126, 155, 163, 178
   See also custom
Sittengesetz   83, 157
solitude   178, 180, 181
Sollen   90, 102, 123, 146, 147, 152, 158–60, 163, 171, 172, 179, 180
soul   27, 55, 72, 81, 89, 90, 95–97, 99, 107, 108, 211, 212, 215, 234, 248, 252, 265
sovereign, sovereignty   8, 56, 81, 82, 87, 126, 154, 157–60, 168, 214
spectator   4, 94, 190, 193, 196, 213, 219, 226
Spiel   25, 46, 57, 60, 84, 187, 250
   See also play

Subject Index — **301**

spirit   14, 23, 63, 65, 124, 137, 191, 241, 247, 253, 276
  See also Geist
Spiritualization (*Vergeistigung*)   64, 79, 81, 84, 87, 109, 199
spontaneity   3, 42, 55–57, 61, 191, 192, 214, 227, 245
Steigerung   8, 42, 51, 55, 124, 210, 228, 264
stimulant, stimulate (*Reiz*)   1, 3, 14, 15, 18, 28, 37–39, 41, 43, 47–49, 56, 57, 59, 61, 65, 66, 70, 73, 74, 78–80, 83, 85, 86, 104, 123, 126, 129, 132, 144, 145, 147–50, 152, 175–77, 209, 217, 227, 229, 234, 236, 237, 266, 267
  See also Reiz, provocation
strength   8, 23, 26, 28, 33–37, 79, 103, 127, 131, 136, 178, 181, 226, 229, 254, 266, 267, 278
stupidity   63, 64
subjection   118, 125, 126, 154, 174–76, 183
subjectivity, subjective, subject-position   5, 20, 42, 60–62, 80, 107, 128, 207, 208, 211, 212, 215, 217, 219, 244, 270–74, 278
sublimation   3, 21, 84, 237, 246–52
substance   271
Succession (*Nachfolge*)   16, 113, 114, 116, 118–20, 123, 128, 129, 132, 133, 140
  See also *Nachfolge*
suffering   51, 52, 90, 180, 182, 223–25, 253, 254, 259
supplement   11, 12, 15, 16, 19, 22, 67, 91–93, 97–104, 127, 129, 199, 202, 205, 206, 231, 232, 244
  See also correlative

talent   47, 115, 117, 121, 122, 125, 151
  See also Begabung
taste, *Geschmack*   4, 18, 19, 65, 75, 113–19, 125, 161, 169, 184–86, 194, 197–210, 264, 265, 275
teleology   6, 224, 232
tension (dynamic)   2, 5, 14, 60, 62, 65, 69, 72, 154, 178, 217, 227, 245
therapy   4, 20, 21, 220–24, 227–44, 246, 249, 250
time (temporality)   11, 14, 25, 29, 67, 69, 70, 76, 113, 123, 127, 135, 152, 163, 165, 166, 218, 226, 239, 257, 273
times, the (present)   106, 163, 165, 166
Todkrieg   21, 261–63

tradition   16, 113, 114, 116, 118, 119, 121, 122, 126, 146
tragedy, tragic   1, 13, 19, 29, 30, 34, 38, 46, 52, 56, 67, 68, 72, 75, 77, 86, 88, 91–93, 98, 99, 135, 185, 193, 194, 203, 209, 211, 213, 223, 224, 228, 242, 256, 258, 259, 274
transcendent   8, 18, 19, 40, 96, 154, 158, 160, 163, 164, 167, 213
transference, (metaphorical, analytic), transposition, *Übertragung*   15, 20, 26, 52, 63, 71, 73, 83–87, 114, 128, 134, 143, 145, 150, 172, 179, 189, 214, 228, 233–35, 237–42, 245, 249, 250, 253
  See also metaphor
transformation (agonal, therapeutic)   20, 25, 27, 53, 54, 63–66, 73, 83, 85, 86, 92, 138, 141–45, 149, 165, 171, 176, 227–29, 232–41, 243, 247, 249, 253, 254, 258, 265, 271, 274
transvaluation, *Umwert(h)ung*   2–4, 7–9, 13–15, 19–23, 26, 34, 42, 50, 54, 63, 66, 68–71, 73–77, 80, 89–93, 100, 155, 178, 184–86, 188, 197, 198, 204, 209, 210, 220–22, 225–27, 229, 230, 232–37, 240, 241, 243–46, 248, 250–54, 256, 260, 261, 279–81
Trieb   47, 58, 82, 84, 93, 113, 138, 139, 157, 159, 160, 199, 201, 249
  See also drive
truth   9, 11, 12, 26, 27, 40, 64, 71, 72, 74, 78, 79, 92, 93, 96, 100, 105, 107, 165, 198, 230, 264
truthfulness, *Wahrhaftigkeit*   71, 136, 164, 165, 204, 207
Tugend   131, 157, 181, 182, 260, 264, 265
  See also virtue
type, *Typus*   8, 24, 34, 51, 55, 77, 82, 115, 145, 150, 155, 170, 172, 173, 180–83, 186, 193, 223, 256, 261

Umwertung   3, 4, 7, 22, 54, 66, 220, 255–57, 260, 261, 268, 273, 274, 276–79
unconscious   20, 54, 63, 71, 88, 233, 234, 237–44, 246
unification, unifying, unity   17, 19, 21, 50, 72, 92, 111, 113, 136, 137, 142, 146, 154, 163, 168, 171, 176, 188–91, 194, 212, 218, 244, 245, 274
  See also Einheit

unleashing   10, 29, 44, 55–57, 59, 190, 194
unmeasured   38, 39, 48, 53, 59, 63, 191, 212, 216, 228

valued   21, 80, 149, 198, 211
values   3, 4, 7–9, 11, 13–17, 21, 23–32, 34, 38, 39, 41, 42, 53–55, 59, 62–64, 66–70, 74, 76–78, 81, 82, 86, 89, 92, 100, 112, 114, 150, 155, 156, 158, 162, 163, 168, 171, 177, 184, 185, 209, 210, 212, 215, 220, 221, 226, 227, 230, 232, 234, 240, 241, 248, 252, 253, 256–58, 260–69, 275, 277
vengefulness   21, 23, 33, 48, 224, 225, 227, 234, 238, 240, 241, 259
   See also revenge, *Rache*
Verehrung   16, 87, 127, 229
   See also reverence
Verhängniss   269
   See also fatalism
Verneinung   53, 63, 257
   See also negation, no-saying
Vernichtung   25, 35, 36, 48, 52, 53, 63, 79, 81, 90, 109, 113, 158, 159, 208, 226, 229, 230, 257, 263, 266, 272, 273, 278
   See also annihilation, destruction
Vernichtungskampf   4, 6, 14, 15, 25, 38, 39, 48, 49, 52–54, 58, 63–65, 83–85, 90, 103, 109, 163, 171, 185, 191, 212, 214, 216, 228, 235
Versuch, attempt   9, 77, 101, 155, 248, 261, 275
   See also attempt
victory   1–6, 19, 25, 30, 33–35, 37–40, 45, 46, 48, 52, 58, 61–63, 65, 74–76, 78, 80, 85, 86, 106, 187, 189, 191, 194, 196, 197, 208, 209, 211–13, 217, 218, 226, 228, 230, 231, 242, 253, 257, 260, 261, 265–68, 272, 273, 279
   See also Sieg
violence   3, 4, 13, 18, 23, 24, 26, 28, 31, 32, 44, 45, 48–51, 90, 113, 178, 233, 253
   See also Gewalt
virtù, virtuosity   214, 219, 260
virtue   11, 31, 39, 44, 67, 72, 81, 89, 95, 109, 110, 116, 119, 131, 149, 156, 181, 221, 260, 264, 265
   See also Tugend
Visibility (of the soul)   42, 55, 212, 215

Volk   60, 111, 142, 144, 146, 148, 150, 182, 183, 200
   See also people
Vollkommenheit   172, 180

Wachsthum   142, 174, 175, 180, 182, 262
   See also growth
Wahn   27, 56, 87, 150, 165, 204
war   1, 2, 11, 13–15, 19, 21, 23–25, 27, 32–39, 43, 44, 46, 48, 49, 52–54, 63, 64, 66, 73, 79–81, 83–86, 88, 89, 103, 107, 109, 124, 127, 139, 141, 166, 168, 171, 187, 188, 190, 191, 233, 235, 241, 244, 250, 256–66, 268–75, 277
   See also Krieg
war-praxis   13, 21, 23, 27, 28, 32, 33, 35, 77, 78, 255, 256, 263, 266–68, 270, 277, 278
Werte   7, 10, 62, 82, 88, 158, 163, 164, 185, 186, 220, 255–57, 261, 263, 273
Wetteifer   44, 55, 57, 131, 152
Wettspiel der Kräfte   13, 14, 24, 25, 37, 38, 56, 57, 60, 65, 75, 80, 103, 209, 215, 227, 253
Wettstreit   24
Widerspruch   24, 48, 82, 142, 176, 183, 261, 262
will, *Wille*   9, 11, 20, 45, 67, 71, 72, 79, 83, 87, 88, 106, 127, 164, 169, 183, 212, 219, 224, 226, 245, 248, 255, 259, 266, 272
will (free will, will to truth, to health)   8, 9, 11, 14, 20, 36, 45, 52, 63, 66, 67, 69, 71–74, 79, 86, 87, 90, 92, 146, 158, 168–70, 173, 178, 181–83, 212, 214, 216–18, 221, 222, 226, 235, 237, 245, 248, 258, 259, 272, 274, 276
will to power, *Wille zur Macht*   2, 3, 6–8, 24, 108, 109, 154, 162, 242, 260, 268, 272
win   62, 75, 76, 80, 124, 125, 194, 196, 203, 208, 217, 272
wisdom   15, 18, 19, 53, 83, 94, 95, 97–102, 124, 174, 181, 182, 186, 199–203, 205, 206, 209, 255, 256, 274
Weisheit   8, 53, 83, 174, 182, 183, 200, 201
Wissenschaft, Wissenstrieb   15, 19, 79, 90, 91, 93, 98, 104, 136, 143, 146, 147, 150, 159, 199–202, 205, 206, 222
   See also science

yes-saying   9, 10, 21, 91, 92, 104, 110, 236, 255–57, 259, 270–74
   See also life-affirmation

Zeit   135, 152, 162, 165, 166
    See also time
Zustimmung   76, 77, 195, 203, 209, 217, 230
    See also consensus

Zweck   117, 187, 258
    See also goal

www.ingramcontent.com/pod-product-compliance
Lightning Source LLC
Chambersburg PA
CBHW062136160426
43191CB00014B/2303